统计工作是经济工作重要组成部分，数字要准确真实，更好发挥湖南统计年鉴乃至整个统计工作对于我省经济和社会的服务功能，为发展湖南经济做出新的贡献

王茂林

中共湖南省委书记、省人大常委会主任王茂林题词：“统计工作是经济工作重要组成部分，数字要准确、真实，更好发挥湖南统计年鉴乃至整个统计工作对于我省经济和社会的服务功能，为发展湖南经济做出新的贡献。”

充分发挥"湖南统计年鉴"的作用，如实宣传湖南改革开放成就。

杨正午

中共湖南省委副书记、省人民政府省长杨正午题词："充分发挥'湖南统计年鉴'的作用，如实宣传湖南改革开放成就。"

发扬求实精神
办好统计年鉴

题赠湖南统计年鉴

文选德 一九九八年三月十二日

中共湖南省委常委、省委宣传部部长文选德题词："发扬求实精神，办好统计年鉴。"

宣传湖南的窗口
投资环境的指南

周伯华
九八年元月

中共湖南省委常委、省人民政府常务副省长周伯华题词:“宣传湖南的窗口,投资环境的指南。”

《湖南统计年鉴》是我省最
权威的數据工具書，是各级党
政部门和经济工作者進行科
学决策的重要依据。

周時昌

一九九八年
二月十二日

湖南省人民政府副省长周时昌题词："《湖南统计年鉴》是我省最权威的数据工具书，是各级党政部门和经济工作者进行科学决策的重要依据。"

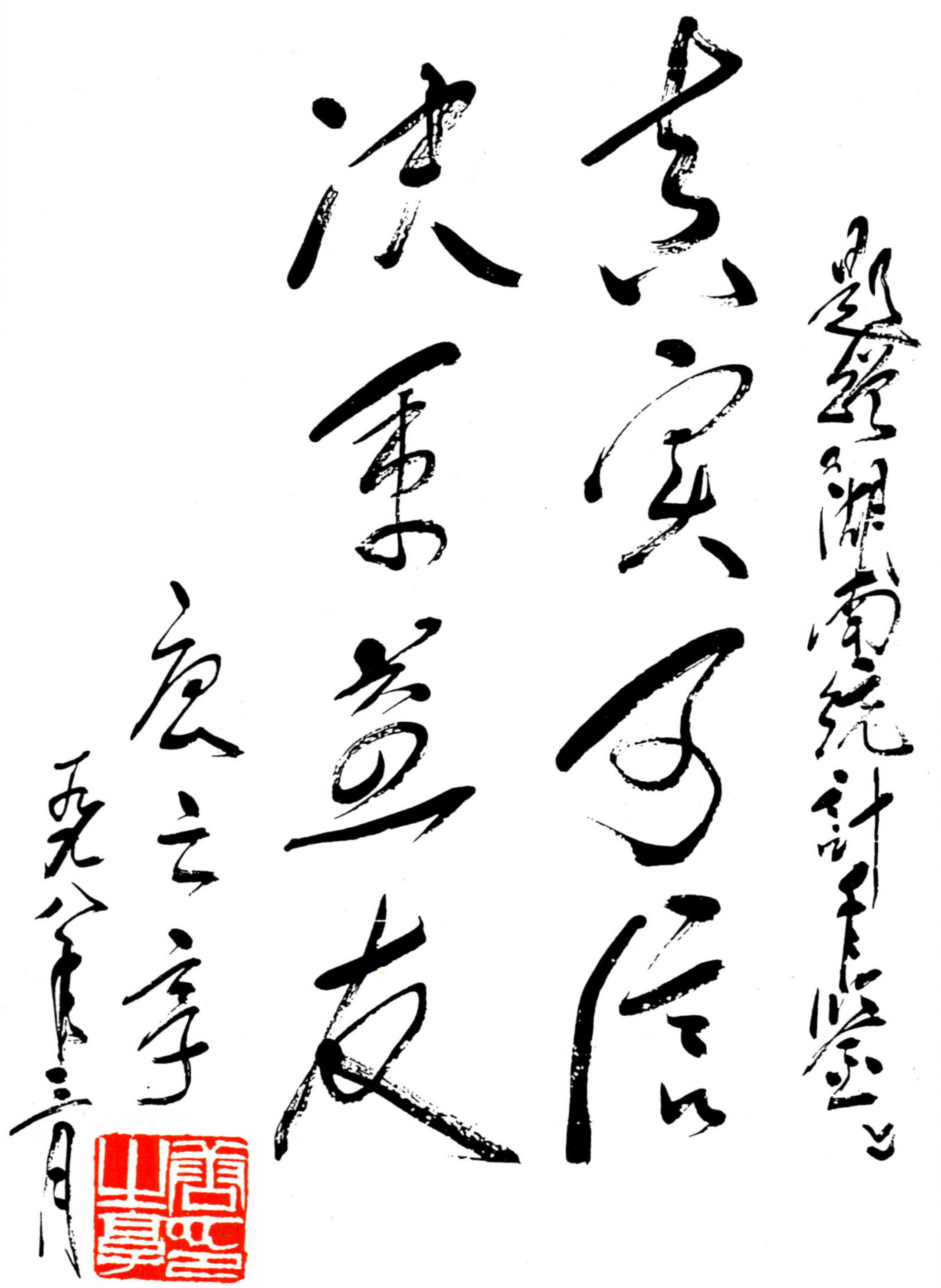

湖南省人民政府副省长唐之享题词："真实可信，决策益友。"

办好《湖南统计年鉴》
为振兴农村经济服务

庞道沐

湖南省人民政府副省长庞道沐题词：“办好《湖南统计年鉴》，为振兴农村经济服务。”

《湖南统计年鉴》全面、准确、详细地展示了湖南的投资环境是对外经济工作者和外商投资者必备工具书。

贺同新

98.3.13

湖南省人民政府副省长贺同新题词：“《湖南统计年鉴》全面、准确、详细地展示了湖南的投资环境，是对外经济工作者和外商投资者必备工具书。”

《湖南统计年鉴》全面、准确、详细地展示了湖南的省情省力，是了解认识湖南，宣传推介湖南的必备工具书。

郑茂清
九八、三、二十五

湖南省人民政府副省长郑茂清题词：“《湖南统计年鉴》全面、准确、详细地展示了湖南的省情省力，是了解认识湖南，宣传推介湖南的必备工具书。”

交通银行
长沙分行

交通银行长沙分行是交通银行在湖南的第一分支机构。该行恪守"一流的服务质量、一流的工作效率、一流的银行信誉"的办行宗旨，经过近十个年头的风雨求索，走出了一条具有自己特色的商业银行发展之路，到目前为止，全行资产总额达40余亿元，各项人民币存款余额达28亿元，各项人民币贷款达19亿元；外汇存款余额达3206万美元，外汇贷款余额达2422万美元。取得了良好的经济效益和社会效益。

China Communication Bank Changsha Branch(CCBCB)is the first branch of Communication Bank in Hunan. Sticking to the principle of "best service, efficient work, keeping promises",employees of CCBCB have worked hard in the past decade and developed their characteristic way to manage and administer commercial bank. Up to date, CCBCB has owned more than 4 billion youn capital, 2.8 billion yuan RMB deposit balance, 1.9 billion yuan RMB credit balance and US$32.06 million foreign exchange deposit balance, US$ 24.22 million foreign exchange credit balance and created favorable economic and social benefits.

行长谭哲在全行实施"文明形象工程"动员大会上讲话

交通银行长沙分行办公大楼

建行湖南省分行行长彭茂吾（右）来电力专业分行检查指导工作。左为电力专业分行行长陈二尧。

中国建设银行湖南电力专业分行成立于1988年。下设19个营业网点，拥有资产总额78.2亿元。1997年底，各项存款余额达24.7亿元，信贷贷款余额 28.9亿元，实现利润7069万元，各项经营指标在全省建行系统名列前茅。近十年来，该行经办国家建设投资60.2亿元，代理国家开发银行委托贷款55.2亿元，确保了国家重点工程东江、五强溪、凌津滩水电站建设资金供应。1990年以来连续八年保持了省委、省政府授予的“文明建设先进单位”荣誉称号。

建行湖南电力专业分行党组成员

China Constructional Bank Hunan Electric Power Branch(CCBHEPB) was established in 1988. It has 19 subsidiaries and 7,820 million yuan fixed assets. By the end of 1997,various deposit balances reached 2.47 billion yuan, credit balance reached to 2.89 billion yuan, 70.69 million yuan profit was created and various targets were perfectly completed. CCBHEPB successfully managed 6.02 billion yuan national construction investment and 5.52 billion yuan trust credits of China Developing Bank, thereby guaranteed the supplying of construction funds of national key projects including Dongjiang power station, Wuqiangxi power station and Lingjingtan power station. From 1990 to 1998, CCBHEPB held the honorary title of “advanced unit of construction system” that awarded by Hunan Provincial Party Committee and government .

建行湖南电力专业分行支持建设的国家“九五”重点建设项目——凌津滩水电站

中国建设银行 China Construction Bank

中国建设银行湖南电力专业分行

建行湖南电力专业分行营业部拓址开业

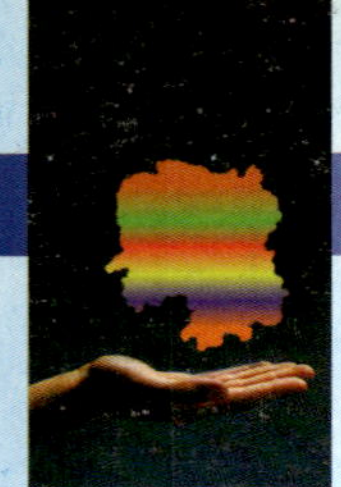

明　星　企　业

湖南賓館 HUNAN HOTEL

Hunan Hotel is located by the beautiful lake of Changsha Martyr's Park. With the fascinating natural scenery, the hotel is circled by luxuriantly green woods entirely and the environment is elegant, quite, and peaceful. It owns 422 various graded rooms, 1,000 seats, 36 meeting rooms, 14 restaurants that can accommodate 1,400 people at the same time and 18 superfine cook. Restaurants of Hunan Hotel are full of various delicious Chinese style food. The hotel also is an ideal place for social activities, business, entertainment and all kinds of banquet. Sticking to the principle of "pursuing perfection" and with the best environment, facilities and service, Hunan Hotel warmly welcome guests from home and abroad.

党委书记、总经理: 罗宏书

多功能会议室

标准间

餐厅

湖南宾馆座落于长沙市烈士公园人工湖畔，环境十分优雅，整个宾馆拥在葱茏翠绿的迷人景色之中。宾馆拥有高、中、低档客房422间，1000个床位，各种会议室36个，餐厅14个，特级厨师18名，可同时容纳1400人就餐。宾馆内设夜总会、酒吧、美容、按摩、传真、票务等服务设施和项目。有着近四十年接待历史的湖南宾馆将以一流的环境、一流的设施、一流的服务恭候各界朋友光临。

湖南宾馆，真诚服务到永远

湖南省机关事务管理局

局长：曹其明

湖南省机关事务管理局坚持为领导服务、为省直机关服务、为基层工作服务。1997 年生产接待单位实现收入1.02亿元，实现利润992万元，完成计划的118%，上交税金598.4万元，经济实体实现收入9476万元，比上年增长74.04%，上缴税金460.13万元，比上年增加59.37%。湖南省机关事务管理以"改革、发展、管理、保障"为宗旨，着力进行机关后勤体制改革、企事业单位内部改革和住房制度改革，努力实现后勤工作再上新台阶。

Hunan Governmental Affairs Administrative Bureau insists on serving the leader, office and grass-roots units, in 1997, the receptional department's income and profit respectively are 102 million yuan and 9.92 million yuan, in which profits increased 11.8% than the plan;the economic department's income are 94,76 million yuan, increased by 74.04% than the previous year. With the principle of "reform, development, administration and guarantee", Hunan Administrative Organization will emphasize in carrying out the reform of rear service system, office structure and housing system, in order to make great progress.

湖南省工商行政管理局

局长：欧阳松

湖南工商行政管理把监管与服务有机结合，充分发挥职能作用，为改革、发展和稳定作出了显著贡献。1997年新注册内资企业24801户，新登记外商投资企业337家；个体私营经济达1824755户、从业人员472.85万人；新注册商标2394件，认定著名商标186件；查处药品回扣案291件，假冒伪劣商品案3432件，案值1.4亿元；新命名省级“重合同、守信用”企业117家。1997年被省委、省政府办公厅评为政务信息工作先进单位。

The administrative function of Hunan Industrial and Commercial Administrative Department (HICAD) is combined by supervision and service. It has made great contribution to the reform, development and stabitlity of the society. In 1997, 24,801 domestic enterprises, 337 joint ventures, 1,824,755 private enterprises were registered; 4,728,500 people were employed; 2,394 trade marks were registered; 186 famous trademarks were verified; 291 drug's rebating cases, 3,432 false merchandise cases which valued 140 million yuan were investigated, 117 enterprises were named as provincial excellent units.In 1997, HICAD was awarded the title of “governmental information service advanced unit” by the General Office of Hunan government.

欧阳松局长就打击假冒伪劣产品接受记者采访

我省工商系统全面展开打击假酒的专项行动。

国家工商局局长王众孚(左)在副省长周时昌(中)的陪同下到湖南省工商局检查工作

湖南邮电业在改革开放的大潮中迅猛发展。到1997年底，全省已建成长途数字传输、程控电话、无线寻呼、移动电话、数据通讯、会议电视网、多媒体、信息服务等七大现代电信通信网络；6条省际长途干线和省内长途干线；光缆总长达4万公里，数字微波总长达7611公里。1997年湖南电信和邮政的用户满意度评分列全国同行第一名和第三名。

Racing against time and going along with the reforming and open trends, Hunan post and telecommunications has been developing rapidly . By the end of 1997 , seven morden networks of telecommunications and communications which include long-distance digital transmission,programme-control telephones, wirless calls, mobile telephones, numerical communications, conference television-nets and multimedium-system informative servies has been set up. otherthan , six inter-provincial or provincial long-distance trunk-lines has been built . Total length of photo-cable has come up to 40,000 kilmeters and total length of numerical microwaves has reached to 7611 kilometers .In 1997 , the place of Hunan telecommunications and post were in the first place and the third place in China.

湖南省邮电管理局

省委、省政府领导视察湖南邮电

集中监视、监控系统

多媒体通信

With the energetic support of Hunan government, the tourism of Hunan has become an important profitable part of national economy. In 1997, more than 301,600 foreign tourists and 40 million inland tourists were received in Hunan ,increased respectively by 31.89% and 25% than last year,US$140 million foreign exchange and 6.8 billion yuan income was created, increased respectively by 40% and 30.89% than last year.3 billion yuan was invested in tourism construction in 1997. With the coming of 98 Huaxia Tour and the orientation of luxurious journey, the tourism of Hunan will surely meet with the brightest possible future.

武陵源风光

猛洞河漂流

局长：张济民

南岳大庙圣帝殿雄姿

岳阳君山团湖泛舟采莲

世界之窗一瞥

湖南省旅游局

在省委省政府高度重视和大力支持下，湖南旅游业已成为湖南国民经济新的增长点。1997年接待入境旅游者30.16万人次，比上年增加31.39%，外汇收入1.4亿美元，增加40%；接待国内旅游者4000万人次，增加25%，国内旅游收入68亿元，增加30.8%。围绕'98华夏城乡游大力实施旅游精品战略，湖南旅游业将蓬勃向上再创佳绩。

湖南省劳动和社会保障厅

省委常委、常务副省长周伯华、省人大常委会副主任罗桂求与厅长谷新珊、副厅长邓玉来及长沙市市长杜远明在街头检查指导社会保险宣传工作

湖南省劳动和社会保障厅是湖南省人民政府综合管理全省劳动和社会保障工作的职能部门。建国以来共安排了613.8万城镇新成长的劳动力就业。全省现已开办有形的劳动力市场148家。1986年到1997年全省累计支出失业救济金21371.1万元，各级劳动部门共接纳失业职工27.81万人，失业职工分流安置再就业率为47.43%，全省已建立再就业服务中心139个，托管下岗失业人员3.42万人。1996年湖南省劳动和社会保障厅被评为“全国劳动系统先进集体”。

厅党组书记、厅长谷新珊接受人民日报记者采访

团结协作的厅党组一班人

Hunan Labour and Society Securing Department (HLSSD) is a functional department of Hunan Provincial Government that administers the labour and society securing work of the whole province. It has provided employment chances for 6.138 million people in cities from the founding day of the country and set up 148 labour markets. From 1986 to 1997,the expenditure of unemployment relief payment of Hunan amounted to 213.711 million yuan, 278.1 thousand jobless people were arranged jobs again,the reemployment rate of the jobless people reached to 47.43%,139 reemployment service were established and responsible for 34.2 thousand jobless people. In 1996,HLSSD was honored the title of “advanced unit of national labour system” .

省职业介绍服务中心吸引了众多的劳动者

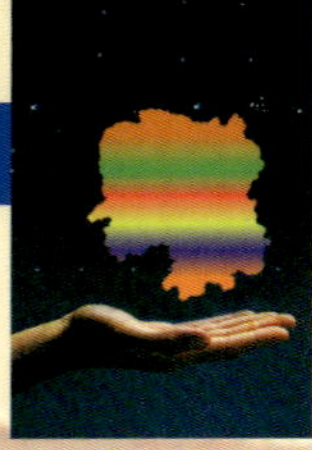

改革开放以来，湖南省交通事业取得令人瞩目的成绩。公路基础设施整体水平明显提高。到1997年底，全省公路总里程达到59761公里，高级、次高级路面里程达到15242公里，其中水泥路面达到2869公里。全省营运车辆15.4万辆，完成客运量7.3亿人次，货运量4.1亿吨；全省航道建养投资达到7543万元。利用世行贷款9000万美元，总投资近20亿元的株洲至衡阳湘江千吨级航道整治工程现已启动。目前全省航道里程10050公里。

Since the reform and open-door policy was implemented,Hunan Transport Department has made great achievements.By the end of 1997,the total mileage of road of Hunan has reached to 59,761 km.the mileage of first-class and second-class road has reached to 15,242km.(with 2869km. cement road). With 154 thousand vehicles, it has completed the passager transported volume of 730 millon and goods transported volume of 410 millon tons in Hunan. At the same time,the investment for the construction of channel has reached to 75.43 million yuan and the dredging project of the Zhuzhou-Hengyan waterways with 2 billion yuan investment(90 million loan from the World Bank) has started. At present, the waterway's mileage of Hunan province is 10,050km.

李安厅长向记者畅谈交通发展前景

湖南省交通厅

長潭高速公路

正在建设中的国家重点工程——湘江航运二期大源渡枢纽工程

1998年4月，湘耒高速公路世界银行贷款、转贷协议在长沙签订

省长杨正午(左)在村支部书记邓启发(右)的陪同下视察龙洞村

湖南红旗村——浏阳市龙洞村

龙洞村地处连云山脉东麓的深山区，340 户农户 1290 人，人均耕地 0.5 亩。在改革的时代，这个昔日的穷山窝发生了翻天覆地的变化。1997年实现工农业总产值1.03亿元，人均纯收入 7065 元。村办集体企业 6 家，固定资产 2322 万元，企业职工 750 人。全村电话装机达 200 门。近年来，全村无赌博、吸毒现象，无刑事案件发生，被评为全省“村民自治模范村”、“红旗村”。

Longdong village is situated in the east of Lianyun mountain range of Liuyang. It has 340 families with 1290 peasants. The average cultivated area is 0.5mu each person. With the great reform of China, an earth-shaking change has taken place in Longdong village, In 1997, the total output value of the village amounted to 103 million yuan, the average income reached to 7,065 yuan each person. Longyang village has 6 collective enterprises with 23.22 million yuan fixed assets and 750 employees. 200 telephones has been installed in Longyang village. In recent years, the gambling, drug taking behaviour and criminal cases have been stamped out in Longyang village and it has been awarded the honorary titles of “model village of self-government “and “Hongqi Village”.

湖南省公安厅交通管理局

湖南省公安

▲党委书记、政委：李火烽

▲党委副书记、局长、总队长：杨建农

▲省委书记、省人大常委会主任王茂林、省委副书记郑培民等领导亲切接见"五一"劳动奖章获得者、长沙市交通民警吴贱安。

湖南省公安厅交通警察总队于1987年3月27日正式成立，至今已走过了十一年的光辉历程。

十一年的历史，是一部我省广大交通民警在省委、省政府和省公安厅的正确领导下，紧紧依靠人民群众，负重前进，顽强拼博，同心同德，开拓创新的历史；是一部我省交通民警为湖南改革开放和经济建设保驾护航的历史；是一部我省广大交通民警用忠诚、智慧、汗水甚至生命印证国务院改革道路交通管理体制英明正确的历史。如今，这支队伍已成为我省两个文明建设的重要力量，成为党和人民可以充分信赖的一支政治坚定、纪律严明、作风顽强、执法公正的有战斗力的文明之师。

全省现有交通民警7023名，是建队初期的两倍多。全省公安交警队伍由建队初期的13个支队、33个交警队发展到现在的15个支队、133个大队、313个中队，形成了总队、支队、大队、中队的"三级管理、四级网络"的管理模式。十一年来，全省交警系统先后有5人荣获全国公安系统英雄模范称号，有19人荣获全国优秀人民警察称号，有3人荣获全国"五一"劳动奖章，长沙市公安局交警支队车管所被授予97年度全国"五一"劳动奖状，是我省目前唯一获此殊荣的优秀集体，还有一大批先进集体和个人被记功、嘉奖。先后有15名交通民警光荣牺牲，663人因公负伤。广大交警战严寒，斗酷暑，吃尘土，闻噪声，在马路上恪尽职守，在红绿灯下奉献青春，用汗水和鲜血谱写了一曲曲壮丽的凯歌。特别是1995年"学济南交警"以来，认真贯彻江总书记"严格执法，热情服务"的题词精神，不断"内强素质，外树形象"，给三湘大地带来了一股文明新风，产生了良好的"交警效应"。

十一年来，我省交通运输事业发展迅猛。目前，全省拥有机动车近110多万辆，驾驶员160多万名，公路里程5.95万公里。机动车和驾驶员分别是1986年的3.1倍和8倍，而公路里程只是1986年的1.06倍。在机动车增长的情况下，万车事故率从1986年的399次／万车下降到1997年的94.55次／万车，万车死亡率从1986年的66.2人／万车下降到1997年的30.07人／万车。

展望未来，任重道远。我们要坚定不移地坚持邓小平同志建设有中国特色社会主义理论和党的基本路线，坚持"抓班子、带队伍、促工作、保平安"的工作思路，以"维护社会稳定，服务经济建设，确保安全畅通"为中心，向改革要效益，向科技要警力，向执法要形象，全面提高队伍整体素质，创一流，上台阶，努力实现道路交通管理的法制化、规范化、现代化和社会化目标，为湖南经济发展和两个文明建设创造一个"安全、有序、畅通"的交通环境，不负党和人民的重托。

（供稿：马丽萍）

▲主席像前宣个誓，要为警徽添光彩。

厅交通警察总队

▲1998年7月14日，省委副书记郑培民(左二)，省委常委、省政法委书记、省公安厅厅长李贻衡(右二)，冒着酷暑，来到长沙街头和长益高速公路，对执勤交警进行慰问。

▲1997年6月9日，省委、省政府、省人大、省政法委领导文选德、唐之享、朱东阳等以及厅领导接见全省交警系统英模报告团的全体代表。

▲总队机关每周星期一庄严的升旗仪式。

▲与有线电视台合办的《平安走天下》栏目于1998年4月26日正式开播。

▲锻炼身体，保卫人民。1998年6月2日，公安厅机关广播操比赛，交通管理局获一等奖。

▲整治马路上的腐败，先从自己做起。总队机关干警上路检查治理警车、警灯、警报器。

▲冰天雪地橄榄绿。

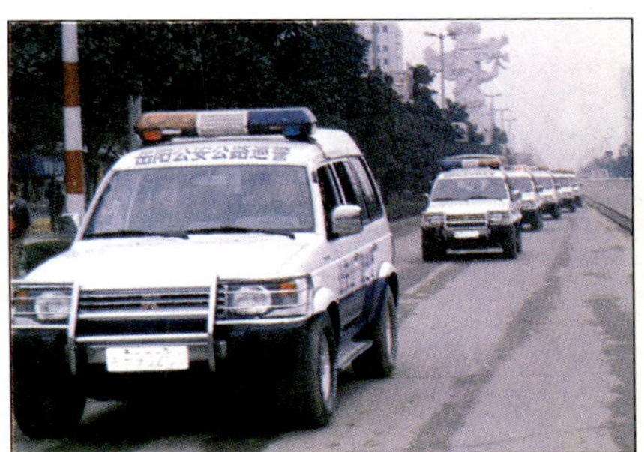

▲装备精良的公路巡逻队。

娄底地区

中共娄底地委副书记、行署专员陈润儿同志要求财政工作实现“三个转变”：从注重聚财转变到既要聚财更要生财上来，从注重节支转变到既要节支又要“优支”上来，从注重“管家”转变到既“管家”更要“当家”上来。

By improving the village and town financial system continuously and regulating the administration of extra-budgetary funds, the financial bureau of Loudi has ensured the steady increase of the financial income of the whole region. In 1997, the local financial income of Loudi has made a breakthrough at 600 million yuan, increased by 10.18% than the previous year and the balance reached to 2.06 million yuan. Up to 1997, the revenue and expenditure of Loudi financial bureau were balanced for 20 years, therefore, the financial bureau was highly praised by the leaders of national Financial Ministry.

财政部扶贫项目之一——湖南新大实业有限公司

全区财源建设工作会议，掀起了新的财源建设高潮。

财政局

团结、精干、高效、廉洁的局领导班子。右四为局长、党组书记赵更效。

娄底地区财政局从改革入手，不断完善乡镇财政体制，规范预算外资金管理，调节财源结构，确保了全区地方财政收入的稳定增长。1997年，全区地方财政收入首次突破6亿元大关，比上年增长10.18%，收支两抵净结余206万元，顺利实现了连续20年财政收支平衡，得到了国家财政部领导同志的高度赞扬。

财政理论研究成果

组稿：赵爱群

局长：邹大华

党委书记：汪威吉

衡阳市交通局

衡山湘江大桥雄姿

在改革开放新时期，衡阳市交通局以建立综合运输体系为方向，以完善运输市场为目标，以加强交通基础设施为重点，以深化企业内部改革为中心，发挥公路运输为主力，水陆运输为优势，专业运输为骨干的作用，初步实现了交通运输业的协调、稳步发展，建立了以城市为中心向外幅射，以县乡为重点向外扩展，以107、322国省道为主骨架，以湘耒水为主通道，以万吨级港站为主枢纽，城乡相通，水陆衔接、干支直达的交通运输网络，为发展衡阳经济，促进两个文明建设，发挥了基础性的先导和纽带作用。

Hengyang Transport Bureau is in charge of the transport construction and administration of four counties, 2 cities and 2 districts. It has set up many departments to administer highway, transportation, levy, channel, rural road, staff school and local railway. Hengyang Transport Bureau has 33 transport enterprises (10 of them directly under the municipality). The total road mileage of Hengyang is 5,680km., among which 2 are national roads, 8 are provincial roads and 95 are county and rural roads. Hengyang has 7 navigable rivers with total length of 1,775km., 22 harbors, 149 wharves, 268 ferries, 74 bus stations, 28,963 vehicles and 2,830 ships. All of these facilities have taken the heavy responsibility of transportation of the whole city. With the orientation of building comprehensive transportation system, the goal of consummating transportation market and strengthening transport infrastructure, the focal object of deepening the structural reform of enterprises and developing highway transportation, Hengyang Transport Bureau has established a highly developed transport network. It has made great contribution to the development of Hengyang's economy and the construction of the double civilizations.

文明、美观、畅通的107国道衡阳段

港口码头建设面貌焕然一新

衡阳市交通天凤大厦

文明执法的交警队伍

衡阳汽车站远眺

组稿：毛智安　涂国华

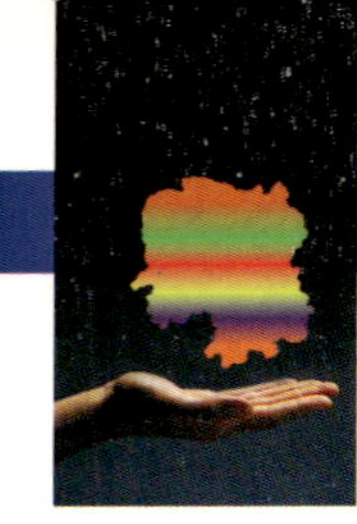

麓 山 国 际

▲爱尔兰都柏林市友人访问时与校长们留影(左一为陈绪常校长、右一为舒明华校长)

▲独轮车表演，展示“麓山娃”的风貌

▲省卫视台“六一”晚会上，“麓山娃”表演《同在蓝天下》的场景

实验学校

▲特长课——手风琴

▲学生们正在上机操作

麓山国际实验学校是直属市教委领导的一所进行“学校国有、校长负责”，“经费自筹，办学自主”体制改革实验的寄宿制学校。学校面临湘江，背依麓山，交通便捷，环境优美，师资力量雄厚，教学设备设施齐全。学校现有中、小学教学班级40个，在校学生1600多人，学校全部建成后将占地近200亩，班级总数达80个，在校学生3000多人。学校以“学会生存、学会关心”为校训，主张“和谐发展”，“因材施教”“先成人，后成才”的办学方针，是面向21世纪培养人才的现代化学校。

校址：长沙市望月湖七片

电话：(0731)8855754

传真：(0731)8855764

电子邮件：Lsxx@public.cs.hn.cn

Lushan International Experimental School is a boarding school that implementing the reform of “headmaster responsible system” and “educational funds raised by itself and decide for itself”, It is directed by Changsha Educational Committee. With graceful environment and convenient transport, the school has an experienced teaching staff and a great variety of teaching equipments at the same time. At present, the school has 40 middle and primary classes and more than 1600 students. The built-up constructional area of the school will take up nearly 200 mu land and the total amount of the classes and students will respectively reach to 80 and 3000 as soon as the school has been completely constucted. Insisting on the principle of “learn to live, learn to care for others”, “harmonious development”, “teach students in accordance with their aptitude” and “first to be an human being, then to be a talented person”, Lushan International Experimental School is a modern school that developing talented people for the 21st century.

Address: 7# district of Wangyuehu, Changsha

Telephone: (0731) 8855754

Fax: (0731) 8855764

E-mail: Lsxx@ public.cs.hn.cn

◀ 科技兴趣小组的同学在做科技实验

▲‘97之夏，“麓山娃”代表湖南省赴深圳布吉镇参加全国无线电测向比赛

▲“素质展示活动”时科技制作一角

总　组　稿：叶双秋

供稿、摄影：殷建军

戴伍军

彭　云

长沙县

▲县委书记：彭可平

▲县长：王支农

长沙县地处省会长沙市东郊，总面积1997平方公里，辖20个乡（镇）495个行政村，74.1万人，74.1万亩耕地。1997年，全县国内生产总值达64.4亿元。粮食总产量、肉类总产量、乡镇企业总产值分别进入全国单项百强行列。实现了乡乡通标准油路，村村通程控电话。被湖南省委、省政府授予湖南省“小康县”称号。

Changsha county is located in the east suburb of Changsha city. With the total areas of 1997 square kilomters, 741 thousand population and cultivated land,Changsha county has jurisdication over 20 towns and 495 villages. In 1997, the GNP of the county has reached to 6.44 billion yuan, at the same time, the total output of grain and meat and the output value of township enterprises are respectively among the top 100 of China. Highways radiate in all directions and telephones are greatly popularized in Changsha county. Changsha county was honored the title of “rich county” by Hunan Provincial Povrty Cominittee and the government.

▲粮食生产自1996年连续两年实现成建制过吨粮。（图为丰收在望的杂交稻）

▲农村人民生活质量不断提高，居住条件得到改善。（图为黄花镇一农家住宅）

▲乡镇企业快速健康发展，主要经济指标连续11年居湖南全省之首。（图为江背镇银河水泥厂和河田水泥厂）

湖南省长沙经济开发区位于长沙市东郊星沙镇，地处319国道 与107国道及京珠高速公路交汇处，距长沙市中心和火车站8公里，距黄花国际机场6公里，规划面积20平方公里，第一期开发面积14平方公里。开发区鼓励工业、 高新技术及服务业的投入，亦欢迎外商投资者自带项目对开发区内的土地进行成片开发。长沙经济开发区热忱欢迎海内外有识之士来此大展鸿图！

▲城镇安居工程步伐加快(图为星沙镇居民文明小区)

◀农业基础设施建设初具规模,水利工程供水量达4.62亿立方米。(图为春华渡槽)

▲通讯便捷,村村通程控电话,邮政投递到户。(图为可提供10万门程控电话,21层的县邮电大楼)

▲老有所养,老有所乐,20个老年康乐中心,敬老院遍布全县。(图为跳马乡敬老院)

卫生事业获湖南省“卫生三项建设先进县”后,再攀新高峰。(图为正在兴建的县人民医院全景)

▲教育工作获全国“两基工作先进县”后,97年又被评定为全国19个实施素质教育试点工作县之一。(图为星沙中学微机室)

组稿:张之伟、谭建国

湖南省长沙经济技术开发区远眺

长沙市芙蓉区

长沙市委书记阳宝华上任伊始即视察芙蓉区的特种养殖业

区委书记：董学生

区长：胡进安

区政府常务会议专题研究小康建设工作

著名乡镇企业——银河电脑公司生产的电脑

五星特种养殖有限公司甲鱼养殖温棚及该公司养殖的蜗牛

被省政府授予“种植大王”称号的黄建国同志建起的蔬菜大棚已硕果累累

长沙市芙蓉区地处湘江东岸，横跨浏阳河，从长沙市繁华闹市中心向东辐射扩展，面积40.8平方公里，人口30万，下辖8个街道办事处，4个乡镇场。该区依托长沙钟灵毓秀的自然环境，惟楚有才的人文历史，开放竞争的市场经济，多姿多彩的社会氛围，集历史人文之壮美，汇现代经济之繁华于一身，素有湖南省会长沙的“窗口”之称。

Changsha Furong District is situated in the east bank of Xiangjiang river and extends from the center of Changsha city to the east. With total areas of 40.8 square kiometers and 300 thousand population, Furong district administers 8 streets and 4 towns and villages. With abundant natural resources, brilliant culture and history, good social atmosphere and prosperous economy, Furong district is called the “window” of Changsha.

社区服务初具规模——这是位于韭菜园街道的社区服务中心一角

水利建设事业蒸蒸日上——图为长善垸防汛抗洪指挥中心的洪水电脑自动监控示意图

小康不小康，关键在住房——马王堆乡新合村农民新居好气派

社会综合治理初见成效——朝阳街人民新村治安小区一瞥

受到高度评价的马王堆乡新桥村村务公开监督栏

总组稿：贺岱权
组　稿：陈春旗
赵昌海
李素泉
马仁村
胡国强
倪伯齐
王　勇
摄　影：周志强

长沙市岳麓区

长沙市人民政府副市长、中共长沙市岳麓区委书记
向　力　力

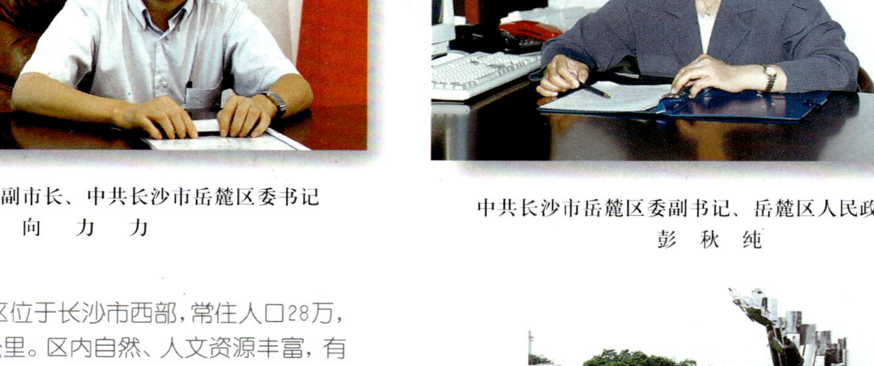

中共长沙市岳麓区委副书记、岳麓区人民政府区长
彭　秋　纯

长沙市岳麓区位于长沙市西部，常住人口28万，总面积145平方公里。区内自然、人文资源丰富，有岳麓山、湘江、桔子洲、爱晚亭、岳麓书院、西汉古王城等名胜古迹。科研教育发达。区内有30余所大专院校和科研院所，各类专业技术人员10万余人，有国家级长沙高新技术产业开发区，规模居全国之首的麓南超硬材料科技市场，形成了高新技术产业群。经济高速发展，社会全面进步。近年，全区工业、商业、财税收入分别以50%、60%、80%的年增率高速发展，农业向产业化快步推进，全区计划生育、城市管理、社会治安、社区服务等几十项工作走在全市、全省甚至全国前列。

岳麓广场

咸嘉农民安置小区

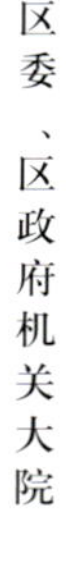

区委、区政府机关大院

1995年3月，江泽民总书记视察龙王港大堤并参加抢修大堤劳动。

Yuelu Distrct is sitruated in the west of Changsha city. It has 280,000 inhabitants. The total area of Yuelu district is 145 square kilometers . With abundant natural and cultural resources, Yuelu District owns a lot of scenic spots including Yuelu Mountain, Xiangjiang River, Juzizhou Islet, Aiwan Pavilion, Yuelu Academy, Xihan kingdom and so on. Yuelu District is famous for its flourishing scientific education. It has more than 30 universities and institutions and 100,000 various technicians. Changsha High-technology Development Zone and the top Lulan Hard Materials Scientific Market are also located there. In recent years, the economy of Yuelu District has been greatly developed. The income of industry, commerce and tax respectively increased by 50%,60% and 80% annually. The birth control plan, city administration , public security and service of Yuelu District have been perfectly completed by the local government.

桃花无公害蔬菜精品基地

北鹿南养获得成功

组稿：文志龙
摄影：周志强

精品葡萄基地喜获丰收

花卉基地初具规模

名楼新区 小康风范

岳阳楼

岳阳楼区是岳阳市政治、经济、文化中心。区内有名扬天下的岳阳楼、君山岛；驰名中外的湘莲、毛尖、君山银针茶。1996年全区社会总产值50.42亿元，国民生产总值20.22亿元，农村人平纯收入3007元，乡镇企业总产值44.5亿元，财政收入1.17亿元。区内已形成八大商贸区及以机电、化工、服装、建材、饲料、食品为主的工业格局。

岳阳楼区

▲蔡家村塑料大棚

◀外国友人参观渔民新村

▲新建的居民住宅区

组稿：李显平、黄　伟、夏　阳

区委书记：胡　亦

区长：陈国荣

区长办公会专题研究农业开发

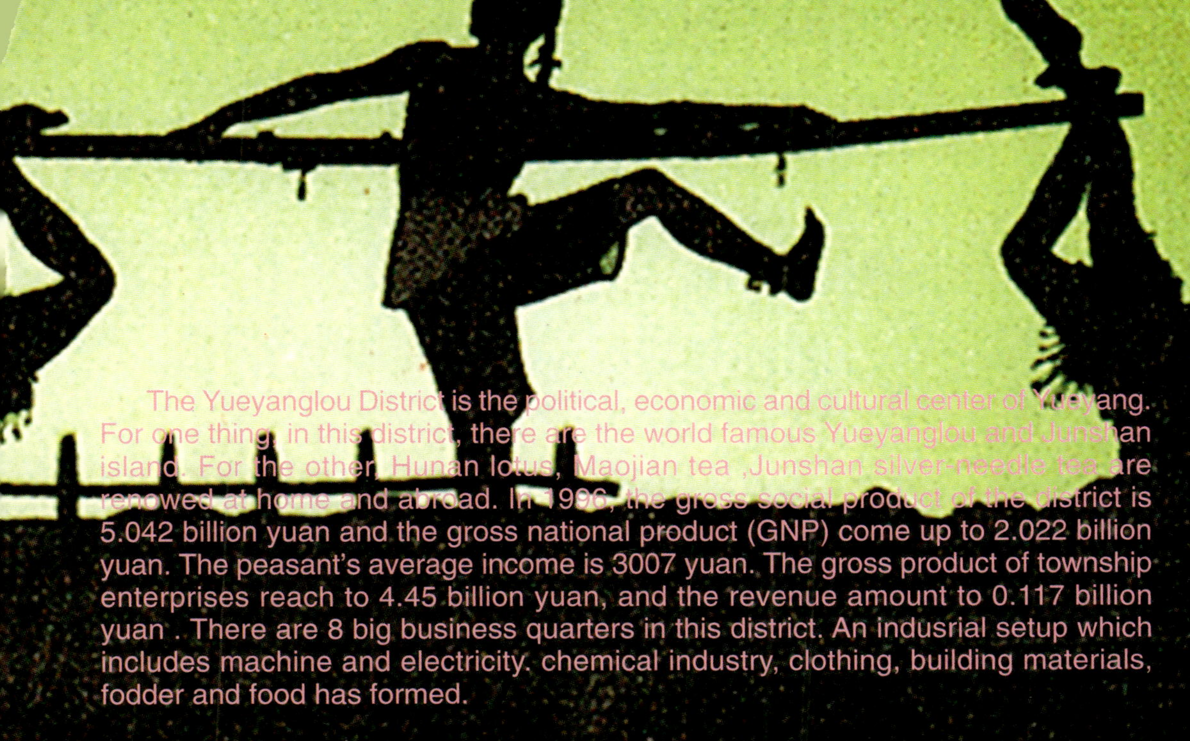

The Yueyanglou District is the political, economic and cultural center of Yueyang. For one thing, in this district, there are the world famous Yueyanglou and Junshan island. For the other, Hunan lotus, Maojian tea ,Junshan silver-needle tea are renowed at home and abroad. In 1996, the gross social product of the district is 5.042 billion yuan and the gross national product (GNP) come up to 2.022 billion yuan. The peasant's average income is 3007 yuan. The gross product of township enterprises reach to 4.45 billion yuan, and the revenue amount to 0.117 billion yuan . There are 8 big business quarters in this district. An indusrial setup which includes machine and electricity. chemical industry, clothing, building materials, fodder and food has formed.

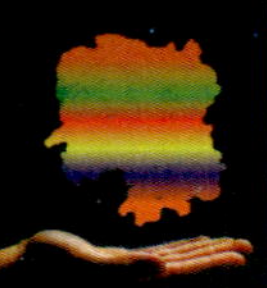

衡阳市南岳区

南岳大庙圣帝殿雄姿

Nanyue district was established in 1984. It administers four villages and towns and has 181.5 square kilometers land and 51 thousand population. With the advantage of its beautiful landscape, Nanyue district has emphasized in developing tourism integrated with agriculture and prosperous scene present everywhere in the villages of Nanyue district. In 1997, the annual net income per peasant of Nanyue district has amounted to 2,654 yuan.

图为主管农业的副区长杨铁桥同志(右一)在大型商品粮建设基地现场指导工作

南岳镇万福村村民旷华南家居一角

南岳区于1984年建区，现辖四个乡镇，总面积181.5平方公里，总人口5.1万人，其中农业人口3.3万人。该区结合旅游区特点，大办旅游农业，农业综合开发成效显著，农村一片安居乐业、社会清明、人寿年丰景象。1997年，该区农民人均纯收入达2654元。

区委书记万一(右一)与区长刘运发在一起研究农村小康工作

图为南岳引进外资300万元兴建的华渝生物工程公司一角

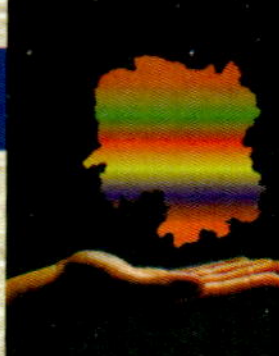

攸县位于株洲南部，辖14个建制镇，16个乡，总人口74.0万人。1996年被命名为全省第一批小康县和全省十个双文明先进县(市)。1997年，全县国内生产总值完成37.02亿元，提前四年实现翻两番目标；财政收入实现1.46亿元，农民人均纯收入达到2599元，人均居住面积51平方米，楼房比重达96%，电视普及率达89%，通电话的村达70%，卫生饮水、用电、通路均达100%，五保户生活得到保障。农民受教育程度显著提高，实现了教育“双基”达标，城乡居民生活质量明显提高，生活环境改善。沐浴着改革开放的春风，攸县已发展成为湘东地区的一颗明珠。

Youxian county is situated in the south of Zhuzhou region with 740,000 population, it has jurisdication over 14 towns, 16 villages. In 1997, the GNP(Gross National Products), financial income and peasant's annual average net income of Youxian county respectively reached to 3.702 billion yuan, 146 million yuan and 2,599 yuan. Tap water and electricity are popularized in peasant's family, education and people's life quality also have been greatly developed in Youxian county. It has been awarded the titles of “rich county of Hunan” and “one of the double civilization advanced county in Hunan”. Followed with the step of the great reform of China, Youxian county has gradually developed to be a brilliant pearl of the east of Hunan.

株洲市攸县

书记：陈立新

县长：龙国华

组稿：李建球　苏寿泉　徐常文　曾叶新

位于上云桥镇内的居民住宅区——龙形花园

攸县精细化工厂生产的“桃水牌”氟化钠产品远销欧洲、东南亚等国家和地区

牲猪是攸县农村经济的支柱产业。1997年全县出栏牲猪94万头

攸县商城——湘东地区最大的农产品集贸市场

常德市武陵区

武陵区是常德市政治、经济、文化中心。面积270平方公里，现辖6乡1镇5个街道办事处，人口36万人。改革开放以来，全区全力实施“兴工、强农、壮大三产”的发展战略，国民经济取得长足发展。1997年完成国民生产总值10.5亿元，财政总收入达7207万元，农民人平纯收入3070元，成为全省第一批小康达标区。

区南坪中学

区张家台村办企业——金桥大市场

区委书记：吴让见

区长：韦绍斌

Wuling district is the political, economic and cultural centre of Changde. The area of Wuling is about 270 square kilometers. It has jurisdiction over 6 townships or towns and 5 street offices, and have a population of 360,000 people. Since the reform and open-door policy was carried out in China, a series of developed strategies including “prosper industry, develop agriculture and strengthen the 3rd productions” have been implemented and national economy has made considerable progress. In 1997, the gross national product (GNP) came up to 1.05 billion yuan and the gross revenue amounted to 72.07 million yuan. The peasants’ average income is 3,070 yuan. Wuling district has become one of the comfortable areas in Hunan.

甘露寺蔬菜批发大市场

区委书记：姜玉泉

区长：肖先培

区党政领导班子共商发展大计

Hetang district is the east entrance of Zhuzhou-the largest railway hub of sourthern China. It has total areas of 159 square kilometer and 200 thousand population. In 1997, Hetang district's GNP and total output value of industry has respectively amounted to 470 million yuan and 1.02 billion yuan and gradually formed a lot of key industry including machinery, chemical, electrical appliance, construction materials and packing. The private enterprises and agriculture have been prosperously developed and its total output value respectively amounted to 390 million yuan and 121.39 million yuan, at the same time, the total grain output has reached to 38580 tons and the total local financial income has amounted to 85.65 million yuan in 1997. Hengtang district was honored the title of "rich district" by Hunan Provincial Party Committee and the government.

株洲市荷塘区

株洲市荷塘区是中国南部最大铁路枢纽株洲市的东大门。全区总面积159平方公里，总人口20万人。1997年国内生产总值4.7亿，工业总产值10.2亿元，逐步形成了机械、化工、电器、建材、纸质包装等支柱产业；私营经济蓬勃发展总产值达3.9亿元；农业总产值12139万元，粮食总产量38580吨；地方财政总收入8565万元。是省委、省政府首批命名的"小康区"。

繁荣的农贸市场

荷塘区骨干乡镇企业——株洲市水玻璃厂

政府机关大楼

社会力量办学的中坚

长沙电脑专修学院

院长：肖训球教授

座落在苍松翠柏之中的长沙电脑学院

第一电脑教学室

该院是经省教委批准的社办全日制高等院校。现有固定资产60万元，在校学生600人。开设计算机应用、计算机信息管理、计算机通信、电子技术、工商(电脑)管理、工业电器自动化等中专、大专、本科及研究生专业课程。创办14年来为国家培养中专、大专、本科及研究生毕业生3000余名。历年被省、市教委多次评为先进单位、先进集体、一类院校及优秀院校。1997年该院被列入“高等教育国家学历文凭考试”湖南省首批试点院校。

院址：长沙市德雅村　　电话：(0731)4221642
邮编：410003

Changsha Computer College is a full-time college that ratified by Hunan Education Committee. It has 600 thousand yuan fixed assets and 600 students. The college set up specialized subjects of computer application, computer information administration, electric technology,business computer administration, electrical automation and so on. It's been 14 years since Changsha Computer College was established, and it has developed more than 3,000 undergraduate and postgraduate students. Changsha Computer College has been honored the titles of “advanced unit” and “first-class college” by Hunan Education Committee for many times. In 1997, Changsha Computer College was chosen to be the experimental college of “national diploma examination”.

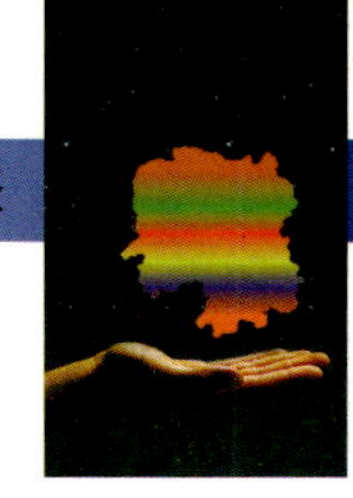

湖南中山进修大学

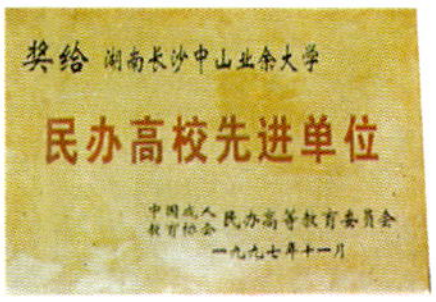

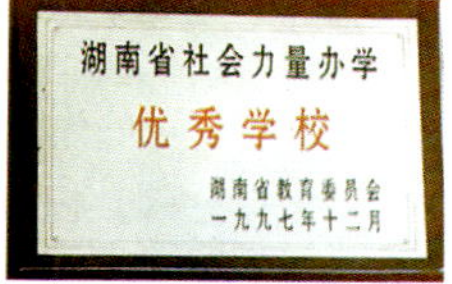

Hunan Zhongshan College is ratified by Hunan Education Committee and established in 1978. It has 1.1 million yuan fixed assets and 1,461 students. The college has set up specialized subjects of Party administration, economy administration, external economy, trade English, law, accountant, secretary and public relations, printing, computer application and developed 57,361 students.

Founder: Wang Xianyao

Vice Chairman: HuangDong, Liu Chongde, Dai Haichun, Liao Jinchi

Headmaster: Liao Jinchi

Vice Headmaster: Yang Zhaoqiu,Liang Shijie Liu Dongsong

Address: Shaoshan North Road 129#, Changsha

Tel: (0731) 4118788 4117334

PC: 410011

湖南中山进修大学(前身为湖南长沙中山业余大学)1978年经省教育局批准创办。现有固定资产110万元，在校学生1461人。学校开设党政管理、经济管理、涉外经济、经贸英语、法律、会计、文秘公关、印刷、计算机应用等专业。创始人王显耀，副董事长黄栋、刘重德、戴海春、廖经池，校长廖经池，副校长杨照球、梁士洁、刘冬生。历届毕业生57361人。

校址：长沙市韶山北路129号

电话：(0731)4118788 4117334

邮编：410011

校长：廖经池教授

语音室一角

电脑教学室

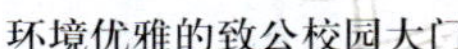

环境优雅的致公校园大门

拥有最先进的多媒体语言教学系统

100 台以多媒体为主体的微机群

湖南衡阳致公科技专修学院

湖南衡阳致公卫生职业中专学校

湖南衡阳致公科技专修学院1988年经省教委批准创办。现有固定资产500万元，在校学生1046人。开设大中专医士、妇幼医士、护士、英语、家政管理、针灸推拿医士、计算机应用、自动化电气设备、市场营销、高护、法律等专业。该院由中国致公党衡阳市委员会举办，校长吴楚良，副校长周品珊、朱广泰。历届毕业生1126人。

院址：衡阳市江东区蒋家山1号

电话：(0734)8350403　8350286

邮编：421002

Hunan Hengyang Zhigong Science and Technology College is situated at Jiangjiashan 1# of Hengyang city. It is ratified by Hunan Education Committee and established in 1988. At present, the college has 5 million yuan fixed assets and 1046 students. It has set up specialized subjects of medical science, nursing, English, household administration, acupuncture, computer application, auto electrical equipment, sale, law and so on and developed 1126 graduates. Zhigong Science and Technology College is directed by China Zhigong Party Hengyang Committee. Mr.WuChuliang is the headmaster and Ms.ZhouPinshan and Mr.ZhuGuangtai are the vice headmasters.

以 70 台光学显微机组成的病理微寄实验室

致公校园

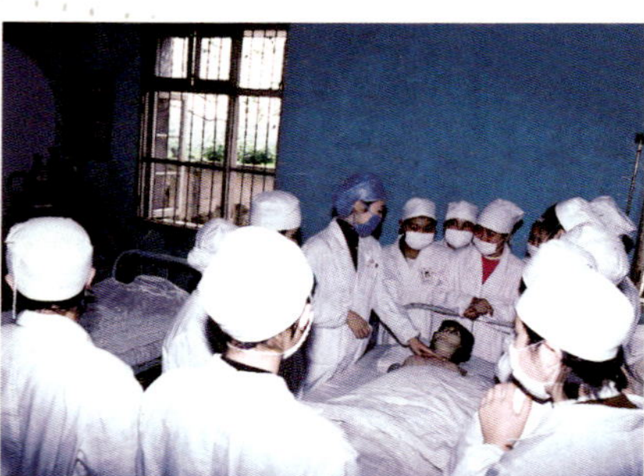

基础护理示教室的教师在上课

湖南省社会力量办学
优秀学校
湖南省教育委员会
一九九七年十二月

岳阳科技进修大学

岳阳科技进修大学系港澳侨胞集资，1993年经省教委批准创办的一所全日制社办高等学校。现有固定资产1050万元，在校学生517人，专兼职教师56名，开设经贸英语、电子技术、企业国贸管理、计算机财会、计算机应用大专课程和经济文秘管理、计算机应用中专课程以及研究生课程班、留学生预科班。该校设北师大硕士课程进修班湖南教学点、北大岳阳函授站、北航湖南远距离教学点、省电大附属中专学校直属教学点。1997年学校被评为全国优秀民办高校，是高等教育学历文凭考试试点院校。

Yueyang Science and Technology College is a full-fime college that ratified by Hunan Education Committee. It was established in 1993 and sponsored by overseas Chinese. It has 10.5 million yuan fixed assets, 517 students, 56 teachers and set up specialized subjects of trade English, electrial technology, business administration, computerized accountant, computer application and economic secretary administration. The college has set up post-graduate course, preparatory course for students preparing to study abroad, Masters' vocational course of Beijing Normal University Hunan teaching center, Yueyang correspondence center of Beijing University, Hunan teaching center of Beijing Aviation University and teaching center of the training school attached to Hunan Radio and Television University. In 1997, Yueyang Science and Technology College was chosen to be the advanced nongovernmental college and experimental college of "national diploma examination".

Honorary Headmaster: Liu Aiqing Liu Haifan
Consultant: LiuJinSheng
Headmaster: Yan Dunwang
Executive Vice Headmaster: Wu Guoxun
Vice Headmaster:Tan Xiushan
Vice Office Director: Xie XianRu
Dean's Office Director: He Zuoren
Students' Office Director: PanNianzhu
Rear-Service Office Director: Li Dayu
Address: Bazimen, Baling Eest Road, Yueyang
Tel: (0730)8711407 8711266

新生军训

学校礼仪队

多媒体语音教学室

名誉校长：刘爱琴　刘海藩
常年顾问：刘金声
校　　长：鄢敦望
常务副校长：邬国勋
副 校 长：谈秀山
办公室副主任：谢先儒
教务处主任：何卓仁
学生处主任：潘念祖
总务处主任：李达钰
地址：岳阳市巴陵东路八字门
电话：(0730)8711407　8711266

校长：鄢敦望

湖南省体育专修学院
湖南娄底小龙武术中专学校

副院长蒋次琰(左)、院长郝钢(中)、常务副院长孔令模在一起共商学院发展大计。

Loudi Xiaolong Wushu Training School is ratified by Hunan Education Committee and established in 1992. It takes up 500mu land and the constructional area has reached to 26,790m^2. The school has 5 million yuan fixed assets, 400 students and 48 teachers (20 of them have middle or senior professional titles). It has set up specialized subjects of wushu, public security, security personnel, computer, secretary and judo. For six years since it was established, the school attended provincial wushu game four times and won a team champion and a team second, at the same time, obtained 6 gold medals, 8 silver medals and 5 brass medals. The school has developed 3,000 graduates for society. In 1997, it was chosen as the first-class nongovernmental school. The school has been classified in the enrollment plan of Hunan in 1998.

Address: Wolongshan, west district, Loudi, Hunan
Tel: (0731) 8616836
PC: 417009

该校1992年经省教委批准创办，占地面积500亩，建筑面积26790平方米，现有固定资产500万元，在校学生400人，教师48人，其中20人具有高中级职称。学校开设武术、公安、保卫、电脑文秘、柔道、保安等专业。建校六年来，四次参加省级以上的武术散手比赛，夺得男女团体冠军和亚军各一次，共获金牌6枚、银牌8枚、铜牌5枚，为社会输送各种需求人才3000名。1997年被评为省属社办一类优良学校，1998年已列入湖南省招生计划。

校址：湖南娄底西区卧龙山
电话：(0738)8616836
邮编：417009

威武的校门

实战军事演练

散手训练

精诚团结的院领导集体

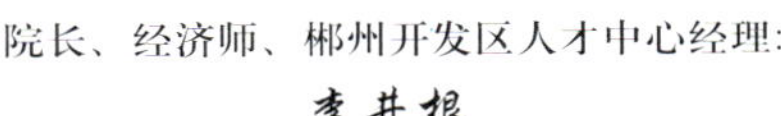

院长、经济师、郴州开发区人才中心经理:
李井根

郴州创业专修学院

校园新貌

Hunan Chengzhou Chuangye College is ratified by Hunan Education Committee and directed by Chengzhou Economy and Technology Developing Zone. With broad campus, peaceful enviroment and a great variety of educational facilites and equipments, the college also has a strong teaching staff of 6 professors, 32 lecturers and specialized subjects of computer information administration, English, public relations and secretary, Chinese literature, computer application, computerize accountant, machinery electronics, electronics and electrial appliance. Hunan Chengzhou Chuangye College has been chosen as "qualified college" and won the title of "first-class college" in the annual evaluation of Hunan Education Committee in 1997.

该院是经省教委批准，由郴州市经济技术开发区人才中心主办的一所全日制学校。校园宽敞、环境幽静，拥有标准、全新的教学楼、宿舍楼、体育运动场和高档次的计算机实验中心，电会模拟实验室、机电实验车间、电子实验室、闭路电视及广播教学系统。学院有正副教授6人，讲师32人，以大、中专学历教育为主。开设计算机信息管理、英语、公关文秘、汉语言文学、计算机应用、电算会计、机电一体化、电子、电器等专业。学院历年被教委评为“合格学校”，1997年省教委年检评估中获“一类学校”称号。

院址：郴州市经济技术开发区内
电话:(0735)2155162
邮编：423000

电脑教学中心

田径比赛

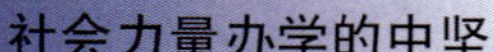

院董事会在学习《社会力量办学条例》

院长、董事长：夏良

该院1988年经省教委批准创办，占地35亩，建筑面积7000多平方米，固定资产520多万元，在校学生600人。学院教学设施配套成龙，师资力量雄厚，教学管理科学，校园环境优美。招生专业：计算机、机电、家电、电算会计、市场营销、烹饪、食品加工、英语、电焊工艺、服装设计、旅游文秘。学生毕业由省教委颁发相应的大、中专文凭，国家承认学历。办学10年来，为国家培养高、中级合格人才3200多人，就业率达95%以上，其中中专毕业生有255人考入中央民族学院、湖南师大、湖南财经学院、湖南农学院等大学深造。

院址：怀化市鹤城区城北南路光明里28号

电话：(0745)2764365　　邮编：418000

怀化英才高等专修学院

微机操作室

校园一角

学生上街宣传《社会力量办学条例》

Hunan Huaihua Yingcai College is ratified by Hunan Education Committee and established in 1988. It takes up 35mu land and the constructional area has reached to 7,000m². The college has more than 5.2 million yuan fixed assets and 600 students. It has set up specialized subjects of computer, machinery electronics, household appliances, computerize accountant, sale, cookery, food processing, English, electric welding, dress designing and travelling secretary. The students' diploma are issued by Hunan Education Committee and acknowledged by the state. It's been 10 years since Hunan Huaihua Yincai College was established and it has developed more than 3,200 graduates. The employment rate of the graduates has amounted to 95% and 255 of them were enrolled by Central Institute for Nationalities, Hunan Normal University, Hunan Finance and Economics Institute and Agriculture Institute for further education.

沅陵工业技术成人中专

该校是经省教委批准，由沅陵县经委主办的一所全日制中专学校。现有固定资产34.6万元，在校学生410人。开设机电、家电维修、电算会计、法律四个专业，附设成人大专函授班和经济管理文秘专业。具有高级职称的教师5人，中级职称和大专毕业以上的青年教师12人。办学6年来毕业学生510人，学校推荐就业率达85%，连续四年被上级教育部门评为办学先进单位。

校址：沅陵县城关镇溪子口

电话:(0745)4222048

邮编：419600

校长、高级会计师：孙久礼

Yuanling Industrial Technology Training School (YITTS) is a normal training school that ratified by Hunan Education Committee and directed by Yuanling Economy Committee. It has 346 thousand yuan fixed assets and 410 students in school. YITTS has set up specialized subjects of machinery electronics, household appliances repair, computerize accountant, law, economy administration, secretary and adult correspondence class.It has 5 senior teachers and 12 young teachers with college educational background. It's been 6 years since YITTS was established and it has developed 510 graduates. The recommending employment rate of YITTS has amounted to 85% and it was honored to be educational advanced unit by higher euducational department for four years.

校园一瞥

机电班在实习

电算会计班在进行电脑操作

家电班在街上进行义务维修

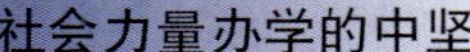

湖南中山财经进修学院

省市领导到校视察。从左至右：原省政协主席刘正、副省长潘贵玉、长沙市副市长张伟玞、原市教委主任杨道正、原省教委主任季益贵

前排自左至右：常务副董事长徐特安、副董事长袁征益、名誉董事长汪浩、董事长徐行方、周振海。后排：副董事长彭焱生、龚业隆、李炳炎、周宏斌、副校长蔡士德、校长陈满清

湖南中山财经进修学院1979年经教委批准创办。现有固定资产30万元，在校生202人，学院开设会计、统计、企业管理、工商管理、金融、法律、旅游、财税、股票等专业。名誉董事长汪浩，创始人董事长徐行方，院长陈满清，副院长蔡士德。历届毕业生7400人。

院址：长沙市蔡锷北路民主东街22号

电话：(0731)4315221　　邮编：410005

Hunan Zhongshan Economy College is ratified by Hunan Education Committee and established in 1979. It has 300 thousand yuan fixed assets and 202 students. The college has set up specialized subjects of accountant, statistics, enterprise administration, business administration, finance, travelling, tax and stock and developed 7400 graduates

Honorary Chairman: WangHao

Chairman: Xu Xingfang

Headmaster: Chen Manqing

Vice Headmaster: Cai Shide

Address: Mingzhu East Street 22#, Caier Road, Changsha

Tel: (0731)-4315221

PC: 410005

图书阅览室

电脑室一角

院长带领学生拍摄电影《桑植起义》

武术专业课

长沙武术中专学校

长沙武术中专学校是1997年经省教委审批和直属领导的全日制学校。现有固定资产40万元，在校学生400人。学校环境优雅、设施齐全、具有现代化的训练教学场所；师资力量雄厚，有一大批高级文武教师和教练；开设武术、影视驾驶、礼仪、电脑等专业。学校以习武为主，兼以修文、文武并重和兼学职业技术的方式培养人才，先后有600人学成毕业安排了工作。

地址：望城县城雷锋西路166号

电话:(0731)8063458

邮编：410200

Changsha Wushu Training School was established in 1992. It is ratified and directed by Hunan Education Committee. The school has 400 thousand fixed assets and 400 students in school. With graceful enviornment, complete facilities, modernized teaching and training arena, and an experienced teaching staff, the school has set up wushu,driving, etiquette and computer specialized subjects. Changsha Wushu Training School emphasizes in wushu training and deals with vocational education concurrently. It has developed 600 graduates and all of them found satisfactory jobs.

Headmaster: Shun Liangping

Address: Leifeng West Road 166#, Wangcheng county

Tel: (0731) 8063458

PC: 410200

省委、省军区首长检阅该校学生

校长：孙亮平

长沙黄埔外语进修学院

该院创办于1990年，系省教委批准举办的一所以英语专业为主的社会高等学院。学院教学设备先进、生活设施齐全，并有一支教学经验丰富的教师队伍。办学八年，年年评为长沙市先进助学单位。1997年省教委年终评估为一类学校，并被列入湖南省高等教育学历文凭试点院校。毕(结)业学生1325人被推荐到北京、深圳、广州、中山、长沙等地工作，赢得了教育行政部门、用人单位、学生和家长的赞誉。

院址：长沙市青园路
电话：(0731)5582272
邮编：410004

Changsha Huangpu Foreign Language College is a nongovernmental college that ratified by Hunan Education Committee. The college has advanced teaching equipments, complete life facilities and an experienced teaching staff. It's been eight yeas since Huangpu Foreign Language College was established and it has been honored to be advanced educational unit continuously. In 1997, it was evaluated to be the first-class college and chosen to be one of the experimental college of "national diploma examination" by Hunan Education Committee. 1,325 graduates were recommended to work in Beijing, Shengzhen, Guangzhou, Zhongshan and Changsha etc. and the college has been highly appreciated by educational administration department, corporation and factory, students and parents.

◀ 邓树林院长(右)和唐进副院长在一起共商学院发展大计

▲电脑教学室

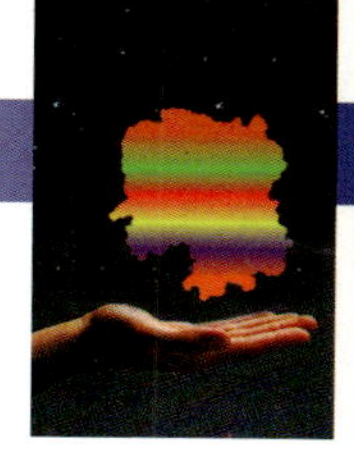

衡阳光明成人中等专业学校

精诚团结的校领导集体

衡阳光明成人中等专业学校1981年经教委批准创办。现有固定资产1000万元，在校学生1240人。学校开设计算机应用、电子电器、汽修、服装制作与设计、旅游服务、电脑文秘、市场营销、电会等专业。创始人陈植森，董事长王超然，校长高杨鑫，副校长黄炳华，校长助理刘祖光、刘培德。历届毕业生43284人。

校址：衡阳市江东区蒋家山1号
电话：(0734)8350630
邮编：421008

电脑教学中心　　光明学校全景中一角　　图书室一角

Hengyang Guangming Adult Training School is ratified by Hunan Education Committee and established in 1981. It is situated at Jiangjiashan 1#, Jiangdong district of Hengyang and has 10 million yuan fixed assets and 1,240 students in school. The school has set up specialized subjects of computer application, electronics and electrical appliance, automobile repairing, dress designing, travelling service, secretary, sale and computerized accountant and developed 43,284 graduates.

Founder: Chen Zhisen
Chairman: Wang Chaoran
Headmaster: GaoYangxin
Vice Headmaster:Huang Binhua
Assistant Headmaster: Liu Zhuguang, Liu Peide
Tel: (0734)8350630
PC:421008

世界粮食计划

倒虹吸管工程

杉木林

公路

排灌分家综合片

署在中国湘西

世界粮食计划署无偿援助的武陵山区乡村基础设施建设项目（项目编号3779），自1991年11月起在湘西花垣、保靖、永顺三县正式实施。在改善农业生产条件和农村运输条件，提高农民素质，保持农业生态平衡等方面已取得显著成效。

The World Food Programme assistants Wuling mountainous area for infrastrucure with no pay(Project No.3779). It has been carried out in Huayuan, Baojing and Yongshun counties of Xiangxi since Novmber, 1991. It has achevied a lot in improving agricultral production conditions, countryside transportation and competence level of farmers, and in keeping the balance of nature.

旱改水全景

渡槽

湖南 3779 项目中综合治理后的全景

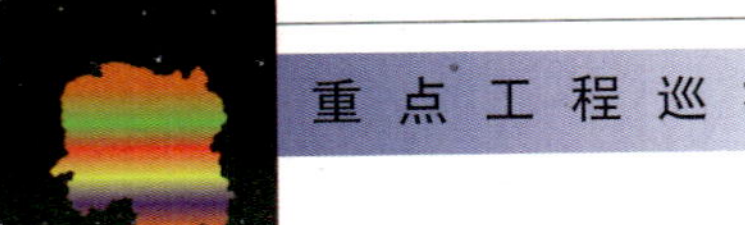

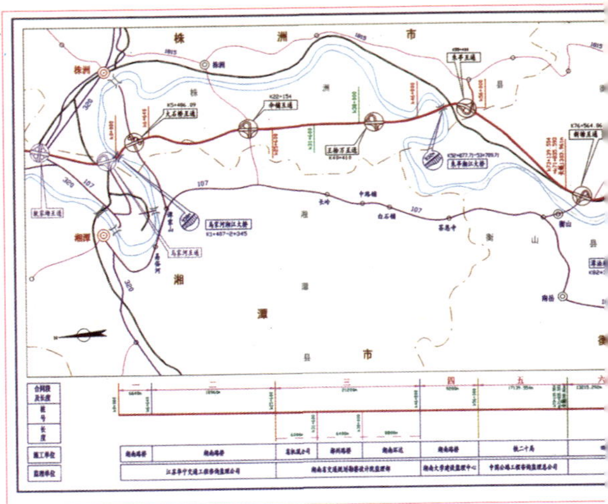

王茂林(左三)、周伯华(左二)、颜永盛(左六)等省市领导为湘耒高速公路奠基。

省交通厅厅长李安在开工典礼上致词

1997年4月25日，“施工监理合同签字仪式”在衡阳花园宾馆举行。

公司经理杨志达(左二)陪同交通厅张清华工程师(右一)，省交通厅马其伟副厅长(右二)、世界银行官员尼克松先生(左一)到施工现场检查考察。

湘耒路
听取监理工

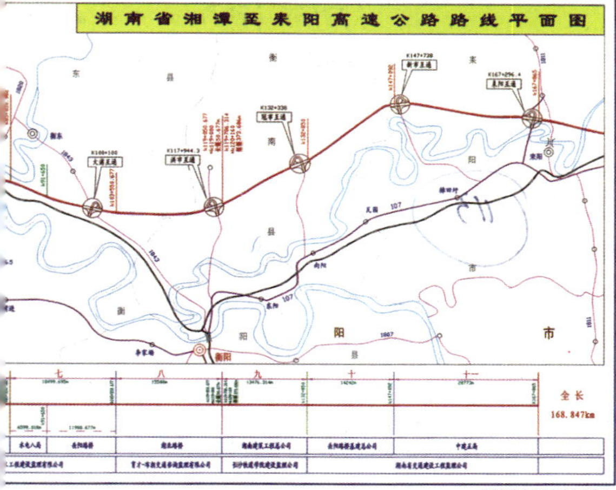

Xianglei Expressway is the component of the "Hunan-Guangzhou Expressway" project and also a section of the national key "JINZHU" expressway. It starts in Jijiahe of Xiangtan district and ends in Chengjiaping of Leiyang district. The whole length of Xianglei expressway is 168.847km. and the designed speed is 120km. per hour. Xianglei expressway's total investment is 4.142 billion yuan, among which 200 million yuan loan from the World Bank. It is the important economic artery of Hunan and its construction will also promote the all-round development of steel, construction materials and transportation industry. Xianglei expressway project is undertaken by Xianglei Expressway Construction Developing Co.Ltd.

湘耒高速公路是广东至湖南高速公路走廊项目的组成部分，也是国家南北主干线京珠高速公路的一段，它起于长潭高速公路的终点湘潭马家河，止于耒阳市以东的陈家坪，全长168.847公里，设计时速120公里，总投资41.42 亿元，其中世行贷款2亿美元。该路是湖南省的重要经济干线，它的建设对湖南及沿线各市、县的经济建设和经济发展起着举足轻重的作用，将带动钢材业、建材业、运输业、旅游业等三产业的全面发展。该项目由湖南省湘耒高速公路建设开发有限公司负责建设经营管理。（供稿：李剑雄）

公司经理杨志达(右二)率领公司副经理余超良(右一)、赵平(左二)、熊瑞文(左一)等在工地进行检查考核。

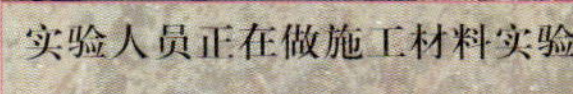

实验人员正在做施工材料实验

理代表吴亚中同志(右二)在施工现场
工报施工监理情况。

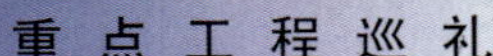

东洞庭湖南大防洪堤

In 1997, the second stage project of harnessing Dongting lake has been examined and approved by the central government. The investment will rearch 5.95 billion yuan, and the earth and stone work will be 0.39 billion cubic metre. As eight narvy ships from Dutch working on the lake, dyke building, channel harnessing, electric irrigation renewing and flood safty area constructing, this project will come into a fully practical stage.

1997年洞庭湖二期治理工程初步设计通过国家审批，预计总投资59.5亿元，工程总土石方3.9亿立方米。随着8条荷兰进口大型挖泥船进入洞庭湖通疏清淤，洞庭湖二期治理已进入全面实施阶段。

汉寿岩汪湖电排站

大东口水闸

局长 周松鹤

洞庭湖防洪蓄洪工程局

湖南世行贷款粮食流通项目分布在长沙、岳阳、益阳、常德等四个粮食产销量大的城市。总投资26327万元，其中世行贷款1467万美元。到1999年项目全面竣工，每年通过城陵矶中转调出发运到省外和国外的大米达82万吨；通过城陵矶中转接收从东北调入的玉米、大豆，国外进口的小麦达60万吨。全省将形成较为完整的粮食流通网络。

The world bank loan project on Hunan grain circulation is underway in four cities, i.e. Changsha, Yueyang, Yiyang and Changde, where are major grain production and marketing districts. The investment for this project will be 263.27 million yuan. In this investment, World Bank will invest USD 14.67 million.

By 1999 of completion for the project, the capacity of allocation and transportation will reach 820 million kg rice through chenglinji to outside Hunan province and abroad, and 600 million kg corn, soybean from northeast China and wheat from abroad to Hunan. Therefore, the net work for grain circulation will be formed integratedly in Hunan.

1995年1月，省市领导参加岳阳城陵矶粮食专用码头开工典礼并为工程奠基。

周时昌副省长与世行第11次监理团副团长奈伯格先生亲切会谈。

岳阳城陵矶3000吨粮食专用码头

岳阳城陵矶20000吨容量立筒库

长常高速公路

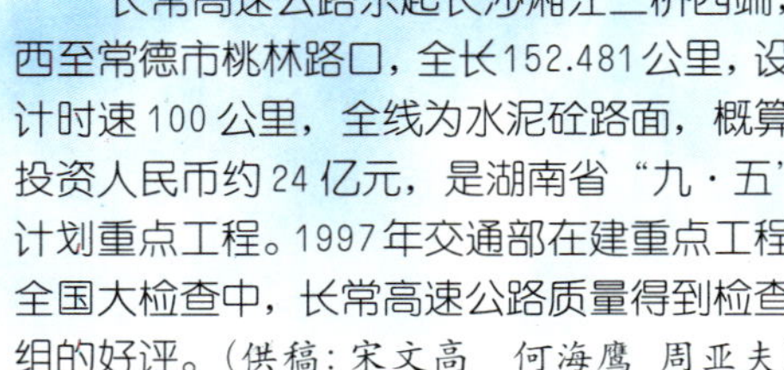
长常高速公路东起长沙湘江二桥西端，西至常德市桃林路口，全长152.481公里，设计时速100公里，全线为水泥砼路面，概算投资人民币约24亿元，是湖南省“九·五”计划重点工程。1997年交通部在建重点工程全国大检查中，长常高速公路质量得到检查组的好评。(供稿：宋文高　何海鹰　周亚夫)

Chang-chang express way is from the west side of the second bridge of Xiangjiang river to Taolin road of Changde. With cement road surface, the express way's whole length is 152.481km, the designed speed is 100km. per hour and the budgetary investment is about 2.4 billion yuan. It is the key project of national "Jiuwu" plan. Chang-chang express way was highly praised by Transport Department in the examination of national key projects in 1997.

石长铁路全线胜利铺通

由铁道部和湖南省共同投资建设的石长铁路，全长264公里，途经常德、益阳、宁乡等12个市县(区)，设计为国家Ⅰ级路网干线，设计修正概算为33.0965亿元。设计运输能力：近期(2000年)年货运量为1700万吨，客车6对；远期(2005年)年货运量为1900万吨，客车8对。石长铁路1995年被列入国家重点建设项目，由石长铁路有限责任公司按照《公司法》经营管理。公司连续三年被省政府评为“重点建设项目责任目标管理先进单位”，并授予“企业精神文明建设优秀成果奖”。

总经理：刘自湖

Shichang Railway constructional project is jointly invested by Ministry of Railway of China and Hunan province. With the whole length of 264km., Shichang railway is via 12 districts including Changde, Yiyang and Ningxiang. Shichang railway is designed to be the first-class national railway network line and the budget is 3.30965 billion yuan. The designed transportation capacity of Shichang railway is: up to the year of 2000, the annual volume of rail freight is 17 million tons and with 6 pairs of coaches; up to the year of 2005, the annual volume of rail freight is 19 million tons and with 8 pairs of coaches.In 1995, Shichang Railway was classified as the national focal construction project and administered by SRC(Shichang Railway Co. Ltd.) according to the COMPANY ACT. SRC was given the title of “advanced unit” by Hunan provincial government for three years and was awarded”excellent cultural and ideological progress of enterprise” prize.

石长铁路有限责任公司

为了人民的健康
——湖南省人民医院

院党委书记、副院长莫春华(左)与院长刘信赋

湖南省人民医院始建于1912年，现设52个临床、医技科室，床位1000张，现有固定资产1.8亿元，其中大型仪器设备价值4500万元；职工1200人，其中副高以上专业技术职称人员111人。1997年投资1亿多元建成的湖南重点工程项目——门诊、住院大楼，建筑面积39224平方米，楼内装有中央空调、中心给氧、中心吸引、呼叫系统和综合智能布线系统。日门诊量可达2500人次。该院1995年被卫生部授予“三级甲等医院”。

Hunan People's Hospital was established in 1912. It has 52 medical departments, 1000 beds, 180 million yuan fixed assets (the high standard medical equipment valued 45 million yuan), 111 senior technicians among 1200 employees. In 1997, Hunan People's Hospital invested more than 100 million yuan to build a large clinical building. With 39,224m^2 constructional areas, the building is equipped with central air conditioning and central oxygen supplying system, central aspirator, calling system and comprehensive intelligent wiring system. More than 2,500 outpatients can be received each day by the new clinical building. In 1995, Hunan People's Hospital was granted "third-class Grade A hospital" by Public Health Ministry of China.

省委常委、省人大常委会副主任王克英、省卫生厅副厅长刘爱华在医院基建工地现场办公

新门诊、住院大楼全景

大源渡枢纽的千吨级船闸

湘江航运建设二期工程系国家重点工程建设项目，是我国内河首批利用世行贷款项目之一。工程总投资18.95亿元，其中世行贷款9000万美元。该工程旨在改善株洲至衡阳182公里湘江航道，使之与已建成的株洲至城陵矶257公里千吨级航道相衔接，从而形成由衡阳经株洲、湘潭、长沙、岳阳、城陵矶到长江的水运主通道。

The second stage project of Xiangjiang river shipping construction is a national key project, and one of first item utilizing World Bank loan. The investment of the project is 1.895 billion yuan. In this investment, World Bank will invest USD 90 million. This project aim at improving 182 km. channel of Xiangjiang river from Zhuzhou to Hengyang which make a linkage with 257 km. channel of one million kilogram from Zhuzhou to Chenglinji. Therefore, the main shipping channel will be formed from Hengyang via Zhuzhou, Xiangtan, Changsha, Yueyang, Chenglinji to Yangzi river.

交通部副部长胡希捷在省交通厅李安厅长陪同下视察大源渡枢纽工地

省委书记王茂林在大源渡工地指导工作

世界银行中国业务部驻中国代表处局长、首席代表黄青川先生一行到大源渡工地检查项目实施情况

湘江航运建设二期工程

正在施工的大源渡枢纽大坝和电站厂房

湖南国贸金融中心位于长沙市中心芙蓉路228号，由中外合资湖南湘迪置业发展有限公司开发建设，总投资2.2亿元，总建筑面积9.7万平方米，主楼50层，高150米，集商贸、金融、办公、商住、娱乐、餐饮于一体，被誉为“三湘第一楼”。

Hunan International Trade and Financial Center is located at Furong Road 228# of Changsha. It is developed by Hunan Xiangdi Co. Ltd. With the total investment of 220 million yuan, the total constructional area of 97,000m², 50 stories with 150 meters high, an organic whole of trade, finance, office, residence, entertainment and restaurant, Hunan International Trade and Financial Center is honored to be the "No. 1 building" of Hunan.

湘迪置业发展有限公司

湖南省公路桥梁建设总公司

胜利完成铜陵长江公路大桥，雄居国内路桥施工单位前列的湖南省公路桥梁建设总公司是国内最具影响的国家一级路桥施工企业。公司下辖20个分公司，现有职工3500人，各类机械设备3600多台套，现值4亿元。1997年完成建安产值9亿元。享有湖南省“AAA”信誉称号。数十次荣获国家、省、部级科技进步成果奖及优质工程项目奖，为全国500家最大经营规模建筑企业中的百强企业。

Hunan Road and Bridge Construction Corporation(HRBCC) is a first-class state-owned enterprise with eminent fame. It has successfully finished building Tongling bridge recently. HRBCC has 20 subsidiaries, 3,500 employees and more than 3,600 set of various mechanic equipments which valued 400 million yuan. The output value of HRBCC amounted to 900 million yuan in 1997. HRBCC enjoyed"AAA" honorary title in Hunan and won dozens of medals and prizes awarded by the state, ministry and province. HRBCC is one of the best enterprises among 500 large-scaled construction corporations of China.

衡阳市金果农工商实业股份有限公司

衡阳市金果农工商实业股份有限公司是全国供销系统在深交所首批上市公司，拥有22家分公司和子公司，员工10000余人，总股本1.04亿股。公司以推动农业产业化为己任，坚持“一业为主，多业并举；一地为主，多地发展；国内为主，跨国经营”的方针，企业资本迅速扩张，经营规模不断壮大，1997年实现销售总额2.38亿元，利润2802万元，上缴税金1283万元，比上年同期分别增长49.5%、82.4%和368%，被评为全国供销合作系统先进集体。

董事长兼总经理：胡振斌

Hengyang Jingguo Limited-liability Co. Ltd. (HJLCL) is the transactional company of Shengzhen Stock Exchange. It has 22 subsidiaries and more than 10,000 employees and the total capital stock is 104 million shares. Insisting on the policy of “stressing agriculiture and domestic market, developing other business and overeas market simultaneously” and expanding the sale scale continuously, HJLCL created 238 million yuan sales volume, 28.02 million yuan profit and 12.38 million yuan tax in 1997, respectively increased by 49.5%,82.4%,368% than the previous year . At the same time, HJLCL was granted “advanced unit” by China Supply and Marketing Cooperative Department.

省长杨正午（中）、副省长周伯华（左四）在金果公司视察。

省委副书记储波（前排右一）在公司检查指导工作。

1997年5月22日，董事长兼总经理胡振斌接过深圳证券交易所赠送的金锤，敲响了“金果实业”A股上市的钟声。

董事长兼总经理：王锡炳

湖南酒鬼酒股份有限公司

敲响湘酒鬼A股上市金钟

公司主要生产和销售湘泉酒、酒鬼酒系列白酒及陶瓷、包装等配套产品。产品畅销全国和东南亚欧美市场，先后五次荣获世界及国际博览会金奖，同时获得“国产精品”、“名牌消费品”、“世界名牌消费品”、“湖南著名商标”等荣誉称号。

1997年底，公司拥有总资产9.27亿元，其中固定资产2.60亿元，流动资产6.67亿元；实现销售收入41026万元，比上年增长47%，经济效益居同行业前列。1997年“湘酒鬼”股票被深交所选为成份指数样本股。

Hunan Jiuguijiu Limited-Liability Corporation is mainly manufacturing and marketing the “XIANG QUAN” alcohol, “JIUGUIJIU” alcohol series, ceramics and package. The products of the corporation are in great demand all over the country and foreign market and were successively awarded the gold medal of international fairs, at the same time, they won the honorary titles of “domestic excellent products”, “famous consumer goods”, “world famous consumer goods”, “Hunan famous trade-mark” etc. By the end of 1997, Jiuguijiu Limited-liability Corporation has owned 927 million yuan capital (260 million yuan fixed assets and 667 million yuan floating capital). It has created 410.26 million yuan marketing income in 1997, increased by 47% than the previous year and made great economic benefits. In the same year, “Xiangjiugui” stock was chosen as the sample stock by Shenzhen Stock Exchange.

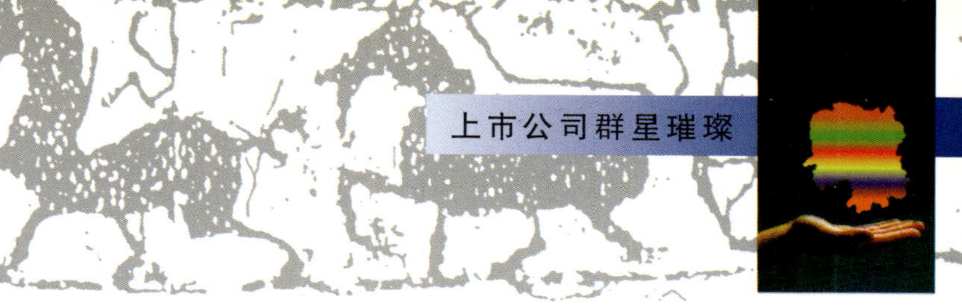

五一文

湖南五一文实业股份有限公司

湖南五一文实业股份有限公司是湖南省文化用品、现代办公设备经营领域中的主导企业，系1996年度A股上市公司，下辖11个分支机构。本着“永不满足、高度负责”的企业精神，根据市场的发展变化，不断创新经营策略。公司由借款一万元起步、发展，截至1997年12月底止，企业总资产达5.07亿元，净资产为2.4亿元。1997年商品销售额达4.89亿元，实现利润3135.96万元，经济效益居全省同行业前茅；长期以来，公司致力于“推进文明、服务社会”；“拥有文化、拥有明天”，五一文专用宣传语已为社会各界所熟悉；曾荣获“全国五一劳动奖状”、“全国优秀集体商业企业”、“湖南省商业企业十佳”等多种荣誉，连续六年获得长沙市文明单位称号、连续两年获得省级文明单位称号，在全省、全国均具较高知名度。

长沙五一文化用品商场 位于省会长沙市的中心商业特区五一广场，五个营业层面，经营文化用品与现代办公设备，系全国最大的文化用品零售商店。商场同时是公司文化用品连锁经营的总部，已在长沙、株洲、湘潭、岳阳、常德、衡阳开设八家连锁店。

五一文北斗星商厦 是长沙北城最大的多功能商厦，建筑面积3.9万平方米，十层营业面积共2.8万平方米。商厦具有浓郁的文化氛围、舒适的休闲环境和自1996年元月开业以来已树立起“以文兴商”的独特形象。

五一文快速彩印公司 是1995年初设立的从事制版印刷、实行产销一体化的新型企业。凭借人才与设备等诸多优势和追求完美的精神，已为省内外许多知名企业及文化、新闻、出版单位设计、印制高档优质的宣传品。

董事长：范涤尘

湖南海利化工股份有限公司是湖南在上海第一家高科技股份制上市公司。1997年公司实施"产品经营和资本经营并重"的发展思路，全年主营业务收入23438.38万元，实现利润总额3352.80万元，分别比上年增长31.54%和19.30%；产品出口创汇198.86万美元，比上年增加21.70%。近年来，公司先后荣获"全国高新技术百强企业"、"国家火炬计划重点高新技术企业"、"湖南省十强高新技术企业"等荣誉称号。

省长杨正午、副省长潘贵玉到海利视察

湖南海利化工股份有限公司

Hunan Haili Chemical Industry Limited-liability Company (HHCILC) is the first high-technology stock transactional company appeared on the Shanghai stock market in Hunan. In 1997, HHCILC implemented the policy of "lay equal stress on both sales administration and capital management" and obtained income of 234,383,800 yuan and profit amounted to 33,528,000 yuan, increased respectively by 31.54% and 19.3% than the previous year. HHCILC's export income was US$1,988,600 in 1997, increased by 21.7% than the last year. Because of its extraordinary achievements, HHCILC was awarded a lot of honorary title including "one of the 100 most powerful high-technology enterprises" and "key high-technology enterprise of national 'torch plan'" and "one of the ten top high-technology enterprises of Hunan" etc. in recent years.

科研生产开发基地

全国优秀新农药克百威
海利主导产品：

湖南古汉集团是一个融科、工、贸于一体，跨地区、跨行业、多层次、多元化发展的大型企业集团，是以独家生产中国中药名牌产品“古汉养生精”等八大剂型，四十个品种的中成药和系列保健饮料而著称的上市公司。公司现有员工2019人，各类专业技术人员302人，占员工总数的15%。截止1997年底，公司拥有总资产37315万元，1997年实现利润总额为2839万元。

Hunan Guhan Group(HGG) is a large, comprehensive and diversified enterprise and an organic whole of science, industry and trade. It is also a stock transactional company and famous for its well-known brand "GU HAN YANG SHENG JING"and forty kinds of Chinese herbal medicine and health beverage series. HGG has 302 technicians among 2019 employees. By the end of 1997, HGG has owned 373.15 million yuan fixed assets and created 28.39 million yuan profit in 1997.

董事长兼总经理：申甲球

湖南古汉集团股份有限公司

全国“五一”劳动奖章获得者、长沙市文物工作队队长、副研究员：宋少华

1997年9月，李鹏总理在省委领导陪同下，在北京展览馆参观长沙三国吴简

长沙市文物工作队
长沙市文物考古研究所

宋少华向中国社科院考古研究所的专家介绍望城坡古坟院西汉长沙王后渔阳墓的发掘情况

文物工作者在长沙走马楼三国吴简发掘现场工作

长沙市文物工作队暨长沙市文物考古研究所隶属于长沙市文化局。现有各类高、中级技术人员和考古专业人才30余人，并负责管理“八路军驻湘通讯处旧址”、“湖南自修大学旧址”两处纪念馆。1993年发掘西汉长沙王后渔阳墓获得’93全国十大考古新发现。1996年发掘长沙走马楼三国孙吴纪年简牍获得’96全国十大考古新发现，被誉为世纪性考古成果，并被评为双文明先进单位，授予保护发掘长沙三国吴简先进集体。

Changsha Relics Investigation Group viz. Changsha Relics & Archaeology Institution is under the jurisdication of Changsha Culture Bureau. It has more than 30 technicians and archaeological experts and is engaged in the administration work of the “communicational site of the former BALU Army” and the “site of the former Hunan Self-study University.” The discovery of “Yuyang grave of Changsha Queen in Xihan dynasty of China” was awarded “one of the top ten discoveries of China in 1993”. In 1996, the discovery of “Changsha Zoumalou’s tablet chronological record of Shunwu in Sanguo period” was highly appraised and awarded “one of the top ten discoveries of China in 1996.” Changsha Relics & Archaeology Institution has been awarded the “double civilization advanced unit” for many times and honored to be the advanced unit of protecting and discovering the “Shuwu tablet chronological record”.

长沙市文物工作队（文物考古研究所）领导班子（中为宋少华）

宋少华向中央、省里领导汇报长沙三国吴简的整理工作

宋少华向国务委员、军委副主席迟浩田将军汇报长沙吴简的发掘整理工作

科 研 奇 葩

1991年3月16日，江泽民总书记视察湖南杂交水稻研究中心（右为中心主任袁隆平）

1994年12月16日，李鹏总理视察杂交水稻研究中心

国家杂交水稻工程技术研究中心

该中心由著名科学家“杂交水稻之父”袁隆平院士任主任，现有中高级科技人员81人。是全国三系杂交水稻科研攻关和“863”两系杂交稻课题的主持单位。“中心”主任袁隆平院士荣获我国第一个特等发明奖和联合国、美国、日本等8项国际大奖。近十年来，“中心”共取得科技成果50多项，其中获国家级奖4项，部、省级奖10多项。

National Hybrid Rice Research Center(NHRRC) has 81 senior technicians and scientists. Professor Yuan Nongping, the famous academician and “father of hybrid rice” is the chairman. NHRRC is engaged in the national scientific research item of three-line hybrid rice and two-line hybrid rice problem of national “863” plan. The chairman Yuan Nongping has won the first top grade invention prize of China and eight international prizes that awarded by United Nations, America and Japan etc. In recent years, NHRRC has obtained more than 50 achievements in scientific research, 4 of them was awarded national prizes and 10 of them was awarded Ministry and provincial prize.

长沙马王堆蔬菜批发交易市场

马王堆蔬菜批发交易市场占地55亩，1991年正式投入营运。该市场坚持“以平衡市场、服务长沙蔬菜供应为己任，立足引进、培育和调控”创出了一条企业办市场的新路。目前，年成交量6亿多公斤，创利润400多万元。1997年李岚清副总理将市场建设模式在全国蔬菜流通体制改革会上向全国推介。1998年该市场被定为国家级市场，被省财办授予十佳文明市场。

Mawangdui Vegetable Terminal Market takes up 55mu land and was in operation in 1991. With the goal of supplying the vegetable of changsha and making balanceable market, the principle of “introducing, cultivating, controlling”, Mawangdui Vegetable Terminal market has developed its characteristic management way. At present, the annual volume of business of the market has amounted to more than 600 million kg. and created over 4 million yuan profit. In 1997, vice premier LiLanqing recommended the constructional mode of Mawangdui Vegetable Terminal Market to the whole country in the conference of national vegetable circulating structure reform. Mawnagdui Vegetable Terminal Market has been defined as the “national market” and awarded “one of the top market”, by Hunan Financial Department.

长沙市委书记阳宝华视察市场

市场领导班子，右四为总经理王正坤，右五为书记沈绍桂。

明星企业

建市三年 成就辉煌

——郴州市

Chengzhou is the southern entrance of Hunan province. It has 19,400 square km. areas and 4,447,600 population, and has jurisdiction on 2 districts, 1 city and 8 counties. Since the the strategic policy of "opening to the world, emphasizing on agriculture, promoting industry and applying science" was implimented in 1994 ,the position of Chengzhou's GNP (Gross National Product) moved up from the 12 place of 1994 to the 10 place of Hunan in 1997 and fulfilled the economic strategic plan 3 years ahead of time. In 1997 , the GNP of Chengzhou amounted to 18.951 billion yuan, increased by 43.2% than 1994. The annual growth rate of Chengzhou' s GNP exceeds 1.2% compared with the average growth rate of Hunan province. As for the comprehensive evaluation of the development of economy and society, Chengzhou situated in the second place for two years in the scope of Hunan province.

市委书记：梅克保

市长：龙定鼎

郴州是湖南的"南大门"，土地总面积1.94万平方公里，辖2区1市8县，总人口444.76万人。自1994年确立"开放兴郴，重农富民，兴工强市，科教兴业"的发展战略以来，全市国内生产总值在全省的位次由1994年的第12位上升到第10位，提前三年实现了国内生产总值翻两番的战略目标。1997年，全市国内生产总值达189.51亿元，比1994年增长43.2%，比全省平均增幅高1.2个百分点，经济和社会发展综合评价，郴州连续两年位居全省第二名。

省委书记王茂林(右一)视察桂阳优质烟基地

省长杨正午(右一)视察郴州城市规划

风景秀丽的郴州城

湖南省长沙经济技术开发区位于长沙市东郊星沙镇，地处319国道与107国道及京珠高速公路交汇处，距长沙市中心和火车站8公里，距黄花国际机场8公里。规划面积20平方公里，第一期开发面积14平方公里。开发区鼓励工业，高新技术及服务业的投入，亦欢迎外商投资者自带项目对开发区内的土地进行成片开发。长沙经济技术开发区热忱欢迎海内外有识之士来此大展鸿图。

Changsha Economic and Technological Development Zone is located in Xingsha Town, east suburb of Changsha. 319 national road, 107 national road and Jinzhu expressway are converged on Xingsha town. It is about 8km. apart from Huanghua international airport and 8km. apart from the center of Changsha city and railway station. The planed area of the zone is 20 square kilometer and the first phase of the developing area is 14 square kilometer. The development zone encourage investments on industry, high-technology and service and welcome foreign investors to exploit land in development zone for their own project. Changsha Economic and Technological Development Zone is waiting for the investors from home and abroad to come to creat brilliant achivements.

主任：汤定一

长沙经济技术开发区

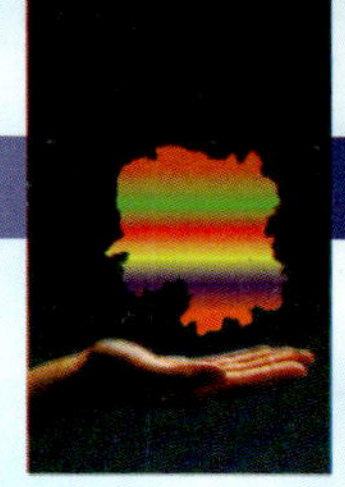

中国投资银行长沙分行

分行领导集体。右二为行长王晓东

中国投资银行长沙分行是中国投资银行按照经济区划和规模经济原则在湖南地区设置的一级分行，是以承担世界银行、亚洲开发银行工业信贷转贷业务为主的金融机构。先后筹资2亿余美元，重点支持了湖南省机械、电子、纺织、化工、建材、包装、外贸等行业60多个项目的基础建设、技术改造、出口创汇。该行实施“客户战略”，靠金融产品、服务品牌、经营特色打入市场，开展多元化的银行服务，为振兴三湘经济做出更大的贡献。

China Investment Bank Changsha Branch(CIBCB) is a first-class financial organization that set up in Hunan according to the principle of economic zone classification and economy scale, it mainly deals with the business of industrial credit and loan transference of World Bank and Asia Developing Band. CIBCB has raised more than US$200 million to support the infrastructure construction, technical innovation and export of over 60 projects in machinery, electronics, construction materials, package and foreign trade field etc. Relying on the best service and characteristic management, implementing “customer strategy” and developing diversified banking service, CIBCB will do much more contribution to promote the economy of Hunan.

Hunan Tobacco Corporation, a member of China's tobacco corporation , is a corporate enterprise which undertakes supplying and marketing, personnel, financial and material, also of domestic and international trade integrated tnanageinent mode for the administration of Hunan tobacco industry . In 1997, it produced cigarette of 2.234 million boxes, tobacco leaves of 200 million kg, increased by 92.31 percent than the last year. 20,659 boxes of cigarette and 31,800 kg tobacco leaves was exported and the export value hit USD 3.24 million. Tax and net profit hit 7.2 billion yuan , up 12.5 per cent over last year, ranking second in developed China's industry during last seven years.

湖南省烟草专卖局局长
湖南省烟草公司经理
张登武

烟草专家在湖南烟叶基地考察

优质烟叶

湖南省烟草公司是隶属中国烟草总公司，对全省烟草行业产供销、人财物、内外贸实行统一管理的法人企业。1997年，共生产卷烟223.4万箱，生产收购烟叶20万吨，比上年增长92.31%，出口卷烟2.0659万箱，出口烟叶31.8吨，创汇342万美元。实现工商税利 72亿元，比上年增长12.5%，连续七年居全国同行第二位。

现代化卷接包车间

湖南盐业集团

省委常委、常务副省长周伯华(左二)视察湖南盐业并作重要讲话。左一为集团董事长陈保民、左三为集团党委书记吴忆萍、左四为集团总经理胡红江

集团总部大门

湖南盐业集团是经湖南省人民政府批准组建的科、工、贸一体化、运输、原材料、加工业配套的大型企业集团，其综合经济实力处于全国同行业领先水平。集团以深化企业改革为动力，立足于盘活现有企业资产存量，合理配置资源，以资产联结为纽带，建立母子公司体系，将企业改革、改组、改造和加强企业管理有机结合，形成高起点、高技术、专业化、大规模、高效益的生产经营格局。到2000年，集团资产达到24亿元，年销售额达30亿元，确保了2000年湖南达到消除碘缺乏之病的阶段目标。

集团控股公司之一、湖南最大的制盐企业——湘澧盐矿

集团控股公司之一——湘衡盐矿

集团独资兴建的晶鑫大酒店

Hunan Salting Group(HSG) was ratifed to be estabished by Hunan provincial government.It is a large organic whole of science,industry and commerce and also deals with the business of transportation,raw materials and processing.The comprehensive economic capability of HSG stands in the forefront among the competitors of China.With the deepening of the enterprise's reform,HSG kept a foothold on digesting stock in hand and disposing resources rationally. At the same time,HSG built a link system between parent company and subsidiaries,and combined the reform, reorganization with the management of enterprises organically, therefore, formed a large-scaled, efficient,specilized and high-technological manufacturing and managing pattern of enterprise.Up to the year of 2000,the capital and annual sales volume of HSG will be respectively amounted to 2.4 billion yuan and 3 billion yuan,at the same time,the iodine deficiency disease in Hunan will be eradicated on the whole.

省委副书记郑培民来厂视察工作

零陵卷烟厂是国有大二型企业。现有职工2500人，固定资产5.89亿元，初具年产卷烟50万箱的能力。主要产品“红豆”系列、“芝城”系列以及传统名优产品“九嶷”、“金婚”等畅销全国20多个省市，其中“红豆”是全国49种名优卷烟品牌和“湖南省著名商标”。1997年，实现销售收入15.18亿元，实现税利7.1亿元。该厂先后荣获“全国先进基层党组织”、“全国五一劳动奖状”、“全国模范职工之家”称号。

Lingling Cigarette Factory is the state-owned second-class enterprise.It has 2500 employees,589 million yuan fixed assets and the annual production capability of 500,000 cases of cigarette.The "HONGDOU","ZHICHENG","JIUYI"and"JINHUN" series of Lingling Cigarette Factory are the well-known brands and on sale in over 20 provinces and cities of China."HONGDOU"is one of the top cigarette brand of China and has won the title of "Hunan famous trademark".In 1997,Lingling Cigarette Factory's total sales income amounted to 1.518 billion yuan and created 710 million yuan tax and profit.Lingling Cigarette Factory has been successively awarded the titles of "national advanced basic Party branch", "WUYI certificate of merit"and "national model family of workers".

环境秀丽的厂区

厂长、党委书记：武俊瑶

湖南零陵卷烟厂

湖南雪峰水泥集团有限公司

公司董事长兼党委书记：王德元

公司是国家大型一类企业，全国300家重点企业之一。现有员工3000余人，资产总额5.8亿元。1975年投产至今，已为国家生产高标号水泥1029万吨，创利税3.5亿元。生产的雪峰牌水泥曾先后荣获湖南省首批名牌产品、部优产品、中华水泥精品、全国重点建筑质量与服务双满意产品第一名、国家级免检产品等殊荣。被广泛用于葛洲坝、亚运村、衡广复线、广州市地铁等多项重点工程建设，并在广东岭澳核电站中标，成为我国首家能生产核电站建设专用水泥的企业。

地址：湖南省新化县西河镇
电话：(0738) 3527220 3527340
传真：(0738) 3527000

CJCCC QUALITY CERTIFICATE

质量体系认证证书

注册号：2297B029

兹证明

湖南雪峰水泥集团有限公司

湖南省新化县西河镇

邮政编码：417821

质量体系符合标准

GB/T 19002-1994 idt ISO 9002：1994

该质量体系适合于下述产品

425/525 普通硅酸盐水泥　425/525 矿渣硅酸盐水泥
525 中热硅酸盐水泥　525 道路硅酸盐水泥
425 低热矿渣硅酸盐水泥

颁证日期：1997年12月25日
有效日期：1997年12月25日～2000年12月24日

中国建材质量体系认证中心

签发人
中心主任（签名）

国家认可注册号 Registration Number SC22

Hunan Xuefeng Cement Group is the national first-class corporation and one of the top 300 enterprises of China. It has more than 3,000 employees with 580 million yuan capital. Up to date, it has manufactured 10.29 million high-grade cement and created 350 million yuan tax and profit. The"XUEFENG"cement has won a lot of honorary titles including "Hunan famous brand", "national best cement", "satisfactory quality and service product" and "P.W.E product", and it was widely used in the construction of GEZHOUBAN, YAYUNCHUN, HENGGUANG railway and Guangzhou subway and so on. Hunan Xuefeng Cement Group has won the bid of Guangdong Lingao nuclear power station and become the first enterprise that manufacturing the special cement for the comstruction of nuclear power station in China.

Address:Xihe Town,Xinhua County,Hunan
Tel:(0738)3527220 3527340
Fax:(0738)3527000

厂区远眺

煤炭工业部部长王森浩、湖南省委书记王茂林在局视察。

资兴矿务局是国家大二型企业。现有地质储量1.64万吨。具备年洗煤120万吨，炼焦22万吨，水泥20万吨，砖4600万块，发电8000万千瓦时，磁化肥4000吨，酒精和冰醋酸各5000吨的生产能力。拥有各类产品100余种，年产值超过5亿元，形成产煤、煤炭深加工、发电、化工、建材多业协调发展的格局。先后被国务院、国家经贸委、煤炭部授予"全国工交系统先进单位"、"安全生产先进单位"、"质量标准化矿务局"等荣誉称号。

资兴矿务局局长：欧资源。

资兴矿务局

资兴矿务局机关大院。

以煤为本，多业并举，非煤产业不断发展壮大。图为产值达2亿元/年的煤电焦化总厂一隅。

矿务局骨干矿井、国家"八五"重点技改项目、1997年创利润1000万元的周源山煤矿。

Zixing Mineral Plant is a national second-class enterprise. It has 164 million tons reserves and the annual capability of producing 1.2 million tons coal washing, 220 thousand tons coke, 200 thousand tons cement, 46 million pieces of brick, 80,000,000 KW electricity, 4,000 tons magnetic fertilizer, 5,000 tons alcohol and 5,000 tons glacial acetic acid. Zixing Mineral Plant owns more than 100 various products and the annual output value exceeds 500 million yuan, it has formed a coordinated growth pattern of developing coal, coal processing, electric energy production, chemical industry and constructional materials simultaneously. Zixing Mineral Plant successively won the honorary titles of "advanced unit of national industry department", "advanced unit of safety production" and "the standardize mineral plant" that respectively awarded by the State Council, National Economy and Trade Committee and Ministry of Coal Industry.

湖南华菱钢铁集团有限责任公司董事长：陈运兴

湖南华菱钢铁集团有限责任公司总经理：李效伟

湖南华菱钢铁集团有限责任公司是由湘潭钢铁公司、涟源钢铁集团有限公司和衡阳钢管厂三家企业组建的特大型国有独资企业集团。现有员工5.7万人，各类专业技术人员1.2万人，资产总额94.6亿元，拥有270万吨钢、226万吨成品钢材年综合生产能力。公司将以资本营运为重点，以市场为导向、以效益为中心，集中力量发展市场短缺的无缝钢管、优质线材、板带材、新型型材和有色金属深加工产品。

Hunan Hualing Steel Group is a large-scaled, state-owned enterprise that composed by Xiangtan Steel Corporation, Lianyuan Steel Corporation and Hengyang Steel-Tube Factory .It has 12,000 various technicians among 57,000 employees, 9.46 billion yuan capital and annual production capability of 2.7 million tons steel and 2.26 million tons finished steel products. Directed by the market and focused on economic benefit, Hunan Hualing Steel Group will emphasize in managing capital and devote major efforts to developing greatly demanded seamless steel tube, steel sheet, new pattern steel products and processing products of nonferrous metal.

湖南华菱钢铁集团有限责任公司

湖南省人民政府为湖南华菱钢铁集团有限责任公司授牌仪式会场实况

湖南五凌水电开发有限责任公司

湖南五凌水电开发有限责任公司是由湖南省电力公司、湖南省经济建设投资公司、华中电力集团公司发起组建。拥有沅水干流及支流的水电资源开发权和湖南核电开发权。拥有五强溪水电站(120KW)和凌津滩水电站(27万KW)资产所有权和经营权,总资产约为103亿元人民币。国务院已将其列为国家水电滚动综合开发的试点单位。

1996年4月杨正午省长陪同邹家华副总理视察凌津滩

周伯华副省长等有关领导在五强溪大坝合影

五强溪电站大坝

凌津滩大江截流

Hunan Wulin Water and Electricity Developing Co.Ltd. (HWWEDCL) is invested by Hunan Electric Power Corporation, Hunan Economic Construction Investing Corporation and Huazhong Electric Power Group. It has the water and electricity exploiting power of the trunk stream and tributary of Yuanshui River and developing priority of Hunan nuclear power. HWWEDCL owns Wuqiangxi hydropower station (1.2 million KW) and Linjintan hydropower station (270 thousand KW) with 10.3 billion yuan fixed assets. The State Council has put HWWEDCL as one of the experimental unit of national water and electricity comprehensive developing project.

明　星　企　业

以中山商业大厦、中山路百货大楼、中山大酒店三大企业为核心的中山集团，是目前全国最大商业零售企业之一，中国商业股份制企业经济联合会成员单位，湖南省大中型百货商店联合会理事长单位，全国联合服务一体化活动湖南省唯一定点服务单位，湖南省家喻户晓的“中华老字号”明星企业。曾多次荣获“全国物价十佳”、省市“消费者最满意商店”、“质量信得过商店”、“特级(AAA)信用优良企业”。是湖南省首家销售过亿元单位。

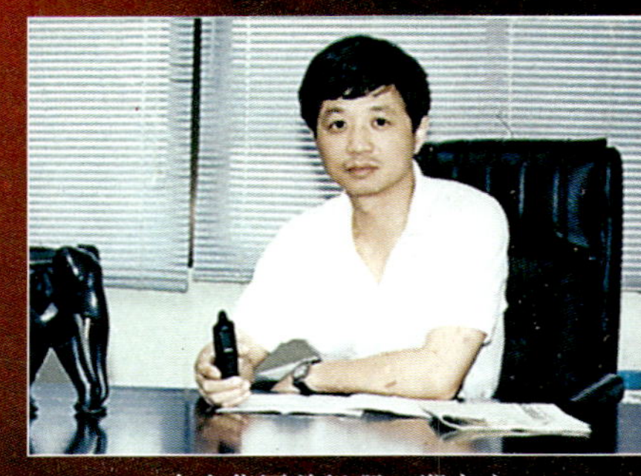

中山集团总经理：郑文立

长沙中山集团股份有限公司

Changsha Zhongshan Group(CZG) is composed by Zhongshan Commercial Building, Department Store of Zhongshan Road and Zhongshan Hotel. It is one of the largest retailing store of China, member of China Stock Company Economic Union, board chairman of Hunan Department Store Union, member of national service activity and a star enterprise of Hunan. CZG was granted the honorary titles of “one of the top favorable commodity prices enterprises of China”, “customer satisfactory store”, “good-quality store” and “AAA credit store” for many times. It is also the first enterprise with which sales volume exceed 100 million yuan in Hunan.

国家新闻出版署署长于友先(左二)、省委常委、省委宣传部部长文选德(左一)等听取总经理颜长庚(左三)对"湖南图书城"建设的汇报。

精诚团结的领导班子。总经理颜长庚(左四)、党委书记黄鹤楼(左五)。

Hunan Xinhua Bookstore(HXB) and Hunan Book and Video Publishing Corporation(HBVPC) were established on AUG,1949. It has 5,100 employees, 462 retailing shops and 380 million yuan fixed assets, and the annual output value amounted to 3 billion yuan. HXB and HBVPC invested 150 million yuan to build Hunan Books Center. With 34,000m^2 constructional area and 90 meter's height, Hunan Books Center is a national high-standard and multifunctional book circulation center. In 1997, Hunan Xinhua Bookstore won the honorary title of "advanced unit of press and publishing system".

湖南省新华书店、湖南省书刊音像发行总公司成立于1949年8月，现有员工5100余人，售书网点462处，固定资产3.8亿元，年总产值近30亿元。投资1.5亿元兴建的"湖南图书城"总建筑面积3.4万平方米，高90米，是一座高标准、多功能、全方位、现代化的国家级图书流通中心。1997年省新华书店获得全国新闻出版系统先进集体和全国"三下乡"活动先进集体的殊荣。

湖南省新华书店
湖南省书刊音像发行总公司

中南地区最大的图书储运基地

近年来荣获的奖旗、奖杯、奖牌

湖南图书城

湖南省建筑工程集团总公司

湖南省建筑工程集团总公司是全省最大的具有勘察设计、建筑安装、大型土石方机械施工、工程建设监理和房地产开发等综合能力的大型企业集团，是建设部确定的全国重点发展33家大型建安企业之一。企业现有职工4.3万人，各类专业技术人员7000余人，生产经营资本19.2亿元，年生产施工能力达30亿元以上。有300余项工程荣获国家和省市颁发的优质工程奖。

Hunan Architecture Engineering Group (HAEG) is one of the largest enterprises in Hunan. It mainly deals with business of architecture prospecting and designing, research and education, personnel training, construction and installation, road and bridge building, concrete structure manufacturing, machinery equipment producing and renting out, constructional materials marketing, engineering management and real estate exploiting. HAEG belongs to the national first-class enterprise and has the power in undertaking foreign contracted projects. Recently, HAEG is confirmed to be one of the 33 key national largest construction enterprises by Construction Ministry of China. HAEG administers 76 enterprises and institutions and has 43,000 employees, more than 7000 various technicians, 1.92 billion yuan floating capital and the annual constructional capacity amounted to 3 billion yuan. At the same time, more than 300 projects of HAEG were honored the title of "best-quality project" by the province and state.

省样板工程——省人民银行综合楼

总经理、法人代表：王茂鑫

湘潭电厂一号机组

长沙市十佳工程——长沙天心阁

湖南金狮啤酒有限公司总资本5.3亿元人民币，拥有世界当代一流的先进生产技术和设备，是湖南省经济活力百强企业，经济效益居全省同行业之首。1997年销售收入2亿元，利税4千多万元。主要生产“白沙”系列啤酒(白沙、白沙王、金白沙)，“白沙液”系列白酒，“白沙”系列食品饮料、矿泉水。“白沙”啤酒为省产名牌，并列为免检产品。“白沙液”白酒为国家名酒，远销首都及东北各省。

总经理：谭桂林

全国政协副主席赵南起(左)、湖南省政协主席刘夫生(右)来公司检查指导工作

先进的啤酒生产线

Hunan Jingsi Beer Co.Ltd.(HJBCL) has 530 million yuan fixed assets and owns the first class advanced technology and equipments of the world. It is one of the 100 key enterprises of Hunan. In 1997, HJBCL created 200 million yuan sales volume and more than 40 million profit and tax. HJBCL mainly manufactures “BAISHA” beer series, “BAISHAYE” alcohol series and “BAISHA” beverage series. “BAISHA” beer is a famous brand of Hunan and classified as P.W.E(Pass Without Examination) products. “BAISHAYE” alcohol is a national famous brand and on sale everywhere of China.

“白沙”系列产品

湖南金狮啤酒有限公司

湖南省经济建设投资公司

湖南省经济建设投资公司是湖南省基本建设投资经营性基金的管理机构。公司实行总经理负责制，下属四个全资子公司，十个合资公司和五个办事处。截至1997年底，公司总资产达89.2亿元，已实现净资产70亿元。随着国家投资体制改革的不断深化，公司将努力朝着多元化、集团化的大型投资控股公司方向发展。

Hunan Economic Construction Investing Corporation (HECIC) is an infrastructure foundation administrative institution of Hunan. HECIC adopted general manager responsible system and has developed 4 subsidiaries, 10 joint ventures and 5 agencies. By the end of 1997, the total capital and the net property of HECIC respectively were 8.92 billion yuan and 7 billion yuan. With the deepening of China's investment system reform, HECIC will make great efforts to develop to be a large-scaled, diversified and grouped investment-holding corporation.

正在施工的省投资大厦雄姿

长沙市五水厂净化水池远眺

湖南省第六工程公司现承担着省投资大厦及统计干部培训中心大型建设项目。该项目总高140米、建筑总面积55000m²。该工程1995年破土动工，在项目经理部经理黄正明为首的项目班子的精心施工和管理下，工程进度和质量均达到较好的水准，主体工程被有关部门评为优良。该项目经理部施工的贺龙体育馆、长沙市五水厂工程均被评为省样板工程。

Hunan Sixth Engineering Corporation is undertaking the contracted project of Hunan Investing building and Training Center for statistics cadres. With total height of 140 meters and 55,000m² constructional areas, the project started in 1995. Under the strict construction and administration of the management department which led by the manager Huang Zhengming, the tempo and quality of the project are well guaranteed and the principal part of the project has been awarded the " excellent" title by relevant administrative units. The completed projects including Helong Gymnasium and Changsha Fifth Waterworks that undertaken by this menagement department have been chosen to be the "sample project of Hunan".

投资大厦项目经理部经理：黄正明

湖南省第六工程公司投资大厦项目经理部

湖南省进出口集团有限公司——中国最大型进出口企业之一

湖南省进出口集团有限公司

湖南省进出口集团有限公司系国有大一型流通企业。主营进出口业务，并开展易货贸易、对外经济技术合作和兴办化工、轻工、服装、工艺品、房地产、旅游服务、商业运输等多种企业。总资产 27 亿元，年进出口总额逾 2 亿元，列湖南省第一位。

地址：湖南省长沙市三湘中路
电话：(0731)4720660　4722087　4402386
电报：1102 长沙　　电传：98178 HPIEC CN
传真：0731-4720984　　邮编：410001
电子邮件：hubieg @ public.cs.cn

Hunan Import and Export Corporation is the state-owned and first-class circulative enterprise. It mainly deals with businesses of importing and exporting and develops barter trade, economic and technological cooperation with foreign countries, chemical industry, light industry, clothing, handicraft article, real estate, travelling service and commercial transportation etc. simultaneously. With 2.7billion yuan capital and 200 million yuan annual import and export total amount, Hunan Import and Export Corporation tightly holds the first place in the foreign trade field of Hunan.

Address:Sanxiang Road, Changsha, Hunan
Tel: (0731)4720660　4722087　4402386
Cable: 1102 Changsha　Telex: 98178　HIPIEC CN
Fax: (0731)4720984　PC: 410001
E-mail: hubieg @ public. cs. cn

法人代表：李炳文

Changsha Sifang Real Estate Corporation (CSREC) passed the evaluation of Hunan Construction Committee on Jan. 1995 and authorized to be a second-class comprehensive exploitation corporation of China. CSREC is contracting of the project of exploiting the land of Huoxing and Sifangping economic development zone. Huoxing's constructional scale is 82.65 ha .and will transfer 46.7ha land, erect 60 apartment houses (180,000m^2 built-up areas) and build 21,000 commercial district. Sifangping's constructional scale is 197.828ha. and is entering the early stages of exploitation. With the aim of serving and flourishing city construction, the spirit of "unity, practicality, creativity, struggle", CSREC will exert itself to make progress in real estate developing field.

长沙四方房地产开发公司1995年元月通过省建委公司资质审查，确定为国家二级综合开发企业。现承建火星开发区和四方坪开发区的土地综合开发任务。火星小区建设规模共82.65公顷，转让土地46.7公顷，自建房屋60栋，建筑面积18万M^2，建成商业网点 2.1 万 M^2；四方坪小区建设规模 197.828 公顷，目前已进入小区前期开发。公司以“兴湘富市、服务城建”为宗旨，以“团结、务实、创新、拼搏”为公司精神，努力在房地产综合开发领域中再创辉煌。

开发区一角

湖南统计年鉴

STATISTICAL YEARBOOK OF HUNAN

1998

（总第16期）

湖南省统计局　编

Edited by

HuNan Province Statistical Bureau

中国统计出版社

China Statistical Publishing House

(京)新登字 041 号

图书在版编目(CIP)数据

湖南统计年鉴 1998/湖南省统计局编
北京:中国统计出版社,1998.7
ISBN 7—5037—2723—3
Ⅰ.湖…
Ⅱ.湖…
Ⅲ.统计资料—湖南—1998—年鉴
Ⅳ.C832.64—54
中国版本图书馆 CIP 数据核字(98)第 11014 号

中国统计出版社出版
Published by China Statistical Publishing House
(北京复外三里河月坛南街 75 号 100826)
湖南五一文快速彩印公司印刷
*
787×1092 毫米　16 开本　39 印张　93.6 万字
1998 年 7 月第 1 版　1998 年 7 月长沙第 1 次印刷
印数:1—4000

ISBN 7—5037—2723—3/C.1525
国内定价:180.00 元

编 者 说 明

一、《湖南统计年鉴—1998》是一部全面反映湖南省全省国民经济和社会发展情况的资料性年刊。收录了全省及各地、市、县1997年经济和社会发展方面的大量统计数据，以及历史重要年份和1978年以来的全省主要统计数据。是一本党政部门、企事业单位、经济研究工作者、教学科研人员及来湘投资者的重要工具书。

二、《湖南统计年鉴—1998》在保持过去历年统计年鉴结构联贯资料可比的基础上，做了部分补充和调整。增加了适应经济建设、市场经济和新国民经济核算体系及报表制度中的新内容，增加了企业间、省市间的资料联系与可比。

三、全书内容：卷首为《1997年湖南省国民经济和社会发展统计公报》，紧接21部分，即：1.行政区划和自然状况；2.综合；3.国民经济核算；4.人口和劳动工资；5.固定资产投资；6.财政、金融、保险；7.物价指数；8.人民生活；9.城市建设、环境保护；10.农业；11.工业；12.建筑业；13.运输和邮电；14.国内、外贸易，对外经贸和旅游；15.教育和科技；16.文化、体育、卫生；17.党群政法和社会福利；18.各地、市、县主要经济和社会统计指标；19.各地、市、县主要指标排序；20.各行业按主要指标企业排序；21.各省市主要经济和社会统计指标。

四、本《年鉴》资料大部分来自年度统计报表，一部分来自抽样调查。各地、市、县主要经济和社会统计指标是据其当年各地的统计年报资料整理的；各省、市、自治区的年度引用数据是根据国家统计局反馈资料加工的；有些专业性很强的指标是由省有关业务厅局年报提供的；土地面积、森林资源、河流湖泊状况是按照有关部门近年来普查资料整理的。

五、本《年鉴》中价值指标均按当年价格计算，指数均按可比价格计算，如有变化表后即有说明。

六、本《年鉴》是按照《中国统计年鉴》的大体框架和规范要求编辑的。统一使用《中国统计年鉴》指标解释。统一采用国际度量衡标准计量单位。统一使用《中国统计年鉴》规范符号。

“……”表示数据不足本表最小单位数；“#”表示其中的主要项；“空格”表示指标数据不详或无该项统计数据；“※”表示表下有注释。

Preface

Statistical Yearbook of Hunan 1998 is an annual statistics publication, which reflects various aspects of HuNan province's social and economic development. The book covers very comprehensive daca series for 1995 and some selected data series for historically important years and the years since 1978 at provincial level and local levels of prefecture, city and county. therefor, It is a important reference book for party and government departments, enterprises units, economy research worker, teacher, and investment units come to Hunan.

Some parts of the book Was adjusted appropriately to maintain the Continuity to Compare With yearbook published before. Some new data suitable to economic construction, market economy and new SNA Were added , meanwhile, We think it is helpful to make a comparison between enterprises and provinces.

The book contains the following twenty—one parts, 1. Administrative Division and Natural Conditions; 2. General Survey; 3. National Economy Accounting. 4. Population, Employment and Wage; 5. Investment in Fixed Assets; 6. Public Finance, Banking, Insurance; 7. Price Indices; 8. People's Iivelihood; 9. Construction of Cities, Environmental Protection; 10. Agriculture; 11. Industry; 12. Construction; 13. Transportation, Post and Telecommunication Services; 14. Domestic Trade, Foreign Trade and Tourism; 15. Education and Science; 16. Culture, Sports, Public Health; 17. Party and Mass, Politics and Law, Social Welfare; 18. Main Economic and Social Statistics Indicators by Prefecture, City and County; 19. Ranking of Main Indicators by prefeture, City and County; 20 Ranking of Enterprises by Main Indicators by Sectors; 21. Main Economic and Social Statistics Indicators by provinces.

The major data sources of this book are annual statistical reports, and some from sampling surveys. Main economic and social statistics indicators by prefecture, city and county are arranged according to their annual statistical reports. Annual data of provinces, autonomous regions, and cities directly under central government are quoted from data returned by State Statistical Bureau. Area of total land, Forest resources, Rivers and lakes condition are arranged according to census by the department concerned in recent years.

All of the value indicators in this book are calculated by the same years' prices, All of the indices are calculated by fixed price. Explanatory notes are provided behind the list in which if there are changes.

This book is edited according to the frame and standard of Statistical Yearbook of China. The indicator explanatory notes are edited according to Statistical Yearbook of China, and the units of measurement are internationally standard measurement units; The notations are standard notations of Statistical Yearbook of China.

…not large enough to be rounded into the least unit.

\#　of which: major items

" "　data not available

※　see footnotes below

《湖南统计年鉴》顾问

杨正午	省委副书记、省长
文选德	省委常委、省委宣传部部长
戚和平	省委常委、省委组织部部长
周时昌	副省长
唐之享	副省长
庞道沐	副省长
贺同新	副省长
郑茂清	副省长

Hunan Statistics Yearbook Consultants

Yang Zhengwu	deputy general secretary of Hunan Provincial Party Committee;governor of Hunan province
Weng Xuande	executive member of Hunan Provincial Party Committee; minister of Propaganda Department of Hunan Provincial Party Committee
Qi Heping	executive member of Hunan Provincial Party Committee; minister of Organization Department of Hunan Provincial Party Committee
Zhou Shichang	Deputy governor of Hunan province
Tang Zhixiang	Deputy governor of Hunan province
Pang Daomu	Deputy governor of Hunan province
He Tongxin	Deputy governor of Hunan province
Zheng Maoqing	Deputy governor of Hunan province

《湖南统计年鉴》理事会

张兴福	省煤炭工业局局长
林国悌	省机械工业局局长
刘学文	省乡镇企业局局长
王啸云	省医药管理局局长
曹其明	省政府机关事务管理局局长
廖林生	省物价局副局长
但德池	省政府外事办公室主任
赵世荣	省委农村工作部副部长、省政府农村工作办公室副主任
杨学金	省技术监督局局长
刘孝纯	省新闻出版局副局长
张济民	省旅游局局长
李火烽	省公安厅交通管理局、省公安厅交通警察总队党委书记兼政委
杨建农	省公安厅交通管理局、省公安厅交通警察总队党委副书记、局长、总队长
左连生	省农业科学院党委书记
张松业	湖南行政学院常务副院长
黄湘平	省证券监督管理委员会主任
吴新民	省农业机械管理局局长
朱振基	省工商业联合会党组书记
冯湘保	省妇女联合会副主席
唐德元	中国国际贸易促进委员会湖南省分会会长
张登武	省烟草专卖局局长、中国烟草总公司湖南省公司经理
余柏青	省档案局局长
周成村	长沙海关副关长
张学文	湖南进出口商品检验局副局长
汪明藻	中国民航湖南省管理局局长
熊道善	中国南方航空(集团)湖南公司总经理
张秀发	省邮电管理局局长
徐联初	中国人民银行湖南省分行副行长

黄长元　　中国农业发展银行湖南省分行行长
王金贤　　中国工商银行湖南省分行行长
王德振　　中国农业银行湖南省分行行长
朱世强　　中国农业银行湖南省分行副行长
仇为发　　中国银行湖南省分行行长
彭茂吾　　中国建设银行湖南省分行行长
谢石洞　　中保人寿保险有限公司湖南省分公司总经理
胡水安　　中国平安保险股份有限公司长沙分公司副总经理
王永中　　中国平安保险股份有限公司长沙分公司副总经理
殷之时　　湖南储备物资管理局局长
杨映璜　　核工业中南地质局局长
赵永海　　航空航天工业部湖南航天管理局局长
史秋生　　省机电设备招标局、省机械设备成套局局长
罗　毅　　中国有色金属工业长沙公司经理
陈明宪　　省公路桥梁建设总公司总经理
康健民　　潇湘电影制片厂厂长
孙明初　　省劳动服务公司党委书记
李杨辉　　省建筑工程集团总公司副总经理
李静安　　省经济建设投资公司总经理
吴琨琪　　省黄金工业总公司总经理
王玉林　　三湘集团有限公司副董事长
孙朝东　　省食品工业集团总公司总经理
王逸时　　省纺织工业集团总公司总经理
陈保民　　省轻工集团总公司总经理
方大鹏　　省二轻工业集团总公司总经理
吴　必　　省商业集团总公司总经理
徐春生　　湖南华升工贸进出口(集团)公司总经理
谢迪安　　省金环进出口总公司总经理
马明全　　中国建筑第五工程局局长

Hunan Statistics Yearbook Board of directors

Lin Guoti	director of Hunan Machinery Industry Bureau
Liu Xuewen	director of Hunan Town and Township Enterprises Bureau
Wang Xiaoyun	director of Hunan Medicine Administration Bureau
Cao Qiming	director of Hunan Governmental Affairs Administrative Bureau
Liao Linsheng	deputy director of Hunan Commodity Prices Bureau
Dan Dechi	director of Foreign Affairs Office of Hunan Provincial Government
Zhao Shirong	deputy minister of Countryside Administration Department of Hunan Provincial Party Committee; deputy director of Countryside Administration Office of Hunan Provincial Government
Yang Xuejin	director of Hunan Technology Supervision Bureau
Liu Xiaochun	deputy director of Hunan News and Publication Bureau
Zhang Jimin	director of Hunan Tour Bureau
Li Huofeng	secretary of Party Committee and Commander of Transport Administrative Bureau and Traffic Police Division of Hunan Public Security Department
Yang Jianlong	deputy secretary of Party Committee of Transport Administrative Bureau and Traffic Police Division of Hunan Public Security Department
Zuo Liansheng	secretary of Party Committee of Hunan Agriculture Institution
Zhang Songye	executive deputy president of Hunan Administration Institution
Huang Xiangping	director of Hunan Stock Supervision and Administration Committee
Wu Xinming	director of Hunan Agricultural Machinery Administration Bureau
Zhu Zhenji	Party secretary of Hunan Industry and Commerce Union
Feng Xiangbo	deputy chairman of Hunan Women's Union
Tang Deyuan	chairman of China International Trade Promoting Committee Hunan Branch
Zhang Dengwu	director of Hunan Tobacco Monopolized Bureau; general manager of China Tobacco Corporation Hunan Branch
Yu Boqing	director of Hunan Archives Bureau
Zhou Chengchun	deputy director of Changsha Customs Office
Zhang Xuewen	deputy director of Hunan Import and Export Commodity Inspection Bureau
Wang Mingzao	director of Hunan Administration Bureau of China Civil Aviation
Xiong Daoshan	general manager of China South Aviation Group Hunan Branch
Zhang Xiufa	director of Hunan Posts and Telecommunications Bureau
Xu Lianchu	deputy president of People's Bank of China Hunan Branch
Huang Changyuan	president of China Agriculture Developing Bank Hunan Branch
Wang Jinxian	president of China Industrial and Commercial Bank Hunan Branch

Wang Dezhen	president of China Agriculture Bank Hunan Branch
Zhu Shiqiang	deputy president of China Agriculture Bank Hunan Branch
Qiu Weifa	president of Bank of China Hunan Branch
Peng Maowu	president of China Construction Bank Hunan Branch
Xie Shidong	general manager of China Life Insurance Company Hunan Branch
Hu Shuian	deputy general manager of China Safty Insurance Company Changsha Branch
Wang Yongzhong	deputy general manager of China Safty Insurance Company Changsha Branch
Ying Zhishi	director of Hunan Reserves Administration Bureau
Yang Yinghuang	director of Zhongnan Geological Bureau of Nuclear Industry
Zhao Yonghai	director of Hunan Space Administration Bureau
Shi Qiusheng	director of Hunan Machinery Equipment Set Bureau; director of Hunan Machinery and Electric Equipment Bid Bureau
Luo Yi	manager of China Nonferrous Metal Industry Corporation Changsha Branch
Chen Mingxian	general manager of Hunan Road and Bridge Construction Corporation
Kang Jianmin	director of Xiaoxiang Film Producing Factory
Sun Mingchu	secretary of Party Committee of Hunan Labour and Service Corporation
Li Yanghui	deputy general manager of Hunan Construction and Engineering Group
Li Jingan	general manager of Hunan Economic Construction Investing Corporation
Wu Kunqi	general manager of Hunan Gold Industrial Corporation
Wang Yulin	vice president of Sanxiang Group
Sun Chaodong	general manager of Hunan Food Industry Group
Wang Yishi	general manager of Hunan Textile Industry Group
Chen Baomin	general manager of Hunan Light Industry Group
Fang Dapeng	general manager of Hunan Second Light Industry Group
Wu Bi	general manager of Hunan Commercial Group
Xu Chunsheng	general manager of Hunan Huasheng Industry and Trade Import and Export Group
Xie Dian	general manager of Hunan Jinhuan Import and Export Corporation
Ma Mingquan	director of China Fifth Construction Engineering Bureau

《湖南统计年鉴—1998》编辑委员会

主任委员：	陈作贵				
副主任委员：	刘志荣	马　勇	邱运斌		
	肖春林	周菊华	傅绍良		
	吴星明	雷树标	江利国		
委员：	（以姓氏笔划为序）				
	王泉德	冯文金	卢光祖	刘业荣	刘家和
	刘顺国	江金生	宋今来	李建平	李机生
	许明德	苏寿泉	陈竹君	陈建军	杨国健
	周雪余	罗　华	张松青	张世平	张　岳
	钟宝森	徐　朋	高　勇	黄志奇	傅依群
	蒋丽芳	谭蒲辉	戴乐平		
责任编辑：	钟宝森				
出版发行：	王忠好				
英文翻译：	戴乐平				
公报：	戴乐平	曾斌求	颜宏晖		

《湖南统计年鉴—1998》资料整理人员

张雍雍	周曙东	唐双全	张昭红	邓　艳	杨新民
周新华	李生春	吴　超	蒋丽芳	向延华	顾　虹
李　群	彭建霞	刘征宇	梁已香	周杰韩	郑红梅
张映欣	唐素芳	刘昕毅	张吉世	张　翔	邹廉喜
王建春	张志群	张启华	刘华娟	肖首雄	蔡宏宇
陈智勇	陈良米	管恩学	朱菊云	蔡冬娥	石　梅
马爱霞	杨鸿雁	贺　震	阳小林		

《湖南统计年鉴—1998》编务部

主　　任：王忠好

编　　辑：张学军　　黄承瑜　　龚行健

　　　　　王作文　　崔国强

广告采编：周志强　　石雁平　　郑立奇

　　　　　卜功华　　黄　倩

美术编辑：俞　峰

文字广告：张新沙

英文编辑：周　青

目　录
CONTENTS

三、国民经济核算
chapter 3 NATIONAR ECONOMIC HCCOUNTINY

四、人口和劳动工资

Chapter 4 POPULATION，EMPLOYMENT AND WAGE

五、固定资产投资
Chapter 5 INVESTMENT IN FIXED ASSETS

六、财政、金融、保险
Chapter 6 PUBLIC FINANCE, BANKING, INSURANCE

七、物价指数
Chapter 6 PRICE INDICES

八、人民生活
Chapter 8 PEOPLE'S LIVELIHOOD

九、城市建设、环境保护
Chapter 9 CONSTRUCTION OF CITIES，ENVIRONMENTAL PROTECTION

十、农业
Chapter 10 AGRICULTURE

十一、工　业
Chapter 11 INDUSTRY

十二、建筑业
Chapter 12 CONSTRUCTION

十三、运输、邮电
Chapter 13 TRANSPORTATION, POST AND TELECOMMUNICATION SERVICES

十四、国内、外贸易、对外经济和旅游
Chapter 14 DOMESTIC TRADE, FOREIGN TRADE, FOREIGN ECONOMY AND TOURISM

十六、文化、体育、卫生

Chapter 16 CULTURE, SPORTS, PUBLIC HEALTH

十七、党群、政法和社会福利

Chapter 17 PARTY AND MASS, POLITICS AND LAW, SOCIAL WELFARE

十八、各地、市、县主要经济和社会统计指标
Chapter 18 MAIN ECONOMIC AND SOCIAL STATISTICS INDICATORS BY PREFECTURE, CITY AND COUNTY

二十一、各省市主要经济和社会统计指标

Chapter 21 MAIN ECONOMIC AND SOCIAL INDICATORS BY PROVINCES

附:企业简介

附:社会办学力量的中坚简介:

1997年湖南省
国民经济和社会发展的统计公报

湖南省统计局

（1998年2月24日）

1997年，香港回归和党的“十五大”召开，为国民经济和社会发展提供了良好的政治环境。全省人民在省委、省政府的领导下，按照“稳中求进”的总体要求，抓住机遇，克服困难，大力推进两个根本性转变，各项改革稳步推进，国民经济和各项社会事业发展取得新的进步。初步统计，全年全省国内生产总值2993亿元，比上年增长10.8%。其中，第一产业851.01亿元，增长6.1%；第二产业1171.71亿元，增长13.5%；第三产业970.28亿元，增长11.5%。整体上看，国民经济呈现适度增长和低通胀的格局，经济运行环境进一步改善，经济生活中出现了一些积极变化。但由于长期积累的体制问题和结构矛盾在短期内难以得到根本性缓解，在市场需求约束增强的情况下，国民经济整体素质和效益仍然不高，失业下岗人员增加。

一、农业和农村经济

农业和农村经济在结构调整中保持了较快的发展势头。

1997年全省农业以市场为导向，以效益为中心，以科技为手段，以农村产业化建设为途径，加快了农村经济由单一结构向多元化结构、由传统农业向现代农业的转变进程，农村经济呈现新的发展格局。全年农业总产值1322.27亿元，比上年增长8.3%。

主要农产品产量获得历史上少有的好收成。1997年我省在稳定粮食生产的前提下，重点发展优质稻和旱粮生产，适度扩大经济作物面积，在粮食总量增产的同时，其他经济作物也获得好收成。全年粮食总产量2876.99万吨，比上年增长6.5%；棉花产量25.57万吨，增长34.8%。畜牧水产继续增产。全年出栏肉猪5837.6万头，比上年增长9.5%；水产品产量突破百万吨大关，达110.76万吨，增长7.4%；蔬菜、牛、羊、家禽等都有较大幅度增长，为丰富城乡居民菜篮子做出了重要贡献。

农业产业化进程加快。1997年全省把农业产业化作为建设农业强省的重大举措来抓，农业产业化基地建设加快，特色农业逐渐成为地方经济的支柱产业，龙头企业得到进一步发展和壮大，重点新建扩建了十大农产品市场，市场辐射日益扩大。

农村产业结构调整力度加大。1997年全省重点扶植10个县100万亩连片中高档优质稻的开发，烤烟基本上实现良种化，三元杂交猪增加184万头，特种水产养殖面积比上年增加20.4万亩。造林与丘岗山地开发相结合，提前实现"十年绿化湖南"的目标，森林覆盖率达51.4%。农村产业结构出现了积极变化。养殖业产值达614.25亿元，占农业总产值的比重由上年的43.3%提高到46.6%。农产品的优质品率达39%，比上年提高3个百分点。农业生产条件继续改善。年末农业机械总动力1692.84万千瓦，比上年增长4.7%。据省乡镇企业局按新口径统计，乡镇企业总产值3000亿元，增长34.9%，其中集体经济增长23.4%，私有经济增长49%。

扶贫攻坚力度加大，成效显著。1997年，全省共抽调1.1万名机关干部定点、到村、入户扶贫帮困。全省共计投入扶贫资金9.86亿元，比上年增长45.9%，是近十年来数额最多、增幅最大的一年。年内有浏阳等6县(市、区)摘掉了贫困帽子，全省有90万贫困人口基本解决温饱问题，贫困人口由上年的352万人减少到262万人，31个贫困县普遍实现增产增收，3500个特困村人均增加纯收入200元。全省已有19个县(市、区)首批跨入小康行列。

农村经济面临的主要问题是：品种结构不合理，加工转化能力低，农民增产增收难同步。

二、工业和建筑业

工业生产保持适度稳定增长，产销衔接水平有所提高，经济效益略有好转。

1997年，在市场需求约束不断加强、生产经营环境依旧困难的情况下，全省工业企业积极加强内部管理，调整产品结构，狠抓产销衔接和扭亏增盈，工业经济呈现生产稳定增长、经济效益逐步好转的态势。全年工业增加值1023.86亿元，增长14.5%；工业总产值3855.82亿元，增长21.4%，其中乡及乡以上工业总产值1898.94亿元，增长12.1%。在乡及乡以上工业企业中，非国有经济发展较快，国有经济与非国有经济的比重由上年的54.7∶45.3调整为50.2∶49.8。大中型企业的主体地位加强。全省21800家独立核算工业企业产品销售率为96.28%，比上年提高1.25个百分点；工业经济效益综合指数为74%，提高2个百分点；实现利税150.08亿元，增长24.9%；盈利企业盈利额47.17亿元，增加7.61亿元；亏损企业亏损额47.51亿元，减亏2.06亿元，企业盈亏相抵后净亏损减少9.67亿元，扭亏增盈初见成效。

产业结构调整取得新进展，瓶颈产业得到加强。伴随着市场竞争和结构调整，大批低值高耗的小企业经过改制改组实现产业升级或破产关闭，科技含量高、效益好的产品得到扶持和加强。摩托车、电子、空调等产品大幅度增长；纺织行业经过几年的调整已取得初步成效，产品产量增长加快；受投资需求增长减缓和企业开工不足的影响，部分能源、原材料及投资类机电产品生产仍未扭转下降局面。

企业改革稳步推进。进一步加强了"优化资本结构"城市试点。在先期株洲、长沙两市进入全国试点城市的基础上，1997年扩充了湘潭、岳阳两市。试点城市利用国家的优惠政策，在"增资、减债、分流、破产"实施再就业方面进展顺利，列入兼并破产和职工再就业工作计划的企业中，已有21户破产终结，14户被兼并，44户实施减人增效。已报批核销银行呆坏帐准备金12.02亿元，占限定我省额度的119.7%。通过再就业服务中心，安置下岗职工21436人。继续推进现代企业制度试点，试点企业由55户扩大到107户，针对先行试点的55户建制试点企业确定了不同的改制类型，明确了国有资产投资主体，公司制框架及企业内部相互制衡的法人治理结构基本形成。实施大公司、大集团发展战略迈出可喜一步，省市两级已组建重点企业集团500个，重组资产300亿元。国有小型企业改革面达69%，涌现出一批转换了机制、放出了效益的典型地市和企业。股份制企业改造取得新进展。

工业经济面临的主要问题是：工业经济运行整体质量不高，国有企业亏损严重，生产能力闲置较多，企业两极分化有所加剧。

建筑业生产经营有一定增长。全省各级政府和主管部门加强了对建筑市场的清理整顿和监督管理，建立健全了投招标制度。积极进行转换企业经营机制和现代企业制度试点，增强了企业的竞争能力，使我省建筑业逐步走入法制化、规范化的轨道。全省国有建筑业企业在激烈的市场竞争中，努力开拓，全年完成建筑业总产值125.22亿元，增长0.9%；国有建筑业增加值36.8亿元，减少3%。劳动生产率53148元/人，增长4.1%；房屋建筑施工面积1191.9万平方米，减少7.3%；房屋建筑竣工面积397.2万平方米，减少15%。

三、固定资产投资

投资结构逐步趋向合理，投资总量依然不足。初步统计，全社会固定资产投资713.34亿元，增长5.1%，其中国有及其股份经济完成投资421.94亿元，增长0.3%。国有及股份制经济投资额中，基本建设投资268.13亿元，增长5.6%；更新改造投资109.07亿元，下降9.2%；房地产开发投资30.06亿元，下降17.5%。固定资产投资率为23.8%，比上年下降1.8个百分点。农业投资比重有所提高。农林牧渔业国有投资2.64亿元，增长166.7%。基础设施和基础产业的投资得到加强，水利、交通、能源、邮电等基础产业的发展加快。水利国有投资8.8亿元，增长8.6%；交通运输业、仓储、邮电通信业投资120.06亿元，增长3.8%；电力煤气水生产及供应业投资60.73亿元，增长6.6%。

重点建设基本完成任务。全年31个重点建设项目投资133.05亿元，超额完成年计划2个百分点，重点建设投资占全省国有固定资产投资的31.54%。洞庭湖一期治理通过验收，江垭水利工程实现拦洪，湘潭电厂1号机组投产发电，五强溪和石门电厂送出工程全部建成，长沙至益阳高等级公路已具备通车条件，南华渡大桥建成通车，石长铁路全线铺通，湘黔复线株娄段投入使用。全年新增主要生产能力：发电装机43万千瓦，22万伏变电容量120万千伏安，输电线路548公里；程控交换机容量61万门，传输光缆7969公里；高压锅炉管16.5万吨，连铸钢坯83.5万吨，高档纸5万吨，彩色显像管136万支，摩托车10万辆，城市供水52.5万吨。

固定资产投资中的主要问题是：投资总量不足，更新改造投资下降，工农业实业性大项目少，有些项目资金到位差，全省固定资产投资增幅步入九十年代来的最低谷。固定资产投资的效益也不理想。固定资产交付使用率为58.6%，下降12.6个百分点；项目投产率49.9%，房屋竣工率为45.6%，分别下降7.5和1.4个百分点。

四、交通邮电

交通设施不断改善，对国民经济发展的瓶颈制约作用进一步缓解。1997年交通运输业实现增加值164.05亿元，比上年增长11.6%；新增公路里程207公里，其中汽车专用公路38公里。全年交通运输完成货物周转量998.6亿吨公里，比上年下降3%；完成旅客周转量592.16亿人公里，增长10%。

电话业务稳步发展，移动通信高速增长，数据通信迅速崛起，网络建设步伐加快。全年邮电通信业实现增加值31.33亿元，增长30.2%，完成邮电业务总量55.6亿元，增长30.2%，全省所有的县(市)均进入长话自动网。年内新增移动电话用户28.1万户，增长112.9%，无线寻呼达157.7万户，比上年增长35.4%。

五、国内贸易和市场物价

商业体制改革稳步推进，经营方式不断创新，商品市场运行平稳。1997年，全省消费品市场货丰价稳，居民消费心理稳定，消费淡旺季节差异逐渐缩小。全年实现社会消费品零售总额1037.66亿元，比上年增长9.5%，扣除物价因素实际增长9.2%，增幅比上年上升1.7个百分点，其中国有及国有控股经济实现消费品零售额214.35亿元，比上年增长0.04%；非国有经济零售额823.31亿元，增长12.3%。农村零售额的比重为30.5%，比上年降低0.4个百分点。全省批发零售贸易企业购进商品总额1296.7亿元，增长6.8%，销售总额为1357.15亿元，增长4.2%。生产资料市场稳中偏淡。全省批零贸易业生产资料销售额540.44亿元，下降6.2%。农资在进口化肥增多、国产化肥超产、农民生产资金紧张等多种因素的影响下，供求关系发生较大变化。全年全省贸易业销售农业生产资料54.63亿元，下降12.7%，其中供销社系统销售42.41亿元，下降8.6%。

市场物价涨幅平稳回落。1997年我省在宏观经济环境进一步趋向宽松，绝大多数商品呈现买方市场特征，有效需求相对不足，价格管理加强的形势下，全省商品零售价格总水平和居民消费价格总水平比上年分别上涨0.3%和2.8%，均大大低于年初确定的6%和8%的控制目标。工业生产和投资市场价格走势平稳，主要工业品出厂价格下降0.8%，原材料、燃料、动力购进价格上涨0.1%，固定资产投资价格上涨1.8%。农村市场价格降幅较大，农业生产资料价格下降2.1%，农副产品收购价格下降4.7%。保持物价稳定是我省宏观调控多年企盼的结果，但农副产品价格下降过多，不利于农业生产和农村市场的繁荣；工业产品价格下降，与企业不断积聚的成本上升压力难以调和；服务项目价格涨幅居高不下，加重了企业和消费者的负担。

六、对外经济与旅游

对外贸易略有增加。1997年我省继续实施“开放带动”战略，努力适应国际竞争环境和国家外贸政策的调整，以经济效益为中心，加大出口力度，全年进出口总额达32.83亿美元，比上年增长2.2%,其中出口23.29亿美元,增长5%。三资、生产(工贸)企业、地县外贸三个出口新增长点势头强劲,共出口11.33亿美元,增长27.5%。港澳、日本、美国仍是我省最大的贸易伙伴。进出口贸易存在的主要问题是:规模较小,进口少,发展后劲不足,全省获得外贸进出口权的493家企业中约三分之一没有进出口实绩。

利用外资大幅度增长。1997年,省委、省政府把招商引资工作放在经济工作中的突出位置,招商引资的软、硬条件不断改善,外商来湘投资活跃,实际到位外资增长较快。全年合同外资12.93亿美元,增长37.8%;实际利用外资13.57亿美元,增长20.6%,其中外商直接投资9.17亿美元,增长30.4%。外商投资结构发生变化,独资企业明显增加,合资企业减少。全年新注册登记的三资企业中,合资企业比上年减少65家,合作企业、外商独资企业分别增加18家和40家。新批外资平均项目金额由上年的161万美元提高到225万美元,增长39.8%。但利用外资总体规模仍然偏小,外商投资企业地区分布不平衡。

对外经济合作发展较快。1997年,全省对外承包工程、劳务合作、设计咨询合同金额2.26亿美元,增长62.9%,完成营业额0.83亿美元,增长14.3%;年末在外人数2584人,增长46.4%。

对外技术进出口稳定发展。1997年全省签定技术进出口合同项目150个,比上年增长13.6%,合同金额2.9亿美元,增长1%。其中技术进口项目90个,增长4.7%,金额2.27亿美元,增长0.4%。

旅游事业取得新的突破。1997年共接待外国人、华侨、港澳台旅游人数30.16万人次,比上年增长31.9%;旅游创汇1.4亿美元,增长40%。随着接待条件改善,旅客在湘逗留时间人均由3天延长到3.2天,人平每天消费为155美元,比上年增加8.2美元,增长5.6%。大旅游开发热潮正在兴起,一批规模大、水平高的旅游项目相继建成。总投资近3亿元的长沙世界之窗已于10月份开园,投资8000万元的天子山索道10月投入营运,投资近亿元开发的南岳水帘洞景区6月对外开放。国内旅游方兴未艾。年内接待国内旅客4000万人次,比上年增长25%;国内旅游收入68亿元,增长30.8%。

七、金融与保险

金融形势基本稳定,宏观调控能力有所加强。1997年金融机构通过整顿金融秩序,灵活操作各种金融工具,优化信贷结构,推动了产业结构调整和社会资源的合理配置。

存款增势放慢,银行信用总量与上年基本持平。国家银行累计净回笼现金36.04亿元,比上年多回笼13.95亿元。年末金融机构各项存款余额1769.91亿元,比年初增加173.88亿元,增长10.9%;金融机构各项贷款余额2123亿元,比年初增加215.59亿元,增长11.3%。贷款投放虽然偏紧,但加上承兑汇票等年内信用总量与上年基本持平。贷款投放重点支持了农副产品收购、国有大中型企业和农业资金的投入。农发行和农行共发放农副产品收购贷款84.86亿元,比上年多增加38.56亿元。资本市场发展平稳,一级证券市场扩容速度加快。年末共有A股上市公司18家,年内新增6家。股市筹资45亿元,加上配股共筹资50亿元。

保险事业继续发展，公民投保意识有所增强。全省保险机构业务承保金额 3730.62 亿元，其中财产承保金额 2770.45 亿元，人身险保额 960.17 亿元；保险费业务收入 31.25 亿元，其中人身险收入 19.16 亿元，分别增长 41.4%和 81.3%；保险业务支出 14.85 亿元，下降 11.6%，其中财产险赔款支出 7.18 亿元，人身险支出 6.69 亿元，退保金额 0.96 亿元。

八、科学技术和教育

科技工作取得新的进展。科研机构和科技队伍稳步发展。年末全省拥有县以上独立核算自然科学研究机构 179 所，社会人文科学研究机构 2 所，科技信息与文献机构 13 所。全省地方国有单位各类专业技术人员 94.47 万人，比上年增长 5.5%。“‘121’跨世纪人才工程”进展顺利，在湘两院院士增至 16 人。年末享受政府特殊津贴的科技人员达 1423 人。民营科技企业已成为我省一个新的经济增长点，远大空调、三一集团、迅达集团等六家企业年销售收入超亿元。

高科技产业迅速发展。全省高新技术产品产值 202.17 亿元，实现利税总额 19.72 亿元，分别比上年增长 17.3%和 28.4%。新材料、生物工程、电子与信息、机电一体化、新能源与环保五大高新技术已初步形成产业群体。全年有 14 项高科技项目列入国家级火炬计划，另有 2 项纳入国家火炬计划重点项目，2 个高科技企业列为国家 火炬计划重点企业，创智软件园列为国家火炬计划四大软件产业基地之一。长沙高新区“一区四园”方案经国家科委批准，已进入实施阶段。高科技产业“百亿工程”正式启动，首批安排 1000 万元支持的 10 个高科技项目已签实施协议。

五大科技工程发展态势喜人。水稻大面积增产示范工程，即开展水稻全程技术服务产业化尝试取得重大成果；重要研究基地建设工程发展态势良好，年末已建成 21 个省级重点实验室；杂交水稻工程完成了早 S/D34、香 125S/D68 等两系法杂交稻新组合；长沙“湘云鲫(鲤)中试基地”建成；“草食动物产业化配套技术研究与示范”等重大科研项目都取得重大进展。

科技成果不断涌现。全省取得各类科技成果 900 项，有 22 项获得国家奖励，309 项获省科技进步奖，其中居国际先进水平的 47 项，国内领先水平的 143 项。

专利工作稳步发展，知识产权保护力度加大。全省受理专利申请约 3100 件，专利授权量 1350 件，累计专利申请量和授权量均居全国第八位。首批 26 家企事业单位知识产权保护工作试点基本完成。

技术市场活跃。全省签订各类技术合同 14878 个，合同成交金额 16.1 亿元，分别比上年增加 8.6%和 15%。

地质勘查和测绘事业稳步发展。全省发现具有良好开发前景的新矿 5 处，完成标准钻探工作量 18150 米，1：200000 区域重力调查 8322 平方公里，各项地质工作计划全面完成。测绘部门全年完成测绘工作量 16.2 万工日，测绘产值工作量 878.63 万元，增长 7.5%；出版地图 61 种，增长 38.6%。

产品质量监测工作力度加大，气象“卫星遥感测试”水平提高，地震、水文等部门为我省经济建设发展也发挥着越来越大的作用。

教育事业稳步、健康、协调发展。全省各级各类在校学生1209.23万人，比上年增长3.6%。脱盲人数37.04万人，增加8.8万人。普及九年义务教育取得新的进展，累计有88个县(市、区)和大型农场通过国家“双基”达标验收，人口覆盖率达61%，比上年提高32.3个百分点；小学适龄儿童入学率为98.6%，小学生年辍学率为0.6%，比上年下降0.5个百分点，小学毕业生升学率为95.7%；初中生年辍学率为3.7%，比上年下降1.3百分点，中小学素质教育开始推行。中等职业教育进一步发展，招生数和在校生数分别占高中阶段教育招生和在校生总数的55.9%和54.9%(不含技工学校)；全省高等学校招生99787人，其中普通高校45111人，比上年增加3022人，成人高校招生54676人，增加4275人。此外，社会各界采用多渠道、多形式培养了大批技术工人，满足了市场经济发展的需要。

教师质量进一步提高。全省各级各类学校专任教师61.92万人，比上年增长2.8%。其中小学专任教师学历合格率94.5%，提高3.5个百分点；初中专任教师合格率80.5%，提高4.8个百分点。

九、文化卫生和体育

公益性文化事业健康发展。1997年，全省有博物馆、纪念馆60个，公共图书馆115个，档案馆200个，馆藏案卷810万卷。各类艺术表演团体89个，文化馆和群众艺术馆138个，发行各种电影新片120部，全省农村文化站巩固率在90%以上。

文艺创作喜获丰收。花鼓戏《红藤草》、巴陵戏《弃花翎》等一批戏剧作品分别获中宣部“五个一工程”奖、文化部第七届文华新剧目奖、剧作奖、新节目奖。

广播、电视事业稳步发展。1997年，我省广播电视节目送上卫星，实现了零的突破，八地市广播电视数字微波实现联网，湖南人民广播电台系列台之一——湖南交通广播电台开播。全省广播电台每日增加播音时间50小时45分钟，广播人口综合覆盖率78.6%；无线电视台每周平均增加播出时间196小时12分钟，电视人口综合覆盖率87.5%。

新闻出版工作成效显著。《精神之火》、《九亿农民健康教育读本》等一批精品、名牌图书分别获中宣部第六届“五个一工程”奖、第三届国家图书奖。出版业结构调整取得重要成果。图书品种数量得到合理控制，图书重版率达57.3%。报纸出版量比上年增长5%，期刊出版量增长2.9%。湘版读物的市场份额进一步扩大，在第八届全国书市上，湘版图书占70%。出版市场整顿取得明显成效。

医疗卫生工作取得新的成绩。90.6%的县(市、区)达到初级卫生保健合格标准。卫生下乡重新得到重视，全省组织下乡医疗队539支，医务人员5000人次，赠送医疗设备和药品，200多万元，为农民义务治病75万人次。预防保健工作得到加强。全省传染病发病率比上年下降5%，连续四年未发现脊髓灰质炎野毒株感染病例，丝虫病已经消灭，六个市以县为单位基本消灭了麻风病，全省爱婴医院由上年的184所增加到378所，28个城市爱卫工作达标上等，有9个城市进入省级以上卫生城市行列；全省孕产妇死亡率、婴儿死亡率和5岁以下儿童死亡率进一步下降。各级卫生部门对1.7万家基层医药卫生单位用药情况进行了严格检查，查处制售假劣药品案件3700起，发现并处理不合格药品18万种次。

体育事业成绩显著。在重大国际体育比赛中，我省运动员获金牌12枚，银牌5枚，铜牌5枚；在全国体育比赛中，获金牌35.5枚，银牌27枚，铜牌33.5枚；有8人46次破17项亚洲纪录，8人56次破17项世界纪录。在第八届全运会上，我省运动员获金牌17.5枚，银牌10枚，铜牌13.5枚，金牌名次由上届的第九位前移到第八位，总分由上届的第十二位前移到第十位。在全民健身计划的推动下，体育健身活动逐步走进千家万户。全省经常参加体育活动的人口占全部人口的比重达32.1%，比上年提高1.1个百分点。实施体育锻炼标准的学校占全部学校的比重由上年的69%上升到70.2%，体育达标学生由160万人增加到165.2万人。

十、人口与劳动就业

计划生育工作取得新的成绩。全省计划生育率为93.98%，比上年提高2.11个百分点。人口继续呈低速增长，据抽样调查，1997年人口出生率为12.59‰，死亡率为6.99‰，自然增长率为5.6‰，较上年均有所下降。据此推算，全省年末总人口为6465万人，比上年净增37万人。城镇人口1629万人，占总人口的25.2%。

人口老龄化的速度加快。年末全省65岁及以上老年人口达441.5万人，较上年增加10.2万人，占总人口的6.83%，接近7%的世界“老龄社会”水平。

劳动力结构有所调整，下岗职工继续增加。年末全省从业人员3550万人，其中第一产业占54.7%，下降2.1个百分点；第二产业占24.1%，第三产业占21.2%，分别上升1.1和1个百分点。城乡个体私营经济从业人员457万人，增加30万人。全年职工工资总额315亿元，比上年增长5.2%。年末下岗职工80万人，比上年末增加33万人，登记失业率为3.9%。

十一、人民生活与环境保护

城镇居民收入增长平缓、差距扩大。1997年，全省城镇居民人均可支配收入5209.8元，比上年增长3.1%，扣除物价因素实际增长0.1%。高低收入户可支配收入之比由上年的3.62∶1扩大到4.17∶1。消费结构趋向合理。城镇居民人均消费支出4317.12元，比上年增长5.3%，扣除物价因素实际增长2.2%；恩格尔系数由上年的48.5%下降到45.7%；衣着消费比重由12.4%下降到11.5%；交通与通信、娱乐文教、居住等消费支出增长较快，分别增长31.4%、25.1%和18.3%。部分下岗职工家庭生活困难的问题比较突出。

农民收入增加较多。1997年全省农民人均纯收入达2037.06元，比上年增加244.81元，增长13.7%，扣除物价因素实际增长8.9%。收入结构发生可喜变化。现金收入占纯收入比重由上年的61.6%提高到64.9%，实物收入占纯收入比重由38.4%下降到35.1%。在总的纯收入中，一产业纯收入比重由上年的64.2%下降为62.6%，二产业由17.2%上升为18%，三产业由14.5%上升为16%，其他非生产性纯收入比重由4.1%下降为3.4%。全省农民人均生活消费支出1815.79元，比上年增加79.08元，增长4.6%。其中，食品、居住、交通通信、文教娱乐用品及服务支出分别增长5.1%、5.5%、18.6%和6%。

城乡居民居住条件继续改善。年末城镇居民人均居住面积9.2平方米，农村居民人均房屋面积27.37平方米，分别比上年增加0.7平方米和0.49平方米。住房质量明显改善。城镇居民住房成套率提高；农村住房中砖木结构和钢筋混凝土结构的比重为91.2%，其中钢筋混凝土结构的比重比上年上升1.6个百分点。

社会福利、劳动保险事业得到发展。年末全省社会福利院床位3.57万张，比上年增长1.2%；收养2.82万人，增长1.5%。各级政府加大了解困工作力度，全省筹集解困资金4.49亿元，使困难企业职工得到救济。年内受到社会救助的城乡困难户和社会福利企业困难职工人数93.80万人次，增长4.8%，救助金额5.54亿元，增长6%。社会统筹和个人相结合的养老保险办法正在实施。全省已参加养老保险统筹的职工392.5万人、离退休人员103.6万人，覆盖面为66.1%。全省建立社会保障网络的乡镇为26%，比上年提高2个百分点。

环境保护工作成效明显。1997年我省环境法制建设进一步加强，环境宣传教育不断深入。各级领导和人民群众环保意识增强，因污染事故而引起的人民群众来信来访与索赔的人次增多，大中型建设项目“三同时”（环保设施应与主体工程同时设计、同时施工、同时竣工使用）执行率保持100%。绿色工程部分项目已经启动，城市环境综合整治工作进展较快。全省建成烟尘控制区497平方公里，噪声达标区190平方公里，城市气化率、饮用水质达标率、绿化覆盖率、工业废水处理率、工业固体废物综合治理率等均有所提高；省政府与各地签订的责任目标的98个办实事项目，90%以上已竣工验收；电力、煤炭、化工、冶金、有色等行业加大了工业污染治理力度，全省应取缔关停的1389家企业已基本关停到位。但环保经费投入不足，“三废”排放量仍在增加，大气污染和酸雨污染没有明显改观，环境治理工作任重道远。

公安、检察、法院为维护社会稳定，确保改革开放和经济建设顺利进行作出了积极贡献。1997年，全省公安机关共破获各类刑事案件50128起，其中重特大案件20050起；全省91个县市开通了智能型110报警服务台或报警电话。检察机关侦查各类经济犯罪案件2526起，涉及县处级及以上干部104人，万元以上经济大案2339件，挽回直接经济损失3.49亿元。全年全省刑事案件较上年下降6%。

注：1. 本公报各项统计数据为初步统计数；

2. 各项指标对比基数均为《湖南统计年鉴1997》公布的年报统计数。

城乡居民居住条件继续改善。年末城镇居民人均居住面积9.2平方米，农村居民人均住房面积27.37平方米，分别比上年增加0.7平方米和0.19平方米。住房质量明显改善，城镇居民住房成套率提高，农村住房中砖木结构和钢筋混凝土结构的比重为91.2%，其中钢筋混凝土结构的比重比上年上升1.6个百分点。

社会福利、劳动保险事业得到发展。年末全省社会福利院床位3.37万张，比上年增长1.2%；收养2.89万人，增长1.6%。各级政府加大了解困工作力度，全年筹集解困资金4.19亿元，使困难企业职工得到帮助。年内受到社会救助的城乡困难户和社会福利企业困难职工人数193.80万人次，增长4.8%，救助金额5.54亿元，增长6%。"社会统筹和个人相结合的养老保险制度"正在实施。全省已参加养老保险统筹的职工392.5万人，离退休人员103.6万人，覆盖面为86.1%。全省建立社会保障网络的乡镇为269，比上年提高2个百分点。

环境保护工作成效明显。1997年我省环境法制建设进一步加强，环境宣传教育不断深入，全社会和人民群众的环境意识增强，因污染事故而引起的人民群众来信来访与去年相比大大减少。大中型建设项目"三同时"（环保设施应与主体工程同时设计、同时施工、同时竣工使用）执行率保持100%。绿色工程部分项目已经启动，城市环境综合整治工作进展较快。全省建成烟尘控制区497平方公里，噪声达标区130平方公里，城市气化率、饮用水源达标率、绿化覆盖率、工业废水达标率、工业固体废物综合利用率等均有所提高。省政府与各地签订的责任目标的95个治理项目90%以上已竣工验收；电力、煤炭、化工、冶金、有色等行业加大了工业污染治理力度，全省限期治理的1589家企业已基本治理到位。但环保经费投入不足，"三废"排放量仍在增加，大气污染和酸雨污染没有明显改观，环境治理工作任重道远。

公安、检察、法院为维护社会稳定、确保改革开放和经济建设顺利进行作出了积极贡献。1997年，全省公安机关共破获各类刑事案件50123起，其中重特大案件20050起；全省91个县市开通了智能型"110"报警服务台或报警电话。检察机关立案各类经济犯罪案件2526起，涉及县处级以上干部104人，万元以上的大案2289件，挽回直接经济损失3.49亿元。全年全省刑事案件数比上年下降9.3%。

注：1.本公报各项统计数据为初步统计数。

2.各项指标对比基数均为《浙江统计年鉴1997》公布的年报统计数。

一、行政区划和自然状况

ADMINISTRATIVE DIVISION AND NATURAL CONDITIONS

1—1 行 政 区 划

Administrative Division

年 份	地州数	省辖市数	地州辖市数	县数	省辖市区数	镇数	乡数
1949	11	2		77	8	104	1681
1950	11	2	6	77	13	126	8287
1951	11	2	7	78	11	146	10306
1952	6	1	7	86	5	209	19485
1953	6	1	8	86	6	263	15611
1954	7	1	8	86	6	270	15330
1955	7	1	8	86	6	246	15345
1956	7	2	7	86	5	179	2966
1957	7	2	7	86	5	205	2974
1958	7	2	8	86	5	94	1184
1959	7	2	8	78	4	110	1158
1960	7	2	8	78	5	99	1263
1961	7	2	14	85	5	158	3480
1962	9	2	8	85	6	160	3545
1963	9	2	5	86	6	171	3549
1964	10	2	5	86	6	173	3532
1965	10	2	5	87	6	175	3461
1966	10	2	5	88	7	182	3351
1967	10	2	5	88	7	175	3318
1968	11	2	5	88	7	157	3182
1969	11	2	6	89	7	162	3272
1970	11	2	6	89	10	158	3315
1971	11	2	6	89	10	157	3316
1972	11	2	6	89	10	158	3317
1973	11	2	6	89	10	161	3318
1974	11	2	6	89	9	161	3319
1975	11	2	7	89	9	162	3324
1976	11	2	7	89	9	165	3324
1977	12	3	7	90	13	163	3326
1978	12	3	7	90	13	154	3295
1979	12	3	10	90	13	148	3297
1980	12	5	9	90	22	155	3321
1981	11	5	9	89	22	185	3331
1982	11	5	11	87	22	196	3340
1983	9	6	10	88	22	230	3340
1984	9	6	12	86	27	513	3090
1985	9	6	14	84	27	544	3011
1986	7	6	16	82	27	581	2895
1987	7	6	18	80	26	585	2903
1988	6	8	17	78	30	596	2889
1989	6	8	17	78	30	621	2807
1990	6	8	18	78	29	628	2801
1991	6	8	18	78	29	639	2784
1992	6	8	19	77	26	663	2773
1993	6	8	20	76	26	748	2689
1994	5	9	20	74	28	769	2658
1995	4	10	19	73	30	899	1406
1996	3	11	17	73	32	950	1360
1997	3	11	18	72	32	979	1327

1—1 续表 (1997年底)

地市	地州数	省辖市数	地州辖市数	县数	省辖市区数	镇数	乡数	市、县(市辖区)名称
全省	3	11	18	72	32	979	1327	
长沙市		1	1	3	5	70	45	长沙市区(芙蓉区、天心区、岳麓区、开福区、雨花区)、浏阳市、长沙县、望城县、宁乡县
株洲市		1	1	4	4	57	85	株洲市区(荷塘区、石峰区、泸淞区、天元区)、醴陵市、株洲县、攸县、茶陵县、炎陵县
湘潭市		1	2	1	2	34	26	湘潭市区(雨湖区、岳塘区)、湘乡市、韶山市、湘潭县
衡阳市		1	2	5	5	103	77	衡阳市区(江东区、城南区、城北区、郊区、南岳区)、耒阳市、常宁市、衡阳县、衡南县、衡山县、衡东县、祁东县
邵阳市		1	1	8	3	78	118	邵阳市区(双清区、大祥区、北塔区)、武冈市、邵东县、新邵县、邵阳县、隆回县、洞口县、新宁县、绥宁县、城步苗族自治县
岳阳市		1	2	4	3	88	86	岳阳市区(岳阳楼区、云溪区、君山区)、汨罗市、临湘市、岳阳县、平江县、湘阴县、华容县
常德市		1	1	6	2	96	114	常德市区(武陵区、鼎城区)、津市市、安乡县、汉寿县、澧县、临澧县、桃源县、石门县
张家界市		1		2	2	29	18	张家界市区(永定区、武陵源区)、慈利县、桑植县
益阳市		1	1	3	2	62	60	益阳市区(资阳区、赫山区)、沅江市、南县、桃江县、安化县
郴州市		1	1	8	2	79	172	郴州市区(北湖区、苏仙区)、资兴市、桂阳县、永兴县、宜章县、嘉禾县、临武县、汝城县、桂东县、安仁县
永州市		1		9	2	108	80	永州市区(芝山区、冷水滩区)、东安县、道县、宁远县、江永县、江华瑶族自治县、蓝山县、新田县、双牌县、祁阳县
娄底地区	1		3	2		52	31	娄底市、冷水江市、涟源市、双峰县、新化县
怀化地区	1		2	10		71	249	怀化市、洪江市、黔阳县、沅陵县、辰溪县、溆浦县、麻阳苗族自治县、新晃侗族自治县、芷江侗族自治县、会同县、靖州苗族侗族自治县、通道侗族自治县
湘西土家族苗族自治州	1		1	7		52	166	吉首市、泸溪县、凤凰县、花垣县、保靖县、古丈县、永顺县、龙山县

注:1997年国务院通知怀化地区撤销改怀化市,因移交衔接诸事未妥,故1997年年报仍按原制综合上报。

1—2 人口和自然资源

Population and Natural Resources

项　　目	单　　位	1997 年
一、人　口		
年底人口数	万人	6465.00
人口密度	人/平方公里	305.24
二、土　地		
土地面积	万平方公里	21.18
耕地	万公顷	323.01
三、气　候		
年平均降水量	毫米	1427
年降水总量	亿立方米	3022
四、森　林		
森林面积	万公顷	750.14(11252 万亩)
森林覆盖率	%	51.4
林木蓄积量	万立方米	24504.47
五、水文、水利		
5 公里以上河流	条	5341
5 公里以上河流长度	万公里	9
河川年径流总量	亿立方米	2085
淡水总面积	万公顷	135.38(2030.64 万亩)
#可养殖面积	万公顷	34.67(520 万亩)
#已放养面积	万公顷	29.12(436.87 万亩)
天然水资源总量	亿立方米	1998.2
地表水资源总量	亿立方米	1565.2
地下(浅层)水量	亿立方米	433.0
水力资源蕴藏量	万千瓦	1532.45
#可开发量	万千瓦	1083.84
六、矿产资源(保有储量)		
煤	亿吨	30.34
铁矿石	亿吨	8.82
磷矿石	亿吨	17.32
盐	亿吨	35.65

注：1、本表第 2—5 项为过去清查数，有待进一步普查和勘测。

2、河川径流量＝省内各水系年径流量(1623)＋客水＋地下水(6.5)。

1—3 土 地 状 况

Land Characteristics

项　目	1997年面积		占总面积的%
	万公顷	万　亩	
总　面　积	2118.29	31774.35	100
1、按地形分			
山地	1084.72	16270.80	51.2
盆地	294.12	4411.73	13.9
平原	277.86	4167.90	13.1
丘陵	326.22	4893.28	15.4
水面	135.37	2030.64	6.4
2、按地高分			
50米以下	210.65	3159.76	9.9
50—100米	235.27	3529.03	11.1
100—300米	491.74	7376.09	23.2
300—500米	478.36	7175.34	22.6
500—800米	390.48	5857.19	18.5
800—1000米	220.58	3308.73	10.4
1000米以上	91.21	1368.21	4.3
3、按特征分			
耕地	323.01	4845.15	15.2
森林	750.14	11252.10	35.4
宜林荒山	33.84	507.60	1.6
疏林	41.63	624.45	2.0
灌木	162.98	2444.70	7.7
未成林造林地	54.32	814.80	2.6
淡水总面积	135.38	2030.70	6.4
其他	616.99	9254.85	29.1

注：为使用方便，面积列出公顷数与万亩数。

1—4 主要山脉基本情况

Major Mountain Ranges

名称	平均高度(米)	最高峰(米)
雪峰山	1500	2021(城步县二宝顶)
武陵山	500—1200	2098.7(石门县壶瓶山)
南岭山脉 (指大庾岭、骑田岭、 萌渚岭、都庞岭、越城岭)	1000—1500	2009(道县韭菜岭)
幕阜山—罗霄山	1000	2052(炎陵县斗笠顶) 2041.1(桂东县八面山)

1—5 主要河流基本情况

Major Rivers

名称	河长(公里)	#省内	河流条数(条)	流域面积(平方公里)	#省内	省内年径流量(亿立方米)	水力资源蕴藏量(万千瓦)	#可开发量
各水系合计			5341		211829	1623.0	1532.45	1083.84
湘江	856	670	2157	94660	85383	664.9	470.70	318.29
资水	713	630	771	28142	26738	217.4	201.03	147.71
沅江	1033	568	1491	89163	51066	393.3	537.51	460.21
澧水	388	388	326	18496	15505	131.2	152.46	137.11
洞庭湖水系			432		27269	157.7	140.20	13.65
鄱阳湖水系			16		683	44.6	3.12	0.58
珠江水系			148		5185	13.9	27.43	6.29

注:1、河流条数指河长 5 公里以上的河流数,河长共 9 万公里。

2、资水河长以夫夷水作水源计算。

3、据 1986 年勘定,洞庭湖面积为 2691 平方公里。

1—6 主要城市平均气温(1997年)

Monthly Average Temperature of Major Cities

单位:摄氏度

城　　市	1月	2月	3月	4月	5月	6月	7月
长　　沙	5.5	7.3	12.7	16.8	24.2	25.3	28.0
株　　洲	5.9	7.5	13.1	17.0	24.2	25.2	28.0
湘　　潭	5.9	7.2	12.7	16.6	23.9	24.8	27.6
衡　　阳	6.9	8.0	13.8	17.4	25.0	25.7	28.1
邵　　阳	6.4	7.3	13.0	16.6	23.5	24.6	26.6
岳　　阳	5.8	7.7	12.3	16.8	24.3	25.7	28.1
常　　德	5.5	7.2	12.0	16.6	24.1	25.5	27.6
张 家 界	6.4	7.5	11.9	16.5	22.9	24.6	26.5
益　　阳	5.5	6.8	12.1	17.9	23.9	25.2	27.5
郴　　州	7.7	9.0	14.6	17.3	24.8	25.6	27.7
永　　州	7.4	8.0	13.9	17.3	24.3	25.1	27.3
娄　　底	6.3	7.2	12.8	16.6	24.1	24.9	27.1
怀　　化	5.8	6.5	12.3	16.1	22.7	24.4	26.6
吉　　首	6.0	6.9	12.2	16.1	22.4	24.2	26.6

城　　市	8月	9月	10月	11月	12月	全 年	附:上年平均
长　　沙	29.0	21.6	19.3	12.2	7.4	17.4	17.6
株　　洲	28.7	21.5	19.5	12.4	7.5	17.5	17.5
湘　　潭	28.6	21.3	19.2	12.1	7.3	17.3	17.1
衡　　阳	28.6	21.9	19.7	13.1	7.9	18.0	18.1
邵　　阳	28.1	21.2	18.6	12.4	7.4	17.1	16.9
岳　　阳	29.4	22.3	19.8	12.3	7.1	17.6	17.5
常　　德	29.8	22.5	19.5	12.0	7.1	17.5	17.4
张 家 界	29.0	22.6	18.8	12.5	7.5	17.2	17.0
益　　阳	28.9	21.5	19.2	11.7	6.9	17.3	17.3
郴　　州	27.6	21.5	19.9	13.9	8.5	18.2	17.7
永　　州	27.8	21.4	19.4	13.2	7.8	17.7	17.2
娄　　底	28.9	21.7	19.2	12.4	7.4	17.4	17.4
怀　　化	28.2	21.1	17.8	12.3	7.2	16.8	16.8
吉　　首	28.5	21.6	18.0	12.3	7.6	16.9	16.7

1—7 主要城市降水量(1997年)

Monthly Precipitation of Major Cities

单位:毫米

城市	1月	2月	3月	4月	5月	6月	7月
长沙	55	92	128	208	178	411	141
株洲	50	95	128	207	166	138	136
湘潭	46	94	108	176	182	209	123
衡阳	78	117	210	115	250	239	202
邵阳	66	101	151	125	228	224	167
岳阳	69	91	38	116	134	155	113
常德	84	91	58	123	157	110	155
张家界	64	75	54	82	160	126	217
益阳	62	129	122	201	138	133	284
郴州	118	145	235	263	183	167	138
永州	106	114	180	207	195	133	174
娄底	45	99	124	222	196	161	232
怀化	53	76	96	137	226	221	114
吉首	59	70	74	241	203	80	167

城市	8月	9月	10月	11月	12月	全年	附:上年全年
长沙	52	161	71	206	118	1821	1396
株洲	56	177	108	169	89	1519	1475
湘潭	47	164	108	148	100	1505	1323
衡阳	185	172	128	74	117	1887	1452
邵阳	118	123	183	120	72	1678	1284
岳阳	8	76	57	148	127	1132	1641
常德	32	61	62	154	99	1186	1187
张家界	33	86	50	67	73	1087	1601
益阳	126	168	37	135	163	1698	1517
郴州	231	241	90	81	121	2013	1343
永州	119	126	108	66	126	1654	1146
娄底	52	142	114	151	83	2521	1416
怀化	73	117	183	51	64	1411	1615
吉首	45	126	86	65	61	1277	1362

1—8 主要城市日照时数(1997年)

Monthly Sunshine Hours of Major Cities

单位:小时

城　市	1月	2月	3月	4月	5月	6月	7月
长　沙	93	29	45	94	199	160	169
株　洲	84	31	62	77	183	142	159
湘　潭	93	37	49	72	184	145	172
衡　阳	75	31	63	61	178	105	159
邵　阳	88	37	68	88	189	152	152
岳　阳	92	26	24	67	146	121	146
常　德	108	52	56	115	218	185	179
张家界	83	22	33	86	156	139	139
益　阳	104	34	45	93	171	152	148
郴　州	78	40	72	69	187	149	142
永　州	89	31	56	71	172	124	144
娄　底	94	39	64	94	195	150	157
怀　化	57	33	49	76	171	130	141
吉　首	65	23	28	40	164	148	93

城　市	8月	9月	10月	11月	12月	全年	附：上年全年
长　沙	226	120	139	111	48	1433	1485
株　洲	199	118	117	112	35	1319	1280
湘　潭	261	125	134	127	38	1437	1552
衡　阳	194	126	101	101	27	1221	1312
邵　阳	253	118	84	110	27	1366	1452
岳　阳	261	152	129	118	37	1319	1575
常　德	302	181	114	130	63	1703	1543
张家界	255	159	98	80	22	1272	1255
益　阳	259	127	130	112	43	1418	1306
郴　州	144	108	115	106	21	1231	1400
永　州	211	134	101	107	14	1254	1511
娄　底	248	133	117	119	30	1440	1471
怀　化	258	133	90	92	29	1259	1367
吉　首	300	150	89	75	25	1200	1395

二、综合

GENERAL SURVEY

2—1 国民经济和社会发展总量与速度指标

Principal Indicators and Develop Speed of National Economy and Development

指　　标	1995年	1996年	1997年	1997年为下列年(%)		年均增长速度	
				1995年	1996年	八五期间	1996—1997年
人口与就业							
一、人口(万人)							
年底总人口	6392.00	6428.00	6465.00	101.5	100.6	0.78	0.76
市镇人口	1550.99	1606.95	1629.00	105.0	101.4	7.52	2.48
乡村人口	4841.01	4821.05	4836.00	99.9	100.3	—0.92	—0.05
男性人口	3322.27	3339.25	3356.43	101.0	100.5	0.76	0.51
女性人口	3069.73	3088.75	3108.57	101.3	100.6	0.79	0.63
二、就业(万人)							
从业人员数	3467.31	3514.16	3560.29	103.0	101.3	1.91	1.50
#职工人数	597.50	596.84	597.48	100.0	100.1	1.6	0
城镇失业人员数	27.40	29.72	29.02	105.9	97.6	11.5	2.91
宏观经济							
一、国民核算(亿元)							
国内生产总值	2195.70	2647.16	2993.00	124.8	110.8	11.0	11.7
第一产业	685.30	793.98	855.75	112.7	106.1	5.0	6.1
第二产业	815.82	1008.43	1166.97	133.0	113.5	15.9	15.3
第三产业	694.58	844.75	970.28	125.5	111.5	12.3	12.0
国内支出总额	2195.70	2647.16	2993.00	124.8	110.8	11.0	11.7
#最终消费	1396.88	1753.27	1956.22	122.9	108.0	5.8	10.9
居民消费	1108.78	1409.44	1540.67	121.5	106.2	5.6	10.2
政府消费	228.10	343.83	415.55	128.1	115.1	6.8	13.2
资本形成总额	800.50	895.30	1021.39	127.6	114.1	18.5	14.7
固定资本形成总额	534.12	678.32	725.73	135.9	107.0	18.7	14.4
存货增加	266.38	216.98	295.66	111.0	136.3	18.2	15.4
二、固定资产投资(亿元)							
全社会固定资产投资总额	524.01	678.33	688.36	131.4	129.4	33.4	14.6
#国有单位	316.90	375.27	353.97	111.7	94.3	34.5	5.7
集体单位	39.83	79.25	84.48	212.1	106.6	26.4	45.6
个体经济	120.34	178.58	195.17	162.6	109.3	24.7	27.4

2—1 续表 1

指 标	1995 年	1996 年	1997 年	1997 年为下列年(%)		年均增长速度	
				1995 年	1996 年	八五期间	1996—1997 年
三、财政(亿元)							
地方财政收入	108.16	130.36	137.16	126.8	105.2	9.1	12.6
地方财政支出	173.94	217.74	230.82	132.7	106.0	16.8	15.2
四、物价总指数(上年=100)							
商品零售价格总指数	115.5	105.2	100.3	105.5	100.3	13.5	2.72
居民消费价格总指数	119.0	107.7	102.8	110.7	102.8	15.0	5.23
农副产品收购价格总指数	117.2	104.9	95.3	99.9	95.3	12.6	—0.03
五、利用外资(万美元)							
签订利用外资协议额	174427	93670	129295	74.1	138.0	46.1	—13.9
实际利用外资额	87104	112530	135777	155.9	120.7	29.6	24.9
产 业							
一、农业							
耕地面积(千公顷)	3249.7	3239.4	3230.1	99.40	99.71	—0.38	—0.30
农林牧渔业从业人员(万人)	2114.71	2089.33	2074.12	98.08	99.27	—0.95	—0.97
农林牧渔业总产值(亿元)	1046.97	1226.32	1322.26	117.4	108.3	5.9	8.4
#农作物种植业	543.16	608.71	617.75	110.5	108.3	2.8	5.1
林业	42.58	45.71	47.98	104.7	101.5	5.1	2.3
牧业	369.34	460.82	538.02	125.6	109.2	10.1	12.1
副业	36.76	40.67	42.40	119.5	106.9	6.1	9.3
渔业	54.93	70.41	76.10	133.1	110.4	12.4	15.4
主要农产品产量(万吨)							
粮食	2752.09	2820.62	2876.99	104.5	102.0	0.4	2.2
棉花	22.35	18.96	25.57	114.4	134.9	13.2	7.0
油料	112.04	118.12	129.26	115.4	109.4	9.2	7.4
苎麻	5.83	4.67	4.87	83.5	104.3	18.3	—8.6
黄红麻(熟麻)	0.36	0.30	0.36	100.0	120.0	—28.1	
烤烟	7.88	13.75	22.48	285.3	163.5	—6.8	68.9
茶叶	6.14	5.49	5.55	90.4	101.1	—3.6	—4.9
柑桔	101.50	89.59	134.14	132.2	149.7	16.8	15.0
猪牛羊肉	317.37	366.46	404.02	127.3	110.2	10.9	12.8
水产品	85.78	98.26	110.76	129.1	112.7	10.1	13.6

2—1　续表 2

指　　标	1995 年	1996 年	1997 年	1997 年为下列年(%)		年均增长速度	
				1995 年	1996 年	八五期间	1996—1997 年
二、工业							
工业总产值(亿元)	2451.47	3280.58	3817.15	155.2	120.5	18.4	24.6
#国有	1022.13	962.70	945.82	104.1	102.7	6.3	2.0
集体	757.91	1131.51	1273.52	148.4	117.9	22.9	21.8
#轻工业	1043.61	1457.22	1705.77	153.5	119.2	18.1	23.9
重工业	1407.86	1823.36	2111.38	172.2	121.5	18.6	31.2
主要工业产品产量							
布(亿米)	4.89	4.65	4.40	90.0	94.6	1.0	-5.2
机制纸及纸板(万吨)	94.02	103.41	94.39	100.4	91.3	7.7	0.2
糖(万吨)	6.31	5.85	7.72	122.3	131.9	-1.9	10.6
自行车(万辆)	6.67	1.42	1.66	24.9	116.9	-37.5	-50.1
缝纫机(万架)	10.03	7.86	4.16	41.5	52.9	-8.6	-35.6
家用电冰箱(万台)	22.28	3.72	7.61	34.2	204.6	-2.6	-41.5
电视机(万部)	24.73	14.86	15.64	63.2	105.2	-14.1	-20.5
录放音机(万台)	38.58	22.53	73.90	191.6	328.0	-7.6	38.4
原煤(万吨)	5564.51	5989.05	4409.84	79.2	73.6	10.5	-11.0
发电量(亿千瓦小时)	332.94	339.09	345.96	103.9	102.0	10.6	1.9
钢(万吨)	175.60	189.45	243.73	138.8	128.7	5.2	17.8
成品钢材(万吨)	154.54	167.52	199.03	128.8	118.8	5.1	13.5
水泥(万吨)	2196.02	2300.28	2208.66	100.6	96.0	17.0	0.3
独立核算工业企业财务指标							
年底固定资产原价(亿元)	1282.75	1419.85	1657.74	129.2	116.8	21.8	13.7
年底固定资产净值	907.38	936.84	1098.71	121.1	117.2	22.9	10.0
利润和税金总额	90.96	135.51	150.24	165.2	110.9	10.0	28.5
三、建筑业							
建筑业企业人数(万人)	60.97	75.94	81.22	133.2	107.0		15.4
建筑业总产值(亿元)	188.28	278.38	296.50	157.5	106.5		25.5
施工房屋面积(万平方米)	4507	4662	4720	104.7	101.2		2.3
竣工房屋面积	2313	2393	2280	98.6	95.3		-0.7
四、交通运输							
货运量(万吨)	49853	50420	48946	98.2	97.1	5.7	-0.9
#铁路	5017	4893	4536	90.4	92.7	1.0	-4.9
公路	41272	42191	41340	100.2	98.0	6.8	0.1
水运	3531	3301	3034	93.6	91.9	1.9	-3.3

2—1 续表 3

指标	1995 年	1996 年	1997 年	1997 年为下列年(%)		年均增长速度	
				1995 年	1996 年	八五期间	1996—1997 年
客运量(万人)	71566	76377	79250	110.7	103.8	5.7	5.2
＃铁路	4135	3892	4488	108.5	115.3	3.5	4.2
公路	65971	71087	73233	111.0	103.0	6.1	5.4
水运	1375	1298	1357	98.7	104.5	—2.6	—0.7
五、邮电通信业							
邮电业务总量(万元)	314794	427332	522447	165.9	122.3	47.9	28.8
函件(万件)	34412	29556	21979	63.9	74.4	11.4	—20.1
报刊期发数(万份)	1485	1223	1369	92.2	111.9	8.7	—3.9
交换机容量(万门)	273.75	358.53	411.08	150.2	114.7	58.3	22.5
城市	205.65	267.05	298.59	145.2	111.8	63.2	20.5
农村	68.10	91.48	112.49	165.2	123.0	47.5	28.5
电话机(万部)	163.10	234.89	265.28	162.6	112.9	59.8	27.5
城市	132.24	186.48	198.95	150.4	106.7	62.3	22.7
农村	30.86	48.41	66.33	214.9	137.0	51.0	46.6
六、国内商业							
社会消费品零售总额(亿元)	837.41	947.40	1041.60	124.4	109.9	23.2	11.5
七、对外经济贸易和旅游							
进出口总额(亿美元)	29.17	32.12	32.83	112.5	102.2	25.4	6.1
进口额	8.20	9.94	9.54	116.3	96.0	43.2	7.9
出口额	20.97	22.18	23.29	111.1	105.0	21.1	5.4
国际旅游							
来湘旅游人数(万人次)	17.73	22.87	30.16	170.1	131.9	15.8	30.4
旅游外汇收入(万美元)	6499	10180	14004	215.5	137.6	45.3	46.8
八、金融保险(亿元)							
国家银行各项存款	831.35	1097.21	1204.36	144.9	109.8	21.1	20.4
国家银行各项贷款	944.82	1188.69	1340.17	141.8	112.7	15.4	19.1
城市信用社各项存款	70.68	88.48	55.95	79.2	63.2		—11.0
城市信用社各项贷款	43.99	56.12	35.92	81.7	64.0		—9.6
农村信用社各项存款	320.36	389.25	438.71	136.9	112.7	37.3	17.0
农村信用社各项贷款	212.88	256.45	276.83	130.0	107.9	38.7	14.0
财产保险承保额	2080.33	2862.07	2770.42	133.2	96.8	22.4	15.4
人身保险期末承保人数(万人)			1912.96				
人身保险期末承保额(亿元)			1140.39				

2—1　续表 4

指　　　标	1995 年	1996 年	1997 年	1997 年为下列年（%）		年均增长速度	
				1995 年	1996 年	八五期间	1996—1997 年
教育、科技、文化							
一、教育							
专任教师数(人)							
普通高等学校	15307	15683	15894	103.8	101.3	1.2	1.9
中等学校	189679	198674	207135	109.2	104.3	2.6	4.5
小学	297967	298500	299453	100.5	100.3	—0.6	0.2
在校学生(万人)							
普通高等学校	13.04	13.57	14.37	110.2	105.9	8.1	5.0
中等学校	323.95	347.63	370.14	114.3	106.5	3.3	6.9
小学	736.65	765.91	787.13	106.9	102.8	1.2	3.4
教育事业费支出(亿元)	31.58	35.50	37.92	120.1	106.8		9.6
二、科技							
科学家、工程师人数(人)	10425	8771	8580		97.8		
科技三项及科学事业费支出(亿元)	2.21	2.83	3.48	157.4	122.9	16.6	25.5
技术市场技术交易成交额	5.08	6.19	7.87	154.9	127.1	36.0	24.5
三、文化							
出版数量							
图书(万册)	33677	39393	37494	111.3	95.2	0.9	5.5
杂志	7768	7844	7686	98.9	98.0	8.3	0.5
报纸(万份)	62425	63585	68726	110.1	108.1	3.8	4.9
故事影片产量(部)	6	6	3	50.0	50.0		
电视节目每周播出时间(时：分)	1291：04	1537：50	1734:02	134.3	112.7	14.3	15.9
家庭、生活、环境							
一、家庭							
家庭总户数(万户)	1785.31	1799.97	1798.83	100.76	99.94	2.5	0.38
城镇居民平均每户家庭人口(人)	3.19	3.19	3.14	98.43	98.43	—0.8	—0.8
农村居民平均每户常住人口	4.19	4.07	4.02	95.94	98.778	—0.9	—2.1
二、婚姻(万对)							
结婚数	43.77	42.92	41.48	94.8	96.6	—4.4	—2.7
离婚数	6.33	6.69	5.39	85.2	80.6	11.2	—7.3
三、居住(平方米/人)							
城市居民人均居住面积	7.75	8.06	8.66	111.7	107.4	2.3	5.7
农村居民人均住房面积	25.57	26.88	27.37	107.0	101.8	2.8	3.4

注：1996 年及以后科学家工程师人数系指从事科技活动的人数，与以前各年不可比。

2—1 续表5

指 标	1995年	1996年	1997年	1997年为下列年(%)		年均增长速度	
				1995年	1996年	八五期间	1996—1997年
四、生活							
城市居民人均可支配收入(元)	4705.2	5052.1	5209.7	100.5	100.3	7.5	0.25
农村居民人均纯收入	1425.16	1792.25	2037.06	117.9	108.9	3.3	8.60
城乡储蓄存款余额(亿元)	880.35	1179.52	1255.28	142.6	106.4	31.7	19.41
五、工资福利							
工资总额(亿元)	282.05	299.57	314.91	101.4	102.3	4.7	0.69
职工平均工资(元)	4797	5100	5326	100.3	101.6	3.1	0.15
职工劳保福利费(亿元)	86.81	102.29	108.70	125.2	106.3	19.0	11.90
离休、退休、退职职工人数(万人)	138.23	145.67	145.82	105.5	100.1	6.5	2.71
离退休退职职工劳保福利费(亿元)	59.28	70.63	76.18	128.5	107.9	25.6	13.36
六、卫生							
医院(个)	3879	3423	3349	86.3	97.8	—1.5	—7.1
医生(万人)	8.46	8.77	9.00	106.4	102.6	0.5	3.1
医院床位数(万张)	13.52	13.36	13.47	99.6	102.4	0.2	—0.2
七、市政建设							
自来水供应量(亿吨)	31.78	29.14	34.01	107.0	116.7	—0.6	3.4
下水道长度(公里)	2928	3209	3274	111.8	102.0	12.2	5.7
城市煤气供气量(万立方米)	69984	74915	94860	135.5	126.6	—4.3	16.2
石油液化气用量(万吨)	11.65	12.13	13.78	118.3	113.6	28.5	8.7
公共汽车总数(辆)	6871	7092	7551	109.9	106.5	24.0	4.8
公交客运总量(万人次)	92334	81756	93053	100.8	113.8		0.4
绿地面积(千公顷)	23.66	24.87	25.81	109.1	103.8	8.7	4.4
八、环境、灾害							
治理污染资金使用额(亿元)	3.77	3.15	2.18	57.8	69.2	16.5	—23.9
环境污染事故数(次)	301	214	362	120.3	169.2	7.3	9.7
环境污染事故罚款金额(万元)	35	33.2	43.2	123.4	130.1	1.8	11.1
火灾发生数(次)	1128	1087	2467	218.7	227.6	—9.2	47.9
火灾损失(万元)	6824	5271	7666	112.3	145.4	25.0	6.0
交通事故发生数(次)	10361	10994	10401	100.4	94.6	—1.4	0.2
交通事故损失(万元)	6203	6967	6586	106.2	94.5	36.4	3.0

2—2 国民经济和社会发展效益指标

Beneficial Indexes of Nationd Economy and Social Development

指　　标	单　　位	1995年	1996年	1997年
人口与就业				
人口出生率	‰	13.02	12.81	12.59
人口死亡率	‰	7.15	7.20	6.99
人口自然增长率	‰	5.87	5.61	5.60
就业者负担人口	人	1.67	1.95	1.64
城镇失业率	%	3.8	3.9	3.9
宏观经济				
全社会劳动生产率	元/人	6394	7583	8461
第一产业	元/人	3304	3905	4285
第二产业	元/人	10965	12879	14473
第三产业	元/人	11275	12533	13216
人均国内生产总值	元	3470	4130	4643
全社会固定资产投资相当于国内生产总值	%	23.87	25.62	23.00
国有经济项目投产率	%	57.2	57.90	58.28
国有经济固定资产交付使用率	%	64.0	71.90	76.30
基本建设固定资产交付使用率	%	57.64	65.10	61.97
基本建设项目建成投产率	%	56.76	57.10	56.57
地方财政收入相当于国内生产总值	%	4.93	4.92	4.58
地方财政支出相当于国内生产总值	%	7.92	8.23	7.71
工农商品综合比价(以上年为100)	%	99.6	100.2	105.4
实际利用外资相当于签订利用外资额	%	49.94	120.13	105.0
产　　业				
农业人均耕地面积	公顷	0.0671	0.0672	0.0499
农业从业者人均耕地面积	公顷	0.157	0.162	0.161
农业从业者人均农业总产值	元	5038	5834	6352
每公顷耕地农业机械总动力	千瓦	4.71	4.99	5.24
每公顷耕地用电量	千瓦小时	1158	1201	1290
每公顷耕地化肥施用量	公斤	517	516	543
每公顷耕地生产的农业产值	元	32214	37849	40936

2—2 续表1

指标	单位	1995年	1996年	1997年
每一农业从业者农产品产量				
粮食	公斤	1326	1351	1382
棉花	公斤	10.76	9.48	12.33
油料	公斤	53.97	59.08	62.32
肉类	公斤	152.90	183.31	194.79
水产品	公斤	41.53	49.15	53.40
每公顷播种面积农产品产量				
粮食	公斤	5380	5494	5581
棉花	公斤	1206	1090	1448
油料	公斤	1258	1252	1352
独立核算工业企业效益				
固定资产利税率	%	9.70	9.54	9.96
全部资金利税率	%	8.14	7.59	7.16
产值利税率	%	9.07	8.17	8.63
国有独立核算工业企业效益				
固定资产利税率	%	9.08	9.03	8.03
资金利税率	%	8.33	5.65	6.81
产值利税率	%	10.78	12.02	11.57
建筑业技术装备率	元/人	4014	3710	3954
建筑业动力装备率	千瓦/人	4.2	3.9	4.1
建筑业产值利税率	%	3.9	4.3	4.1
建筑业全员劳动生产率	元/人	36707	36773	36506
运输业运输铁路网密度	公里/万平方公里	123	123	123
运输业公路网密度	公里/万平方公里	2792	2792	2822
邮电通信业城镇百人拥有电话机数	部	8.53	11.60	12.25
农村百人拥有电话机数	部	0.64	1.00	1.37
按全省计算人均消费品零售额	元	1319	1477	1615
进出口总额相当于国内生产总值	%	11.10	10.07	9.10
每一来湘旅游客人次支出	美元	366	445	464
银行存款相当于国内生产总值	%	37.86	41.45	40.24
银行贷款相当于国内生产总值	%	43.03	44.90	44.78

2—2 续表 2

指　　标	单　位	1995 年	1996 年	1997 年
教育、科技、文化				
学龄儿童入学率	%	98.0	98.2	98.5
小学升学率	%	90.6	93.6	95.7
中学升学率	%	47.7	53.0	50.0
学校教师负担学生人数				
高等学校	人	8.5	8.6	9.0
普通中等学校	人	15.9	16.3	16.6
小学学校	人	24.7	25.7	26.3
当年教育事业费	亿元	31.58	35.50	37.92
教育事业费相当于国内生产总值	%	1.44	1.34	1.27
科技三项及科学事业费相当于国内生产总值	%	0.10	0.11	0.12
每百万人有电影放影单位	个	101	79	91
每百万人有艺术表演团体	个	1.39	1.37	1.33
每百万人有公共图书馆	个	1.83	1.80	1.78
家庭、生活、环境				
离婚率	‰	2.00	2.08	1.67
职工保险福利相当于工资比	%	30.78	34.14	34.50
离退休职工相当于在职工人数比	%	23.1	24.4	24.4
每万人口中医院数	个	0.61	0.53	0.52
医生数	人	13.32	13.64	13.90
医院床位数	张	21.28	20.79	20.84
医院病床使用率	%	64.60	65.00	56.68
城市自来水普及率	%	97.7	97.74	97.79
城市用气普及率	%	55.5	64.7	65.7
每万人绿地面积	公顷	4.3	4.5	4.7
平均每起火灾损失	万元	6.05	4.85	3.11
平均每起交通事故损失	万元	0.60	0.63	0.63
平均每起环境污染事故罚款	万元	0.12	0.16	0.12

2—3 国民经济主要比例关系

Principal Relations of Major Economic Indicators

单位:%

指　　标	1995年	1996年	1997年
一、国内生产总值比例			
第一产业	31.2	30.0	28.6
第二产业	37.2	38.1	39.0
#工业	31.8	32.9	34.1
建筑业	5.3	5.2	4.9
第三产业	31.6	31.9	32.4
#运输邮电业	6.0	6.4	6.5
商业	9.6	9.3	9.0
二、国内支出总额比例			
资本形成总额	36.5	33.8	34.1
固定资本形成总额	66.7	75.8	71.1
存货增加	33.3	24.2	28.9
最终消费	63.6	66.2	65.4
居民消费	79.4	80.4	78.8
农民	60.8	63.6	63.0
非农业居民	39.2	36.4	37.0
政府消费	20.6	19.6	21.2
三、全社会固定资产投资的资金来源比例			
国家预算内投资	3.81	1.93	2.67
国内贷款	19.32	18.72	15.75
债　券	0.14	0.78	0.02
利用外资	6.26	4.22	4.48
自筹投资	52.73	54.39	61.55
其他投资	17.74	19.96	15.53
四、固定资产投资中农轻重投资比例（国有经济）			
农　业	0.3	0.26	0.6
轻 工 业	6.1	4.56	4.7
重 工 业	34.2	32.08	29.5
#能源工业	19.4	16.93	20.4
运输、邮电、仓储业	26.0	30.49	32.7
五、地方财政收入比例			
工商税收	60.5	58.0	59.7
国有企业所得税	6.3	4.9	5.0
国有企业上交利润	0.7	1.7	0.7
国有企业亏损补贴	−4.2	−4.0	−3.1
六、地方财政收入相当于国内生产总值	4.93	4.92	4.58
七、工农业总产值中农轻重比例			
农　业	29.9	27.2	25.7
轻工业	29.8	32.8	33.2
重工业	40.3	40.5	41.1

2—3　续表　　　　　　　　　　　　　　　　　　　　　　　　单位：%

指　　标	1995 年	1996 年	1997 年
八、农业总产值中农林牧副渔比例			
农作物种植业	51.9	49.7	46.7
林　业	4.1	3.7	3.6
牧　业	35.3	37.6	40.7
副　业	3.5	3.3	3.2
渔　业	5.2	5.7	5.8
九、工业总产值中轻重工业比例			
轻工业	42.6	44.4	44.7
重工业	57.4	55.6	55.3
十、轻工业总产值内部比例			
以农产品为原料	73.5	66.0	65.4
以非农产品为原料	26.5	34.0	34.6
十一、重工业总产值内部比例			
采掘工业	13.2	21.7	22.1
原料工业	43.0	30.9	30.1
加工工业	43.8	47.4	47.8
十二、旅客运量比例			
铁路	5.8	5.1	5.7
公路	92.2	93.1	92.4
水运	1.9	1.7	1.7
民用航空	0.1	0.1	0.2
十三、货运量比例			
铁路	10.1	9.7	9.3
公路	82.8	83.7	84.5
水运	7.1	6.5	6.2
十四、货物周转量比例			
铁路	72.0	70.6	69.2
公路	22.6	23.6	24.5
水运	5.4	5.8	6.3
十五、全社会消费品零售总额比例			
市	51.1	49.9	50.2
县	19.9	19.2	19.7
县以下	29.0	30.9	30.1
国有经济	25.5	21.6	19.1
集体经济	14.0	12.7	12.7
私营经济	1.6	2.0	2.4
个体经济	39.0	43.0	44.6
联营经济	0.1	0.1	0.1
股份制经济	1.0	1.3	1.8
外商投资经济	0.1	0.1	0.1
港澳台投资经济			0.1
其他经济	18.6	19.0	19.1

2—4 平均每天主要社会经济活动

Selected Indicators of Average Daily Social and Economic Activities

指 标	单 位	1995 年	1996 年	1997 年
一、全省每天创造的财富				
国内生产总值	亿元	6.02	7.25	8.20
工农业总产值	亿元	9.59	12.35	14.08
农业总产值	亿元	2.87	3.36	3.62
工业总产值	亿元	6.72	8.99	10.46
地方财政收入	万元	2963	3572	3758
布	万米	134	122	120
机制纸及纸板	吨	2576	2833	2586
原 煤	万吨	15.25	16.41	12.08
发 电 量	万千瓦小时	9121	9290	9478
原油加工量	吨	9500	9447	9773
钢	吨	4811	5190	6678
成品钢材	吨	4234	4590	5453
水 泥	万吨	6.02	6.30	6.05
粮 食	万吨	7.54	7.73	7.88
棉 花	吨	612	519	701
油 料	吨	3070	3236	3541
苎 麻	吨	160	128	133
烤 烟	吨	216	377	616
茶 叶	吨	168	150	152
柑 桔	吨	2781	2454	3675
猪牛羊肉	吨	8695	10040	11069
水产品	吨	2364	2692	3035
对外贸易进出口总额	万美元	799.18	880.00	899.45
进口总额	万美元	224.66	272.33	261.37
出口总额	万美元	574.52	607.67	638.08
二、全省每天消费				
城乡居民消费总额	亿元	3.05	3.87	4.22
平均每人消费额	元	4.80	6.02	6.55
三、其他经济活动				
邮电业务总量	万元	862.45	1167.07	1431.36
出版图书	万册	92.27	107.93	102.72
出版杂志	万册	21.28	21.49	21.06
出版报纸	万份	171	174	188
邮寄函件	万份	94.28	81.40	60.22
四、全省每天人口变动和婚姻				
出 生	人	2266	2256	2230
死 亡	人	1244	1268	1238
结 婚	对	1199	1176	1136
离 婚	对	173	183	148

2—5 人均主要工农业产品产量

Per Capita Output of Major Agricultural and Industrial Products

指　标	单　位	1990 年	1995 年	1996 年	1997 年
粮食	公斤	444	439	423	446
棉花	公斤	2.0	3.6	3.0	4.0
食用植物油	公斤	4.9	7.2	7.3	8.3
甘蔗	公斤	20.9	22.5	20.0	27.1
烤烟	公斤	1.8	1.2	2.2	3.5
茶叶	公斤	1.2	1.0	0.9	0.9
水果	公斤	9.3	18.6	16.4	23.8
#柑桔	公斤	7.6	16.1	14.0	20.8
猪牛羊肉	公斤	31.0	50.6	57.3	62.7
#猪肉	公斤	31.0	49.2	55.3	60.1
禽蛋	公斤	4.6	7.4	9.2	9.7
水产品	公斤	8.7	13.7	15.4	17.2
纱(混合数)	公斤	1.93	2.32	1.94	2.06
布(混合数)	米	7.67	7.73	7.25	6.83
针棉织品(折用纱量)	公斤	0.35	0.12	0.09	0.12
丝织品	米	0.16	0.04	0.01	0.01
机制纸及纸板	公斤	10.70	14.86	16.18	14.64
自行车	辆/百人	1.19	0.11	0.02	0.03
合成洗涤剂	公斤	0.74	0.95	1.03	0.98
原盐	公斤	7.55	9.43	9.75	10.69
糖	公斤	1.14	1.00	0.92	1.20
卷烟	箱/百人	4.37	3.95	4.05	3.62
原煤	吨	0.56	0.88	0.94	0.68
原油加工量	公斤	52.83	54.80	53.96	55.33
发电量	千瓦小时	332.22	526.17	529.00	536.66
生铁	公斤	25.32	31.68	33.34	41.06
钢	公斤	22.44	27.75	29.65	37.81
钢材	公斤	19.86	24.42	26.21	30.87
水泥	吨	0.17	0.35	0.36	0.34
合成氨	公斤	21.20	24.93	27.59	26.47
农用化肥(折纯量)	公斤	19.78	24.14	24.86	23.39
#氮肥	公斤	15.25	17.87	19.52	18.93
农药(原药折纯量)	公斤	0.35	0.72	0.63	0.65

2—6 改革开放前后主要指标对比

Composition Between The Mujorindieators Before Reform and The Major Indicators After Refom

	单 位	绝 对 数			1978年为1949年%	1997年为1978年%	平均每年增长%	
		1949年	1978年	1997年			1950—1978年	1979—1997年
一、国内生产总值	亿元	17.65	146.99	2993.00	329.0	514.7	6.8	9.0
人均国内生产总值	元	59	286	4643	234.1	409.4	4.8	7.7
二、国有单位固定资产投资	亿元	0.17※	14.71	353.97	7433.2	2406.3	17.3	18.2
国有单位新增固定资产	亿元	0.16※	10.56	269.20	5612.5	2549.2	16.1	18.6
三、地方财政收入	亿元	2.15	27.98	137.16	1301.4	490.2	9.6	8.7
地方财政支出	亿元	0.79	24.46	230.82	3096.2	943.7	13.0	12.5
四、职工年底人数	万人	40.67	363.78	597.48	894.1	164.2	8.1	2.6
职工工资总额	亿元	1.13	20.16	314.91	1784.7	271.7	10.8	5.4
职工年平均工资	元	279	563	5326	201.5	163.3	2.5	2.6
居民消费水平	元/人	53	183	2390	180.7	270.7	2.1	5.4
城乡居民储蓄存款余额	亿元	0.02	5.50	1255.28	275倍	228倍	22.2	33.1
五、农业总产值	亿元	15.84	81.91	1322.26	337.1	259.8	4.4	5.2
粮食产量	万吨	640.45	2087.90	2876.99	316.5	137.8	4.2	1.7
棉花产量	万吨	0.70	7.56	25.57	1002.0	338.2	8.6	6.6
油料产量	万吨	7.22	19.71	129.26	263.0	655.8	3.5	10.4
猪牛羊肉产量	万吨	7.98	69.02	404.02	804.9	585.4	7.7	9.7
水产品产量	万吨	4.34	11.87	110.76	263.5	933.1	3.5	12.5
六、工业总产值	亿元	3.18	142.78	3817.15	4198.9	1209.3	14.3	14.0
轻工业产值	亿元	2.64	55.78	1705.77	1707.1	1404.2	10.7	14.9
重工业产值	亿元	0.54	87.00	2111.38	174倍	1083.7	20.2	13.4
布产量	亿米	0.57	3.02	4.40	509.8	145.7	5.9	2.0
机制纸及纸板产量	万吨	0.03	19.38	94.39	525倍	487.0	25.0	8.7
原煤产量	万吨	79.06	2671.98	4409.84	3009.7	165.0	12.9	2.7
发电量产量	亿千瓦/时	0.19	93.54	345.96	402倍	369.9	23.8	7.1
铁	万吨	0.32	86.69	264.69	270倍	305.3	22.1	6.1
钢	万吨	0.03※	62.44	243.73	20倍	390.3	31.3	7.4
工业全员劳动生产率	元/人	2495	9200	39048	450.5	424.4	5.5	7.9
七、货物同转量	亿吨公里	13.53※	304.73	998.64	1992.3	327.7	11.8	6.4
旅客周转量	亿人公里	7.81※	101.12	592.16	1204.7	585.6	9.6	9.7
邮电业务总量	万元	270	4598	522447	1403.2	113倍	10.3	28.3
八、社会商品零售总额	亿元	6.53※	68.84		964.2		8.8	
社会消费品零售总额	亿元	6.45※	53.73	1041.60	833.0	1938.6	8.2	16.9
对外进出口总额	亿美元	0.09※	1.59	32.83	1766.7	2064.8	11.2	17.8
进口总额	亿美元	0.02※	0.27	9.54	1350.0	35倍	10.1	20.6
出口总额	亿美元	0.07※	1.32	23.29	1885.7	1764.4	11.5	16.3

注:有※有数是1950年数,但进出口总额数是1951年,钢是1952年数。邮电业务总量只有当年使用的不变价格数。

2—7 法人单位、产业活动单位数

Number of Institutional Llnits and Establishncents by Types of Ownership and Regions

单位:个

项目	法人单位数			多产业法人单位的产业活动单位数
	小计	单产业法人单位	多产业法人单位	
总计	190938	176623	14315	112676
按经济类型分:				
国有经济	40986	30589	10397	79908
集体经济	64304	61297	3007	31135
私营经济	29811	29765	46	171
联营经济	1692	1685	7	55
股份制经济	636	592	44	213
外商投资经济	552	542	10	45
中外合资经济	422	415	7	30
中外合作经济	72	69	3	15
外商独资经济	58	58		
港澳台投资经济	527	513	14	55
港澳台与大陆合资经济	403	393	10	41
港澳台与大陆合作经济	37	36	1	4
港澳台独资经济	87	84	3	10
其他经济	52430	51640	790	1094
按地区:				
长沙市	17418	16143	1275	10581
株洲市	12295	11414	881	6668
湘潭市	8113	7359	754	4538
衡阳市	20576	19367	1209	9534
邵阳市	20896	19172	1724	14664
岳阳市	12283	14393	890	7001
常德市	15775	14519	1256	8924
张家界市	4120	3705	415	2708
益阳市	11733	10972	761	6758
郴州市	13635	18541	1094	8197
永州市	19217	18146	1071	9374
娄底地区	12603	11946	657	5691
怀化地区	15395	13967	1428	11970
湘西自治州	6879	5979	900	6068

注:1. 2—7,2—8,2—9,2—10 由基本单位普查办公室提供。

2. 湖南省第一次基本单位普查的标准时点是 1996 年 12 月 31 日。

3. 法人单位(INSTITUTIONAL UNIT):指依法成立,有自己的名称、组织机构和场所,能独立承担民事责任;独立拥有和使用(或授权使用)资产,有权与其他单位签订合同;会计上独立核算,能够编制资产负债表的单位。产业活动单位(ESTABLISHMENT):指在一个场所从事一种或主要从事一种社会经济活动;相对独立组织生产或业务活动;能够掌握收入和支出等业务资料的单位。

2—8 按行业大类分组的法人、产业活动单位数

Number of Institutional Llnits and Establishncents by Industries

单位:个

行 业 类 别	法 人 单 位 数			多产业法人单位的产业活动单位数
	小 计	单产业法人单位	多产业法人单位	
总 计	190938	176623	14315	112676
一、农、林、牧、渔业	6082	5741	341	6419
农业	1902	1788	114	611
林业	1850	1761	89	494
畜牧业	216	206	10	89
渔业	606	586	20	88
农、林、牧、渔服务业	1508	1400	108	5137
二、采掘业	13479	13379	100	402
煤炭采选业	6435	6378	57	85
石油和天然气开采业				
黑色金属矿采选业	706	701	5	20
有色金属矿采选业	1525	1502	23	73
非金属矿采选业	4470	4461	9	94
其他矿采选业	34	34		1
木材及竹材采运业	309	303	6	129
三、制造业	54289	53495	794	5066
食品加工业	6877	6828	49	577
食品制造业	1290	1267	23	297
饮料制造业	1403	1383	10	126
烟草加工业	26	12	14	16
纺织业	913	885	28	124
服装及其他纤维制品制造业	1069	1049	20	112
皮革、毛皮、羽绒及其制品业	1048	1037	11	57
木材加工及竹、藤、棕、草制品业	2964	2954	10	134
家具制造业	1607	1601	6	106
造纸及纸制品业	1741	1723	18	126
印刷业、记录媒介的复制	1105	1064	41	296
文教体育用品制造业	320	315	5	64
石油加工及炼焦业	129	126	3	11
化学原料及化学制品制造业	2169	2088	81	292
医药制造业	214	199	15	68
化学纤维制造业	73	67	6	12
橡胶制品业	211	206	5	33
塑料制品业	1204	1184	20	163
非金属矿物制品业	16721	16646	75	706
黑色金属冶炼及压延加工业	455	436	19	62

2—8 续表1 单位:个

行 业 类 别	法人单位数			多产业法人单位的产业活动单位数
	小 计	单产业法人单位	多产业法人单位	
有色金属冶炼及压延加工业	698	681	17	65
金属制品业	2268	2239	29	261
普通机械制造业	2430	2366	64	229
专用设备制造业	1193	1146	47	165
交通运输设备制造业	1549	1489	60	436
武器弹药制造业	12	6	6	6
电气机械及器材制造业	1021	972	49	233
电子及通信设备制造业	253	225	28	51
仪器仪表及文化、办公用机械制造业	163	149	14	57
其他制造业	3163	3152	11	181
四、电力、蒸汽、热水的生产和供应业	1780	1679	101	731
电力、蒸汽、热水的生产和供应业	1410	1336	74	674
煤气生产和供应业	16	13	3	6
自来水的生产和供应业	354	330	24	51
五、建筑业	8267	7952	315	951
土木工程建筑业	7824	7537	287	742
线路、管道和设备安装业	226	208	18	137
装修装饰业	217	207	10	72
六、地质勘查业、水利管理业	772	624	148	1025
地质勘查业	74	41	33	71
水利管理业	698	583	115	954
七、交通运输、仓储及邮电通信业	2147	1755	392	4199
铁路运输业	7	3	4	338
公路运输业	900	787	113	361
管道运输业				
水上运输业	213	161	52	104
航空运输业	2	2		
交通运输辅助业	720	636	84	1437
其他交通运输业	4	4		4
仓储业	139	119	20	265
邮电通信业	162	43	119	1690
八、批发和零售贸易、餐饮业	15910	12723	3187	19748
食品、饮料、烟草和家庭用品批发业	3930	2839	1091	4892
能源、材料和机械电子设备批发业	2869	2514	355	1891
其他批发业	1001	696	305	1824
零售业	6834	5491	1343	9996

2—8 续表 2

单位：个

行业类别	法人单位数			多产业法人单位的产业活动单位数
	小计	单产业法人单位	多产业法人单位	
商业经纪与代理业	25	25		5
餐饮业	1251	1158	93	1140
九、金融、保险业	4348	3113	1235	8950
金融业	4061	2830	1231	8937
保险业	287	283	4	13
十、房地产业	1033	972	61	296
房地产开发与经营业	866	832	34	102
房地产管理业	140	115	25	171
房地产经纪与代理业	27	25	2	23
十一、社会服务业	2867	2684	183	2243
公共设施服务业	708	645	63	283
居民服务业	331	314	17	261
旅馆业	689	625	64	701
租赁服务业	12	11	1	11
旅游业	124	116	8	28
娱乐服务业	122	119	3	139
信息、咨询服务业	564	556	8	481
计算机应用服务业	23	22	1	28
其他社会服务业	294	276	18	311
十二、卫生、体育和社会福利业	4214	3793	421	2529
卫生	3727	3327	400	2296
体育	57	46	11	34
社会福利保障业	430	420	10	199
十三、教育、文化艺术及广播电影电视业	8127	5872	2255	42492
教育	6912	4769	2143	40714
文化艺术业	799	751	48	690
广播电影电视业	416	352	64	1088
十四、科学研究和综合技术服务业	1080	980	100	523
科学研究业	255	207	48	137
综合技术服务业	825	773	52	386
十五、国家机关、政党机关和社会团体	64745	60332	4413	15946
国家机关	10386	6896	3490	14682
政党机关	1420	1344	76	87
社会团体	1292	1210	82	412
基层群众自治组织	51647	50882	765	765
十六、其他行业	1798	1529	269	1156
其他行业	1798	1529	269	1156

2—9 企业法人单位数及构成情况

Corporations and Lst Composition

单位:个

指　　标	企业法人单位数	比　例　%
总　　计	105699	100.0
按经济类型分:		
国有经济	13060	12.3
集体经济	59039	55.9
私营经济	29739	28.1
联营经济	1687	1.6
股份制经济	619	0.6
外商及港澳台投资经济	1055	1.0
其他经济	500	0.5
按从业人员规模分:		
7 人以下	17863	16.9
8—19 人	40914	38.7
20—49 人	24409	23.1
50—99 人	10112	9.6
100—299 人	8737	8.3
300—499 人	1765	1.7
500—999 人	1152	1.1
1000—4999 人	686	0.6
5000 人及以上	61	…
按营业收入规模分:		
50 万元以下	63389	60.0
50—100 万元	13968	13.2
100—500 万元	19834	18.7
500—1000 万元	3798	3.6
1000—5000 万元	3778	3.6
5000 万元以上	932	0.9

2—10 企业法人和营利性产业活动单位按行业分组情况

The Distribution of Corporations and Profit－making Establishments Among Various Sectors

单位:个

行　业(门　类)	企业法人单位数	比例%	营利性产业活动单位数	比例%
总　　计	105699	100.0	146910	100.0
农、林、牧、渔业	4161	3.9	5964	4.1
采掘业	13479	12.8	13740	9.4
制造业	54213	51.3	58289	39.7
电、气、水的生产和供应业	1711	1.6	2245	1.5
建筑业	8192	7.8	8817	6.0
地质勘查业、水利管理业	18	…	335	0.2
交通运输、仓储及邮电通讯业	1795	1.7	4672	3.2
批发和零售贸易、餐饮业	15585	14.7	32092	21.8
金融、保险业	3886	3.7	11367	7.7
房地产业	743	0.7	831	0.6
社会服务业	1282	1.2	2573	1.8
卫生、体育和社会福利业	42	…	604	0.4
教育、文化艺术及广播电影电视业	94	0.1	4412	3.0
科学研究和综合技术服务业	209	0.2	350	0.2
其他行业	289	0.3	619	0.4

2—11 城乡个体工商业基本情况(1997年)

Basic Statistics Individuals Industry and Commerce in Crban and Rural Areas

项目	户数(户)		从业人员(人)		注册资金(万元)	
	小计	#城镇	小计	#城镇	小计	#城镇
合计	1800927	715452	4294156	1734193	1656926	713972
农林牧渔业	43497	7463	111150	35657	60621	42318
#农林牧渔服务业	24431	5970	54158	31674	49587	40140
采掘业	6016	817	30593	3587	16942	3731
制造业	203565	68508	602658	185778	212547	75202
建筑业	2815	1120	12083	4812	6923	2982
交通运输、仓储业	219162	79839	425304	160816	490461	177161
#仓储业	1697	1213	3942	2463	2172	1249
批发零售贸易、餐饮业	1078541	444773	2562954	1102671	722238	330320
#餐饮业	144218	69697	376859	196910	90590	50722
社会服务业	217247	100387	489955	215405	130578	73589
#日用品修理业	69943	27630	137769	49839	32872	16428
旅馆业	15372	7895	37753	19370	12293	6679
娱乐服务业	24434	14538	57504	36924	30550	20647
其他行业	30084	12545	59459	25467	16616	8669

项目	总产值(万元)		销售总额或营业收入(万元)		社会消费品零售额(万元)	
	小计	#城镇	小计	#城镇	小计	#城镇
合计	2379521	916646	7375451	3446507	4134135	2116352
农林牧渔业	161970	59212	106190	76892	33836	23550
#农林牧渔服务业			101122	75574	30903	22668
采掘业	136306	55096				
制造业	1984854	770497			420534	211403
建筑业	96391	31841				
交通运输、仓储业			1495032	552517		
#仓储业			5778	3755		
批发零售贸易、餐饮业			4820120	2246501	3185191	1555394
#餐饮业			684996	402350	453032	264921
社会服务业			834176	512108	442682	298036
#日用品修理业			183919	88424	81595	42010
旅馆业			61027	36157	27674	16953
娱乐服务业			259561	219121	164369	150767
其他行业			119933	58489	51892	27969

补充资料:1、外省(市、区)来本地经营 67857 户; 2、个人合伙经营 66297 户,资金 113126 万元,总产值 122766 万元,销售总额或营业收入 458651 万元,社会消费品零售额 338156 万元; 3、出口创汇折人民币 1587 万元; 4、个体工商户从事第一产业增加值 47513 万元,第二产业增加值 395015 万元,第三产业增加值 1067690 万元。

2—12 城乡私营企业生产经营情况(1997年)

Basic Statistics of Production and Operation on Private Enterprises in Urban and Rural Areas

项目	合计			城镇			农村		
	总产值(万元)	销售总额或营业收入(万元)	社会消费零售总额(万元)	总产值(万元)	销售总额或营业收入(万元)	社会消费零售总额(万元)	总产值(万元)	销售总额或营业收入(万元)	社会消费零售总额(万元)
合计	1822940	1151009	832958	747789	711285	502510	1075151	439724	330448
农林牧渔业	32213	16950	4967	6999	3069	1086	25214	13881	3881
#农林牧渔服务业		5068	2434		1144	467		3924	1967
采掘业	108934		11961	28642		1371	80292		10590
制造业	1542456		212918	606813		86835	935643		126083
建筑业	139337			105335			34002		
交通运输、仓储业		31907			21421			10486	
#仓储业		352						352	
批发零售贸易、餐饮业		943642	525741		576062	365295		367580	160446
#餐饮业		18498	13404		14672	9922		3826	3482
社会服务业		109180	47487		84440	31789		24740	15698
#日用品修理业		4097	2396		3633	2092		464	304
旅馆业		1741	922		1579	778		162	144
娱乐服务业		7625	5588		7064	5309		561	279
其他行业		49330	29884		26293	16134		23037	13750

补充资料:私营企业出口创汇 5808 万元人民币。

2—13 外商投资工商登记基本情况(1997年末)

Basic Individuals of Registered Enterprises With Foreign Capital

项目	年末企业数(个)	#投资1000—3000万美元	#投资3000万美元以上	累计投资总额(万美元)	企业注册资本(万美元)	#外方
合计	2756	121	28	745348	463265	268296
按企业类型分:						
中外合资	1803	66	17	429117	280996	133054
中外合作	283	41	9	203827	113967	66940
外商投资	670	14	2	112403	68302	68302
按行业分:						
农林牧渔业	54			5617	3978	3212
采掘业	35	1		4210	2494	2125
制造业	1708	57	17	412541	264714	139938
电力煤气及水的生产和供应业	15	5	3	49227	19641	15395
建筑业	97	18	3	67025	34925	23243
地质勘查业、水利管理业	1			180	126	113
交通运输仓储邮电通信业	49	3		14103	11144	6382
批发零售贸易餐饮业	49			4717	3268	1847
金融保险业						
房地产业	309	13	2	94095	60057	39369
社会服务业	421	23	3	90846	61250	35968
卫生、体育和社会福利业	3			115	110	51
教育、文化艺术广播电影电视业	9	1		2355	1314	520
科学研究和综合技术服务业	5			318	247	135
其他行业	1					

2—14 城乡私营企业

Basic Statistics on Private Enterprises

项　　目	单位	合　计	农林牧渔业	农林牧渔服务业	采掘业	制造业	建筑业
总户数	户	23828	413	27	766	11003	441
#分支机构	户	909	13	3	11	159	6
投资者总人数	人	71900	1062	61	4826	31294	1560
雇工人数	人	362408	5251	250	19177	189509	17844
注册资本金	万元	1032500	33264	1233	19329	357101	92348
城镇户数	户	15504	137	13	109	5172	307
投资者人数	人	46148	387	36	306	15028	1136
雇工人数	人	22316	1676	104	1951	92954	13038
注册资金	万元	827156	25594	637	4014	225860	84334
农村户数	户	8324	276	14	657	5831	134
投资者人数	人	25752	675	25	4520	16266	424
雇工人数	人	139192	3575	146	17226	96555	4806
注册资金	万元	205344	7670	596	15315	131241	8014
独资企业户数	户	8543	179	9	187	5188	86
投资者人数	人	8543	179	9	187	5188	86
雇工人数	人	120849	2050	82	5168	79084	1371
注册资金	万元	152958	6539	268	4361	84495	3928
合资企业户数	户	7049	139	2	457	3987	86
投资者人数	人	29772	549	4	3793	16562	338
雇工人数	人	117581	1766	28	11565	68252	3344
注册资金	万元	172758	4471	130	10840	91456	3521
有限责任公司							
户　　数	户	8236	95	16	122	1828	269
投资者人数	人	33585	334	48	846	9544	1136
雇工人数	人	123978	1435	140	2444	42173	13129
注册资金	万元	706784	22254	835	4128	181150	84899
按公司法范围的公司							
户　　数	户	6268	79	15	47	1159	214
投资者人数	人	22030	244	44	194	5510	867
雇工人数	人	88687	1014	125	1697	25659	10904
注册资金	万元	619758	20586	776	2501	155020	77024

补充资料：1、雇工 100—499 人的企业 198 户，雇工 500 人以上的企业 13 户，私营企业集团计 27 户；

3、出口创汇私营企业 152 户；

基本情况(1997年)

in Urban and Rural Areas

交通运输仓储业	仓储业	批发、零售贸易餐饮业	餐饮业	社会服务业	日用品修理业	旅馆业	娱乐服务业	其他行业
187	1	9219	254	1361	98	41	123	438
1		659	6	49	1		2	11
1022	3	27205	486	3451	195	90	290	1480
2874	8	105882	2644	17027	911	474	1559	4844
7239	3	418301	5091	77494	1354	1356	4189	27424
117		8124	188	1185	80	36	117	353
629		24428	391	3048	147	83	268	1186
1980		92739	2031	14993	758	428	1508	3885
4887		384735	4202	71793	1288	868	3935	25939
70	1	1095	66	176	18	5	6	85
393	3	2777	95	403	48	7	22	294
894	8	13143	613	2034	153	46	51	959
2352	3	33566	889	5701	66	488	254	1485
58		2281	130	466	59	18	63	98
58		2281	130	466	59	18	63	98
439		25263	1279	6472	511	216	626	1002
1134		39644	1905	11037	575	543	1981	1820
63		1836	96	345	29	15	39	136
484		6288	263	1250	98	45	140	508
864		25322	1072	4847	280	140	649	1621
2230		47955	1920	8892	462	365	1205	3392
66	1	5102	28	550	10	8	21	204
480	3	18636	93	1735	38	27	87	874
1571	8	55297	293	5708	120	118	284	2221
3874	3	330702	1266	57565	317	448	1003	22212
41		4169	8	462	8	5	13	97
256		13247	34	1424	34	24	53	288
1046		42950	78	4576	113	62	200	841
2857		292473	350	54499	282	289	814	14798

2、注册资本金100—500万元的企业971户，注册500万元以上的企业245户；

4、乡镇企业217031户，投资者384577人，雇工人数728870，注册资本2000万元。

2—15 进出口商品检验概况

A Survey of Commodity Inspection on Imports and Exports

单位:万美元

	总计	农副产品	纺织品	轻工产品	五金及工矿产品	化工产品	机械产品	其他
一、出口商品								
1993年检验批数	25475	8291	1989	7802	2332	3382	1492	187
商品金额	63096	22049	7270	6213	13718	8983	4176	687
批合格率	99.88	98.40	99.55	99.12	99.53	98.17	99.87	
1994年检验批数	30328	8382	3235	9686	3015	4492	1370	148
商品金额	68335	24212	9137	6577	14780	9162	3088	379
批合格率	98.89	98.20	99.94	98.93	99.34	98.66		
1995年检验批数	26800	6875	3317	9441	2785	3139	1191	52
商品金额	75865	21442	9650	7490	21192	12440	3565	86
批合格率	98.84	98.79	99.55	99.01	98.13	97.99	99.66	
1996年检验批数	24026	6472	2558	8548	2340	3064	1020	24
商品金额	73773	22163	6526	6132	21350	12794	4767	41
批合格率	98.51	98.92	98.79	98.75	97.82	96.77		
1997年检验批数	22070	6188	2043	7534	2470	2884	903	48
商品金额	71733	12361	5336	5987	30831	11077	6079	62
批合格率	98.73	98.76	99.17	98.95	98.34	97.82	99.67	
二、进口商品								
1993年检验批数	635	23	19	10	87	27	466	3
商品金额	20086	287	1041	226	2957	940	14563	72
批合格率	59.06	47.83	89.47	70.00	93.10	85.19	50.00	
1994年检验批数	787	54	32	22	74	45	553	7
商品金额	30314	1567	2104	359	3050	1070	21986	142
批合格率	66.20	88.89		86.36	85.14	86.67	56.78	
1995年检验批数	565	19	24	14	28	28	448	4
商品金额	22141	852	1529	330	2377	649	16331	73
批合格率	52.74	89.47	83.33	50.00	75.00	75.00	46.87	50.00
1996年检验批数	639	11	56	21	37	16	498	
商品金额	21063	666	2525	461	486	164	16761	
批合格率	58.69	54.55	96.43	95.24	91.89	68.75	50.20	
1997年检验批数	563	9	27	6	63	17	436	5
商品金额	15983	439	469	70	735	119	14104	47
批合格率	71.40	77.78			93.65	88.24	64.91	

注:1. 本表由湖南省商检局提供。

2. 进出口商品检验批数是以一份检验单为一批。

2—16 进出口商品类章检验情况(1997 年)

Basic Statistics of Commodity Classificatory Impection of Import and Exports

金额:万美元

类章	品名	出口		进口	
		检验金额	不合格金额	检验金额	不合格金额
	总计	71733	741	15983	1818
第一类	活动物;动物产品	2956	1	1	
02 章	肉及食用杂碎	2102			
03 章	鱼、甲壳动物、软体动物及其他水生无脊椎动物	23			
04 章	乳品;蛋品;天然蜂蜜;其他食用动物产品	59	1		
05 章	其他动物产品	772		1	
第二类	植物产品	3952	41		
07 章	食用蔬菜、根及块茎	52	3		
08 章	食用水果及坚果;甜瓜或柑桔属水果的果皮	701	7		
09 章	咖啡、茶、马黛茶及调味香料	1415	3		
10 章	谷物	1519	28		
11 章	制粉工业产品;麦芽;淀粉;菊粉;面筋	16			
12 章	含油子仁及果实;杂项子仁及果实;工业用或药用植物;稻草、秸杆及饲料	242			
14 章	编结用植物材料;其他植物产品	7			
第三类	动、植物油、脂及其分解产品;精制的食用油脂;动、植物蜡				
	动、植物油、脂、及其分解产品;精制的食用油脂;动、植物	564	20	18	
15 章	蜡	564	20	18	
第四类	食品;饮料、酒及醋;烟草、烟草及烟草代用品的制品	3397	41	416	242
16 章	肉、鱼、甲壳动物、软体动物及其他水生无脊椎动物的制品	14			
17 章	糖及糖食	1			
19 章	谷物、粮食粉、淀粉或乳的制品;糕饼点心	6			
20 章	蔬菜、水果、坚果或植物其他部分的制品	2145	41		
21 章	杂项食品	102			
22 章	饮料、酒及醋	4			
23 章	食品工业的残渣及废料;配制的动物饲料	24		416	242
24 章	烟草、烟草及烟草代用品的制品	1101			
第五类	矿产品	330	1	290	88
25 章	盐、硫磺;泥土及石料;石膏料、石灰及水泥	250	1		
26 章	矿砂、矿渣及矿灰	80		276	88
27 章	矿物燃料、矿物油及其蒸馏产品;沥青物质;矿物蜡			14	
第六类	化学工业及其相关工业的产品	10905	257	1	1
28 章	无机化学品;贵金属、稀土金属、放射性元素及其同位素的有机及无机化合物	8280	224	1	1
29 章	有机化学品	263	29		
30 章	药品	196			
31 章	肥料	176			
32 章	鞣料浸膏及染料浸膏;鞣酸及其衍生物;染料、颜料及其他着色料;油漆及清漆;油灰及其他类似胶粘剂;墨水、油墨	70			

2—16 续表 1

金额:万美元

类 章	品 名	出口		进口	
		检验金额	不合格金额	检验金额	不合格金额
33 章	精油及香膏;芳香料制品及化妆盥洗品	177			
36 章	炸药;烟火制品;火柴;引火合金;易燃材料制品	1517	3		
38 章	杂项化学产品	226	1		
第七类	塑料及其制品;橡胶及其制品	172		118	
39 章	塑料及其制品	34		107	
40 章	橡胶及其制品	138		11	
第八类	生皮、皮革、毛皮及其制品;鞍具及挽具;旅行用品、手提包及类似品;动物肠线(蚕胶丝除外)制品	1439	2		
41 章	生皮(毛皮除外)及皮革	197			
42 章	皮革制品;鞍具及挽具;旅行用品、手提包及类似容器;动物肠线(蚕胶丝除外)制品	1242	2		
第九类	木及木制品;木炭软木及软木制品;稻草、秸杆、针茅或其他编结材料制品;篮筐及柳条编结品	53		4	
44 章	木及木制品;木炭	51		4	
46 章	稻草、秸杆、针茅或其他编结材料制品;篮筐皮柳条编结品	2			
第十类	木浆及其他纤维状纤维素浆;纸及纸板的废碎品;纸、纸板及其制品	1		53	
47 章	木浆及其他纤维状纤维素浆;纸及纸板的废碎品			4	
48 章	纸及纸板;纸浆、纸或纸板制品	1		49	
第十一类	纺织原料及纺织制品	5336	33	469	
50 章	蚕丝	2			
51 章	羊毛、动物细毛或粗毛,马毛纱线及其机织物	7			
52 章	棉花	516		58	
53 章	其他植物纺织纤维;纸纱线及其机织物	1722			
54 章	化学纤维长丝			403	
55 章	化学纤维短纤	22		8	
56 章	絮胎、毡呢及元纺织物;特种纱线;线、绳、索、缆及其制品	9			
58 章	特种机织物;簇绒织物;花边;装饰带;刺绣品	5			
60 章	针织物及钩编织物	10			
61 章	针织或钩编的服装及衣着附件	327	2		
62 章	非针织或非钩编的服装及衣着附件	2558	25		
63 章	其他纺织制成品;成套物品;旧衣着及旧纺织品;碎织物	158	6		
第十二类	鞋、帽、伞、杖、鞭及其零件;已加工的羽毛及其制品;人造花;人发制品	1425	27	2	
64 章	鞋靴、护腿、和类似品及其零件	1424	27		
65 章	帽类及其零件			2	
67 章	已加工羽毛、羽绒及其制品;人造花;人发制品	1			
第十三类	石料、石膏、水泥、石棉、云母及类似材料的制品;陶瓷产品;玻璃及其制品	4561	31	15	

2—16 续表 2 金额:万美元

类 章	品 名	出口 检验金额	出口 不合格金额	进口 检验金额	进口 不合格金额
68 章	石料、石膏、水泥、石棉、云母及类似材料的制品	156			
69 章	陶瓷产品	4387	31	15	
70 章	玻璃及其制品	18			
第十四章	天然或养殖珍珠、宝石或半宝石、贵金属、包贵金属及其制品;仿首饰;硬币				
71 章	天然或养殖珍珠、宝石或半宝石、贵金属、包贵金属及其制品;仿首饰;硬币				
第十五类	贱金属及其制品	30501	287	445	49
72 章	钢铁	3303	218	312	48
73 章	钢铁制品	571	2	72	1
74 章	铜及其制品	118		9	
76 章	铝及其制品	165		50	
78 章	铅及其制品	7			
79 章	锌及其制品	20431	39		
80 章	锡及其制品	766			
81 章	其他贱金属、金属陶瓷及其制品	4680	28		
82 章	贱金属工具、器具、利口器、餐匙、餐叉及其零件	449			
83 章	贱金属杂项制品	11		2	
第十六类	机器、机械器具、电气设备、及其零件;录音机及放声机、电视图像、声音的录制和重放设备及其零件、附件	3575		13081	1426
84 章	核反应堆、锅炉、机械器具及零件	998		12065	1156
85 章	电机、电气设备及其零件;录音机及放声机、电视图像、声音的录制和重放设备入其零件、附件	2577		1016	270
第十七类	车辆、航空器、船舶及有关运输设备	2475		207	
86 章	铁道及电车道机车、车辆、及其零件;铁道及电车道轨道固定装置及其零件、附件;各种机械(包括电动机械)交通信号设备	2273			
87 章	车辆及其零件、附件,但铁道及电车道车辆附除外	122		207	
89 章	船舶及浮动结构体	80			
第十八类	光学、照相、电影、计量、检验、医疗或外科用仪器及设备、精密仪器及设备;钟表;乐器;上述物品的零件、附件	29		816	12
90 章	光学、照相、电影、计量、检验、医疗或外科用仪器及设备、精密仪器及设备;上述物品的零件、附件	29		816	12
第二十类	杂项制品	62		47	
94 章	家具、寝具、褥垫、弹簧床垫、软坐垫及类似的填充制品;未列名灯具及照明装置;发光标志、发光名牌及类似品;活动房屋	36		2	
95 章	玩具、游戏品、运动用品及其零件、附件	13		45	
96 章	杂项制品	13			

注:本表资料来源湖南商检局年度报表。

2—17 贫困县市基本情况(1997年)

Basic Statistics on Poverty Counties and Cities

县　市	总人口(万人)	农业人口(万人)	国内生产总值(万元)	农业总产值(万元)	工业总产值(万元)	财政收入(万元)	粮食产量(万吨)	农民人均纯收入(元)
1. 永　顺	47.41	42.32	80217	62131	58440	3564	18.95	1027.83
2. 保　靖	27.47	24.13	41075	28215	38551	1687	8.90	1062.07
3. 平　江	97.19	89.14	245199	169037	256935	8089	44.81	1280.49
4. 桑　植	42.15	37.43	68555	44085	80475	4367	14.35	1090.30
5. 新　化	126.20	114.01	302146	169412	264756	9361	45.06	1005.30
6. 沅　陵	63.25	51.97	241310	104603	231727	8712	22.55	1023.68
7. 花　垣	26.08	22.69	48422	31687	48367	2841	10.28	1018.26
8. 安　化	94.35	82.70	240026	123457	305718	7946	28.06	985.22
9. 隆　回	107.11	100.10	244122	161608	141492	9654	42.54	1267.81
10. 新　田	36.87	33.80	81618	60300	105903	3145	12.86	1009.29
11. 城　步	24.85	20.92	50279	37975	71603	3196	9.27	1228.31
12. 桂　东	16.85	14.99	33493	22512	38199	1609	5.00	1064.88
13. 汝　城	36.02	32.59	101352	58868	122906	5668	12.74	1144.95
14. 古　丈	13.38	11.15	23984	16522	11329	995	3.80	974.85
15. 泸　溪	26.79	22.81	54351	37017	41402	2101	7.98	953.18
16. 凤　凰	35.80	32.21	69905	36848	40483	3452	11.99	1046.54
17. 通　道	21.33	19.29	41985	35184	57927	3426	8.00	976.67
18. 江　华	43.88	39.68	107783	109322	86725	4201	15.13	1260.55
19. 龙　山	50.85	45.77	109809	72986	107949	5521	17.86	1093.17
20. 麻　阳	35.16	31.48	78432	56337	86229	4364	12.07	1268.73
21. 慈　利	67.02	60.07	148003	100792	161816	7763	27.52	1576.67
22. 宜　章	54.13	47.23	190762	88442	407720	8740	20.05	2003.80
23. 新　晃	24.99	22.04	79102	34829	61373	3280	9.59	1293.81
24. 炎　陵	17.61	14.95	62966	42297	65205	3982	11.78	1745.14
25. 茶　陵	58.12	51.83	172211	137881	247582	7438	31.20	1936.35
26. 吉　首	26.05	14.92	142752	38049	169915	5500	5.37	1508.21
27. 石　门	70.30	59.80	235879	145023	228640	8268	27.90	1691.85
28. 芷　江	34.48	30.50	98399	70675	103223	4895	16.07	1752.13
29. 永定区	40.14	30.72	96111	75049	74050	5126	16.50	1587.54
30. 浏阳市	133.01	120.58	527287	254905	790658	21465	70.12	2442.32
31. 武陵源区	4.46	2.64	14000	7013	6828	3792	1.37	1589.39

注:1—10为国开发(1994)5号通知列入扶贫的10县;11—31为湘政发(1994)29号文件中增加省定扶贫县市21个。

2—18 “三资”企业投资基本情况(1997年)

Basic Statistics on Investment of “Three Types of Capital” Enterprises

类别	合同数（个）	协议投资（万美元）	实际投资（万美元）	年末实有企业数（个）	本年新增企业（个）	年末从业人员（人）
总计	407	86013	91702	2756	337	282915
中外合资企业	167	24536	47460	1803	131	191610
中外合作企业	57	35186	19208	283	52	49202
外商独资企业	183	26291	23034	670	154	42103
1、按国民经济行业分组						
农、林、牧、渔业	26	5701	3033	54	19	
采掘业			729	35	7	
制造业	240	42046	48069	1708	179	
#纺织业	12	696	1750	93	8	
石油加工及炼焦业				5	2	
化学原料及化学制品制造业	30	2781	3349	172	24	
普通机械制造业	7	888	11060	53	5	
交通运输设备制造业				91	3	
电气机械及器材制造业				75	5	
电子及通信设备制造业				100	9	
电力、煤气及水的生产和供应业			1686	15	2	
建筑业	22	23005	14550	97	22	
地质勘查业、水利管理业				1		
交通运输、仓储及邮电通信业	2		562	49	5	
批发和零售贸易、餐饮业	22	1422	1179	49	8	
房地产业	72	11893	10822	309	21	
社会服务业(宾馆)	17	1313	9629	421	73	
卫生、体育和社会福利业			82	3	1	
教育、文艺及广播电影电视业	6	633	609	9		
科学研究和综合技术服务业			50	5		
其他			702	1		
2、按国别、地区分组						
亚洲	335	54262	74578	2428	294	
#香港	210	35950	42470	1693	183	
澳门	9	2338	1277	59	6	

2—18 续表 (1997 年)

类别	合同数（个）	协议投资（万美元）	实际投资（万美元）	年末实有企业数（个）	本年新增企业（个）	年末从业人员（人）
台湾	74	6750	10688	477	64	
日本	8	2020	3651	55	7	
菲律宾	4	72	115	9	3	
泰国	2	131	958	17	3	
马来西亚	8	2554	2280	28	5	
新加坡	13	2290	5627	44	12	
印度尼西亚				9		
韩国	6	2037	7182	17	7	
非洲						
欧洲	8	384	1392	65	9	
#德国	1	14	15	9	1	
法国	1	47		1		
意大利	1	12	107	6	1	
荷兰	2	134	108	7	3	
英国	1	12	723	23	3	
挪威				4		
奥地利				1		
拉丁美洲	18	21164	9211	22	6	
#巴拿马				3		
维尔京群岛				14	6	
北美洲	40	7728	5909	219	25	
加拿大	10	1425	809	36	6	
美国	30	6303	5100	183	19	
大洋洲	6	2475	612	22	3	
澳大利亚	5	1801	504	21	3	
新西兰				1		
其他						

2—19 洞庭湖区主要经济、社会指标

Major Economic Indicators and Social Indicators of The DongTing Lake Area

指　　标	单　位	1997年全省总计	洞庭湖区合计		
			1995年	1996年	1997年
总户数	万户	1798.83	414.91	428.59	434.11
总人口	万人	6465.00	1430	1472.80	1482.62
#农业人口	万人	5249.94	1133.34	1125.65	1214.03
农村劳动力	万人	2774.69	631.08	624.94	624.75
农作物总播种面积	千公顷	8008.98	2411.47	2370.79	2423.41
#粮食	千公顷	5155.26	1391.54	1376.09	1407.4
棉花	千公顷	176.54	141.78	129.23	132.86
油料	千公顷	956	366.48	380.58	387.74
粮食总产量	万吨	2876.99	776.89	758.02	864.18
#稻谷	万吨	2617.84	743.63	718.46	818.85
小麦	万吨	32.11	2.13	2.19	2.57
薯类	万吨	109.87	17.26	20.08	21.45
棉花总产量	万吨	25.53	18.45	13.78	20.28
油料总产量	万吨	129.25	47.18	50.50	52.6
#油菜籽	万吨	104.77	43.61	46.26	48.53
苎麻总产量	万吨	4.82	4.97	3.88	3.82
甘蔗总产量	万吨	174.56	100.98	82.79	130.47
蚕茧总产量	吨	1136	2075	1298	887
茶叶总产量	吨	55493	26212	23025	23707
水产品产量	吨	1107610	437363	491692	566557
生猪存栏头数	万头	3632.01	907.67	845.5	863.11
生猪出栏头数	万头	6096.02	1455.16	1457.06	1588.71
农业机械总动力	千瓦	16928396	5593287	5815943	5986894
农用排灌动力机械	台	827362	285548	336101	349148
	千瓦	4137717	1792681	1861261	1906267
大中型拖拉机	台	4622	3648	3588	3480
	千瓦	201817	145579	158137	155681
小型及手扶拖拉机	台	196586	61942	60425	60610
	千瓦	1768758	5400425	534805	556735
农用运输车	辆	47033	9258	9017	8403
	千瓦	985380	167003	160220	168873
年末耕地面积	千公顷	3230.1	981.20	972.83	969.78
农业总产值(1990年不变价)	万元	6807910	1861223	1940351	2145737
#农　业	万元	3478101	970057	954005	1090656
林　业	万元	351755	45860	55238	51338
牧　业	万元	2448345	620591	672541	713446
渔　业	万元	529709	214715	258567	290297

三、国民经济核算

NATIONAL ECONOMIC ACCOUHTING

3—1 总　产　出

Gross Output

单位:亿元

年份	总产出	第一产业	第二产业	工业	建筑业	第三产业	运输邮电业	商业	其他
1952	39.34	23.79	9.09	8.19	0.90	6.46	1.32	2.79	2.35
1953	42.63	23.71	11.39	10.10	1.29	7.53	1.92	3.90	1.71
1954	43.86	21.97	13.54	11.94	1.60	8.35	2.05	4.48	1.82
1955	49.24	25.83	14.47	12.11	2.36	8.94	2.39	4.50	2.05
1956	53.66	25.67	17.19	14.65	2.54	10.80	2.72	5.73	2.35
1957	66.03	32.88	19.74	16.99	2.75	13.41	3.08	5.46	4.87
1958	86.51	31.68	39.51	32.41	7.10	15.32	4.16	5.70	5.46
1959	103.48	29.79	52.35	42.63	9.72	21.34	7.01	7.60	6.73
1960	113.37	27.78	62.58	48.85	13.73	23.01	6.90	8.45	7.66
1961	76.77	26.29	31.72	28.56	3.16	18.76	4.20	6.59	7.97
1962	80.42	33.61	28.56	26.42	2.14	18.25	3.62	6.90	7.84
1963	80.55	31.92	31.43	28.21	3.22	17.20	4.30	4.70	8.20
1964	94.08	38.05	38.19	32.38	5.81	17.84	5.46	5.20	7.18
1965	107.35	42.70	45.55	38.90	6.65	19.10	5.93	5.35	7.82
1966	123.98	47.87	55.52	47.94	7.58	20.59	6.61	5.92	8.06
1967	120.70	50.35	49.33	42.98	6.35	21.02	6.16	6.24	8.62
1968	118.55	55.79	41.80	36.72	5.08	20.96	5.09	5.88	9.99
1969	134.39	55.30	55.51	47.83	7.68	23.58	6.24	7.07	10.27
1970	162.14	58.22	78.40	68.94	9.46	25.52	7.16	7.71	10.65
1971	177.75	60.29	90.37	77.35	13.02	27.09	8.01	8.28	10.80
1972	194.62	64.84	99.73	87.05	12.68	30.05	8.89	9.26	11.90
1973	216.29	70.82	113.61	100.63	12.98	31.86	9.60	10.22	12.04
1974	202.91	72.33	97.37	83.66	13.71	33.21	8.56	10.59	14.06
1975	234.10	76.06	120.60	105.34	15.26	37.44	9.25	11.23	16.96
1976	233.23	76.44	118.53	104.52	14.01	38.26	8.72	11.54	18.00
1977	256.72	77.59	138.02	124.44	13.58	41.11	10.12	12.76	18.23
1978	289.79	81.91	160.32	142.78	17.54	47.56	11.40	14.45	21.71
1979	347.74	109.18	186.04	164.12	21.92	52.52	12.12	16.05	24.35
1980	376.14	111.14	206.57	177.85	28.72	58.43	12.60	17.81	28.02
1981	408.13	126.36	214.61	187.02	27.59	67.16	12.68	19.77	34.71
1982	449.11	142.71	235.37	205.78	29.59	71.03	13.63	22.68	34.72
1983	498.03	158.16	261.66	221.15	40.51	78.21	15.14	22.84	40.23
1984	562.67	171.26	299.00	255.06	43.94	92.41	18.54	28.72	45.15
1985	698.36	198.44	372.89	314.68	58.21	127.03	26.00	40.52	60.51
1986	810.42	222.68	437.15	368.88	68.27	150.59	28.44	48.42	73.73
1987	980.08	253.39	540.92	456.74	84.18	185.77	32.68	58.96	94.13
1988	1239.59	303.01	690.19	581.85	108.34	246.39	43.09	80.03	123.27
1989	1390.89	337.48	768.85	680.09	88.76	284.56	51.37	85.79	147.40
1990	1571.34	397.42	809.86	712.67	97.19	364.06	56.35	136.70	171.01
1991	1777.40	425.58	928.67	803.71	124.96	423.15	70.50	157.16	195.49
1992	2247.41	471.22	1184.05	1006.79	177.26	592.14	90.01	232.92	269.21
1993	2938.67	563.47	1685.35	1438.92	246.43	689.85	142.87	289.82	257.16
1994	4110.56	792.90	2243.62	1925.35	318.27	1074.04	227.34	393.00	453.70
1995	5282.23	1046.97	2854.10	2451.47	402.63	1381.16	283.72	506.55	590.89
1996	6810.23	1226.32	3984.05	3474.15	509.90	1599.86	324.74	590.37	684.75
1997	7676.38	1322.26	4586.11	4023.38	562.73	1768.01	375.85	649.63	742.53

3—2 总产出构成

Composition of Gross Output

（以总产出为100）　　单位：%

年　份	总产出	第一产业	第二产业	工　业	建筑业	第三产业	运　输邮电业	商　业	其　他
1952	100.0	60.5	23.1	20.8	2.3	16.4	3.4	7.1	6.0
1953	100.0	55.6	26.7	23.7	3.0	17.7	4.5	9.1	4.0
1954	100.0	50.1	30.9	27.2	3.6	19.0	4.7	10.2	4.1
1955	100.0	52.5	29.4	24.6	4.8	18.2	4.9	9.1	4.2
1956	100.0	47.8	32.0	27.3	4.7	20.1	5.1	10.7	4.4
1957	100.0	49.8	29.9	25.7	4.2	20.3	4.7	8.3	7.4
1958	100.0	36.6	45.7	37.5	8.2	17.7	4.8	6.6	6.3
1959	100.0	28.8	50.6	41.2	9.4	20.6	6.8	7.3	6.5
1960	100.0	24.5	55.2	43.1	12.1	20.3	6.1	7.5	6.8
1961	100.0	34.2	41.3	37.2	4.1	24.4	5.5	8.6	10.4
1962	100.0	41.8	35.5	32.9	2.7	22.7	4.5	8.4	9.7
1963	100.0	39.6	39.0	35.0	4.0	21.4	5.3	5.8	10.2
1964	100.0	40.4	40.6	34.4	6.2	19.0	5.8	5.5	7.6
1965	100.0	39.8	42.4	36.2	6.2	17.8	5.5	5.0	7.3
1966	100.0	38.6	44.8	38.7	6.1	16.6	5.3	4.8	6.5
1967	100.0	41.7	40.9	35.6	5.3	17.4	5.1	5.2	7.1
1968	100.0	47.1	35.3	31.0	4.3	17.7	4.3	5.0	8.4
1969	100.0	41.1	41.3	35.6	5.7	17.5	4.6	5.3	7.6
1970	100.0	35.9	48.4	42.5	5.8	15.7	4.4	4.8	6.6
1971	100.0	33.9	50.8	43.5	7.3	15.2	4.5	4.7	6.1
1972	100.0	33.3	51.2	44.7	6.5	15.4	4.6	4.8	6.1
1973	100.0	32.7	52.5	46.5	6.0	14.7	4.4	4.7	5.6
1974	100.0	35.6	48.0	41.2	6.8	16.4	4.2	5.2	6.9
1975	100.0	32.5	51.5	45.0	6.5	16.0	4.0	4.8	7.2
1976	100.0	32.8	50.8	44.8	6.0	16.4	3.7	4.9	7.7
1977	100.0	30.2	53.8	48.5	5.3	16.0	3.9	5.0	7.1
1978	100.0	28.3	55.3	49.3	6.1	16.4	3.9	5.0	7.5
1979	100.0	31.4	53.5	47.2	6.3	15.1	3.5	4.6	7.0
1980	100.0	29.5	54.9	47.3	7.6	15.5	3.3	4.7	7.4
1981	100.0	31.0	52.6	45.8	6.8	16.5	3.1	4.8	8.5
1982	100.0	31.8	52.4	45.8	6.6	15.8	3.0	5.0	7.7
1983	100.0	31.8	52.5	44.4	8.1	15.7	3.0	4.6	8.1
1984	100.0	30.4	53.1	45.3	7.8	16.4	3.3	5.1	8.0
1985	100.0	28.4	53.4	45.1	8.3	18.2	3.7	5.8	8.7
1986	100.0	27.5	53.9	45.5	8.4	18.6	3.5	6.0	9.1
1987	100.0	25.9	55.2	46.6	8.6	19.0	3.3	6.0	9.6
1988	100.0	24.4	55.7	46.9	8.7	19.9	3.5	6.5	9.9
1989	100.0	24.3	55.3	48.9	6.4	20.5	3.7	6.2	10.6
1990	100.0	25.3	51.5	45.4	6.2	23.2	3.6	8.7	10.9
1991	100.0	23.9	52.2	45.2	7.0	23.8	4.0	8.8	11.0
1992	100.0	21.0	52.7	44.8	7.9	26.3	4.0	10.4	12.0
1993	100.0	19.2	57.4	49.0	8.4	23.5	4.9	9.9	8.8
1994	100.0	19.3	54.6	46.8	7.7	26.1	5.5	9.6	11.0
1995	100.0	19.8	54.0	46.4	7.6	26.1	5.4	9.6	11.2
1996	100.0	18.0	58.5	51.0	7.5	23.5	4.8	8.7	10.1
1997	100.0	17.2	59.7	52.4	7.3	23.0	4.9	8.5	9.7

3—3 总产出发展速度

Growth Rate of Gross Output

（上年 =100）　　　　　　　　　　　　　　　　　　单位:%

年 份	总产出	第一产业	第二产业	工 业	建筑业	第三产业	运输邮电业	商 业
1952	100.0	121.3	151.9	132.3	236.8	100.0	129.3	107.7
1953	108.2	100.1	130.6	129.1	143.3	112.1	150.4	130.1
1954	101.3	91.7	120.3	119.3	127.9	107.2	107.3	114.0
1955	115.1	118.5	111.8	105.8	154.5	110.2	118.8	99.5
1956	109.6	97.4	126.4	128.8	114.9	121.1	112.7	127.2
1957	117.6	120.1	111.8	112.6	107.5	121.4	113.2	91.4
1958	130.3	104.1	204.6	176.2	258.1	113.7	134.0	104.0
1959	117.0	91.9	130.0	132.4	119.3	137.5	173.6	133.2
1960	105.2	84.7	117.1	112.3	140.5	105.3	96.6	109.8
1961	59.9	84.8	47.1	53.5	22.5	66.0	57.6	55.6
1962	97.7	119.3	85.1	87.0	67.5	90.1	84.4	92.4
1963	103.2	94.2	111.2	109.2	135.6	106.0	125.8	81.1
1964	117.4	113.9	124.5	118.6	180.7	109.7	123.0	132.3
1965	115.5	104.4	126.1	127.9	114.5	112.2	109.6	105.0
1966	118.4	111.7	127.1	129.0	114.0	108.0	110.8	111.0
1967	97.2	105.1	91.0	91.9	83.8	101.9	92.1	105.4
1968	95.6	107.5	81.8	82.0	80.1	109.9	81.3	94.1
1969	116.8	97.9	139.4	138.1	151.0	106.1	124.2	120.3
1970	124.3	105.0	142.3	144.6	123.3	100.9	116.6	109.1
1971	110.9	99.9	116.2	115.5	137.6	109.6	112.4	107.3
1972	110.2	106.6	112.3	114.7	97.4	111.0	111.7	112.1
1973	109.3	108.3	110.8	112.0	102.4	106.0	107.5	110.3
1974	92.5	102.1	83.5	80.7	105.6	104.2	87.4	103.6
1975	117.4	104.6	128.4	131.2	111.3	112.9	109.6	106.3
1976	98.6	100.4	96.5	97.1	91.8	102.1	92.9	102.7
1977	111.2	101.5	118.4	121.2	96.9	107.4	116.9	110.5
1978	114.8	110.2	117.0	115.6	130.3	115.8	113.2	113.2
1979	110.4	106.3	112.9	112.1	120.0	108.7	106.6	109.5
1980	105.8	98.1	109.8	108.0	123.6	104.8	102.6	104.8
1981	105.6	106.1	103.2	104.0	98.4	112.9	98.8	109.2
1982	108.7	110.1	109.2	109.6	106.3	104.4	108.3	112.8
1983	108.9	105.0	111.4	107.8	137.6	108.2	110.3	107.6
1984	110.7	105.7	112.2	112.6	104.3	115.1	122.3	121.9
1985	114.5	104.9	116.1	116.4	114.3	125.9	140.3	127.0
1986	110.6	105.4	112.1	113.0	106.3	113.6	111.6	114.1
1987	113.3	103.3	116.2	116.9	111.4	117.8	109.2	110.1
1988	111.0	100.5	114.6	115.3	110.0	112.6	118.7	107.8
1989	104.3	105.1	103.1	106.7	76.6	107.2	109.7	90.8
1990	103.9	101.9	104.7	105.0	100.9	103.8	109.4	91.2
1991	109.5	103.9	111.9	111.2	117.3	110.5	112.9	110.4
1992	114.5	103.8	120.0	119.9	121.5	113.6	121.5	132.4
1993	116.4	105.3	121.0	123.2	105.8	116.5	119.6	109.4
1994	118.0	106.4	120.0	120.8	113.8	123.5	110.8	109.0
1995	114.4	110.2	116.9	117.2	114.6	111.3	108.1	111.6
1996	122.4	108.4	131.8	133.4	117.1	108.9	112.7	108.7
1997	114.0	108.3	115.7	116.4	108.1	113.4	113.5	106.7

3—4 总 产 出 指 数

Indices of Gross Output

(以 1952 年为 100)

单位:%

年 份	总产出	第一产业	第二产业			第三产业		
				工 业	建筑业		运 输 邮电业	商 业
1952	100.0	100.0	100.0	100.0	100.0	100.0	100.0	100.0
1953	108.2	100.1	130.6	129.1	143.3	112.1	150.4	130.1
1954	109.6	91.8	157.1	154.0	183.3	120.2	161.3	148.4
1955	126.2	108.7	175.7	163.0	283.3	132.4	191.6	147.7
1956	138.3	105.9	222.0	209.9	325.6	160.4	216.0	187.8
1957	162.6	127.2	248.2	236.2	350.0	194.7	244.5	171.7
1958	211.9	132.4	507.9	416.3	903.3	221.4	327.7	178.6
1959	247.9	121.7	660.2	551.3	1077.7	304.4	568.9	237.9
1960	260.8	103.1	773.1	619.0	1514.3	320.5	549.6	261.1
1961	156.2	87.4	364.1	331.3	340.4	211.5	316.8	145.3
1962	152.6	104.3	309.9	288.4	229.7	190.6	267.2	134.3
1963	157.5	98.2	344.6	314.8	311.5	202.0	336.1	108.9
1964	184.9	111.8	429.0	373.4	562.9	221.6	413.4	144.1
1965	213.6	116.7	541.0	477.6	644.7	248.7	452.9	151.3
1966	252.9	130.4	687.6	616.0	734.9	268.6	501.7	167.9
1967	245.8	137.0	625.7	565.9	615.8	273.7	462.2	177.0
1968	235.0	147.3	511.8	464.1	493.1	300.8	375.6	166.7
1969	274.4	144.2	713.5	640.9	744.5	319.1	466.4	200.7
1970	341.1	151.4	1015.3	926.6	917.7	350.7	543.7	218.8
1971	378.3	151.3	1179.8	1070.5	1262.9	384.4	610.9	234.8
1972	416.9	161.4	1324.9	1227.8	1230.1	426.6	682.4	263.1
1973	455.7	174.7	1468.0	1374.8	1259.9	452.2	733.6	290.3
1974	421.5	178.4	1225.8	1109.9	1330.4	471.2	641.2	300.8
1975	494.8	186.5	1573.9	1456.6	1480.3	532.0	702.5	319.8
1976	487.9	187.2	1518.8	1414.6	1359.2	543.2	652.9	328.3
1977	542.6	190.0	1798.3	1714.1	1317.5	583.4	763.0	362.9
1978	622.9	209.5	2104.0	1981.4	1716.6	675.6	863.9	410.9
1979	687.6	222.7	2375.4	2220.8	2060.1	734.3	921.0	450.0
1980	727.5	218.4	2608.1	2398.2	2546.6	769.6	944.5	471.5
1981	768.2	231.6	2691.6	2493.0	2504.9	868.8	933.6	514.7
1982	835.1	255.1	2939.3	2732.4	2663.9	907.1	1010.9	580.6
1983	909.4	267.9	3274.3	2946.3	3666.3	981.5	1115.1	624.9
1984	1006.7	283.1	3673.8	3347.1	3825.3	1129.7	1363.9	762.0
1985	1152.7	297.0	4265.3	3894.3	4371.0	1422.2	1913.4	967.7
1986	1274.9	313.2	4781.4	4401.3	4647.3	1615.7	2136.1	1103.8
1987	1444.4	323.5	5556.6	5144.4	5177.6	1903.3	2331.9	1214.8
1988	1603.3	325.2	6367.2	5931.2	5695.4	2143.1	2768.0	1309.6
1989	1672.3	341.8	6564.5	6328.6	4362.7	2297.4	3036.5	1189.1
1990	1737.5	348.3	6873.1	6647.7	4401.9	2384.7	3321.9	1084.5
1991	1902.6	361.9	7691.0	7302.2	5163.4	2635.1	3750.4	1197.3
1992	2178.4	375.6	9229.2	8863.3	6273.6	2993.5	4556.8	1585.2
1993	2535.7	395.5	11167.3	10919.6	6637.4	3487.2	5449.9	1734.2
1994	2992.1	420.8	13400.8	13190.9	7553.4	4306.7	6038.5	1890.3
1995	3423.0	463.7	15665.5	15459.7	8656.2	4793.3	6527.6	2109.6
1996	4189.8	502.7	20647.1	20623.2	10136.4	5219.9	7356.6	2293.1
1997	4776.4	544.4	23888.7	24005.4	10957.4	5919.4	8349.7	2446.7

3—5 国内生产总值 (1952—1977)

Gross Domestic Product

单位:亿元

年份	国民生产总值	国内生产总值	第一产业	第二产业	工业	建筑业	第三产业	运输邮电业	商业	其他	人均国内生产总值(元/人)
1952	27.81	27.81	18.72	3.43	2.94	0.49	5.66	1.10	2.50	2.06	86
1953	30.29	30.29	18.48	4.28	3.53	0.75	7.53	1.64	3.54	2.35	91
1954	30.51	30.51	17.03	5.13	4.22	0.91	8.35	1.77	3.98	2.60	90
1955	35.83	35.83	21.13	5.76	4.25	1.51	8.94	2.07	3.83	3.04	104
1956	37.93	37.93	20.56	6.57	5.19	1.38	10.80	2.38	4.83	3.59	109
1957	45.20	45.20	26.41	7.45	5.94	1.51	11.34	2.71	4.51	4.12	127
1958	55.85	55.85	26.65	16.63	12.40	4.23	12.57	3.51	4.58	4.48	154
1959	61.95	61.95	23.60	21.57	16.57	5.00	16.78	5.45	6.04	5.29	168
1960	64.07	64.07	20.58	25.47	19.22	6.25	18.02	5.42	6.60	6.00	176
1961	46.64	46.64	20.78	11.69	10.25	1.44	14.17	3.20	4.95	6.02	132
1962	51.19	51.19	27.17	10.59	9.46	1.13	13.43	2.73	4.93	5.77	144
1963	48.08	48.08	25.11	11.37	10.31	1.06	11.60	3.25	2.82	5.53	131
1964	57.36	57.36	30.41	15.60	13.50	2.10	11.35	2.57	3.45	5.33	153
1965	65.32	65.32	34.00	19.17	16.86	2.31	12.15	2.98	3.68	5.49	170
1966	72.73	72.73	37.30	22.16	19.67	2.49	13.27	3.14	4.41	5.72	184
1967	73.51	73.51	40.07	19.89	17.46	2.43	13.55	3.03	4.54	5.98	181
1968	75.67	75.67	44.85	17.31	15.03	2.28	13.51	2.92	4.22	6.37	181
1969	81.26	81.26	44.08	21.98	19.39	2.59	15.20	3.37	5.20	6.63	189
1970	93.05	93.05	44.62	31.98	28.83	3.15	16.45	3.96	5.67	6.82	211
1971	99.10	99.10	46.31	35.33	30.35	4.98	17.46	4.34	5.63	7.49	218
1972	107.01	107.01	47.73	39.91	34.31	5.60	19.37	4.89	6.68	7.80	230
1973	115.80	115.80	51.91	43.35	37.92	5.43	20.54	5.01	7.23	8.30	244
1974	108.17	108.17	53.17	34.87	29.21	5.66	20.13	4.34	6.98	8.81	223
1975	118.40	118.40	54.97	41.96	35.58	6.38	21.47	4.92	7.29	9.26	239
1976	118.53	118.53	55.07	41.47	34.95	6.52	21.99	4.83	7.17	9.99	236
1977	129.17	129.17	55.95	49.59	43.14	6.45	23.63	5.33	8.06	10.24	254

3—6 国内生产总值构成 (1952—1977)

Composition of Gross Domestic Product

(以国内生产总值为100)　　单位:%

年 份	国内生产总 值	第一产业	第二产业	工 业	建筑业	第三产业	运 输 邮电业	商 业	其 他
1952	100.0	67.3	12.3	10.6	1.8	20.4	4.0	9.0	7.4
1953	100.0	61.0	14.1	11.7	2.5	24.9	5.4	11.7	7.8
1954	100.0	55.8	16.8	13.8	3.0	27.4	5.8	13.0	8.5
1955	100.0	59.0	16.1	11.9	4.2	25.0	5.8	10.7	8.5
1956	100.0	54.2	17.3	13.7	3.6	28.5	6.3	12.7	9.5
1957	100.0	58.4	16.5	13.1	3.3	25.1	6.0	10.0	9.1
1958	100.0	47.7	29.8	22.2	7.6	22.5	6.3	8.2	8.0
1959	100.0	38.1	34.8	26.7	8.1	27.1	8.8	9.7	8.5
1960	100.0	32.1	39.8	30.0	9.8	28.1	8.5	10.3	9.4
1961	100.0	44.6	25.1	22.0	3.1	30.4	6.9	10.6	12.9
1962	100.0	53.1	20.7	18.5	2.2	26.2	5.3	9.6	11.3
1963	100.0	52.2	23.6	21.4	2.2	24.1	6.8	5.9	11.5
1964	100.0	53.0	27.2	23.5	3.7	19.8	4.5	6.0	9.3
1965	100.0	52.1	29.3	25.8	3.5	18.6	4.6	5.6	8.4
1966	100.0	51.3	30.5	27.0	3.4	18.2	4.3	6.1	7.9
1967	100.0	54.5	27.1	23.8	3.3	18.4	4.1	6.2	8.1
1968	100.0	59.3	22.9	19.9	3.0	17.9	3.9	5.6	8.4
1969	100.0	54.2	27.0	23.9	3.2	18.7	4.1	6.4	8.2
1970	100.0	48.0	34.4	31.0	3.4	17.7	4.3	6.1	7.3
1971	100.0	46.7	35.7	30.6	5.0	17.6	4.4	5.7	7.6
1972	100.0	44.6	37.3	32.1	5.2	18.1	4.6	6.2	7.3
1973	100.0	44.8	37.4	32.7	4.7	17.7	4.3	6.2	7.2
1974	100.0	49.2	32.2	27.0	5.2	18.6	4.0	6.5	8.1
1975	100.0	46.4	35.4	30.1	5.4	18.1	4.2	6.2	7.8
1976	100.0	46.5	35.0	29.5	5.5	18.6	4.1	6.0	8.4
1977	100.0	43.3	38.4	33.4	5.0	18.3	4.1	6.2	7.9

3—7 国内生产总值发展速度 (1952—1977)

Growth Rate of GDP

(上年＝100)

单位：%

年 份	国民生产总值	国内生产总值	第一产业	第二产业	工业	建筑业	第三产业	运输邮电业	商业
1952	100.0	100.0	100.0	100.0	100.0	100.0	100.0	100.0	100.0
1953	108.4	108.4	99.9	131.5	127.7	153.1	128.1	150.7	131.7
1954	98.2	98.2	89.9	120.1	120.0	121.3	110.1	109.6	111.6
1955	118.5	118.5	122.8	120.3	107.6	178.5	106.6	116.5	95.4
1956	105.4	105.4	96.4	119.3	128.7	92.9	120.7	116.6	126.2
1957	115.1	115.1	121.4	111.7	112.4	109.6	103.4	115.3	89.6
1958	119.8	119.8	101.3	206.3	184.1	292.6	110.3	126.1	101.5
1959	108.8	108.8	86.7	126.5	134.6	104.0	134.2	157.4	131.6
1960	99.0	99.0	79.7	115.9	113.6	124.1	105.2	98.7	108.2
1961	64.5	64.5	91.6	43.4	49.5	22.8	64.8	58.5	53.9
1962	103.0	103.0	122.9	85.6	86.6	78.7	88.7	85.6	89.6
1963	96.4	96.4	91.1	107.9	110.6	85.7	97.2	118.7	67.1
1964	118.8	118.8	115.5	141.0	135.8	195.1	103.0	79.2	144.6
1965	113.1	113.1	104.3	129.1	131.9	109.2	110.9	115.2	108.8
1966	112.8	112.8	109.1	119.9	121.4	107.9	109.2	105.0	119.9
1967	100.3	100.3	107.4	91.1	90.4	97.6	101.8	96.4	103.0
1968	98.6	98.6	108.7	83.9	82.8	94.0	99.4	96.0	92.9
1969	110.6	110.6	97.2	133.7	136.2	113.4	112.6	115.6	123.2
1970	117.6	117.6	100.9	147.0	149.8	121.4	106.2	117.6	108.9
1971	105.6	105.6	100.6	111.6	107.7	156.8	102.8	109.5	99.3
1972	108.0	108.0	101.8	114.4	114.7	112.5	110.8	112.4	118.7
1973	106.8	106.8	108.0	106.0	107.4	97.2	105.5	102.4	107.1
1974	92.6	92.6	102.4	78.7	75.2	104.3	98.4	86.7	97.6
1975	110.4	110.4	102.9	123.7	126.0	112.2	106.6	113.3	104.8
1976	99.5	99.5	100.1	97.3	96.4	102.5	102.2	98.1	98.2
1977	109.6	109.6	101.5	121.1	125.1	98.9	107.3	110.3	112.5

3—8 国内生产总值(1978—1997)

Gross Domestic Product

单位:亿元

年份	国民生产总值	国内生产总值	第一产业	第二产业	工业	建筑业	第三产业	运输邮电业	商业
1978	146.99	146.99	59.83	59.82	51.94	7.88	27.34	5.91	9.71
1979	178.01	178.01	79.40	68.42	59.23	9.19	30.19	6.47	10.85
1980	191.72	191.72	81.14	76.99	65.31	11.68	33.59	6.77	11.73
1981	209.68	209.68	93.29	77.78	67.19	10.59	38.61	6.93	13.42
1982	232.52	232.52	107.99	82.51	71.31	11.20	42.02	7.61	12.81
1983	257.43	257.43	117.79	93.37	78.84	14.53	46.27	8.16	12.56
1984	287.29	287.29	128.28	104.34	90.79	13.55	54.67	9.30	15.40
1985	349.95	349.95	147.72	127.08	110.05	17.03	75.15	13.23	22.94
1986	397.68	397.68	165.28	143.31	124.30	19.01	89.09	15.00	27.60
1987	469.44	469.44	187.09	172.45	149.67	22.78	109.90	20.13	34.56
1988	584.07	584.07	217.03	221.28	190.40	30.88	145.76	24.12	46.61
1989	640.80	640.80	234.31	238.15	212.21	25.94	168.34	26.81	45.48
1990	744.44	744.44	279.09	249.98	220.69	29.29	215.37	32.27	62.94
1991	833.30	833.30	301.02	281.95	242.96	38.99	250.33	41.68	73.91
1992	997.70	997.70	323.91	347.89	295.38	52.51	325.90	51.29	104.96
1993	1278.28	1278.28	383.68	488.98	417.52	71.46	405.62	72.47	123.71
1994	1694.42	1694.42	532.89	618.07	525.77	92.30	543.46	99.63	167.75
1995	2195.70	2195.70	685.30	815.82	699.03	116.79	694.58	132.39	211.37
1996	2647.16	2647.16	793.98	1008.43	871.11	137.32	844.75	168.88	245.95
1997	2993.00	2993.00	855.75	1166.97	1019.12	147.85	970.28	195.38	270.12

3—8 续表　　　　(1978—1997)　　　　单位:亿元

年份	金融保险业	房地产业	社会服务业	卫生体育福利业	教育文艺广播电视业	科学研究综合技术服务业	国家政党机关和社会团体	其他	人均国内生产总值(元/人)
1978	2.55	2.03	0.62	1.05	3.21	0.20	1.86	0.20	286
1979	2.50	2.10	0.68	1.24	3.72	0.28	2.10	0.25	343
1980	2.70	2.32	0.83	1.54	4.46	0.31	2.63	0.30	365
1981	3.60	3.56	0.95	1.72	4.83	0.36	2.89	0.35	394
1982	5.02	3.96	1.06	1.96	5.60	0.39	3.21	0.40	430
1983	5.66	5.18	1.17	2.33	6.40	0.49	3.87	0.45	470
1984	6.53	5.76	1.58	2.58	7.57	0.57	4.88	0.50	519
1985	8.85	7.84	3.34	2.87	9.13	0.68	5.67	0.60	626
1986	12.55	7.93	3.39	3.26	10.80	0.84	6.75	0.97	703
1987	15.94	8.53	3.91	3.84	12.61	0.99	8.14	1.25	818
1988	20.91	9.96	6.55	5.08	17.61	3.99	10.93		999
1989	26.94	11.00	8.73	6.04	21.61	6.07	13.86	1.80	1074
1990	31.01	16.25	10.84	7.98	17.43	7.36	26.51	2.78	1228
1991	38.26	17.73	10.88	9.02	19.14	7.45	29.08	3.18	1357
1992	49.01	20.57	16.52	11.35	23.02	9.41	34.72	5.05	1613
1993	63.47	25.73	18.54	14.08	27.55	10.93	43.96	5.18	2053
1994	73.60	32.30	24.84	20.72	42.37	15.78	59.70	6.77	2701
1995	90.15	40.90	29.39	25.47	55.99	19.86	79.98	9.08	3470
1996	105.14	57.37	33.11	33.84	67.21	8.62	99.78	24.85	4130
1997	119.22	65.75	39.66	40.62	80.27	10.23	119.35	29.68	4643

3—9 国内生产总值构成(1978—1997)

Composition of GDP

(以国内生产总值为100)

单位:%

年 份	国内生产总值	第一产业	第二产业	工 业	建筑业	第三产业	运输邮电业	商 业
1978	100.0	40.7	40.7	35.3	5.4	18.6	4.0	6.6
1979	100.0	44.6	38.4	33.3	5.2	17.0	3.6	6.1
1980	100.0	42.3	40.2	34.1	6.1	17.5	3.5	6.1
1981	100.0	44.5	37.1	32.0	5.1	18.4	3.3	6.4
1982	100.0	46.4	35.5	30.7	4.8	18.1	3.3	5.5
1983	100.0	45.8	36.3	30.6	5.6	18.0	3.2	4.9
1984	100.0	44.7	36.3	31.6	4.7	19.0	3.2	5.4
1985	100.0	42.2	36.3	31.4	4.9	21.5	3.8	6.6
1986	100.0	41.6	36.0	31.3	4.8	22.4	3.8	6.9
1987	100.0	39.9	36.7	31.9	4.9	23.4	4.3	7.4
1988	100.0	37.2	37.9	32.6	5.3	25.0	4.1	8.0
1989	100.0	36.6	37.2	33.1	4.0	26.3	4.2	7.1
1990	100.0	37.5	33.6	29.6	3.9	28.9	4.3	8.5
1991	100.0	36.1	33.8	29.2	4.7	30.0	5.0	8.9
1992	100.0	32.5	34.9	29.6	5.3	32.7	5.1	10.5
1993	100.0	30.0	38.3	32.7	5.6	31.7	5.7	9.7
1994	100.0	31.4	36.5	31.0	5.4	32.1	5.9	9.9
1995	100.0	31.2	37.2	31.8	5.3	31.6	6.0	9.6
1996	100.0	30.0	38.1	32.9	5.2	31.9	6.4	9.3
1997	100.0	28.6	39.0	34.1	4.9	32.4	6.5	9.0

3—9　续表　(1978—1997)　单位:%

年　份	金　融保险业	房地产业	社　会服务业	卫生体育福利业	教育文艺广播电视业	科学研究综合技术服务业	国家政党机关和社会团体	其　他
1978	1.7	1.4	0.4	0.7	2.2	0.1	1.3	0.1
1979	1.4	1.2	0.4	0.7	2.1	0.2	1.2	0.1
1980	1.4	1.2	0.4	0.8	2.3	0.2	1.4	0.2
1981	1.7	1.7	0.5	0.8	2.3	0.2	1.4	0.2
1982	2.2	1.7	0.5	0.8	2.4	0.2	1.4	0.2
1983	2.2	2.0	0.5	0.9	2.5	0.2	1.5	0.2
1984	2.3	2.0	0.5	0.9	2.6	0.2	1.7	0.2
1985	2.5	2.2	1.0	0.8	2.6	0.2	1.6	0.2
1986	3.2	2.0	0.9	0.8	2.7	0.2	1.7	0.2
1987	3.4	1.8	0.8	0.8	2.7	0.2	1.7	0.3
1988	3.6	1.7	1.1	0.9	3.0	0.7	1.9	0.0
1989	4.2	1.7	1.4	0.9	3.4	0.9	2.2	0.3
1990	4.2	2.2	1.5	1.1	2.3	1.0	3.6	0.4
1991	4.6	2.1	1.3	1.1	2.3	0.9	3.5	0.4
1992	4.9	2.1	1.7	1.1	2.3	0.9	3.5	0.5
1993	5.0	2.0	1.5	1.1	2.2	0.9	3.4	0.4
1994	4.3	1.9	1.5	1.2	2.5	0.9	3.5	0.4
1995	4.1	1.9	1.3	1.2	2.5	0.9	3.6	0.4
1996	4.0	2.2	1.3	1.3	2.5	0.3	3.8	0.9
1997	4.0	2.2	1.3	1.4	2.7	0.3	4.0	1.0

3—10 国内生产总值发展速度(1978—1997)

Growth Rate of GDP

(以上年为100)

单位:%

年 份	国民生产总值	国内生产总值	第一产业	第二产业	工 业	建筑业	第三产业	运输邮电业	商 业
1978	116.4	116.4	111.7	121.8	121.6	123.3	115.5	110.7	120.4
1979	109.1	109.1	106.8	111.4	111.3	112.1	109.0	109.3	110.1
1980	105.2	105.2	98.9	111.0	109.7	119.9	105.5	104.5	102.5
1981	105.5	105.5	107.0	100.2	101.4	92.7	113.3	102.6	112.6
1982	109.4	109.4	113.0	106.0	106.1	105.0	107.5	109.6	94.0
1983	109.2	109.2	103.7	116.7	114.8	130.2	108.2	107.2	95.8
1984	109.4	109.4	106.6	109.7	113.0	89.8	115.6	113.9	119.3
1985	112.0	112.0	103.7	113.6	114.3	108.7	127.2	140.6	134.8
1986	108.1	108.1	105.2	107.7	108.5	101.6	114.1	112.6	114.6
1987	109.3	109.3	102.9	112.8	113.3	108.6	114.0	127.1	113.8
1988	108.2	108.2	97.7	115.0	115.3	112.6	112.6	120.4	108.9
1989	103.6	103.6	105.7	101.2	103.0	79.3	105.0	97.3	90.6
1990	104.0	104.0	103.2	104.6	104.5	106.1	103.8	113.7	83.7
1991	107.9	107.9	105.6	108.5	107.4	116.7	110.5	118.6	112.0
1992	112.4	112.4	103.5	121.1	121.2	120.4	114.1	112.8	110.0
1993	113.1	113.1	104.3	119.2	121.1	105.5	116.1	125.2	110.8
1994	111.0	111.0	105.4	116.3	116.9	111.7	110.3	110.6	109.0
1995	110.9	110.9	106.5	114.7	114.7	114.6	110.4	116.3	109.1
1996	112.6	112.6	106.2	117.2	117.8	112.3	112.6	117.8	109.0
1997	110.8	110.8	106.1	113.5	114.5	104.4	111.5	115.0	109.5

3—10 续表 (1978—1997) 单位:%

年份	金融保险业	房地产业	社会服务业	卫生体育福利业	教育文艺广播电视业	科学研究综合技术服务业	国家政党机关和社会团体	其他
1978	115.3	104.0	100.0	113.4	115.8	115.1	116.9	100.0
1979	96.5	101.7	101.9	115.9	113.6	137.9	111.2	125.0
1980	97.8	110.4	104.8	113.5	110.0	103.7	115.3	112.0
1981	131.0	146.4	151.3	110.4	106.6	114.5	108.2	116.7
1982	137.3	110.3	110.2	112.1	114.3	105.8	109.1	111.4
1983	110.1	128.5	128.5	116.0	111.8	124.7	117.7	112.8
1984	111.9	110.0	108.8	107.9	114.9	114.0	122.7	106.6
1985	122.1	128.4	125.9	100.9	109.5	109.0	106.1	110.6
1986	135.3	100.9	97.4	109.4	113.0	118.6	113.7	157.7
1987	114.9	105.0	99.4	107.0	106.2	107.4	109.8	118.3
1988	104.6	109.5	149.8	107.1	112.6	131.1	108.5	112.4
1989	150.6	86.7	122.5	113.6	117.5	146.3	120.8	101.8
1990	109.0	109.0	104.3	110.2	107.3	108.9	110.4	115.3
1991	115.5	106.1	100.0	107.8	104.9	100.0	106.0	107.6
1992	130.3	110.6	116.7	104.4	106.3	108.7	116.8	107.8
1993	121.3	124.0	107.1	116.8	113.1	108.4	113.3	101.0
1994	105.7	112.0	107.4	117.9	123.2	125.5	109.2	104.6
1995	106.0	114.7	102.4	106.5	104.4	104.4	116.0	116.2
1996	110.6	117.1	107.1	126.3	114.1	117.5	110.3	106.6
1997	110.3	110.2	111.3	112.4	114.9	113.0	111.1	108.1

3—11 国内生产总值指数

Gross Domestic Product Indices

(1978=100)

单位:%

年 份	国民生产总值	国内生产总值	第一产业	第二产业	工 业	建筑业	第三产业	运输邮电业	商 业
1978	100.0	100.0	100.0	100.0	100.0	100.0	100.0	100.0	100.0
1979	109.1	109.1	106.8	111.4	111.3	112.1	109.0	109.3	110.1
1980	114.8	114.8	105.6	123.6	122.1	134.4	115.0	114.2	112.9
1981	121.0	121.0	113.0	123.9	123.8	124.6	130.4	117.2	127.1
1982	132.4	132.4	127.7	131.3	131.4	130.8	140.2	128.4	119.4
1983	144.6	144.6	132.5	153.3	150.8	170.3	151.7	137.7	114.4
1984	158.2	158.2	141.2	168.1	170.4	153.0	175.4	156.8	136.5
1985	177.2	177.2	146.4	191.0	194.7	166.3	223.0	220.5	184.0
1986	191.7	191.7	154.1	205.8	211.3	168.9	254.5	248.3	210.9
1987	209.5	209.5	158.5	232.2	239.4	183.5	290.0	315.6	240.0
1988	226.7	226.7	154.9	267.0	276.1	206.6	326.6	379.9	261.4
1989	234.9	234.9	163.8	270.2	284.3	163.8	342.9	369.1	236.8
1990	244.3	244.3	169.1	282.7	297.1	173.8	355.9	420.3	198.2
1991	263.6	263.6	178.5	306.7	319.1	202.8	393.3	498.5	222.0
1992	296.3	296.3	184.8	371.5	386.8	244.2	448.7	562.3	244.2
1993	335.1	335.1	192.7	442.8	468.4	257.6	520.9	704.0	270.6
1994	372.0	372.0	203.1	515.0	547.6	287.7	574.6	742.0	295.0
1995	412.5	412.5	216.3	590.7	628.1	329.7	634.3	863.3	321.8
1996	464.5	464.5	229.7	692.3	739.9	370.3	714.2	1017.0	350.8
1997	514.7	514.7	243.7	785.8	847.2	386.6	796.3	1169.6	384.1

3—11 续表1 (1978=100) 单位:%

年份	金融保险业	房地产业	社会服务业	卫生体育福利业	教育文艺广播电视业	科学研究综合技术服务业	国家政党机关和社会团体	其他
1978	100.0	100.0	100.0	100.0	100.0	100.0	100.0	100.0
1979	96.5	101.7	101.9	115.9	113.6	137.9	111.2	125.0
1980	94.4	112.3	106.8	131.5	125.0	143.0	128.2	140.0
1981	123.6	164.4	161.6	145.2	133.2	163.7	138.7	163.4
1982	169.7	181.3	178.1	162.8	152.3	173.2	151.4	182.0
1983	186.9	233.0	228.8	188.8	170.2	216.0	178.1	205.3
1984	209.1	256.3	248.9	203.8	195.6	246.3	218.6	219.3
1985	255.4	329.1	313.4	205.6	214.2	268.4	231.9	242.5
1986	345.5	332.0	305.0	224.9	242.0	318.4	263.7	382.4
1987	397.0	348.6	303.4	240.7	257.0	341.9	289.5	452.4
1988	415.2	381.7	454.5	257.8	289.4	448.3	314.1	508.5
1989	625.3	331.0	556.8	292.8	340.0	655.8	379.5	517.7
1990	681.6	360.8	580.7	322.7	364.8	714.2	419.0	596.9
1991	787.2	382.8	580.7	347.8	382.7	714.2	444.1	642.3
1992	1025.7	423.4	677.7	363.1	406.8	776.3	518.7	692.4
1993	1244.2	525.0	725.8	424.1	460.1	841.5	587.7	699.3
1994	1315.1	588.0	779.5	500.0	566.8	1056.1	641.8	731.5
1995	1394.0	674.4	798.2	532.5	591.8	1102.6	744.5	850.0
1996	1541.8	789.7	854.9	672.5	675.2	1295.6	821.2	906.1
1997	1700.6	870.2	951.5	755.9	775.8	1464.0	912.4	979.5

3—11 续表 2　　(1952=100)　　单位:%

年 份	国民生产总值	国内生产总值	第一产业	第二产业	工 业	建筑业	第三产业	运输邮电业	商 业
1952	100.0	100.0	100.0	100.0	100.0	100.0	100.0	100.0	100.0
1953	108.4	108.4	99.9	131.5	127.7	153.1	128.1	150.7	131.7
1954	106.4	106.4	89.8	157.9	153.3	185.7	141.1	165.2	147.0
1955	126.1	126.1	110.3	190.0	165.0	331.5	150.4	192.5	140.2
1956	132.9	132.9	106.4	226.8	212.3	308.1	181.6	224.5	176.9
1957	153.0	153.0	129.2	253.3	238.6	337.6	187.8	258.8	158.5
1958	183.4	183.4	130.8	522.4	439.3	987.8	207.0	326.3	160.9
1959	199.5	199.5	113.4	660.9	591.3	1027.3	277.9	513.6	211.7
1960	197.5	197.5	90.4	765.8	671.7	1274.9	292.1	506.9	229.1
1961	127.4	127.4	82.8	332.0	332.5	290.7	189.1	296.5	123.5
1962	131.3	131.3	101.7	284.3	287.9	228.8	167.7	253.8	110.6
1963	126.5	126.5	92.7	306.7	318.4	196.1	163.0	301.3	74.2
1964	150.3	150.3	107.1	432.6	432.6	382.6	167.9	238.6	107.3
1965	170.1	170.1	111.7	558.4	570.3	417.8	186.1	274.9	116.7
1966	191.9	191.9	121.9	669.8	692.3	450.8	203.2	288.6	139.9
1967	192.5	192.5	130.9	610.1	625.8	440.0	206.9	278.2	144.1
1968	189.8	189.8	142.2	512.0	518.2	413.6	205.6	267.1	133.9
1969	210.0	210.0	138.2	684.2	705.8	469.0	231.5	308.8	165.0
1970	247.0	247.0	139.5	1005.8	1057.3	569.4	245.9	363.1	179.7
1971	261.0	261.0	140.3	1122.5	1138.7	892.8	252.7	397.6	178.4
1972	281.8	281.8	142.8	1283.9	1306.1	1004.4	280.0	446.9	211.8
1973	300.9	300.9	154.2	1361.2	1402.8	976.3	295.4	457.6	226.8
1974	278.8	278.8	157.9	1071.5	1054.9	1018.3	290.6	396.7	221.4
1975	307.6	307.6	162.4	1325.9	1329.2	1142.5	309.9	449.5	232.0
1976	306.0	306.0	162.5	1290.1	1281.3	1171.1	316.9	441.0	227.8
1977	335.3	335.3	165.0	1562.0	1602.9	1158.2	340.0	486.4	256.3
1978	390.3	390.3	184.3	1903.0	1949.8	1427.7	392.8	538.3	308.6
1979	425.7	425.7	196.8	2119.1	2169.4	1600.1	428.2	588.3	339.8
1980	448.0	448.0	194.6	2352.0	2380.0	1918.7	451.9	614.8	348.3
1981	472.4	472.4	208.3	2357.8	2414.0	1779.3	512.1	630.5	392.2
1982	516.7	516.7	235.4	2498.9	2561.8	1868.4	550.6	690.8	368.7
1983	564.4	564.4	244.2	2917.3	2939.9	2432.2	595.9	740.7	353.2
1984	617.4	617.4	260.2	3198.9	3321.7	2184.7	688.9	843.8	421.4
1985	691.8	691.8	269.9	3634.5	3795.5	2375.4	875.9	1186.1	568.0
1986	748.1	748.1	284.0	3916.1	4119.2	2414.5	999.7	1335.2	650.9
1987	817.8	817.8	292.2	4418.7	4668.6	2622.1	1139.2	1697.3	740.7
1988	884.9	884.9	285.5	5081.5	5382.9	2952.5	1282.7	2043.5	806.6
1989	916.8	916.8	301.8	5142.5	5544.4	2341.3	1346.8	1988.3	730.8
1990	953.1	953.1	311.6	5380.0	5793.9	2484.2	1397.9	2260.7	611.7
1991	1028.4	1028.4	329.0	5837.3	6222.6	2899.1	1544.7	2681.2	685.1
1992	1155.9	1155.9	340.5	7074.8	7541.8	3490.5	1762.5	3024.4	753.6
1993	1307.3	1307.3	355.1	8433.2	9133.1	3682.5	2046.3	3786.5	835.0
1994	1451.1	1451.1	374.3	9807.8	10676.6	4113.4	2257.1	4187.9	910.2
1995	1609.3	1609.3	398.6	11249.6	12246.1	4713.9	2491.8	4870.5	993.0
1996	1812.1	1812.1	423.3	13184.5	14425.9	5293.7	2805.8	5737.4	1082.4
1997	2007.8	2007.8	449.1	14964.4	16517.7	5526.6	3128.5	6598.0	1185.2

3—12 国内生产总值构成项目表(一)(1978－1983)

Structure of Gross Domestic Product

单位:亿元

指　　　标	1978	1979	1980	1981	1982	1983
国内生产总值	146.99	178.01	191.72	209.68	232.52	257.43
劳动者报酬	91.13	113.89	120.77	134.16	152.04	165.48
固定资产折旧	12.78	14.02	16.27	17.82	18.47	22.44
生产税净额	19.26	20.81	22.52	23.61	24.35	28.09
营业盈余	23.82	29.29	32.16	34.09	37.66	41.42
第一产业	59.83	79.40	81.14	93.29	107.99	117.79
(一)农业增加值	59.83	79.40	81.14	93.29	107.99	117.79
劳动者报酬	55.70	74.60	75.92	87.52	101.27	110.62
固定资产折旧	1.50	1.80	2.15	2.20	2.50	2.70
生产税净额	1.73	1.80	1.57	1.67	1.72	1.87
营业盈余	0.90	1.20	1.50	1.90	2.50	2.60
第二产业	59.82	68.42	76.99	77.78	82.51	93.37
劳动者报酬	22.07	24.60	27.83	27.33	29.84	33.43
固定资产折旧	6.66	6.49	7.90	7.88	7.76	9.44
生产税净额	15.16	16.45	18.13	18.70	19.45	21.79
营业盈余	15.93	20.88	23.13	23.87	25.46	28.71
(二)工业增加值	51.94	59.23	65.31	67.19	71.31	78.84
劳动者报酬	14.98	16.35	17.27	17.82	20.19	22.08
固定资产折旧	6.21	6.09	7.48	7.45	7.35	8.90
生产税净额	15.05	16.32	17.98	18.64	19.29	21.09
营业盈余	15.70	20.47	22.58	23.28	24.48	26.77
(三)建筑业增加值	7.88	9.19	11.68	10.59	11.20	14.53
劳动者报酬	7.09	8.25	10.56	9.51	9.65	11.35
固定资产折旧	0.45	0.40	0.42	0.43	0.41	0.54
生产税净额	0.11	0.13	0.15	0.06	0.16	0.70
营业盈余	0.23	0.41	0.55	0.59	0.98	1.94
第三产业	27.34	30.19	33.59	38.61	42.02	46.27
劳动者报酬	13.36	14.69	17.02	19.31	20.93	21.43
固定资产折旧	4.62	5.73	6.22	7.74	8.21	10.30
生产税净额	2.37	2.56	2.82	3.24	3.18	4.43
营业盈余	6.99	7.21	7.53	8.32	9.70	10.11
(四)运输邮电业增加值	5.91	6.47	6.77	6.93	7.61	8.16
劳动者报酬	2.26	2.48	2.74	2.80	3.08	3.30
固定资产折旧	1.09	1.20	1.02	1.03	1.08	1.16
生产税净额	0.28	0.31	0.43	0.44	0.49	0.53
营业盈余	2.28	2.48	2.58	2.66	2.96	3.17
(五)商业增加值	9.71	10.85	11.73	13.42	12.81	12.56
劳动者报酬	4.71	5.36	5.78	6.74	6.48	4.68
固定资产折旧	0.57	0.74	1.00	1.16	1.09	1.67
生产税净额	2.08	2.24	2.36	2.63	2.45	3.60
营业盈余	2.35	2.51	2.59	2.89	2.79	2.61

3—12 续表 (1978—1983) 单位:亿元

指 标	1978	1979	1980	1981	1982	1983
(六)金融保险业增加值	2.55	2.50	2.70	3.60	5.02	5.66
劳动者报酬	0.20	0.33	0.34	0.69	0.86	1.06
固定资产折旧	0.06	0.03	0.07	0.08	0.08	0.09
生产税净额	0.00	0.00	0.01	0.15	0.22	0.28
营业盈余	2.29	2.14	2.28	2.68	3.86	4.23
(七)房地产业增加值	2.03	2.10	2.32	3.56	3.96	5.18
劳动者报酬	0.02	0.03	0.03	0.03	0.04	0.04
固定资产折旧	2.01	2.07	2.29	3.53	3.92	5.14
生产税净额						
营业盈余						
(八)社会服务业增加值	0.62	0.68	0.83	0.95	1.06	1.17
劳动者报酬	0.46	0.49	0.62	0.71	0.82	0.90
固定资产折旧	0.08	0.10	0.11	0.13	0.13	0.15
生产税净额	0.01	0.01	0.02	0.02	0.02	0.02
营业盈余	0.07	0.08	0.08	0.09	0.09	0.10
(九)卫生体育福利业增加值	1.05	1.24	1.54	1.72	1.96	2.33
劳动者报酬	0.88	1.04	1.32	1.47	1.68	2.02
固定资产折旧	0.17	0.20	0.22	0.25	0.28	0.31
生产税净额						
营业盈余						
(十)教育文艺广播电视业增加值	3.21	3.72	4.46	4.83	5.60	6.40
劳动者报酬	3.14	2.97	3.66	4.01	4.76	5.50
固定资产折旧	0.07	0.75	0.80	0.82	0.84	0.90
生产税净额						
营业盈余						
(十一)科学研究和综合技术服务业增加值	0.20	0.28	0.31	0.36	0.39	0.49
劳动者报酬	0.14	0.20	0.21	0.25	0.27	0.34
固定资产折旧	0.06	0.08	0.10	0.11	0.12	0.15
生产税净额						
营业盈余						
(十二)国家政党机关和社会团体增加值	1.86	2.10	2.63	2.89	3.21	3.87
劳动者报酬	1.36	1.55	2.03	2.27	2.56	3.16
固定资产折旧	0.50	0.55	0.60	0.62	0.65	0.71
生产税净额						
营业盈余						
(十三)其他增加值	0.20	0.25	0.30	0.35	0.40	0.45
劳动者报酬	0.19	0.24	0.29	0.34	0.38	0.43
固定资产折旧	0.01	0.01	0.01	0.01	0.02	0.02
生产税净额						
营业盈余						

3—12 国内生产总值构成项目表(二)(1984—1989)

Structure of Gross Domestic Product

单位:亿元

指　　标	1984	1985	1986	1987	1988	1989
国内生产总值	287.29	349.95	397.68	469.44	584.07	640.80
劳动者报酬	186.96	225.99	257.04	296.68	373.76	415.54
固定资产折旧	24.22	28.23	31.36	36.75	44.58	50.52
生产税净额	32.91	40.48	45.86	60.44	87.95	99.88
营业盈余	43.20	55.25	63.42	75.57	77.78	74.86
第一产业	128.28	147.72	165.28	187.09	217.03	234.31
(一)农业增加值	128.28	147.72	165.28	187.09	217.03	234.31
劳动者报酬	120.46	140.17	156.57	176.45	202.12	218.00
固定资产折旧	2.92	2.20	2.48	2.82	4.01	4.61
生产税净额	2.10	2.25	2.73	3.08	5.56	5.93
营业盈余	2.80	3.10	3.50	4.74	5.34	5.77
第二产业	104.34	127.08	143.31	172.45	221.28	238.15
劳动者报酬	37.55	44.89	53.12	66.94	94.42	100.70
固定资产折旧	10.23	12.02	13.30	15.55	18.83	20.80
生产税净额	25.74	30.85	34.85	41.35	61.79	68.63
营业盈余	30.82	39.32	42.04	48.61	46.24	48.02
(二)工业增加值	90.79	110.05	124.30	149.67	190.40	212.21
劳动者报酬	26.42	30.84	36.67	47.79	68.81	78.99
固定资产折旧	9.80	11.23	12.49	14.74	17.77	19.64
生产税净额	24.84	29.91	33.92	39.77	59.34	66.36
营业盈余	29.73	38.07	41.22	47.37	44.48	47.22
(三)建筑业增加值	13.55	17.03	19.01	22.78	30.88	25.94
劳动者报酬	11.13	14.05	16.45	19.15	25.61	21.71
固定资产折旧	0.43	0.79	0.81	0.81	1.06	1.16
生产税净额	0.90	0.94	0.93	1.58	2.45	2.27
营业盈余	1.09	1.25	0.82	1.24	1.76	0.80
第三产业	54.67	75.15	89.09	109.90	145.76	168.34
劳动者报酬	28.95	40.93	47.35	53.29	77.22	96.84
固定资产折旧	11.07	14.01	15.58	18.38	21.74	25.11
生产税净额	5.07	7.38	8.28	16.01	20.60	25.32
营业盈余	9.58	12.83	17.88	22.22	26.20	21.07
(四)运输邮电业增加值	9.30	13.23	15.00	20.13	24.12	26.81
劳动者报酬	4.45	7.85	9.01	7.81	10.27	13.39
固定资产折旧	1.17	1.64	2.05	3.25	3.62	5.11
生产税净额	0.53	0.55	0.87	3.29	4.01	3.24
营业盈余	3.15	3.19	3.07	5.78	6.22	5.07
(五)商业增加值	15.40	22.94	27.60	34.56	46.61	45.48
劳动者报酬	7.94	11.98	12.60	15.39	22.36	24.36
固定资产折旧	1.57	1.73	2.75	3.19	3.57	3.77
生产税净额	3.56	5.22	5.04	9.47	11.49	14.72
营业盈余	2.33	4.01	7.21	6.51	9.19	2.63

3—12 续表 (1984—1989) 单位：亿元

指　　标	1984	1985	1986	1987	1988	1989
(六)金融保险业增加值	6.53	8.85	12.55	15.94	20.91	26.94
劳动者报酬	1.61	2.07	3.16	3.36	6.33	8.29
固定资产折旧	0.14	0.17	0.26	0.34	0.35	0.41
生产税净额	0.93	1.26	1.97	2.77	4.42	6.22
营业盈余	3.85	5.35	7.16	9.47	9.81	12.02
(七)房地产业增加值	5.76	7.84	7.93	8.53	9.96	11.00
劳动者报酬	0.05	0.06	0.13	0.13	0.20	0.25
固定资产折旧	5.71	7.78	7.80	8.38	9.68	10.66
生产税净额				0.02	0.03	0.04
营业盈余					0.05	0.05
(八)社会服务业增加值	1.58	3.34	3.39	3.91	6.55	8.73
劳动者报酬	1.13	2.50	2.40	2.81	5.26	7.09
固定资产折旧	0.15	0.21	0.15	0.19	0.33	0.41
生产税净额	0.05	0.35	0.40	0.45	0.57	0.92
营业盈余	0.25	0.28	0.44	0.46	0.39	0.31
(九)卫生体育福利业增加值	2.58	2.87	3.26	3.84	5.08	6.04
劳动者报酬	2.23	2.51	2.97	3.46	4.70	5.66
固定资产折旧	0.35	0.36	0.29	0.38	0.38	0.38
生产税净额						
营业盈余						
(十)教育文艺广播电视业增加值	7.57	9.13	10.80	12.61	17.61	21.61
劳动者报酬	6.58	8.03	9.55	11.12	15.52	19.51
固定资产折旧	0.99	1.10	1.25	1.49	2.09	2.10
生产税净额						
营业盈余						
(十一)科学研究和综合技术服务业增加值	0.57	0.68	0.84	0.99	3.99	6.07
劳动者报酬	0.41	0.50	0.66	0.78	2.86	4.24
固定资产折旧	0.16	0.18	0.18	0.21	0.51	0.66
生产税净额					0.08	0.18
营业盈余					0.54	0.99
(十二)国家政党机关和社会团体增加值	4.88	5.67	6.75	8.14	10.93	13.86
劳动者报酬	4.08	4.85	5.93	7.22	9.72	12.55
固定资产折旧	0.80	0.82	0.82	0.92	1.21	1.31
生产税净额						
营业盈余						
(十三)其他增加值	0.50	0.60	0.97	1.25		1.80
劳动者报酬	0.47	0.58	0.94	1.21		1.50
固定资产折旧	0.03	0.02	0.03	0.03		0.30
生产税净额				0.01		
营业盈余						

3—12 国内生产总值构成项目表(三)(1990-1997)

Structure of Gross Domestic Product

单位:亿元

指 标	1990	1991	1992	1993	1994	1995	1996	1997
国内生产总值	744.44	833.30	997.70	1278.28	1694.42	2195.70	2647.16	2993.00
劳动者报酬	458.40	505.93	548.15	722.76	1057.86	1479.29	1729.81	1960.74
固定资产折旧	58.88	75.18	100.15	132.90	177.69	240.05	341.55	407.76
生产税净额	90.91	127.90	131.28	147.71	249.26	225.68	266.55	317.20
营业盈余	136.25	124.29	218.12	274.91	209.61	250.68	309.25	307.30
第一产业	279.09	301.02	323.91	383.68	532.89	685.30	793.98	855.75
(一)农业增加值	279.09	301.02	323.91	383.68	532.89	685.30	793.98	855.75
劳动者报酬	260.14	280.30	298.08	350.68	472.10	590.90	694.35	753.53
固定资产折旧	4.74	6.23	7.73	10.67	11.12	20.59	27.92	31.27
生产税净额	8.26	8.08	9.32	8.88	11.70	15.20	24.01	19.90
营业盈余	5.95	6.41	8.78	13.45	37.97	58.61	47.70	51.05
第二产业	249.98	281.95	347.89	488.98	618.07	815.82	1008.43	1166.97
劳动者报酬	112.51	125.30	119.44	195.29	313.66	477.48	543.51	643.78
固定资产折旧	22.36	27.72	39.58	51.19	91.23	108.30	141.40	180.33
生产税净额	69.36	102.80	100.14	108.62	187.88	135.25	172.03	212.89
营业盈余	45.75	26.13	88.73	133.88	25.30	94.79	151.49	129.97
(二)工业增加值	220.69	242.96	295.38	417.52	525.77	699.03	871.11	1019.12
劳动者报酬	90.23	97.22	84.26	142.99	243.75	387.91	443.43	535.52
固定资产折旧	20.95	25.24	37.00	46.06	83.42	100.70	132.23	167.92
生产税净额	64.81	96.52	94.36	100.36	176.40	122.56	154.07	193.42
营业盈余	44.70	23.98	79.76	128.11	22.20	87.86	141.38	122.26
(三)建筑业增加值	29.29	38.99	52.51	71.46	92.30	116.79	137.32	147.85
劳动者报酬	22.28	28.08	35.18	52.30	69.91	89.57	100.08	108.26
固定资产折旧	1.41	2.48	2.58	5.13	7.81	7.60	9.17	12.41
生产税净额	4.55	6.28	5.78	8.26	11.48	12.69	17.96	19.47
营业盈余	1.05	2.15	8.97	5.77	3.10	6.93	10.11	7.71
第三产业	215.37	250.33	325.90	405.62	543.46	694.58	844.75	970.28
劳动者报酬	85.75	100.33	130.63	176.79	272.10	410.91	491.95	563.43
固定资产折旧	31.78	41.23	52.84	71.04	75.34	111.16	172.23	196.16
生产税净额	13.29	17.02	21.82	30.21	49.68	75.23	70.51	84.41
营业盈余	84.55	91.75	120.61	127.58	146.34	97.28	110.06	126.28
(四)运输邮电业增加值	32.27	41.68	51.29	72.47	99.63	132.39	168.88	195.38
劳动者报酬	8.47	10.84	14.00	36.39	65.67	90.79	106.88	121.42
固定资产折旧	6.13	8.01	10.57	19.48	12.56	29.24	56.41	64.98
生产税净额	2.31	2.90	3.68	7.94	14.52	15.96	12.12	14.34
营业盈余	15.36	19.93	23.04	8.66	6.88	—3.60	—6.53	—5.36
(五)商业增加值	62.94	73.91	104.96	123.71	167.75	211.37	245.95	270.12
劳动者报酬	21.81	27.85	37.89	44.73	60.66	127.66	150.49	164.09
固定资产折旧	5.25	5.99	7.92	9.37	12.70	19.76	32.76	36.03
生产税净额	6.86	8.71	11.40	13.44	18.22	37.34	36.35	40.39
营业盈余	29.02	31.36	47.75	56.17	76.17	26.61	26.35	29.61

3—12 续表　　(1990—1997)　　单位:亿元

指　　标	1990	1991	1992	1993	1994	1995	1996	1997
(六)金融保险业增加值	31.01	38.26	49.01	63.47	73.60	90.15	105.14	119.22
劳动者报酬	2.36	2.95	6.74	8.22	13.32	16.73	18.65	20.83
固定资产折旧	0.50	1.12	2.16	2.69	3.84	4.55	5.91	6.29
生产税净额	3.26	3.66	4.06	5.66	7.45	10.63	9.61	15.63
营业盈余	24.89	30.53	36.05	46.90	48.99	58.24	70.97	76.47
(七)房地产业增加值	16.25	17.73	20.57	25.73	32.30	40.90	57.37	65.75
劳动者报酬	0.90	1.00	1.29	1.65	2.75	3.11	2.74	3.22
固定资产折旧	13.97	15.44	18.32	22.81	26.97	34.21	51.61	59.01
生产税净额	0.02	0.16	0.24	0.36	1.37	1.70	1.35	1.56
营业盈余	1.36	1.13	0.72	0.91	1.21	1.88	1.67	1.96
(八)社会服务业增加值	10.84	10.88	16.52	18.54	24.84	29.39	33.11	39.66
劳动者报酬	4.35	4.85	6.05	6.79	9.10	10.77	12.13	13.52
固定资产折旧	0.65	1.31	1.63	1.83	2.45	2.90	3.27	3.57
生产税净额	0.79	1.17	1.46	1.63	7.39	8.74	9.85	10.83
营业盈余	5.05	3.55	7.38	8.29	5.90	6.98	7.86	11.74
(九)卫生体育福利业增加值	7.98	9.02	11.35	14.08	20.72	25.47	33.84	40.62
劳动者报酬	5.45	7.70	9.28	11.51	16.64	21.91	27.12	32.54
固定资产折旧	0.40	0.90	1.08	1.34	2.01	3.39	4.05	4.79
生产税净额		0.02	0.05	0.06	0.07	0.04	0.16	0.24
营业盈余	2.13	0.40	0.94	1.17	2.00	0.13	2.51	3.05
(十)教育文艺广播电视业增加值	17.43	19.14	23.02	27.55	42.37	55.99	67.21	80.27
劳动者报酬	13.50	14.73	18.08	21.64	36.14	47.82	58.38	69.83
固定资产折旧	2.15	3.37	4.12	4.93	5.18	7.31	7.43	8.83
生产税净额		0.20	0.28	0.34	0.35	0.16	0.22	0.32
营业盈余	1.78	0.84	0.54	0.64	0.70	0.70	1.18	1.29
(十一)科学研究和综合技术服务业增加值	7.36	7.45	9.41	10.93	15.78	19.86	8.62	10.23
劳动者报酬	5.06	5.50	6.77	7.62	12.26	15.92	6.20	7.35
固定资产折旧	1.08	1.24	1.90	2.20	2.50	2.62	1.18	1.41
生产税净额	0.05	0.16	0.46	0.54	0.31	0.52	0.30	0.34
营业盈余	1.17	0.55	0.28	0.57	0.71	0.80	0.94	1.13
(十二)国家政党机关和社会团体增加值	26.51	29.08	34.72	43.96	59.70	79.98	99.78	119.35
劳动者报酬	22.43	23.41	28.78	36.44	53.21	73.05	92.75	110.99
固定资产折旧	1.34	3.50	4.66	5.90	6.49	6.32	6.69	7.88
生产税净额		0.04	0.19	0.24		0.14	0.14	0.24
营业盈余	2.74	2.13	1.09	1.38		0.47	0.20	0.24
(十三)其他增加值	2.78	3.18	5.05	5.18	6.77	9.08	11.18	14.27
劳动者报酬	1.42	1.50	1.75	1.80	2.35	3.15	5.88	7.51
固定资产折旧	0.31	0.35	0.48	0.49	0.64	0.86	1.02	1.31
生产税净额							0.04	0.06
营业盈余	1.05	1.33	2.82	2.89	3.78	5.07	4.24	5.39

3—13 国内生产总值(支出法)

GDP(in Expenditure Approach)

单位:亿元

年份	国内生产总值	最终消费	居民消费	农业居民	非农业居民	政府消费
1952	27.81	24.87	24.12	20.98	3.14	0.75
1953	30.29	26.30	25.44	21.61	3.83	0.86
1954	30.51	26.61	25.46	21.43	4.03	1.15
1955	35.83	29.84	28.52	24.26	4.26	1.32
1956	37.93	32.23	30.56	25.28	5.28	1.67
1957	45.20	34.18	32.42	26.31	6.11	1.76
1958	55.85	36.98	35.16	27.57	7.59	1.82
1959	61.95	37.16	34.76	24.93	9.83	2.40
1960	64.07	37.96	35.47	24.92	10.55	2.49
1961	46.64	41.38	39.12	28.36	10.76	2.26
1962	51.19	45.28	43.51	33.32	10.19	1.77
1963	48.08	40.92	39.32	28.50	10.82	1.60
1964	57.36	43.61	41.32	30.59	10.73	2.29
1965	65.32	47.29	45.18	33.84	11.34	2.11
1966	72.73	51.61	49.26	37.93	11.33	2.35
1967	73.51	54.81	52.56	40.95	11.61	2.25
1968	75.67	55.30	53.27	41.60	11.67	2.03
1969	81.26	55.90	53.52	42.09	11.43	2.38
1970	93.05	58.04	55.60	43.54	12.06	2.44
1971	99.10	62.19	59.04	45.36	13.08	3.15
1972	107.01	67.40	63.76	47.81	15.95	3.64
1973	115.80	71.30	67.28	50.71	16.57	4.02
1974	108.17	74.50	69.54	51.98	17.56	4.96
1975	118.40	76.87	72.16	53.89	18.27	4.71
1976	118.53	78.41	73.13	53.94	19.19	5.28
1977	129.17	86.16	79.74	60.13	19.61	6.42
1978	146.99	100.83	93.93	70.87	23.06	6.90
1979	178.01	118.77	109.67	83.37	26.30	9.10
1980	191.72	136.94	125.42	93.15	32.27	11.52
1981	209.68	155.72	142.77	107.33	35.44	12.95
1982	232.52	174.68	159.45	121.93	37.52	15.23
1983	257.43	195.09	178.56	137.91	40.65	16.53
1984	287.29	218.09	199.24	152.95	46.29	18.85
1985	349.95	263.11	240.71	182.85	57.86	22.40
1986	397.68	290.14	265.54	196.12	69.42	24.60
1987	469.44	328.34	298.85	218.93	79.92	29.49
1988	584.07	399.15	364.37	256.19	108.18	34.78
1989	640.80	439.54	393.49	270.81	122.68	46.05
1990	744.44	564.70	454.90	314.05	140.85	109.80
1991	833.30	621.93	500.84	340.27	160.57	121.09
1992	997.70	725.60	582.91	379.23	203.68	142.69
1993	1278.28	885.05	706.55	442.35	264.20	178.50
1994	1694.42	1113.62	883.46	534.34	349.12	230.16
1995	2195.70	1396.88	1108.78	674.09	434.69	288.10
1996	2647.16	1753.27	1409.44	896.48	512.96	343.83
1997	2993.00	1956.22	1540.67	970.95	569.72	415.55

3—13 续表

单位:亿元

年 份	资本形成总额	固定资产形成总额	存货增加	货物和服务净出口
1952	1.63	1.24	0.39	1.31
1953	2.69	1.93	0.76	1.30
1954	3.10	2.41	0.69	0.80
1955	5.36	1.93	3.43	0.63
1956	5.09	3.28	1.81	0.61
1957	7.99	3.81	4.18	3.03
1958	18.84	14.06	4.78	0.03
1959	24.54	16.43	8.11	0.25
1960	21.39	17.98	3.41	4.72
1961	3.69	4.62	−0.93	1.57
1962	0.89	2.73	−1.84	5.02
1963	6.83	3.91	2.92	0.33
1964	11.39	8.46	2.93	2.36
1965	12.69	9.39	3.30	5.34
1966	16.31	11.20	5.11	4.81
1967	13.93	9.41	4.52	4.77
1968	12.69	7.52	5.17	7.68
1969	16.78	10.81	5.97	8.58
1970	27.05	18.54	8.51	7.96
1971	33.51	22.12	11.39	3.40
1972	28.60	18.23	10.37	11.01
1973	28.24	19.00	9.24	16.26
1974	24.50	19.32	5.18	9.17
1975	26.36	21.31	5.05	15.17
1976	24.80	19.33	5.47	15.32
1977	28.00	17.83	10.17	15.01
1978	42.41	27.68	14.73	3.75
1979	41.82	29.81	12.01	17.42
1980	40.02	32.76	7.26	14.76
1981	41.19	27.95	13.24	12.77
1982	50.53	34.07	16.46	7.31
1983	56.63	43.89	12.74	5.71
1984	59.06	42.15	16.91	10.14
1985	92.19	58.14	34.05	−5.35
1986	115.02	75.57	39.45	−7.48
1987	139.84	91.79	48.05	1.26
1988	184.75	114.73	70.02	0.17
1989	169.41	83.19	86.22	31.85
1990	184.12	122.82	61.30	−4.38
1991	224.80	160.49	64.31	−13.43
1992	301.76	228.29	73.47	−29.66
1993	414.73	330.54	84.19	−21.50
1994	581.52	422.61	158.91	−0.72
1995	800.50	534.12	266.38	−1.68
1996	895.30	678.32	216.98	−1.41
1997	1021.39	725.73	295.66	15.39

3—14 最 终 消 费 构 成 项 目

Structure of Final Consumption Expenditure

单位：亿元

年 份	最终消费	居民消费	农业居民	自给性消费	商品性消费	文化生活服务性消费	住房及水电消费
1978	100.83	93.93	70.87	46.07	19.35	1.91	3.54
1979	118.77	109.67	83.37	47.76	28.51	1.85	5.25
1980	136.94	125.42	93.15	50.67	33.72	1.77	6.99
1981	155.72	142.77	107.33	53.77	42.82	2.48	8.26
1982	174.68	159.45	121.93	62.42	46.58	0.49	12.44
1983	195.09	178.56	137.91	62.06	56.82	3.03	16.00
1984	218.09	199.24	152.95	69.44	63.17	3.82	16.52
1985	263.11	240.71	182.85	81.13	89.85	2.87	9.00
1986	290.14	265.54	196.12	82.54	100.88	3.56	9.14
1987	328.34	298.85	218.93	85.01	117.40	6.38	10.14
1988	399.15	364.37	256.19	89.98	145.58	8.94	11.69
1989	439.54	393.49	270.81	90.88	154.75	11.81	13.37
1990	564.70	454.90	314.05	136.03	152.46	12.44	13.12
1991	621.93	500.84	340.27	145.00	166.39	14.44	14.44
1992	725.60	582.91	379.23	153.78	173.94	35.72	15.79
1993	885.05	706.55	442.35	173.97	203.25	46.55	18.58
1994	1113.62	883.46	534.34	218.72	239.01	54.05	22.56
1995	1396.88	1108.78	674.09	256.35	311.44	70.56	35.74
1996	1753.27	1409.44	896.48	346.21	367.75	121.20	61.32
1997	1956.22	1540.67	970.95	351.51	410.07	147.95	61.42

3—14 续表 单位:亿元

年份	非农业居民	商品性消费	文化生活服务性消费	住房及水电消费	政府消费
1978	23.06	20.96	1.59	0.51	6.90
1979	26.30	23.90	1.82	0.58	9.10
1980	32.27	29.40	2.19	0.68	11.52
1981	35.44	32.36	2.34	0.74	12.95
1982	37.52	34.07	2.59	0.86	15.23
1983	40.65	37.16	2.56	0.93	16.53
1984	46.29	42.40	2.83	1.06	18.85
1985	57.86	51.75	4.77	1.34	22.40
1986	69.42	61.92	6.29	1.21	24.60
1987	79.92	70.46	7.64	1.82	29.49
1988	108.18	97.08	8.95	2.15	34.78
1989	122.68	109.30	9.82	3.56	46.05
1990	140.85	125.82	11.06	3.97	109.80
1991	160.57	142.58	13.50	4.49	121.09
1992	203.68	169.99	27.59	6.10	142.69
1993	264.20	221.65	35.39	7.16	178.50
1994	349.12	282.11	54.49	12.52	230.16
1995	434.69	362.77	56.61	15.31	288.10
1996	512.96	418.38	50.01	44.57	343.83
1997	569.72	439.82	80.04	49.86	415.55

3—15 最终消费发展速度及指数

Growth Rate and Indices of Final Consumption Expenditure

单位:%

年 份	以上年为100					以1952年为100				
	最终消费	居民消费	农业居民	非农业居民	政府消费	最终消费	居民消费	农业居民	非农业居民	政府消费
1952						100.0	100.0	100.0	100.0	100.0
1953	97.3	97.0	94.8	111.2	108.8	97.3	97.0	94.8	111.2	108.8
1954	100.5	99.5	99.1	101.9	127.0	97.8	96.5	93.9	113.3	138.2
1955	111.0	110.9	112.2	103.7	113.8	108.5	107.0	105.4	117.5	157.2
1956	103.9	103.0	100.2	119.4	123.4	112.8	110.2	105.6	140.3	194.0
1957	101.2	101.1	98.6	113.8	103.8	114.1	111.5	104.1	159.7	201.4
1958	106.8	107.0	102.7	125.4	104.5	121.9	119.3	107.0	200.2	210.5
1959	100.5	98.8	91.2	129.2	131.9	122.5	117.8	97.5	258.7	277.6
1960	96.8	96.9	94.2	103.7	95.3	118.6	114.2	91.9	268.3	264.6
1961	79.1	80.0	85.4	68.1	65.4	93.8	91.3	78.5	182.7	173.0
1962	101.0	102.7	107.6	89.1	70.9	94.7	93.8	84.4	162.8	122.7
1963	101.8	101.6	96.3	119.9	105.3	96.4	95.3	81.3	195.2	129.2
1964	115.7	114.0	116.8	106.3	158.0	111.6	108.7	95.0	207.5	204.1
1965	118.9	119.9	120.6	117.7	101.3	132.7	130.3	114.5	244.2	206.8
1966	109.4	109.1	111.6	101.4	115.6	145.1	142.1	127.8	247.6	239.0
1967	104.3	104.8	105.7	101.5	95.1	151.4	149.0	135.1	251.3	227.3
1968	100.3	100.8	101.0	100.1	89.2	151.8	150.1	136.5	251.6	202.8
1969	101.6	100.9	101.7	98.0	118.5	154.3	151.3	138.8	246.5	240.3
1970	104.5	104.6	104.2	106.1	103.2	161.2	158.5	144.6	261.6	247.9
1971	107.1	106.0	103.8	114.0	129.2	172.7	168.0	150.1	298.2	320.3
1972	107.7	107.4	105.0	115.0	115.1	185.9	180.4	157.6	342.9	368.7
1973	105.4	105.1	105.4	104.2	110.4	196.0	189.6	166.1	357.3	407.1
1974	102.0	100.9	99.9	103.7	120.5	199.9	191.3	165.9	370.5	490.5
1975	103.5	104.1	104.1	104.2	95.2	206.9	199.2	172.7	386.1	467.0
1976	100.6	99.9	98.4	103.9	110.4	208.1	199.0	170.3	401.2	515.5
1977	110.4	109.6	111.9	103.1	122.1	229.8	218.1	190.6	413.6	629.5
1978	112.5	112.9	111.0	118.7	107.7	258.5	246.2	211.6	490.9	677.9
1979	112.3	110.8	110.3	112.2	131.4	290.3	272.8	233.4	550.8	890.8
1980	108.9	108.5	109.2	106.5	112.8	316.2	296.0	254.8	586.6	1004.8
1981	111.2	111.3	113.0	106.5	109.9	351.6	329.4	288.0	624.8	1104.3
1982	111.8	111.3	113.4	105.0	116.5	393.0	366.6	326.5	656.0	1286.5
1983	107.5	107.7	108.8	104.2	104.7	422.5	394.8	355.3	683.5	1347.0
1984	108.9	108.8	108.3	110.2	110.6	460.1	429.6	384.8	753.3	1489.8
1985	108.3	108.4	107.6	111.3	106.6	498.3	465.7	414.0	838.4	1588.1
1986	104.5	104.5	101.8	113.3	104.3	520.7	486.6	421.5	949.9	1656.4
1987	102.3	102.1	101.2	104.5	104.5	532.7	496.9	426.5	992.6	1730.9
1988	98.3	98.2	95.6	105.4	99.4	523.7	487.9	407.7	1046.2	1720.5
1989	97.7	96.8	97.0	96.2	107.9	511.6	472.3	395.5	1006.5	1856.5
1990	105.9	105.0	101.7	113.8	114.0	541.8	495.9	402.2	1145.4	2116.4
1991	105.4	105.3	104.1	108.0	106.0	571.1	522.2	418.7	1237.0	2243.4
1992	103.9	103.5	101.4	108.3	105.4	593.3	540.5	424.6	1339.7	2364.5
1993	105.3	104.5	100.7	112.2	108.9	624.8	564.8	427.5	1503.1	2575.0
1994	105.8	105.9	100.6	115.5	105.6	661.0	598.1	430.1	1736.1	2719.2
1995	108.6	108.7	109.2	107.8	108.4	717.9	650.2	469.6	1871.5	2947.6
1996	113.8	114.4	120.7	104.4	111.3	817.0	743.8	566.8	1953.8	3280.7
1997	108.0	106.2	105.7	107.3	115.1	882.4	790.0	599.1	2096.4	3776.1

3—16 居民消费水平

Per Capita Consumption

年份	按当年价计算			以上年为100			以1952年为100		
	居民消费水平(元)	农业居民	非农业居民	居民消费水平(元)	农业居民	非农业居民	居民消费水平(元)	农业居民	非农业居民
1952	75	71	113				100.0	100.0	100.0
1953	77	72	130	94.6	92.9	104.5	94.6	92.9	104.5
1954	75	70	123	97.2	97.6	91.9	92.0	90.7	96.0
1955	83	78	130	108.9	110.0	103.5	100.1	99.7	99.4
1956	88	80	156	101.9	99.3	115.8	102.0	99.0	115.1
1957	91	82	167	99.2	97.4	105.2	101.2	96.5	121.1
1958	97	86	172	103.6	102.5	104.1	104.9	98.9	126.1
1959	94	79	183	97.6	91.7	106.1	102.3	90.7	133.7
1960	98	80	199	98.3	95.6	104.9	100.6	86.7	140.3
1961	111	92	230	82.1	86.2	77.5	82.6	74.7	108.7
1962	122	106	248	102.3	105.2	101.2	84.5	78.6	110.0
1963	107	87	272	98.7	92.9	123.9	83.4	73.0	136.3
1964	110	92	263	111.2	114.0	103.8	92.7	83.2	141.5
1965	118	99	274	117.0	117.5	115.8	108.5	97.8	163.9
1966	125	107	268	106.0	108.3	99.5	115.0	105.9	163.0
1967	129	113	269	101.9	102.7	99.3	117.2	108.8	161.9
1968	127	111	271	98.1	97.9	100.3	115.0	106.5	162.4
1969	125	108	277	98.2	98.2	102.2	112.9	104.6	166.0
1970	126	109	289	101.8	101.2	105.0	114.9	105.8	174.3
1971	130	111	305	103.2	101.6	105.9	118.6	107.5	184.5
1972	137	114	339	104.9	102.8	109.6	124.4	110.6	202.3
1973	141	119	343	102.7	103.1	101.6	127.8	114.0	205.5
1974	143	119	354	98.8	97.9	100.8	126.3	111.6	207.1
1975	146	121	360	102.2	102.3	101.9	129.0	114.2	211.1
1976	146	120	371	98.3	97.0	102.1	126.8	110.7	215.5
1977	157	132	374	108.3	110.6	101.7	137.4	122.5	219.2
1978	183	154	427	111.7	110.0	115.4	153.4	134.7	252.9
1979	211	181	454	109.6	110.0	104.5	168.2	148.2	264.3
1980	239	201	523	107.3	108.8	100.1	180.4	161.2	264.6
1981	268	229	552	109.9	112.0	102.4	198.3	180.6	270.9
1982	295	257	567	109.5	111.8	101.7	217.2	201.9	275.5
1983	326	287	603	106.2	107.4	102.4	230.6	216.8	282.1
1984	360	317	650	107.7	108.0	104.3	248.4	234.2	294.3
1985	430	379	751	107.3	107.6	102.9	266.5	252.0	302.8
1986	469	404	866	103.3	101.1	108.9	275.3	254.7	329.8
1987	521	446	969	100.7	100.0	101.6	277.2	254.7	335.0
1988	623	514	1256	96.4	94.2	101.0	267.2	239.9	338.4
1989	660	534	1372	100.0	103.6	91.8	267.2	248.6	310.6
1990	750	611	1533	103.6	100.0	111.9	276.9	248.6	347.6
1991	816	654	1714	104.0	102.9	105.9	288.0	255.8	368.1
1992	942	726	2106	102.7	101.1	104.9	295.8	258.6	386.1
1993	1134	849	2598	103.9	100.8	106.6	307.3	260.7	411.6
1994	1408	1027	3260	105.0	100.8	109.6	322.7	262.8	451.1
1995	1752	1294	3884	107.8	109.0	103.2	347.9	286.5	465.5
1996	2199	1710	4395	113.0	119.9	100.1	393.1	343.5	466.0
1997	2390	1851	4746	105.6	105.7	104.3	415.1	363.1	486.0

3—17 分经济类型资本形成总额

Gross Capital Formation by Ownership

单位:亿元

年 份	资本形成总额	固定资产形成总额	国有经济	集体经济	其他经济	存货增加	国有经济	集体经济	其他经济
1978	42.41	27.68	20.21	4.65	2.82	14.73	9.41	4.52	0.80
1979	41.82	29.81	20.69	4.77	4.35	12.01	6.76	4.37	0.88
1980	40.02	32.76	20.67	4.39	7.70	7.26	3.32	2.53	1.41
1981	41.19	27.95	15.60	4.81	7.54	13.24	7.26	3.43	2.55
1982	50.53	34.07	21.50	5.04	7.53	16.46	8.76	5.35	2.35
1983	56.63	43.89	19.49	4.56	19.84	12.74	4.64	4.41	3.69
1984	59.06	42.15	19.47	4.76	17.92	16.91	6.43	7.07	3.41
1985	92.19	58.14	29.07	7.97	21.10	34.05	17.26	10.79	6.00
1986	115.02	75.57	36.73	10.13	28.71	39.45	21.18	11.56	6.71
1987	139.84	91.79	45.71	13.86	32.22	48.05	26.38	13.65	8.02
1988	184.75	114.73	56.91	15.49	42.33	70.02	40.40	16.59	13.03
1989	169.41	83.19	44.76	8.49	29.94	86.22	54.40	20.26	11.56
1990	184.12	122.82	69.68	13.31	39.83	61.30	33.29	19.37	8.64
1991	224.80	160.49	96.46	19.80	44.23	64.31	42.62	13.48	8.21
1992	301.76	228.29	145.66	31.59	51.04	73.47	46.62	15.95	10.90
1993	414.73	330.54	210.81	46.06	73.67	84.19	32.41	10.75	41.03
1994	581.52	422.61	250.96	56.55	115.10	158.91	76.88	52.29	29.74
1995	800.50	534.12	316.90	39.83	177.39	266.38	87.52	53.31	125.55
1996	895.30	678.32	375.27	79.25	223.80	216.98	58.58	31.29	127.11
1997	1021.39	725.73	371.79	95.75	258.19	295.66	36.27	97.22	162.17

3—18 按三次产业分的资本形成总额

Gross Capital Formation by Type of Industry

单位:亿元

年 份	资本形成总额	固定资产形成总额	存货增加	第一产业 资本形成总额	固定资产形成总额	存货增加
1978	42.41	27.68	14.73	4.59	3.43	1.16
1979	41.82	29.81	12.01	4.74	3.73	1.01
1980	40.02	32.76	7.26	3.58	3.31	0.27
1981	41.19	27.95	13.24	1.49	1.40	0.09
1982	50.53	34.07	16.46	2.36	1.60	0.76
1983	56.63	43.89	12.74	1.40	1.67	−0.27
1984	59.06	42.15	16.91	4.37	1.56	2.81
1985	92.19	58.14	34.05	2.71	1.45	1.26
1986	115.02	75.57	39.45	6.28	1.51	4.77
1987	139.84	91.79	48.05	6.37	2.48	3.89
1988	184.75	114.73	70.02	5.24	3.56	1.68
1989	169.41	83.19	86.22	13.70	2.41	11.29
1990	184.12	122.82	61.30	7.99	3.45	4.54
1991	224.80	160.49	64.31	12.01	3.91	8.10
1992	301.76	228.29	73.47	16.97	8.45	8.52
1993	414.73	330.54	84.19	37.00	15.73	21.27
1994	581.52	422.61	158.91	87.04	69.37	17.67
1995	800.50	534.12	266.38	160.92	95.46	65.46
1996	895.30	678.32	216.98	98.26	28.64	69.62
1997	1021.39	725.73	295.66	166.81	32.15	134.66

3—18 续表 单位:亿元

年 份	第二产业			第三产业		
	资本形成总额	固定资产形成总额	存货增加	资本形成总额	固定资产形成总额	存货增加
1978	20.15	17.68	2.47	17.67	6.57	11.10
1979	18.85	17.83	1.02	18.23	8.25	9.98
1980	16.23	15.36	0.87	20.21	14.09	6.12
1981	16.25	14.53	1.72	23.45	12.02	11.43
1982	21.84	18.09	3.75	26.33	14.38	11.95
1983	26.11	24.49	1.62	29.12	17.73	11.39
1984	38.97	23.94	15.03	15.72	16.65	—0.93
1985	38.93	32.73	6.20	50.55	23.96	26.59
1986	58.05	47.08	10.97	50.69	26.98	23.71
1987	69.19	59.48	9.71	64.28	29.83	34.45
1988	92.67	75.03	17.64	86.84	36.14	50.70
1989	101.59	56.24	45.35	54.12	24.54	29.58
1990	110.18	78.61	31.57	65.95	40.76	25.19
1991	116.64	99.02	17.62	96.15	57.56	38.59
1992	134.41	119.42	14.99	150.38	100.42	49.96
1993	199.25	127.78	71.47	178.48	187.03	—8.55
1994	200.99	145.74	55.25	293.49	207.50	85.99
1995	232.28	158.33	73.95	407.30	280.33	126.97
1996	277.68	205.55	72.13	519.36	444.13	75.23
1997	351.47	215.69	135.78	503.11	477.89	25.22

3—19 国内生产总值(支出法)构成

Composition of GDP(in Expenditure Approach)

单位:%

年份	以国内生产总值为100			以最终消费为100		以居民消费为100	
	最终消费	资本形成总额	货物和服务净出口	居民消费	政府消费	农业居民	非农业居民
1978	68.6	28.9	2.6	93.2	6.8	75.4	24.6
1979	66.7	23.5	9.8	92.3	7.7	76.0	24.0
1980	71.4	20.9	7.7	91.6	8.4	74.3	25.7
1981	74.3	19.6	6.1	91.7	8.3	75.2	24.8
1982	75.1	21.7	3.1	91.3	8.7	76.5	23.5
1983	75.8	22.0	2.2	91.5	8.5	77.2	22.8
1984	75.9	20.6	3.5	91.4	8.6	76.8	23.2
1985	75.2	26.3	—1.5	91.5	8.5	76.0	24.0
1986	73.0	28.9	—1.9	91.5	8.5	73.9	26.1
1987	69.9	29.8	0.3	91.0	9.0	73.3	26.7
1988	68.3	31.6	0.0	91.3	8.7	70.3	29.7
1989	68.6	26.4	5.0	89.5	10.5	68.8	31.2
1990	75.9	24.7	—0.6	80.6	19.4	69.0	31.0
1991	74.6	27.0	—1.6	80.5	19.5	67.9	32.1
1992	72.7	30.2	—3.0	80.3	19.7	65.1	34.9
1993	69.2	32.4	—1.7	79.8	20.2	62.6	37.4
1994	65.7	34.3	0.0	79.3	20.7	60.5	39.5
1995	63.6	36.5	—0.1	79.4	20.6	60.8	39.2
1996	66.2	33.8	0.0	80.4	19.6	63.6	36.4
1997	65.4	34.1	0.5	78.8	21.2	63.0	37.0

3—19 续表

单位：%

年份	以资本形成总额为100		以固定资产形成总额为100			以存货增加为100		
	固定资本形成总额	存货增加	国有经济	集体经济	其他经济	国有经济	集体经济	其他经济
1978	65.3	34.7	73.0	16.8	10.2	63.9	30.7	5.4
1979	71.3	28.7	69.4	16.0	14.6	56.3	36.4	7.3
1980	81.9	18.1	63.1	13.4	23.5	45.7	34.8	19.4
1981	67.9	32.1	55.8	17.2	27.0	54.8	25.9	19.3
1982	67.4	32.6	63.1	14.8	22.1	53.2	32.5	14.3
1983	77.5	22.5	44.4	10.4	45.2	36.4	84.6	20.0
1984	71.4	28.6	46.2	11.3	42.5	38.0	41.8	20.2
1985	63.1	36.9	50.0	13.7	36.3	50.7	31.7	17.6
1986	65.7	34.3	48.6	13.4	38.0	53.7	29.3	17.0
1987	65.6	34.4	49.8	15.1	35.1	54.9	28.4	16.7
1988	62.1	37.9	49.6	13.5	36.9	57.7	23.7	18.6
1989	49.1	50.9	53.8	10.2	36.0	63.1	23.5	13.4
1990	66.7	33.3	56.7	10.8	32.4	54.3	31.6	14.1
1991	71.4	28.6	60.1	12.3	27.5	66.3	21.0	12.8
1992	75.7	24.3	63.8	13.8	22.4	63.5	21.7	14.8
1993	79.7	20.3	63.8	13.9	22.3	38.5	12.8	48.7
1994	72.7	27.3	59.4	13.4	27.3	48.4	32.9	18.7
1995	66.7	33.3	59.3	7.5	33.2	32.9	20.0	47.1
1996	75.8	24.2	55.3	11.7	33.0	27.0	14.4	58.6
1997	71.1	28.9	51.2	13.2	35.6	12.3	32.8	54.9

3—20 资本形成总额发展速度及指数

Growth Rate and Indices of Gross Capital Formation

单位：%

年 份	以上年为100			以1952年为100		
	资本形成总额	固定资本形成总额	存货增加	资本形成总额	固定资本形成总额	存货增加
1952				100.0	100.0	100.0
1953	162.2	159.4	191.3	162.2	159.4	191.3
1954	115.0	126.3	87.5	186.5	201.3	167.4
1955	172.8	84.5	514.0	322.3	170.1	860.5
1956	102.1	178.4	52.4	329.1	303.5	450.7
1957	149.8	113.9	222.0	493.0	345.7	1000.5
1958	253.3	388.3	114.4	1248.7	1342.3	1144.9
1959	125.1	113.2	166.6	1562.1	1519.4	1907.1
1960	86.5	106.0	40.0	1351.5	1610.6	762.6
1961	15.9	23.1		214.9	372.0	
1962	23.3	56.7		49.9	211.0	
1963	696.2	142.7		347.4	301.0	534.0
1964	180.9	227.1	103.6	630.5	683.6	553.4
1965	119.4	120.8	114.1	752.8	825.8	631.5
1966	130.6	122.6	161.0	983.1	1012.5	1016.6
1967	85.4	85.6	87.8	839.6	866.7	892.5
1968	85.0	76.8	108.3	713.7	665.6	966.7
1969	140.9	151.2	121.5	1005.5	1006.4	1174.4
1970	169.6	177.2	149.1	1705.4	1783.3	1751.5
1971	127.3	124.6	135.0	2171.0	2222.0	2363.8
1972	86.2	84.3	91.3	1871.4	1873.2	2158.4
1973	97.9	101.8	87.4	1832.1	1906.9	1885.4
1974	84.7	95.2	54.0	1551.8	1815.4	1018.3
1975	113.5	115.8	99.6	1761.3	2102.2	1014.7
1976	90.4	87.9	105.6	1592.2	1847.8	1072.0
1977	110.3	95.2	188.6	1756.2	1759.1	2022.5
1978	154.2	156.3	148.0	2708.0	2749.5	2992.9
1979	98.0	106.2	75.9	2653.9	2920.0	2270.6
1980	96.1	105.9	58.4	2550.4	3092.3	1327.0
1981	95.8	84.2	176.5	2443.2	2603.7	2342.7
1982	122.7	122.4	123.7	2997.9	3186.9	2898.9
1983	113.5	125.0	75.4	3402.6	3983.6	2186.4
1984	99.6	93.9	130.4	3389.0	3740.6	2850.1
1985	138.0	125.6	185.8	4676.8	4698.2	5295.1
1986	119.7	123.6	110.1	5598.1	5807.0	5828.1
1987	113.7	113.7	113.3	6365.0	6602.6	6602.0
1988	114.1	109.7	127.4	7262.5	7243.0	8409.8
1989	81.2	68.6	113.3	5897.1	4968.7	9525.7
1990	88.1	90.9	86.0	5195.4	4516.6	8192.1
1991	115.4	121.4	103.4	5995.5	5483.2	8470.6
1992	117.3	122.1	106.1	7032.7	6694.9	8987.3
1993	117.2	123.2	101.1	8242.3	8248.2	9086.2
1994	119.7	112.6	143.2	9866.0	9287.5	13011.4
1995	123.0	114.5	145.1	12135.2	10634.2	18879.5
1996	115.1	124.5	95.8	13967.6	13239.6	18086.6
1997	114.4	105.1	139.0	15978.9	13914.8	25140.4

3—21 各地、市全社会总产出及指数(1997年)

Gross Output of Society and Its Indices by Prefecture, City and County

地　市	总产出(万元)	第一产业	第二产业	#工　业	#建筑业	第三产业	#交通运输仓储邮电业	#批发零售贸易餐饮业	总产出指数以上年为100
长沙市	13682724	1114485	7962843	6574290	1388553	4605396	481259	2354786	117.8
株洲市	7071130	749052	4763877	4310751	453126	1558201	416333	510002	117.6
湘潭市	4313736	584913	2629423	2342154	287269	1099400	258400	330430	119.5
衡阳市	7187135	1468959	4401411	4032714	368697	1316765	339851	343564	118.9
邵阳市	5078255	1345207	2757591	2537801	219790	975457	143992	262749	119.8
岳阳市	8056550	1357945	4956401	4434095	522306	1742204	426160	447930	117.0
常德市	7253863	1627799	4041343	3531481	509862	1584721	199405	546996	108.3
张家界市	1025814	226939	451185	323156	128029	347690	81191	100074	113.5
益阳市	4336528	860760	2311359	2005194	306165	1164409	340059	363410	113.6
郴州市	5072629	858694	3136735	291566	221073	1077200	298372	330234	127.2
永州市	5075980	1252235	2818166	2508317	309849	1005579	326248	452735	121.7
娄底地区	3970184	638899	2562976	2370683	192293	768309	249875	191528	112.1
怀化地区	3925913	812981	1988516	1839801	148715	1124416	316553	300328	118.2
湘西自治州	1300334	323500	656240	574588	81652	320594	88081	105784	104.3

3—22 各地、市国内生产总值项目构成(1997年)

Item Composition of Gross Domestic Products by Prefecture, City and County

单位:万元

地　市	国内生产总值	劳动者报酬	固定资产折旧	生产税净额	营业盈余
长沙市	4828691	2563382	530831	652165	1082313
株洲市	2397033	1388691	314985	283314	410043
湘潭市	1875000	1082605	218862	180543	392990
衡阳市	2643541	1974759	241455	149279	278048
邵阳市	2046973	1391314	200944	185117	269598
岳阳市	2795623	1641341	451110	354332	348840
常德市	2831623	1798307	260612	457655	315049
张家界市	475513	292744	57221	48470	77078
益阳市	1730754	1119953	265657	149794	195350
郴州市	1895096	1194427	224709	305758	170202
永州市	2138027	1375509	175714	271199	315605
娄底地区	1660841	1078420	155483	122248	304690
怀化地区	1900695	1089684	212755	167549	430707
湘西自治州	570515	399336	52952	75668	42559

3—23 各地、市国内生产总值及构成(1997年)

Gross Domestic Products and Its Composition by Prefecture, City and County

地 市	国内生产总值(万元)	第一产业	第二产业	# 工 业	# 建筑业	第三产业	# 运输邮电业	# 商 业	人均国内生产总值(元)
长沙市	4828691	687320	2075005	1670486	404519	2066366	331106	682888	8476
株洲市	2397033	491597	1155827	1027390	128437	749609	217866	192204	6557
湘潭市	1875000	371431	824000	702000	122000	679569	105500	145510	6801
衡阳市	2643541	902091	899373	787277	112096	842077	214479	197929	3832
邵阳市	2046973	868752	598265	518047	80218	579956	67826	148348	2888
岳阳市	2795623	866303	1018464	923995	94469	910856	254095	228360	5505
常德市	2831623	1073300	1019340	874145	145195	738983	83888	202388	4787
张家界市	475513	140111	136040	100192	35848	199362	41344	60044	3107
益阳市	1730754	560146	574249	479338	94911	596359	142381	167241	3880
郴州市	1895096	550074	694007	634823	59184	651015	176856	175024	4276
永州市	2138027	802124	720042	630127	89915	615861	142421	199584	3887
娄底地区	1660841	426968	773730	707958	65772	460143	142163	101253	4246
怀化地区	1900695	613734	611875	555533	56342	675086	211809	153080	4000
湘西自治州	570515	206829	191457	170588	20869	172229	36985	48084	2259

3—24 各地、市国内生产总值及其行业增加值(1997年)

Gross Domestic Products and Its Added—Value by Sector by Prefecture, City and County

地 市	国内生产总值(万元)	农 业	工 业	建筑业	运输邮电业	商饮业	其 他
长沙市	4828691	687320	1670486	404519	331106	682888	1052372
株洲市	2397033	491597	1027390	128437	217866	192204	339539
湘潭市	1875000	371431	702000	122000	105500	145510	428559
衡阳市	2643541	902091	787277	112096	214479	197929	429669
邵阳市	2046973	868752	518047	80218	67826	148348	363782
岳阳市	2795623	866303	923995	94469	254095	228360	428401
常德市	2831623	1073300	874145	145195	83888	202388	452707
张家界市	475513	140111	100192	35848	41344	60044	97974
益阳市	1730754	560146	479338	94911	142381	167241	286737
郴州市	1895096	550074	634823	59184	176856	175024	299135
永州市	2138027	802124	630127	89915	142421	199584	273856
娄底地区	1660841	426968	707958	65772	142163	101253	216727
怀化地区	1900695	613734	555533	56342	211809	153080	310197
湘西自治州	570515	206829	170588	20869	36985	48084	87160

3—25 各地、市国内支出总额(1997年)

Gross Domestic Expenditures by Prefecture,City and County

地 市	国内支出总 额(万元)	总消费	总投资	净出口	投资率(%)	消费率(%)
长沙市	4828691	2541219	1810829	476643	37.5	52.6
株洲市	2367416	1246953	865083	255380	36.5	52.7
湘潭市	1875000	1113955	719900	41145	38.4	59.4
衡阳市	2643541	1984876	676719	—18054	25.6	75.1
邵阳市	2029133	1624882	409271	—5020	20.2	80.1
岳阳市	2795623	1448099	1348615	—1091	48.2	51.8
常德市	2778702	1804334	895773	78595	32.2	64.9
张家界市	470823	292719	180085	—1981	38.2	62.2
益阳市	1730754	1274947	483896	—28089	28.0	73.7
郴州市	1895096	1426593	329475	139028	17.4	75.3
永州市	2138027	1449462	655396	33169	30.7	67.8
娄底地区	1660841	1069723	581883	9235	35.0	64.4
怀化地区	1900695	1360774	349965	189956	18.4	71.6
湘西自治州	570515	468977	106350	—4812	18.6	82.2

3—26 各地、市国内支出总额结构(1997年)

Structure of gross Domestic Expenditures by Prefecture,City and County

单位:万元

地 市	总投资				总消费					
	绝对数		比重(%)		绝对数				比重(总消费=100)	
	固定资产	库存增加	固定资产	库存增加	居民消费	农民	非农业居民	社会消费	居民消费	社会消费
长沙市	1324035	486794	73.1	26.9	2191730	1043896	1147834	349489	86.2	13.8
株洲市	525220	339863	60.7	39.3	1055997	630367	425630	190956	84.7	15.3
湘潭市	498400	221500	69.2	30.8	941000	551235	389765	172955	84.5	15.5
衡阳市	525738	150981	77.7	22.3	1658762	1043119	615643	326114	83.6	16.4
邵阳市	308109	101162	75.3	24.7	1504486	1093154	411332	120396	92.6	7.4
岳阳市	661898	686717	49.1	50.9	1329204	807899	521305	118895	91.8	8.2
常德市	696189	199584	77.7	22.3	1617584	1008498	609086	186750	89.6	10.4
张家界市	108584	71501	60.3	39.7	263243	190914	72329	29476	89.9	10.1
益阳市	401144	82752	82.9	17.1	1106754	776603	330151	168193	86.8	13.2
郴州市	312391	17084	94.8	5.2	1163081	643924	519157	263512	81.5	18.5
永州市	416465	238931	63.5	36.5	1211168	918177	292991	238294	83.6	16.4
娄底地区	317057	264826	54.5	45.5	921832	601009	320823	147891	86.2	13.8
怀化地区	246876	103089	70.5	29.5	1135617	695823	439794	225157	83.5	16.5
湘西自治州	95584	10766	89.9	10.1	375919	242758	133161	93058	80.2	19.8

四、人口和劳动工资

POPULATION, EMPLOYMENT AND WAGE

4—1 人 口 数(年底数)

Number of Population Over The Years

单位:万人

年 份	总户数(万户)	总人口	总人口中		总人口中		总人口中	
			男	女	市 镇	乡 村	非农业人口	农业人口
1978	1167.53	5165.91	2684.80	2481.11	593.86	4572.05	552.39	4613.52
1980	1197.88	5280.95	2740.40	2540.55	671.05	4609.90	626.89	4654.06
1985	1334.54	5622.49	2928.44	2694.05	915.90	4706.59	796.63	4825.86
1986	1407.45	5695.73	2966.85	2728.88	963.15	4732.58	806.71	4889.02
1987	1485.85	5782.61	3012.59	2770.02	1003.28	4779.33	843.15	4939.46
1988	1562.45	5915.68	3079.65	2836.03	1044.12	4871.56	880.05	5035.63
1989	1623.00	6013.62	3130.76	2882.86	1049.25	4964.37	908.00	5105.62
1990	1661.65	6110.89	3178.31	2932.58	1072.46	5038.43	929.29	5181.60
1991	1697.69	6166.33	3208.42	2957.91	1147.86	5018.47	944.83	5221.50
1992	1725.72	6207.78	3231.73	2976.05	1217.74	4990.04	989.05	5218.73
1993	1745.47	6245.58	3249.20	2996.38	1205.95	5039.63	1044.84	5200.74
1994	1765.67	6302.58	3279.07	3023.51	1356.56	4946.02	1096.75	5205.83
1995	1796.19	6392.00	3322.27	3069.73	1550.99	4841.01	1148.65	5243.35
1996	1799.97	6428.00	3339.25	3088.75	1606.95	4821.05	1185.76	5242.24
1997	1798.83	6465.00	3356.43	3108.57	1629.00	4836.00	1215.06	5249.94

注:1995 年以后各年全省总人口数及构成系根据人口变动抽样调查资料推算数。其余各年均为年报数。

4—2 人口出生率、死亡率、自然增长率

Birth Rate, Death Rate and Natural Growth Rate of Population

年 份	出生率(‰)	死亡率(‰)	自然增长率(‰)
1978	17.40	7.01	10.39
1980	17.68	6.88	10.80
1985	18.16	6.47	11.69
1986	19.90	6.30	13.60
1987	23.62	7.07	16.55
1988	23.32	6.82	16.50
1989	22.91	7.07	15.84
1990	23.93	7.23	16.70
1991	20.50	7.30	13.20
1992	16.70	7.30	9.40
1993	14.08	7.13	6.95
1994	13.88	7.03	6.85
1995	13.02	7.15	5.87
1996	12.81	7.20	5.61
1997	12.59	6.99	5.60

4—3 四次全国人口普查人口基本情况

Population Status of Four Censuses

指　　标	单位	1953 年	1964 年	1982 年	1990 年
总户数	万户	836.11	916.20	1233.88	1573.79
家庭户	万户			1227.89	1564.88
集体户	万户			5.99	8.91
总人口	万人	3322.69	3718.23	5401.05	6065.80
男	万人	1752.64	1931.70	2805.23	3149.76
女	万人	1570.05	1786.53	2595.82	2916.04
育龄妇女(15—49 岁)	万人	750.73	819.43	1301.08	1607.99
各年龄组人口					
0—6 岁	万人	669.02	706.05	701.81	869.47
7—14 岁	万人	519.19	768.91	1131.16	826.93
劳动年龄人口	万人	1720.75	1878.68	2936.91	3618.26
男 60、女 55 岁以上人口	万人	319.57	285.00	503.39	628.16
民族人口					
汉族	万人	3254.67	3589.80	5180.92	5583.42
少数民族	万人	68.02	128.43	220.13	482.38
15 岁以上婚姻人口					
未　婚	万人			1009.86	1099.89
有配偶	万人			2271.76	2963.86
丧　偶	万人			262.16	278.87
离　婚	万人			24.31	26.77
6 岁以上文化程度人口					
大学本科	万人		}9.77	}24.56	20.72
大学专科	万人				48.27
中专	万人		}40.99	}353.64	81.82
高中	万人				404.79
初中	万人		160.27	932.53	1370.42
小学	万人		1256.03	2325.78	2552.16
不识字或识字很少	万人		1255.57	1173.52	822.76
#文盲、半文盲人口	万人		1255.57	894.48	742.56
在业人口	万人			2827.75	3489.74
不在业人口	万人			740.34	879.65
市镇县人口					
市	万人	134.97	161.31	507.43	765.62
镇	万人	157.57	160.79	260.00	328.20
县	万人	3030.15	3396.13	4633.62	4971.98

注:1.劳动年龄人口指男 16—59 岁,女 16—54 岁人口。

2.各年龄组人口缺 15 岁人口和年龄不详人口,加总不等于总人口。

3.由于四次普查所设指标不同,故此表空栏处均表示该年度普查无此调查项目。

4.1964 年人口普查时,6—12 岁不在校儿童没有调查其相当的文化程度,故各项文化程度人口加总不等于 6 周岁及以上人口数。

5.文盲、半文盲人口是指 15 岁及以上年龄不识字或识字很少的人口,由于缺乏详细资料,1964 年人口普查的文盲、半文盲人口是指 6 岁及以上年龄不识字或识字很少人口。

4—4 人口变动调查主要数据

Main Indicators form Population Varied Investigation

	单位	合计		男		女	
		1996年	1997年	1996年	1997年	1996年	1997年
一、按户别分							
总户数	户	12319	12161				
家庭户	户	12297	12142				
集体户	户	22	19				
二、按户别分的人口数							
总人口	人	44059	43017	22816	22076	21243	20941
家庭户人口	人	43906	42871	22699	21960	21207	20911
集体户人口	人	153	146	117	116	36	30
三、按户口所在地分							
1. 住本地，户口在本地	人	42664	41455	22127	21320	20537	20135
2. 住本地半年以上，户口在外地	人	1156	1399	580	677	576	722
3. 住本地不满半年，离开户口地半年以上	人	91	34	54	14	37	20
4. 住本地，户口待定	人	148	129	55	65	93	64
四、按受教育程度分							
6岁及以上人口	人	40796	40288	21034	20595	19762	19693
不识字或识字很少	人	4930	3885	1396	1072	3534	2813
小学	人	18907	18266	9623	9220	9284	9046
初中	人	12298	13161	7140	7301	5158	5860
高中	人	3922	4165	2379	2469	1543	1696
大专及以上	人	739	811	496	533	243	278
五、按婚姻状况分							
15岁及以上人口	人	32773	32433	16846	16464	15927	15969
未婚	人	6693	6371	4297	3986	2396	2385
初婚有配偶	人	23068	23091	11381	11382	11687	11709
再婚有配偶	人	675	551	317	261	358	290
离婚	人	279	259	192	183	87	76
丧偶	人	2058	2161	659	652	1399	1509

注：本表为人口变动抽样调查数。1996年抽样比为0.69‰，1997年抽样比为0.67‰。

4—5 全省人口平均预期寿命

Expectancy of Life for Total Population

年龄别(岁) X	X年龄死亡概率 Q_x	死亡人数 D_x	尚存人数 l_x	平均生存人年数 L_x	总人年数 T_x	平均预期寿命(岁) e_x^0
0	0.04120	4120	100000	72600	6892031	68.92
1	0.00403	387	95880	95686	6819431	71.12
2	0.00181	173	95493	95407	6723745	70.41
3	0.00239	228	95320	95206	6628338	69.54
4	0.00123	117	95092	95034	6533132	68.70
5	0.00072	68	94975	94941	6438098	67.79
6	0.00085	81	94907	94867	6343157	66.84
7	0.00085	80	94826	94786	6248290	65.89
8	0.00125	118	94746	94687	6153504	64.95
9	0.00094	89	94627	94583	6058818	64.03
10	0.00124	117	94539	94480	5964235	63.09
11	0.00042	40	94421	94401	5869754	62.17
12	0.00039	37	94382	94363	5775353	61.19
13	0.00050	47	94345	94321	5680990	60.22
14	0.00057	53	94297	94271	5586669	59.25
15	0.00065	61	94244	94213	5492398	58.28
16	0.00102	96	94183	94135	5398184	57.32
17	0.00078	73	94087	94050	5304050	56.37
18	0.00189	178	94014	93925	5209999	55.42
19	0.00193	181	93836	93746	5116074	54.52
20	0.00195	183	93655	93564	5022328	53.63
21	0.00121	113	93472	93416	4928765	52.73
22	0.00208	194	93360	93263	4835349	51.79
23	0.00168	156	93166	93087	4742086	50.90
24	0.00312	290	93009	92864	4648999	49.98
25	0.00230	213	92719	92612	4556135	49.14
26	0.00272	251	92506	92380	4463523	48.25
27	0.00182	168	92254	92170	4371143	47.38
28	0.00210	193	92086	91989	4278973	46.47
29	0.00262	241	91893	91772	4186983	45.56
30	0.00195	179	91652	91562	4095211	44.68
31	0.00199	182	91473	91382	4003648	43.77
32	0.00211	193	91291	91194	3912267	42.85
33	0.00096	88	91098	91054	3821072	41.94
34	0.00177	161	91011	90930	3730018	40.98
35	0.00342	311	90849	90694	3639088	40.06
36	0.00249	225	90539	90426	3548394	39.19
37	0.00294	265	90313	90181	3457968	38.29
38	0.00289	260	90048	89918	3367787	37.40
39	0.00292	262	89788	89657	3277869	36.51
40	0.00487	436	89526	89308	3188213	35.61
41	0.00257	229	89090	88975	3098905	34.78
42	0.00296	263	88861	88729	3009930	33.87
43	0.00197	175	88598	88510	2921200	32.97
44	0.00411	364	88423	88241	2832690	32.04
45	0.00299	263	88059	87928	2744449	31.17
46	0.00301	264	87796	87664	2656521	30.26
47	0.00286	250	87532	87407	2568857	29.35

注:生命表数据系根据1995年1%人口变动抽样调查资料整理。

4—5　　续表

年龄别（岁）X	X年龄死亡概率 Q_x	死亡人数 D_x	尚存人数 l_x	平均生存人年数 L_x	总人年数 T_x	平均预期寿命（岁）e_x^0
48	0.00534	466	87282	87049	2481451	28.43
49	0.00586	509	86816	86561	2394402	27.58
50	0.00675	583	86307	86016	2307840	26.74
51	0.00464	398	85724	85525	2221825	25.92
52	0.00845	721	85326	84966	2136300	25.04
53	0.00690	584	84605	84313	2051334	24.25
54	0.00443	372	84021	83835	1967021	23.41
55	0.00690	577	83649	83361	1883186	22.51
56	0.00811	674	83072	82735	1799825	21.67
57	0.00722	595	82398	82101	1717090	20.84
58	0.01046	856	81803	81375	1634989	19.99
59	0.01119	906	80947	80495	1553614	19.19
60	0.01273	1019	80042	79532	1473119	18.40
61	0.01680	1327	79023	78359	1393587	17.64
62	0.01507	1171	77696	77110	1315227	16.93
63	0.01876	1435	76525	75807	1238117	16.18
64	0.02265	1700	75089	74239	1162310	15.48
65	0.01923	1411	73389	72683	1088071	14.83
66	0.02693	1938	71978	71009	1015388	14.11
67	0.02442	1711	70040	69184	944380	13.48
68	0.02418	1652	68329	67503	875195	12.81
69	0.04110	2740	66677	65307	807693	12.11
70	0.03695	2362	63936	62755	742386	11.61
71	0.03758	2314	61574	60417	679631	11.04
72	0.04172	2473	59261	58024	619213	10.45
73	0.06185	3512	26788	55032	561189	9.88
74	0.05177	2758	53276	51897	506157	9.50
75	0.05428	2742	50517	49146	454261	8.99
76	0.06745	3222	47775	46164	405114	8.48
77	0.06373	2839	44553	43133	358950	8.06
78	0.06759	2819	41714	40304	315817	7.57
79	0.08539	3321	38894	37234	275512	7.08
80	0.08396	2987	35573	34080	238279	6.70
81	0.09802	3194	32586	30989	204199	6.27
82	0.09642	2834	29392	27975	173209	5.89
83	0.11985	3183	26558	24967	145234	5.47
84	0.09588	2240	23375	22255	120267	5.15
85	0.14592	3084	21135	19593	98011	4.64
86	0.12766	2304	18051	16899	78418	4.34
87	0.14493	2282	15747	14606	61519	3.91
88	0.14940	2012	13465	12459	46913	3.48
89	0.21306	2440	11453	10233	34455	3.01
90	0.20619	1858	9013	8084	24222	2.69
91	0.40000	2862	7155	5724	16138	2.26
92	0.21359	917	4293	3834	10414	2.43
93	0.17476	590	3376	3081	6580	1.95
94	0.24390	679	2786	2446	3499	1.26
95^+	0.18182	383	2106	1053	1053	0.50

4—6 从业人员人数(年底数)

Laborers

单位:万人

年 份	从业人员人 数	按经济类型分						
		职工人数	国有单位	城镇集体单 位	其他经济类型单位	城镇个体、私营企业劳 动 者	农村社会劳 动 者	其他社会劳 动 者
1978	2280.05	363.78	282.06	81.72		0.35	1915.92	
1980	2399.95	409.16	316.80	92.36		1.81	1988.98	
1981	2449.46	426.88	332.46	94.42		3.43	2019.15	
1982	2541.05	441.48	344.41	97.07		5.21	2094.36	
1983	2594.37	447.81	348.97	98.84		9.72	2136.84	
1984	2672.86	460.71	340.94	119.75	0.02	13.18	2198.97	
1985	2728.71	475.15	352.73	122.34	0.08	16.19	2237.37	
1986	2808.87	492.79	367.31	125.25	0.23	18.44	2297.64	
1987	2904.10	515.22	386.34	128.60	0.28	24.72	2364.16	
1988	2998.64	530.20	401.75	128.14	0.31	30.75	2437.69	
1989	3091.37	536.64	411.34	124.81	0.49	30.43	2524.30	
1990	3158.42	551.03	422.28	128.07	0.68	31.94	2575.45	
1991	3222.43	567.07	435.66	130.35	1.06	32.52	2622.84	
1992	3278.83	579.74	447.88	130.43	1.43	39.93	2659.16	
1993	3345.61	588.87	454.26	126.70	7.91	60.42	2675.75	20.57
1994	3400.29	589.48	459.14	121.57	8.77	106.51	2685.54	18.76
1995	3467.31	597.50	466.00	119.13	12.37	133.86	2717.38	18.57
1996	3514.16	596.84	471.55	114.47	10.82	166.21	2732.35	18.76
1997	3560.29	597.48	471.52	110.48	15.48	200.36	2744.33	18.12
长 沙 市	341.89	89.92	66.77	19.40	3.75	25.02	225.35	1.60
株 洲 市	197.50	45.84	34.30	9.38	2.16	6.65	144.00	1.01
湘 潭 市	162.84	36.99	27.62	8.40	0.97	11.04	114.33	0.48
衡 阳 市	366.75	60.07	46.90	12.07	1.10	16.50	289.02	1.16
邵 阳 市	399.34	45.76	35.16	8.71	1.89	19.95	332.22	1.41
岳 阳 市	259.98	54.21	43.63	9.27	1.31	17.05	186.69	2.03
常 德 市	319.87	48.13	37.89	9.70	0.54	21.56	249.03	1.15
张家界市	80.71	10.22	8.08	1.84	0.30	3.40	66.78	0.31
益 阳 市	249.96	40.93	31.34	8.62	0.97	13.04	194.81	1.18
郴 州 市	243.74	34.15	28.90	4.37	0.88	13.28	195.23	1.08
永 州 市	301.47	32.75	27.81	4.52	0.42	12.89	254.65	1.18
娄底地区	223.04	34.68	28.32	6.07	0.29	17.62	169.44	1.30
怀化地区	260.19	33.38	26.90	5.69	0.79	14.19	211.13	1.49
湘西自治州	135.27	17.53	14.98	2.44	0.11	5.90	111.65	0.19
未列入地区单位	2.27					2.27		
广铁公司	13.32	10.87	10.87					2.45
铁 五 局	0.77	0.67	0.67					0.10
总后非企业	1.38	1.38	1.38					

4—7 按三次产业分的从业人员

Distribution of Laborers in Primary, Secondary and Tertiary Industries

年份	从业人员（万人）				构成（以合计为100）		
		第一产业	第二产业	第三产业	第一产业	第二产业	第三产业
1978	2280.05	1788.17	305.37	186.51	78.4	13.4	8.2
1980	2399.95	1846.46	339.06	214.43	77.0	14.1	8.9
1981	2449.46	1887.54	339.52	222.40	77.0	13.9	9.1
1982	2541.05	1955.49	350.79	234.77	77.0	13.8	9.2
1983	2594.37	1966.48	361.77	266.12	75.8	13.9	10.3
1984	2672.84	1971.93	413.98	286.93	73.8	15.5	10.7
1985	2728.71	1946.85	458.68	323.18	71.4	16.8	11.8
1986	2808.87	1969.64	494.51	344.72	70.1	17.6	12.3
1987	2904.10	2011.35	531.70	361.05	69.3	18.3	12.4
1988	2998.64	2050.72	550.38	397.54	68.4	18.4	13.2
1989	3091.37	2104.60	550.26	436.51	68.1	17.8	14.1
1990	3158.42	2176.70	553.83	427.89	68.9	17.5	13.6
1991	3222.43	2219.82	570.35	432.26	68.9	17.7	13.4
1992	3278.83	2213.42	613.57	451.84	67.5	18.7	13.8
1993	3345.61	2140.76	679.22	525.63	64.0	20.3	15.7
1994	3400.29	2076.14	731.01	593.14	61.1	21.5	17.4
1995	3467.31	2071.61	756.54	639.16	59.8	21.8	18.4
1996	3514.16	1994.90	810.38	708.88	56.8	23.0	20.2
1997	3560.29	1998.59	802.25	759.45	56.1	22.5	21.4

4—8 从业人员年平均人数及指数

Average Annual Persons and Its Indexes of Laborers

年份	年平均人数（万人）		指数（以1978年为100）	
	从业人员	物质生产部门从业人员	从业人员	物质生产部门从业人员
1985	2700.78	2550.59	120.1	118.6
1986	2768.79	2606.24	123.2	121.2
1987	2855.96	2684.69	127.0	124.9
1988	2951.37	2763.93	131.3	128.6
1989	3045.01	2839.37	135.4	132.1
1990	3124.90	2908.41	139.0	135.3
1991	3190.43	2971.70	141.9	138.2
1992	3250.63	3028.90	144.6	140.9
1993	3312.22	3093.78	147.3	143.9
1994	3372.95	3124.95	150.0	145.4
1995	3433.80	3180.95	152.7	148.0
1996	3490.74	3218.35	155.3	149.7
1997	3537.23	3248.56	157.3	151.1

4—9 按类型分的从业人员

Employment by Type

单位:万人

类别	城乡合计		城镇		乡村	
	1996年	1997年	1996年	1997年	1996年	1997年
一、从业人员总计	3514.16	3560.29	781.81	815.96	2732.35	2744.33
(一)按就业身份分						
全部职工	596.84	597.48	596.84	597.48		
再就业的离退休人员	9.23	10.63	9.23	10.63		
私营业主	6.59	7.19	3.75	4.62	2.84	2.57
个体户主	173.33	180.09	65.54	71.55	107.79	108.54
私营企业和个体从业人员	247.39	285.57	96.92	124.19	150.47	161.38
乡镇企业从业人员	303.99	253.26			303.99	253.26
农村从业人员	2167.26	2218.58			2167.26	2218.58
其他从业人员	9.53	7.49		7.49	9.53	
(二)按经济类型分						
国有经济	487.94	486.58	487.94	486.58		
集体经济	2587.86	2585.03	116.61	113.19	2471.25	2471.84
私营经济	41.38	43.43	22.80	26.94	18.58	16.49
个体经济	385.93	429.42	143.41	173.42	242.52	256.00
联营经济	0.41	0.40	0.41	0.40		
股份制经济	4.53	8.64	4.53	8.64		
外商投资经济	3.34	3.64	3.34	3.64		
港、澳、台投资经济	2.59	2.96	2.59	2.96		
其他经济	0.18	0.19	0.18	0.19		
(三)按国民经济行业分						
农、林、牧、渔业	1999.08	2003.03	38.92	42.32	1960.16	1960.71
采掘业	65.19	63.67	28.95	27.65	36.24	36.02
制造业	591.30	580.20	228.33	225.20	362.97	355.00
电力、煤气及水的生产和供应业	10.43	10.61	10.43	10.61		
建筑业	140.36	141.25	37.78	37.26	102.58	103.99
地质勘查业、水利管理业	6.49	6.52	6.49	6.52		
交通运输、仓储及邮电通信业	109.22	119.14	49.76	52.91	59.46	66.23
批发和零售贸易、餐饮业	315.32	348.31	180.60	200.69	134.72	147.62
金融、保险业	16.42	18.11	12.56	14.05	3.86	4.06
房地产业	1.92	2.14	1.92	2.14		
社会服务业	57.32	65.46	32.03	37.76	25.29	27.70
卫生、体育和社会福利业	28.19	28.92	20.95	21.88	7.24	7.04
教育、文化艺术和广播电影电视业	77.30	79.58	70.14	72.26	7.16	7.32
科学研究和综合技术服务业	5.39	5.40	5.39	5.40		
国家机关、政党机关和社会团体	76.31	77.17	51.35	52.05	24.96	25.12
其他行业	13.92	10.78	6.21	7.26	7.71	3.52

4—10 各行业从业人数及构成(1997年底)

Laborers and Its Composition by Sector

行业	从业人员(万人)	职工	城镇个体、私营企业劳动者	农村社会劳动者	其他社会劳动者	构成(以从业人员为100) 职工	城镇个体、私营企业劳动者	农村社会劳动者	其他社会劳动者
总计	3560.29	597.48	200.36	2744.33	18.12	16.8	5.6	77.1	0.5
农、林、牧、渔业	2003.03	37.65	3.77	1960.71	0.90	1.9	0.2	97.9	
采掘业	63.67	26.83	0.58	36.02	0.24	42.1	0.9	56.6	0.4
制造业	580.20	194.25	29.38	355.00	1.57	33.4	5.1	61.2	0.3
电力、煤气及水的生产和供应业	10.61	10.45			0.16	98.5			1.5
建筑业	141.25	33.55	1.90	103.99	1.81	23.8	1.3	73.6	1.3
地质勘查业、水利管理业	6.52	6.51			0.01	99.8			0.2
交通运输、仓储及邮电通信业	119.14	33.77	16.34	66.23	2.80	28.3	13.7	55.6	2.4
批发和零售贸易、餐饮业	348.31	78.12	121.99	147.62	0.58	22.4	35.0	42.4	0.2
金融、保险业	18.11	12.84		4.06	1.21	70.9		22.4	6.7
房地产业	2.14	2.10			0.04	98.1			1.9
社会服务业	65.46	13.93	23.34	27.70	0.49	21.3	35.7	42.3	0.7
卫生、体育和社会福利业	28.92	21.67		7.04	0.21	75.0		24.3	0.7
教育、文化艺术和广播电影电视业	79.58	64.76		7.32	7.50	81.4		9.2	9.4
科学研究和综合技术服务业	5.40	5.33			0.07	98.7			1.3
国家机关、政党机关和社会团体	77.17	51.57		25.12	0.48	66.8		32.6	0.6
其他行业	10.78	4.15	3.06	3.52	0.05	38.5	28.4	32.6	0.5

4—11 城乡劳动力资源与分配

Resources and Distribution of Labor Force in Urban and Rural Areas

单位:万人

类别	城乡合计		城镇		乡村	
	1996年	1997年	1996年	1997年	1996年	1997年
年末劳动力资源总计	4166.02	4154.99	831.38	858.40	3334.64	3296.59
#当年新增加劳动力	95.95	105.99	18.91	19.92	77.04	86.07
1.年末16岁以上全部人数	4678.82	4653.34	943.58	970.74	3735.24	3682.60
#不计入劳动力资源的人数	514.24	501.26	112.76	112.89	401.48	388.37
2.机械变动差额跨地区调整数(±)	1.44	2.91	0.56	0.55	0.88	2.36
经济活动人口	3543.88	3589.31	811.53	844.98	2732.35	2744.33
1.从业人员	3514.16	3560.29	781.81	815.96	2732.35	2744.33
2.失业人员	29.72	29.02	29.72	29.02		
非经济活动人口	622.14	565.68	19.85	13.42	602.29	552.26
#16岁以上在校学生	110.28	110.95	67.99	65.31	42.29	45.64
家务劳动者	361.20	251.41	10.57	5.96	350.63	245.45

4—12 全部职工年末人数和平均人数(1997年)

Staff and Workers in The End of Year and Average Annual Persons in Urban Collective－Owned Units

单位:万人

	年末人数				平均人数			
	全部职工	国有单位	城镇集体单位	其他经济类型	全部职工	国有单位	城镇集体单位	其他经济类型
总计	597.48	471.52	110.48	15.48	591.31	467.23	108.94	15.14
长沙市	89.92	66.77	19.40	3.75	88.83	66.18	19.07	3.58
株洲市	45.84	34.30	9.38	2.16	45.48	34.13	9.21	2.14
湘潭市	36.99	27.62	8.40	0.97	37.04	27.75	8.31	0.98
衡阳市	60.07	46.90	12.07	1.10	59.56	46.56	11.92	1.08
邵阳市	45.76	35.16	8.71	1.89	45.16	34.65	8.64	1.87
岳阳市	54.21	43.63	9.27	1.31	54.32	43.72	9.30	1.30
常德市	48.13	37.89	9.70	0.54	47.55	37.46	9.55	0.54
张家界市	10.22	8.08	1.84	0.30	9.92	7.92	1.74	0.26
益阳市	40.93	31.34	8.62	0.97	40.79	31.26	8.57	0.96
郴州市	34.15	28.90	4.37	0.88	33.82	28.67	4.31	0.84
永州市	32.75	27.81	4.52	0.42	32.24	27.34	4.48	0.42
娄底地区	34.68	28.32	6.07	0.29	33.47	27.47	5.74	0.26
怀化地区	33.38	26.90	5.69	0.79	33.11	26.63	5.68	0.80
湘西自治州	17.53	14.98	2.44	0.11	17.24	14.71	2.42	0.11
其他	12.92	12.92			12.78	12.78		

4—13 各行业全部职工及女职工人数(1997年底)

Staff and Workers and Female Staff and Workers by Sector

单位:万人

行业	全部职工	国有	城镇集体	其他经济类型	女职工人数	国有	城镇集体	其他经济类型
总计	597.48	471.52	110.48	15.48	229.07	173.96	48.12	6.99
农、林、牧、渔业	37.66	36.52	1.13	0.01	14.90	14.68	0.22	
采掘业	26.83	25.97	0.58	0.28	6.89	6.62	0.18	0.09
制造业	194.25	136.35	46.27	11.63	82.94	54.09	23.70	5.15
电力、煤气及水的生产和供应业	10.45	10.12	0.15	0.18	3.68	3.54	0.05	0.09
建筑业	33.55	19.01	14.38	0.16	6.25	4.10	2.11	0.04
地质勘查业、水利管理业	6.51	6.25	0.26		1.69	1.64	0.05	
交通运输、仓储及邮电通信业	33.77	26.04	7.65	0.08	9.40	7.39	1.99	0.02
批发和零售贸易、餐饮业	78.12	48.32	28.20	1.60	38.03	22.98	14.23	0.82
金融、保险业	12.83	8.34	4.09	0.40	5.41	3.34	1.86	0.21
房地产业	2.10	1.83	0.08	0.19	0.79	0.70	0.03	0.06
社会服务业	13.93	10.93	2.07	0.93	6.93	5.30	1.12	0.51
卫生、体育和社会福利业	21.67	17.49	4.18		11.82	9.87	1.95	
教育、文化艺术和广播电影电视业	64.76	64.52	0.24		25.38	25.27	0.11	
科学研究和综合技术服务业	5.33	5.28	0.05		1.87	1.86	0.01	
国家机关、政党机关和社会团体	51.57	51.17	0.40		11.50	11.29	0.21	
其他行业	4.15	3.39	0.75	0.01	1.59	1.29	0.30	

4—14 各行业城镇个体劳动者人数

Urban Individual Laborers by Sector

单位:万人

年 份	合 计	工 业	建筑业	交通运输仓储业	批发零售餐饮业	社会服务业	其它行业
1995	133.86	19.55	0.76	8.95	86.69	15.18	2.73
1996	166.21	27.33	0.99	12.52	102.10	19.48	3.79
1997	200.36	29.96	1.90	16.34	121.99	23.34	6.83

注:城镇个体劳动者中包括城镇私营企业的资料。

4—15 城 镇 新 就 业 人 数

Newly Employed Persons in Urban Areas

单位:万人

年 份	城镇新就业人数合计	主 要 来 源				就 业 去 向			
		从城镇招收	从农村招收	大中专技校毕业生	其 他	国 有	城镇集体	从事个体劳动	其他经济类型
1995	30.62	6.85	4.27	8.69	10.81	21.08	4.64	3.24	1.66
1996	27.17	4.94	3.13	8.97	10.13	17.92	3.35	4.98	0.92
1997	26.49	4.10	2.91	9.07	10.41	17.28	3.19	4.91	1.11

4—16 城 镇 失 业 人 员 及 失 业 率

Job—Waiting Persons and Job—Waiting Rate in Urban Areas

年 份	城镇失业人员(万人)	失业青年(万人)	占城镇失业人员(%)	失 业 率(%)
1995	27.40	123.41	85.4	3.8
1996	29.72			3.9
1997	29.02			3.9

4—17 职业介绍服务机构及劳动力交流情况

Swrvice Organization of Occupafion Introducfion and Labor Force Exchanges

项 目	1997年	项 目	1997年
职业介绍服务机构(个)	1501	劳动力交流	
劳动部门办	1264	求职登记人数(万人)	112.72
省 级	1	#本年登记	45.85
地市级	15	本年内介绍成功人数	40.85
县市级	130	1.失业人员	12.00
乡镇街道	1118	#失业六个月及以上	6.75
非劳动部门办	237	2.城镇在业人员	3.38
#企业、事业单位	60	3.农村劳动力	23.32
社会团体	20	4.其 他	2.15

4—18 其他经济类型单位各行业职工年末人数

Year End Staff and Workers in Other Ownership Units by Sector

单位:人

类别	1990 年	1995 年	1996 年	1997 年
总计	6757	123671	108196	154785
按经济类型分				
联营经济		2748	3998	3904
股份制经济		58958	44221	85121
外商投资经济		31719	33064	34920
港澳台投资经济	709	26827	25152	28967
其他经济	6048	3419	1761	1873
按行业分				
农林牧渔业			65	106
采掘业		1079	1288	2795
制造业	4832	100666	79755	116272
电力、煤气及水的生产和供应业		2181	2564	1747
建筑业		444	685	1606
地质勘查业、水利管理业				
交通运输、仓储及邮电通信业	60		1042	798
批发和零售贸易、餐饮业	201	11724	13237	16013
金融、保险业		677	1194	4103
房地产业		1454	1163	1915
社会服务业	1664	5393	7171	9339
卫生、体育和社会福利业				
教育、文化艺术和广播电影电视业				
科学研究和综合技术服务业		46	6	40
国家机关、政党机关和社会团体				
其他行业		7	26	51

4—19 合同制职工人数

Contractual Staff And Worders

年份	年末人数(万人)				比重(以全部职工为100)			
	合计	国有	城镇集体	其他经济类型	合计	国有	城镇集体	其他经济类型
1990	83.36	74.99	8.19	0.18	15.1	17.8	6.4	26.5
1995	176.65	145.53	25.33	5.79	29.6	31.2	21.3	46.8
1996	246.40	205.66	34.35	6.39	41.3	43.6	30.0	59.1
1997	251.94	204.47	38.23	9.24	42.2	43.4	34.6	59.7

4—20 职工工资总额及年平均工资

Total Wage Bill of Staff and Workers and Its Indexes

年　　份	全部职工	国有单位	城镇集体单位	其他经济类型单位
一、工资总额(亿元)				
1978	20.33	16.29	4.04	
1979	23.39	18.50	4.89	
1980	28.73	23.09	5.64	
1981	30.09	24.17	5.92	
1982	32.46	26.13	6.33	
1983	34.48	27.71	6.77	
1984	41.69	32.28	9.41	
1985	49.30	38.36	10.93	0.01
1986	58.80	45.97	12.81	0.02
1987	70.14	55.16	14.94	0.04
1988	87.38	69.78	17.54	0.06
1989	96.78	78.66	18.02	0.10
1990	108.97	88.92	19.91	0.14
1991	119.67	97.57	21.91	0.19
1992	143.69	118.37	24.96	0.36
1993	181.84	148.64	29.51	3.69
1994	238.22	198.56	34.76	4.90
1995	282.05	233.48	41.12	7.45
1996	299.57	251.74	41.59	6.24
1997	314.91	265.53	40.70	8.68
二、年平均工资(元)				
1978	563	589	474	
1979	628	644	580	
1980	718	746	625	
1981	725	748	643	
1982	750	772	670	
1983	780	803	700	
1984	922	965	800	
1985	1059	1111	912	1270
1986	1220	1281	1043	1078
1987	1400	1470	1190	1483
1988	1688	1777	1407	1966
1989	1836	1945	1475	2125
1990	2014	2141	1593	2089
1991	2152	2278	1727	2361
1992	2526	2686	1966	2852
1993	3142	3324	2379	4970
1994	4104	4388	2910	5762
1995	4797	5082	3525	6259
1996	5100	5412	3724	5897
1997	5326	5683	3736	5733

4—21 职工实际工资总额指数

Total Wage Indices for Staff and Workers

	以1978年为100			以上年为100			
	全部职工	国有单位	城镇集体单位	全部职工	国有单位	城镇集体单位	其他经济类型单位
1978	100.0	100.0	100.0	106.1	121.5	72.3	
1980	121.4	121.8	120.0	108.6	109.9	101.5	
1985	168.1	163.2	187.5	105.7	106.2	103.9	
1990	213.5	217.4	196.3	111.9	112.3	99.4	139.2
1991	223.1	227.0	205.5	104.5	104.4	104.7	129.1
1992	236.0	242.6	206.3	105.8	106.9	100.4	166.9
1993	255.9	261.1	209.0	108.4	107.5	101.2	878.3
1994	267.3	278.1	196.3	104.5	106.5	93.9	105.9
1995	268.0	276.9	196.6	100.3	99.6	100.1	128.7
1996	265.6	278.6	185.4	99.1	100.6	94.3	78.1
1997	269.6	283.7	175.4	102.3	102.6	95.2	135.3

4—22 职工年平均工资指数

Average Annual Wage Indices for Staff and Workers

	货币工资指数				实际工资指数			
	全部职工	国有单位	城镇集体单位	其他经济类型单位	全部职工	国有单位	城镇集体单位	其他经济类型单位
以1978年为100								
1990	357.7	363.5	336.1		141.4	143.7	132.9	
1991	382.2	386.8	364.3		144.0	145.9	137.2	
1992	448.7	456.0	414.6		148.9	151.6	137.6	
1993	558.2	564.3	501.9		158.6	160.7	142.6	
1994	729.0	745.0	613.9		165.1	168.7	139.0	
1995	852.0	862.7	743.4		164.6	166.7	143.7	
1996	905.9	918.8	785.7		163.3	165.5	141.5	
1997	946.0	964.9	788.2		164.7	168.0	137.2	
以上年为100								
1990	109.7	110.1	108.0	98.3	109.0	109.4	107.3	97.7
1991	106.9	106.4	108.4	115.2	101.7	101.2	103.1	109.6
1992	117.4	117.9	113.8	118.6	103.4	103.9	100.3	104.5
1993	124.4	123.8	121.0	174.3	106.5	106.0	103.6	149.4
1994	130.6	132.0	122.3	115.9	104.2	105.3	97.6	92.4
1995	116.9	115.8	121.1	108.6	99.0	98.1	102.5	92.0
1996	106.3	106.5	105.6	94.2	99.2	99.3	98.5	87.9
1997	104.4	105.0	100.3	97.2	101.6	102.1	97.6	94.6

4—23 职工工资增长情况

Increase in Total Wage Bill of Staff and Workers

项　　目	1995年	1996年	1997年
工资总额(亿元)	282.05	299.57	314.91
国有经济	233.48	251.74	265.53
城镇集体经济	41.12	41.59	40.70
其他经济类型单位	7.45	6.24	8.68
1.奖金和计件超额工资	40.71	39.26	39.13
国有经济	34.70	34.38	34.55
城镇集体经济	4.54	3.80	3.42
其他经济类型单位	1.47	1.08	1.16
2.各种津贴和补贴	42.85	44.69	53.43
国有经济	38.48	40.40	48.68
城镇集体经济	3.89	3.71	4.04
其他经济类型单位	0.48	0.58	0.71
平均工资(元)	4797	5100	5326
国有经济	5082	5412	5683
城镇集体经济	3525	3724	3736
其他经济类型单位	6259	5897	5733
平均奖金和计件超额工资(元)	692	668	662
国有经济	755	739	740
城镇集体经济	273	340	314
其他经济类型单位	1237	1024	768
平均津贴和补贴(元)	729	761	904
国有经济	837	869	1042
城镇集体经济	234	333	371
其他经济类型单位	404	549	472

注:本表均按货币工资计算。

4—24 职工平均工资增长速度

Average Annual Wage Increase Rate for Staff and Workers

单位:%

时　　期	年均增长速度		时　　期	年均增长速度	
	货币工资	实际工资		货币工资	实际工资
“一五”时期	10.0	6.2	“六五”时期	8.1	4.1
“二五”时期	−0.5	−9.8	“七五”时期	13.7	1.8
1963—1965年	2.6	8.1	“八五”时期	19.0	3.1
“三五”时期	−0.8	−1.1	“九五”时期		
“四五”时期	0.8	0.9	1996年	6.3	−0.8
“五五”时期	5.9	2.9	1997年	4.4	1.6

4—25 各行业职工工资总额及年平均工资(1997年)

Total Wage Bill and Average Annual Wage of Staff and Workers by Sector

行业	工资总额(万元)			平均工资(元)		
	全省	国有	城镇集体	全省	国有	城镇集体
总计	3149149	2655343	407009	5326	5683	3736
一、农、林、牧、渔业	145509.3	141007.4	4437.6	3904	3901	3958
1.农业	102860.1	102699.1	146.5	3854	3855	3573
2.林业	12497.3	12433.2	64.1	3290	3294	2616
3.畜牧业	2186.7	2080.1	56.8	3845	3878	2185
4.渔业	3573.6	3385.6	188.0	3491	3555	2637
5.农、林、牧、渔服务业	24391.6	20409.4	3982.2	4695	4817	4155
二、采掘业	124388.5	121740.6	1671.4	4629	4669	3212
三、制造业	890801.8	678738.5	150898.2	4604	4981	3294
四、电力、煤气及水的生产和供应业	89885.7	85696.8	1122.7	8742	8605	7884
五、建筑业	182312.3	121643.8	59664.3	5631	6639	4293
1.土木工程建筑业	161891.9	106357.2	55350.7	5366	6294	4180
2.线路、管道和设备安装业	19466.6	14940.5	3852.8	9496	11036	6580
3.建筑物的装修装饰业	953.8	346.1	460.8	5950	4847	6583
六、地质勘查业、水利管理业	35156.6	33898.7	1257.9	5425	5408	5945
1.地质勘查业	15126.1	15126.1		5405	5405	
2.水利管理业	20030.5	18772.6	1257.9	5440	5410	5945
七、交通运输、仓储及邮电通信业	248532.4	225298.0	22651.5	7249	8487	2957
1.铁路运输业	107486.2	107486.2		11833	11833	
2.公路运输业	36657.4	27020.4	9577.4	3828	4100	3234
3.管道运输业						
4.水上运输业	8833.7	2298.9	6464.6	2340	3163	2130
5.航空运输业	1309.9	1309.9		11790	11790	
6.交通运输辅助业	37598.4	31899.4	5699.0	6122	6857	3826
7.其他交通运输业	124.9	59.9		9913	8557	
8.仓储业	4239.4	3977.0	211.5	5467	5424	6026
9.邮电通信业	52282.5	51246.3	699.0	10868	11037	5051
八、批发和零售贸易、餐饮业	313297.0	208887.9	95410.6	4065	4386	3421
1.食品、饮料、烟草和家庭用品批发业	117577.6	90489.8	26240.6	4397	4671	3623
2.能源、材料和机械电子设备批发业	41480.1	33871.1	5971.7	4434	4452	4072
3.其他批发业	29554.4	13430.2	15733.3	4296	5799	3485
4.零售业	113005.5	63059.8	45111.0	3649	3901	3239
5.商业经纪与代理业	442.6	363.1	31.0	3799	3549	3605
6.餐饮业	11236.8	7673.9	2323.0	3748	3718	3201
九、金融、保险业	110920.2	74783.8	32846.8	8724	9001	8185
1.金融业	103890.0	68572.4	32846.8	8760	9081	8185
2.保险业	7030.2	6211.4		8232	8199	
十、房地产业	12839.1	11156.7	429.9	6257	6236	5687
1.房地产开发与经营业	6030.7	4426.2	364.0	6281	6222	5732
2.房地产管理业	6384.6	6321.0	51.6	6262	6257	7068
3.房地产代理与经纪业	423.8	409.5	14.3	5870	6076	2979

4—25 续表1 (1997年)

行业	工资总额（万元）			平均工资（元）		
	全省	国有	城镇集体	全省	国有	城镇集体
十一、社会服务业	78047.1	63344.6	8355.7	5702	5913	4073
1.公共服务业	41119.0	37817.7	2275.4	6061	6123	5043
2.居民服务业	3854.4	2182.2	1483.7	5156	6062	4062
3.旅馆业	21224.1	15683.1	1258.4	5493	5373	4079
4.租赁服务业	810.6	799.5	11.1	7772	7838	4826
5.旅游业	1689.9	955.2	578.3	5389	4926	5709
6.娱乐服务业	1554.7	784.5	127.8	6387	5785	5705
7.信息、咨询服务业	3718.3	2412.9	1305.4	4728	7149	2907
8.计算机应用服务业	165.2	137.4	27.8	5697	5608	6178
9.其他社会服务业	3910.9	2572.1	1287.8	4799	5554	3710
十二、卫生、体育和社会福利业	151253.5	130693.7	20559.8	7085	7586	4989
1.卫生	145669.8	125200.5	20469.3	7082	7606	4985
2.体育	1615.5	1615.5		7923	7923	
3.社会福利保障业	3968.2	3877.7	90.5	6865	6888	6033
十三、教育、文化艺术和广播电影电视业	381412.5	379885.6	1526.9	6035	6033	6413
1.教育	357229.7	356120.4	1109.3	6020	6015	8091
#(1)普通高等教育	31993.3	31993.3		7971	7971	
(2)普通中学	118171.1	118113.1	58.0	5853	5853	7073
(3)小学校	157069.3	157047.3	22.0	5505	5505	7857
2.文化艺术业	12201.6	11878.6	323.0	6735	6886	3730
3.广播电影电视业	11981.2	11886.6	94.6	5847	5842	6569
十四、科学研究和综合技术服务业	39813.3	39453.6	336.0	7472	7473	7417
1.科学研究	21104.0	21098.6	3.0	7273	7275	2727
(1)自然科学研究	18610.5	18605.1	3.0	7121	7124	2727
(2)社会科学研究	789.1	789.1		6762	6762	
(3)其他科学研究	1704.4	1704.4		9927	9927	
2.综合技术服务业	18709.3	18355.0	333.0	7709	7715	7534
(1)气象	1329.3	1329.3		7105	7105	
(2)地震	97.3	97.3		6950	6950	
(3)测绘	1197.0	1197.0		6980	6980	
(4)技术监督	2635.6	2613.6	22.0	7010	6999	8462
(5)海洋环境						
(6)环境保护	2339.5	2190.3	149.2	6627	6595	7139
(7)技术推广和科技交流服务业	1350.0	1282.7	67.3	6076	6036	6938
(8)工程设计业	8788.7	8685.0	82.4	9469	9482	9258
(9)其他综合技术服务业	971.9	959.8	12.1	5560	5558	5762
十五、国家机关、政党机关和社会团体	320046.9	317735.1	2311.8	6307	6311	5761
#国家机关	300663.7	299327.8	1335.9	6311	6310	6401
政党机关	15302.5	15302.5		6305	6305	
十六、其他行业	24932.8	21378.6	3528.8	6043	6321	4775
#企业管理机构	15365.6	12021.1	3335.0	6032	6512	4769

4—26 国有经济各行业职工工资总额及构成(1997年)

Total Wage Bill of Staff and Workers and Its Composition in State－Owned Units by Sector

行业	工资总额	计时和计件标准工资	奖金和计件超额工资	津贴和补贴
一、总计(万元)	2655343.4	1668705.8	345536.3	486764.2
农、林、牧、渔业	141007.4	103208.6	7836.5	12214.5
采掘业	121740.6	88584.7	13184.0	15385.5
制造业	678738.5	470007.9	110442.8	60383.8
电力、煤气及水的生产和供应业	85696.8	48176.1	21171.4	12582.6
建筑业	121643.8	74962.1	21476.9	16566.5
地质勘查业、水利管理业	33898.7	20612.5	2461.2	9643.7
交通运输、仓储及邮电通信业	225298.0	120582.3	45004.9	49470.7
批发和零售贸易、餐饮业	208887.9	150604.1	27703.6	18712.9
金融、保险业	74783.8	30296.8	5411.2	34341.2
房地产业	11156.7	6256.9	1190.1	3150.6
社会服务业	63344.6	38335.9	7932.4	13227.7
卫生、体育和社会福利业	130693.7	65614.5	23060.7	37069.5
教育、文化艺术和广播电影电视业	379885.6	229835.6	28602.8	101149.0
科学研究和综合技术服务业	39453.6	21806.8	5703.8	10735.2
国家机关、政党机关和社会团体	317735.1	186399.4	22043.3	87899.8
其他行业	21378.6	13421.6	2310.7	4231.0
二、构成(以总额为100)	100.0	62.8	13.0	18.3
农、林、牧、渔业	100.0	73.2	5.6	8.7
采掘业	100.0	72.8	10.8	12.6
制造业	100.0	69.2	16.3	8.9
电力、煤气及水的生产和供应业	100.0	56.2	24.7	14.7
建筑业	100.0	61.6	17.7	13.6
地质勘查业、水利管理业	100.0	60.8	7.3	28.4
交通运输、仓储及邮电通信业	100.0	53.5	20.0	22.0
批发和零售贸易、餐饮业	100.0	72.1	13.3	9.0
金融、保险业	100.0	40.5	7.2	45.9
房地产业	100.0	56.1	10.7	28.2
社会服务业	100.0	60.5	12.5	20.9
卫生、体育和社会福利业	100.0	50.2	17.6	28.4
教育、文化艺术和广播电影电视业	100.0	60.5	7.5	26.6
科学研究和综合技术服务业	100.0	55.3	14.5	27.2
国家机关、政党机关和社会团体	100.0	58.7	6.9	27.7
其他行业	100.0	62.8	10.8	19.8

4—27 全部职工和离休、退休、退职人员劳保福利费

Total Value of Insurance and Welfare Funds of On—Job Staff and Workers, Retirees and Resigned Workers

单位:亿元

年份	劳保福利费用总额	国有单位			城镇集体单位			相当于工资总额%		
		合计	职工	离退休、退职人员	合计	职工	离退休、退职人员	全省	国有	城镇集体
1995	86.81	74.92	24.26	50.66	11.05	2.92	8.13	30.8	32.1	26.9
1996	102.29	88.93	28.21	60.72	12.4	3.03	9.37	34.1	35.3	29.8
1997	108.70	95.38	29.15	66.23	12.48	2.97	9.51	34.5	35.9	30.7

注:劳保福利费用总额中包括其他经济类型单位的资料。

4—28 国有单位职工劳保福利费及构成(1997年)

Value of Insurance and Welfare Funds and Its Composition of Staff and Workers in State—Owned Units

	劳保福利费用总额	医疗卫生费	文体宣传费	集体福利设施费及集体福利事业补贴	冬季取暖补贴	其他
一、总计(万元)	291548.7	150259.2	13559.4	67537.2	15770.1	44422.8
农、林、牧、渔业	10314.9	4925.5	623.5	2643.4	675.1	1447.4
采掘业	15321.1	7822.7	493.7	4189.4	559.7	2255.6
制造业	67396.1	34110.4	2607.8	19020.7	2489.4	9167.8
电力、煤气及水的生产和供应业	10914.0	5941.3	539.2	2138.8	487.4	1807.3
建筑业	10047.6	5482.6	332.7	1954.2	521.5	1756.6
地质勘探业、水利管理业	3600.4	1861.0	170.8	752.5	303.8	512.3
交通运输、仓储及邮电通讯业	21472.8	8971.9	1226.2	5151.7	1171.0	4952.0
批发和零售贸易、餐饮业	22731.4	12047.7	800.2	4664.1	1544.6	3674.8
金融、保险业	12293.2	6850.6	717.0	2426.9	856.2	1442.5
房地产业	1421.9	651.7	100.1	288.2	120.4	261.5
社会服务业	16542.7	12496.7	238.9	1678.5	448.3	1680.3
卫生、体育和社会福利业	20363.7	11442.6	933.9	4263.4	1100.1	2623.7
教育、文化艺术和广播电影电视业	27879.4	13003.3	1576.8	7035.8	1795.0	4468.5
科学研究和综合技术服务业	6808.1	3296.0	527.6	1381.9	375.9	1226.7
国家机关、政党机关和社会团体	38005.6	18599.7	2186.9	8424.0	2801.5	5993.5
其他行业	6435.8	2755.5	484.1	1523.7	520.2	1152.3
二、构成(以费用总额为100)	100.00	51.54	4.65	23.16	5.41	15.24
农、林、牧、渔业	100.00	47.75	6.05	25.63	6.54	14.03
采掘业	100.00	51.06	3.22	27.35	3.65	14.72
制造业	100.00	50.61	3.87	28.22	3.70	13.60
电力、煤气及水的生产和供应业	100.00	54.44	4.94	19.60	4.46	16.56
建筑业	100.00	54.57	3.31	19.45	5.19	17.48
地质勘探业、水利管理业	100.00	51.69	4.74	20.90	8.44	14.23
交通运输、仓储及邮电通讯业	100.00	41.78	5.71	23.99	5.46	23.06
批发和零售贸易、餐饮业	100.00	53.00	3.52	20.52	6.79	16.17
金融、保险业	100.00	55.73	5.83	19.74	6.97	11.73
房地产业	100.00	45.83	7.04	20.27	8.47	18.39
社会服务业	100.00	75.54	1.44	10.15	2.71	10.16
卫生、体育和社会福利业	100.00	56.19	4.59	20.94	5.40	12.88
教育、文化艺术和广播电影电视业	100.00	46.64	5.65	25.24	6.44	16.03
科学研究和综合技术服务业	100.00	48.41	7.75	20.30	5.52	18.02
国家机关、政党机关和社会团体	100.00	48.94	5.75	22.17	7.37	15.77
其他行业	100.00	42.82	7.52	23.68	8.08	17.90

4—29 离休、退休、退职人员年末人数

Year—End Number of Retirees and Resigned Workers

年份	离休、退休、退职人数（万人）	国有单位	城镇集体单位	离休、退休、退职人数为职工%	国有单位	城镇集体单位
1995	138.23	107.52	29.74	23.1	23.1	25.0
1996	145.67	114.48	30.18	24.4	24.3	26.4
1997	145.82	116.10	28.81	24.4	24.6	26.1

4—30 离休、退休、退职人员劳保福利费

Value of Insurance and Welfare Funds of Retirees and Resigned Workers

年份	劳保福利费用总额（万元）	国有单位	城镇集体单位	人均劳保福利费（元）	国有单位	城镇集体单位
1995	592837.0	506584.9	81260.4	4289	4712	2732
1996	706296.7	607182.4	93671.0	4976	5470	3127
1997	761849.7	662307.5	95127.1	5227	5745	3225

注：劳保福利费用合计中包括其他经济类型单位的资料；人均劳保福利费按离退休人员计算。

4—31 国有单位离休、退休、退职人员劳保福利费及构成

Value of Insurance and Welfare Funds and Its Composition of Retirees and Resigned Workers in State—Owned Units

类别	劳保福利费（万元）		构成（以总计为100）	
	1996年	1997年	1996年	1997年
总计	607182.4	662307.5	100.0	100.0
离休金	29602.4	32346.9	4.9	4.9
退休金	447552.6	501866.0	73.7	75.8
退职生活费	4446.7	5000.8	0.7	0.7
医疗卫生费	70060.1	79582.5	11.5	12.0
交通费补贴	2823.5		0.5	
丧葬抚恤救济费	8296.7		1.4	
其他	44400.4	43511.3	7.3	6.6

五、固定资产投资

INVESTMENT IN FIXED ASSETS

5—1 全社会固定资产投资

Total Investment in Fixed Assets

类　别	1995 年	1996 年	1997 年	1997 年为上年%
投资总额(亿元)	524.01	678.33	688.36	101.5
按经济类型分				
国有经济	316.90	375.27	353.97	94.3
集体经济	39.83	79.25	84.48	106.6
城镇	16.22	15.39	11.79	76.6
农村	23.61	63.86	72.69	113.8
个体经济	120.34	178.58	195.17	109.3
城镇	13.94	16.02	26.60	166.0
农村	106.40	162.56	168.57	103.7
联营经济	0.85	0.56	0.89	158.9
股份制经济	14.45	11.05	19.31	174.8
外商投资经济	23.47	21.38	23.33	109.1
港澳台投资经济	7.46	10.95	8.37	76.4
其他经济	0.71	1.29	2.84	220.2
按管理渠道分				
基本建设	217.52	253.92	258.01	101.6
更新改造	92.02	120.14	107.26	89.3
房地产开发	50.84	40.22	34.02	84.6
其他投资	163.63	264.05	289.07	109.5
按资金来源分				
国家预算内投资	19.95	13.12	18.37	140.0
国内贷款	101.24	126.98	108.41	85.4
债券	0.72	5.28	0.13	2.5
利用外资	32.81	28.62	30.86	107.8
自筹投资	276.30	368.93	423.71	114.8
#股票	0.61	0.34	0.69	202.9
其他资金	92.99	135.40	106.88	78.9
按构成分				
建筑安装工程	363.26	456.53	491.22	107.6
设备、工具、器具购置	106.51	138.84	126.45	91.1
其他费用	54.24	82.96	70.69	85.2
按隶属关系分				
中央	142.58	174.70	162.66	93.1
地方	364.02	480.27	503.83	104.9
其他	17.41	23.36	21.87	93.6
按用途分:住宅	180.99	206.59	224.43	108.6
房屋建筑面积(万平方米)				
施工面积	8338.70	12627.96	10289.91	81.5
竣工面积	6360.57	10582.17	8674.84	82.0
#住宅	5115.43	8918.35	7012.41	78.6

注:1997 年固定资产投资额中,不含 50 万元及以下基本建设、更新改造和其他项目投资 12.37 亿元。为上年%均按可比数计算(下同)。

5—2 各种分组的全社会固定资产投资及构成(1997 年)

Selected Breakdowns of Total Investment in Fixed Assets and Its composition

类别	全省总计	国有	#基本建设	#更新改造	集体	#农村	个体	#农村	其他
一、绝对数									
投资总额(亿元)	688.36	353.97	238.01	89.42	84.48	72.69	195.17	168.57	54.74
1.按资金来源分									
国家预算内投资	18.37	16.11	15.26	0.69	2.21	2.18			0.05
国内贷款	108.41	81.90	54.63	22.39	16.95	14.96			9.56
债　　券	0.13	0.12	0.06	0.04	0.01				
利用外资	30.86	15.12	12.78	1.31	4.13	4.04			11.61
自筹投资	423.71	178.31	112.06	55.97	36.45	31.40	195.17	168.57	13.78
#股　票	0.69	0.49	0.21	0.28					0.20
其他资金	106.88	62.41	43.22	9.02	24.73	20.11			19.74
2.按构成分									
建安工程	491.22	233.57	184.28	27.86	56.91	47.85	170.37	143.77	30.37
设备、工具、器具购置	126.45	84.87	28.83	54.76	21.64	20.19	3.03	3.03	16.91
其他费用	70.69	35.53	24.90	6.80	5.93	4.65	21.77	21.77	7.46
3.按用途分:#住宅	224.43	45.92	33.38	2.59	13.94	9.52	156.75	136.17	7.82
房屋建筑面积(万 m^2)									
施工面积	10289.91	2273.22	1770.15	212.50	1026.80	838.51	6525.39	6037.70	464.50
竣工面积	8674.84	1142.72	892.27	115.45	853.69	745.05	6525.39	6037.70	153.04
#住宅	7012.41	621.07	459.12	45.90	260.76	198.09	6040.32	5669.55	90.26
二、构成(%)									
投资总额	100.0	100.0	100.0	100.0	100.0	100.0	100.0	100.0	100.0
1.按资金来源分									
国家预算内投资	2.7	4.6	6.4	0.8	2.6	3.0			0.1
国内贷款	15.8	23.1	22.9	25.0	20.1	20.6			17.5
债　　券	0.02	0.3	0.03	0.04	0.01				
利用外资	4.5	4.3	5.4	1.5	4.9	5.5			21.2
自筹投资	61.5	50.4	47.1	62.6	43.1	43.2	100.0	100.0	25.2
#股　票	0.1	0.1	0.1	0.3					0.4
其他资金	15.5	17.6	18.2	10.1	29.3	27.7			36.0
2.按构成分									
建安工程	71.3	66.0	77.4	31.2	67.4	65.8	87.3	85.3	55.5
设备、工具、器具购置	18.4	24.0	12.1	61.2	25.6	27.8	1.5	1.8	30.9
其他费用	10.3	10.0	10.5	7.6	7.0	6.4	11.2	12.9	13.6
3.按用途分:#住宅	32.6	13.0	14.0	2.9	16.5	13.1	80.3	80.8	14.3

注:其他含联营经济、股份制经济、中外合资经营、中外合作经营、外资、与大陆合资经营、与大陆合作经营、港澳台独资等经济。

5—3 各行业基本建设投资(1997年)

Capital Construction Investment by sector

单位:亿元

	合计	农林牧渔业	采掘业	制造业	电力煤气及水的生产和供应业	建筑业	地质勘查业和水利管理业	交通运输仓储和邮电通信业
全省	258.01	2.09	1.49	21.57	57.00	1.93	9.59	70.88
长沙市	52.24	0.97	0.01	1.12	3.65	0.56	0.52	9.09
株洲市	9.26			1.12	0.66	0.09	0.18	1.03
湘潭市	22.06			3.78	15.37	0.09	0.13	0.27
衡阳市	10.22	0.30	0.78	0.60	0.94	0.20	0.20	1.59
邵阳市	9.53	0.07	0.05	0.41	1.36	0.35	0.55	2.69
岳阳市	18.90	0.10	0.05	10.32	0.11	0.03	0.91	3.20
常德市	23.82	0.06	0.11	1.60	9.21	0.04	1.91	2.90
张家界市	9.60		0.04	0.03	7.35		0.01	0.79
益阳市	9.68	0.19		0.22	1.80	0.01	1.31	2.67
郴州市	10.95	0.09	0.37	0.40	1.80	0.16	0.05	1.50
永州市	9.27	0.11	0.07	1.11	1.19	0.01	0.17	1.25
娄底地区	5.82	0.03	0.01	0.48	0.42	0.11	0.24	1.24
怀化地区	10.28	0.13	0.01	0.18	5.59	0.28	0.06	0.27
湘西自治州	3.85	0.02		0.21	0.28		0.06	0.42
不分地区	52.53				7.25		3.31	41.96

	批发零售贸易和餐饮业	金融保险业	房地产业	社会服务业	卫生体育和社会福利业	教育文化艺术广播电影电视业	科学研究和综合技术服务业	国家机关政党机关和社会团体	其他行业
全省	14.04	5.66	0.94	18.15	4.94	25.74	1.26	21.28	1.45
长沙市	6.56	1.84	0.66	5.92	1.15	12.81	0.73	5.75	0.90
株洲市	1.30	0.24		1.88	0.19	1.07	0.37	1.12	
湘潭市	0.24	0.14	0.08	0.49	0.09	0.60	0.01	0.64	0.13
衡阳市	0.52	0.06		1.24	0.37	1.69	0.05	1.57	0.09
邵阳市	0.54	0.20	0.02	0.46	0.21	1.05	0.01	1.48	0.08
岳阳市	0.31	0.10	0.02	1.37	0.27	0.76		1.28	0.06
常德市	0.84	1.33		1.30	0.59	1.99	0.04	1.89	0.02
张家界市	0.14	0.03		0.64	0.04	0.24		0.29	
益阳市	0.44	0.12	0.10	1.46	0.14	0.56	0.02	0.63	
郴州市	0.94	0.42	0.05	1.17	0.81	1.51		1.68	0.01
永州市	0.62	0.29		0.41	0.40	1.55	0.04	2.05	0.03
娄底地区	0.72	0.31	0.02	0.87	0.13	0.52		0.74	
怀化地区	0.44	0.22		0.49	0.36	0.71		1.51	0.02
湘西自治州	0.43	0.36		0.45	0.18	0.67		0.66	0.11
不分地区									

5—4 各行业基本建设新增固定资产(1997年)

Newly Increased Fixed Assets through Capital Construction by Sector

单位:亿元

	合计	农林牧渔业	采掘业	制造业	电力煤气及水的生产和供应业	建筑业	地质勘查业和水利管理业	交通运输仓储和邮电通信业
全省	159.88	0.99	2.43	19.34	35.20	1.47	5.30	29.50
长沙市	25.46	0.05	0.03	1.88	2.31	0.05	0.04	3.22
株洲市	10.16	0.02		1.16	0.16	0.13	1.41	1.24
湘潭市	4.57			0.37	1.88	0.10		0.34
衡阳市	6.58	0.25	0.17	0.70	0.15	0.17	0.19	0.82
邵阳市	7.21	0.05	0.03	0.43	0.78	0.34	0.17	2.03
岳阳市	17.31	0.08	0.05	12.04	0.04	0.03	0.53	0.67
常德市	22.67	0.09		0.69	10.94	0.05	1.95	1.41
张家界市	2.70		0.02		1.54		0.01	0.15
益阳市	5.64	0.17		0.19	0.29	0.01	0.69	2.16
郴州市	11.77	0.07	2.08	0.40	1.32		0.04	1.30
永州市	7.47	0.11	0.05	0.90	1.55	0.01	0.12	1.01
娄底地区	4.26	0.03		0.18	0.38	0.14	0.05	1.31
怀化地区	7.67	0.05		0.25	3.75	0.45	0.08	0.35
湘西自治州	3.55	0.02		0.16	0.18			0.57
不分地区	22.86				9.94		0.01	12.91

	批发零售贸易和餐饮业	金融保险业	房地产业	社会服务业	卫生体育和社会福利业	教育文化艺术广播电影电视业	科学研究和综合技术服务业	国家机关政党机关和社会团体	其他行业
全省	8.65	6.03	0.32	9.67	5.70	16.35	1.40	17.03	0.51
长沙市	2.91	1.26	0.01	1.83	1.77	5.53	0.79	3.58	0.20
株洲市	1.25	0.07		2.18	0.18	0.80	0.45	1.11	
湘潭市	0.18	0.27	0.06	0.29	0.17	0.41	0.01	0.47	0.01
衡阳市	0.34	0.03		0.32	0.23	1.78	0.05	1.34	0.04
邵阳市	0.33	0.28	0.08	0.18	0.18	1.13	0.02	1.17	0.02
岳阳市	0.30	0.04	0.03	1.54	0.15	0.80		0.94	0.05
常德市	0.98	2.02		0.62	0.89	1.60	0.01	1.42	
张家界市	0.20	0.02		0.22	0.04	0.26		0.24	
益阳市	0.26	0.06	0.09	0.37	0.13	0.60	0.03	0.58	0.01
郴州市	0.70	0.63	0.03	1.12	0.78	1.28		2.01	0.01
永州市	0.44	0.20		0.03	0.38	0.84	0.04	1.75	0.04
娄底地区	0.30	0.63	0.02	0.29	0.14	0.28		0.51	
怀化地区	0.11	0.34		0.20	0.40	0.43		1.21	0.06
湘西自治州	0.34	0.17		0.48	0.26	0.58		0.70	0.09
不分地区									

5—5 基本建设项目个数、项目投产率(1997年)

Capital Construction projects, Rate of projects Put into Operation

	投资额(亿元)	施工项目(个)	全部建成投产项目(个)	项目建成投产率(%)	新增固定资产(亿元)	固定资产交付使用率(%)
全省总计	258.01	4221	2388	56.57	159.88	61.97
(一)按地市分						
长沙市	52.24	369	151	40.92	25.46	48.74
株洲市	9.26	290	178	61.38	10.16	109.67
湘潭市	22.06	156	73	46.79	4.57	20.73
衡阳市	10.22	398	220	55.28	6.58	64.44
邵阳市	9.53	429	258	60.14	7.21	75.68
岳阳市	18.90	283	189	66.78	17.31	91.63
常德市	23.82	482	237	49.17	22.67	95.16
张家界市	9.60	98	61	62.24	2.70	28.13
益阳市	9.68	227	154	67.84	5.64	58.22
郴州市	10.95	451	306	67.85	11.77	107.49
永州市	9.27	287	198	68.99	7.47	80.54
娄底地区	5.82	196	94	47.96	4.26	73.14
怀化地区	10.28	309	142	45.95	7.67	74.61
湘西自治州	3.85	226	124	54.87	3.55	92.23
不分地区	52.53	20	3	15.00	22.86	43.52
(二)按行业分						
1.农林牧渔业	2.09	80	50	62.50	0.99	47.34
2.采掘业	1.49	34	14	41.18	2.43	163.03
3.制造业	21.57	292	157	53.77	19.34	89.63
4.电力煤气及水生产供应业	57.00	212	104	49.06	35.20	61.76
5.建筑业	1.93	49	32	65.31	1.47	76.32
6.地质勘查业水利管理业	9.59	125	57	45.60	5.30	55.26
7.交通运输、仓储及邮电通信业	70.88	460	266	57.83	29.50	41.62
8.批发和零售贸易餐饮业	14.04	427	228	53.40	8.65	61.57
9.金融保险业	5.66	162	86	53.09	6.03	106.63
10.房地产业	0.94	23	13	56.52	0.32	33.39
11.社会服务业	18.15	315	128	40.63	9.67	53.30
12.卫生体育和社会福利业	4.94	248	135	54.44	5.70	115.40
13.教育文化艺术和广播电影电视业	25.74	755	480	63.58	16.35	63.53
14.科学研究和综合技术服务业	1.26	53	25	47.17	1.40	111.07
15.国家机关、政党机关和社会团体	21.28	942	590	62.63	17.03	80.00
16.其他行业	1.45	44	23	52.27	0.51	34.48

5—6 各种分组的更新改造投资(1997年)

Technical Updates and Transformation Investment by Various Characterisfics

单位:亿元

	投资额	按构成分			按建设性质分		
		建筑安装工程	设备工器具购置	其他费用	#新建	#扩建	#改建
全省	107.26	33.90	65.40	7.96	5.95	50.39	46.94
长沙市	25.05	6.11	17.35	1.59	3.33	13.06	6.56
株洲市	8.40	3.54	4.50	0.36	1.07	2.67	4.40
湘潭市	5.14	1.57	2.98	0.59	0.03	2.40	2.62
衡阳市	7.77	1.98	4.41	1.38	0.28	4.66	2.51
邵阳市	1.56	0.49	1.01	0.05		0.58	0.68
岳阳市	15.14	7.11	7.18	0.84	0.11	3.01	11.73
常德市	7.61	1.47	5.65	0.49	0.01	4.28	3.32
张家界市	0.96	0.43	0.49	0.04	0.04	0.67	0.24
益阳市	2.77	0.54	2.11	0.12		1.60	0.72
郴州市	5.03	2.09	2.65	0.30	0.11	2.24	2.61
永州市	2.84	0.50	2.31	0.04		0.79	2.04
娄底地区	5.63	1.84	3.08	0.71	0.22	2.00	3.41
怀化地区	4.14	1.21	2.68	0.25	0.71	2.49	0.92
湘西自治州	2.67	1.04	1.42	0.21	0.04	1.33	1.25
不分地区	12.55	3.97	7.58	1.00		8.61	3.94

	按资金来源分					按隶属关系分	
	国家预算内资金	国内贷款	利用外资	自筹资金	其他投资	中央项目	地方项目
全省	0.69	24.39	8.42	59.27	14.45	60.40	35.71
长沙市	0.06	2.88	6.66	9.30	6.15	9.77	5.23
株洲市		1.84	0.70	4.88	0.98	6.04	2.03
湘潭市		1.16		2.85	1.13	0.93	4.21
衡阳市	0.02	1.35	0.28	4.87	1.25	3.49	4.00
邵阳市		0.42		0.79	0.32	0.60	0.92
岳阳市	0.51	3.76		9.09	1.78	11.21	3.92
常德市	0.03	3.15		4.31	0.12	4.54	3.07
张家界市	0.01	0.04	0.23	0.48	0.20	0.37	0.32
益阳市	0.02	0.89	0.05	1.43	0.38	1.45	1.32
郴州市	0.02	1.62	0.19	2.46	0.74	3.15	1.83
永州市		1.85		0.93	0.06	2.07	0.78
娄底地区		1.00	0.01	3.73	0.89	2.10	3.53
怀化地区		2.11	0.18	1.61	0.24	0.98	3.05
湘西自治州	0.02	1.03	0.02	1.39	0.21	1.14	1.51
不分地区		1.29	0.10	11.15		12.55	

5—7 更新改造完成投资及新增固定资产(1997年)

Technical Updates and Transformation and Nemly increased Fixed Assets

	投资额(亿元)	施工项目(个)	全部建成投产项目(个)	项目建成投产率(%)	新增固定资产(亿元)	固定资产交付使用率(%)
全省总计	107.26	1335	791	59.25	110.05	102.60
(一)按地市分						
长沙市	25.05	175	86	49.14	25.07	100.09
株洲市	8.40	117	67	57.26	9.32	110.97
湘潭市	5.14	61	37	60.66	14.15	275.31
衡阳市	7.77	139	79	56.83	13.78	177.35
邵阳市	1.56	86	58	67.44	1.47	94.43
岳阳市	15.14	128	95	74.22	9.20	60.80
常德市	7.61	82	45	54.88	7.37	96.85
张家界市	0.96	21	19	90.48	1.36	141.72
益阳市	2.77	84	52	61.90	2.57	92.65
郴州市	5.03	118	75	63.56	5.10	101.46
永州市	2.84	42	20	47.62	2.02	70.85
娄底地区	5.63	71	33	46.48	7.24	128.57
怀化地区	4.14	92	50	54.35	3.87	93.45
湘西自治州	2.67	75	48	64.00	2.30	86.07
不分地区	12.55	44	27	61.36	5.23	41.69
(二)按行业分						
1.农林牧渔业	0.09	7	4	57.14	0.05	57.08
2.采掘业	2.21	103	49	47.57	1.53	69.34
3.制造业	61.89	637	319	50.08	75.82	122.50
4.电力煤气及水生产供应业	3.47	119	75	63.03	2.85	82.03
5.建筑业	0.40	11	7	63.64	0.42	103.16
6.地质勘查业水利管理业	0.12	3	2	66.67	0.05	45.61
7.交通运输、仓储及邮电通信业	37.14	413	310	75.06	27.19	73.19
8.批发和零售贸易餐饮业	0.22	7	4	57.14	0.21	94.43
9.金融保险业						
10.房地产业						
11.社会服务业	0.96	11	9	81.82	1.25	130.04
12.卫生体育和社会福利业	0.03	1			0.02	46.38
13.教育文化艺术和广播电影电视业	0.26	10	7	70.00	0.27	103.43
14.科学研究和综合技术服务业	0.02	2				
15.国家机关、政党机关和社会团体	0.15	7	4	57.14	0.16	106.94
16.其他行业	0.29	4	1	25.00	0.25	85.49

5—8 工业企业更新改造按企业规模分主要指标(1997年)

Major Indicators of Technical Updating and Transformation Investment by Scale of Industrial Enterprises

单位:万元

指标名称	合计	特大型	大型	中型	小型
实际需要的投资	1791518	157133	1085593	271445	277347
本年完成投资	675744	92595	348378	104738	130033
按构成分:					
1.建筑工程	148306	17031	65727	28665	36883
2.安装工程	86735	35256	31346	13028	7105
3.设备、工具器具购置	375120	35947	205623	55082	78468
#用于更新的设备	138054	35947	60900	18709	22498
按用途分:					
1.增产	356918	60027	151391	64817	80683
2.节约能源	28247	5497	9983	2011	10756
3.其他节约	3539	257	589	394	2299
4.增加品种	139930	1666	102846	20996	14422
5.提高产品质量	75378	14693	50493	6842	3350
6.三废治理	12174	6828	2496	909	1941
7.其他	60733	3627	30580	9792	16734
在总计中:住宅	9953		6703	1944	1306
按建设性质分:					
1.新建	55874		3230	21860	30784
2.扩建	232193		130650	48609	52934
3.改建	363773	92595	207222	29021	34935
4.单纯建造生活设施	449			449	
5.单纯购置	21116		6732	4599	9785
本年新增固定资产	801968	50412	538750	83312	129494
施工项目个数(个)	859	32	327	222	278
#本年新开工	420	16	127	115	162
本年投产项目个数(个)	443	27	142	119	155
本年房屋施工面积(平方米)	1209082	23196	620152	271583	294151
#住宅	276759		202001	49228	25530
本年竣工房屋面积(平方米)	760430	10686	371211	165553	212980
#住宅	188553		127135	43008	18410
本年竣工房屋价值(万元)	75236	1171	35746	12399	25920
#住宅	11246		7435	2770	1041

5—9 国有经济固定资产投资及构成

Investment in Fixed Assets of State-Owned Units

年份	固定资产投资总额	基本建设	更新改造	房地产开发	其他	新增固定资产	基本建设	更新改造	房地产开发	其他
绝对数（亿元）										
1978	14.71	13.51	1.20			10.56	9.65	0.91		
1980	20.32	15.53	4.79			15.24	11.98	3.26		
1981	18.67	12.92	5.75			14.11	9.81	4.30		
1982	25.34	17.62	7.72			18.22	12.48	5.74		
1983	25.06	14.21	10.50		0.35	18.85	10.42	8.16		0.27
1984	29.39	16.90	11.09		1.40	21.09	10.94	9.08		1.07
1985	43.86	25.58	16.20		2.08	30.66	16.91	12.19		1.56
1986	50.40	28.00	20.17		2.23	33.55	19.33	13.94		0.28
1987	60.98	32.47	25.44		3.07	46.68	25.97	19.88		0.83
1988	72.97	38.03	31.42		3.52	56.80	32.77	20.94		3.09
1989	62.94	37.34	24.28		1.32	43.86	24.50	18.22		1.14
1990	72.01	43.11	25.24	2.14	1.52	47.27	25.68	18.81	1.37	1.41
1991	94.85	56.10	32.45	3.20	3.10	82.36	50.75	27.20	2.19	2.22
1992	149.72	90.89	49.17	7.42	2.24	117.07	75.01	36.25	4.05	1.76
1993	203.17	122.75	61.72	15.12	3.58	125.96	69.83	45.07	7.75	3.31
1994	251.21	162.99	70.63	13.81	3.78	154.80	92.09	51.48	7.66	3.57
1995	316.90	209.70	79.85	21.61	5.74	202.81	117.55	68.57	11.88	4.81
1996	375.27	245.10	104.67	17.50	8.00	269.99	163.23	86.82	13.12	6.82
1997	353.97	238.01	89.42	15.79	10.75	269.20	156.86	93.81	11.16	7.37
构成（%）										
1978	100.0	91.8	8.2			100.0	91.4	8.6		
1980	100.0	76.4	23.6			100.0	78.6	21.4		
1981	100.0	69.2	30.8			100.0	69.5	30.5		
1982	100.0	69.5	30.5			100.0	68.5	31.5		
1983	100.0	56.7	41.9		1.4	100.0	55.3	43.3		1.4
1984	100.0	57.5	37.7		4.8	100.0	51.9	43.0		5.1
1985	100.0	58.3	36.9		4.8	100.0	55.1	39.8		5.1
1986	100.0	55.6	40.0		4.4	100.0	57.6	41.6		0.8
1987	100.0	53.3	41.7		5.0	100.0	55.6	42.6		1.8
1988	100.0	52.1	43.1		4.8	100.0	57.7	36.9		5.4
1989	100.0	59.3	38.6		2.1	100.0	55.7	41.5		2.6
1990	100.0	59.9	35.0	3.0	2.1	100.0	54.3	39.8	2.9	3.0
1991	100.0	59.1	34.2	3.4	3.3	100.0	61.6	33.0	2.7	2.7
1992	100.0	60.7	32.8	5.0	1.5	100.0	64.0	31.0	3.5	1.5
1993	100.0	60.4	30.4	7.4	1.8	100.0	55.4	35.8	6.2	2.6
1994	100.0	64.9	28.1	5.5	1.5	100.0	59.5	33.3	4.9	2.3
1995	100.0	66.2	25.2	6.8	1.8	100.0	58.0	33.8	5.8	2.4
1996	100.0	65.3	27.9	4.7	2.1	100.0	60.4	32.2	4.9	2.5
1997	100.0	67.2	25.3	4.5	3.0	100.0	58.3	34.8	4.1	2.7

5—10 国有经济各种分组的固定资产投资

Selected Breakdowns of Investment in Fixed Assets of State－Owned Units

指　　标	1995 年	1996 年	1997 年	1997 年为上年%
投资总额(亿元)	316.90	375.27	353.97	94.3
一、按资金来源分				
国家预算内投资	18.36	11.41	16.11	141.2
国内贷款	77.34	85.46	81.90	95.8
债　　券	0.69	5.23	0.12	2.3
利用外资	23.18	11.73	15.12	128.9
自筹投资	144.00	189.43	178.31	94.1
#股　票	0.05	0.17	0.49	288.2
其他投资	53.33	72.01	62.41	86.7
二、按隶属关系分				
中央项目	141.13	171.71	161.75	94.2
地方项目	175.14	203.07	192.04	94.6
其　　它	0.63	0.49	0.18	36.7
三、按规模分				
大中型	97.77	117.60	94.16	80.1
小　型	219.13	257.67	259.81	100.8
四、按构成分				
建筑安装工程	194.80	230.90	233.57	101.2
设备、工具、器具购置	81.38	91.06	84.87	93.2
其他费用	40.72	53.31	35.53	66.6
五、按建设性质分				
新建	125.46	129.16	125.78	97.4
扩建	107.46	132.65	115.35	87.0
改建	58.83	81.62	80.96	99.2
六、按国民经济主要行业门类分				
#农业	0.83	0.98	2.16	220.4
工业	127.58	137.49	121.03	88.0
#能源工业	61.33	63.54	72.21	113.6
运输邮电业	82.25	114.41	115.96	101.4
新增固定资产(亿元)	202.81	269.99	269.20	99.7
房屋建筑面积(万平方米)				
施工面积	2631.38	2428.61	2273.22	93.6
竣工面积	1337.96	1248.39	1142.72	91.5
#住宅	747.66	708.41	621.07	87.7

5—11 国有经济各行业固定资产投资和新增固定资产(1997年)

Investment in Fixed Assets and Newly Increased Fixed Assets of State—Owned Units by Sector

行业	固定资产投资额			新增固定资产		
	合计	# 基本建设	# 更新改造	合计	# 基本建设	# 更新改造
一、绝对数(亿元)						
全省总计	353.97	238.01	89.42	269.20	156.86	93.81
1.农、林、牧、渔业	2.16	1.89	0.09	0.99	0.79	0.05
2.采掘业	3.72	1.49	2.21	3.98	2.43	1.53
3.制造业	62.09	16.69	45.33	78.59	18.34	60.18
4.电力、煤气及水生产和供应业	55.23	52.48	2.71	37.60	34.72	2.85
5.建筑业	2.37	1.93	0.40	1.93	1.47	0.42
6.地质勘查业、水利管理业	9.75	9.59	0.12	5.39	5.30	0.05
7.交通运输、仓储及邮电通信业	115.96	70.67	36.86	61.44	29.38	27.19
8.批发和零售贸易、餐饮业	11.20	10.96	0.22	8.33	8.10	0.21
9.金融、保险业	5.46	5.44		5.87	5.81	
10.房地产业	16.21	0.42		11.47	0.32	
11.社会服务业	16.95	15.24	0.73	11.50	9.36	0.65
12.卫生、体育和社会福利业	5.04	4.91	0.03	5.78	5.68	0.02
13.教育、文化艺术和广播电影电视业	22.74	22.42	0.26	16.63	16.31	0.27
14.科学研究和综合技术服务业	1.27	1.25	0.02	1.38	1.38	
15.国家机关、政党机关和社会团体	21.79	21.19	0.15	17.52	16.96	0.16
16.其他行业	2.04	1.44	0.29	0.81	0.51	0.25
二、构　成(%)						
全省总计	100.00	100.00	100.00	100.00	100.00	100.00
1.农、林、牧、渔业	0.61	0.79	0.10	0.37	0.50	0.05
2.采掘业	1.05	0.63	2.47	1.48	1.55	1.63
3.制造业	17.54	7.01	50.69	29.19	11.69	64.15
4.电力、煤气及水生产和供应业	15.60	22.05	3.03	13.97	22.13	3.04
5.建筑业	0.67	0.81	0.45	0.72	0.94	0.45
6.地质勘查业、水利管理业	2.75	4.03	0.13	2.00	3.38	0.05
7.交通运输、仓储及邮电通信业	32.76	29.69	41.22	22.82	18.73	28.98
8.批发和零售贸易、餐饮业	3.16	4.60	0.25	3.09	5.16	0.22
9.金融、保险业	1.54	2.29		2.18	3.70	
10.房地产业	4.58	0.18		4.26	0.20	
11.社会服务业	4.79	6.40	0.82	4.27	5.97	0.69
12.卫生、体育和社会福利业	1.42	2.06	0.03	2.15	3.62	0.02
13.教育、文化艺术和广播电影电视业	6.42	9.42	0.29	6.18	10.40	0.29
14.科学研究和综合技术服务业	0.36	0.53	0.02	0.51	0.88	
15.国家机关、政党机关和社会团体	6.16	8.90	0.17	6.51	10.81	0.17
16.其他行业	0.58	0.61	0.32	0.30	0.33	0.27

5—12 国有经济房屋建设指标(1997年)

Indicators of Building Construction of State－Owned Units

	单位	合计	基本建设	更新改造	房地产开发	其他固定资产投资
施工房屋面积	万平方米	2273.22	1770.15	186.01	312.43	4.64
#住宅	万平方米	1096.28	766.97	91.46	236.56	1.29
竣工房屋面积	万平方米	1142.72	892.27	98.10	149.69	2.65
#住宅	万平方米	621.07	459.12	45.05	116.72	0.19
竣工房屋价值	万元	845627	647918	91182	104705	1822
#住宅	万元	385048	276069	34045	74773	161
房屋建筑面积竣工率	%	50.27	50.41	52.74	47.91	57.11
#住宅	%	56.65	59.86	49.26	49.34	14.73
竣工房屋单位面积造价	元/平方米	740.01	726.15	929.48	699.48	687.55
#住宅	元/平方米	619.98	601.30	755.72	640.62	847.37

5—13 国有经济各行业项目个数、项目投产率及固定资产交付使用率

Number of Projects, Rate of Projects Put into Operation and Rate of Fixed Assets

(1997年)

地市名称	施工项目个数(个)	全投项目个数(个)	项目投产率(%)	固定资产交付使用率(%)
全省总计	5575	3249	58.28	76.30
长沙市	492	217	44.11	69.02
株洲市	406	258	63.55	115.57
湘潭市	227	120	52.86	77.26
衡阳市	537	310	57.73	115.42
邵阳市	505	307	60.79	78.36
岳阳市	403	284	70.47	78.76
常德市	550	280	50.91	96.45
张家界市	111	76	68.47	44.32
益阳市	310	210	67.74	65.49
郴州市	545	367	67.34	108.30
永州市	355	246	69.30	82.83
娄底地区	269	130	48.33	102.67
怀化地区	384	183	47.66	81.04
湘西自治州	297	171	57.58	88.78
不分地区	184	90	48.91	42.17

注:施工、全投项目及项目投产率未包括房地产开发统计资料。

5—14 国有经济基本建设投资

Investment in Capital Construction of State—Owned Units

类　　别	1995年	1996年	1997年
一、投资总额(亿元)	209.7	245.10	238.01
1.按资金来源分			
国家预算内投资	17.27	10.92	15.26
国内贷款	48.20	52.62	54.63
债　　券	0.59	5.20	0.06
利用外资	15.56	10.03	12.78
自筹投资	96.72	119.66	112.06
其他投资	31.36	46.67	43.22
2.按隶属关系分			
中央项目	94.05	104.32	101.76
地方项目	115.45	140.48	136.15
其　　它	0.20	0.30	0.10
3.按构成分			
建筑安装工程	147.49	178.65	184.28
设备、工具、器具购置	33.62	24.66	28.83
其他费用	28.59	41.79	24.90
4.按建设性质分			
#新建	101.46	110.07	110.26
扩建	66.01	69.31	69.83
改建	19.42	37.81	32.64
5.按用途分			
农林牧渔业用	1.49	2.55	3.88
工业建筑业用	66.81	68.71	60.66
商业交通及其他产业用	107.67	75.32	74.97
住　　宅	33.73	36.88	33.38
6.按大中小类型分			
#大中型项目	79.74	91.03	82.96
小型项目	128.81	152.90	153.68
7.按国民经济行业主要门类分			
#农业	0.71	0.86	1.89
工业	73.85	73.32	70.66
轻工业	7.25	6.78	5.01
重工业	66.60	66.54	65.65
#能源工业	54.75	56.02	58.79
运输邮电仓储业	53.66	70.68	70.67
二、新增固定资产(亿元)	117.55	163.23	156.86
三、建设项目个数(个)			
施工项目	5304	5178	4118
#大中型项目	52	55	54
全部建成投产项目	3026	2981	2354
#大中型项目	5	6	11
四、房屋建筑面积(万平方米)			
施工面积	1876.10	1822.08	1770.15
#住宅	897.79	925.77	766.97
竣工面积	1023.02	966.33	892.27
#住宅	541.93	543.13	459.12

5—15 国有经济基本建设项目计划总投资完成情况

Situation Completed of Investment in Capital Construction of Projects of State-Owned Units

指　　标	1995年	1996年	1997年
基本建设项目			
计划总投资(亿元)	726.28	874.96	991.16
自开始建设至本年底累计完成投资(亿元)	462.13	565.59	589.61
#本年完成投资	209.70	245.10	238.01
#本年新开工项目投资	49.52	65.74	48.97
累计新增固定资产	195.32	272.49	249.89
未完工程投资	247.28	249.28	285.52
全部建成尚需投资(亿元)	372.40	392.05	464.69
未完工程占用率(%)	117.9	101.7	120.0
建设周期(年)	3.42	3.54	4.16
基本建设大中型项目			
计划总投资(亿元)	430.67	418.44	549.41
自开始建设至本年底累计完成投资(亿元)	229.77	286.49	289.53
#本年完成投资	80.70	91.03	90.63
#本年新开工项目投资	1.66	7.76	2.16
累计新增固定资产	72.60	123.68	108.73
未完工程投资	144.19	129.15	151.98
全部建成尚需投资(亿元)	200.90	178.73	279.97
未完工程占用率(%)	178.7	141.9	167.7
建设周期(年)	4.85	4.60	6.06

5—16 国有经济重点行业固定资产投资

Investment in Fixed Assets in Key Sector of State-Owned Units

年　份	农　业	轻工业	重工业	#能源工业	运输邮电仓储业
投资额(亿元)					
1995	0.83	19.35	108.23	61.33	482.25
1996	0.98	17.10	120.39	63.54	114.41
1997	2.16	16.74	104.29	72.21	115.96
构成(%)					
1995	0.3	6.1	34.2	19.4	26.0
1996	0.3	4.6	32.1	16.9	30.5
1997	0.6	4.7	29.5	20.4	32.7
基建投资额(亿元)					
1995	0.71	7.25	66.60	54.75	53.66
1996	0.86	6.78	66.54	56.02	70.68
1997	1.89	5.01	65.65	58.79	70.67
构成(%)					
1995	0.3	3.5	31.8	26.1	25.6
1996	0.4	2.8	27.1	22.9	28.8
1997	0.8	2.1	27.6	24.7	29.7

5—17 国有经济按用途分的更新改造投资

Technical Updating and Transformation Investment by Purpose of State－Owned Units

项　　目	更改投资(万元)		构　　成(%)	
	1996年	1997年	1996年	1997年
总　　计	1046729	894232	100.0	100.0
1.增产	407962	290698	40.0	32.5
2.节约能源	15158	20756	1.4	2.3
3.其他节约	5300	3539	0.5	0.4
4.增加品种	110751	90201	10.6	10.1
5.提高产品质量	68562	79565	6.6	8.9
6.三废治理	13621	11314	1.3	1.3
7.其他	425375	398159	40.6	44.5
在总计中:#住宅	22131	25917	2.1	2.9

5—18 新增生产能力(1997年)

Newly Increased Production Capacity in 1997

生产能力(或效益)名称	计量单位	全省总计	国有经济	基本建设	国有经济	更新改造	国有经济
原煤开采	万吨/年	39.40	39.40	30.00	30.00	9.40	9.40
洗　煤	万吨/年	30.00	30.00			30.00	30.00
焦　炭	万吨/年	10.00	10.00			10.00	10.00
铁矿石原矿开采	万吨/年	15.50	15.50			15.50	15.50
炼　钢	万吨/年	110.00	110.00			110.00	110.00
转炉钢	万吨/年	110.00	110.00			110.00	110.00
连　铸	万吨/年	65.00	65.00			65.00	65.00
铁合金	吨/年	4800	3000			4800	3000
钢　材	万吨/年	33.50	33.50			33.50	33.50
按加工工艺划分的钢材							
热轧钢材	万吨/年	33.50	33.50			33.50	33.50
按品种分							
无缝钢管	万吨/年	16.50	16.50			16.50	16.50
金属丝及其制品	吨/年	1100					
铅锌选矿:①处理原矿	万吨/年	7.30	7.30			7.30	7.30
铅冶炼	吨/年	15000	15000			15000	15000
其中:电解铅	吨/年	15000	15000			15000	15000
锡冶炼	吨/年	500	500			500	500
铝加工	吨/年	3000					
发电机组容量	万千瓦	50.68	44.18	48.48	42.48	1.70	1.70
水力发电	万千瓦	19.48	12.98	17.28	11.28	1.70	1.70
火力发电	万千瓦	31.20	31.20	31.20	31.20		

注:本表中不含房地产开发投资、农村集体投资及城乡个体投资新增能力资料。

5—18 续表1

生产能力(或效益)名称	计量单位	全省总计	国有经济	基本建设	国有经济	更新改造	国有经济
输电线路长度(11万伏及以上)	公里	1041.47	1041.47	1027.10	1027.10	14.37	14.37
变电设备能力(11万伏及以上)	万千伏安	250.80	250.80	132.15	132.15	118.65	118.65
水　泥	万吨/年	203.20	183.40	37.00	37.00	157.40	146.40
卫生陶瓷	万件/年	10.00				10.00	
胶合板	万立方米/年	1.85	1.85			1.85	1.85
纤维板	万立方米/年	6.00	3.00			6.00	3.00
硫　酸	吨/年	80258	80258			80258	80258
纯　碱	吨/年	4000	4000			4000	4000
电　石	吨/年	2000					
合成氨	吨/年	57000	57000			57000	57000
农用氮、磷、钾化学肥料	吨/年	35738	35738			35738	35738
氮　肥	吨/年	31116	31116			31116	31116
其中:农用尿素	吨/年	9200	9200			9200	9200
农用碳酸氢铵	吨/年	9916	9916			9916	9916
磷　肥	吨/年	4122	4122			4122	4122
其中:普通过磷酸钙	吨/年	2502	2502			2502	2502
钾　肥	吨/年	500	500			500	500
化学农药	吨/年	38920	7920	2000	2000	36920	5920
丙　烯	吨/年	44000	44000			44000	44000
冰醋酸	吨/年	5000	5000			5000	5000
塑料树脂及共聚物	吨/年	10000	5000			10000	5000
合成纤维单体	吨/年	10000	10000			10000	10000
合成纤维聚合物	吨/年	5000	5000			5000	5000
化学原料药	吨/年	5.00	5.00			5.00	5.00
化学药制剂	吨/年	2.60	2.60			2.60	2.60
中成药	吨/年	1231	591			1231	591
拖拉机械制造	台/年	5000	5000			5000	5000
大中型拖拉机制造	台/年	5000	5000			5000	5000
民用船舶制造	艘/年	3.00	3.00			3.00	3.00
	万综合吨/年	0.09	0.09			0.09	0.09
彩色显像管	万只/年	136				136	
电子计算机外部设备	台/年	300000	300000			300000	300000
化学纤维	吨/年	17000	16000	13000	13000	3000	3000
其中:合成纤维	吨/年	13000	13000	13000	13000		
棉纺锭	万锭	1.40	1.40			1.40	1.40
食用植物油	日处理原料:吨	217.00	217.00	40.00	40.00	177.00	177.00
	日精炼油:吨	58.00	58.00	10.00	10.00	48.00	48.00

5—18 续表 2

生产能力(或效益)名称	计量单位	全省总计	国有经济	基本建设	国有经济	更新改造	国有经济
糖　果	吨/年	30.00					
酒	吨/年	66210	16060			46210	16060
啤　酒	吨/年	65000	15000			45000	15000
白　酒	吨/年	1060	1060			1060	1060
其他酒	吨/年	150				150	
卷　烟	万箱/年	4.70	4.70			4.70	4.70
机制纸浆	万吨/年	0.46	0.46			0.46	0.46
机制纸及纸板	万吨/年	0.96	0.46			0.46	0.46
汽、挂车购置	辆	1006	859	190	189	461	461
载货汽车购置	辆	52.0	43	4	4	36	36
载客汽车购置	辆	832	697	81	81	417	417
小汽车购置	辆	111	108	103	102	4	4
其它汽车购置	辆	11	11	2	2	4	4
增建铁路第二线交付运营里程	公里	74.70	74.70	74.70	74.70		
电气化铁路主线正线交付运营里程	公里	318	318	318	318		
新建公路	公里	213.47	213.47	174.32	174.32	15.45	15.45
改建公路	公里	1386.13	1386.13	627.43	627.43	42.66	42.66
其中:一级公路	公里	25.00	25.00	10.80	10.80		
新建独立公路桥梁	延长米	2397.00	2397.00	2397.00	2397.00		
	座	9.00	9.00	9.00	9.00		
船舶购置	艘	6.00	6.00				
	载重量:吨位	220.00	220.00				
	拖轮功率:千瓦	65.60	65.60				
新(扩)建客、货运站	个	7.00	6.00	7.00	6.00		
	平方米	22308	17308	22308	17308		
长途电缆	延长公里	1246	1246			1246	1246
新建微波电路	公里	8	8			8	8
市内电话自动交换机	门	344161	329161	50132	50132	294029	279029
长途自动电话交换设备	路端	41010	41010			41010	41010
耕地面积	万亩	0.30	0.30	0.30	0.30		
造林面积	万亩	1.00	1.00	1.00	1.00		
水库容量(总库容)	亿立方米	1.14	1.14	1.14	1.14		
有效灌溉面积	万亩	13.93	13.93	12.33	12.33		
除涝面积	万亩	19.70	19.70	19.60	19.60		
排灌装机	万千瓦	8.21	8.21	8.00	8.00	0.21	0.21
商业石油库	万立方米	0.38	0.38	0.38	0.38		
粮食仓库	万公斤	8912	7712	5182	3982	2000	2000
	平方米	42747	41347	29502	28102	2500	2500

生产能力(或效益)名称	计量单位	全省总计	国有经济	基本建设	国有经济	更新改造	国有经济
商业饮食服务网点	处	253	186	191	182	3	3
	平方米	707600	461837	473858	453128	7225	7225
高等院校:学生席位	个	6358	6358	6358	6358		
建筑面积	平方米	40444	40444	40444	40444		
中等学校:学生席位	个	142677	141077	140757	139477		
建筑面积	平方米	544975	534709	536295	530095		
小学校:学生席位	个	91038	91038	91038	91038		
建筑面积	平方米	273706	273706	273706	273706		
其他学校:学生席位	个	5101	5101	5101	5101		
建筑面积	平方米	51206	51206	51206	51206		
公共图书馆:藏书量	万册(件)	53	53.20	53.20	53.20		
阅览室座席	个	80	80	80	80		
建筑面积	平方米	2400	2400	2400	2400		
影剧院:座席	个	1667	1667	1667	1667		
	平方米	10797	10797	10797	10797		
文化馆	平方米	1000	1000	1000	1000		
医院病床	张	3254	2987	2987	2987		
宾馆、旅馆、招待所客房数	间	2629	2156	2318	2014	142	142
宾馆、旅馆、招待所客户数	平方米	111294	91331	98321	85481	5850	5850
办公用房	平方米	1238239	1134525	1114697	1094005	37596	37596
厂　房	平方米	620110	418032	106613	91634	474618	326398
仓　库	平方米	62912	51296	58332	50296	1000	1000
商业用房	平方米	582329	359267	368862	353012	4505	4505
科学研究实验用房	平方米	80794	77431	77684	75521	1910	1910
城市自来水供水能力	万吨/日	69.71	69.71	67.51	67.51	2.20	2.20
城市自来水管道长度	公里	35.60	35.60	32.00	32.00	2.00	2.00
城市液化石油气储气能力	吨	503	503	500	500	3	3
城市公共交通车辆购置	辆	42	42			42	42
城市道路扩建长度	公里	43.50	43.00	20.50	20.00		
城市道路扩建面积	万平方米	40.87	40.57	29.27	28.97		
城市排水管道铺设长度	公里	0.54	0.54	0.54	0.54		
城市污水处理能力	万吨/日	4.80	4.80			4.80	4.80
城市永久性桥梁	座	1.00	1.00	1.00	1.00		
城市防洪堤长度	公里	174.08	174.08	170.08	170.08		
煤　炭	吨/年	46000	46000			46000	46000
电　力	万千瓦小时/年	60	60			60	60

5—19 基本建设大中型、更新改造限额以上及重点项目基本情况(1997年)

Basic Statistics on Investment in Capital Construction of Large and Medium Projects, and Technical Uppdating and Transformation in Above—norm

项目名称	开工时间(年·月)	投产时间(年·月)	计划总投资(万元)	累计完成投资(万元)	本年完成投资(万元)	新增能力或效益
一、基本建设大中型项目						
湖南医科大学附属第三医院门诊楼、住院楼	1989.11	1997.02	10573	10883	21	医院病床600张
长沙市四水厂扩建工程	1992.10	1997.02	12000	18542	1814	城市自来水供水能力20万吨/日
☆湖南省广播电视中心	1994.11		29000	28139	13139	
湘潭大学校舍建设	1975.01		8000	7523	280	
湘潭市自来水公司一水厂扩建工程	1994.12	1997.12	2350	2350	157	城市自来水供水能力20万吨/日
湘潭市湘江三大桥			20373	259	259	
☆湖南金迪化纤公司扩建聚酯工程	1995.06		108742	41972	33446	
☆湘潭发电厂B厂火力发电	1996.07		330676	200400	152433	
湘潭师范学院校舍建设	1985.05		3350	8057	538	
湘潭县邮电局邮电综合楼	1997.01		2138	400	400	
湖南江雁机械厂增压器工程	1993.11	1997.06	4520	4520		
衡南县近尾洲水电站	1994.10		46300	19100	8470	
湖南省白沙矿务局大岭矿井	1992.12		6830	14265	4980	
隆回县六都寨水库灌区工程	1991.10		19790	14520	4202	
邵阳城步县白云水电站	1991.01		33280	22063	4394	
邵阳市大圳灌区工程	1965.10		12300	10077		
☆岳阳巴陵石化公司帘子布工程	1994.12	1997.12	138910	131200	6850	化学纤维13000吨/年
岳阳巴陵石油化工公司原油加工工程	1995.12		70939	63100	48810	
岳阳巴陵石油化工公司烧碱系列工程	1996.06		132950	30930	23000	
岳阳市铁山灌区工程	1977.11		26276	36407	1513	
☆岳阳城陵矶粮食专用码头	1995.01		17021	11050	6327	
☆岳阳华能电厂二期扩建工程			455000	8391	110	
☆岳阳洞庭大桥	1996.12		52027	19139	15139	
常德市邮电局邮电枢纽中心基建工程			9970	2213	2000	
常德市沅江公铁两用桥(公路桥部分)	1996.02		20385	7366	3066	
常德市恒安纸业有限公司厂房建设	1997.03		24943	6344	6344	
常德市石龟山大桥	1994.11		6479	6510	1087	
澧县渔洲水电站	1991.11		19600	18514	1956	发电机组容量0.64万千瓦
湖南嘉丰建材公司30万吨特种水泥一期工程	1996.05		4802	1550		
☆桃源县凌津滩水电站	1994.11		324000	136500	82500	
桃源县沅水大桥	1995.10		5000	4856	2872	
☆湖南石门电厂一期工程	1992.05	1997.12	237660	267500	3	发电机组容量30万千瓦
张家界市渔潭水电站	1991.01		41708	33662	20860	发电机组容量6万千瓦
☆江垭水利枢纽工程	1992.08		246000	133916	38079	
桑植县贺龙水库电站工程	1992.02	1997.12	23186	23244	11499	发电机组容量2.55万千瓦
湖南无纺布厂聚脂油毡基胎及脱险搬迁工程	1993.08		15433	17660	240	

5—19 续表1

项目名称	开工时间(年·月)	投产时间(年·月)	计划总投资(万元)	累计完成投资(万元)	本年完成投资(万元)	新增能力或效益
☆益阳电厂			358842	19817	15914	
☆益阳资江二桥	1992.10		18342	17636	1136	新建公路2公里
汝城县满天星水电站	1992.02	1997.12	15222	14770	3852	发电机组容量3万千瓦
资兴矿务局黄牛岭矿等扩建工程	1983.07	1997.05	19874	24388	844	原煤开采30万吨/年
冷水滩市宋家洲潇湘水电站	1993.10		45200	33913	3725	
湖南华达机械总厂整体脱险搬迁二期工程	1985.12		11176	9049	458	
怀化市二水厂建设工程	1993.07		10343	10046	1945	城市自来水供水能力10万吨/日
☆五强溪水电站	1986.09		39636	34428	34428	
沅陵县高滩水电站	1992.09		56701	55745	9884	
辰溪县火电厂2X25MW火力发电机组扩建工程	1993.04		10908	11011	1909	
☆洞庭湖区二期治理工程	1996.10		220139	60268	33059	
☆襄石复线湖南段	1994.11		37519	17200	8000	
☆武广铁路电气化湖南段	1993.08		791107	43637	18000	
五强溪220KV送出工程	1993.12	1997.12	96053	96053	30853	输电线路长度(11万伏及以上)452公里
石门电厂220KV送出工程	1993.12	1997.12	70786	70786	26786	输电线路长度(11万伏及以上)269公里
☆浙赣复线湖南段	1983.07		201754	203016	24049	
☆湘黔线部分复线及电气化湖南段	1980.01		339026	416838	60000	增建铁路第二线交付运营里程74.7公里
☆湘江航运建设二期工程	1995.12		189524	83000	35200	
☆石长铁路	1993.08		330965	288509	79000	
湖南省邮电管理局呼和—北海光缆(湖南段)	1996.11		20178	7122	5550	
☆凌津滩水电站220KV送出工程	1997.01		30771	4992	4992	输电线路长度(11万伏及以上)23.5公里
☆湘潭电厂B厂送出工程	1997.01		57554	9906	9906	输电线路长度(11万伏及以上)38.6公里
二、更新改造限额以上项目						
湖南计算机股份有限公司金融终端开发	1995.06	1997.12	8609	8609	2039	电子计算机外部设备30万台/年
湖南制药厂制剂大楼	1993.09		8027	2000	165	
乐金曙光电子有限公司彩管一期工程	1996.08	1997.08	56590	56590	49892	彩色显像管136万只/年
湖南长发发动机有限公司CF4G15技改工程	1991.12		4167	3174	45	
湖南省浦沅集团有限公司“双加”工程	1995.12		8143	5739	1752	
株洲硬质合金厂硬质合金老系统改造	1994.06	1997.12	17950	18138	2785	
中国南方航空动力机械公司发动机生产线	1995.12		5643	5066	543	
中国南方航空动力机械公司双加工程1303K厂房	1996.03	1997.12	19883	19883	11787	厂房8750平方米
株洲南方热电有限公司热电厂工程	1997.10		18990	7600	7600	
株洲冶炼厂铅烟气综合治理			54602	3600	100	
湖南省湘江氮肥厂“四六”合成氨技改	1997.07		11724	6218	6218	
株洲湘瑞塑料建材有限公司塑料门窗工程	1995.12		11467	9096	2530	
湘潭市邮电局图像通信工程	1996.04		8165	3296	2208	
☆湘潭钢铁公司1号转炉工程	1995.01	1997.12	46973	44404	12669	炼钢100万吨/年
☆湘潭钢铁公司1号3号连铸机	1995.01		19832	19376	1582	连铸50万吨/年

5—19 续表 2

项目名称	开工时间(年·月)	投产时间(年·月)	计划总投资(万元)	累计完成投资(万元)	本年完成投资(万元)	新增能力或效益
南方通用电气集团公司 154T 国产化	1993.11		4400	2643	144	
南方通用电气集团公司双加工程	1996.01		6600	3643	1493	
湘潭电化集团公司 3000 吨/年碱性电解二氧化硫	1997.05		5019	2652	2652	
韶峰水泥集团公司一号窑技改工程	1994.12	1997.12	72189	68648	6490	水泥 70 万吨/年
衡阳有色冶金机械总厂采冶车间改造	1990.12		3500	3534	42	
☆衡阳钢管有限公司电站用高压锅	1992.11	1997.09	80759	92482	16654	钢材 16.5 万吨/年
南岳油泵嘴有限公司合营生产喷油泵技改	1992.12		17000	11389	989	
衡阳现代电器设备集团发展大型变压器	1992.06	1997.12	3737	3737	647	厂房 2818 平方米
水口山矿务局康家湾技术改造	1986.01		6535	6841	657	
邵阳市自来水公司西水东调工程	1995.06		8540	5960	210	
岳阳市纸业集团有限公司 5.1 万吨系列胶印书刊纸技改	1995.12		19989	20563	10445	
常德华特制罐有限公司特型三片罐生产线	1995.12		5800	3850	50	
湖南省桃源县水泥集团 400t/d 熟料回转窑生产线	1995.11	1997.07	8856	8756	3356	水泥 15 万吨/年
石门县水泥一厂扩改工程	1994.06	1997.12	9347	9347	2230	水泥 21 万吨/年
湖南特种水泥厂三线扩建工程	1997.06		7744	5500	5500	
沅江纸厂红麻浆系统工程	1993.07		5600	4850	584	
郴州化工集团公司磷铵装置改造	1995.04	1997.06	6000	6272	1937	硫酸 4 万吨/年
郴州金亚实业有限公司山河电站	1996.10		5700	1520	1064	
湖南华达机械总厂汽车空调压缩机技术改造	1988.05		13708	9305	1209	
娄底彩色水泥厂15万吨特种水泥生产线	1995.01		6850	5946	1250	
冷水江市钢铁总厂炼钢工程	1992.11		10500	11285	1020	炼钢 10 万吨/年
冷水江市钢铁总厂烧结改造	1994.04		5200	2927		
冷水江市耐火材料总厂高级硅砖机技术改造	1995.01		7745	6399	1078	
怀化华峰电子集团公司三线调整搬迁	1987.05		5500	4784	36	
湖南莱孚铝业有限公司电解铝	1995.07		7000	1500	1500	
湖南林都中密度纤维板公司技改工程	1997.02	1997.12	5700	5400	5400	纤维板 3 万立方米/年
湖南湘维有限公司聚乙烯醇生产线扩建	1995.11	1997.12	14961	15011	7711	合成纤维聚合物 5000 吨/年
湘西湘泉酒总厂湘泉四期扩建	1993.06	1997.12	13851	14414	3683	酒 1000 吨年
三、省其他重点项目						
☆湖南省人民医院门诊病房楼	1993.05		10795	9880	2750	
☆湖南国际金融大厦有限公司	1993.10		46426	27992	8053	
☆长沙—益阳一级汽车专用公路	1995.12		114200	88181	45566	
☆长沙市环线工程	1994.12		147600	168436	27193	
☆湘耒高速公路	1996.12		414272	60105	45048	
☆益阳—常德高速公路	1996.12		118000	39537	32167	
☆湖南省职工教育培训中心	1996.01		10000	5155	3335	
☆长沙第二长途电信大楼	1994.12		55648	40098	15019	

注：带“☆”的为省列重点建设项目。

5—20　城镇集体各行业项目个数、投资额及新增固定资产（1997年）

Number of Projects, Investment and Newly Increased Fixed Assets of Urban Collective－Owned Units by Sector

指标名称	施工项目个数（个）	全投项目个数（个）	固定资产投资（万元）	新增固定资产（万元）
全省总计	452	301	117850	104728
一、农林牧渔业	9	1	1443	400
二、采掘业	4	3	296	290
三、制造业	111	77	21863	22044
食品加工业	2	2	127	374
食品制造业	2	2	174	174
纺织业	5	4	1200	1140
服装及其他纤维制品制造业	3	1	428	637
木材加工及竹、藤、棕、草制品业	2		269	
家具制造业	1	1	15	130
造纸及纸制品业	5	4	747	685
印刷业、记录媒介复制业	2	1	265	205
石油加工及炼焦业				
化学原料及化学制品制造业	15	12	3452	2545
医药制造业	2	1	298	186
橡胶制品业	1	1	70	70
塑料制品业	2	1	59	54
非金属矿物制品业	13	11	2002	2930
黑色金属冶炼及压延加工业	3	2	820	880
有色金属冶炼业及压延加工业	2	2	305	505
金属制品业	7	4	1107	1185
普通机械制造业	7	4	785	852
专用设备制造业	4	2	863	443
交通运输设备制造业	6	4	2029	1739
电气机械及器材制造业	9	6	1333	1346
电子及通信设备制造业	3		649	
四、电力、煤气及水的生产和供应业	3	1	705	475
#电力、蒸汽、热水的生产和供应业	1	1	275	275
煤气生产和供应业				
五、建筑业	36	29	3992	4588
六、地质勘查业、水利管理业	5	2	660	366
七、交通运输、仓储及邮电通信业	21	11	4459	3742
八、批发和零售贸易、餐饮业	98	66	23941	18213
九、金融、保险业	103	73	18260	18666
十、房地产业			33267	27786
十一、社会服务业	10	8	2622	2805
十二、卫生、体育和社会福利业	17	10	1928	1690
十三、教育、文化艺术及广播电影电视业	7	4	689	612
十四、科学研究和综合技术服务业	2	2	113	113
十五、国家机关、政党机关和社会团体	14	7	2327	1561
十六、其他行业	12	7	1285	1377

注：施工、全投项目个数中未含房地产开发项目。

5—21 房地产开发情况(1997 年)

Real Estate Development

	开发公司个数(个)	#国有经济	#集体经济	#外商投资经济	#港澳台投资经济	年平均职工人数(人)
全省总计	569	277	69	87	13	14344
长沙市	146	60	18	35	4	3954
株洲市	61	22	6	6	1	1431
湘潭市	37	20	5	3	3	1008
衡阳市	63	27	7	18	2	1820
邵阳市	49	22	12	4		1007
岳阳市	29	13	1	6		996
常德市	52	26	9	5	1	1138
张家界市	2	1	1			20
益阳市	19	10	3	2		447
郴州市	35	18	4	4	2	618
永州市	28	20		1		663
娄底地区	11	7	1	1		359
怀化地区	27	23	2			627
湘西自治州	10	8		2		256

	经营总收入(万元)	土地转让收入	商品房屋销售收入	房屋出租收入	其他收入	本年缴纳税费	本年实现利润
全省总计	192080	20212	157012	2839	12017	10784	—17733
长沙市	62824	6305	52028	553	3938	4380	—7896
株洲市	16355	812	13938	36	1569	877	—2742
湘潭市	14055	414	11842	78	1721	756	—1656
衡阳市	27009	1751	24603	160	495	1179	—1561
邵阳市	8160	814	6970	200	176	419	—817
岳阳市	13197	2678	8947	566	1006	845	277
常德市	15459	1860	13330	108	161	778	—1894
张家界市	558		345	30	183	27	—28
益阳市	3785		3767	16	2	128	—202
郴州市	12267	144	10485	229	1409	600	—1051
永州市	7291	2209	4754		328	270	257
娄底地区	2681	343	2007		331	203	217
怀化地区	6386	2706	2516	681	483	269	—891
湘西自治州	2053	176	1480	182	215	53	254

5—22 房地产开发统计主要指标(1997年)

Main Statistics Indicators of Real Estate Devolopment

金额单位:万元

指标名称	合计	按经济类型分			按隶属关系分		
		国有	集体	其他	中央	地方	其他
计划总投资	1617572	640857	121906	854809	9126	1275632	332814
实际需要的总投资	1711637	688237	126855	896545	13017	1354626	343994
累计完成投资	943170	361648	68647	512875	11267	752345	179558
累计新增固定资产	426586	180932	40723	204931	1943	367803	56840
本年底未完工程累计投资	491650	174831	26077	290742	9224	375590	106836
本年计划投资	438911	200695	41581	196635	4467	357105	77339
本年完成投资	340151	157871	33267	149013	3767	287493	48891
1.按构成分:							
①建筑工程	254461	121374	26821	106266	2691	218353	33417
②安装工程	17571	5413	1053	11105	278	13976	3317
③设备、工具器具购置	10160	4331	670	5159	35	9003	1122
2.按工程用途分:							
①住　宅	191633	98852	21980	70801	2257	165018	24358
②办公楼	35863	10640	2230	22993	838	30399	4626
③商业营业用房	50543	18185	3703	28655	315	41575	8653
④其　他	62112	30194	5354	26564	357	50501	11254
房地产开发企业本年资金来源	465848	242311	37317	186220	4359	398962	62527
国内贷款	105872	58296	12332	35244	1012	93647	11213
债券	20	20				20	
自筹资金	118836	60926	10382	47528	172	100161	18503
本年土地开发投资	36187	16434	2744	17009	220	26343	9624
本年新增固定资产	250449	111587	27786	111076	1643	218231	30575
本年施工房屋面积(平方米)	7045604	3124266	639022	3282316	70719	5881281	1093406
#:住宅	4994989	2365643	504348	2124998	35327	4205522	754140
本年竣工房屋面积(平方米)	2937089	1496932	337530	1102627	31937	2590883	314269
#:住宅	2283531	1167158	275678	840695	20284	2012082	251165
本年竣工房屋价值	232995	104705	27016	101274	1643	201855	29497
#:住宅	166045	74773	19697	71575	988	141673	23384
土地开发面积(公顷)	147.62	78.85	10.69	58.08	0.29	132.35	14.97
商品房销售额	153274	76989	12393	63892	786	134394	18094
商品房销售建筑面积(平方米)	1478985	824786	126428	527771	10808	1320944	147233

5—23 商品房屋销售情况(1997 年)

Sales of Commerocal Houses

	实际销售商品房屋面积(平方米)	#住宅	个人购买商品房住宅(平方米)	商品房屋销售额(万元)	#住宅
全省总计	1478985	1314883	1073386	153274	122054
长沙市	278262	248290	199680	51558	41441
株洲市	128552	123464	72983	12385	11556
湘潭市	147595	129985	116792	12018	9197
衡阳市	240559	212652	185396	23011	17356
邵阳市	85622	62845	41443	6888	4278
岳阳市	130852	129499	124299	8897	8701
常德市	155975	145157	130695	13804	11795
张家界市	6100	6100	6100	345	345
益阳市	44333	39183	36051	3763	2900
郴州市	90472	67613	35603	9922	5733
永州市	86139	81739	60639	4753	4159
娄底地区	26079	20943	20943	1967	1489
怀化地区	38618	32586	27935	2483	2052
湘西自治州	19827	14827	14827	1480	1052

5—24 房地产开发建设房屋建筑面积和造价(1997 年)

Floor Space of Building and Cost of Renl Estate Development

	施工房屋面积(平方米)	竣工房屋面积(平方米)	房屋建筑面积竣工率(%)	竣工房屋价值(万元)	竣工房屋造价(元/平方米)
全省总计	7045604	2937089	41.69	232995	793.29
长沙市	2572961	852796	33.14	98096	1150.29
株洲市	757512	265653	35.07	19856	747.44
湘潭市	579015	248451	42.91	13810	555.84
衡阳市	993179	347721	35.01	23165	666.20
邵阳市	461595	194159	42.06	12647	651.37
岳阳市	247722	241374	97.44	14217	589.00
常德市	428034	205579	48.03	14157	688.64
张家界市	9090	6100	67.11	345	565.57
益阳市	115142	61078	53.05	3638	595.63
郴州市	283988	136597	48.10	8859	648.55
永州市	270690	189226	69.91	10464	552.99
娄底地区	124230	62035	49.94	4889	788.10
怀化地区	152322	80716	52.99	4844	600.13
湘西自治州	50124	45604	90.98	4008	878.87

5—25 城镇集体单位固定资产投资和房屋建筑面积(1997年)

Investment in Fixed Assets and Floor Space of Buildingsof Urban Collective—Owned Units

	本年完成投资(万元)				房屋建筑面积(万平方米)			
	合计	建筑安装工程	设备工具器具购置	其他费用	施工面积	#住宅	竣工面积	#住宅
全省总计	117850	90582	14559	12709	188.29	101.89	108.64	62.67
长沙市	30978	25701	2904	2373	36.18	18.51	20.54	12.60
株洲市	8148	5735	790	1623	9.88	5.51	8.40	4.81
湘潭市	11080	8238	1814	1028	17.59	9.02	11.63	5.95
衡阳市	9871	7003	2392	476	27.69	17.36	9.39	6.37
邵阳市	9703	7573	1200	930	17.12	10.41	8.36	4.41
岳阳市	6985	4651	1392	942	7.79	3.05	5.95	2.41
常德市	13793	10826	1696	1271	21.51	12.77	13.25	8.15
张家界市	1525	803	1	721	1.31	0.11	0.39	
益阳市	5933	3957	677	1299	8.24	4.92	5.76	4.12
郴州市	8846	7258	625	963	16.19	8.80	10.82	6.44
永州市	4606	3904	284	418	9.75	4.33	6.88	3.54
娄底地区	1353	1171		182	5.14	1.65	1.11	0.45
怀化地区	2721	2113	407	201	5.02	3.51	2.75	1.91
湘西自治州	2308	1649	377	282	4.89	1.94	3.41	1.51

5—26 城镇和工矿区私人建房情况(1997年)

Building Construction by Individuals in Cities and Towns and in Industrial and Mining Areas

	城镇、工矿区个数(个)	本年竣工房屋建筑面积(平方米)		本年竣工房屋价值(万元)		建房户数(户)
		合计	其中:住宅	合计	其中:住宅	
全省总计	1014	487.69	370.77	266034	205850	20955
长沙市	53	68.59	51.17	36002	22713	3284
株洲市	57	28.32	28.12	9958	9846	996
湘潭市	44	22.24	18.59	9018	7745	1421
衡阳市	106	30.72	28.53	11641	10605	2168
邵阳市	80	41.86	33.71	16363	12973	1532
岳阳市	88	34.52	33.55	10716	9497	1745
常德市	91	40.36	39.66	17813	17293	2102
张家界市	35	10.82	9.32	4256	3921	805
益阳市	62	18.83	12.72	7753	5388	921
郴州市	66	31.40	9.91	3487	3617	618
永州市	122	69.87	59.83	19918	17911	3339
娄底地区	72	12.90	11.52	4640	4198	486
怀化地区	85	20.22	10.23	7990	4495	803
湘西自治州	53	15.79	13.78	5680	4554	735

5—27 农村全社会固定资产投资

Total Investment in Fixed Assets in Rural Areas

项　目	1995年	1996年	1997年
一、固定资产投资总额(亿元)	130.85	227.40	243.42
1.按经济类型分：国　有	0.83	0.98	2.16
集　体	23.62	63.86	72.69
个　人	106.40	162.56	168.57
2.按行业分：农林牧渔业	91.32	28.58	28.81
工　业	15.68	37.99	34.29
建筑业	1.43	4.47	5.4
水利管理业	0.25	0.61	
运输邮电业	14.29	11.36	8.07
文教卫生、社会福利	2.27	7.68	7.87
二、房屋建筑竣工面积总计(万平方米)	4352.98	8623.96	6792.42
国　有	9.90	10.47	9.67
集　体	260.37	646.86	745.05
个　人	4082.71	7966.63	6037.70
总计中：住宅	3900.18	7679.82	5873.39
国　有	5.41	5.21	5.75
集　体	58.98	147.14	198.09
个　人	3835.79	7527.47	5669.55

5—28 国有农林牧渔业固定资产投资及新增固定资产

Investment in Fixed Assets and Newly Inereased Fixed Assets of State—Owned Units of Farming, Forest, Animal Husbandry, Fishery

单位:万元

行　业	固定资产投资总额		新增固定资产	
	1996年	1997年	1996年	1997年
总　计	9769	21639	8934	9923
1.农　业	3283	5981	1637	4764
2.林　业	2310	1461	2446	1332
3.畜牧业	1027	2404	1123	935
4.渔　业	324	205	116	220
5.农林牧渔服务业	2825	11588	3612	2672

5—29 国有农林牧渔业基本建设、更新改造投资及新增固定资产

Investment in Capital Construction, Tehnical Updating and Transformation and Newly Increased Fixed Assets of State-Owned Units of Farming, Forest, Animal Husbandry, Fishery

单位:万元

行业	固定资产投资总额		新增固定资产	
	1996年	1997年	1996年	1997年
一、基本建设	8600	18877	7537	7893
1.农业	2781	3619	1198	3054
2.林业	2074	1461	1988	1332
3.畜牧业	1027	2404	1123	935
4.渔业	255	5	98	100
5.农林牧渔服务业	2463	11388	3130	2472
二、更新改造	62	852	182	500
1.农业		852		500
2.林业				
3.畜牧业				
4.渔业				
5.农林牧渔服务业	62		182	

5—30 国有农林牧渔业投资额施工投产项目和固定资产交付使用率(1997年)

Investment, Projects Put into Operation and Rate of Fixed Assets Turned over to Uses of State-Owned Units of Farming, Forest, Animal Husbandry, Fishery

行业	投资额合计(万元)	#住宅	施工项目个数	全部建成投产项目个数	项目投产率(%)	固定资产交付使用率(%)
总计	21639	3678	91	58	63.74	45.86
1.农业	5981	946	29	23	79.31	79.65
2.林业	1461	926	18	9	50.00	91.17
3.畜牧业	2404	123	9	6	66.67	38.89
4.渔业	205		2			107.32
5.农林牧渔服务业	11588	1683	33	20	60.61	23.06

5—31 国有工业施工、投产项目及项目投产率(1997年)

Projects Under Construction, Put Into Operation and Rate of Projects Put Into Operation of State－Owned Industrial Enterprises

指标名称	施工项目个数(个)	全投项目个数(个)	项目投产率 (%)
总计	1238	649	52.42
采掘业	138	64	46.38
煤炭采选业	74	29	39.19
石油和天然气开采业			
黑色金属矿采选业	6	6	100.00
有色金属矿采选业	49	24	48.98
非金属矿采选业	8	4	50.00
其他矿采选业			
木材及竹材采运业	1	1	100.00
制造业	777	405	52.12
食品加工业	35	26	74.29
食品制造业	11	6	54.55
饮料制造业	20	13	65.00
烟草加工业	65	22	33.85
纺织业	22	18	81.82
服装及其他纤维制品制造业	2	2	100.00
皮革、毛皮、羽绒及其制品业	1	1	100.00
木材加工及竹、藤、棕、草制品业	7	5	71.43
家具制造业	2	2	100.00
造纸及纸制品业	37	15	40.54
印刷业、记录媒介的复制	16	9	56.25
文教体育用品制造业	1	1	100.00
石油加工及炼焦业	36	29	80.56
化学原料及化学制品制造业	126	64	50.79
医药制造业	18	9	50.00
化学纤维制造业	7	5	71.43
橡胶制品业	4	2	50.00
塑料制品业	1	1	100.00
非金属矿物制品业	92	54	58.70
黑色金属冶炼及压延加工业	35	16	45.71
有色金属冶炼及压延加工业	32	16	50.00
金属制品业	7	5	71.43
普通机械制造业	47	19	40.43
专用设备制造业	51	24	47.06
交通运输设备制造业	53	25	47.17
武器弹药制造业	2	1	50.00
电气机械及器材制造业	31	11	35.48
电子及通信设备制造业	8	3	37.50
仪器仪表及文化、办公用机械制造业	7	1	14.29
其他制造业	1		
电力、煤气及水的生产和供应业	323	180	55.73
电力、蒸汽、热水的生产和供应业	245	141	57.55
煤气生产和供应业	7	3	42.86
自来水的生产和供应业	71	36	50.70

5—32 国有工业固定资产投资及新增固定资产(1997年)

Investment in Fixed Assets and Newly Increased Fixed Assets of State—Owned Industrial Enterprises

指标名称	固定资产投资完成额(万元)	新增固定资产(万元)	固定资产交付使用率(%)
全省总计	1210327	1201651	99.28
采掘业	37175	39794	107.05
煤炭采选业	24396	29052	119.09
石油和天然气开采业			
黑色金属矿采选业	908	926	101.98
有色金属矿采选业	10629	8819	82.97
非金属矿采选业	1132	832	73.50
其他矿采选业			
木材及竹材采运业	110	165	150.00
制造业	620871	785899	126.58
食品加工业	13096	10180	77.73
食品制造业	1032	613	59.40
饮料制造业	10800	10522	97.43
烟草加工业	49622	41918	84.47
纺织业	11761	11102	94.40
服装及其他纤维制品制造业	370	370	100.00
皮革、毛皮、羽绒及其制品业	164	164	100.00
木材加工及竹、藤、棕、草制品业	5553	20927	376.86
家具制造业	1000	1000	100.00
造纸及纸制品业	18753	12923	68.91
印刷业、记录媒介的复制	3313	3197	96.50
文教体育用品制造业	50	50	100.00
石油加工及炼焦业	145380	60152	41.38
化学原料及化学制品制造业	107769	149628	138.84
医药制造业	7354	4287	58.29
化学纤维制造业	11206	18376	163.98
橡胶制品业	511	716	140.12
塑料制品业	765	765	100.00
非金属矿物制品业	44857	100299	223.60
黑色金属冶炼及压延加工业	67527	200329	296.67
有色金属冶炼及压延加工业	20460	41976	205.16
金属制品业	1687	1577	93.48
普通机械制造业	14678	12143	82.73
专用设备制造业	23567	21858	92.75
交通运输设备制造业	41899	40401	96.42
武器弹药制造业	323	273	84.52
电气机械及器材制造业	11747	8485	72.23
电子及通信设备制造业	3329	9585	287.92
仪器仪表及文化、办公用机械制造业	2213	2093	94.13
其他制造业	85		
电力、煤气及水的生产和供应业	55281	375958	68.07
电力、蒸汽、热水的生产和供应业	515017	340314	66.08
煤气生产和供应业	3510	330	9.40
自来水的生产和供应业	33754	35314	104.62

5—33 国有运输仓储邮电通信业投资额

Investment of State—Owned Units of Transportation, Storehouse, Postal and Telecommunication Services

单位:万元

类别	1996年			1997年		
	合计	#商业运邮用	#住宅	合计	#商业运邮用	#住宅
交通运输仓储邮电通信业	1144141	1027668	49476	1159593	1037696	55930
1.铁路运输业	333224	310579	19381	292260	254677	28487
2.公路运输业	233054	207843	5034	273437	261166	6556
3.管道运输业				58		58
4.水上运输业	733	382	230	640	177	313
5.航空运输业	11399	8825	2574	1364	1364	
6.交通运输辅助业	110922	61849	7747	172195	118220	6005
7.其他交通运输业	5230	5111	70	5843	5803	2
8.仓储业	8616	6341	746	6718	1784	2028
9.邮电通信业	440963	426738	13694	407078	394505	12481

5—34 国有运输仓储邮电通信业项目投产率和固定资产交付使用率

Rate of Projects Put Into Operation and Rate of Fixed Assets Turned Over to Uses of State—Owned Units of Transportation, Postal and Telecommunication Services

类别	1996年				1997年			
	施工项目个数(个)	全部建成投产项目个数(个)	项目投产率(%)	固定资产交付使用率(%)	施工项目个数(个)	全部建成投产项目个数(个)	项目投产率(%)	固定资产交付使用率(%)
交通运输仓储邮电通信业	1200	704	58.7	68.2	1053	685	65.1	53.0
1.铁路运输业	173	57	32.9	15.4	52	27	51.9	56.0
2.公路运输业	219	99	45.2	103.4	295	154	52.2	28.1
3.管道运输业					1	1	100.0	100.0
4.水上运输业	10	6	60.0	82.7	8	5	62.5	141.7
5.航空运输业	2	1	50.0	114.6	1			
6.交通运输辅助业	231	153	66.2	48.4	193	123	63.7	53.0
7.其他交通运输业	6	3	50.0	6.1	2	1	50.0	1.8
8.仓储业	32	18	56.3	72.3	33	23	69.7	165.1
9.邮电通信业	527	367	69.6	93.9	468	351	75.0	66.4

六、财政、金融、保险

PUBLIC FINANCE, BANKING, INSURANCE

6—1 地方财政收支总额

Total Local Finacial Revenue and Expenditures

年份（地市）	总收入	#企业收入	#各项税收	总支出	#基本建设支出	#支援农村生产支出及农业事业费	#文教科学卫生事业费	#行政管理费
年份（亿元）								
1978	28.98	9.68	17.17	24.46	7.62	3.57	4.33	1.88
1980	29.86	9.58	19.53	23.71	4.86	3.44	6.68	2.66
1981	31.40	9.10	21.49	21.39	3.00	3.07	6.81	2.90
1982	30.33	5.11	24.48	23.26	3.12	2.95	7.91	3.03
1983	29.27	2.25	26.16	25.31	3.48	3.26	8.79	3.58
1984	32.85	2.74	29.12	30.04	4.43	3.21	9.86	4.87
1985	39.19	1.61	36.83	40.09	4.60	4.01	12.53	5.20
1986	47.65	4.08	42.26	54.29	5.80	4.52	14.22	5.54
1987	54.38	4.37	48.36	55.93	4.65	3.09	14.88	6.22
1988	56.54	—0.47	54.25	64.89	5.21	5.88	18.30	6.13
1989	68.86	—1.48	64.88	74.23	5.44	6.91	20.69	6.43
1990	70.07	—3.70	67.33	80.08	5.60	8.17	21.92	6.82
1991	80.52	—0.91	74.14	88.58	6.16	8.81	24.47	7.80
1992	92.78	—0.78	84.90	99.10	6.23	9.86	28.42	11.03
1993	127.56	—0.66	116.31	132.03	7.73	12.89	32.96	13.18
1994	85.89	2.70	65.04	151.49	7.89	13.74	42.54	17.79
1995	108.16	2.74	78.05	173.94	9.65	14.55	47.87	21.46
1996	130.36	2.30	88.00	217.74	13.33	17.09	53.70	24.27
1997	137.16	2.72	105.75	230.82	13.78	17.66	58.75	26.20
地市（万元）								
长沙市	256384	10792	192890	280728	20381	20135	51444	34190
株洲市	105634	4490	75846	131002	6501	9055	27702	16062
湘潭市	51806	—1144	39109	66982	526	4937	13979	9656
衡阳市	102171	—43	61342	139829	653	9730	33369	23412
邵阳市	85154	1615	50729	129437	394	9514	32515	20006
岳阳市	93422	5320	69745	136619	9810	15164	29711	16249
常德市	99988	5080	74435	142806	880	14104	35274	23344
张家界市	24807	215	17510	46813	225	3172	9972	6476
益阳市	49764	1113	35938	86134	780	8464	21677	14988
郴州市	98348	1700	60966	128866	1952	9450	31517	18564
永州市	72114	—12	48568	111591	2639	7672	29887	17830
娄底地区	57630	1780	39511	85771	1952	6330	19941	12266
怀化地区	76098	3986	49362	115791	38	10698	32344	20750
湘西自治州	32077	2784	22930	101968	552	7750	20112	13145

6—2 地方财政收入构成(1997年)

Local Finacial Revenue and Its Composition

科目	财政收入（万元）	科目	财政收入（万元）
一、工商税收类	818836	工业部门小计	5150
增值税	209125	#冶金工业	498
营业税	283549	煤炭工业	−6200
个人所得税	91667	石油化学工业	658
外商投资企业和外国企业所得税	3834	电力工业	1925
城市维护建设税	95617	化学工业	1485
车船税	3284	机械工业	1300
房产税	33049	电子工业	27
屠宰税	19751	建筑材料工业	438
资源税	5646	农机工业	27
土地使用税	21866	轻工业	3732
印花税	11563	纺织工业	356
固定资产投资方向调节税	38476	医药企业	384
工商税收税款滞纳金、罚款收入	720	森林工业	505
二、农牧业税和耕地占用税类	170727	建筑工程企业小计	181
农牧业税	112737	交通、邮电部门小计	−24
农业特产税	42229	#交通企业	176
耕地占用税	8547	邮电企业	−200
契税	7214	农林水等部门小计	−293
三、企业所得税类	67967	商业企业小计	−2169
四、国有企业上缴利润类	9601	粮食企业小计	−22433
五、国有企业计划亏损补贴类	−42334	外贸企业小计	166
六、基本建设贷款归还收入类		文教企业小计	1270
七、其他收入类	103353	电影企业	−365
#事业收入	11743	出版企业	1856
其他收入	75594	其他文教企业	−221
八、所得税退税类	−11915	其他部门小计	45283
九、罚没收入、行政性收费收入类	255322	#预算外企业	2419
海关罚没收入	800	集体企业	20279
工商罚没收入	7383	私营企业	1659
政法罚没收入	79062	地方股份制企业	4557
公安行政收费收入	10233	其他企业	11974
其他罚没收入	55645	附：上交中央财政合计	1178228
其他行政性收费收入	84257	1.消费税	550178
		2.75%增值税	628050

6—3 地方财政支出构成

Local Finacial Expenditures and Its Composition

科目	地方财政支出(万元)			构成(%)	
	1996年	1997年	1997年为上年%	1996年	1997年
总计	2177430	2308151	108.56	100.6	100.0
一、基本建设支出	133256	137783	103.4	6.1	6.0
二、企业挖潜改造资金	115772	99220	85.7	5.3	4.3
三、简易建筑费	11559	11994	103.8	0.5	0.5
四、科技三项费用	15411	19447	126.2	0.7	0.8
五、支援农村生产支出	71090	71111	100.0	3.3	3.1
六、农林水气等部门事业费	99809	105453	105.7	4.6	4.6
七、工交事业费	20522	22903	111.6	0.9	1.0
八、商业事业费	4904	7179	146.4	0.2	0.3
九、城市维护费	120508	121088	100.5	5.5	5.2
十、城镇青年就业经费					
十一、文教卫生事业费	525244	460079	87.6	24.1	19.9
#文化事业费	13636	14916	109.4	0.6	0.6
教育事业费	354952	379162	106.8	16.3	16.4
卫生事业费	81521	67408	82.7	3.7	2.9
公费医疗经费	32332	37874	117.1	1.5	1.6
体育事业费	10721	11753	109.6	0.5	0.5
广播电视电影事业费	11945	14837	124.2	0.5	0.6
计划生育事业费	20137	23871	118.5	0.9	1.0
十二、科学事业费	12879	15416	119.7	0.6	0.7
十三、其他部门事业费	134337	156174	116.3	6.2	6.8
十四、抚恤和社会福利救济费	52841	48157	91.1	2.4	2.1
十五、民兵事业费	2170	2134	98.3	0.1	0.1
十六、行政管理费	242749	262008	107.9	11.1	11.6
十七、公检法支出	142838	167301	117.1	6.6	7.2
十八、政策性补贴支出	167881	158106	94.2	7.7	6.8
#粮食加价款	20868	13415	64.3	0.9	0.6
粮油差价补贴	33	3421	103倍		0.1
市镇居民肉价补贴	4805	4556	94.8	0.2	0.2
十九、支援不发达地区支出	23816	42427	178.1	1.1	1.8
二十、其他支出	203916	199359	97.8	9.4	8.6
二十一、专项支出	51304			2.4	
二十二、农业综合开发	19619	24825	126.5	0.9	1.1
二十三、行政事业离退休经费	6144	62055	1010.0	0.3	2.7

注:省财政厅按可比口径计算,1997年度地方财政收入比上年增长9.56%,地方财政支出比上年增长8.56%。

6—4 人民银行机构和人员

Institutions and Personnel of People's Bank

类　别	机　构　数（个）			人　员　数（人）		
	1995 年	1996 年	1997 年	1995 年	1996 年	1997 年
合　计	98	98	98	5856	5881	6042
省分行	1	1	1	423	431	454
地州市分行	14	14	14	2083	2107	2216
县市支行	82	82	82	3157	3159	3197
大中专院校	1	1	1	193	184	175

6—5 商业银行机构与人员（1997 年）

Institutions and Personnel of State－Owned Commercial Bank

类　别	国有商业银行合计					其他商业银行	
		工商银行	农业银行	中国银行	建设银行	交通银行	投资银行
机构合计（个）	5868	1705	2332	653	1178	40	6
一、省分行	7	1	2	2	2		1
#营业部	3		1	1	1		1
二、地市分行	92	11	25	28	28	2	
#营业部	54	13	14	14	13	1	
三、中心支行	8	3	3		2		
四、支　行	537	164	134	87	152	6	2
#专业支行	5				5		
五、办事处	108	20	42	1	45	13	2
六、分理处、营业所	2027	389	1172	183	283	11	
七、储蓄所	3076	1104	954	352	666	8	
#联办、代办储蓄所	118		48		70	2	
人员合计（人）	62725	20773	20342	9049	12561	729	146
一、省分行	2014	316	438	879	381		90
#营业部	245		64	120	61		27
二、地市分行	7420	1743	824	2326	2527	467	
#营业部	1965	944	462		559	89	
三、中心支行	687	357	231		99		29
四、支　行	22839	11414	4466	2302	4657	306	
#专业支行	126				126		27
五、办事处	1651	136	806	34	675	153	
六、分理处、营业所	17273	2572	11070	1930	1701	259	
七、储蓄所	8417	3291	1027	1578	2521	32	
#联办、代办储蓄所	368		140		228	6	

6—6 金融概览

General Survey of Banking

项目	1995年年末余额（亿元）	1996年年末余额（亿元）	1997年	
			年末余额（亿元）	比年初增加（亿元）
一、金融机构各项存款	1389.05	1748.61	1769.91	173.88
#企业存款	357.17	446.14	509.08	43.66
定期	47.58	72.72	112.22	7.05
活期	309.59	373.42	396.86	36.60
储蓄存款	966.27	1179.52	1224.68	127.34
定期	764.65	941.11	960.69	88.41
活期	201.62	238.41	263.99	38.93
二、金融机构各项贷款	1494.03	1880.94	2123.00	215.59
#短期贷款	1176.28	1402.34	1667.21	167.92
#工业贷款	350.63	407.91	446.58	21.57
商业贷款	416.09	491.85	595.83	95.83
建筑贷款	22.24	26.17	52.12	-1.99
农业贷款	104.17	123.51	147.47	23.15
乡镇企业贷款	115.44	130.24	145.26	12.96
中长期贷款	282.28	331.66	341.63	27.90
#基本建设贷款	110.94	82.76	127.44	16.32
技术改造贷款	91.65	104.01	117.81	7.59

6—7 国家银行现金收支分析(1997年)

General Survey of Cash Statistics of Banking Institutions

单位:亿元

收入项目	年累计收入	比去年同期增减(±)	支出项目	年累计支出	比去年同期增减(±)
一、商品销售收入	662.95	-0.43	一、工资性支出	446.54	20.88
#县及县以下	132.84	-20.41	#国家工资支出	227.52	15.32
二、服务企事业收入	226.58	36.15	国家职工奖金支出	44.85	0.70
三、税款收入	38.96	5.71	国家对个人其他支出	95.31	1.84
四、农村信用社收入	98.06	-27.71	部队存款支出	9.30	9.30
五、乡镇企事业收入	45.29	3.12	集体工资奖金支出	45.43	2.83
#商品销售收入	6.88	1.10	集体个人其他支出	24.12	-9.11
服务事业收入	3.01	1.26	二、农副产品采购支出	138.76	21.73
六、城乡个体经营收入	71.49	20.18	三、工矿产品收购支出	73.21	-8.83
七、储蓄存款收入	2434.27	471.21	四、行政企事业管理费支出	231.24	16.69
八、其他金融机构收入	170.12	16.66	五、农村信用社支出	103.54	-38.15
九、汇兑收入	48.53	10.72	六、乡镇企事业支出	51.55	3.44
十、其他收入	478.69	188.66	#工资性支出	5.62	2.23
十一、债券收入	31.24	13.32	七、城乡个体经营支出	66.45	5.74
内部现金收入	1795.84		八、储蓄存款支出	2440.13	495.44
由人行发行库领取现金	466.85		九、其他金融机构支出	115.35	15.91
同业拆入现金	13.73		十、汇兑支出	92.21	12.72
前期业务库存	187.59		十一、其他支出	493.29	174.69
			十二、债券支出	17.88	3.39
			内部现金支出	1787.32	
			交回人行发行库现金	503.14	
			同业拆出现金	16.94	
			本期业务库存	192.68	
收入合计	6770.20		支出总计	6770.20	
投放差额			投放(+)回笼(-)	-36.04	-13.95

6—8 金融机构信贷收支(1997年)

Credit Receipt and Expenditures of Banking Institutions

单位:亿元

负债项目	年末余额	比年初增减额(±)	资产项目	年末余额	比年初增减额(±)
一、各项一般性存款	1769.91	173.88	一、各项贷款	2123.00	215.59
1.企业存款	509.08	43.65	1.短期贷款	1667.21	167.92
活期存款	396.86	36.60	工业贷款	446.58	21.57
#工业存款	74.09	6.62	#工业企业贷款	371.33	19.71
商业存款	37.81	−0.55	集体工业企业贷款	31.05	−1.03
建筑业存款	29.46	−8.39	物资供销企业贷款	35.67	2.48
集体企业存款	15.03	3.71	商业贷款	595.83	95.83
乡镇企业存款	3.04	−0.29	#农副产品贷款	364.17	84.86
定期存款	112.22	7.05	建筑业贷款	52.12	−1.99
2.储蓄存款	1224.68	127.34	农业贷款	147.47	23.15
活期存款	263.99	38.93	乡镇企业贷款	145.26	12.56
定期存款	960.89	88.41	三资企业贷款	14.50	2.25
3.农村存款	34.77	2.44	私营及个体贷款	10.42	−0.98
4.信托类存款	1.38	0.45	贴　现	5.78	1.13
二、代理财政性存款	25.28	5.54	其他短期贷款	249.25	13.99
三、临时存款	37.83	−3.77	2.中长期贷款	341.63	27.90
四、发行金融债券	0.12	−0.64	基本建设贷款	127.44	16.32
#政策性	…	−0.01	技术改造贷款	117.81	7.59
五、国家投资债券	0.02	0.02	其他中长期贷款	96.38	3.99
六、卖出回购证券	0.49	−5.26	3.信托贷款	1.20	0.88
七、向中央银行借款	17.75	−2.44	4.逾期类贷款	51.25	24.40
#再贴现	0.30	−0.85	二、国家投资债券贷款	2.12	−0.15
八、同业往来	136.30	16.79	三、有价证券及投资	51.83	−16.13
1.同业存放款	105.41	24.08	四、存放中央银行一般性存款	226.24	34.27
2.同业拆借	30.89	−7.29	五、在人行存款	96.49	−21.01
九、联行存放款	4937.09	857.28	六、存放中央银行特种存款	0.61	−6.44
#省辖往来	963.50	331.35	七、存放中央银行财政性存款	12.85	−0.36
十、委托存款及委托投资基金	127.96	5.68	八、同业往来	123.27	5.02
1.委托存款	126.49	6.08	存放同业款项	80.43	3.43
2.委托投资基金	1.47	−0.40	拆放同业	42.84	1.59
十一、所有者权益	−42.86	−49.67	九、存放联行款项	4092.13	737.12
实收资本	49.18	−7.73	省辖往来	961.78	342.20
十二、当年结益	−49.22	−34.71	十、应收及预付款项	158.91	33.34
十三、各项准备	8.61	−1.15	十一、代理金融机构贷款	74.88	9.09
十四、应付及暂收款	61.85	−9.14	十二、库存现金	30.48	6.84
十五、其他负债	171.70	69.94	十三、外汇占款	9.83	0.31
			十四、其他资产	200.16	25.08
资金来源总计	7202.82	1022.58	资金运用总计	7202.82	1022.58

6—9 国有商业银行信贷收支(1997 年)

Credit Income and Expenditures of State-Owned Commercial Banks

单位:亿元

负债项目	年末余额	资产项目	年末余额
一、各项一般性存款	1204.36	一、各项贷款	1340.17
1.企业存款	446.39	1.短期贷款	1050.04
活期存款	346.95	工业贷款	437.56
#工业存款	69.74	#工业企业贷款	364.06
商业存款	21.09	物资供销企业贷款	35.53
建筑业存款	29.08	集体工业企业贷款	29.54
集体企业存款	10.21	商业贷款	281.58
乡镇企业存款	3.03	#农副产品贷款	80.45
定期存款	99.44	建筑业贷款	51.27
2.储蓄存款	750.18	农业贷款	54.79
活期存款	177.59	乡镇企业贷款	56.90
定期存款	572.59	三资企业贷款	14.01
3.农村存款	4.76	私营及个体贷款	6.67
4.信托类存款	0.07	贴　现	5.18
二、代理财政性存款	15.55	其他短期贷款	142.08
三、临时存款	29.34	2.中长期贷款	280.15
四、发行金融债券	0.03	基本建设贷款	127.39
五、国家投资债券	0.02	技术改造贷款	117.69
六、卖出回购证券	−1.05	其他中长期贷款	35.08
七、向中央银行借款	14.39	3.信托贷款	
八、同业往来	106.01	4.逾期类贷款	9.98
九、联行存放款	3656.30	二、国家投资债券贷款	2.12
十、委托存款及委托投资基金	10.34	三、有价证券及投资	38.15
十一、代理金融机构贷款基金	71.99	四、存放中央银行一般性存款	155.93
十二、所有者权益	−58.16	五、在人行存款	60.69
十三、当年结益	−34.27	六、存放中央银行特种存款	
十四、各项准备	2.19	七、存放中央银行财政性存款	12.67
十五、应付及暂收款	17.92	八、同业往来	32.06
十六、其他负债	131.53	九、存放联行款项	3165.31
		十、应收及预付款项	122.87
		十一、代理金融机构贷款	72.65
		十二、库存现金	15.14
		十三、外汇占款	9.19
		十四、其他资产	139.51
资金来源总计	5166.49	资金运用总计	5166.49

6—10 城市信用社现金收支情况

Cash Income and Expenditures of Urban Credit Cooperative

单位:亿元

收入项目	1997年 全年收入	1997年 比上年增减额(±)	支出项目	1997年 全年支出	1997年 比上年增减额(±)
一、商品销售收入	41.35	-23.37	一、工资性支出		
二、服务企事业收入	8.90	-5.73	1.集体单位工资支出	8.89	-2.67
三、税款收入	0.87	-0.69	2.集体单位奖金支出	1.53	-0.97
四、乡镇企事业收入	5.26	-1.38	3.集体单位对个人其他支出	4.16	-1.61
五、信用收入	9.23	0.7	二、农副产品采购支出	7.03	-1.17
六、城市个体经营收入	34.92	-7.98	三、工矿产品收购支出	15.87	-12.72
七、储蓄存款收入	216.91	-19.50	四、行政企事业管理费支出	7.88	-5.60
八、债券收入	0.60	-0.31	五、乡镇企事业支出	4.89	-1.82
九、其他收入	24.73	3.32	六、信用支出	10.04	2.93
			七、城乡个体经营支出	28.87	-6.12
			八、储蓄存款支出	192.40	-17.40
			九、债券支出	0.22	-0.35
			十、其他支出	30.14	7.02
收入合计	342.77	-54.94	支出合计	311.92	-40.50
投放差额			回笼差额	-30.85	14.44

6—11 农村信用社现金收支情况

Cash Income and Expenditures of Rural Credit Cooperative

单位:亿元

收入项目	1997年 累计收入	1997年 比上年增减额(±)	支出项目	1997年 全年支出	1997年 比上年增减额(±)
一、集体现金收入	50.35	13.11	一、集体现金支出	49.41	10.27
二、乡镇企业收入	167.19	14.57	#农户分配	0.38	-0.39
三、个人存款收入	756.98	143.82	二、乡镇企事业支出	187.50	14.48
四、农户贷款收入	117.29	1.84	#工资性支出	5.40	-4.57
五、代理业务收入	8.43	0.39	三、个人存款支出	729.46	134.75
#商品销售收入	0.84	0.39	四、农户贷款支出	119.90	-6.42
六、其他收入	138.79	23.62	五、代理业务支出	10.33	1.23
			#农副产品采购支出	1.30	0.71
			六、其他支出	160.04	43.93
收入合计	1239.02	197.34	支出合计	1256.64	198.25
投放差额	17.62	0.90	回笼差额		

6—12 各地市城乡居民储蓄存款年末余额(1997年)

Saving Deposits Balance by Prefecture, City

单位:亿元

	合 计	工商银行	农业银行	中国银行	建设银行	交通银行	城市合作银行	城市信用社	农村信用社
合计	1224.68	277.60	212.41	86.66	162.67	10.83	23.65	41.85	405.79
#活期	263.99	62.26	49.70	16.98	47.01	1.65	7.15	7.20	71.51
定期	960.69	215.34	162.71	69.68	115.66	9.18	16.50	34.65	334.28
长沙	241.43	67.81	36.68	16.32	41.48	8.41	11.63	2.51	56.57
株洲	107.01	25.52	13.80	10.92	12.83		8.03	0.31	35.60
湘潭	88.12	20.51	11.10	11.20	9.50		3.90	0.30	31.40
衡阳	128.19	24.94	23.11	7.84	10.62			13.74	47.93
邵阳	83.26	17.29	14.60	6.18	11.56			2.37	31.25
岳阳	87.19	17.23	15.95	7.53	11.18	2.43		2.92	29.95
常德	82.52	17.99	15.73	5.47	8.85			3.58	30.91
张家界	15.93	3.38	2.94	0.93	2.17			0.30	6.21
益阳	62.20	13.07	12.87	3.99	6.05			3.36	22.86
郴州	79.12	21.21	15.49	4.75	10.69			2.30	24.69
娄底	65.63	11.51	10.37	3.07	10.06			1.15	29.48
永州	65.58	12.55	13.15	1.77	9.60			2.53	25.98
怀化	65.99	15.76	11.05	1.90	11.54			4.59	21.14
自治州	21.27	6.28	5.30	0.57	2.43			0.79	5.90

注:本表城乡居民储蓄存款年末余额未包括外币部分。1997年全省外币储蓄36914万美元,折人民币30.6亿元。

6—13 保险机构与人员

Institutions and Personnel of Insurance System

项　　目	单　　位	1995年	1996年	1997年
一、保险机构数	个	173	361	331
省级公司	个	3	3	4
地市级公司	个	27	55	45
县支公司	个	113	205	282
市辖区办事处	个	48	98	
二、年底实有职工人数	人	5255	6366	

6—14 保险业务(1997年)

Insurance Business

项　　目		单位	合　计	中保公司湖南分公司	平安公司长沙分公司	太平洋保险公司
一、财产保险业务						
保险金额		亿元	2770.42	2364.85	310.28	113.31
保费收入		亿元	12.54	10.42	1.69	0.43
储金有效余额		万元	38237	39234	1380	290
赔付(给付)件数		件	131677	111713	17484	2480
赔款(给付)支出		万元	71859	60526	9090	2244
赔付率		%	57.32	58.07	53.79	52.39
年末决赔	件数	件	10767	7203	5364	
	金额	万元	13898	10443	3453	
二、人身保险						
保　　费		亿元	18.20	14.37	3.16	0.62
本年承保或期末有效合同	人数	万人	1912.96	1732.08	166.24	14.64
	件数	万件	804.52	765.00	22.27	17.24
	保额	亿元	1140.39	673.32	125.66	341.41
退保金给付		万元	23959	9753	6732	7473
满期给付		万元	55047	51803	838	2406
死伤医疗给付		万元	12766	12255	478	33
储金有效余额		万元	6327	518	5739	70
退保率		%	0.13	6.79		
满期给付率		%	0.30	36.05		39
死伤医疗给付率		%	0.07	8.53		0.53

6—15 财产保险金额及构成(1997年)

Premium and It's Composition of Property Insurance

单位:万元

	总计	中保公司湖南分公司	平安公司长沙分公司	太平洋保险公司
总计	27704222	23468533	3102806	1133103
1、财产损失保险	25908421	21847307	2948055	1113329
#企业财产保险	16315075	13789043	1991109	534922
家庭财产保险	2078343	1989881	74238	14224
机动车辆及第三者保险	3228272	2656758	338292	233222
建筑工程质量及责任保险	288107	213643	34008	40456
二、责任保险	1182616	1061031	101815	19770
#产品责任	358404	291608	47026	19770
雇主责任	157275	155244	2031	
公众责任	67007	28694	38313	
三、信用保险				
四、保证保险	219823	166837	52986	
五、农业保险	393361	393358		4
#种植业	382662	382662		
养殖业	10699	10695		4

6—16 人身保险保费构成(1997年)

Premium and It's Composition of Life Insurance

保费:万元

人数:人

	总计	中保公司湖南分公司	平安公司长沙分公司	太平洋保险公司
一、团体保险				
人寿保险保费	102806	86139	12528	4139
参保人数	4931774	4781574	78181	72015
意外伤害保险保费	15649	14662	909	78
参保人数	12800683	11404138	1341410	55144
健康保险保费	4515	4458	57	
参保人数	674628	633102	41526	
二、个人保险				
人寿保险保费	57100	37833	17105	1572
参保人数	551212	373040	163796	14374
意外伤害保险保费	206	206		
参保人数	96132	96132		
健康保险保费	1763	394	984	1957
参保人数	75199	32833	37458	19282
总计 保费	182041	143692	31585	6174
参保人数	19129628	17320819	1662362	146445

七、物价指数

PRICE INDICES

7—1 各种物价总指数

Overall Price Indexes

年　　份	零售物价总指数	职工生活费用价格总指数	农民生活费用价格总指数	农副产品收购价格总指数	农村工业品零售价格总指数	集市贸易价格总指数	工农业商品综合比价指数(以农副产品收购价格总指数为100)
以上年为100							
1978	100.0	99.4		101.7	99.8		98.1
1979	102.0	103.3		127.1	100.0	102.9	78.7
1980	110.8	113.6		111.2	101.4	103.3	91.2
1981	101.7	102.6		107.3	100.5	110.4	93.7
1982	101.7	101.6		103.7	102.0	107.3	98.4
1983	102.4	102.7	100.0	105.4	101.4	104.4	96.2
1984	103.1	103.4	102.9	102.9	103.9	101.1	101.0
1985	111.1	111.9	110.2	111.6	106.1	118.7	95.1
1986	104.8	105.4	105.3	105.7	103.3	104.7	97.7
1987	110.6	111.3	108.8	110.2	109.9	119.3	99.7
1988	125.9	125.7	125.4	123.1	123.6	136.7	100.4
1989	118.1	117.3	119.1	106.8	120.9	110.8	113.2
1990	99.4	100.6	100.2	94.1	99.7	94.1	106.0
1991	104.1	105.1	103.8	94.3	103.1	99.6	109.3
1992	109.5	113.5	107.9	99.1	104.9	107.8	105.9
1993	115.1	117.4	116.4	114.7	114.9	113.9	100.2
1994	124.5	124.8	125.6	144.1	117.2	135.5	81.3
1995	115.5	118.1	119.5	117.2	116.7	125.2	99.6
1996	105.2	107.2	108.2	104.9	105.1	101.1	100.2
1997	100.3	103.0	102.5	95.3	100.4	95.0	105.4
以1978年为100							
1979	102.0	103.3		127.1	100.0	102.9	78.7
1980	113.0	117.3		141.3	101.4	106.3	71.8
1981	114.9	120.3		151.6	101.9	117.4	67.3
1982	116.9	122.2		157.2	103.9	126.0	66.2
1983	119.7	125.5	100.0	165.7	105.4	131.5	63.7
1984	123.4	129.8	102.9	170.5	109.5	132.9	64.3
1985	137.1	145.2	113.4	190.3	116.2	157.8	61.1
1986	143.7	153.0	119.4	201.1	120.0	165.2	59.7
1987	158.9	170.3	129.9	221.6	131.9	197.1	59.5
1988	200.1	214.1	162.9	272.8	163.0	269.4	59.7
1989	236.3	251.1	194.0	291.4	197.1	298.5	67.6
1990	234.9	252.6	194.4	274.2	196.5	280.9	71.6
1991	244.5	265.5	201.8	258.6	202.6	279.8	78.3
1992	267.7	301.3	217.7	256.3	212.5	301.6	82.9
1993	308.2	353.7	253.4	294.0	244.2	343.5	83.1
1994	383.6	441.4	318.2	423.7	286.2	465.4	67.6
1995	443.1	521.3	380.2	496.6	334.0	582.7	67.3
1996	466.1	558.8	411.4	520.9	351.0	589.1	67.4
1997	467.5	575.6	421.7	496.4	352.4	559.6	71.0

7—2 零售物价分类指数(1997年)

Orerall Retail Indexes by Category of Commodities

类别	全省		城市		农村	
	以上年为100	以1978年为100	以上年为100	以1978年为100	以上年为100	以1978年为100
零售价格总指数	100.3	467.5	100.6	440.2	99.8	423.1
一、食品类	98.7	657.2	99.6	202.7	97.9	579.4
1.粮食	94.0	927.6	94.2	786.7	93.9	664.6
2.油脂类	98.9	580.0	100.3	526.2	97.5	789.2
3.肉禽蛋	99.0	777.2	99.4	771.0	98.6	774.3
4.水产品	98.6	747.0	98.2	698.3	99.0	828.7
5.鲜菜	97.9	1335.2	100.5	1243.8	94.2	
6.干菜	95.7	522.0	98.6	504.4	95.1	551.1
7.鲜果	91.1	525.9	93.0	542.6	88.4	291.8
8.干果	106.6	502.1	108.5	528.1	103.9	404.1
9.其他食品类	102.3	475.0	101.8	537.1	102.6	393.8
10.饮食业	106.1		105.9		106.4	
二、饮料、烟酒类	101.3	251.2	102.2	256.0	100.7	200.2
三、服装、鞋帽类	103.4	245.4	104.1	252.2	102.7	248.7
四、纺织品类	101.9	322.5	102.9	332.5	101.0	305.5
五、中、西药品类	102.6	403.6	100.5	380.3	106.2	435.2
六、化妆品类	104.8		103.8		106.9	
七、书报、杂志类	111.1		111.2	1203.3	111.1	1356.1
八、文化体育用品类	103.9	168.9	102.0	164.4	106.7	180.2
九、日用品类	103.6	284.5	103.2	257.5	103.9	316.4
十、家用电器类	95.9	137.9	96.0	142.7	95.8	137.5
十一、首饰类	96.3		95.7		99.6	
十二、燃料类	102.4	482.5	103.2	478.5	101.6	437.5
十三、建筑装璜材料类	97.4		100.8		94.3	
十四、机电产品类	95.0		94.5		97.3	

7—3 农业生产资料价格指数(1997年)

Overall Agricultural Producer Goods Price Indices

类别	以上年价格为100	以1978年价格为100
总指数	97.9	470.6
1.小农具	114.0	517.6
2.饲料	102.1	
3.幼禽家畜	136.0	
4.大牲畜	82.1	
5.半机械化农具	100.1	524.5
6.机械化农具	98.5	289.0
7.化肥	87.9	413.7
8.农药及农药械	98.6	328.4
(1)化学农药	98.6	338.5
(2)农药械	98.6	208.3
9.农用机油	104.9	800.3
10.其他	101.3	419.2

7—4 居民消费价格分类指数(1997 年)

Orerall Retail Indexes by Category of Commodities

类　　别	全省		城市		农村	
	以上年为100	以1978年为100	以上年为100	以1978年为100	以上年为100	以1978年为100
居民消费价格总指数	102.8	436.3	103.0	575.6	102.5	421.7
一、食品	99.3	619.1	100.3	673.7	98.8	542.1
1.粮食	93.5	930.0	94.2	810.8	93.0	648.2
2.淀粉及薯类	97.1		99.0		96.1	
3.干豆类及豆制品	103.9		107.9		101.7	
4.油脂类	98.9	561.7	99.4	516.5	98.2	748.2
5.肉禽及其制品	102.0	827.1	103.1	833.4	101.3	812.8
6.蛋类	83.8		83.3		84.4	
7.水产品类	98.7	749.4	98.9	687.9	98.6	830.7
8.菜类	95.8	1189.6	99.8	1206.9	93.2	
9.调味品	101.6	329.7	101.1	509.4	101.9	340.7
10.糖类	100.1	441.6	101.3	372.3	99.6	438.9
11.烟草类	100.0	242.0	100.2	245.3	99.9	199.9
12.酒和饮料	102.9	217.2	104.6	229.3	102.2	196.9
13.干鲜瓜果类	92.6	511.2	96.3	548.4	88.9	315.0
14.糕点类	104.0	504.1	102.8	572.2	105.5	407.7
15.奶及奶制品	105.4	328.5	101.5	349.4	111.7	301.1
16.其他食品	104.4	227.3	105.2	449.0	103.3	349.2
17.饮食业	105.3		105.4		105.2	
二、衣着	102.8	263.2	103.3	262.9	102.4	259.4
三、家庭设备、用品	102.9	179.0	100.5	220.6	103.9	208.2
四、医疗保健	106.4	415.3	101.3	377.2	107.9	443.1
五、交通和通讯	99.0		95.9		100.6	
六、娱乐、教育、文化用品	103.0	198.2	103.2	183.5	102.6	210.8
七、居住	104.0		109.8		101.8	
八、服务项目	112.5	733.1	114.1	962.4	111.7	980.9
1.电讯费	112.8	438.1	113.2	482.5	111.5	433.8
2.邮费	214.8	860.1	217.2	965.7	214.1	805.0
3.交通费	105.7	617.4	106.5	809.9	105.3	541.9
4.洗理美容费	105.9		108.5		104.8	
5.文娱费	107.9	2629.6	110.0	2580.8	106.6	2764.7
6.学杂保育费	112.5	1605.5	115.4	1602.3	111.3	1565.5
7.修理及其他服务费	109.2	494.9	106.8	512.9	111.7	491.7
8.医疗保健服务	134.5	1812.5	136.5	1545.6	133.3	1614.0

7—5 十三个调查市县价格指数(1997年)

Overall Price Indexes in 13 Cities and Counties Under Investigation

调查点	职工生活费用价格指数	零售物价指数	农业生产资料价格指数	农产品成交价格指数
长沙市	103.5	100.8		93.7
常德市	103.0	99.8		93.8
邵阳市	98.5	98.6		93.5
株洲市	102.5	99.9		93.3
郴州市	102.1	100.2		97.8
岳阳市	103.0	100.5		94.6
怀化市	101.5	99.8		97.0
衡阳市	104.6	104.4		98.6
湘潭市	103.9	99.9		94.3
耒阳市	102.2	99.7	98.5	
道　县	102.0	98.5	98.0	
新化县	102.1	100.7	94.7	
慈利县	102.6	99.4	100.2	

7—6 生活费用价格分类指数

Resident Cost of Living Indexes by Category of Commodities

(以上年价格为100)

项　目	居民生活费用价格指数		职工生活费用价格指数		农民生活费用价格指数	
	1996年	1997年	1996年	1997年	1996年	1997年
总指数	107.7	102.8	107.2	103.0	108.2	102.5
其中:服务项目	112.4	112.5	114.3	114.1	111.7	111.7
电讯费	101.3	112.8	100.2	113.2	105.6	111.5
邮　费	110.2	214.8	109.5	217.2	110.7	214.1
交通费	128.3	105.7	134.0	106.5	127.0	105.3
洗礼美容费	109.8	105.9	110.8	108.5	109.1	104.8
文娱费	113.4	107.9	116.2	110.0	112.1	106.6
学杂保育费	108.0	112.5	114.1	115.4	105.4	111.3
修理及其他服务费	106.6	109.2	106.6	106.8	106.6	111.7
医疗保健服务费	121.2	134.5	114.3	136.5	125.6	133.3

7—7 主要调查城市农贸市场农产品成交价格指数(1997年)

Overall Farm Products Trade Price Indices in Major Cities Under Investigation

(以上年价格为100)

类别	长沙市	常德市	邵阳市	株洲市	郴州市	岳阳市	怀化市	衡阳市	湘潭市
农产品成交价格指数	93.7	93.8	93.5	93.3	97.8	94.6	97.0	98.6	94.3
1.粮食	86.8	92.2	89.2	84.9	97.2	90.6	88.0	101.8	92.9
2.油脂类	97.5	98.9	90.6	95.7	93.8	97.2	99.4	97.1	100.4
3.肉禽蛋	98.4	100.5	95.4	100.4	99.7	99.3	98.8	97.5	99.8
4.水产品	100.7	96.2	99.6	95.8	97.7	105.6	98.3	98.0	96.7
5.鲜菜	91.5	89.9	98.6	89.4	97.4	90.9	98.8	97.5	92.0
6.干菜	74.1	74.1	80.7	81.5	99.7	94.4	89.8	104.7	84.6
7.鲜果	84.0	83.4	87.8	93.6	94.1	89.1	98.7	99.1	88.5
8.干果	108.1	101.8	119.8	101.3	99.0	102.0	115.2	106.1	109.7

7—8 主要调查农村农业生产资料价格指数(1997年)

Overall Agricultual Producer Goods Price Indices in Major Rural Areas Under Investigation

(以上年价格为100)

类别	道县	耒阳市	新化县	慈利县
农业生产资料价格指数	98.0	98.5	94.7	100.2
一、小农具	98.5	139.6	100.0	111.3
二、饲料	97.3	96.2	97.4	115.0
三、幼禽家畜	134.5	131.4	148.1	132.6
四、大牲畜	87.3		78.7	80.4
五、半机械化农具	99.6	100.2	100.0	100.0
六、机械化农具	100.0	101.6	94.6	96.1
七、化肥	86.5	89.1	83.3	91.5
八、农药及农药械	101.6	99.0	94.7	99.1
九、农用机油	121.9	100.9	89.4	106.6
十、其　他	94.5	97.5	98.8	112.6

7—9 农副产品收购价格分类指数(1997年)

Overall Farm and sideline Products Purchasing price Indexes by Category of Commodities

类别及品名	以上年价格为100	以1978年价格为100	类别及品名	以上年价格为100	以1978年价格为100
农副产品收购价格总指数	95.3	496.5	2.禽蛋	94.2	781.8
一、粮食类	91.9	412.3	3.皮张	87.5	549.5
二、经济作物类	97.0	216.3	4.鬃毛	89.0	325.7
1.食用植物油及油料	96.9	344.6	5.其他畜产品	122.9	899.9
2.棉花	99.3	778.2	六、蚕茧蚕丝类		
3.麻	85.5	108.6	七、干鲜果类	59.2	148.3
4.烟叶	88.5	215.6	1.瓜果	54.0	136.7
5.糖料	103.7	580.0	2.干果	73.3	576.9
6.茶叶	112.6	374.0	八、干鲜菜及调味品类	90.3	323.6
三、竹木材类	82.5	1493.0	1.鲜菜	88.6	699.1
四、工业用油漆类	103.7	385.3	2.干菜	94.3	201.4
1.工业用油脂油料	101.9	366.6	九、药材类	95.6	302.3
2.工业用漆胶	110.0	570.5	十、土副产品类	100.9	471.3
五、禽畜产品类	102.1	840.3	十一、水产品类	96.5	99.4
1.肉畜	104.3	847.5	(淡水鲜品)		

7—10 农产品成交价格指数(1997年)

Overall Farm Products Trade Price Indices

类　　别	以上年价格为100	以1978年价格为100
农产品成交价格指数	95.0	559.6
1.粮食	91.7	377.6
(1)细粮	90.0	
(2)粗粮	116.5	
2.食用植物油	95.8	349.0
3.肉禽蛋	99.1	671.2
4.水产品	96.7	596.1
5.鲜菜	93.4	1081.7
6.干菜	87.4	384.2
7.鲜果	87.2	355.6
8.干果	104.1	422.2

7—11 全省物价分月指数(1997年)

Overall Price Indices of the Whole Province by Month

(以上年同期价格为100)

类别	1月	2月	3月	4月	5月	6月	7月	8月	9月	10月	11月	12月
零售价格总指数	103.0	102.8	102.1	101.7	101.2	100.5	99.7	99.0	98.5	97.8	98.8	98.2
一、食品类	102.9	102.1	101.1	101.6	100.2	98.8	97.0	95.8	95.6	95.2	97.4	96.5
#粮食	102.0	102.1	101.2	99.9	97.2	95.0	93.0	85.8	84.2	85.7	90.1	91.5
鲜菜	79.9	88.3	94.4	101.6	96.0	97.3	92.1	89.7	102.9	102.5	114.6	115.5
二、饮料、烟酒类	103.7	102.8	102.2	101.8	100.7	100.7	100.6	100.7	100.5	100.7	100.9	100.7
三、服装、鞋帽类	106.6	105.2	104.9	104.2	103.5	103.5	103.5	103.7	101.2	101.1	101.8	101.4
四、纺织品类	102.1	102.2	103.1	102.2	102.7	102.4	102.6	102.4	101.4	101.1	100.2	100.1
五、中、西药品类	107.4	107.4	106.9	105.8	105.1	105.1	106.0	98.6	97.5	97.2	97.3	97.2
六、化妆品类	104.9	103.5	103.9	104.7	105.1	104.0	104.3	104.3	105.4	105.4	106.8	105.3
七、书报杂志类	121.2	123.8	114.5	115.3	115.2	115.2	109.6	109.3	103.4	102.7	102.5	102.4
八、文化体育用品	106.9	106.6	104.4	105.7	104.8	104.1	104.2	103.5	102.2	101.6	101.3	101.2
九、日用品类	105.2	104.8	104.4	104.4	104.3	103.9	103.4	103.6	102.7	102.3	102.0	101.9
十、家用电器类	97.5	97.6	96.7	96.9	96.9	96.6	96.6	95.7	95.3	93.9	93.8	93.8
十一、首饰类	100.7	100.7	100.6	100.3	97.4	97.4	96.8	96.7	92.0	91.5	90.5	90.5
十二、燃料类	103.7	103.7	103.6	101.8	101.7	101.6	102.4	103.5	103.0	103.4	101.3	99.5
十三、建筑装璜材料类	95.9	97.4	98.0	97.8	96.2	97.3	98.0	97.8	96.5	97.2	99.0	97.6
十四、机电产品类	96.3	95.7	95.1	94.8	94.9	94.9	94.7	94.5	94.9	94.5	94.9	94.8
居民消费价格总指数	105.9	105.1	104.1	103.8	103.6	103.0	102.1	101.4	101.1	100.8	101.4	100.7
一、食品	103.1	102.6	101.6	101.8	100.8	99.1	97.5	97.1	97.1	96.5	97.9	96.9
#粮食	101.5	100.9	100.7	99.8	97.3	94.5	92.4	85.2	83.6	84.9	89.4	91.5
菜类	82.2	89.4	95.2	100.3	96.3	94.4	88.2	88.0	100.1	98.9	108.8	108.3
二、衣着	105.5	104.3	103.7	103.0	102.7	102.8	102.6	102.5	101.4	101.1	101.7	101.7
三、家庭设备、用品	105.3	104.9	104.0	103.9	103.7	103.1	102.5	102.3	101.7	101.5	101.3	100.9
四、医疗保健	109.2	108.6	108.2	108.3	108.1	108.4	110.9	105.5	103.8	102.8	101.5	100.9
五、交通和通讯工具	101.9	101.1	99.4	99.5	99.6	99.2	99.3	99.0	98.4	97.2	96.9	96.9
六、娱乐、教育、文化用品	108.5	111.2	105.5	105.7	105.8	105.8	102.8	102.2	98.2	97.0	96.7	96.4
七、居住	109.1	105.6	104.5	103.6	103.6	104.4	104.0	101.9	101.4	102.2	103.8	103.6
八、服务项目	113.4	111.0	110.8	112.1	112.7	112.8	112.8	113.0	113.4	113.6	113.2	111.7

7—12 主要农产品与工业品交换比价

Price Parity of Principal Agricaltural and Industrial Products

农产品（百公斤）	工业品	1996年	1997年	农产品（百公斤）	工业品	1996年	1997年
稻 谷	食盐（公斤）	120	108	油菜籽	食盐（公斤）	191	183
	白糖（公斤）	26	23		白糖（公斤）	42	39
	白布（米）	22	18		白布（米）	36	31
	洗衣粉（公斤）	28	21		洗衣粉（公斤）	44	36
	化肥（公斤）	63	77		化肥（公斤）	101	130
皮 棉	食盐（公斤）	1165	1158	甘 蔗	食盐（公斤）	22	23
	白糖（公斤）	254	244		白糖（公斤）	5	5
	白布（米）	217	193		白布（米）	4	4
	洗衣粉（公斤）	269	229		洗衣粉（公斤）	5	5
	化肥（公斤）	616	824		化肥（公斤）	12	17
烤 烟	食盐（公斤）	477	423	毛 茶	食盐（公斤）	873	763
	白糖（公斤）	104	89		白糖（公斤）	191	161
	白布（米）	89	71		白布（米）	162	127
	洗衣粉（公斤）	110	84		洗衣粉（公斤）	201	151
	化肥（公斤）	252	301		化肥（公斤）	461	543
黄红麻（熟麻）	食盐（公斤）	251	250	肥 猪	食盐（公斤）	669	648
	白糖（公斤）	55	53		白糖（公斤）	146	137
	白布（米）	47	42		白布（米）	124	108
	洗衣粉（公斤）	58	50		洗衣粉（公斤）	154	128
	化肥（公斤）	133	178		化肥（公斤）	354	461
苎 麻	食盐（公斤）	582	483	鸡 蛋	食盐（公斤）	682	667
	白糖（公斤）	127	102		白糖（公斤）	149	141
	白布（米）	108	80		白布（米）	127	111
	洗衣粉（公斤）	134	96		洗衣粉（公斤）	157	132
	化肥（公斤）	308	344		化肥（公斤）	361	474
				桐 油	食盐（公斤）	790	833
					白糖（公斤）	173	176
					白布（米）	147	139
					洗衣粉（公斤）	182	165
					化肥（公斤）	417	593

7—13 工业品出厂价格指数

Factory Price Indexes of Industrial Products

(以上年价格为100)

行业	指数(%)		
	1995年	1996年	1997年
全部工业品	121.37	105.63	99.2
总计中：生产资料	118.97	103.11	98.6
1.采掘工业	131.32	102.71	102.5
2.原材料工业	119.10	104.50	98.3
3.加工工业	115.50	101.25	98.2
生活资料	126.40	110.65	100.4
1.食品类	132.56	117.05	104.0
2.衣着类	121.10	99.76	93.7
3.一般日用品	121.94	105.27	98.9
4.耐用消费品	104.37	96.64	95.8
按工业部门分:			
1.冶金工业	114.54	97.52	95.4
2.电力工业	117.56	123.27	108.0
3.煤炭及炼焦工业	125.83	106.61	102.3
4.石油工业	119.57	103.43	108.3
5.化学工业	133.42	104.67	92.2
6.机械工业	105.20	99.14	99.1
7.建材工业	101.26	96.36	95.4
8.森林工业	121.06	103.74	92.7
9.食品工业	132.60	117.05	103.3
10.纺织工业	120.84	96.65	93.7
11.缝纫工业	124.18	121.24	94.4
12.皮革工业	119.75	85.25	99.5
13.造纸工业	149.45	110.88	92.0
14.文教艺术用品工业		105.08	93.0
15.其他工业	140.51	103.95	107.1

7—14　主要工业产品分行业出厂价格指数

Major Industrial Products Price Indices by Category of Commodities

（以上年为100）

分组名称	1995年	1996年	1997年
煤炭采选业	127.05	106.84	102.0
石油及天然气开采业			
黑色金属矿采选业	103.58	95.90	102.4
有色金属矿采选业	150.33	89.15	104.6
建筑材料及其它非金属矿采选业	129.41	112.84	98.9
采盐业	96.91	97.48	100.3
木材及竹材采运业	113.54		94.4
自来水生产与供应业	152.05	112.36	115.6
食品制造业	153.26	95.95	90.9
饮料制造业	104.53	99.33	99.6
烟草加工业	115.40	137.67	112.1
饲料工业	138.10	101.44	105.5
纺织业	113.21	97.38	94.1
缝纫业	124.17	121.24	94.4
皮革、毛皮及其制品业	119.75	85.25	99.1
木材加工及竹藤棕草制品业	104.13	102.91	88.3
家具制造业	90.66	88.31	109.4
造纸及纸制品业	149.45	110.88	92.0
文教体育用品制造业		105.08	92.8
电力、蒸气、热水生产和供应业	117.56	123.27	108.0
石油加工业	119.57	103.43	108.3
炼焦、煤气及煤制品业	106.37	102.09	107.6
化学工业	135.18	103.70	90.7
医药工业	115.28	99.80	104.0
化学纤维工业	146.19	86.95	87.8
橡胶制品业	125.05	107.61	96.0
塑料制品业	128.57	105.46	102.0
建筑材料及其它非金属矿制品业	100.94	96.26	95.3
黑色金属冶炼及压延加工业	97.48	101.81	95.9
有色金属冶炼及压延加工业	128.66	92.97	90.0
金属制品业	95.24	96.68	95.9
机械工业	103.86	99.48	101.4
交通运输设备制造业	104.42	101.03	101.7
电力机械及器材制造业	112.62	99.53	95.9
电力及通讯设备制造业	104.72	90.45	85.7
仪器仪表及其它计量器具制造业	99.73	102.22	102.8
工艺美术制造业			

7—15 主要原材料、燃料、动力购进价格指数

Principal Raw and Processed Materials, Fuel, Power Purchasing Price Indexes

(以上年价格为100)

类　　别	1995年	1996年	1997年
全部原材料	117.58	105.67	100.1
一、燃料动力类	112.18	109.29	108.4
二、黑色金属材料类	94.10	100.68	97.9
三、有色金属材料类	131.20	99.91	96.0
四、化工原料类	125.14	102.02	97.1
五、木材及纸浆类	129.37	97.63	94.3
六、建材类	103.04	102.53	102.7
七、非金属矿类	109.59	108.43	100.4
八、农副产品类	138.68	115.04	95.3
九、纺织原料类	123.84	86.30	88.8

7—16 主要原材料、燃料、动力购进产品分行业价格指数

Purchasing Price Indices of Important Raw Material、Fuel Power by Sector

(以上年为100)

分组名称	1997年	分组名称	1997年
煤炭采选业	104.2	医药制造业	107.0
石油天然气采选业		化学纤维制造业	103.0
黑色金属矿采选业	114.0	橡胶制品业	104.2
有色金属矿采选业	105.5	塑料制品业	100.3
非金属矿采选业	104.7	非金属矿物制品业	105.0
木材竹材采选业	96.7	黑色金属冶炼及压延加工业	105.5
食品加工业	106.7	有色金属冶炼及压延加工业	100.2
食品制造业	103.5	金属制品业	103.7
饮制造业	105.0	普通机械制造业	102.2
烟草加工业	101.9	专用设备制造业	100.9
纺织业	102.5	交通运输设备制造业	100.2
服装及其他纤维制品制造业	106.2	电气机械及器材制造业	106.6
皮鞋皮毛羽绒及其制品业		电子及通信设备制造业	103.1
木材加工及竹藤棕草制品业	99.3	仪器仪表及文化办公用机械制造业	107.9
家具制造业	100.0	其它制造业(地毯、首饰、漆器、制伞)	
造纸及纸制品业	102.3	电力蒸气热力生产和供应业	111.2
文教体育用品制造业	107.4	煤气生产和供应业	105.6
石油加工及炼焦业	98.7	自来水生产和供应业	106.7
化学原料及化学制品制造业	104.5		

7—17 固定资产投资和建筑业价格指数

Price Indexes of Investment in Fixed Assets and Construction

(以上年价格为100)

项　　目	1995年	1996年	1997年
一、固定资产投资品价格			
总指数	109.53	104.94	101.8
#建筑安装工程	110.37	108.18	102.1
设备、工具、器具购置	104.67	99.32	98.9
其他投资	114.66	96.19	107.5
二、建筑业			
施工产值指数	109.04	108.18	102.1
直接费用指数	110.64	108.08	101.3
#人工费	133.36	113.11	104.4
材料费	105.60	101.68	100.2
其他费用指数	109.04	113.21	106.0
三、主要材料费用价格指数			
钢　　材	94.29	97.25	98.7
木　　材	109.25	103.77	101.4
水　　泥	104.81	97.65	96.2
地方材料	114.90	101.78	101.1
其他材料	115.47	100.72	105.7

八、人民生活

PEOPLE'S LIVELIHOOD

8—1 人民物质文化生活提高情况

Improvement of People's Material and Cultural Life

指　　　　标	单位	1995年	1996年	1997年
一、就业				
每一农村劳动力负担人数	人	1.60	1.56	1.56
每一城镇就业者负担人数	人	1.67	1.64	1.64
城镇失业率	%	3.8	3.9	3.9
二、农民家庭人均纯收入	元	1425.16	1792.25	2037.06
城镇居民家庭人均可支配收入	元	4075.2	5052.1	5209.7
职工年平均工资(货币)	元	4797	5100	5326
三、全省居民消费水平	元	1752	2199	2390
农民	元	1294	1710	1851
非农业居民	元	3884	4395	4746
四、城乡居民年底储蓄存款余额	亿元	880.35	1179.52	1255.28
平均每人储蓄存款余额	元	1391.42	1840.12	1947.23
五、住房				
农村平均每人住房面积	平方米	25.57	26.88	27.37
城市平均每人居住面积	平方米	7.75	8.06	8.66
六、零售商业饮食业服务业网点				
七、城镇居民每百户拥有自行车	辆	157.5	148.9	137.2
农村居民每百户拥有自行车	辆	103.67	96.54	97.38
城市每万人拥有公共车辆	标台	9.2	8.76	9.13
八、城市公用事业				
自来水普及率	%	97.7	97.74	97.79
煤气、液化气普及率	%	55.5	64.7	65.7
每人拥有公共绿地	平方米	4.3	4.5	4.71
九、城镇居民每百户有彩色电视机	台	86.8	90.2	95.1
农村居民每百户有电视机	台	65.6	65.6	80.66
城镇居民每百户有录音机	台	67.8	71.7	49.1
农村居民每百户有收录机	台	25.6	28.9	19.8
平均每人每年发函件数	件	5.42	4.99	3.68
平均每万人每年订报刊数	份	2338	1370	2141
十、教育				
学龄儿童入学率	%	98.0	98.2	98.6
每万人口有大学生数	人	20.6	21.1	22.23
十一、卫生				
每万人口拥有医院病床数	张	21.28	20.79	20.84
每万人口拥有医生数	人	13.32	13.64	13.90

8—2 城镇居民生活

Urban Household's Life

年份	平均每人每年					每一就业者负担人数（人）	城市人均居住面积（平方米）
	全部收入	可支配收入	可支配收入指数(1978年为100)	消费性支出	#食品		
1978	323.88	323.9	100	289.56	166.1	1.90	3.9
1980	475.92	475.9	125.2	425.52	244.1	1.76	4.3
1985	760.80	760.8	161.8	685.32	366.48	1.88	6.0
1986	904.44	904.4	182.5	775.32	427.90	1.90	6.4
1987	1017.80	1017.8	184.5	871.56	497.10	1.87	6.5
1988	1254.97	1255.0	181.0	1142.70	580.70	1.84	6.9
1989	1492.61	1492.6	183.5	1234	678.30	1.82	7.0
1990	1591.45	1591.5	194.5	1294	720.30	1.80	6.91
1991	1783.24	1783.2	207.3	1446	772.07	1.80	7.07
1992	2172	2166.5	221.9	1732	881.56	1.76	7.41
1993	2822	2816.5	245.8	2194	1049.40	1.73	8.14
1994	3893	3887.6	271.9	3138	1496.80	1.70	7.93
1995	4705	4705.2	278.7	3886	1898.10	1.67	7.75
1996	5060	5052.1	279.2	4098	1986.6	1.64	8.06
1997	5248.9	5209.7	280.1	4317.2	1972.8	1.64	8.66

注：1991年及以前的可支配收入均以全部收入代替。

8—3 农村居民生活

Rural Household's Life

年份	平均每人每年					每一劳动力负担人数	农村人均居住面积（平方米）
	纯收入	纯收入指数(1978年为100)	总支出	生活消费支出	#食品		
1978	142.56	100.0	167.10	140.07	97.93	2.33	10.50
1980	219.72	147.6	236.13	192.95	127.7	2.09	11.15
1985	395.26	239.4	519.85	348.45	219.43	1.69	18.20
1986	439.66	255.9	568.00	386.35	228.96	1.68	19.25
1987	471.30	257.4	639.14	434.75	245.68	1.67	20.00
1988	515.40	244.8	730.06	480.75	266.89	1.65	20.48
1989	558.30	236.5	786.48	516.30	290.35	1.63	21.57
1990	545.69	229.4	780.77	504.60	288.32	1.65	22.27
1991	688.91	234.5	1088.06	655.54	408.21	1.69	22.58
1992	739.42	239.2	1116.06	707.29	438.11	1.67	23.12
1993	851.87	244.5	1306.48	816.55	498.95	1.63	24.56
1994	1155.00	257.0	1766.51	1088.73	665.72	1.60	24.23
1995	1425.16	270.4	2203.36	1367.30	823.91	1.60	25.57
1996	1792.25	292.8	2784.64	1736.71	1025.32	1.56	26.88
1997	2037.06	318.9	2853.42	1815.79	1078.00	1.56	27.37

8—4 城镇居民家庭基本情况

Basic Indicators of Urban Households

	单位	1995 年	1996 年	1997 年
调查户数	户	1000	1000	1000
平均每户家庭人口	人	3.19	3.19	3.14
平均每户就业人口	人	1.91	1.95	1.92
平均每户就业面(包括就业者)	%	59.9	61.1	61.1
平均每人全部年收入	元	4705.2	5059.7	5248.9
#可支配收入	元	4069.6	4280.1	5209.7
国有单位职工工资	元	3326.6	3700.0	3612.4
集体单位职工工资	元	295.2	275.8	323.6
职工从工作单位得到的其他收入	元	241.0	202.5	343.7
个体经营劳动者收入	元	26.0	44.3	35.2
被聘用或留用的离退休人员收入	元	2.6	6.4	12.9
其他就业者收入	元	2.3	2.4	3.8
其他劳动收入	元	94.8	108.9	86.1
财产性收入	元	81.6	86.8	112.0
转移性收入	元	626.5	619.4	668.1
平均每人消费性支出	元	3885.6	4098.3	4317.2
一、食品	元	1898.1	1986.6	1972.8
二、衣着	元	481.1	507.1	497.6
三、家庭设备和日用品	元	370.7	334.1	327.8
四、医疗保健	元	108.7	149.8	161.2
五、交通和通讯	元	206.9	210.6	276.7
六、娱乐、教育和文化	元	408.4	460.9	576.4
七、居住	元	244.3	267.8	316.7
八、杂项商品和服务	元	167.5	181.5	188.1

8—5 城镇居民可支配收入指数

Indexes of Urban Household Annual Living Income

年 份	以上年为100		以1978年为100	
	货币收入	实际收入	货币收入	实际收入
1995	121.0	102.5	1452.6	278.7
1996	107.4	100.2	1560.0	279.2
1997	103.1	100.3	1608.4	280.1

注:实际收入指数,指扣除价格上涨因素后的指数。

8—6 城镇居民1997年调查户基本情况

Basic Indicators of Urban Household Investigated in 1997

项目	单位	居民家庭总平均	按可支配收入高低分组							
			最低收入	更低收入	低收入	中等偏下	中等收入	中等偏上	高收入	最高收入
调查户数	户	1000	100	52	100	200	200	200	100	100
平均每户家庭人口	人	3.14	3.57	3.65	3.30	3.25	3.17	3.03	2.86	2.78
平均每户就业人口	人	1.92	1.89	1.82	1.87	1.89	1.97	1.97	1.92	1.90
平均每户就业面	%	61.1	52.9	49.9	56.7	58.2	62.1	65.0	67.1	68.3
平均每一就业者负担人数	人	1.64	1.89	2.01	1.76	1.72	1.61	1.54	1.49	1.46
平均每人每年可支配收入	元	5209.7	2406.8	2091.5	3290.1	3980.7	4926.7	6138.5	7665.4	10052.9
平均每人每年实际收入	元	5248.9	2437.4	2118.7	3320.3	4014.9	4979.5	6176.8	7703.4	10097.5
平均每人每年消费性支出	元	4317.2	2380.7	2098.7	3035.9	3591.0	4077.2	4967.3	6159.4	7255.8
一、食品	元	1972.8	1337.9	1219.1	1679.9	1791.1	1978.7	2209.7	2334.9	2657.2
#粮食	元	209.7	192.0	187.6	207.9	210.0	213.4	213.1	204.8	222.5
肉禽及制品	元	495.8	352.4	311.7	461.6	450.5	512.4	556.4	559.5	591.4
蛋类	元	58.6	41.5	41.5	57.4	58.9	58.6	59.3	66.7	71.9
水产品类	元	97.9	66.9	55.5	83.8	89.0	103.4	108.9	111.6	124.5
鲜菜	元	192.2	160.8	166.9	178.7	181.2	195.5	207.9	203.2	221.2
奶及奶制品	元	24.0	8.6	6.5	16.0	18.2	23.8	30.4	31.8	45.6
二、衣着	元	497.6	188.4	153.7	298.8	399.2	472.1	623.1	741.8	894.1
#服装	元	306.6	110.8	86.5	175.2	240.7	282.4	382.0	471.2	589.6
三、家庭设备、用品及服务	元	327.8	91.0	63.4	160.8	210.8	227.4	362.4	660.6	914.4
#耐用消费品	元	149.6	21.8	6.6	46.3	88.9	88.7	143.6	356.5	518.0
家庭日用杂品	元	101.5	50.7	44.2	70.6	77.1	95.4	130.9	142.9	167.4
四、医疗保健	元	161.3	76.5	49.3	88.5	120.2	150.0	196.1	246.0	313.8
五、交通和通讯	元	276.7	82.0	62.0	150.9	206.8	267.8	360.4	363.6	587.8
六、娱乐、教育、文化服务	元	576.4	324.8	345.5	342.0	490.8	549.9	633.8	992.4	884.9
耐用消费品	元	130.3	37.8	37.7	38.0	71.9	75.3	184.2	345.1	281.7
教育	元	343.0	258.1	283.5	251.6	351.0	385.5	307.1	446.4	416.6
文化娱乐	元	103.2	28.9	24.3	52.3	67.9	89.1	142.5	200.9	186.7
七、居住	元	316.7	207.7	163.8	227.3	244.8	272.0	341.0	499.8	590.9
#房租	元	72.5	51.1	44.6	59.1	73.1	67.0	71.1	105.9	96.0
水费	元	25.8	19.7	18.6	21.3	23.0	28.0	29.0	30.6	29.0
电费	元	61.2	29.8	28.6	39.1	52.1	60.1	78.8	88.1	86.0
八、杂项商品和服务	元	188.1	72.5	42.0	87.6	127.2	159.3	240.8	320.3	412.6

8—7 城镇居民1997年消费性支出构成

Composition of Consumption Expenditures of Urban Household in 1997

(以消费性支出为100)　　单位:%

项目	居民家庭总平均	按家庭人均生活费收入分组							
		最低收入	更低收入	低收入	中等偏下	中等收入	中等偏上	高收入	最高收入
消费性支出	100	100	100	100	100	100	100	100	100
一、食　品	45.7	56.2	58.1	55.3	49.9	48.5	44.5	37.9	36.6
#粮　食	4.9	8.1	8.9	6.8	5.8	5.2	4.3	3.3	3.1
肉禽及制品	11.5	14.8	16.8	15.2	12.5	12.6	11.2	9.1	8.2
蛋类	1.4	1.7	2.0	1.9	1.6	1.4	1.2	1.1	1.0
水产品类	2.3	2.8	2.6	2.8	2.5	2.5	2.2	1.8	1.7
菜　类	4.8	6.8	8.4	6.3	5.4	5.1	4.5	3.5	3.3
奶制品	0.6	0.4	0.3	0.5	0.5	0.6	0.6	0.5	0.6
二、衣　着	11.5	7.9	7.3	9.8	11.1	11.6	12.5	12.1	12.3
#服　装	7.1	4.7	4.1	5.8	6.7	6.9	7.7	7.6	8.1
三、家庭设备、用品及服务	7.6	3.8	3.0	5.3	5.9	5.6	7.3	10.7	12.6
#耐用消费品	3.5	0.9	0.3	1.5	2.5	2.2	2.9	5.8	7.1
家庭日用杂品	2.4	2.1	2.1	2.3	2.1	2.3	2.6	2.3	2.3
四、医疗保健	3.7	3.2	2.3	2.9	3.3	3.7	3.9	4.0	4.3
五、交通和通讯	6.4	3.5	3.0	5.0	5.8	6.6	7.3	5.9	8.1
六、娱乐、教育、文化服务	13.4	13.6	16.5	11.3	13.7	13.4	12.8	16.1	12.2
(一)耐用消费品	3.0	1.6	1.8	1.3	2.0	1.8	3.7	5.6	3.9
(二)教　育	8.0	10.8	13.5	8.3	9.8	9.5	6.2	7.2	5.7
(三)文化娱乐	2.4	1.2	1.2	1.7	1.9	2.2	2.9	3.3	2.6
七、居　住	7.3	8.7	7.8	7.5	6.8	6.7	6.9	8.1	8.2
#房　租	1.7	2.1	2.1	1.9	2.0	1.6	1.4	1.7	1.3
水　费	0.6	0.8	0.9	0.7	0.6	0.7	0.6	0.5	0.4
电　费	1.4	1.3	1.4	1.3	1.5	1.5	1.6	1.4	1.2
八、杂项商品和服务	4.4	3.1	2.0	2.9	3.5	3.9	4.8	5.2	5.7

8—8 城镇居民平均每人全年购买商品数量(1997年)

Per Capita Purchases of Maior Commodities in Urban Household(1997)

项目	居民家庭总平均	按家庭人均可支配收入分组							
		最低收入	更低收入	低收入	中等偏下	中等收入	中等偏上	高收入	最高收入
粮食(千克)	83.1	81.5	80.6	85.8	85.3	84.9	81.4	77.2	82.4
淀粉及薯类(千克)	6.3	6.3	7.2	6.1	6.1	6.1	6.3	6.3	7.2
大豆(千克)	0.3	0.2	0.2	0.2	0.2	0.3	0.3	0.3	0.3
豆腐(千克)	4.1	4.8	5.4	3.8	3.7	4.5	4.0	3.6	4.6
食用植物油(千克)	6.3	6.5	6.6	6.6	6.0	6.2	6.3	7.2	6.4
食用动物油(千克)	2.6	3.1	2.9	2.6	2.8	2.6	2.6	1.5	2.0
猪肉(千克)	19.8	16.1	14.0	19.1	18.6	19.5	21.7	21.5	23.0
牛肉(千克)	2.0	1.6	1.4	1.7	1.8	2.1	2.2	2.1	2.1
羊肉(千克)	0.3	0.2	0.1	0.2	0.3	0.4	0.4	0.3	0.4
家禽(千克)	6.0	3.8	3.6	5.7	5.3	6.0	7.2	7.2	6.9
蛋类(千克)	7.8	5.6	5.7	7.7	7.9	7.7	7.8	8.7	9.6
鱼(千克)	4.2	3.8	3.4	4.2	4.0	4.0	4.3	4.5	5.5
虾(千克)	0.3	0.1	0.1	0.2	0.3	0.4	0.5	0.4	0.4
鲜菜(千克)	101.2	89.1	90.6	95.9	97.1	102.7	106.6	105.1	113.1
食糖(千克)	1.2	0.9	0.8	1.2	1.1	1.4	1.1	1.2	1.6
糖果(千克)	0.7	0.5	0.4	0.5	0.6	0.7	0.9	1.0	1.0
卷烟(盒)	25.5	17.8	16.2	24.3	24.6	26.3	26.8	26.9	33.0
白酒(千克)	2.4	1.9	1.5	1.8	1.7	2.6	3.0	2.4	3.7
果酒(千克)	0.06	0.02	0.03	0.08	0.04	0.06	0.06	0.08	0.13
啤酒(千克)	2.0	0.5	0.4	1.3	1.7	1.8	2.3	2.0	5.0
其他酒(千克)	0.5	0.5	0.6	0.4	0.6	0.5	0.6	0.7	0.4
鲜瓜果(千克)	53.6	32.2	24.8	44.7	48.9	54.0	62.6	66.5	69.0
糕点(千克)	2.4	1.1	1.1	1.9	2.1	2.6	2.5	3.3	3.9
鲜乳品(千克)	0.4			0.3	0.4	0.5	0.6	0.6	0.6
奶粉(千克)	0.5	0.2	0.1	0.3	0.3	0.5	0.6	0.6	0.9
酸奶(千克)	0.2				0.2	0.2	0.4	0.3	0.4
男士服装(件)	2.1	1.1	0.8	1.2	2.0	2.1	2.3	2.7	3.2
女士服装(件)	3.3	1.5	1.2	2.2	2.8	3.3	3.9	4.7	5.0
儿童服装(件)	0.8	0.5	0.4	0.6	0.6	1.0	1.0	1.0	0.9
棉布(米)	0.2	0.1	0.1		0.2	0.2	0.2	0.4	0.4
棉化纤混纺(米)	0.2	0.1		0.1	0.1	0.2	0.2	0.2	0.4
化纤布(米)	0.8	0.3	0.2	0.5	0.7	0.6	0.8	1.2	1.5
呢绒(米)	0.1					0.1	0.1	0.1	0.1
绸缎(米)	0.1						0.1	0.1	0.2
毛线(千克)	0.3	0.2	0.1	0.2	0.2	0.3	0.3	0.4	0.4

8—9 城镇居民1997年平均每百户拥有耐用消费品数量

Possession of Major Durable Consumer Goods Per 100 Households in 1997

名称	单位	居民家庭总平均	按家庭人均可支配收入分组							
			最低收入	更低收入	低收入	中等偏下	中等收入	中等偏上	高收入	最高收入
毛皮大衣	件	52.4	37.4	31.7	47.2	43.0	43.1	56.6	72.5	82.0
呢大衣	件	192.0	133.5	109.4	144.3	157.7	189.0	207.5	258.2	275.7
毛　毯	条	147.5	129.9	120.8	134.9	142.0	140.2	150.7	176.8	168.1
沙　发	个	192.7	143.7	118.8	150.8	171.8	196.9	204.4	219.4	267.2
大衣柜	个	99.2	104.4	113.2	82.6	95.1	95.3	97.9	112.9	115.2
写字台	张	106.1	95.7	101.1	91.5	100.6	111.7	109.7	116.3	113.2
摩托车	辆	7.9	2.0	0.8	8.3	7.1	7.8	9.1	6.4	14.5
自行车	辆	137.2	107.3	91.2	134.4	124.3	140.8	146.3	147.5	160.2
缝纫机	台	58.1	46.2	56.5	52.9	57.8	56.1	60.8	66.8	65.4
洗衣机	台	94.0	85.0	78.2	94.6	95.0	90.8	92.8	100.2	103.4
电风扇	台	253.0	215.9	201.0	245.2	238.2	253.9	264.4	270.1	286.2
电冰箱	台	81.4	58.8	51.5	70.7	76.0	83.7	89.5	92.2	93.7
彩色电视机	台	95.1	72.7	63.9	95.2	87.1	94.5	101.2	108.4	109.5
影碟机	台	8.6			1.9	5.1	7.3	12.8	18.3	15.0
录放像机	台	19.6	7.1	6.5	11.7	14.3	20.1	25.1	21.8	36.6
家用电脑	台	2.7	2.4	4.7		2.4	1.3	3.7	5.5	4.2
组合音响	套	13.0	4.6	3.4	8.4	9.1	10.8	19.5	21.9	15.8
录音机	台	49.1	40.0	35.2	46.6	43.4	49.6	54.1	53.1	57.8
摄像机	台	0.2							1.3	0.8
照相机	架	31.5	17.3	19.5	23.9	23.3	33.3	35.5	42.3	47.5
钢　琴	架	1.0						1.0	0.8	6.8
其它中高档乐器	件	7.3	1.4	2.7	1.9	2.5	7.7	12.6	6.1	18.2
空调机	台	18.1	3.8	1.1	10.1	10.6	14.6	28.5	26.0	34.1
电炊具	台	48.2	30.1	35.4	37.8	40.1	41.8	61.4	61.7	65.5
淋浴热水器	台	42.5	16.5	13.8	37.2	30.7	31.8	60.4	60.9	64.4
脱排油烟机	台	36.3	19.5	14.7	33.1	27.8	31.4	42.5	53.8	53.2
吸尘器	台	3.6	0.8		3.7	1.3	1.5	4.8	5.4	10.9

8—10 各地市城镇居民家庭生活基本情况(1997年)

Basie Indicators of Urban Household's Life by Prefeeture and City

地　　市	平均每户家庭人口(人)	平均每户就业人口(人)	平均每一就业者负担人数(人)	平均每人现金收入(元)	平均每人可支配收入(元)	平均每人消费性支出(元)	平均每人年存入储蓄数(元)
长沙市	3.13	1.93	1.62	7844.3	6232.1	5528.5	533.8
株洲市	3.05	1.90	1.61	7112.2	5799.6	4719.2	697.8
邵阳市	3.16	2.01	1.57	5102.5	4317.2	3608.0	400.9
岳阳市	3.19	2.06	1.55	7611.0	6317.0	4837.3	741.4
常德市	3.02	1.97	1.53	5788.3	5175.5	4067.9	415.0
郴州市	3.14	1.98	1.59	6767.5	5239.2	4930.8	811.8
怀化市	3.21	1.90	1.69	5351.6	4538.0	3767.6	311.8
衡阳市	3.18	1.67	1.90	5249.2	4699.6	3723.0	702.1
湘潭市	3.11	1.88	1.65	6565.7	5464.9	4411.7	460.8
益阳市	3.16	2.10	1.50	5175.1	4822.8	3693.5	532.4
娄底市	3.36	1.98	1.70	6451.4	5574.5	4301.6	890.8
吉首市	3.60	2.20	1.64	6256.1	4653.8	3755.9	943.4
张家界市	3.27	1.47	2.22	4460.9	4083.6	2726.0	91.1
资兴市	2.88	1.27	2.27	5521.1	4547.5	3809.2	471.4
冷水江市	3.46	2.18	1.59	5580.4	3832.7	3016.2	1015.9
冷水滩市	3.24	2.00	1.62	3357.5	3239.0	2594.6	486.2
津　市	3.18	1.90	1.67	3854.6	3440.9	2918.9	265.9
芝山区	2.88	2.06	1.40	4366.0	4092.4	3307.7	359.6
道　县	3.04	1.76	1.73	4542.1	3763.7	2927.4	663.6
耒　阳	3.04	1.50	2.03	6159.7	4819.2	3422.4	1236.5
新　化	.41	1.94	1.76	4870.9	4122.2	3453.5	539.2
慈　利	3.28	1.96	1.67	6265.3	4872.7	3371.2	644.2
南　县	3.34	2.06	1.62	5784.6	5276.6	3501.4	242.6
临湘市	3.48	2.04	1.71	4711.9	4151.9	2921.8	1004.8
溆浦县	3.34	2.14	1.56	4909.6	3854.8	3059.5	151.1
武冈市	3.34	1.96	1.70	5204.3	3788.4	3043.9	522.1
攸　县	3.40	2.14	1.59	5000.9	4389.5	3345.5	535.1
凤凰县	4.20	2.33	1.80	4035.6	3664.8	2519.5	231.6

8—11 各地市城镇居民平均每人全年家庭收入来源(1997 年)

Urban Household Annual per Captita Sources of Income by prefecture and City

单位:元

地 市	可支配收 入	实际收入	国有单位职工收入	国有单位职工工资	集体单位职工收入	集体单位职工工资	其他经济类型单位职工收入	转移收入
长沙市	6232.1	6285.4	4979.4	4621.6	349.1	334.0		723.2
株洲市	5799.6	5840.8	4112.2	3742.9	130.9	122.6	105.1	771.6
邵阳市	4317.2	4359.5	3430.0	3191.3	205.1	196.8	91.8	566.2
岳阳市	6317.0	6321.1	4881.8	4491.2	588.6	536.0	31.8	642.8
常德市	5175.4	5199.5	3464.8	3194.9	536.4	494.0	88.8	722.2
郴州市	5239.2	5278.6	4101.0	3901.0	345.6	326.4		654.2
怀化市	4538.0	4550.8	3658.3	3516.7	393.8	189.6	63.4	429.6
衡阳市	4699.6	4756.6	2916.1	2520.6	124.7	117.4	1.6	1392.5
湘潭市	5464.9	5503.4	3564.1	3418.0	523.1	517.1	160.7	922.6
益阳市	4822.8	4898.0	4286.8	4270.0	19.8	19.8		330.0
娄底市	5574.5	5613.5	3894.7	3370.0	151.9	142.2		1253.2
吉首市	4653.8	4973.4	3851.4	3345	85.3	83.6	16.0	722.8
张家界市	4083.6	4277.3	1633.2	1512.7	120.8	120.8		1104.2
资兴市	4547.5	4569.4	2458.4	1970.5	203.2	198.4	244.8	1490.8
冷水江市	3832.7	3847.9	3140.0	2892.6	253.6	242.2		167.9
冷水滩区	3239.0	3239.8	1957.0	1907.0	488.8	438.8		193.3
津 市	3440.9	3442.8	1606.8	1498.9	615.1	582.5		712.8
芝山区	4092.4	4095.0	3443.4	3293.0	484.3	432.5	0.2	77.3
道 县	3763.7	3813.8	2753.9	2367.2	211.2	208.0		515.5
耒阳市	4819.3	4837.2	3396.7	2924.4	219.2	179.5		1077.5
新化县	4122.2	4172.6	2818.3	2661.2	272.4	266.4		802.8
慈利县	4872.7	4943.2	2941.4	2313.8	1094.2	894.4		525.7
南 县	5276.6	5342.1	3666.1	3481.1	293.8	289.1		1054.7
临湘市	4151.9	4175.9	3525.1	2955.8	116.5	113.6	16.7	238.4
溆浦县	3854.8	3901.0	2841.2	2576.9	118.6	115.2	113.0	299.4
武冈市	3788.4	3850.0	2110.6	1804.2	598.4	523.1	4.8	644.8
攸 县	4389.5	4432.1	3017.5	2390.5	770.2	620.4	4.7	282.8
凤凰县	3664.8	3704.0	2695.9	2452.7	204.5	202.9	1.3	613.0

8—12 城镇居民家庭平均每人全年现金收入和支出(1997年)

Annual Cash Revenue and Expenditures of Urban Household Per Capita

单位:元

项　　目	金　额	项　　目	金　额
期初手存现金	249.6	4.收回借出款	45.4
可支配收入	5209.7	5.收回储蓄性保险本金	2.5
现金收入	6349.6	6.兑售有价证券	10.1
一、实际收入	5248.9	7.赊购	0.1
1.国有单位职工收入	3928.5	8.为购置房屋从银行贷款	
2.集体经济单位职工收入	351.2	9.其他借贷收入	35.4
3.其他经济类型单位职工工资	40.2	现金支出	6276.3
4.个体经营者的净收入	30.1	一、实际支出	5301.7
5.个体被雇者收入	5.1	1.消费性支出	4317.2
6.离退休再就业者收入	12.9	2.非消费性支出	977.9
7.其他就业者收入	3.8	贷款利息	
8.其他劳动收入	86.1	个人所得税	1.4
9.财产性收入	112.0	其他各种税	0.8
利　息	74.7	各种非储蓄性保险支出	2.5
红　利	9.5	赡养支出	146.2
其他财产租金收入	27.8	赠送支出	650.3
10.转移收入	668.1	购房建房支出	134.3
离退休金	285.4	其他非消费支出	42.4
价格补贴	0.3	3.家庭副业生产支出	6.6
赡养收入	23.5	二、储蓄借贷支出	974.6
赠送收入	275.7	1.存入储蓄款	561.3
亲友搭伙费	35.3	2.存入储蓄会款	11.6
记帐补贴	31.2	3.归还借款	97.9
出售财物收入	7.7	4.借出款	29.4
其　他	9.0	5.储蓄性保险支出	52.2
11.家庭副业生产收入	11.0	6.购置有价证券	115.5
二、储蓄借贷收入	1100.7	7.预　购	
1.提取储蓄存款	717.0	8.归还购置住房的银行贷款	0.3
2.提取储金会款	22.4	9.其他借贷支出	106.4
3.借入款	267.8	期末手存现金	322.9

8—13 农村居民家庭基本情况

Basic Indicators of Rural Household

项　　目	单位	1995 年	1996 年	1997 年
调查村数	个	370	370	381
已通电话村所占比重	%	53.5	59.7	72.4
已通公路村所占比重	%	97.3	97.6	97.6
有学校的村所占比重	%	95.1	93.5	94.2
有卫生站的村所占比重	%	72.7	76.5	77.4
有邮电所(点)的村所占比重	%	23.5	34.3	35.4
有有线广播的村所占比重	%	42.2	39.2	39.9
调查户数	户	3700	3700	3810
调查户人口(常住人口)	人	15493	15064	15306
平均每户常住人口	人	4.19	4.07	9790
平均每户整半劳动力	人	2.62	2.61	2.57
平均每个劳动力负担人口	人	1.60	1.56	1.56
农户饮用安全卫生水所占户数比重	%	43.8	49.0	
每百个常住人口中职工人数	人	0.65	0.72	0.72
每百个常住人口中乡村企业从业人数	人	1.41	1.17	1.25
每百个常住人口中在外从事其他劳动人数	人	4.77	4.95	5.93
平均每人经营耕地面积	亩	1.25	1.42	1.20
平均每人经营山地面积	亩	0.58	0.54	0.61
平均每人经营水面面积	亩	0.04	0.04	0.04
平均每户年末拥有生产性固定资产原值	元	1376.34	2348.72	2507.72
平均每百个劳动力中:				
文盲或半文盲	人	6.65	5.17	4.62
小学程度	人	43.47	40.61	39.67
初中程度	人	38.88	43.07	44.70
高中程度	人	10.19	9.97	9.80
中专程度	人	0.63	0.91	1.00
大专以上	人	0.18	0.28	0.21
平均每个劳动力受教育年限	年	7.43	7.63	7.73
按纯收入分组户数占调查户比重				
100 元以下	%	0.03		
100—200 元	%	0.03	0.03	0.05
200—300 元	%	0.19	0.03	
300—400 元	%	0.65	0.24	0.13
400—500 元	%	1.22	0.27	0.16
500—600 元	%	2.30	0.92	0.55
600—800 元	%	7.75	2.70	2.05
800—1000 元	%	12.11	6.46	4.15
1000—1200 元	%	14.00	10.95	7.45
1200—1300 元	%	8.00	5.41	4.46
1300—1500 元	%	13.95	10.92	9.82
1500—1700 元	%	10.16	12.46	10.89
1700—2000 元	%	11.92	14.65	15.12
2000—2500 元	%	10.54	18.78	19.48
2500—3000 元	%	4.59	8.51	11.05
3000—3500 元	%	1.49	3.54	6.14
3500—4000 元	%	0.49	2.00	3.62
4000—4500 元	%	0.24		2.26
4500—5000 元	%	0.24	0.38	1.02
5000 元以上	%	0.11	0.86	1.60

8—14 农村居民主要农、牧产品出售情况

Sales of Major Farming, Animal Husbandry Products per Rural Household

项目	单位	1995年	1996年	1997年
粮食	公斤/人	104.85	130.47	120.19
棉花	公斤/人	2.74	2.57	5.02
油料	公斤/人	6.03	7.02	8.29
麻类	公斤/人	0.60	0.73	0.64
糖料	公斤/人	7.46	3.34	4.13
烟叶	公斤/人	2.00	4.75	8.22
蔬菜	公斤/人	24.82	31.46	45.73
果用瓜	公斤/人	6.94	11.29	7.95
水果	公斤/人	14.77	20.36	27.72
茶叶	公斤/人	0.12	0.24	0.17
猪肉	公斤/户	192.20	219.58	206.99
羊肉	公斤/户	0.26	0.82	1.25
家禽	公斤/户	4.43	4.58	6.65
禽蛋	公斤/户	4.50	5.04	4.50
鱼虾	公斤/户	19.79	14.96	20.79
蜂蜜	公斤/户	0.01	…	…
蚕茧	公斤/户	0.07	…	…

8—15 农村居民平均每人总收入及总支出

Annual per Capita Revenue and Expenditures of Rural Household

单位:元

项目	1995年	1996年	1997年
平均每人总收入	2235.35	2794.28	3060.92
一、基本收入	2160.40	2706.94	2971.75
1.劳动者报酬收入	268.00	352.07	459.97
(1)在集体组织中得到的报酬收入	35.04	46.04	56.70
(2)在企业劳动得到的收入	211.09	276.53	363.72
#在乡村企业劳动得到的报酬收入	46.41	38.06	52.31
在其他企业劳动得到的报酬收入	164.68	178.08	229.11
(3)在其他单位劳动得到的报酬收入	21.87	29.50	39.55
2.家庭经营收入	1892.40	2354.87	2511.79
二、转移性和财产性收入	74.96	87.34	106.43
平均每人总支出	2203.36	2784.64	2853.42
一、家庭经营费用支出	669.27	813.07	837.18
二、购置生产用固定资产支出	35.71	61.29	45.60
三、交纳税款	39.71	45.71	47.69
四、上交集体承包任务	33.16	31.20	25.07
五、集体提留和摊派	32.45	59.33	51.68
六、生活消费支出	1367.30	1736.71	1815.79
七、其他非借贷性支出	25.76	37.33	30.41
#寄给、带给在外人口	1.63	2.41	1.42
赠送农村外部亲友	2.11	3.00	3.73
其他支出	17.79	23.21	18.00

8—16 农村居民平均每人纯收入来源构成

Rural Household Per Capita Net Income by Source

单位:元

项　　目	1995 年	1996 年	1997 年
平均每人纯收入	1425.16	1792.25	2037.06
一、按纯收入来源分			
(一)基本收入	1363.89	1719.18	1968.52
1.劳动者的报酬收入	268.00	352.07	459.97
(1)在集体组织中得到报酬收入	35.04	46.04	56.07
(2)在企业劳动得到的收入	211.09	276.53	363.72
(3)在其他单位劳动得到的报酬收入	21.87	29.50	39.55
2.家庭经营纯收入	1095.89	1367.11	1508.55
(1)农业收入	627.31	769.02	792.01
(2)林业收入	14.28	27.76	21.88
(3)牧业收入	201.30	240.40	312.64
(4)渔业收入	27.12	25.87	33.25
(5)手工业收入	28.85	47.42	47.47
(6)采集捕猎收入	18.38	26.40	26.77
(7)工业收入	21.17	21.50	29.98
(8)建筑业收入	55.98	86.59	95.23
(9)运输业收入	20.18	30.00	39.10
(10)商业收入	35.70	36.38	42.70
(11)饮食业收入	2.03	2.29	2.52
(12)服务业收入	17.43	28.35	32.54
(13)其他家庭经营收入	26.16	25.13	32.46
(二)转移性收入和财产性收入	61.27	73.07	68.54
二、按纯收入性质分			
(一)生产性纯收入	1363.89	1719.18	1935.98
(二)非生产性纯收入	61.27	73.07	101.08
三、按现金和实物分			
(一)现金纯收入	845.35	1104.65	1321.23
(二)实物纯收入	579.91	687.60	715.83

8—17 农民人均纯收入指数

Indices of Net Income of Rural Household Per Capita

年　份	以上年为 100		以 1978 年为 100	
	按当年价格计算	扣除价格因素	按当年价格计算	扣除价格因素
1995	123.4	105.2	999.7	270.4
1996	125.8	108.3	1257.2	292.8
1997	113.7	108.9	1428.9	318.9

8—18 农村居民家庭平均每人生活消费支出

Rural Household per Capita Living Expenditures

	1995 年	1996 年	1997 年
生活消费支出	1367.30	1736.71	1815.79
按消费类别分:			
食　品	823.91	1025.32	1078.00
#主食	322.18	391.50	355.93
副食	362.86	441.40	489.41
其他食品	92.12	119.39	129.81
衣　着	73.51	96.04	89.97
居　住	192.42	229.74	242.55
家庭设备用品及服务	68.79	84.74	83.73
医疗保健	35.78	58.66	58.16
交通通讯	26.29	38.70	45.89
文教娱乐用品及服务	128.84	176.96	187.61
其他商品及服务	17.75	26.55	29.88
按消费性质分:			
货币性消费			
食　品	346.51	435.29	477.37
衣　着	73.00	95.13	89.48
居　住	178.16	210.13	225.10
家庭设备用品及服务	68.77	84.74	83.73
医疗保健	35.78	58.66	58.16
交通通讯	26.29	38.70	45.89
文教娱乐用品及服务	128.84	176.96	187.61
其他商品及服务	17.75	26.55	29.88
实物性消费			
食　品	477.40	590.03	600.63
衣　着	0.51	0.91	0.49
居　住	14.26	19.61	17.45
家庭设备用品及服务	0.02		
医疗保健			
交通通讯			
文教娱乐用品及服务			
其他商品及服务			

8—19 农村居民平均每人现金收入

Rural Household Per Capita Cash Revenue

单位:元

项　　目	1995年	1996年	1997年
平均每人现金收入	1873.35	2471.13	2699.93
一、基本收入	1364.70	1740.68	2010.69
1.劳动者报酬收入	267.35	351.60	459.42
(1)在集体组织中得到的报酬收入	34.78	45.63	56.29
(2)在企业劳动得到的收入	210.69	276.47	363.58
(3)在其他单位劳动得到的报酬收入	21.87	29.50	39.55
2.家庭经营现金收入	1097.35	1389.08	1551.27
(1)出售产品收入	857.40	1060.78	1184.82
#出售种植业产品收入	276.27	384.26	389.21
出售牧业产品收入	500.66	577.80	679.91
(2)工业加工费的现金收入	25.56	20.20	20.03
(3)建筑业的现金收入	59.85	94.50	96.89
(4)运输业的现金收入	34.90	49.71	66.72
(5)商业的现金收入	44.0	56.65	62.24
(6)饮食业的现金收入	3.00	4.91	5.18
(7)服务业的现金收入	20.29	34.59	37.57
(8)其他家庭经营现金收入	52.35	67.76	77.81
二、转移性和财产性收入	150.59	203.42	207.61
三、储蓄借贷现金收入	358.07	527.03	481.63
1.银行信用社得到的贷款	35.26	65.02	56.06
2.借入款	204.49	272.03	273.19
3.收回借出款	74.14	111.09	89.36
4.从银行信用社取回存款	43.34	75.93	62.48
5.转让股票收入			
6.收回投资款	0.82	2.96	0.54

8—20 农村居民平均每人现金支出

Rural Household Per Capita Cash Expenditures

单位:元

项 目	1995年	1996年	1997年
平均每人现金支出	1832.79	2376.57	2578.52
一、生产费用支出	498.56	620.18	662.75
1.家庭经营费用支出	462.85	558.88	617.15
#种植业生产支出	184.93	226.73	215.94
牧业生产支出	198.83	231.39	299.04
2.购置生产用固定资产支出	35.71	61.29	45.60
二、交纳税款	35.22	39.52	45.82
三、上交集体承包任务	30.07	29.06	24.47
四、集体提留和摊派	32.45	59.33	51.68
五、生活消费支出	875.11	1126.16	1197.23
六、其他非借贷性支出	121.59	201.84	205.97
#寄给、带给在外人口	1.63	2.41	1.36
赠送农村以外亲友	2.10	2.93	3.23
其他支出	11.32	19.75	17.05
七、储蓄借贷现金支出	239.79	300.49	390.61
#归还银行信用社贷款	26.67	44.53	42.94
借出款	26.91	39.72	33.50
归还款	101.59	140.07	174.30
存入银行信用社款	82.70	73.07	134.29
支出投资款	1.92	3.09	5.57

8—21 农村居民平均每人全年主要消费品消费量

Rural Household Per Capita Annual Consumption of Major Consumer Goods

指　　标	单位	1996年	1997年	指　　标	单位	1996年	1997年
棉布	米	0.22	0.12	蛋类及蛋制品	公斤	2.53	2.99
化纤布	米	1.85	1.66	奶和奶制品	公斤	0.03	0.03
呢绒	米	0.03	0.27	水产品	公斤	4.69	5.38
绸缎	米	0.01	…	(1)鱼类	公斤	4.48	4.50
毛线及毛线织品	公斤	0.09	0.08	(2)虾类	公斤	0.04	0.03
棉布服装	件	0.07	0.04	(3)贝类	公斤	0.02	0.02
化纤布服装	件	1.17	1.10	(4)澡类	公斤	0.08	0.77
呢绒服装	件	0.02	0.01	(5)其他水产品	公斤	0.08	0.06
绸缎服装	件	0.01	…	糖类	公斤	1.98	1.83
皮鞋	双	0.23	0.23	(1)食糖	公斤	1.40	1.34
胶鞋、球鞋	双	0.67	0.62	(2)糖果	公斤	0.57	0.49
床褥单	条	0.04	0.04	(3)其他	公斤	0.02	…
肥皂	块	1.00	0.88	酒和饮料	公斤	10.43	8.78
洗衣粉	公斤	1.16	1.18	(1)白酒	公斤	4.62	5.34
粮食(原粮)	公斤	298.71	289.68	(2)啤酒	公斤	1.04	1.04
#(1)小麦	公斤	2.99	2.59	(3)果酒	公斤	0.05	0.04
(2)稻谷	公斤	286.09	280.64	(4)其他酒	公斤	1.55	1.18
(3)玉米	公斤	0.87	0.90	(5)汽水、可乐	公斤	0.06	0.05
(4)高粱	公斤	0.09	0.14	(6)茶叶	公斤	0.21	0.21
(5)薯类	公斤	5.85	2.93	(7)其他饮料	公斤	0.99	0.92
豆类	公斤	1.97	1.61	糕点	公斤	1.13	1.04
#大豆	公斤	1.95	1.59	干鲜瓜果类	公斤	19.89	21.73
豆制品	公斤	3.30		(1)苹果	公斤	2.23	2.68
蔬菜	公斤	137.18	142.79	(2)梨	公斤	0.48	0.70
(1)鲜菜	公斤	136.77	142.36	(3)香蕉	公斤	0.11	0.20
(2)干菜	公斤	0.41	0.44	(4)柑桔	公斤	6.23	9.56
调味品	元	7.13	10.44	(5)菠萝	公斤	0.01	0.01
油脂类	公斤	8.27	9.05	(6)葡萄	公斤	0.07	0.05
(1)植物油	公斤	3.58	4.55	(7)桃	公斤	0.28	0.25
(2)动物油	公斤	4.69	4.50	(8)柿子	公斤	0.05	0.01
肉禽及其制品	公斤	19.47	19.80	(9)西瓜	公斤	7.23	5.43
#(1)猪肉	公斤	16.71	16.15	(10)其他	公斤	3.21	2.84
(2)牛肉	公斤	0.19	0.35	坚果及果仁制品	公斤	0.08	0.79
(3)羊肉	公斤	0.05	0.07	(1)坚果和果仁	公斤	0.06	0.78
(4)家禽	公斤	2.26	3.00	(2)坚果和果仁制品	公斤	0.02	0.01
(5)肉禽制品	公斤	0.15	0.12				

8—22 农村居民平均每百户年末拥有耐用消费品数量

Rural Household Year－End Possession of Durable Consumer Goods Per 100 Households

品 名	单位	1996年	1997年	品 名	单位	1996年	1997年
自行车	辆	96.54	97.38	沙发	个	35.54	37.69
缝纫机	架	39.81	41.02	大衣柜	个	115.70	115.80
钟	只	39.70	48.19	写字台	张	100.27	102.41
手表	只	120.05	120.71	收音机	台	10.14	10.37
电子表	只	20.43	23.02	黑白电视机	台	69.14	69.45
电风扇	台	120.32	128.03	彩色电视机	台	7.84	11.21
洗衣机	台	6.00	6.98	收录机	台	18.84	19.82
电冰箱	台	2.30	3.43	照像机	台	0.76	0.76
摩托车	辆	2.78	4.44				

8—23 农村居民住房情况

Rural Household Livng Conditions

指 标	单 位	1995年	1996年	1997年
平均每户年末使用房屋间数	间	5.20	4.87	5.05
平均每人新建房屋面积	平方米	0.94	1.63	1.03
#砖木结构面积	平方米	0.74	0.97	0.56
钢筋混凝土面积	平方米	0.18	0.64	0.43
楼房面积	平方米	0.46	0.69	0.46
平均每人年末住房面积	平方米	25.57	26.88	27.37
#砖木结构面积	平方米	19.72	19.70	19.62
钢筋混凝土面积	平方米	2.44	4.80	5.33
年末每间房屋价值	元	1197.02	2282.14	2498.58

8—24 农村居民拥有生产性固定资产

Comprehensive Appraise on “Comparatively Well off”Level in Rual Areas

	1990年	1995年	1996年	1997年
一、按原值计算(每户拥有)				
合　　计(元)	791.82	1376.34	2348.72	2507.72
1. 役畜、产品畜	243.66	335.69	487.98	494.57
2. 大中型铁木农具	93.18	151.61	266.77	271.20
3. 农林牧渔机械	67.32	150.87	234.24	256.80
4. 工业机械	47.40	90.48	89.55	110.92
5. 运输机械	80.41	205.46	318.98	328.28
6. 生产用房	232.55	417.15	858.52	961.50
7. 其他	27.30	25.08	92.69	84.46
二、按实物统计(每百户拥有)				
汽　车(辆)	0.16	0.23	0.46	0.42
大中型拖拉机(台)	0.05	0.07	0.24	0.19
小型和手扶拖拉机(台)	1.43	2.07	2.95	3.10
机动脱粒机(台)	1.01	4.33	8.33	8.30
胶轮大车(辆)	0.42	0.49	1.05	0.88
胶轮手推车(辆)	7.70	10.04	10.76	10.39
抽水机(台)	2.00	3.94	5.11	4.92
水　泵(台)	2.51	5.89	8.47	9.14
机动船(条)	0.08	0.08	0.34	0.30
役　畜(头)	35.30	31.02	28.89	29.84
产品畜(头)	26.19	29.15	25.66	28.45

九、城市建设 环境保护

CONSTRUCTION OF CITIES, ENVIRONMENTAL PROTECTION

9—1 城市公用事业基本情况

Basic Statistics on Urban Public Utilities

	单 位	1995 年	1996 年	1997 年
一、城市个数	个	28	29	29
省辖市	个	11	11	12
县级市	个	17	18	17
二、城市规模				
12 个省辖市区年末总人口	万人			1004.04
12 个省辖市区面积	平方公里			16135
#建成区面积	平方公里			501
三、房屋建筑				
固定资产投资(12 个省辖市)	亿元			268.18
#住宅投资	亿元			46.26
本年实有住宅居住面积	万平方米	4816	5351	5355.01
人均住宅居住面积	平方米	7.75	8.06	8.66
四、自来水				
年末自来水生产能力	万吨/日	1207	1151	1179
年末供水管道长度	公里	4581	5879	6616
全年供水总量	亿吨	31.78	29.14	34.01
#生活用水量	亿吨	8.18	7.79	8.89
平均每人生活用水	吨/年	121.0	110.41	117.10
用水普及率	%	97.7	97.7	97.79
五、公用煤气、液化气				
煤气供气总量	万立方米	69984	74915	94860
煤气管道长度	公里			811
液化石油气(家庭用量)	吨	116518	121293	137752
用气普及率	%	55.5	64.7	65.70
六、邮电、通讯、电力				
邮电业务总量(按 1990 年不变价计算)	亿元	20.48	27.72	29.28
年末电话机数	万部	112.49	135.89	124.91
年末无线寻呼用户	万户			90.58
年末移动电话	万部			29.05
年末邮电局(所)数	处		2864	1576
全年用电量	亿千瓦小时	167.19	172.98	113.21
#工业用电	亿千瓦小时	119.13	127.49	80.07
城乡居民生活用电	亿千瓦小时	24.39	27.14	20.24

注：1. 怀化改地级市因机构未理顺仍按上年建制报年报。

2. 本表资料来源于省建委正式年报，包括地级市、县级市共 29 个。

3. 表中二、六两部分，1997 年数为 12 个省辖市数，与前两年不可比。

9—1 续表

	单 位	1995 年	1996 年	1997 年
七、市政工程				
铺装道路长度	公里	3570	4132	4275
铺装道路面积	万平方米	3129	3816	4025
平均每人拥有道路面积	平方米	5.3	6.22	6.32
立交桥数量	座			83
城市下水道长度	公里	2928	3209	3274
城市污水厂日处理能力	万吨/日	38.7	52.15	58.15
城市污水处理率	%	6.1	11.04	19.32
城市路灯	万盏	5.20	5.74	6.64
防洪堤长度	公里			591.69
八、公共车辆				
年末实有公共汽车	辆	6871	7092	7551
平均每万人拥有公共车辆	标台	9.2	8.76	9.13
营运线路长度	公里			2712
运客总数	万人次	92334	81756	93053
出租汽车	辆	12525	13693	15671
九、园林绿化				
园林绿地总面积	公顷	23661	24866	25807
公共绿地面积	公顷			3003
人平公共绿地面积	平方米	4.3	4.5	4.71
公园个数	个	97	100	105
公园面积	公顷	2183	2290.01	2448
苗圃面积	公顷			752.6
十、环境卫生				
清扫面积	万平方米	1976	2062.71	2344
生活垃圾清运量	万吨	249	274.78	294.07
粪便清运量	万吨	26	28.36	27.21
垃圾无害化处理能力	吨/日			100.00
垃圾粪便无害化处理率	%	43.9	26.29	29.54
环卫机械数量	辆	943	1013	1110
公共厕所	座	2751	2611	2596

9—2 废水、废气、粉尘与工业固体废物排放及处理情况

Statistics on Discharge and Treatment of Waste Water, Waste Gas, Dust and Industrial Residue

指　　标	单　位	1995年	1996年	1997年
一、工业废水处理设施				
汇总工业企业数	个	1704	2829	3528
治理设施数	套	3849	2708	2736
治理设施设备原价	万元	126649	167911	151374.1
二、工业废水排放				
工业废水排放总量	万吨	145251	144946	149538.84
工业废水排放达标率	%	56	57.1	52.5
三、工业废水处理				
工业废水处理量	万吨	144893	150617	145213.48
工业废水处理回用量	万吨	70462	78476	72165.07
工业废水处理排放达标量	万吨	39719	37275.51	44210.86
工业废水处理率	%	83.2	84.6	77.5
四、工业废气排放总量	亿标立方米	3466	3520	3718.61
燃料燃烧过程中废气排放量	亿标立方米	1893	1976	1843.25
#经过消烟除尘的	亿标立方米	1720	1728	1596.47
生产工艺过程中废气排放量	亿标立方米	1573	1544	1875.36
#经过净化处理的	亿标立方米	1182	1224	1504.64
五、工业粉尘排放量	万吨	27.1	27.3	94.5
工业粉尘回收量	万吨	125.4	117.2	149.5
六、工业固体废物产生、排放及处理情况				
1.工业固体废物产生量	万吨	1853	1801	2188.31
2.工业固体废物处置量	万吨	474	182	251.43
工业固体废物处置率	%	25.6	10.0	11.4
3.工业固体废物贮存量	万吨	717	810	938.08
工业固体废物贮存率	%	38.7	44.9	42.0
4.工业固体废物综合利用量	万吨	767	776	911.33
工业固体废物综合利用率	%	41.4	43.0	41.6
5.工业固体废物排放量	万吨	46	52	142.90
6.历年工业固体废物堆存总量	万吨	25840	22521	23951.03
七、“三废”综合利用产品产值	万元	98301	98223	98797.0
“三废”综合利用利润	万元	25214	16500	25823.4

注:汇总企事业单位数仅指“废水处理设施”项的汇总数,不是“废水排放及处理”项的汇总数。

9—3 工业污染治理情况

Statistics on Treatment of Pollution in Enterprises and Institutions

项　　目	单位	1995年	1996年	1997年
一、污染治理资金来源总计	万元	37656	20488.7	21761.0
#1.基本建设资金	万元	12625	3312.9	1229.1
2.更新改造资金	万元	14035	3980.6	801.3
3.综合利用利润留成	万元	812	2197.2	1243.3
4.环保补助资金	万元	6623	1173.2	1768.6
5.贷　款	万元	5174	3750.9	3933.8
6.其　　他	万元	3561	6073.9	12784.9
二、污染治理资金使用总计	万元	37656	31545.2	21761.0
1.治理废水	万元	14111	20688.7	12526.3
2.治理废气	万元	17480	6784.8	6903.4
3.治理固体废物	万元	3885	2814.8	727.9
4.治理噪声	万元	1384	179.6	261.2
5.其　　他	万元	796	1077.3	1342.2
三、污染治理概况				
1.当年安排治理项目	个	1664	365	310
2.当年竣工项目	个	1405	373	387
#治理废水	个	499	131	148
治理废气	个	545	162	169
治理固体废物	个	153	35	32
治理噪声	个	128	17	11
3.排污费收支情况				
交纳排污费单位	个	22470		
征收排污费	万元	18949		
4.污染情况				
污染事故	次	301	214	362
污染赔款总额	万元	420	2296.5	2752.1
污染罚款总额	万元	35	33.2	43.2

9—4 12个地级市城市基本情况(1997年)

Basic Statistics on Pant of City Which 12 Prefecture－Level Cities

指标名称	单位	地区（包括市辖县）	市区（不包括市辖县）
一、人口、劳动力及土地面积			
年末总人口	万人	5792.96	1004.04
其中：非农业人口	万人	1100.5	518.59
年末全部从业人员数	万人	3457.04	600.64
其中：城镇个体劳动者	万人	228.1	85.78
土地面积	平方公里	188627	16135
其中：建成区面积	平方公里		501
二、综合经济			
(一)国内生产总值(当年价格)	万元	27558569	9826855
第一产业	万元	7926983	877194
第二产业	万元	10326487	4570000
其中：工业增加值	万元	8903353	3843459
第三产业	万元	9305099	4379661
(二)农业			
农林牧渔业总产值(当年价格)	万元	12265749	1471663
年末实有耕地面积	千公顷	2941	328
蔬菜产量	万吨	1207.38	224.21
水果产量	吨	1434921	167582
猪肉产量	吨	3553018	397730
牛羊肉产量	吨	144988	12685
牛羊奶产量	吨	5696	2143
禽蛋产量	吨	598179	88567
禽肉产量	吨	443001	67821
水产品产量	吨	1056709	185188
(三)工业			
乡及乡以上工业企业及生产单位数	个	24771	7426
其中：国有经济	个	4154	1631
集体经济	个	18797	5186
私营经济	个	997	197
工业总产值(当年价格)	万元	35554432	12852804
其中：乡及乡以上工业总产值	万元	17444104	9259138
其中：国有经济	万元	8553202	6073680
集体经济	万元	7107888	2183967
私营经济	万元	364165	101976
全部独立核算工业企业经济指标			
工业增加值(生产法)	万元	4979396	2753390
流动资产年平均余额	万元	8949630	5684266
固定资产原价合计	万元	14303984	9182696
固定资产净值年平均余额	万元	9375314	5897313
产品销售收入	万元	14107448	8265702
其中：产品销售税金及附加	万元	659945	538274

9—4 续表1

指标名称	单位	地区（包括市辖县）	市区（不包括市辖县）
本年应交增值税	万元	725244	459893
利润总额	万元	228229	216603
(四)交通运输、邮电通信、电力			
铁路客运量	万人	4204.693	2656.53
铁路货运量	万吨	4484	2513
民用运输车辆拥有量	辆	572680	210729
公路客运量	万人	72436.33	42632.32
公路货运量	万吨	32745	19256
水运客运量	万人	1112.41	244.64
水运货运量	万吨	3575	1230
年末邮电局(所)数	处	12043	1576
邮电业务总量	万元	498757	292763
电话交换机装机总容量	门	3948942	2014530
年末电话机数	部	2585536	1249119
年末无线寻呼用户数	户	1472930	905847
年末移动电话用户数	户	482210	290468
全年用电量	万千瓦小时	2405749	1132062
其中:工业用电	万千瓦小时	1624214	800681
城乡居民生活用电	万千瓦小时	418443	202402
(五)批发零售贸易与外经、旅游			
批发零售贸易业商品销售总额	万元	12424220	8047148
社会消费品零售总额	万元	9603983	4698830
外国和港澳台地区在华直接投资			
新签协议(合同)数	个	509	278
客商协议投资额	万美元	115039	66054
客商实际投资额	万美元	85100	60150
旅游者人数	人	38010400	
其中:境外旅游者人数	人	172150	
旅游收入	万元	664941	
其中:外汇收入	万元	88463	
(六)固定资产投资			
固定资产投资完成额	万元	5271532	2681766
其中:住宅建设	万元	1273311	462593
房地产开发投资完成额	万元	328530	301575
其中:商品住宅	万元	192563	178571
全年新增固定资产	万元	3632635	1832762
全年施工住宅建筑面积(包括商品房)	万平方米	3189.63	1131.66
全年竣工住宅建筑面积(包括商品房)	万平方米	2527.12	747.43
商品房屋销售建筑面积	万平方米	144.2	122.31
商品房屋销售额	万元	150860	135601

9—4 续表 2

指 标 名 称	单 位	地 区（包括市辖县）	市 区（不包括市辖县）
三、教育、科技、文化、卫生			
在校学生总数	万人	1047	207
其中：高等学校	人	138231	136857
中等专业学校	人	217263	185340
普通中学	万人	294.02	52.63
小学	万人	701.89	110.45
成人高等教育学校在校学生数	人	68858	64573
成人中等教育学校在校学生数	人	139737	107119
各类专业技术人员数	万人	103.33	53.841
其中：中级技术职称以上人员	万人	35.44	20.57
剧场、影剧院数	个	185	61
公共图书馆总藏量	千册、件	13267	7457
医院、卫生院数	个	3925	936
医院、卫生院床位数	张	121506	48206
医生数	人	73694	28299
四、财政、金融、保险			
中央财政预算内收入	万元	473203	251061
地方财政预算内收入	万元	1115690	513775
其中：工商税收	万元	619185	351733
地方财政预算内支出	万元	1516598	684558
其中：科学事业费支出	万元	6499	4436
教育事业费支出	万元	308646	83751
金融机构数	个	8637	2251
其中：保险机构数	个	312	118
年末金融机构存款金额	万元	16061582	9033655
其中：城乡居民储蓄年末余额	万元	11065997	5634309
年末金融机构各项贷款余额	万元	17731576	9727751
承保额	万元	33104422	17065799
保费	万元	269756	141191
已决赔款	万元	89328	43798
五、人民生活			
住宅建筑面积	万平方米		8850.83
住宅使用面积	万平方米		6333.59
全部职工平均人数	万人	531.57	257.65
社会福利院数	个	990	99
社会福利院床位数	张	21620	4982
六、社会治安			
交通事故件数	件		4624
刑事案件发案数	件		27149
犯罪人数	人		21027

9—5 湖南东线各城市基本情况(一)(1997年)

Basic Statistics on Eastern Cities in Hunan Include Counties under The Jurisdiction of The Municipal Government （包括市辖县）

指标名称	单位	长沙市	株洲市	湘潭市	衡阳市	岳阳市	郴州市
一、人口、劳动力及土地面积							
年末总人口	万人	571.91	365.65	276.18	692.42	510.35	444.76
其中:非农业人口	万人	170.98	87.63	71.4	131.73	94.71	80.41
年末总户数	万户	164.78	97.83	81.15	181.99	151.88	121.99
年末全部从业人员数	万人	379.02	207.5	165.9	368.95	352.5	243.62
其中:城镇个体劳动者	万人	21.55	4.75	12.8	16.5	24.22	13.24
(1)农、林、牧、渔业	万人	150.88	99.8	85.3	205.7	207.4	153.48
(2)采掘业	万人	1.51	1.5	1.3	5.36	3.6	9.46
(3)制造业	万人	68.33	41.7	27.2	51.5	40.4	15.42
(4)电力、煤气及水的生产和供应业	万人	0.71	0.8	0.4	1.01	0.5	0.95
(5)建筑业	万人	25.41	11	13.4	19.59	18	1.28
(6)地质勘查业、水利管理业	万人	1.08	0.4	0.3	0.71	0.4	0.52
(7)交通运输、仓储及邮电通信业	万人	12.3	8.3	4.3	13.38	12.7	6.65
(8)批发和零售贸易、餐饮业	万人	50.22	25.2	13.6	39.13	46.64	25.2
(9)金融、保险业	万人	3.26	1.4	1	2.19	1.27	1.29
(10)房地产业	万人	0.39	0.1	0.1	0.34	0.14	0.15
(11)社会服务业	万人	10.94	3.2	2.2	7.68	7.93	5.26
(12)卫生、体育和社会福利业	万人	3.31	1.3	1.1	2.53	1.62	1.4
(13)教育、文化艺术和广播电影电视业	万人	11.91	3.9	3.4	6.78	4.8	5.64
(14)科学研究和综合技术服务业	万人	2.71	0.5	0.2	0.37	0.3	0.18
(15)国家机关、政党机关和社会团体	万人	6.16	3	2.3	4.63	3.9	4.38
(16)其他行业	万人	29.9	5.4	9.8	8.05	2.9	12.36
城镇失业人员年末数	人	28700	15201	11320	55600	59028	15000
土地面积	平方公里	11819	11420	5015	15310	15019	19388
二、综合经济							
(一)国内生产总值(当年价格)	万元	4828691	2397033	1875000	2643541	2795623	1895096
第一产业	万元	687320	491597	371431	902091	866303	550074
第二产业	万元	2075005	1155827	824000	899373	1018464	694007
其中:工业增加值	万元	1670486	1027390	702000	787277	923995	634823
第三产业	万元	2066366	749609	679569	842077	910856	651015
(二)农业							
农林牧渔业总产值(当年价格)	万元	1114485	749052	584913	1468954	1357948	864476
年末实有耕地面积	千公顷	244	160	122	306	287	207
蔬菜产量	万吨	173.29	84.85	58	129.09	104.78	69.79
水果产量	吨	39559	36465	8403	88021	55938	94837

9—5 续表1 (包括市辖县)

指标名称	单位	长沙市	株洲市	湘潭市	衡阳市	岳阳市	郴州市
猪肉产量	吨	383970	213572	224363	483954	409000	279152
牛羊肉产量	吨	9232	5407	988	7665	4254	7052
牛羊奶产量	吨	2738	45	172	70	281	39
禽蛋产量	吨	40129	25763	22050	116451	56595	13942
禽肉产量	吨	21572	19426	7817	54853	35236	23984
水产品产量	吨	75529	39177	53000	151349	225481	43271
(三)工业							
乡及乡以上工业企业及生产单位数	个	3838	1800	1643	2682	1944	1807
其中:国有经济	个	541	259	167	413	385	279
集体经济	个	2442	1450	1386	2152	1468	1409
私营经济	个	686	12	61	26	22	35
股份制经济	个	6	8	6	15	10	5
外商及港澳台投资经济	个	143	53	23	50	49	48
工业总产值(当年价格)	万元	6008035	3528681	2342194	3977847	4435869	2965897
其中:乡及乡以上工业总产值	万元	3620568	2002825	1435060	1621283	2597987	996652
其中:国有经济	万元	1599622	1208213	751011	764455	1401941	459406
集体经济	万元	1443444	573885	608841	730745	859007	465637
私营经济	万元	248264	5285	23674	5108	21337	2425
股份制经济	万元	51399	66694	21925	55403	25205	16604
外商及港澳台投资经济	万元	271308	142827	29609	55048	290497	41725
其中:轻工业	万元	1962176	406785	405406	541172	931362	259474
全部独立核算工业企业经济指标							
工业增加值(生产法)	万元	1142219	514608	315424	442194	766655	291738
流动资产年平均余额	万元	1960894	1233565	878930	847309	1071632	520821
固定资产原价合计	万元	2331723	1691689	1501034	1431713	2096712	1043634
固定资产净值年平均余额	万元	1530494	1108960	922974	961873	1167917	787715
产品销售收入	万元	2960591	1804654	1029462	1307073	2264473	881331
其中:产品销售税金及附加	万元	267858	26842	7480	24219	10622	62760
本年应交增值税	万元	180299	102274	46541	47133	109875	45186
利润总额	万元	76455	11694	35550	448	17498	2903
(四)交通运输、邮电通信、电力							
铁路客运量	万人	794	521.41	152	550.28	526.29	202.7
铁路货运量	万吨	262	512	429	375	612	768
民用运输车辆拥有量	辆	72656	35872	18898	31475	98014	79751
公路客运量	万人	7210	4960.13	3095	5662	7206.2	9798
公路货运量	万吨	4784	4500	2487	2276	1581	6386
水运客运量	万人	24	2.01	4	97	107.4	127
水运货运量	万吨	684	250	133	560	450	170
民用航空货邮运量	吨	9875					
民用航空客运量	万人	172					
年末邮电局(所)数	处	745	221	175	961	205	1595
邮电业务总量	万元	142291	39765	26873	42000	51041	27034
电话交换机装机总容量	门	995947	297654	241030	364822	333834	280454

9—5 续表 2 (包括市辖县)

指标名称	单位	长沙市	株洲市	湘潭市	衡阳市	岳阳市	郴州市
年末电话机数	部	553560	210793	154235	248800	230274	153762
年末无线寻呼用户数	户	408975	120000	75388	142354	136749	86036
年末移动电话用户数	户	184907	40000	22902	22298	42101	24456
全年用电量	万千瓦小时	379048	328749	269171	218976	221306	235287
其中:工业用电	万千瓦小时	190771	269743	229731	150639	161519	154317
城乡居民生活用电	万千瓦小时	109368	25078	27286	36490	35087	63394
(五)批发零售贸易与外经、旅游							
批发零售贸易业商品销售总额	万元	5583421	734309	793297	968787	723435	685071
社会消费品零售总额	万元	2050280	876030	548067	948150	995402	787754
外国和港澳台地区在华直接投资							
新签协议(合同)数	个	82	20	22	115	65	95
客商协议投资额	万美元	13060	6307	2033	17375	17269	36704
客商实际投资额	万美元	29086	6209	4029	11096	8725	5681
年末实有企业数	个	1150	153	155	347	411	173
年末从业人员数	人	37801	16964	16000	14325	10902	5983
旅游者人数	人	24045530	12462	1500000	421576	3825124	1500000
其中:境外旅游者人数	人	45530	2409	2000	3939	65124	14000
旅游收入	万元	396000	4425	18500	86000	49594	13000
其中:外汇收入	万元	70560	112	8620	823	5567	754
(六)固定资产投资							
固定资产投资完成额	万元	1239759	347574	499086	513922	542430	303682
其中:住宅建设	万元	281600	127460	183728	168264	73681	72392
房地产开发投资完成额	万元	157374	27328	17113	19999	19240	11779
其中:商品住宅	万元	83309	18189	14380	10587	15290	6563
全年新增固定资产	万元	620944	350547	202075	452736	461092	295920
全年施工住宅建筑面积(包括商品房)	万平方米	296.29	459.63	109.3	300.18	189.84	307.6
全年竣工住宅建筑面积(包括商品房)	万平方米	135.57	394.28	83.83	227.87	174.15	269.3
商品房屋销售建筑面积	万平方米	27.83	12.86	14.76	24.06	13.09	9.93
商品房屋销售额	万元	52028	12385	12018	23011	8897	10485
三、教育、科技、文化、卫生							
学校总数	个	3357	2398	1631	4304	3579	3357
其中:高等学校	个	20	2	5	6	2	2
中等专业学校	个	47	12	14	13	11	7
普通中学	个	379	239	215	494	400	342
小学	个	2779	2145	1359	3724	3082	3005
专任教师总数	人	62140	30403	25334	54272	42308	38504
其中:高等学校	人	8595	765	2092	1312	403	357
中等专业学校	人	3543	1331	829	818	680	578
普通中学	人	19905	11049	9341	19015	16900	14028
小学	人	26302	15696	11859	31457	22814	23541
在校学生总数	万人	114	69	55	125	91	88
其中:高等学校	人	72020	6807	19655	12736	3748	3035
中等专业学校	人	76808	18963	19837	15681	11574	12690

9—5 续表 3 （包括市辖县）

指 标 名 称	单 位	长沙市	株洲市	湘潭市	衡阳市	岳阳市	郴州市
普通中学	万人	30.94	19.6	16	35.87	25.37	25
小学	万人	64.3	46.79	33.81	83.16	62.24	61.2
成人高等教育学校在校学生数	人	28616	3533	4736	6977	7086	3680
成人中等教育学校在校学生数	人	55936	3885	5806	12470	9165	8092
各类专业技术人员数	万人	21.7	7.97	7.45	15.25	9.05	5.75
其中：中级技术职称以上人员	万人	8.08	3.15	2.48	5.33	2.81	1.82
国有独立科技机构中从事科技活动人员数	人	9173	1015	511	43	678	357
全日制高等院校从事科技活动人员数	人	2567	675	112	69	15	
企业从事科技活动人员数	人	11266	12361	8210	4887	3301	1695
剧场、影剧院数	个	11	18	12	31	9	6
公共图书馆总藏量	千册、件	4708	846	756	1228	666	481
医院、卫生院数	个	246	194	116	354	217	294
医院、卫生院床位数	张	18240	9544	7258	14441	8570	9932
医生数	人	11526	4743	4749	10181	6328	5090
四、财政、金融、保险							
中央财政预算内收入	万元	119610	67614	22596	44578	41001	27941
地方财政预算内收入	万元	256384	105634	51806	102171	93422	98348
其中、工商税收	万元	177138	66876	33071	45630	56174	42739
地方财政预算内支出	万元	280728	131002	66982	139829	136619	128866
其中：科学事业费支出	万元	1771	439	404	400	351	927
教育事业费支出	万元	42967	26883	14047	28536	25690	27563
金融机构数	个	418	248	146	1438	1207	912
其中：保险机构数	个	21	26	22	35	25	41
年末金融机构存款余额	万元	4495625	1520100	1086050	1641000	1235068	1054170
其中：城乡居民储蓄年末余额	万元	2414290	1070054	881707	1282000	871912	791247
年末金融机构各项贷款余额	万元	3792409	1447200	1140149	1672000	1880132	1043178
承保额	万元	8864985	3286900	3692064	2808973	5463780	2157305
保费	万元	57601	28000	18559	26251	21414	19508
已决赔款	万元	19244	6600	12893	8025	5853	5258
五、人民生活							
职工保险福利费用总额	万元	73450	30094	23812	30611	21870	18244
年末离休、退休、退职人员数	万人	26.07	12.31	11.3	16.57	10.53	8.01
离休、退休、退职人员保险福利费用总额	万元	163420	70234	57108	77290	39755	47653
社会福利院数	个	128	87	144	195	19	2
社会福利院床位数	张	4680	2115	2341	6322	623	176

9—5 湖南东线各城市基本情况(二)(1997年)

Basic Statistics on Eastern Cities in Hunan Non－Include Counties under The Jurisdiction of The Municipal Government （不包括市辖县）

指标名称	单位	长沙市	株洲市	湘潭市	衡阳市	岳阳市	郴州市
一、人口、劳动力及土地面积							
年末总人口	万人	163.44	71.19	64.62	77.5	82.95	61.24
其中:非农业人口	万人	132.43	51.67	50.58	57.59	43.47	26.88
年末总户数	万户	49.71	20.99	19.6	23.34	30.16	17.83
年末全部从业人员数	万人	91.32	43.83	45.82	46.93	55.56	33.59
其中:城镇个体劳动者	万人	14.94	2.37	11.8	5.71	11.4	2.13
(1)农、林、牧、渔业	万人	2.2	6.96	5.25	5.6	15.78	16.18
(2)采掘业	万人	0.03	0.18	0.82	0.36		1.54
(3)制造业	万人	27.62	18.24	18.34	12.39	16.38	5.04
(4)电力、煤气及水的生产和供应业	万人	0.5	0.52	0.33	0.48	0.33	0.39
(5)建筑业	万人	8.19	4.06	2.84	1.34	3.15	0.65
(6)地质勘查业、水利管理业	万人	0.8	0.28	0.22	0.26		0.43
(7)交通运输、仓储及邮电通信业	万人	4.8	2.63	2.03	3.16	3.93	1.58
(8)批发和零售贸易、餐饮业	万人	23.01	5.2	8.4	13.61	10.18	3.43
(9)金融、保险业	万人	1.46	0.67	0.56	0.95	0.31	0.48
(10)房地产业	万人	0.35	0.09	0.09	0.23	0.09	0.1
(11)社会服务业	万人	6.91	1.28	1.53	1.84	1.29	0.86
(12)卫生、体育和社会福利业	万人	2.28	0.49	0.61	1.34	0.89	0.46
(13)教育、文化艺术和广播电影电视业	万人	5.85	1.12	1.58	1.81	0.84	1.13
(14)科学研究和综合技术服务业	万人	2.61	0.44	0.17	0.21	0.29	0.09
(15)国家机关、政党机关和社会团体	万人	3.9	1.17	1.23	1.19	1.56	1.11
(16)其他行业	万人	0.81	0.5	1.82	2.16	0.54	0.12
城镇失业人员年末数	人	23300	7745	9259	16900	29676	1680
土地面积	平方公里	556	428	334	559	1044	2178
其中:建成区面积	平方公里	110	57	44	55	54	24
二、综合经济							
(一)国内生产总值(当年价格)	万元	3021813	1181518	918472	676669	1112182	451371
第一产业	万元	64427	39847	26340	37217	60486	54060
第二产业	万元	1328853	702124	511427	304769	572196	217096
其中:工业增加值	万元	1025844	624308	438060	235865	526017	198960
第三产业	万元	1628533	439547	380705	334683	479500	180215
(二)农业							
农林牧渔业总产值(当年价格)	万元	104941	62495	43978	61611	171145	99192
年末实有耕地面积	千公顷	12	10	5	10	33	24
蔬菜产量	万吨	35.57	13.16	10	18.04	12.51	13.77
水果产量	吨	2299	1639	1014	12381	9789	8465

9—5(二) 续表1 (不包括市辖县)

指标名称	单位	长沙市	株洲市	湘潭市	衡阳市	岳阳市	郴州市
猪肉产量	吨	40385	18144	21268	17239	47352	33220
牛羊肉产量	吨	133	446	110	387	351	1925
牛羊奶产量	吨	1636		168	53	273	
禽蛋产量	吨	1239	1215	819	2140	4126	1436
禽肉产量	吨	1287	4435	1176	1696	4530	3549
水产品产量	吨	11225	3932	3433	7725	49578	7103
(三)工业							
乡及乡以上工业企业及生产单位数	个	1747	652	860	798	460	453
其中:国有经济	个	390	123	106	162	181	106
集体经济	个	1175	472	674	578	216	284
私营经济	个	52	9	61	16	22	30
股份制经济	个	5	5	1	10	10	4
外商及港澳台投资经济	个	118	31	18	20	31	27
工业总产值	万元	2602271	1865512	1240622	1034836	1984144	741275
其中:乡及乡以上工业总产值	万元	2116904	1512806	1001976	665542	1718269	437622
其中:国有经济	万元	1395832	1095698	585297	433444	1191666	279762
集体经济	万元	530824	224380	355705	170774	219648	122017
私营经济	万元	43663	4650	23674	5009	21337	1368
股份制经济	万元	26959	47548	13192	31475	25205	14228
外商及港澳台投资经济	万元	118380	126069	24108	19774	260413	20246
其中:轻工业	万元	1200197	180463	290125	195982	469771	144681
全部独立核算工业企业经济指标							
工业增加值	万元	786882	381840	203006	129219	482779	138772
流动资产年平均余额	万元	1404983	1009224	678438	461248	760517	249555
固定资产原价合计	万元	1664404	1378448	1216407	762185	1802416	428082
固定资产净值年平均余额	万元	1087334	911339	747505	515574	972339	313822
产品销售收入	万元	1923468	1449135	718759	550236	1517951	428674
其中:产品销售税金及附加	万元	249444	19706	3424	3333	1627	54149
本年应交增值税	万元	122505	86544	31990	15753	76241	23064
利润总额	万元	50377	17571	31195	19064	7883	20987
(四)交通运输、邮电通信、电力							
铁路客运量	万人	749	392.12	90.45	338.5	326.18	186.58
铁路货运量	万吨	203	378	227	168	478	529
民用运输车辆拥有量	辆	58124	22375	10497	7013	29050	22360
公路客运量	万人	6436	2175.41	2101	1754	5121.2	7229.46
公路货运量	万吨	4028	1928	1381	1125	1546	4712
水运客运量	万人	24	1.01	4		51.4	
水运货运量	万吨	220	201	133	43	128	
民用航空货邮运量	吨	9875					
民用航空客运量	人	1720000					
年末邮电局(所)数	处	334	78	55	52	50	92
邮电业务总量	万元	113228	27054	17581	28560	26835	12334
电话交换机装机总容量	门	752398	200000	158000	221177	132500	97411

9—5(二)　续表 2　　　　　　(不包括市辖县)

指　标　名　称	单　位	长沙市	株洲市	湘潭市	衡阳市	岳阳市	郴州市
年末电话机数	部	425297	131517	104542	96500	91190	65038
年末无线寻呼用户数	户	323273	76758	53041	101677	77357	48947
年末移动电话用户数	户	136628	23128	15071	14527	22445	13189
全年用电量	万千瓦小时	208492	233986	140092	127921	117181	59125
其中:工业用电	万千瓦小时	93112	222054	120371	79865	91419	39649
城乡居民生活用电	万千瓦小时	78001	11749	15184	18450	17881	17483
(五)批发零售贸易与外经、旅游							
批发零售贸易业商品销售总额	万元	4835067	417211	600513	473133	280537	408929
社会消费品零售总额	万元	1564902	473432	311225	466276	510929	346722
外国和港澳台地区在华直接投资							
新签协议(合同)数	个	64	13	20	73	23	29
客商协议投资额	万美元	10448	5709	1988	5887	14330	13747
客商实际投资额	万美元	23268	6209	3112	4215	7813	2570
年末实有企业数	个	920	119	137	158	30	79
年末从业人员数	人	30240	12947	15200	9159	6015	2356
(六)固定资产投资							
固定资产投资完成额	万元	809150	218422	320740	234300	341261	114201
其中:住宅建设	万元	155353	52082	38067	31903	34010	33384
房地产开发投资完成额	万元	155408	25261	15938	17800	18238	8676
其中:商品住宅	万元	83309	16908	13205	9177	14288	5292
全年新增固定资产	万元	505469	222597	127007	198927	274318	104283
本年施工住宅建筑面积(包括商品房)	万平方米	269.29	114.96	95.2	158.53	54.49	75.61
本年竣工住宅建筑面积(包括商品房)	万平方米	119.33	69.23	63.3	99.95	50.25	58.93
商品房屋销售建筑面积	万平方米	27.83	10.99	12.86	21.44	11.5	8.18
商品房屋销售额	万元	52028	10982	10166	21167	7990	8634
三、教育、科技、文化、卫生							
学校总数	个	551	233	209	306	332	407
其中:高等学校	个	20	2	5	6	2	2
中等专业学校	个	44	10	12	10	10	5
普通中学	个	91	49	37	54	66	53
小学	个	317	172	133	203	230	339
专任教师总数	人	26810	8958	9047	8713	8976	2878
其中:高等学校	人	8595	765	2092	1204	403	357
中等专业学校	人	3280	1174	735	541	680	385
普通中学	人	5542	2523	2429	2604	3322	1041
小学	人	6851	2955	2864	3394	4092	1127
在校学生总数	万人	38	13	14	16	15	13
其中:高等学校	人	72020	6807	19655	11362	3748	3035
中等专业学校	人	70624	16984	18210	11684	11391	11109
普通中学	万人	7.65	3.53	3	4.04	4.15	3.56

9—5(二) 续表 3 (不包括市辖县)

指标名称	单位	长沙市	株洲市	湘潭市	衡阳市	岳阳市	郴州市
小学	万人	13.3	6.85	5.7	8.31	9.06	7.11
成人高等教育学校在校学生数	人	25104	3533	4736	6977	7086	3680
成人中等教育学校在校学生数	人	54736	1944	5806	5176	9165	4985
各类专业技术人员数	万人	17.91	5.2	5.2	7.87	4.51	1.95
其中:中级技术职称以上人员	万人	7.03	2.6	1.81	3.18	1.43	0.62
国有独立科技机构中从事科技活动人员数	人	9173	789	445	12	587	269
全日制高等院校从事科技活动人员数	人	2567	675	112	63	15	
企业从事科技活动人员数	人	11090	10907	7021	3784	3137	258
剧场、影剧院数	个	8	6	4	8	3	2
公共图书馆总藏量	千册、件	4350	391	454	563	231	147
医院、卫生院数	个	94	37	43	68	35	11
医院、卫生院床位数	张	12009	6334	4254	6443	3093	2276
医生数	人	7619	2877	1942	2495	1547	821
四、市政公用事业							
年末实有铺装道路面积	万平方米	771	305	222	279	269	133
城市下水道总长度	公里	606	352	323	257	219	89
水厂综合生产能力	万吨/日	106	240	203	90	109	41
全年供水总量	万吨	34600	45895	50763	33365	17277	7507
生活用水量	万吨	19958	7079	9155	14147	4541	3881
生活用水人口	万人	150	58.8	59.45	74.5	45.9	23.78
其中:非农业用水人口	万人	130	52.5	51.1	56.6	37	22.74
煤气(人工、天然气)供气总量	万立方米	1379	2321	38724	1026	30	
其中:家庭用量	万立方米	1137	1906	1805	774	24	
家庭用煤气人口	人	96000	187000	132260	28400	11000	
液化石油气供气总量	吨	32685	18608	14112	10760	17332	6200
其中:家庭用量	吨	31609	18608	11922	10060	11474	5800
家庭用液化气人口	人	783000	298100	322100	229000	241000	178000
年末实有公共汽(电)车营运车辆数	辆	1832	574	350	233	614	401
全年公共汽(电)车客运总量	万人次	31156	7835	4873.4	4806	6370	3818
年末实有出租汽车数	辆	4800	1531	542	1266	2287	330
园林绿地面积	公顷	4299	1887	3900	1457	2199	666
其中:公共绿地面积	公顷	833	288	157	101	196	184
建成区绿化覆盖面积	公顷	3120	2177	1746	1666	1991	923
工业废水排放总量	万吨	2833	8821	21947	4618	13230	6441
工业废水处理排放达标量	万吨	2457	5853	1952	3346	6170	5164
工业废水处理量	万吨	2342	8307	14733	4254	16131	6008
工业废水处理回用量	万吨	902	4666	11062	2745	8118	324
工业二氧化硫去除量	吨	32859	25901	3868	19226	59359	288
工业二氧化硫排放量	吨	18929	5116	28356	17511	19634	4782
环境噪声达标面积	平方公里	72	28	9	48	10	20
生活垃圾粪便清运量	万吨	73	15	12	30	10	13

9—5(二)　续表 4　　　　(不包括市辖县)

指 标 名 称	单 位	长沙市	株洲市	湘潭市	衡阳市	岳阳市	郴州市
生活垃圾粪便无害处理量	万吨	45	15	16	43	10	14
五、财政、金融、保险							
中央财政预算内收入	万元	79875	50668	14393	21264	28412	10168
地方财政预算内收入	万元	181665	63482	27315	34694	46902	31659
其中:工商税收	万元	132531	44334	20537	22121	36197	18162
地方财政预算内支出	万元	179519	77542	35933	52496	65753	45813
其中:科学事业费支出	万元	1576	360	323	253	210	595
教育事业费支出	万元	19684	5999	5075	5651	7016	6974
金融机构数	个	164	82	13	402	291	231
其中:保险机构数	个	13	9	11	16	12	9
年末金融机构存款金额	万元	3596500	996189	602510	1031946	628067	324065
其中:城乡居民储蓄年末余额	万元	1927568	652733	489146	806189	358643	279425
年末金融机构各项贷款余额	万元	3185624	964800	725795	995440	917233	418210
承保额	万元	6637000	2587354	3293998	1263350	190114	822760
保费	万元	43086	21000	13336	14328	11285	7328
已决赔款	万元	12935	3217	7395	3888	2510	2301
六、人民生活							
住宅建筑面积	万平方米	2232	999	1145	787.55	706	358
住宅使用面积	万平方米	1562	549	846.5	551.28	592.2	287
居住人口(与使用面积口径一致)	万人	130.2	53.5	51.07	56.6	53	25.8
全部职工平均人数	万人	68.16	28.13	26.58	26.86	22.01	6.28
全部职工工资总额	万元	447508	167909	149205	131512	14846	71000
居民人均可支配收入	元	6232	5800	5465	4699	6317	5239
居民人均消费支出	元	5528	4719	4412	3725	4837	4931
(1)食品	元	2404	2103	1993	2009	2217	2129
(2)衣着用品	元	646	511	511	386	556	549
(3)家庭设备、用品及服务	元	395	244	294	215	492	589
(4)医疗保健	元	186	178	157	113	218	224
(5)交通和通讯	元	413	301	300	215	261	234
(6)娱乐、教育、文化服务	元	845	739	615	396	667	820
(7)居住	元	399	463	300	192	194	166
(8)杂项商品和服务	元	240	180	242	199	232	220
居民消费价格指数(以上年为100)	%	103.5	102.5	103.9	104.6	103	102.1
商品零售价格指数(以上年为100)	%	100.8	99.9	99.9	104.4	100.5	100.2
职工保险福利费用总额	万元	62482	22083	18703	19675	5122	7400
年末离休、退休、退职人员数	万人	20.42	7.58	10.4	9.48	3.13	2.76
离休、退休、退职人员保险福利费用总额	万元	136669	47545	52652	9485	11816	17266
社会福利院数	个	19	4	15	11	1	1
社会福利院床位数	张	1940	340	472	733	150	146
七、社会治安							
交通事故件数	件	180	108	2007	389	848	134
刑事案件发案数	件	4548	3886	3634	602	6931	1125
犯罪人数	人	3698	3945	512	750	4889	252

9—6 湖南西部地区城市基本情况(1997年)

Basic Statistics on Western Cities in Hunan

指标名称	单位	张家界市		怀化市	
		包括市辖县	不包括市辖县	包括市辖县	不包括市辖县
一、人口、劳动力及土地面积					
年末总人口	万人	153.77	44.6	476.62	21.41
其中:非农业人口	万人	22.91	11.24	87.84	20.93
年末总户数	万户	46.78	14.12	128.98	7.65
年末全部从业人员数	万人	95.34	20.93	311.5	19.82
其中:城镇个体劳动者	万人	3.17	2.17	55.3	13.73
(1)农、林、牧、渔业	万人	56.3	11.66	195.6	0.12
(2)采掘业	万人	0.8	0.1	10.6	
(3)制造业	万人	5	1.11	21.5	1.64
(4)电力、煤气及水的生产和供应业	万人	0.5	0.11	1.7	0.3
(5)建筑业	万人	2.3	1.02	2.7	0.66
(6)地质勘查业、水利管理业	万人	0.2	0.2	1	0.07
(7)交通运输、仓储及邮电通信业	万人	2.3	0.82	7.8	0.5
(8)批发和零售贸易、餐饮业	万人	6.3	2.2	36.1	9.43
(9)金融、保险业	万人	0.3	0.11	1.3	0.3
(10)房地产业	万人	0.04		0.1	0.05
(11)社会服务业	万人	1.6	0.65	10.4	2.47
(12)卫生、体育和社会福利业	万人	0.4	0.11	2.9	0.35
(13)教育、文化艺术和广播电影电视业	万人	1.7	0.61	7.9	1.26
(14)科学研究和综合技术服务业	万人	0.1	0.1	0.2	0.08
(15)国家机关、政党机关和社会团体	万人	1.3	0.6	4.8	2.09
(16)其他行业	万人	16.2	1.53	6.9	0.5
城镇失业人员年末数	人	10201	4000	53000	8300
土地面积	平方公里	9563	2736	27624	24
其中:建成区面积	平方公里		14		22
二、综合经济					
(一)国内生产总值(当年价格)	万元	475513	110111	1900695	281531
第一产业	万元	140111	52386	613734	2000
第二产业	万元	136040	15459	611875	76954
其中:工业增加值	万元	100192	11539	555533	55785
第三产业	万元	199362	42266	675086	202577
(二)农业					
农林牧渔业总产值(当年价格)	万元	226939	82062	812981	
年末实有耕地面积	千公顷	88	25	243	
蔬菜产量	万吨	25.57	8.38	82.11	
水果产量	吨	72253		220494	

注:怀化市数为调整为地级市的怀化市数。

9—6 续表1

指标名称	单位	张家界市		怀化市	
		包括市辖县	不包括市辖县	包括市辖县	不包括市辖县
猪肉产量	吨	63448	18503	228342	
牛羊肉产量	吨	5634	2658	20274	
牛羊奶产量	吨			171	
禽蛋产量	吨	8027	1280	11093	
禽肉产量	吨	4016	1491	34038	
水产品产量	吨	5309	1898	23481	
(三)工业					
乡及乡以上工业企业及生产单位数	个	469	131	2189	225
其中:国有经济	个	87	36	475	107
集体经济	个	367	88	1656	98
私营经济	个	1	1	12	3
股份制经济	个	7	6	19	9
外商及港澳台投资经济	个	2		17	6
工业总产值	万元	323169	80878	1711083	254541
其中:乡及乡以上工业总产值	万元	125429	37862	961153	139078
其中:国有经济	万元	68198	24246	429415	54095
集体经济	万元	45728	8802	442299	40340
私营经济	万元	47	47	3445	1283
股份制经济	万元	9012	4178	54218	14899
外商及港澳台投资经济	万元	1246		28567	27167
其中:轻工业	万元	63464	17830	324916	52711
全部独立核算工业企业经济指标					
工业增加值	万元	55501	26320	164039	31224
流动资产年平均余额	万元	38741	34051	358956	78568
固定资产原价合计	万元	92101	68336	730000	230000
固定资产净值年平均余额	万元	69188	51935	525331	168223
产品销售收入	万元	54081	38229	577723	141681
其中:产品销售税金及附加	万元	6753	506	12087	1214
本年应交增值税	万元	3270	2085	22479	5436
利润总额	万元	5814	261	9303	7171
(四)交通运输、邮电通信、电力					
铁路客运量	万人	126.313	97	971.7	246.1
铁路货运量	万吨	89	46	1000	290
民用运输车辆拥有量	辆	7748	817	27509	8250
公路客运量	万人	1704	440	6087	1826
公路货运量	万吨	617	220	905	181
水运客运量	万人			81	0.3
水运货运量	万吨	8		51	6
民用航空货邮运量	吨	640	640		
民用航空客运量	人	206400	206400		
年末邮电局(所)数	处	109	47	1042	18
邮电业务总量	万元	9370	5516	25447	8377
电话交换机装机总容量	门	75828	13200	267497	66144

9—6　续表 2

指　标　名　称	单　位	张家界市		怀　化　市	
		包括市辖县	不包括市辖县	包括市辖县	不包括市辖县
年末电话机数	部	53000	23185	168194	46182
年末无线寻呼用户数	户	26307	13732	75918	29468
年末移动电话用户数	户	7391	4210	20666	8709
全年用电量	万千瓦小时	22658	5534	143781	37205
其中:工业用电	万千瓦小时	9035	1257	71375	18469
城乡居民生活用电	万千瓦小时	8690	3627	8274	2141
(五)批发零售贸易与外经、旅游					
批发零售贸易业商品销售总额	万元	171172	73746	669045	183885
社会消费品零售总额	万元	147379	65372	536278	101778
外国和港澳台地区在华直接投资					
新签协议(合同)数	个	4	4	22	10
客商协议投资额	万美元	1982	500	1996	900
客商实际投资额	万美元	675	324	3050	2083
年末实有企业数	个	61	21	94	45
年末从业人员数	人	1400	920	4000	2500
旅游者人数	人	2076588		1660000	
其中:境外旅游者人数	人	21272		2000	
旅游收入	万元	41649		21200	
其中:外汇收入	万元			60	
(六)固定资产投资					
固定资产投资完成额	万元	128029	20052	221776	44355
其中:住宅建设	万元	12088	310	51339	15400
房地产开发投资完成额	万元	598	330	9597	3839
其中:商品住宅	万元	268	268	3749	1687
全年新增固定资产	万元	48509	11476	182612	27392
全年施工住宅建筑面积(包括商品房)	万平方米	8.34	4.25	157.72	47.32
全年竣工住宅建筑面积(包括商品房)	万平方米	6.26	3.25	129.28	38.78
商品房屋销售建筑面积	万平方米	0.61	0.61	3.86	1.93
商品房屋销售额	万元	345	345	2483	1117
三、教育、科技、文化、卫生					
学校总数	个	1569	388	4383	380
其中:高等学校	个	1	1	1	1
中等专业学校	个	1	1	7	4
普通中学	个	105	36	380	46
小学	个	1462	350	3995	321
专任教师总数	人	11899	4217	42843	3467
其中:高等学校	人	159	159	263	263
中等专业学校	人	119	119	543	294
普通中学	人	4191	1591	16046	1400
小学	人	7430	2348	25991	1510
在校学生总数	万人	23	8	79	12
其中:高等学校	人	1073	1073	2690	2690
中等专业学校	人	3090	3090	11065	6058

9—6 续表 3

指标名称	单位	张家界市		怀化市	
		包括市辖县	不包括市辖县	包括市辖县	不包括市辖县
普通中学	万人	5.73	1.74	21.02	2.89
小学	万人	16.41	5.03	56.97	7.58
成人高等教育学校在校学生数	人	745	745	792	792
成人中等教育学校在校学生数	人	1089	1089	7971	3000
各类专业技术人员数	万人	1.97	0.82	5.52	1.37
其中:中级技术职称以上人员	万人	0.66	0.28	1.71	0.45
企业从事科技活动人员数	人	392	198	1183	408
剧场、影剧院数	个	16	4	19	8
公共图书馆总藏量	千册、件	166	51	1035	100
医院、卫生院数	个	61	53	414	8
医院、卫生院床位数	张	3051	1283	11100	890
医生数	人	1747	756	5500	2700
五、财政、金融、保险					
中央财政预算内收入	万元	9950		28635	5756
地方财政预算内收入	万元	24807	12677	76098	18691
其中、工商税收	万元	13611	4430	37214	10774
地方财政预算内支出	万元	48613	22432	115791	31217
其中:科学事业费支出	万元	219	4	243	121
教育事业费支出	万元	9967	2811	27673	4265
金融机构数	个	286	22	382	28
其中:保险机构数	个	10	4	32	7
年末金融机构存款金额	万元	223882	72760	913349	274005
其中:城乡居民储蓄年末余额	万元	159307	51807	659858	197858
年末金融机构各项贷款余额	万元	383677	89324	1050355	315100
承保额	万元	109484	109484	1090000	218000
保费	万元	4917	1482	19154	4788
已决赔款	万元	1616	1616	2602	651

十、农业

AGRICULTURE

10—1 农村基层组织与劳动力

Administrative Division and Labor Force in Rural Area

指　　标	单位	1995年	1996年	1997年
一、农村基层组织				
1.乡(镇)政府个数	个	2321	2310	2299
(1)乡政府	个	1406	1360	1348
#民族乡	个	101	101	108
(2)镇政府	个	899	950	951
2.村(居)民委员会个数	万个	4.97	4.98	4.99
#村民委员会	万个	4.77	4.76	4.75
3.村(居)民小组	万个	50.80	50.84	50.94
#村民小组	万个	48.33	49.73	49.78
二、乡村户数、人口、劳动者				
乡村户数	万户	1428.5	1434.89	1431.51
(1)农业户	万户	1371.63	1374.31	1370.15
(2)非农业户	万户	56.87	60.58	66.47
乡村人口	万人	5322.32	5327.56	5334.90
#农业人口	万人	5086.24	5088.30	5095.43
乡村实有劳动力	万人	2756.07	2765.7	2774.69
(1)男劳力	万人	1502.98	1499.94	1505.65
(2)女劳力	万人	1253.09	1265.76	1267.92
#(1)农林牧渔业劳动力	万人	2114.71	2089.33	2074.12
(2)工业劳动力	万人	169.78	175.75	176.95
乡镇办工业	万人	51.11	50.33	50.46
村办工业	万人	43.59	43.83	43.95
村以下办工业	万人	75.08	81.6	82.54
(3)建筑业劳动力	万人	98.89	102.58	103.99
(4)交通运输、仓储、邮电通信业劳动力	万人	38.48	39.67	41.25
(5)批发零售贸易业餐饮业劳动力	万人	59.55	58.84	62.88
(6)金融保险业劳动力	万人	3.62	3.86	4.06
(7)其他非农行业劳动力合计	万人	271.04	295.66	311.44
#外出合同工、临时工	万个	194.26	211.47	200.59
三、农村社会基础设施				
自来水受益村数	万个	0.76	0.76	0.78
通汽车村数	万个	4.14	4.11	4.16
通电话村数	万个	2.50	1.94	2.32

注：乡村劳动力未包括国有农场劳动力。

10—2 农业基本情况

Basic Indicators of Agricultural

年份	农林牧渔业劳动力（万人）	年末实有耕地面积（万公顷）	当年减少耕地面积（万公顷）	农作物播种面积（万公顷）	粮食作物	经济作物	造林面积（万公顷）
1980	1764.83	342.48		790.95	545.13	58.45	24.52
1985	1908.43	334.17		747.71	516.14	72.94	34.40
1986	1929.37	333.05		753.65	521.04	76.71	
1987	1968.58	331.82		747.47	515.09	86.67	
1988	2007.96	332.64		749.62	519.63	84.70	
1989	2061.40	331.86	1.27	774.88	533.05	91.45	
1990	2133.07	331.23	1.16	795.18	536.56	98.99	
1991	2174.96	331.02	0.92	804.02	536.52	110.42	37.17
1992	2169.74	329.59	1.93	796.08	524.36	118.17	37.75
1993	2101.88	327.31	2.81	765.39	468.84	108.94	27.83
1994	2041.28	325.84	2.40	773.05	507.74	116.58	13.44
1995	2114.71	324.97	1.83	784.04	511.56	125.01	10.95
1996	2089.33	323.94	1.86	792.74	513.39	131.00	5.29
1997	2074.12	323.01	1.66	800.90	515.53	136.64	4.29

10—3 农业生产条件

Producer Condition of Agricultual

年份	农用机械总动力（万千瓦）	灌溉面积（千公顷）	化肥施用量（万吨）	农村用电量（万千瓦小时）	每公顷面积产量（公斤）		
					粮食	棉花	油料
1980	588.99	2742.73	361.04	96674	3900	540	570
1985	892.02	2771.18	369.64	150648	4875	990	1005
1986	1059.37	2771.73	432.12	180512	5055	975	930
1987	1053.56	2665.33	457.77	179801	5040	855	1035
1988	1112.91	2670.29	490.07	203523	4875	480	975
1989	1168.47	2674.20	517.88	218573	5025	705	945
1990	1209.17	2676.22	126.09	233704	5025	1020	990
1991	1270.52	2612.70	138.66	257705	5100	1110	1035
1992	1284.37	2681.09	146.18	277089	5115	1215	1065
1993	1374.35	2676.11	148.15	304442	5210	1225	1130
1994	1459.07	2675.09	159.41	330408	5253	1139	1280
1995	1532.54	2680.03	167.91	376414	5380	1206	1258
1996	1616.29	2630.42	167.08	389147	5262	1090	1252
1997	1692.84	2672.38	175.39	416758	5581	1448	1352

注：化肥施用量1989年及以前均为实物量，1990年及以后为折纯量。

10—4 农林牧渔业总产值、指数及构成

Indexes and Composition of Gross Output Value of Agriculture

年份	农林牧渔业总产值	农作物种植业产值	林业产值	牧业产值	副业产值	渔业产值
一、绝对额(按当年价格计算,亿元)						
1988	303.01	140.71	21.79	109.60	17.71	13.20
1989	337.48	164.86	21.67	116.86	18.81	15.28
1990	397.42	219.17	25.89	117.22	22.04	17.10
1991	425.58	234.74	24.59	122.57	23.45	20.23
1992	471.22	248.07	28.12	146.04	25.30	23.69
1993	563.47	298.03	31.37	175.53	27.94	30.60
1994	838.16	446.18	37.75	275.85	33.46	44.92
1995	1046.97	543.16	42.58	369.54	36.76	54.93
1996	1226.32	608.71	45.71	460.82	40.67	70.41
1997	1322.26	618.52	47.98	538.15	41.50	76.10
二、指数(按可比价格计算,%)						
以上年为100						
1988	103.3	95.0	97.7	108.8	121.3	105.0
1989	100.5	106.4	115.0	105.1	90.7	110.4
1990	105.1	100.3	97.4	103.4	111.0	103.0
1991	101.9	103.5	107.3	105.2	102.1	100.3
1992	103.8	100.2	111.8	107.1	105.3	112.4
1993	105.3	103.3	99.1	108.7	105.3	114.6
1994	107.8	103.0	105.3	114.7	112.0	114.4
1995	108.8	104.2	102.3	115.4	106.1	121.4
1996	108.4	102.1	103.2	115.0	111.8	120.7
1997	108.3	108.3	101.5	109.2	106.9	110.4
以1978年为100						
1988	155.2	127.6	106.7	219.9	496.5	393.8
1989	163.2	135.7	122.7	231.1	450.3	434.8
1990	166.2	136.2	119.5	239.0	499.9	447.8
1991	172.7	140.9	128.2	251.4	510.4	449.2
1992	179.2	141.2	143.4	269.3	537.4	504.9
1993	188.7	145.9	142.1	292.7	565.9	578.6
1994	203.4	150.2	149.6	335.8	633.8	661.9
1995	221.3	156.5	153.0	387.5	672.5	803.6
1996	239.9	159.8	157.9	445.6	751.9	969.9
1997	259.8	173.1	160.3	486.6	803.8	1070.8
三、构成(按当年价格计算,%)						
1990	100.0	55.1	5.5	29.5	5.6	4.3
1991	100.0	55.2	5.8	28.8	5.5	4.7
1992	100.0	52.6	6.0	31.0	5.4	5.0
1993	100.0	52.9	5.6	31.1	5.0	5.4
1994	100.0	53.2	4.5	32.9	4.0	5.4
1995	100.0	51.9	4.1	35.3	3.5	5.2
1996	100.0	49.7	3.7	37.6	3.3	5.7
1997	100.0	46.8	3.6	40.7	3.1	5.8

10—5 农林牧渔业分项总产值

Gross Output Value of Farming, Forestry, Animal Husbandry, Fishery

单位:万元

指 标	1996年	1997年	指 标	1996年	1997年
农林牧渔业总产值	12263186	13222561	#谷物副产品	146851	157591
一、农业产值	6491877	6600268	(2)经济作物副产品	23263	24716
(一)种植业产值	6087049	6185232	(二)其他农业	404828	415036
1.主产品产值	5883508	5973117	1.采集野生植物	187858	182915
(1)粮食	3752914	3582277	2.农民家庭兼营商品性工业	216970	232121
①谷物	3541320	3370690	二、林业产值	457142	479802
②豆类	109007	118335	(一)营林	55900	64955
③薯类	102587	93252	(二)林产品	135390	168263
(2)经济作物	845102	978270	(三)村及村以下竹木采伐	265852	246584
①油料	291034	313195	三、牧业产值	4610103	5381490
②棉花	267319	334936	(一)牲畜	3772401	4417666
③麻类	47113	41562	1.大牲畜繁殖、增长、增重	67349	73978
④甘蔗	48650	60806	(1)牛	67136	73709
⑤烟叶	144779	173170	(2)马	156	194
⑥药材类	40202	41818	(3)驴	25	33
⑦其它经济作物	6005	12783	(4)骡	32	42
(3)蔬菜、瓜类	1003410	1119446	2.猪	3666876	4295403
(4)茶、桑、果	185511	200981	3.羊	34819	45265
(5)青饲料、绿肥作物	38089	36538	4.其它	3357	3020
#饲料作物	9206	8440	(二)家禽的饲养	376839	463684
(6)其他农作物	58482	55605	(三)活的畜禽产品	435858	471866
2.副产品产值	203541	212115	(四)捕猎	1869	2494
(1)粮食作物副产品	180278	187399	(五)其它动物饲养	23136	25780
			四、渔业产值	704064	761001

10—6 农村非农行业总产值

Gross Output Value of Non-Agriculture in Rural Area

单位:万元

指 标	1996年	1997年	指 标	1996年	1997年
非农行业总产值	31422039	38114456	三、农村运输业总产值	3109340	3259781
一、农村工业总产值	19859140	24469300	1.乡办运输企业货运产值	97541	106166
1.乡办工业总产值	4667520	5147725	2.村办运输企业货运产值	117445	115053
2.村办工业总产值	3710310	3685794	3.村以下办运输企业货运产值	2894354	3038562
3.村以下办工业总产值	11481310	15635781	四、农村批发零售贸易业、餐饮业总产值	4320920	5086445
二、农村建筑业总产值	4132639	5298930			
1.建筑安装工程产值	3822508	4951487	1.批发零售贸易业产值	3185431	3782089
(1)兴建房屋产值	3038477	3956476	#农村供销社产值	531572	720378
(2)农田水利工程产值	383563	483490	2.餐饮业产值	1135489	1304356
(3)其他建筑安装工程产值	400474	511521	#农村供销社餐饮业产值	60953	103323
2.其他基本建设产值	310131	347443			
#开垦荒地产值	24963	31139			

10—7 农林牧渔业商品产值

Commodity Output Value of Farming, Forestry, Animal Husbandry, Fishery

单位:万元

指　　标	1996年	1997年	指　　标	1996年	1997年
农林牧渔业商品产值	7116581	7928773	#谷物副产品	11599	15544
一、农业商品产值	2772290	2892016	(2)经济作物副产品	1043	978
(一)种植业产值	2524532	2616159	(二)其他农业	247758	275857
1.主产品商品产值	2509272	2597764	1.采集野生植物	30788	35260
(1)粮食	1279659	1207494	2.农民家庭兼营商品性工业	216970	240597
①谷物	1189395	1123353	二、林业商品产值	279407	282372
②豆类	57572	58000	(一)林产品	79915	98241
③薯类	32692	26141	(二)村及村以下竹木采伐	199492	184131
(2)经济作物	632256	752057	三、牧业商品产值	3513165	4125569
①油料	156874	165502	(一)牲畜	2978318	3487805
②棉花	228261	294847	1.大牲畜繁殖、增长、增重	28249	34038
③麻类	45079	39744	(1)牛	28184	33937
④甘蔗	34662	44900	(2)马	42	69
⑤烟叶	131478	156495	(3)驴	11	18
⑥药材类	31729	41280	(4)骡	12	14
⑦其它经济作物	4173	9289	2.猪	2919631	3417317
(3)蔬菜、瓜类	401228	444370	3.羊	27941	33500
(4)茶、桑、果	140891	141360	4.其他	2497	2950
(5)青饲料、绿肥作物	3151	3019	(二)家禽的饲养	241663	324362
#饲料作物	541	479	(三)活的畜禽产品	273196	290077
(6)其他农作物	52087	49464	(四)捕猎	1153	1751
2.副产品产值	15260	18395	(五)其它动物饲养	18835	21574
(1)粮食作物副产品	14217	17417	四、渔业产值	551719	628816

10—8 农林牧渔业增加值(1997年)

Value-added of Farming, Forestry, Animal Husbandry, Fishery

单位:万元

指　　标	合计	农业	种值业	其他农业	农民家庭兼营商品性工业	林业	牧业	渔业
总产值	13222561	6600268	6185232	415036	232121	479802	5381490	761001
中间消耗	4665081	2021586	1900672	120914	105068	116520	2329685	197290
中间物质消耗	4363846	1830640	1723901	106739	93168	92120	2259390	181696
中间非物质部门劳务支出	301235	190946	176771	14175	11900	24400	70295	15594
增加值	8557480	4578682	4284560	294122	127053	363282	3051805	563711

10—9 耕地面积(1997 年)

Cultivated Area

单位:千公顷

指标	耕地	指标	耕地
年初实有耕地面积	3239.4	#改园地	2.88
年内增加耕地面积	7.29	改林地	0.49
1.开荒	3.33	改牧地	0.20
2.围垦	0.06	改渔塘	0.48
3.废弃地利用	1.41	5.灾害毁地	1.61
4.其他	2.49	年末实有耕地面积	3230.10
年内减少耕地面积	16.59	1.水田	2544.79
1.国家建设占地	3.31	2.旱地	685.31
2.乡村集体建设占地	1.19	#水浇地	90.5
3.农民建房占地	1.08	#国有单位耕地面积	78.66
4.农业结构调整占地	5.23		

10—10 农村主要能源及物资消耗(1997 年)

Consumption of Major Energy and Materials in Rural Area

指标	单位	数量	指标	单位	数量
一、农村电气化情况			(2)磷肥	吨	1789714
1.农村用电量	万千瓦小时	416757.8	(3)钾肥	吨	572836
2.年末乡办水电站个数	个	976	(4)复合肥	吨	566908
装机容量	千瓦	294951	2.按折纯量计算	吨	1753883
发电量	万千瓦小时	101238.7	(1)氮肥	吨	972394
3.村及村以下办水电站个数	个	4374	#尿素	吨	485816
装机容量	千瓦	85256	氨水	吨	938
发电量	万千瓦小时	27548.73	碳氨	吨	477961
二、农用化肥施用量			(2)磷肥	吨	241796
1.按实物量计算(总施用量)	吨	6872335	(3)钾肥	吨	285636
每亩播种面积施用量	公斤	57.21	(4)复合肥	吨	254057
(1)氮肥	吨	3942877	三、农用薄膜使用量	吨	35215
#尿素	吨	1064659	#地膜使用量	吨	24074
氨水	吨	7313	地膜覆盖面积	公顷	276210
碳氨	吨	2834935	四、农药使用量	吨	80851
			五、农用柴油	吨	193416

10—11 农田基本建设

Capital Construction On Farmland

单位:千公顷

指标	1996 年	1997 年	指标	1996 年	1997 年
一、农田有效灌溉面积	2667.07	2672.38	机灌	273.38	266.53
#当年实灌	2476.86	2512.59	电灌	850.20	855.69
二、旱涝保收面积	2169.39	2182.52	固定站	850.98	850.72
三、易涝面积	523.93	523.93	流动机	246.27	245.01
四、除涝面积	446.70	448.85	喷滴灌	26.06	26.49
五、机电排灌面积	1260.53	1259.83	纯排面积	136.95	137.61
机电灌溉面积	1123.58	1122.22	六、水轮泵灌溉面积	87.68	87.22

10—12 农业机械年末拥有量

Year-End Possession of Agriculture Machinery

指　　标	单位	1995年	1996年	1997年
农业机械总动力合计	千瓦	15325431	16162947	16928396
1.柴油发动机	千瓦	9941749	10633393	11175311
2.汽油发动机	千瓦	1798702	1956748	2090057
3.电动机	千瓦	3495999	3476417	3581081
4.其他机械	千瓦	88981	96389	81947
一、耕作机械				
大中型拖拉机	混合台	5323	4805	4622
	千瓦	202238	203985	201817
＃轮式拖拉机	混合台	3057	2381	2101
	千瓦	87339	78422	68251
小型及手扶拖拉机	混合台	198013	194389	196586
	千瓦	1748573	1735018	1768758
＃小四轮拖拉机	台	3632	5457	6442
	千瓦	45380	69897	78221
耕整机	台	319022	331687	354982
	千瓦	1098449	1174397	1214913
机耕(滚)船	艘	18043	22814	21742
	千瓦	74031	91767	90444
大中型拖拉机配套农具	部	1266	2896	2206
＃机引犁	部	456	1098	855
机引耙	部	419	873	666
小型拖拉机配套农具	部	34535	43800	42643
＃机引犁	部	9433	10947	13900
机引耙	部	7859	8434	10287
二、农用排灌机械				
农用排灌动力机械	台	681085	767198	827362
	千瓦	3855312	3983306	4137717
＃柴油机	台	447655	478977	513964
	千瓦	1999958	2170256	2308598
电动机	台	226255	278878	303088
	千瓦	1759757	1736520	1753226
汽油机	台	2078	4495	5224
	千瓦	5542	16931	13510
＃农用水泵	台	694948	750447	895963
喷灌机械	套	14131	24329	15956

10—12 续表

指　　标	单位	1995年	1996年	1997年
三、收获机械				
联合收获机	台	18	144	156
	千瓦	622	1132	1563
机动收割机	台	129	364	349
	千瓦	502	37382	37453
机动脱粒机	台	193395	391931	477950
四、畜牧机械				
饲料粉碎机	台	59116	53870	77199
牧草收割机	台	36		3
五、渔业机械				
渔用机动船	艘	9173	8646	9736
	吨	22170	21166	22256
	千瓦	37657	35182	37714
增氧机	台	2543	4100	5041
池塘挖掘机	台	189	311	483
六、农产品加工机械				
农产品加工动力机械	千瓦	2841140	2572889	2499849
#柴油机动力	千瓦	1568405	1326150	1213969
碾米机	部	288210	291797	316116
磨面机	部	31463	27680	28614
弹轧花机	部	22803	15614	17808
榨油机	部	24167	26307	25890
淀粉加工机械	部	27310	43425	54021
揉茶机	部	15850	13847	15790
七、运输机械				
农用载重汽车	辆	56207	56159	58358
	千瓦	4466599	4432608	4669555
#柴油汽车	辆	34319	33884	35343
	千瓦	2624466	2673474	2816472
机动运输船	艘	17434	18162	19417
	吨	229423	230267	234072
	千瓦	167463	164062	172378
农用运输车	辆	55352	48857	47033
	千瓦	925013	1036196	985380
八、其他农用机械				
推土机	台	1982	2013	2123
	千瓦	112965	115556	122133
风力机	台	4	2	1
水稻工厂化育秧设备	套	38	23	66

10—13 农作物生产情况(1997年)

Basic Indicators of Farm Corp Production

指　　标	播种面积 (千公顷)	单　产 (公斤/公顷)	总产量 (吨)
农作物总播种面积	8008.98		
一、粮食	5155.26	5581	28769909
其中:早稻	1651.21	6298	10399453
其中:杂交稻	569.45	6507	3705563
中稻与一季晚稻	514.95	6533	3364038
其中:杂交稻	474.81	6609	3138076
晚稻	1909.64	6763	12414929
其中:杂交稻	1649.52	6528	11202472
小麦	163.05	1970	321133
玉米	171.78	3442	591189
其中:杂交玉米	152.09	3517	534838
大麦	23.79	2346	55809
大豆	205.26	1664	341588
二、油料	956.00	1352	1292581
花生	126.41	1877	237259
油菜籽	820.63	1277	1047912
芝麻	5.59	903	5050
向日葵	0.36	1058	381
其他油料	3.01	657	1979
三、棉花	176.54	1448	255702
四、麻类	25.25	2070	52255
黄红麻	1.09	3292	3588
苎麻	24.16	2014	48667
五、甘蔗	29.62	58923	1745306
六、烟叶	138.28	1720	237879
烤烟	126.8	1773	224755
晒(土)烟	11.48	1143	13124
七、药材	27.15		
八、蔬菜瓜类	604.2		
蔬菜(包括菜用瓜)	525.55		12860022
果用瓜	78.65		1762230
#西瓜	62.56		
九、其他作物:	896.68		
#青饲料	172.62		
绿肥	686.05		
#草籽	39.22		19109
席草			
苇子			532087
莲子			7142
附:国有单位棉花	16.58	1553	25741
国有单位油料	17.13	1155	19779

10—14 林 业 情 况(1997年)

Basic Indicators of Forestry

单位:千公顷

指 标	绝对数	指 标	绝对数
一、当年造林面积总计	42.94	四、零星(四旁)植树(万株)	17479.13
#工程造林	27.38	五、林木种子采集量(吨)	450
竹林	5.64	六、育苗面积	4.65
按主要林种用途分		#本年新育面积	4.13
1.用材林	26.25	七、幼林抚育实际面积	304.65
#速生丰产林	11.31	八、幼林抚育作业面积	424.73
2.经济林	12.99	九、成林抚育面积	269.79
3.防护林	3.62	#中幼林抚育面积	214.71
4.薪炭林	0.04	十、低产林改造面积	99.41
5.特种用途林	0.04	十一、抚育改造出材量	68.07
二、迹地更新面积	43.75	#中幼林改造出材量	42.48
#人工更新面积	40.10	十二、年末实有母树林面积	26.12
三、封山育林面积	2901.97	十三、年末实有种子园面积	6.03
#本年新封	179.54		

10—15 林 产 品 产 量(1997年)

Output of Major Forestry Products

名 称	单 位	数 量	名 称	单 位	数 量
生 漆	公斤	41041	白 果	公斤	241633
油桐籽	吨	50107	杏 仁	公斤	9671
油茶籽	吨	340433	肉 桂	公斤	87687
乌柏籽	吨	1123	黄 柏	公斤	424981
五倍子	吨	1560	杜 仲	公斤	977035
棕 片	吨	7168	白 蜡	公斤	58987
松 脂	吨	16526	杂木棍	万根	7757
竹笋干	吨	10459	桎木条	吨	33275
核 桃	吨	2265	小杂竹	吨	89461
板 栗	吨	14038	楠竹尾	吨	74545
紫 胶	吨	12	村及村以下竹木采伐量		
山苍子	吨	11850	1.木材采伐量	万立方	329.12
香 菇	公斤	1094854	2.竹材	万根	7799.89
花 椒	公斤	140011	#楠竹	万根	4876.41
黑木耳	公斤	616858	篙竹	万根	2253.52
八 角	公斤	9888			

10—16 茶叶、水果生产情况(1997年)

Output of Tea and Fruit

指标	单位	数量	指标	单位	数量
茶叶产量	吨	55493	桃子	吨	42874
红毛茶、红碎茶原料	吨	11622	李子	吨	54841
绿毛茶	吨	26586	梨	吨	23290
乌龙毛茶	吨	369	葡萄	吨	11272
紧压茶原料	吨	6681	红枣	吨	10658
其他茶	吨	10235	鲜柿子(柿饼应折成鲜柿)	吨	6096
水果产量	吨	1532102	枇杷	吨	1902
柑桔	吨	1341400	其他水果	吨	23368
柚子	吨	16401			

10—17 畜牧业主要产品产量(1997年)

Output of Major Animal Husbandry Products

项目	单位	数量	项目	单位	数量
当年出栏猪头数	万头	6096.02	驴肉产量	吨	22
1.出栏肉猪	万头	5837.60	骡肉产量	吨	72
2.出口中仔猪	万头	258.42	马肉产量	吨	45
出售和自宰肉用牛	万头	98.90	禽肉产量	吨	461849
出售和自宰肉用羊	万只	381.04	兔肉产量	吨	972
出售和自宰肉用驴	匹	270	牛奶产量	吨	6394
出售和自宰肉用骡	匹	691	羊毛产量	吨	23
马	匹	504	山羊毛	吨	17
家禽	万羽	31458.15	绵羊毛	吨	6
兔	万只	73.42	蜂蜜产量	吨	5650
当年猪牛羊肉类总产量	吨	4503201	蜂蜡产量	公斤	180295
1.猪肉产量	吨	3875023	禽蛋产量	吨	625046
肉猪产量	吨	3817897	兔毛产量	吨	2
出口中仔猪产量	吨	57126	蚕茧产量	吨	1136
2.牛肉产量	吨	110488	#桑蚕茧	吨	1076
3.羊肉产量	吨	54730			

10—18 畜牧业年末存栏情况(1997年)

Year-End Animals in Stock

项目	单位	合计	能繁母畜	当年生仔畜	项目	单位	合计	能繁母畜	当年生仔畜
大牲畜总头数	头	4965407			3.乳牛	头	3657	2017	603
#从事劳役的	头	3637185			马	匹	24206	4640	1708
牛	头	4937244	1891615	715868	驴	头	2527	746	264
1.耕牛	头	4809901	1860128	701870	骡	头	1430		239
#从事劳役	头	3673447			生猪	万头	3632.01	308.37	
黄牛	头	2876253	1091693	431112	羊	万只	461.31	184.25	
水牛	头	1933648	768435	270758	山羊	万只	460.91		
2.菜牛	头	123686	29470	13395	绵羊	万只	0.4		

10—19 主要农产品产量

Output of Major Farm Products

单位:万吨

年份	粮食	#小麦	#稻谷	棉花	油料	甘蔗	茶叶	水果
1990	2692.67	28.56	2517.26	12.01	72.22	127.76	7.39	56.61
1991	2734.40	34.74	2534.44	14.89	84.29	159.60	7.32	94.86
1992	2680.01	33.29	2482.26	20.31	83.89	171.28	6.93	39.75
1993	2631.37	29.77	2413.71	21.08	79.14	178.41	7.28	85.59
1994	2667.15	32.04	2429.98	23.81	98.22	149.16	6.73	80.75
1995	2752.09	31.02	2515.34	22.35	112.04	141.52	6.14	116.94
1996	2820.62	30.42	2559.03	18.96	118.12	129.17	5.49	105.01
1997	2876.99	32.11	2667.84	25.57	129.26	174.53	5.55	153.21

10—20 畜牧饲养和水产品产量

Number of Livestocks and Output of Aquatic Products

年份	年底大牲畜头数(万头)	#耕牛	年底猪头数(万头)	年底羊只数(万只)	猪牛羊肉(万吨)	水产品(万吨)
1990	400.65	398.24	2798.27	66.46	189.47	53.01
1991	406.28	403.90	2837.45	71.36	199.35	53.16
1992	413.14	410.49	2912.05	79.41	213.94	59.57
1993	416.50	413.72	3016.08	109.22	237.54	68.06
1994	422.43	419.47	3171.80	138.26	272.12	74.14
1995	432.65	428.86	3391.10	214.76	317.36	86.27
1996	471.78	462.38	3545.55	390.23	366.46	98.25
1997	496.54	480.99	3632.01	461.31	404.02	110.76

10—21 自然灾害情况(1997年)

Output of Major Animal Husbandry Products

项目	单位	数量	项目	单位	数量
受灾面积合计	公顷	2023706	病虫	公顷	59370
旱灾	公顷	680570	其他	公顷	4715
水灾	公顷	751644	减产粮食	吨	2574392
风雹灾	公顷	162822	死亡人数	人	389
病虫	公顷	92870	死亡大牲畜	头	167320
其他	公顷	335800	倒塌房屋	间	253992
成灾面积	公顷	1314882	损坏房屋	间	615482
旱灾	公顷	515663	成灾人口合计	人	20178000
水灾	公顷	462087	因灾缺粮数量	吨	783473
风雹灾	公顷	91427	因灾缺粮人口	人	10666952
霜冻	公顷	181620			

10—22 渔业生产情况(1997年)

Basic Indicators of Fishery Production

项目	单位	数量	项目	单位	数量
水产品总产量	吨	1107610	1.池塘养殖	千公顷	196.92
淡水产品捕捞产量	吨	126380	#鱼业专用塘	千公顷	106.17
1.鱼类	吨	105436	2.湖泊养殖	千公顷	59.19
2.虾蟹类	吨	7223	#粗养	千公顷	47.77
3.贝类	吨	7441	3.河沟养殖	千公顷	11.08
4.其他	吨	6280	4.水库养殖	千公顷	92.52
淡水产品养殖产量	吨	981230	#粗养	千公顷	38.29
1.鱼类	吨	948698	5.其他养殖	千公顷	25.22
2.虾蟹类	吨	5746	附:稻田养殖	千公顷	187.96
3.贝类	吨	11963	养殖水面中鱼种池面积	千公顷	10.9
4.其他类	吨	14823	淡水产品中珍珠产量	公斤	72703
淡水养殖面积合计	千公顷	384.93	稻田养殖鱼种面积	千公顷	48.92

10—23 按全省人口平均的主要农产品产量

Per Capita Output of Major Agriculture Products

单位:公斤/人

产品名称	1990年	1995年	1996年	1997年
粮食	444	439	423	446
#稻谷	412	399	400	414
杂粮	7.0	7.5	11.1	13.3
棉花	2.0	3.6	3.0	4.0
食用植物油	4.9	7.2	7.3	8.3
(包括料折油及茶油)				
甘蔗	20.9	22.5	20.2	27.1
烤烟	1.8	1.2	2.2	3.5
茶叶	1.2	1.0	0.9	0.9
水果	9.3	18.6	16.4	23.8
#柑桔	7.6	16.1	14.0	20.8
猪牛羊肉	31.0	50.6	57.3	62.7
#猪肉	31.0	49.2	55.3	60.1
禽蛋	4.6	7.4	9.2	9.7
水产品	8.7	13.7	15.4	17.2

10—24 乡镇集体企业财务评价指标(1997年)

Appraise Indicotors on Finance of Township and Village Enterprises

指标名称	单位	数量
一、基本情况		
1、汇总企业数	个	93837
(1)盈利企业数	个	84560
占汇总企业数比例	%	90.11
净利润总额	万元	635088
(2)亏损企业数	个	9277
占汇总企业数比例	%	9.89
亏损总额	万元	79964
2、本期职工平均人数	人	2500802
3、工资总额	万元	1047103
4、本期人均工资	元/人	4187
5、期末固定资产原值	万元	2894944
6、银行借款余额	万元	1092307
(1)短期银行借款	万元	606637
(2)长期银行借款	万元	485670
二、营业收入增长率	%	－6.90
1、本期营业收入	万元	11056584
2、上年同期营业收入	万元	11876086
三、净利润增长率	%	－8.33
1、本期净利润额	万元	555124
2、上年同期净利润总额	万元	605565
四、税金增长率	%	－5.93
1、本期税金总额	万元	446264
2、上年同期税金总额	万元	474387
五、资本金增长率	%	6.89
1、本期末资本金总额	万元	1641116
2、上年同期末资本金总额	万元	1535289
六、应收款项与应付款项差额(逆差用"－"号表示)	万元	232732
1、本期末应收款项总额	万元	1208677
2、本期末应付款项总额	万元	975945
七、营业收入利润率	%	5.60
1、营业利润	万元	619168
2、营业收入	万元	11056584
八、总资产报酬率	%	17.55
1、利润总额＋利息支出	万元	805306
2、平均资产总额	万元	4588415

10—24 续表

指标名称	单位	数量
九、资本收益率	%	33.83
1、净利润	万元	555124
2、实收资本	万元	1641116
十、资本保值增值率	%	102.44
1、期末所有者权益总额	万元	1836897
2、期初所有者权益总额	万元	1793125
十一、资产负债率	%	63.45
1、负债总额	万元	3188353
2、资产总额	万元	5025250
十二、流动比率	%	105.59
1、流动资产	万元	2553227
2、流动负债	万元	2417962
十三、速动比率	%	67.20
1、速运资产	万元	1624775
2、流动负债	万元	2417962
十四、应收帐款周转率	次	14.35
1、营业收入	万元	11056584
2、平均应收帐款余额	万元	770464
十五、存货周转率	次	9.61
1、产品销售成本	万元	5622928
2、平均存货成本	万元	585301
十六、社会贡献率	%	51.26
1、企业社会贡献总额	万元	2351846
2、平均资产总额	万元	4588415
十七、社会积累率	%	18.98
1、上交国家财政总额	万元	446264
2、企业社会贡献总额	万元	2351846
十八、产品销售率	%	92.14
1、工业销售产值	万元	7346579
2、工业总产值(现行价格)	万元	7972947
十九、固定资产折旧率	%	7.23
1、本期固定资产折旧额	万元	196707
2、固定资产原值平均余额	万元	2719251
二十、人均利税	元/人	3908
1、利税总额	元	977212
2、全部职工平均人数	人	2500802

10—25 农村小康实现程度(1997年)

Degree of Being Fairly Well-off of Rural Area (1997)

指标名称	单位	湖南省		
		数量	实现程度	得分(分)
一、收入分配				
1. 人均纯收入	元	2037.06	68.9	20.67
2. 基尼系数		0.24	40	2
二、物质生活				
恩格尔系数	%	59.37	6.3	0.38
2. 每日每人蛋白质摄入量	克	78.14	100	9
3. 衣着消费支出	元/人	89.97	31.7	0.95
4. 钢木结构住房比重	%	91.16	100	7
三、精神生活				
1. 电视机普及率	台/百户	83.05	100	6
2. 服务消费支出比重	%	17.41	100	6
四、人口素质				
1. 劳动力平均受教育年限	年	7.73	86.5	4.33
2. 农村人口平均预期寿命	岁	69.5	75	3
五、生活环境				
1. 安全卫生水普及率	%	94	100	3
2. 用电户比重	%	99.6	100	3
3. 已通公路的行政村比重	%	91.64	100	3
4. 已通电话的行政村比重	%	53.3	16.5	0.33
六、社会保障与社会安全				
1. 五保人口生活有保障比重	%	71.2	53	2.12
2. 万人刑事案件立案件数	件	9.3	100	4
总计			74.78	74.78

10—26 第一批农村小康县(市、区)综合评价情况

Basic Indicators of County (City. District) of Being Fairly Well—Off Valuated Firstly

	单 位	芙蓉区			天心区		
		数量	实现程度	得分	数量	实现程度	得分
一、收入分配							
1. 人均纯收入	元	3340	100	30	2860	100	30
2. 基尼系数	—	0.295	95	4.8	0.295	95	4.8
二、物质生活							
1. 恩格尔系数	%	48.3	100	6	47	100	6
2. 每人每日蛋白质摄入量	克	78	100	9	78.4	100	9
3. 衣着消费支出	元/人	185.1	100	3	184.5	100	3
4. 钢木结构住房比重	%	100	100	7	100	100	7
三、精神生活							
1. 电视机普及率	台/百户	100	100	6	100	100	6
2. 服务消费支出比重	%	13	100	6	12	100	6
四、人口素质							
1. 劳动力平均受教育年限	年	8.5	100	5	9.5	100	5
2. 农村人口平均预期寿命	岁	71	100	4	71	100	4
五、生活环境							
1. 安全卫生水普及率	%	100	100	3	100	100	3
2. 用电户比重	%	100	100	3	100	100	3
3. 已通公路的行政村比重	%	100	100	3	100	100	3
4. 已通电话的行政村比重	%	100	100	2	100	100	2
六、社会保障与社会安全							
1. 五保人口生活有保障比重	%	100	100	4	100	100	4
2. 万人刑事案件立案件数	件	10	100	4	14	100	4
合 计	—		99.8	99.8		99.8	99.8

	单 位	岳麓区			开福区			雨花区		
		数量	实现程度	得分	数量	实现程度	得分	数量	实现程度	得分
一、收入分配										
1. 人均纯收入	元	3056	100	30	3269	100	30	3256	100	30
2. 基尼系数	—	0.295	95	4.8	0.295	95	4.8	0.295	95	4.8
二、物质生活										
1. 恩格尔系数	%	48.3	100	6	46.1	100	6	46.1	100	6
2. 每人每日蛋白质摄入量	克	75	100	9	78	100	9	78	100	9
3. 衣着消费支出	元/人	184.5	100	3	184.5	100	3	184.5	100	3
4. 钢木结构住房比重	%	90.4	100	7	92.8	100	7	100	100	7
三、精神生活										
1. 电视机普及率	台/百户	99.5	100	6	100	100	6	100	100	6
2. 服务消费支出比重	%	13	100	6	11.1	100	6	11.1	100	6
四、人口素质										
1. 劳动力平均受教育年限	年	9.4	100	5	8.9	100	5	8.5	100	5
2. 农村人口平均预期寿命	岁	71	100	4	70.8	100	4	70.8	100	4
五、生活环境										
1. 安全卫生水普及率	%	100	100	3	100	100	3	99.7	100	3
2. 用电户比重	%	100	100	3	100	100	3	100	100	3
3. 已通公路的行政村比重	%	100	100	3	100	100	3	100	100	3
4. 已通电话的行政村比重	%	100	100	2	100	100	2	100	100	2
六、社会保障与社会安全										
1. 五保人口生活有保障比重	%	100	100	4	100	100	4	100	100	4
2. 万人刑事案件立案件数	件	4	100	4	13	100	4	18.7	100	4
合 计	—		99.8	99.8		99.8	99.8		99.8	99.8

10—26 续表1

	单位	长沙县			望城县			株洲市郊区		
		数量	实现程度	得分	数量	实现程度	得分	数量	实现程度	得分
一、收入分配										
1. 人均纯收入	元	2684	100	30	2317	88.1	26.5	2517	98.5	29.6
2. 基尼系数	—	0.24	40	2	0.22	20	1	0.29	90	4.5
二、物质生活										
1. 恩格尔系数	%	41.6	100	6	51.8	82	4.9	51.2	87.4	5.2
2. 每人每日蛋白质摄入量	克	76.4	100	9	83	100	9	75.6	100	9
3. 衣着消费支出	元/人	146.5	97.9	2.9	148.7	100	3	174.1	100	3
4. 钢木结构住房比重	%	92.9	100	7	99.3	100	7	80.6	100	7
三、精神生活										
1. 电视机普及率	台/百户	95	100	6	78	100	6	100	100	6
2. 服务消费支出比重	%	11.6	100	6	9.9	98.8	5.9	10.8	100	6
四、人口素质										
1. 劳动力平均受教育年限	年	8.6	100	5	8	100	5	8.8	100	5
2. 农村人口平均预期寿命	岁	71.7	100	4	70.2	100	4	70	100	4
五、生活环境										
1. 安全卫生水普及率	%	100	100	3	92	100	3	97.9	100	3
2. 用电户比重	%	100	100	3	99	100	3	100	100	3
3. 已通公路的行政村比重	%	100	100	3	100	100	3	100	100	3
4. 已通电话的行政村比重	%	96.8	100	2	99.5	100	2	85.3	100	2
六、社会保障与社会安全										
1. 五保人口生活有保障比重	%	100	100	4	100	100	4	100	100	4
2. 万人刑事案件立案件数	件	5	100	4	7.3	100	4	6.8	100	4
合计	—		96.9	96.9		91.3	91.3		98.3	98.3

	单位	攸县			雨湖区			岳塘区		
		数量	实现程度	得分	数量	实现程度	得分	数量	实现程度	得分
一、收入分配										
1. 人均纯收入	元	2409	92.9	27.9	3542	100	30	3358.7	100	30
2. 基尼系数	—	0.27	70	3.5	0.26	60	3	0.36	100	5
二、物质生活										
1. 恩格尔系数	%	49.2	100	6	47	100	6	50	100	6
2. 每人每日蛋白质摄入量	克	71.8	88.6	8	73	92.9	8.4	67	71.4	6.4
3. 衣着消费支出	元/人	124.1	73.3	2.2	153.8	100	3	224.8	100	3
4. 钢木结构住房比重	%	99.4	100	7	98	100	7	87	100	7
三、精神生活										
1. 电视机普及率	台/百户	89	100	6	100	100	6	98.6	100	6
2. 服务消费支出比重	%	9.6	95	5.7	11.8	100	6	6.7	58.8	3.5
四、人口素质										
1. 劳动力平均受教育年限	年	7.9	95	4.8	9.1	100	5	8.9	100	5
2. 农村人口平均预期寿命	岁	69.2	60	2.4	70	100	4	73	100	4
五、生活环境										
1. 安全卫生水普及率	%	100	100	3	99.1	100	3	99	100	3
2. 用电户比重	%	100	100	3	100	100	3	100	100	3
3. 已通公路的行政村比重	%	100	100	3	97	100	3	100	100	3
4. 已通电话的行政村比重	%	69.1	95.5	1.9	97	100	2	83	100	2
六、社会保障与社会安全										
1. 五保人口生活有保障比重	%	98.9	100	4	100	100	4	100	100	4
2. 万人刑事案件立案件数	件	9	100	4	2	100	4	6.4	100	4
合计	—		92.4	92.4		97.4	97.4		94.9	94.9

10—26 续表 2

	单位	韶山市			衡阳市郊区			南岳区		
		数量	实现程度	得分	数量	实现程度	得分	数量	实现程度	得分
一、收入分配										
1. 人均纯收入	元	2710	100	30	2636	100	30	2572	100	30
2. 基尼系数	—	0.34	100	5	0.24	40	2	0.19		
二、物质生活										
1. 恩格尔系数	%	48	100	6	32.3	100	6	29.9	100	6
2. 每人每日蛋白质摄入量	克	86	100	9	70	82.1	7.4	99.9	100	9
3. 衣着消费支出	元/人	77	21.6	0.6	169.7	100	3	110.5	58.4	1.8
4. 钢木结构住房比重	%	80	100	7	98.9	100	7	90	100	7
三、精神生活										
1. 电视机普及率	台/百户	97	100	6	90	100	6	92	100	6
2. 服务消费支出比重	%	7.1	63.7	3.8	10.4	100	6	10.4	100	6
四、人口素质										
1. 劳动力平均受教育年限	年	9	100	5	9.2	100	5	8	100	5
2. 农村人口平均预期寿命	岁	72	100	4	70	100	4	70	100	4
五、生活环境										
1. 安全卫生水普及率	%	97.6	100	3	98	100	3	100	100	3
2. 用电户比重	%	99	100	3	100	100	3	100	100	3
3. 已通公路的行政村比重	%	100	100	3	100	100	3	100	100	3
4. 已通电话的行政村比重	%	85	100	2	91	100	2	67.7	88.5	1.8
六、社会保障与社会安全										
1. 五保人口生活有保障比重	%	100	100	4	100	100	4	100	100	4
2. 万人刑事案件立案件数	件	4	100	4	2.8	100	4	4.4	100	4
合　计	—		95.4	95.4		95.4	95.4		93.6	93.6

	单位	衡山县			岳阳楼区			武陵区		
		数量	实现程度	得分	数量	实现程度	得分	数量	实现程度	得分
一、收入分配										
1. 人均纯收入	元	2568	100	30	3007	100	30	2925	100	30
2. 基尼系数	—	0.25	50	2.5	0.25	50	2.5	0.24	40	2
二、物质生活										
1. 恩格尔系数	%	49	100	6	44	100	6	50.3	97	5.8
2. 每人每日蛋白质摄入量	克	77	100	9	107	100	9	77.7	100	9
3. 衣着消费支出	元/人	186.6	100	3	129.4	79.1	2.4	149.5	100	3
4. 钢木结构住房比重	%	90	100	7	99	100	7	100	100	7
三、精神生活										
1. 电视机普及率	台/百户	99	100	6	99	100	6	99.7	100	6
2. 服务消费支出比重	%	21	100	6	9	87.5	5.3	8.2	77.5	4.6
四、人口素质										
1. 劳动力平均受教育年限	年	8.2	100	5	8.6	100	5	8.8	100	5
2. 农村人口平均预期寿命	岁	70	100	4	69	50	2	70.1	100	4
五、生活环境										
1. 安全卫生水普及率	%	98	100	3	100	100	3	95.9	100	3
2. 用电户比重	%	99	100	3	100	100	3	100	100	3
3. 已通公路的行政村比重	%	99	100	3	92.1	100	3	100	100	3
4. 已通电话的行政村比重	%	61	55	1.1	89.5	100	2	100	100	2
六、社会保障与社会安全										
1. 五保人口生活有保障比重	%	100	100	4	100	100	4	100	100	4
2. 万人刑事案件立案件数	件	1	100	4	4.8	100	4	2.3	100	4
合　计	—		96.6	96.6		94.2	94.2		95.4	95.4

十一、工业

INDUSTRY

11—1 工业企业单位数及总产值(1997年)

Number and Gross Output Value of Industrial Enterprises

类别	单位数(个)	工业总产值(亿元)	类别	单位数(个)	工业总产值(亿元)
总计(乡及乡以上工业)	27015	1884.99	食品加工业	1817	139.18
在总计中:			食品制造业	753	26.22
国有经济	4672	945.82	饮料制造业	764	31.56
中央企业	274	414.13	烟草加工业	26	122.50
地方企业	4398	531.69	纺织业	637	75.83
#县属企业	2751	163.80	服装及其他纤维制品制造业	510	14.72
集体经济	20487	751.15	皮革、毛皮及其他制品业	450	23.51
#县属企业	2816	91.38	木材加工及竹藤棕草制品业	1162	30.60
私营经济	1016	44.51	家具制造业	502	13.40
联营经济	76	3.02	造纸及纸制品业	872	48.61
股份制经济	156	43.41	印刷业、记录媒介复制	967	28.96
外商投资经济	240	58.01	文教体育用品制造业	249	5.20
中外合资经营企业	192	39.79	石油加工业及炼焦业	34	84.73
中外合作经营企业	25	14.20	化学原料及化学制品制造业	1435	152.58
外资企业	23	4.02	医药工业	208	20.70
港、澳、台投资经济	260	32.80	化学纤维工业	38	9.59
其他经济	108	6.34	橡胶制品业	157	13.81
在总计中:			塑料制品业	694	22.25
乡属企业	12427	482.70	非金属矿物制品业	4328	184.34
在总计中:			黑色金属冶炼及压延加工业	274	88.91
轻工业	11900	751.98	有色金属冶炼及压延加工业	370	83.10
以农产品为原料	8226	559.27	金属制品业	1082	52.07
以非农产品为原料	3674	192.71	普通机械制造业	1312	71.88
重工业	15115	1133.01	专用设备制造业	736	41.87
采掘工业	2607	127.64	交通运输设备制造业	1096	106.07
原料工业	3708	481.84	电气机械及器材制造业	807	71.42
加工工业	8800	523.53	电子及通讯设备制造业	198	27.68
在总计中:			仪器仪表及文化办公用机械制造业	134	7.90
大型企业	209	616.50	其他制造业	1157	40.14
中型企业	514	179.72	电力蒸汽热水生产和供应业	1249	89.85
小型企业	26292	1088.77	煤气生产和供应业	13	8.98
在总计中:			自来水生产和供应业	338	9.97
煤炭采选业	957	51.34	附:		
黑色金属矿采选业	151	9.79	城(镇)合作经营工业	5374	23.91
有色金属矿采选业	466	37.52	城(镇)个体工业	49141	129.17
非金属矿采选业	796	26.01	农村合作经营工业	28021	129.89
其他矿采选业	14	5.68	农村村办工业	35471	368.58
木材及竹材采运业	253	5.99	农村个体工业	518275	1280.61

注:本表各分组均未包括乡以下,工业总产值按当年价格计算。

11—2 工业总产值、指数及构成

Gross Output Value of Industry and Its Indexes and Composition

年　　份	全部工业总产值	国　有	集　体所有制	#乡　办工　业	#村　办工　业	城乡个体	其他经济类型
一、绝对数(按当年价格计算,亿元)							
1988	581.85	376.29	172.00	52.39	33.76	31.55	2.01
1989	680.09	442.18	192.87	58.21	37.18	41.89	3.15
1990	712.67	455.87	204.73	62.70	42.17	48.57	3.50
1991	803.71	504.36	235.03	74.55	49.64	59.71	4.61
1992	1006.79	594.30	303.90	104.19	71.61	94.88	13.71
1993	1438.92	724.49	451.91	176.16	119.23	192.55	69.97
1994	1925.35	855.74	632.62	238.34	180.31	339.52	97.47
1995	2451.47	1022.13	757.91	297.31	219.11	484.75	186.68
1996	3280.58	962.70	1131.51	452.93	371.70	1045.59	140.78
1997	3817.15	945.82	1273.52	514.77	368.58	1409.78	188.03
二、指数(按可比价格计算,%)							
以上年为100							
1988	115.3	111.5	118.0	122.7	119.4	123.0	258.0
1989	106.7	103.3	108.0	109.3	108.3	130.3	153.4
1990	105.0	103.0	106.5	109.1	111.5	113.6	120.9
1991	111.2	107.8	115.8	122.1	118.4	122.9	129.5
1992	119.9	110.7	128.5	137.4	146.1	156.7	211.5
1993	123.0	103.2	133.9	159.3	140.9	174.7	416.3
1994	120.8	105.4	127.8	129.8	126.6	148.7	157.6
1995	117.2	104.8	110.1	109.9	121.5	142.8	195.2
1996	128.8	104.4	129.8	131.3	150.4	191.2	74.1
1997	120.5	102.7	117.9	120.2	101.3	137.7	138.3
以1978年为100							
1988	299.3	244.8	382.0	440.3	379.0	438.6	1369.3
1989	319.4	252.9	412.6	481.3	410.5	571.5	2100.5
1990	335.5	260.5	439.2	525.1	457.7	649.2	2539.5
1991	373.2	280.9	508.8	641.1	541.9	779.9	3289.7
1992	447.5	310.9	653.8	880.9	791.8	1250.2	6957.7
1993	550.4	320.8	875.4	1403.3	1115.6	2184.2	28964.9
1994	664.9	338.2	1118.7	1821.4	1412.4	3247.9	45648.7
1995	779.3	354.4	1231.7	2001.7	1716.0	4638.0	89106.3
1996	1003.6	370.0	1598.7	2628.2	2580.9	8867.9	66027.8
1997	1209.3	380.0	1884.9	3159.1	2614.5	12211.1	91316.4
三、构成(按当年价格计算,%)							
1990	100.0	64.0	28.7	8.8	5.9	6.8	0.5
1991	100.0	62.8	29.2	9.3	6.2	7.4	0.6
1992	100.0	59.0	30.2	10.3	7.1	9.4	1.4
1993	100.0	50.3	31.4	12.2	8.3	13.4	4.9
1994	100.0	44.4	32.9	12.4	9.4	17.6	5.1
1995	100.0	41.7	30.9	12.1	8.9	19.8	7.6
1996	100.0	29.3	34.5	13.8	11.3	31.9	4.3
1997	100.0	24.8	33.4	13.5	9.7	36.9	4.9

11—3 轻工业、重工业总产值、指数及构成

Gross Output Value of Light and Heavy Industry and Its Indexes and Composition

年 份	轻工业产值	以农产品为原料	以非农产品为原料	重工业产值	采掘工业	原料工业	加工工业
一、绝对数(按当年价格计算,亿元)							
1988	263.39	191.84	71.55	318.46	40.86	115.23	162.37
1989	300.07	216.97	83.10	380.02	49.34	140.38	190.30
1990	316.63	223.45	93.18	396.04	51.28	151.01	193.75
1991	354.00	249.14	104.86	449.71	56.51	179.46	213.74
1992	422.17	291.74	130.43	584.62	68.76	235.04	280.82
1993	561.72	379.90	181.82	877.20	108.95	347.74	420.51
1994	801.37	560.00	241.37	1123.98	168.64	424.98	530.36
1995	1043.61	767.13	276.48	1407.86	186.45	605.31	616.10
1996	1457.22	961.64	495.58	1823.36	396.20	562.86	864.30
1997	1705.77	1115.03	590.74	2111.38	467.54	634.46	1009.38
二、指数(按可比价格计算,%)							
以上年为100							
1988	115.5	115.5	115.6	115.1	114.1	109.1	119.0
1989	103.6	102.9	105.1	109.5	115.0	105.8	110.6
1990	105.1	102.3	111.3	105.0	112.6	106.4	102.9
1991	111.4	110.0	114.7	111.1	109.2	113.9	109.5
1992	116.5	113.1	124.5	122.7	122.0	116.7	127.5
1993	121.0	118.7	125.7	124.6	133.8	113.8	130.0
1994	123.2	125.5	118.6	119.0	138.1	116.7	115.8
1995	118.9	124.3	107.4	115.9	101.0	132.1	110.1
1996	128.8	118.2	155.0	128.8	206.2	98.8	130.6
1997	119.2	117.5	122.4	121.5	121.5	121.0	121.8
以1978年为100							
1988	365.4	363.8	371.5	257.0	169.0	226.7	307.5
1989	378.5	374.3	390.5	281.5	194.4	239.9	340.1
1990	397.6	382.6	434.8	295.6	218.9	255.1	350.1
1991	442.9	420.9	498.9	328.4	239.0	290.6	383.5
1992	516.0	476.1	621.1	403.0	291.6	339.1	488.9
1993	624.3	565.1	780.7	502.1	390.2	385.9	635.6
1994	769.2	709.2	925.9	597.5	538.9	450.4	736.0
1995	914.6	881.6	994.5	692.5	544.3	594.9	810.3
1996	1178.0	1042.1	1541.5	891.9	1122.3	587.8	1058.3
1997	1404.2	1224.5	1886.8	1083.7	1363.6	711.2	1289.0
三、构成(按当年价格计算,%)							
1990	44.4	31.4	13.1	55.6	7.2	21.2	27.2
1991	44.0	31.0	13.0	56.0	7.1	22.3	26.6
1992	41.9	29.0	12.9	58.1	6.8	23.4	27.9
1993	39.0	26.4	12.6	61.0	7.6	24.2	29.2
1994	41.6	29.1	12.5	58.4	8.8	22.1	27.5
1995	42.6	31.3	11.3	57.4	7.6	24.7	25.1
1996	44.4	29.3	15.1	55.6	12.1	17.2	26.3
1997	44.7	29.2	15.5	55.3	12.2	16.6	26.5

11—4 乡及乡以上工业总产值

Gross Output Value of Industry Enterprises at and above Township Level

年份	总产值（亿元）	轻工业	重工业	# 大中型工业	国有	集体	其他	总产值指数（以1978年为100）
1978	138.63	52.65	86.98					100.0
1979	156.47	59.80	96.67					108.0
1980	163.97	68.76	95.21	37.98				142.7
1981	171.89	78.49	93.40	67.49				148.5
1982	188.29	85.33	102.96	76.30				161.9
1983	200.94	89.19	111.75	83.07				173.6
1984	227.60	98.79	128.81	99.77				193.4
1985	288.34	124.74	163.60	128.65				222.2
1986	334.19	148.44	185.75	151.16				247.1
1987	403.18	179.94	223.24	182.00	297.72	103.34	0.82	284.0
1988	506.20	223.65	282.55	229.76	376.29	127.91	2.00	319.2
1989	590.93	253.16	337.77	290.64	442.18	145.61	3.14	335.8
1990	611.67	264.39	347.25	311.77	455.87	152.30	3.50	348.9
1991	684.40	291.18	393.22	347.90	504.36	175.43	4.61	383.7
1992	827.29	329.23	498.06	425.89	594.30	219.27	13.71	440.2
1993	1102.53	386.86	715.67	582.37	724.49	308.08	69.96	505.3
1994	1356.28	509.21	847.07	711.80	855.74	403.07	97.47	610.4
1995	1646.55	630.59	1015.96	840.35	1022.13	486.22	138.20	657.4
1996	1758.70	687.58	1071.12	771.47	962.70	655.22	140.78	711.64
1997	1884.99	751.98	1133.01	796.22	945.82	751.15	188.02	803.66
长沙市	362.06	196.61	165.45	141.03	159.96	138.75	63.35	
株洲市	200.28	40.68	159.60	113.44	120.82	57.39	22.07	
湘潭市	143.51	40.54	102.87	72.67	75.10	60.89	7.52	
衡阳市	162.13	54.12	108.01	65.98	76.45	73.07	12.61	
邵阳市	77.11	35.40	41.71	22.00	29.59	38.12	9.4	
岳阳市	260.25	106.54	153.71	140.98	140.68	83.24	36.33	
常德市	166.87	102.69	64.18	58.30	81.84	79.19	5.84	
张家界市	12.54	6.35	6.19	3.72	6.82	4.57	1.15	
益阳市	76.40	37.63	38.77	17.77	28.69	41.73	5.98	
郴州市	99.67	25.95	73.72	34.22	45.94	46.56	7.17	
永州市	87.93	39.56	48.37	34.77	46.98	34.79	6.16	
娄底地区	107.93	14.80	93.13	58.10	66.65	40.83	0.45	
怀化地区	96.12	32.49	63.63	16.97	42.94	44.23	8.95	
湘西自治州	34.80	20.49	14.31	16.02	25.28	8.46	1.06	

11—5 独立核算工业企业主要指标

Major Indlcators of Industrial Independent Accounting Enterprises

年 份	企业单位数（个）	# 亏损企业	工业总产值（现价）（亿元）	工业增加值（生产法）（亿元）	职工平均人数（万人）	固定资产原价（亿元）	产品销售收入（亿元）	利税总额（亿元）
全部工业								
1978	16419	1810				123.20		24.48
1979								
1980	18670	2597				153.75		31.97
1981	18312	2759				168.77		34.33
1982	18300	2760				182.07		36.18
1983	18379	2049				195.84		39.66
1984	20084	2131	227.60			211.25	219.47	43.45
1985	18204	2107	276.64		204.13	240.16	271.98	53.38
1986	20430	2911	319.88		213.26	269.73	313.30	57.89
1987	20539	3209	387.28		283.17	309.01	382.17	65.52
1988	20991	2834	489.05		286.63	357.97	481.22	80.48
1989	21233	4180	569.10		293.53	409.12	527.14	82.29
1990	21060	5209	586.67		297.37	455.41	540.02	65.37
1991	20803	4358	654.82		305.08	517.29	632.96	74.98
1992	20276	3864	790.54	231.88	313.58	602.21	782.16	89.91
1993	22083	5016	1064.44	323.31	347.88	714.55	1102.25	105.71
1994	22978	4915	1298.22	382.08	314.88	944.41	1120.34	130.54
1995	23931	6210	1370.84	400.52	313.54	1282.75	1340.79	124.37
1996	24250	5408	1659.04	555.66	321.01	1419.85	1477.74	135.51
1997	22910	5632	1740.59	571.22	300.00	1657.45	1520.14	150.24
国有工业								
1978	2986	630	101.69			110.15		19.80
1979			118.49			122.69		24.19
1980	3074	586	129.88			134.61		26.75
1981	3066	688	135.14			146.63		27.53
1982	3123	729	148.25			157.40		29.95
1983	3129	470	158.05			168.49		33.83
1984	3187	345	177.78			180.34	172.47	37.05
1985	3522	362	212.66		145.57	203.94	210.45	44.90
1986	3463	486	242.09		154.01	226.05	239.87	48.60
1987	3568	474	290.04		164.36	255.41	290.19	55.82
1988	3567	461	367.23		168.85	294.81	365.06	67.41
1989	3602	740	429.96		172.61	335.60	402.65	70.44
1990	3608	1261	441.73		176.32	374.01	413.34	56.39
1991	3609	1092	488.04		181.90	426.45	481.56	63.67
1992	3550	1009	575.57	173.98	185.87	474.47	574.09	75.29
1993	3649	1474	700.29	209.65	182.20	532.95	759.42	73.31
1994	3652	1400	823.47	247.32	180.48	719.25	730.74	91.29
1995	3859	1621	843.83	259.97	180.43	1001.31	855.96	90.96
1996	3770	1559	912.85	309.09	182.17	1117.07	886.48	100.91
1997	3036	1540	886.94	299.52	161.86	1276.85	853.10	102.58

11—6 独立核算工业企业各种分组的主要生产指标(1997 年)

Major Indicators of Industrial Independent Accounting Enterprises by Various Characteristics

单位:亿元

指　　标	企业单位数(个)	亏损企业	工业总产值(现价)	工业增加值(生产法)	工业中间投入	本年应付工资	本年应付福利费	全部职工年平均人数(万人)
总　　计	22919	5632	1740.59	571.22	1250.54	146.79	19.97	300.00
国有经济	3036	1540	886.94	299.52	641.45	91.17	13.53	161.86
中央企业	181	93	406.96	160.38	277.38	30.73	4.54	41.00
地方企业	2855	1447	479.98	139.13	364.07	60.44	9.00	120.86
集体经济	18271	3777	673.22	214.08	478.14	45.85	5.11	121.21
私营经济	820	32	38.81	14.70	25.77	1.24	0.18	2.22
联营经济	70	10	2.90	0.82	2.16	0.19	0.03	0.36
股份制经济	142	57	43.35	15.99	29.12	3.27	0.41	6.48
外商投资经济	229	84	57.96	16.24	44.89	3.13	0.46	3.94
中外合资经营企业	182	69	39.79	11.02	31.76	2.58	0.41	3.01
中外合作经营企业	25	9	14.19	4.10	10.25	0.33	0.03	0.49
外资企业	22	6	3.97	1.13	2.87	0.23	0.02	0.44
港、澳、台投资经济	254	114	31.66	7.22	25.68	1.71	0.23	3.22
其他经济	97	18	5.74	2.65	3.33	0.22	0.02	0.71
在总计中:乡属工业	11918	1822	456.14	138.61	328.72	27.38	2.76	68.87
在总计中:								
轻工业	9843	2374	666.32	248.64	447.01	42.55	6.26	99.87
以农产品为原料	6660	1582	492.21	196.44	318.92	28.32	4.51	63.52
以非农产品为原料	3183	792	174.11	52.20	128.09	14.23	1.74	36.35
重工业	13076	3258	1074.27	322.58	803.53	104.24	13.72	200.13
采掘工业	2347	430	120.62	39.92	85.49	19.29	2.51	41.62
原料工业	3318	903	470.54	148.21	352.21	38.26	5.03	57.67
加工工业	7411	1925	483.11	134.45	365.83	46.69	6.18	100.84
在总计中:								
大型企业	209	91	616.50	208.70	447.95	52.79	7.60	75.81
中型企业	514	297	179.72	52.16	137.57	23.41	4.12	45.68
小型企业	22196	5244	944.36	310.35	665.02	70.59	8.25	178.51
煤炭采选业	940	213	50.89	18.58	35.14	12.42	1.73	24.85
黑色金属矿采选业	143	23	9.67	2.56	7.44	0.88	0.14	2.87
有色金属矿采选业	435	65	35.30	10.44	25.68	3.63	0.36	7.78
非金属矿采选业	734	105	24.87	8.49	17.31	2.47	0.28	5.61
其他矿采选业	12	4	0.57	0.19	0.41	0.06		0.11
木材及竹材采运业	119	19	2.65	1.04	1.69	0.26	0.04	0.81
食品加工业	1346	309	111.65	34.59	78.55	3.11	0.35	7.17

11—6 续表1 (1997年) 单位:亿元

指标	企业单位数(个)	亏损企业	工业总产值(现价)	工业增加值(生产法)	工业中间投入	本年应付工资	本年应付福利费	全部职工年平均人数(万人)
食品制造业	504	125	19.47	6.61	13.80	1.28	0.19	4.05
饮料制造业	662	142	28.91	12.13	18.48	2.48	0.21	4.36
烟草加工业	25	4	122.29	74.11	59.30	3.20	0.70	2.81
纺织业	554	220	64.48	19.94	46.61	7.42	1.78	18.94
服装及其他纤维制品制造业	434	107	12.55	3.93	8.99	1.07	0.11	3.41
皮革、毛皮、羽绒及其制品业	410	116	21.86	6.60	16.04	1.25	0.20	3.42
木材加工及竹藤棕草制品业	1052	125	26.57	8.97	18.43	1.64	0.16	4.59
家具制造业	411	48	10.79	4.13	7.03	0.53	0.05	1.56
造纸及纸制品业	788	210	45.50	14.55	33.10	3.68	0.42	8.79
印刷业、记录媒介的复制	732	191	23.50	8.61	15.97	2.19	0.27	4.45
文教体育用品制造业	201	44	4.98	1.38	3.74	0.40	0.05	1.35
石油加工及炼焦业	31	12	84.41	15.00	73.39	4.08	0.57	4.18
化学原料及化学制品制造业	1270	387	144.78	42.34	106.79	11.47	1.63	21.40
医药制造业	167	62	20.39	6.27	15.10	1.73	0.21	3.04
化学纤维制造业	37	7	9.59	1.53	8.42	0.83	0.11	1.28
橡胶制品业	133	45	13.46	3.54	10.31	1.35	0.16	2.80
塑料制品业	594	178	20.44	6.91	14.13	1.44	0.18	4.26
非金属矿物制品业	1412	380	78.22	25.48	56.45	8.23	0.97	18.12
黑色金属冶炼及压延加工业	253	82	87.69	21.85	69.37	7.98	1.00	11.22
有色金属冶炼及压延加工业	347	85	81.84	19.95	65.24	5.63	0.70	7.64
金属制品业	880	234	39.34	10.99	29.57	2.60	0.29	6.54
普通机械制造业	100	49	11.65	3.04	9.15	1.87	0.21	3.98
专用设备制造业	649	199	39.54	12.84	28.62	5.41	0.93	12.58
交通运输设备制造业	788	257	99.45	26.00	77.87	9.17	1.20	14.83
电气机械及器材制造业	663	239	68.60	19.19	51.93	5.07	0.80	11.01
电子及通信设备制造业	185	80	27.04	5.73	22.56	1.91	0.22	4.17
仪器仪表及文化办公用机械制造业	113	52	5.22	0.98	4.47	0.92	0.12	1.92
其他制造业	985	158	33.85	10.89	23.91	2.46	0.29	9.34
电力蒸气热水生产和供应业	1011	145	86.62	49.40	50.13	8.60	1.17	9.20
煤气生产和供应业	10	7	0.87	—0.03	0.94	0.22	0.03	0.33
自来水生产和供应业	312	71	9.89	5.08	5.28	1.58	0.21	2.11

11—7 独立核算工业企业各种分组的资本金与资产(1997年)

Capital Fund and Fixed Assets of Industrial Independent Accounting Enterprises by Various Characteristics

单位:亿元

指 标	流动资产年平均余额	资本金合计	流动资产合计	固定资产原价合计	累计折旧	本年折旧
总 计	1000.87	593.14	1015.67	1657.45	492.04	76.57
国有经济	662.37	380.73	696.05	1276.85	376.60	55.26
中央企业	260.46	172.38	275.34	576.29	166.84	29.41
地方企业	401.92	208.35	420.70	700.56	209.76	25.85
集体经济	239.06	124.78	215.71	237.28	72.20	11.73
私营经济	8.17	5.19	9.39	4.72	1.03	0.28
联营经济	1.28	0.98	1.06	1.28	0.40	0.08
股份制经济	35.02	24.53	35.02	41.97	11.27	2.11
外商投资经济	37.05	39.08	39.35	72.40	25.35	5.59
中外合资经营企业	27.82	31.50	30.93	64.11	23.65	5.11
中外合作经营企业	6.60	5.35	6.74	5.68	1.31	0.30
外资企业	2.63	2.23	1.68	2.61	0.39	0.18
港、澳、台投资经济	16.30	16.04	17.76	20.98	4.87	1.44
其他经济	1.62	1.80	1.35	1.97	0.32	0.08
在总计中:乡属工业	124.10	63.76	108.90	131.62	37.38	6.91
在总计中:轻工业	333.04	178.57	335.40	397.06	114.08	19.33
以农产品为原料	245.77	122.31	248.07	273.26	78.48	13.10
以非农产品为原料	87.27	56.26	87.33	123.79	35.61	6.23
重工业	667.83	414.57	680.27	1260.39	377.96	57.23
采掘工业	62.05	39.52	59.07	97.26	32.47	3.19
原料工业	281.56	199.70	289.47	754.57	221.72	36.91
加工工业	324.22	175.35	331.73	408.56	123.77	17.13
在总计中:大型企业	421.92	251.54	446.57	774.99	267.75	38.52
中型企业	171.28	74.88	175.77	275.38	82.06	11.60
小型企业	407.68	266.72	393.34	607.08	142.23	26.45
煤炭采选业	31.44	22.78	32.11	55.03	17.19	1.70
黑色金属矿采选业	7.07	1.96	6.48	7.59	3.37	0.24
有色金属矿采选业	13.92	9.43	11.98	21.57	7.94	0.77
非金属矿采选业	10.11	5.57	8.82	15.07	4.98	0.55
其他矿采选业	0.10	0.05	0.11	0.12	0.04	0.01
木材及竹材采运业	1.63	1.28	1.56	1.35	0.52	0.08
食品加工业	42.18	16.95	36.10	36.18	8.55	1.54

11—7 续表1 (1997年) 单位:亿元

指标	流动资产年平均余额	资本金合计	流动资产合计	固定资产原价合计	累计折旧	本年折旧
食品制造业	10.43	8.17	11.25	16.80	3.80	0.57
饮料制造业	20.97	11.88	23.55	20.20	4.09	0.75
烟草加工业	62.10	29.77	66.63	60.01	17.60	5.14
纺织业	41.10	18.96	43.15	55.24	18.83	1.76
服装及其他纤维制品制造业	5.58	3.51	5.16	5.36	1.50	0.20
皮革、毛皮、羽绒及其制品业	10.66	5.12	9.71	9.01	2.39	0.31
木材加工及竹藤棕草制品业	12.15	6.54	10.40	16.46	3.41	0.50
家具制造业	2.42	1.20	1.97	2.14	0.66	0.10
造纸及纸制品业	24.47	12.11	24.36	35.26	11.40	1.29
印刷业、记录媒介的复制	10.37	6.46	9.97	16.31	5.33	0.91
文教体育用品制造业	2.44	1.26	2.44	1.96	0.70	0.09
石油加工及炼焦业	36.43	14.47	35.22	102.77	32.57	5.23
化学原料及化学制品制造业	73.49	35.03	74.71	122.44	40.92	5.71
医药制造业	15.38	8.03	16.80	18.46	4.63	0.66
化学纤维制造业	6.08	3.97	6.05	16.55	4.87	0.58
橡胶制品业	7.11	2.74	7.43	8.50	2.48	0.30
塑料制品业	9.77	7.80	9.16	13.08	3.67	0.45
非金属矿物制品业	36.90	24.90	36.22	81.26	25.65	3.71
黑色金属冶炼及压延加工业	56.79	32.02	57.50	107.68	33.40	4.09
有色金属冶炼及压延加工业	41.10	25.06	44.32	57.82	17.76	3.36
金属制品业	18.57	9.25	17.58	17.22	5.34	0.76
普通机械制造业	14.87	7.59	14.67	16.35	4.78	0.60
专用设备制造业	39.27	20.36	38.95	44.75	15.91	1.63
交通运输设备制造业	71.78	43.11	74.00	74.77	22.33	3.58
电气机械及器材制造业	48.45	21.84	49.81	45.14	12.76	1.68
电子及通信设备制造业	24.25	16.54	30.08	32.03	6.71	1.83
仪器仪表及文化办公用机械制造业	5.81	3.42	6.07	6.75	2.09	0.19
其他制造业	9.64	5.10	8.73	6.94	2.34	0.35
电力蒸气热水生产和供应业	75.64	86.80	82.61	350.91	96.35	18.36
煤气生产和供应业	0.82	2.73	0.84	4.07	0.35	0.10
自来水生产和供应业	5.85	11.63	6.66	28.87	6.90	1.99

11—7 续表 2　　(1997 年)　　单位:亿元

指　标	固定资产净值年均余额	流动负债	长期负债	所有者权益
总　计	1098.71	1149.88	558.20	810.79
国有经济	843.32	818.08	450.90	581.08
中央企业	375.92	277.11	241.37	274.83
地方企业	467.40	540.97	209.54	306.24
集体经济	162.99	230.00	72.53	112.28
私营经济	3.58	7.37	0.62	8.12
联营经济	0.91	1.00	0.25	0.85
股份制经济	26.59	33.69	17.01	38.00
外商投资经济	45.62	41.65	10.55	50.64
中外合资经营企业	38.99	32.69	9.77	43.05
中外合作经营企业	4.38	6.81	0.55	5.86
外资企业	2.25	2.15	0.23	1.74
港、澳、台投资经济	14.09	16.69	6.12	18.04
其他经济	1.61	1.41	0.22	1.77
在总计中:乡属工业	94.16	108.10	45.45	63.22
在总计中:轻工业	270.74	380.74	94.97	230.95
以农产品为原料	189.38	279.16	64.09	164.01
以非农产品为原料	81.36	101.58	30.89	66.94
重工业	827.97	769.13	463.22	579.84
采掘工业	70.10	57.42	28.11	53.40
原料工业	484.34	345.98	325.67	292.73
加工工业	273.52	365.73	109.44	233.71
在总计中:大型企业	466.11	471.18	236.99	453.65
中型企业	186.45	228.02	78.95	101.31
小型企业	446.15	450.67	242.25	255.83
煤炭采选业	41.66	30.40	16.49	30.91
黑色金属矿采选业	4.23	7.19	2.37	1.69
有色金属矿采选业	14.79	10.65	5.12	14.05
非金属矿采选业	10.50	8.64	3.65	8.17
其他矿采选业	0.08	0.09	0.08	0.03
木材及竹材采运业	0.93	1.76	0.92	0.95
食品加工业	27.08	42.85	8.43	20.49

11—7 续表 3 (1997 年) 单位:亿元

指　　标	固定资产净值年均余额	流动负债	长期负债	所有者权益
食品制造业	12.49	13.59	4.79	8.37
饮料制造业	15.31	21.48	6.82	17.27
烟草加工业	40.94	66.16	5.90	63.10
纺织业	37.11	60.70	14.00	12.31
服装及其他纤维制品制造业	3.96	6.26	1.10	2.26
皮革、毛皮、羽绒及其制品业	6.56	11.05	2.98	3.30
木材加工及竹藤棕草制品业	11.65	11.67	5.62	7.70
家具制造业	1.58	1.77	0.51	1.38
造纸及纸制品业	22.96	30.01	11.28	13.95
印刷业、记录媒介的复制	10.96	11.23	3.38	8.63
文教体育用品制造业	1.27	2.80	0.39	0.94
石油加工及炼焦业	53.06	41.79	61.20	33.04
化学原料及化学制品制造业	79.07	95.25	35.79	44.50
医药制造业	11.87	15.82	5.58	12.58
化学纤维制造业	9.71	8.78	6.94	4.53
橡胶制品业	6.34	9.09	1.44	3.92
塑料制品业	9.03	11.94	5.45	5.31
非金属矿物制品业	52.63	50.91	33.33	30.02
黑色金属冶炼及压延加工业	64.55	72.67	33.33	59.42
有色金属冶炼及压延加工业	38.25	55.00	8.96	34.59
金属制品业	12.04	18.89	4.83	9.09
普通机械制造业	11.76	18.00	4.86	9.05
专用设备制造业	28.17	41.58	7.46	25.59
交通运输设备制造业	50.46	72.08	16.86	64.62
电气机械及器材制造业	31.50	55.62	8.60	32.42
电子及通信设备制造业	21.84	30.63	15.72	22.24
仪器仪表及文化办公用机械制造业	4.67	8.34	1.58	1.77
其他制造业	4.46	7.85	1.60	4.83
电力蒸气热水生产和供应业	238.77	80.81	170.55	117.58
煤气生产和供应业	3.64	1.71	0.59	2.68
自来水生产和供应业	19.81	7.36	5.06	19.34

11—8 独立核算工业企业各种分组的主要财务指标(1997年)

Major Financial Indicators of Industrial Enterprise with Independent Accountings Systems by Various Characterisrics

单位:亿元

指标	产品销售收入	销售费用	销售税金	销售利润
总计	1520.14	50.28	70.30	168.93
国有经济	853.10	19.61	60.47	103.09
中央企业	410.32	4.73	54.15	47.78
地方企业	442.79	14.89	6.31	55.31
集体经济	505.38	22.33	7.97	45.69
私营经济	21.88	2.71	0.49	3.92
联营经济	2.85	0.26	0.05	0.29
股份制经济	36.57	2.07	0.41	5.12
外商投资经济	67.34	1.72	0.32	7.07
中外合资经营企业	51.68	1.24	0.31	5.64
中外合作经营企业	12.27	0.37		1.05
外资企业	3.39	0.11	0.01	0.37
港、澳、台投资经济	29.19	1.34	0.52	3.45
其他经济	3.83	0.22	0.08	0.30
在总计中:乡属工业	333.84	15.10	5.83	29.06
在总计中:轻工业	557.32	21.80	60.85	57.07
以农产品为原料	423.77	13.89	58.25	40.86
以非农产品为原料	133.55	7.91	2.60	16.21
重工业	962.83	28.48	9.45	111.86
采掘工业	104.15	4.13	1.45	13.13
原料工业	453.22	9.69	3.15	46.78
加工工业	405.45	14.66	4.84	51.95
在总计中:大型企业	611.18	11.51	52.55	83.29
中型企业	168.46	5.82	6.23	16.94
小型企业	740.51	32.94	11.52	68.71
煤炭采选业	45.01	1.44	0.61	6.12
黑色金属矿采选业	9.30	0.22	0.11	0.86
有色金属矿采选业	30.59	1.15	0.31	3.81
非金属矿采选业	19.24	1.27	0.42	2.53
其他矿采选业	0.40	0.11	0.03	0.04
木材及竹材采运业	2.24	0.19	0.08	0.39
食品加工业	90.44	3.37	0.48	5.69

11—8　续表 1　　（1997 年）　　单位:亿元

指　　标	产品销售收　　入	销售费用	销售税金	销售利润
食品制造业	17.49	1.14	0.13	2.17
饮料制造业	24.80	1.42	2.28	3.76
烟草加工业	122.81	1.24	53.42	12.35
纺织业	50.44	1.39	0.34	4.10
服装及其他纤维制品制造业	10.73	0.52	0.13	0.77
皮革、毛皮、羽绒及其制品业	19.56	0.39	0.24	1.21
木材加工及竹藤棕草制品业	19.99	1.33	0.38	1.88
家具制造业	6.91	0.45	0.22	0.60
造纸及纸制品业	37.65	1.09	0.46	4.17
印刷业、记录媒介的复制	19.45	0.57	0.19	3.06
文教体育用品制造业	3.56	0.22	0.04	0.41
石油加工及炼焦业	90.43	0.59	0.01	7.76
化学原料及化学制品制造业	126.47	3.90	0.78	13.91
医药制造业	17.52	2.03	0.14	3.23
化学纤维制造业	9.21	0.24	0.02	1.16
橡胶制品业	11.57	0.43	0.10	1.46
塑料制品业	14.78	0.59	0.22	1.38
非金属矿物制品业	61.12	3.67	1.08	4.67
黑色金属冶炼及压延加工业	86.39	1.53	0.44	8.93
有色金属冶炼及压延加工业	75.51	1.54	0.42	8.17
金属制品业	30.02	1.14	0.33	2.53
普通机械制造业	10.73	0.49	0.08	1.35
专用设备制造业	32.74	1.51	0.28	5.38
交通运输设备制造业	91.21	2.07	2.45	12.25
电气机械及器材制造业	50.14	4.04	0.39	6.97
电子及通信设备制造业	26.65	1.03	0.12	4.37
仪器仪表及文化办公用机械制造业	4.52	0.26	0.02	0.80
其他制造业	22.42	1.22	0.91	1.87
电力蒸气热水生产和供应业	90.99	0.78	0.96	12.29
煤气生产和供应业	0.93	0.08		-0.34
自来水生产和供应业	8.86	0.22	0.11	1.45

11—8 续表 2 (1997 年) 单位:亿元

指　　标	管理费用	财务费用	利润总额	利税总额	应付利润
总　计	131.95	69.08	−1.22	150.24	9.69
国有经济	93.08	44.71	−11.92	102.58	1.14
中央企业	35.17	15.69	8.46	93.42	0.56
地方企业	57.92	29.02	−20.38	9.16	0.58
集体经济	27.53	17.39	4.72	31.68	4.40
私营经济	1.43	0.25	2.30	4.44	1.43
联营经济	0.14	0.06	0.10	0.23	0.05
股份制经济	4.15	1.63	0.86	3.03	0.42
外商投资经济	3.55	3.83	1.24	4.73	0.99
中外合资经营企业	2.67	3.40	0.51	3.80	0.92
中外合作经营企业	0.63	0.33	0.63	0.79	0.02
外资企业	0.25	0.09	0.10	0.13	0.05
港、澳、台投资经济	1.85	1.11	1.45	3.20	1.23
其他经济	0.21	0.10	0.02	0.34	0.03
在总计中:乡属工业	12.19	11.27	7.24	24.27	3.17
在总计中:轻工业	39.84	20.13	7.75	97.93	5.46
以农产品为原料	26.52	14.71	7.59	89.00	3.15
以非农产品为原料	13.32	5.42	0.16	8.93	2.31
重工业	92.11	48.95	−8.97	52.31	4.23
采掘工业	11.61	3.27	1.74	7.98	1.01
原料工业	35.57	23.68	−4.16	28.87	1.17
加工工业	44.93	22.00	−6.55	15.46	2.05
在总计中:大型企业	55.94	26.01	13.03	105.73	1.52
中型企业	23.80	12.62	−14.10	2.14	0.21
小型企业	52.21	30.45	−0.15	42.37	7.95
煤炭采选业	6.17	1.15	0.80	4.24	0.19
黑色金属矿采选业	0.68	0.38	0.04	0.48	0.11
有色金属矿采选业	3.16	1.08	0.61	1.74	0.42
非金属矿采选业	1.62	0.65	0.40	1.75	0.32
其他矿采选业	0.01	0.01	0.02	0.07	0.02
木材及竹材采运业	0.38	0.11	−0.06	0.11	0.02
食品加工业	4.22	2.73	0.42	2.38	0.39

11—8 续表 3 (1997 年) 单位:亿元

指标	管理费用	财务费用	利润总额	利税总额	应付利润
食品制造业	1.32	0.58	0.83	1.91	1.03
饮料制造业	2.39	0.62	1.86	5.84	0.58
烟草加工业	5.32	3.65	5.90	70.43	0.12
纺织业	4.87	2.69	—2.93	—0.52	0.05
服装及其他纤维制品制造业	0.71	0.32	—0.10	0.40	0.05
皮革、毛皮、羽绒及其制品业	0.83	0.66		1.02	0.16
木材加工及竹藤棕草制品业	1.26	1.00	—0.10	1.10	0.18
家具制造业	0.23	0.10	0.28	0.86	0.07
造纸及纸制品业	3.02	1.71	—0.12	2.49	0.15
印刷业、记录媒介的复制	1.87	0.74	0.92	2.18	0.36
文教体育用品制造业	0.42	0.14		0.18	0.02
石油加工及炼焦业	6.83	3.41	—1.55	2.44	
化学原料及化学制品制造业	11.25	5.66	—0.66	4.46	0.42
医药制造业	2.11	1.19	0.18	1.30	0.15
化学纤维制造业	1.00	0.54	—0.22	0.16	0.03
橡胶制品业	1.27	0.45	—0.05	0.45	0.02
塑料制品业	1.36	0.84	—0.45	0.36	0.08
非金属矿物制品业	5.63	4.32	—4.54	0.25	0.24
黑色金属冶炼及压延加工业	6.28	3.71	—0.91	3.05	0.03
有色金属冶炼及压延加工业	5.53	3.22	—0.28	3.49	0.18
金属制品业	2.05	1.22	—0.29	1.26	0.21
普通机械制造业	1.91	0.85	—1.30	—0.70	0.02
专用设备制造业	5.96	2.17	—2.07	0.13	0.07
交通运输设备制造业	9.91	4.05	0.56	7.43	0.31
电气机械及器材制造业	5.52	2.57	0.56	3.48	1.48
电子及通信设备制造业	2.67	1.72	0.52	1.89	0.14
仪器仪表及文化办公用机械制造业	0.98	0.61	—0.41	—0.16	—0.01
其他制造业	1.10	0.49	0.43	2.29	0.18
电力蒸气热水生产和供应业	6.57	6.40	4.05	17.92	0.60
煤气生产和供应业	0.23	0.06	—0.23	—0.18	
自来水生产和供应业	1.73	0.42	—0.32	0.26	0.04

11—9 国有独立核算工业企业主要指标(1997年)

Main Financial Indicators of Industrial Independent Accounting Enterprises by Various Characteristics

单位:亿元

指标	企业单位数(个)	亏损企业	工业总产值(现价)	工业增加值(生产法)	工业中间投入	本年应付工资
总计	3036	1540	886.94	299.52	641.45	91.17
轻工业	1353	666	296.49	127.87	187.13	22.37
以农产品为原料	1040	509	251.08	115.18	152.47	16.60
以非农产品为原料	313	157	45.41	12.69	34.67	5.77
重工业	1683	874	590.45	171.65	454.32	68.80
采掘工业	255	127	42.47	14.75	30.20	11.56
原料工业	556	273	319.65	99.08	244.44	28.60
加工工业	872	474	228.34	57.82	179.67	28.63
煤炭采选业	125	64	24.23	9.17	16.73	8.04
黑色金属矿采选业	10	7	4.04	0.80	3.42	0.32
有色金属矿采选业	56	25	9.58	3.21	6.81	2.30
非金属矿采选业	40	15	5.31	1.98	3.69	1.04
其他矿采选业	1					
木材及竹材采运业	25	15	1.18	0.46	0.77	0.19
食品加工业	356	199	42.69	12.28	31.14	1.76
食品制造业	139	57	4.63	2.00	2.80	0.51
饮料制造业	102	48	14.30	6.84	8.64	1.54
烟草加工业	20	3	121.92	73.95	59.06	3.13
纺织业	128	74	33.94	9.85	25.49	5.68
服装及其他纤维制品制造业	24	9	1.34	0.36	1.00	0.19
皮革、毛皮、羽绒及其制品业	21	8	0.79	0.22	0.61	0.13
木材加工及竹藤棕草制品业	35	20	3.39	0.94	2.71	0.36
家具制造业	2		0.01		0.02	
造纸及纸制品业	71	29	15.69	4.45	12.31	1.79
印刷业、记录媒介的复制	133	61	6.44	2.47	4.34	1.14
文教体育用品制造业	10	3	0.19	0.05	0.15	0.04
石油加工及炼焦业	6	3	83.46	14.60	72.81	4.03
化学原料及化学制品制造业	233	121	79.09	18.48	63.17	7.84
医药制造业	52	23	11.93	3.16	9.32	1.08
化学纤维制造业	4	4	4.51	0.23	4.47	0.38
橡胶制品业	16	8	7.57	1.80	5.92	0.86
塑料制品业	46	23	2.34	0.80	1.62	0.25
非金属矿物制品业	141	80	23.17	7.41	17.49	3.69
黑色金属冶炼及压延加工业	42	24	69.29	17.16	55.19	7.03
有色金属冶炼及压延加工业	42	25	48.41	11.30	39.42	4.09
金属制品业	34	17	3.31	0.68	2.78	0.38
普通机械制造业	30	18	7.77	2.27	5.89	1.46
专用设备制造业	149	92	21.02	6.55	15.50	4.10
交通运输设备制造业	135	76	60.96	16.26	47.76	6.54
电气机械及器材制造业	92	53	25.30	5.93	20.32	2.96
电子及通信设备制造业	57	28	22.02	4.11	18.33	1.26
仪器仪表及文化办公用机械制造业	23	14	2.78	0.84	2.04	0.65
其他制造业	16	7	0.32	0.09	0.24	0.06
电力蒸气热水生产和供应业	235	84	68.86	42.13	38.27	7.40
煤气生产和供应业	9	7	0.86	—0.03	0.94	0.22
自来水生产和供应业	108	47	7.71	4.35	3.79	1.44

11—9 续表 1 (1997 年) 单位:亿元

指 标	本年应付福利费	全部职工年均人数(万人)	固定资产净值年均余额	流动负债	长期负债	所有者权益
总 计	13.53	161.86	843.32	818.08	450.90	581.08
轻工业	3.87	44.03	179.25	245.03	55.35	146.46
以农产品为原料	3.14	32.06	130.09	197.10	38.06	114.90
以非农产品为原料	0.73	11.97	49.15	47.93	17.30	31.56
重工业	9.67	117.83	664.07	573.04	395.55	434.62
采掘工业	1.76	24.09	56.18	42.64	24.07	39.10
原料工业	3.89	37.62	412.21	271.21	294.97	240.03
加工工业	4.02	56.12	195.68	259.20	76.50	155.49
煤炭采选业	1.27	16.03	34.88	23.29	14.61	24.78
黑色金属矿采选业	0.08	1.34	3.35	5.98	2.11	0.98
有色金属矿采选业	0.28	4.50	11.74	8.00	4.53	9.40
非金属矿采选业	0.13	1.96	7.53	5.10	2.49	5.67
其他矿采选业						
木材及竹材采运业	0.03	0.59	0.67	1.44	0.75	0.67
食品加工业	0.22	4.02	16.52	29.52	4.48	11.76
食品制造业	0.06	1.79	6.14	6.99	1.71	2.25
饮料制造业	0.13	2.10	10.30	15.97	4.52	11.32
烟草加工业	0.70	2.75	40.78	65.56	5.90	62.83
纺织业	1.58	13.28	28.05	43.77	9.02	9.06
服装及其他纤维制品制造业	0.02	0.49	1.16	1.46	0.23	0.23
皮革、毛皮、羽绒及其制品业	0.01	0.49	1.64	2.36	0.63	0.20
木材加工及竹藤棕草制品业	0.06	0.99	6.63	6.31	3.64	3.30
家具制造业		0.01	0.02	0.01		0.02
造纸及纸制品业	0.20	3.65	13.60	17.25	7.11	8.87
印刷业、记录媒介的复制	0.13	2.29	5.40	6.10	1.15	2.92
文教体育用品制造业	0.01	0.18	0.38	0.91	0.10	—0.06
石油加工及炼焦业	0.56	4.06	52.91	41.44	61.15	32.98
化学原料及化学制品制造业	1.20	14.41	62.21	69.87	29.66	27.30
医药制造业	0.15	1.87	8.38	11.61	4.20	5.93
化学纤维制造业	0.05	0.63	6.10	5.76	4.89	0.80
橡胶制品业	0.10	1.44	4.31	5.63	0.62	2.92
塑料制品业	0.04	0.89	2.40	3.09	1.16	0.57
非金属矿物制品业	0.44	6.71	27.29	26.05	19.14	21.02
黑色金属冶炼及压延加工业	0.89	9.15	59.16	64.02	30.88	55.60
有色金属冶炼及压延加工业	0.52	5.10	26.67	40.82	7.17	23.90
金属制品业	0.05	0.85	2.97	3.98	1.01	2.39
普通机械制造业	0.17	2.96	9.35	13.92	4.14	5.74
专用设备制造业	0.75	9.18	23.71	33.70	6.24	18.40
交通运输设备制造业	0.82	9.30	38.60	54.16	12.99	46.33
电气机械及器材制造业	0.43	5.81	21.69	34.00	5.34	17.08
电子及通信设备制造业	0.14	2.86	11.58	20.02	8.11	12.74
仪器仪表及文化办公用机械制造业	0.09	1.27	3.47	4.81	0.99	1.56
其他制造业	0.01	0.17	0.27	0.42	0.13	0.20
电力蒸气热水生产和供应业	1.03	7.63	218.46	67.51	162.16	96.69
煤气生产和供应业	0.03	0.33	3.64	1.70	0.59	2.67
自来水生产和供应业	0.19	1.77	18.36	6.64	4.32	18.12

11—9 续表 2 (1997 年) 单位:亿元

指标	流动资产年平均余额	资本金合计	流动资产合计	固定资产原价合计	累计折旧	本年折旧
总计	662.37	380.73	696.05	1276.85	376.60	55.26
轻工业	189.52	93.39	202.30	263.64	77.47	12.74
以农产品为原料	155.42	70.43	168.04	190.06	56.87	9.08
以非农产品为原料	34.10	22.95	34.26	73.59	20.61	3.66
重工业	472.85	287.35	493.75	1013.20	299.13	42.53
采掘工业	40.22	28.57	42.07	79.63	27.69	2.25
原料工业	222.44	160.59	232.15	641.15	180.85	29.55
加工工业	210.19	98.19	219.53	292.42	90.59	10.72
煤炭采选业	23.54	17.45	24.78	46.29	14.94	1.26
黑色金属矿采选业	5.43	1.46	5.33	6.48	3.12	0.17
有色金属矿采选业	7.31	6.85	7.50	17.99	6.98	0.53
非金属矿采选业	4.66	3.26	5.07	11.24	3.78	0.38
其他矿采选业						
木材及竹材采运业	1.19	1.02	1.23	1.01	0.42	0.07
食品加工业	22.67	9.93	23.19	22.88	5.81	0.82
食品制造业	3.65	2.89	3.73	8.22	2.00	0.16
饮料制造业	14.53	4.61	17.96	13.91	2.78	0.47
烟草加工业	60.93	29.51	66.10	59.83	17.55	5.13
纺织业	27.59	10.86	29.35	41.76	14.37	1.13
服装及其他纤维制品制造业	0.67	0.57	0.61	1.40	0.29	0.02
皮革、毛皮、羽绒及其制品业	1.37	1.11	1.35	2.06	0.48	0.03
木材加工及竹藤棕草制品业	4.96	2.40	4.87	9.56	2.00	0.25
家具制造业				0.02		
造纸及纸制品业	12.28	5.79	13.42	21.28	7.27	0.61
印刷业、记录媒介的复制	4.32	2.40	4.35	8.08	3.22	0.40
文教体育用品制造业	0.56	0.10	0.53	0.42	0.10	0.01
石油加工及炼焦业	36.12	14.32	34.92	102.55	32.49	5.22
化学原料及化学制品制造业	47.41	20.94	48.89	97.03	33.48	4.20
医药制造业	9.97	3.42	10.51	13.30	3.59	0.45
化学纤维制造业	3.05	1.65	3.09	9.30	2.97	0.26
橡胶制品业	4.31	1.46	4.49	5.46	1.47	0.15
塑料制品业	1.77	0.97	1.72	3.15	0.85	0.06
非金属矿物制品业	19.25	13.09	19.43	43.05	13.12	1.65
黑色金属冶炼及压延加工业	49.12	28.60	50.37	100.00	31.54	3.70
有色金属冶炼及压延加工业	29.44	15.28	32.52	43.16	15.23	2.51
金属制品业	3.41	1.21	3.39	4.15	1.13	0.13
普通机械制造业	11.36	3.37	11.22	12.89	3.73	0.45
专用设备制造业	29.31	13.43	29.16	37.72	13.56	1.31
交通运输设备制造业	50.40	26.32	52.59	55.58	16.80	2.30
电气机械及器材制造业	26.74	10.18	27.16	30.97	8.61	0.97
电子及通信设备制造业	14.69	6.70	17.19	17.40	4.84	0.90
仪器仪表及文化办公用机械制造业	3.55	1.99	3.64	4.87	1.48	0.13
其他制造业	0.45	0.30	0.45	0.50	0.22	0.01
电力蒸气热水生产和供应业	67.30	80.24	74.24	311.27	75.63	14.95
煤气生产和供应业	0.82	2.73	0.84	4.07	0.35	0.10
自来水生产和供应业	5.03	10.53	5.95	26.88	6.51	1.92

11—9 续表 3 (1997 年) 单位:亿元

指标	产品销售收入	销售税金	销售利润	利润总额	利税总额	应付利润
总计	853.10	60.47	103.09	-11.92	102.58	1.14
轻工业	278.49	56.20	29.37	0.38	75.10	0.25
以农产品为原料	237.14	55.66	23.78	2.89	75.12	0.24
以非农产品为原料	41.36	0.54	5.59	-2.51	-0.02	0.01
重工业	574.61	4.26	73.72	-12.30	27.49	0.89
采掘工业	40.17	0.34	7.16	-0.72	2.11	0.07
原料工业	329.01	1.67	36.15	-2.13	23.42	0.51
加工工业	205.43	2.25	30.42	-9.45	1.95	0.31
煤炭采选业	22.93	0.16	4.02	0.22	2.04	0.04
黑色金属矿采选业	3.98	0.03	0.41	-0.17	0.03	
有色金属矿采选业	9.15	0.06	1.89	-0.49	0.01	0.03
非金属矿采选业	4.92	0.13	1.13	-0.14	0.35	0.01
其他矿采选业						
木材及竹材采运业	1.03	0.06	0.26	-0.11		
食品加工业	38.99	0.10	2.05	-1.15	-0.31	-0.06
食品制造业	4.06	0.03	0.30	-0.36	-0.16	
饮料制造业	12.56	1.74	2.59	1.71	4.62	0.22
烟草加工业	122.38	53.41	12.22	5.80	70.31	0.08
纺织业	29.00	0.17	2.75	-2.22	-0.65	0.01
服装及其他纤维制品制造业	1.05		0.09	-0.03	-0.01	
皮革、毛皮、羽绒及其制品业	0.67			-0.23	-0.18	
木材加工及竹藤棕草制品业	2.79	0.04	0.34	-0.49	-0.19	-0.01
家具制造业						
造纸及纸制品业	14.69	0.09	1.78	-0.35	0.81	-0.01
印刷业、记录媒介的复制	4.96	0.04	0.77	-0.21	0.20	
文教体育用品制造业	0.23		0.01	-0.02	-0.01	
石油加工及炼焦业	89.76	0.01	7.70	-1.52	2.43	
化学原料及化学制品制造业	74.56	0.24	8.17	-2.38	0.42	0.10
医药制造业	10.20	0.07	1.98	-0.16	0.47	0.01
化学纤维制造业	4.55		0.35	-0.35	-0.16	
橡胶制品业	7.20	0.06	0.93	0.03	0.23	
塑料制品业	1.79	0.02	0.17	-0.38	-0.28	
非金属矿物制品业	22.42	0.24	2.68	-1.59	0.38	0.01
黑色金属冶炼及压延加工业	71.21	0.28	8.01	-0.73	2.60	
有色金属冶炼及压延加工业	45.81	0.22	6.04	-0.49	2.03	0.06
金属制品业	2.62	0.07	0.30	-0.24	-0.02	
普通机械制造业	7.45	0.04	1.15	-0.88	-0.45	
专用设备制造业	18.63	0.12	3.53	-2.33	-1.19	0.01
交通运输设备制造业	60.05	1.77	8.70	0.17	5.00	0.09
电气机械及器材制造业	22.95	0.09	2.81	-0.86	0.17	0.01
电子及通信设备制造业	8.83	0.06	1.79	-0.40	0.07	-0.08
仪器仪表及文化办公用机械制造业	2.54	0.01	0.59	-0.35	-0.24	0.01
其他制造业	0.28	0.01	0.03		0.02	
电力蒸气热水生产和供应业	75.73	0.79	9.81	3.92	16.25	0.45
煤气生产和供应业	0.93		-0.34	-0.23	-0.18	
自来水生产和供应业	7.08	0.08	1.20	-0.37	0.13	0.01

11—10 工 业 产 品 产 量

Output of Industrial Products

产品名称	单 位	1995年	1996年	1997年
化学纤维	万吨	4.80	4.07	5.53
纱(混合数)	万吨	14.66	13.42	13.27
#纯棉纱	万吨	9.04	6.91	5.67
布(混合数)	亿米	4.89	4.65	4.40
#纯棉布	亿米	2.04	1.93	1.53
针棉织品(折用纱量)	万吨	0.75	0.58	0.79
毛 巾	万条	8633	6868	7098
袜 子	万双	3895	3818	3719
服 装	万件	6861	10028	8187
毛 线	吨	1407	626	1657
呢 绒	万米	3.00	2.67	
毛 毯	万条	40.55	39.08	45.89
麻 袋	万条	1371	776	1710.53
丝(不包括土丝)	吨	95	56	15.00
丝织品(不包括土丝织品)	万米	274	68	92.78
机制纸浆	万吨	62.01	48.79	66.94
机制纸及纸板	万吨	94.02	103.41	94.39
缝纫机	万架	10.03	7.86	4.16
自行车	万辆	6.67	1.42	1.66
手 表	万只	94.42	42.28	11.32
日用搪瓷制品	吨	3006	6134	7118
日用陶瓷器	亿件	10.64	12.55	12.36
日用精铝制品	吨	1590	3320	3779
※#铝锅	万口	37.17	39.85	96.86
日用玻璃制品	万吨	14.35	12.34	9.43
保温瓶	万个	973.59	1014	1065
自来水笔	万支	1102.16	835.47	271.68
圆珠笔	万支	632.58	278.96	171.70
灯泡	万只	12157	16168	15419
合成洗涤剂	万吨	6.05	6.57	6.32
肥 皂	万吨	2.90	2.11	1.78
牙 膏	万支	3510.15	3325	2582
火 柴	万件	99.65	66.30	67.15
干电池	亿只	2.61	2.10	1.45
大 米	万吨	892	1184	830
原 盐	万吨	59.72	62.30	68.91
糖	万吨	6.31	5.85	7.72
卷 烟	万箱	249.88	258.62	233.39
罐 头	万吨	5.60	4.87	4.69
无酒精饮料	万吨	7.69	7.92	9.54

注:※铝锅中包括精锅压力锅。

11—10 续表1

产品名称	单位	1995年	1996年	1997年
饮料酒	万吨	47.17	51.82	56.29
#白酒(商品量)	万吨	20.57	24.14	29.29
啤酒	万吨	25.48	26.64	26.03
乳制品	吨	2074	2248	2507
#奶粉	吨	2066	2248	2507
味精	吨	4500	3815	3600
食用植物油	万吨	33.11	43.42	36.05
化学原料药(二十四大类)	吨	7444	5457	4021
中成药	吨	13984	11568	12177
配混合饲料	万吨	201.86	205.23	196.54
塑料制品	万吨	16.95	16.53	14.13
皮革	万张	731.39	916.00	694.10
皮鞋	万双	2851	5001.43	2780.35
胶鞋	万双	6293	5154.70	4652.68
家用电冰箱	万台	22.28	3.72	7.61
电风扇	万台	40.16	26.06	16.34
房间空气调节器	台	25144	11380	12321
收音机	万台	16.64	18.66	1.61
收录放机	万台	38.58	22.53	73.90
电视机	万部	24.73	14.86	15.64
#彩色电视机	万部	1.49	1.10	0.41
电子计算机外部设备	万部	5.13	11.75	7.64
原煤	万吨	5564.51	5989.05	4409.84
#烟煤	万吨	1760.34	1798.71	1461.20
无烟煤	万吨	3801.18	4190.35	2948.64
原油加工量	万吨	346.75	344.83	356.70
汽油	万吨	90.38	90.39	94.41
柴油	万吨	104.36	108.16	105.59
发电量	亿千瓦小时	332.94	339.09	345.96
#水电	亿千瓦小时	157.97	166.02	193.00
火电	亿千瓦小时	174.86	173.07	152.96
生铁	万吨	200.46	213.09	264.69
钢	万吨	175.60	189.45	243.73
成品钢材	万吨	154.54	167.52	199.03
#铁道用钢材	万吨	0.97	0.40	0.85
普通大型钢材	万吨	1.83	1.00	2.23
普通中型钢材	万吨	18.15	19.44	28.16
普通小型钢材	万吨	48.39	54.72	52.22
优质型钢材	万吨	13.69	15.87	15.45
线材	万吨	51.94	54.81	76.83
薄钢板	万吨	3.02	3.43	2.15
硅钢片	万吨	0.03		0.25
钢带	万吨	0.23	0.32	0.90
无缝钢管	万吨	14.91	16.83	19.09
焊接钢管	万吨	1.18	0.70	0.90

11—10 续表 2

产品名称	单位	1995年	1996年	1997年
机制焦炭	万吨	185.82	190.38	210.28
煤 气	亿立方米	34.78	21.91	23.68
铁矿石(成品矿)	万吨	101.30	79.04	100.49
水 泥	万吨	2196.02	2300.28	2209
平板玻璃	万重量箱	861.43	765.87	543.49
原木(全社会产量)	万立方米	313.45	301.82	331.27
硫 酸(折100%)	万吨	99.32	98.11	110.37
纯 碱	万吨	10.80	12.87	10.91
烧 碱(折100%)	万吨	21.46	21.23	19.29
合成氨	万吨	157.77	176.34	170.65
农用化肥(折纯量)	万吨	152.78	158.86	150.81
#氮肥	万吨	113.05	124.72	122.03
磷肥	万吨	39.49	34.05	28.30
化学农药(原药)(折纯量)	万吨	4.53	4.01	4.20
电 石	万吨	12.16	12.45	13.81
塑料树脂及共聚物	万吨	5.86	7.09	8.72
合成橡胶	万吨	3.42	4.81	4.97
轮胎外胎	万条	56.92	48.76	22.15
矿山设备	吨	15952	11947	8317
起重设备	吨	39383	10669	19928
冶炼设备	吨	6001	6929	2695
化工设备	吨	8972	11720	8379
发电设备	万千瓦	18.20	20.03	13.26
交流电动机	万千瓦	217.59	182.06	235.47
变压器	万千伏安	420.69	491.21	410.31
泵	万台	51.78	36.48	33.83
金属切削机床	台	3297	1447	1127
锻压机械	台	1195	727	809
汽 车	辆	9895	6634	7569
摩托车	辆	233744	229327	269102
轴 承	万套	4394	3637	2654
小型拖拉机	万台	2.97	1.60	0.65
内燃机	万千瓦	566	639	404
工矿电机车	辆	344	254	208
铁路机车	台	124	98	108
铁路货车	辆	4771	3903	3734
民用钢质船舶	艘	502	165	98
工业锅炉	蒸吨/台	1861/738	3222/2499	2004/645

11—11 按全省人口平均的主要工业品产量

Per Capita Output of Major Industry Products

产品名称	单位	1995 年	1996 年	1997 年
化学纤维	公斤/人	0.76	0.59	0.86
纱(混合数)	公斤/人	2.32	1.94	2.06
#纯棉纱	公斤/人	1.43	1.08	0.88
布(混合数)	米/人	7.73	7.25	6.83
针棉织品(折用纱量)	公斤/人	0.12	0.09	0.12
丝织品(不包括土丝织品)	米/人	0.04	0.01	0.01
机制纸及纸板	公斤/人	14.86	16.18	14.64
缝纫机	架/百人	0.16	0.12	0.06
自行车	辆/百人	0.11	0.02	0.03
手　表	只/百人	1.49	0.66	0.18
日用陶瓷器	件/人	16.82	19.64	19.17
日用精铝制品	公斤/百人	2.51	5.20	5.86
合成洗涤剂	公斤/人	0.95	1.03	0.98
原　盐	公斤/人	9.43	9.75	10.69
糖	公斤/人	1.00	0.92	1.20
卷　烟	箱/百人	3.95	4.05	3.62
家用电冰箱	台/万人	35.21	5.82	11.58
电视机	台/百人	0.39	0.23	0.24
原　煤	吨/人	0.88	0.94	0.68
原油加工量	公斤/人	54.80	53.96	55.33
发电量	千瓦小时/人	526.17	529.00	536.66
生　铁	公斤/人	31.68	33.34	41.06
钢	公斤/人	27.75	29.65	37.81
成品钢材	公斤/人	24.42	26.21	30.87
水　泥	吨/人	0.35	0.36	0.34
平板玻璃	重量箱/人	0.14	0.12	0.08
硫　酸(折 100%)	公斤/人	15.69	15.35	17.12
纯　碱	公斤/人	1.71	2.01	1.69
烧　碱(折 100%)	公斤/人	3.39	3.32	2.99
合成氨	公斤/人	24.93	27.59	26.47
农用化肥(折纯量)	公斤/人	24.14	24.86	23.39
#氮肥	公斤/人	17.87	19.52	18.93
磷肥	公斤/人	6.24	5.33	4.39
化学农药(原药,折纯量)	公斤/人	0.72	0.63	0.65
塑料树脂及共聚物	公斤/人	0.93	1.11	1.35
合成橡胶	公斤/人	0.54	0.75	0.77
汽　车	辆/万人	1.56	1.04	1.17
摩托车	辆/万人	36.94	24.99	41.74

11—12 村办工业主要指标(1997年)

Main Indicators of Village-Run Industrial Enterprises

	企业单位数(个)	现价工业总产值(万元)	销售收入(万元)	产品销售税金及附加(万元)	利润总额(万元)	固定资产原价年末数(万元)
总计	35471	3685794	3349093	56366	206109	653995
轻工业	18348	1505223	1390542	22792	78878	251330
重工业	17123	2180571	1958551	33574	127231	402665
煤炭采选业	2324	333506	301053	7303	24442	63222
黑色金属矿采选业	157	28513	25632	404	1756	3504
有色金属矿采选业	397	73801	70637	1551	4175	8703
非金属矿采选业	3326	352128	307531	5121	20791	53219
其他矿采选业	292	25284	22645	596	1809	8278
木材及竹材采运业	965	56375	49999	872	4130	13038
食品加工业	9637	526356	473319	6923	33216	93960
食品制造业	1450	107861	96795	1310	6606	16457
饮料制造业	691	42998	39995	668	2147	10570
烟草加工业	5	865	808	26	96	191
纺织业	168	32333	29508	536	1657	10652
服装及其他纤维制品制造业	430	43257	27070	536	1986	8013
皮革、毛皮、羽绒及其制品业	182	53236	48701	754	2586	8541
木材加工及竹藤棕草制品业	1816	127144	146861	1727	7655	19283
家具制造业	410	42733	39170	850	2011	7239
造纸及纸制品业	543	82298	73166	1112	3789	15845
印刷业、记录媒介的复制	219	37302	30865	419	1237	7297
文教体育用品制造业	27	4743	4233	113	178	1245
石油加工及炼焦业	46	4868	3868	96	209	992
化学原料及化学制品制造业	421	93870	83627	1133	4333	18323
医药制造业	12	4573	4271	80	84	1787
化学纤维制造业	50	11238	10563	217	932	4530
橡胶制品业	54	9212	8938	113	456	3099
塑料制品业	265	41853	30407	505	1700	7786
非金属矿物制品业	5801	653911	610164	8610	36596	112125
黑色金属冶炼及压延加工业	323	65509	55507	850	3749	13105
有色金属冶炼及压延加工业	164	37896	32986	451	1318	6537
金属制品业	457	85861	74699	950	2827	16284
普通机械制造业	419	95964	87675	1738	4790	22728
专用设备制造业	34	14593	13891	113	1179	1447
交通运输设备制造业	121	23449	22042	383	1232	4969
电气机械及器材制造业	76	27749	25707	180	557	3428
电子及通信设备制造业	150	30137	26685	103	1692	5966
仪器仪表及文化办公用机械制造业	136	26523	24523	349	1227	4328
其他制造业	3303	455953	417366	9055	20159	68827
电力蒸气热水生产和供应业	515	27613	25776	547	2530	7374
煤气生产和供应业	19	568	537	28	72	418
自来水生产和供应业	66	2721	1873	44	200	685

11—13 城乡合作经营工业主要指标

Main Indicators of Cooperative—Run Industrial Enterprises of Cities and Villages

指标	单位	1995年	1996年	1997年
一、城镇合作经营工业				
1.户数	户	1133	2684	5374
2.从业人数	人	17614	37573	52067
3.工业总产值	万元	55164	150243	239038
轻工业产值	万元	21876	69253	103730
重工业产值	万元	33288	80990	135308
4.上交税金	万元	2216	4414	6142
5.自有资金	万元	10254	35141	42394
二、农村合作经营工业				
1.户数	户	15062	19043	28021
2.从业人数	人	188772	224828	265476
3.工业总产值	万元	470613	895569	1298922
轻工业产值	万元	104417	315780	524540
重工业产值	万元	366196	579789	774382
4.上交税金	万元	12388	18319	24748
5.自有资金	万元	84315	133292	142094

11—14 城乡个体工业主要指标

Main Indicators of Individual—Run Industrial Enterprises of Cities and Villages

指标	单位	1995年	1996年	1997年
一、城镇个体工业				
1.户数	户	29372	45140	49141
2.从业人数	人	105004	184856	241544
3.工业总产值	万元	380888	920323	1291694
轻工业产值	万元	266402	562843	773642
重工业产值	万元	114486	357480	518052
4.上交税金	万元	12465	26449	38576
5.自有资金	万元	54510	132828	174424
二、农村个体工业				
1.户数	户	411159	525130	518275
2.从业人数	人	1477317	1988402	1789844
3.工业总产值	万元	4466556	9535615	12806127
轻工业产值	万元	2618355	5153346	6630681
重工业产值	万元	1848201	4382269	6175446
4.上交税金	万元	102167	232427	213678
5.自有资金	万元	632532	1352944	1380411

11—15 重点工业企业产品质量指标

Quality Indicators of Products of Key Industrial Enterprises

项　　目	单 位	1995 年	1996 年	1997 年
一、煤炭工业				
商品煤灰分	%	25.69	26.41	24.16
商品煤含矸率	%	0.55	0.35	1.25
二、电力工业				
周波合格率	%			99.97
三、冶金工业				
生铁合格率	%	99.70	99.55	99.66
平炉钢锭合格率	%	98.54	98.55	98.52
电炉钢锭合格率	%	96.99	97.49	98.31
顶吹转炉钢锭合格率	%	98.73	98.54	99.09
钢材合格率(成材率)	%	96.80	88.21	97.27
焦炭结焦率	%	78.76	78.24	78.38
冶金焦率	%	93.94	93.73	93.68
四、化学工业				
磷矿石品位	%	24	22.54	24.37
普钙有效磷含量	%	12	12.34	12.4
尿素合格率(中型)	%	100	98.86	99.62
电石发气量	升/千克	276	274	269
隔膜法液碱合格率	%	100	100	100
聚氯乙烯合格率	%	100	100	99.81
轮胎外胎综合合格率	%	100	99.22	
顺丁橡胶优级品率	%		93.49	100
硫酸合格率	%	100	100	100
纯碱合格率	%	100	99.61	100
五、机械工业				
铸铁件废品率	%	14.00	13.9	13.02
六、建筑材料工业				
熟料平均标号	号	624.48	571.38	
出厂水泥合格率	%	100	100	
平板玻璃一级品率	%	35.11	36.50	
七、纺织工业				
合成纤维正品率	%	98.83	96.17	97.85
棉纱一等一级以上品率	%	83.40	92.39	92.49
棉布入库一等品率	%	86.43	88.10	76.01
苎麻布入库一等品率	%	94.47	92.94	95.26
棉印染布入库一等品率	%	98.13	93.67	92.33
桑蚕丝正品率	%	100		100
丝织品入库一等品率	%	97.62	97.96	90.50
八、森林工业				
锯材特等品、一等品率	%	31.03	7.7	
胶合板优、一等品率	%	66.41	74.9	90
硬质纤维板优、一等品率	%	70.22	87.2	

11—16 重点工业企业设备利用率及其他指标

Utilitation of Machinery, Equipment and Related Indicators of Key Industrial Enterprises

项　　目	单　位	1995年	1996年	1997年
一、电力工业(部属厂)				
发电设备平均利用小时	小时	4953	4621	4081
水　　电	小时	4454	4054	4052
火　　电	小时	5407	5308	4113
二、冶金工业				
高炉利用系数	吨/立方米·昼夜	1.43	1.38	1.44
平炉利用系数	吨/立方米·昼夜	7.60	8.21	8.51
平炉炉顶寿命	炉	71.07	69	102
平炉每炉冶炼时间	时:分	5:50	5:30	4:50
平炉日历作业率	%	47.39	51.63	46.90
电炉利用系数	吨/百万伏安·昼夜	7.92	7.94	10.97
电炉每炉冶炼时间	时:分	3:44	3:53	3:30
电炉日历作业率	%		50.87	59.59
顶吹转炉利用系数	吨/公称吨·昼夜	43.44	46.69	43.15
顶吹转炉炉衬寿命	炉	530.68	691	1340
顶吹转炉每炉冶炼时间	分	34.63	33.71	29.9
顶吹转炉日历作业率	%	69.62	68.92	82.12
三、化学工业				
触媒容积利用系数:				
硫酸(100%)(大型)	吨/立方米·日	4	3.99	3.65
合成氨(大型)	吨/立方米·日	15		34.79
四、机械工业				
金属切削机床利用率	%	50.69	43.70	45.67
五、建筑材料工业				
回转窑运转率	%	76.74	72.14	
水泥磨运转率	%		58.63	
平板玻璃熔窑熔化能力	千克/平方米·日	2579.41	1147.67	
六、纺织工业				
每千锭时平均产纱量(混合)	千克	17.62	17.40	15.84
棉纺锭设备利用率	%	90.07	91.77	95.53
棉布织机每台时产量(混合)	米	3.67	3.69	3.37
棉布织机设备利用率	%	89.53	91.01	96.94
棉布织机设备运转率	%	92.06	92.32	92.35
苎麻布织机每台时产量	米	3.55	2.53	2.22
丝织机每台时产量	米	1.35	1.83	2.04
七、森林工业				
平均每辆汽车年运材量	立方米		1130	

11—17 重点工业企业物资消耗指标

Material Consumption Indicators of Key Industrial Enterprises

项　目	单　位	1995年	1996年	1997年
一、煤炭工业				
企业原煤耗坑木	立方米/万吨	105.15	90	129.80
原煤耗火药	千克/万吨	2738.62	2759	3025
原煤耗钢材	吨/万吨	7.86	8.50	7.1
原煤综合耗电	千瓦小时/吨	101.71	105.35	
洗精煤回收率	%	74.87	83.13	
二、石油工业				
原油加工耗电	千瓦小时/吨	77.33	76.84	
原油加工耗燃料油	千克/吨	19.92	24.73	
三、电力工业				
发电标准煤耗(湖南电网)	克/千瓦时	455	402	393
发电厂用电率	%	5.35	4.73	4.45
水　电	%	0.35	0.26	0.30
火　电	%	9.10	8.87	8.88
四、冶金工业				
生铁耗铁矿石	千克/吨	1807.23	1813	1812
入炉焦比	千克/吨	637.47	637	603
平炉钢耗钢铁料	千克/吨	1155.92	1158	1137
#生铁	千克/吨	935.38	953	941
电炉钢耗钢铁料	千克/吨	1121.03	1124	1102
#生铁	千克/吨	249.82	255	228
顶吹转炉钢耗钢铁料	千克/吨	1171.37	1119	1120
#生铁	千克/吨	1047.48	1034	1047
全焦耗湿煤	千克/吨	1379.43	1374	1372
电炉钢耗电	千瓦小时/吨	674.63	681	548
电解铝耗直流电	千瓦小时/吨	15837	15467	
电解铝耗氧化铝	千克/吨	1975	1971	
铜选矿回收率	%	91.51	87.75	87.81
铅选矿回收率	%	85.77	86.54	85.68
锌选矿回收率	%	77.29	86.91	86.38
锑选矿回收率	%	91.43	85.67	86.50
锡选矿回收率	%	60.98	61.80	59.60
钨选矿回收率	%	65.90	65.61	74.63
钼选矿回收率	%	81.79		
铜精炼回收率(株冶)	%	99.24	99.90	
粗铅冶炼回收率	%	95.59	95.17	94.67
电锌总回收率(株冶)	%	95.39	89.54	91.86
铅冶炼总回收率	%	94.47	94.06	93.55

11—17 续表

项目	单位	1995年	1996年	1997年
五、化学工业				
合成氨耗入炉焦、白煤(中型)	千克/吨	1385	1261	1212
合成氨耗入炉焦、白煤(小型)	千克/吨	1442	1385	1348
合成氨耗燃料煤(小型)	千克/吨		370	330
合成氨耗电(中型)	千瓦小时/吨	1236	1348	1479
合成氨耗电(小型)	千瓦小时/吨	1319	1312	1285
电石耗电	千瓦小时/吨	3578	3578	3537
隔膜液碱耗直流电(折标)	千瓦小时/吨	2420	2336	2348
硫酸耗硫铁矿	千克/吨	1022	1009	992
硫酸耗电	千瓦小时/吨	109	112	108
聚氯乙烯耗电石	千克/吨	1717	1938	1585
过磷酸钙耗硫酸	千克/吨	2677	2694	2706
六、机械工业				
化铁炉金属炉料耗焦	千克/吨	146.47	132	141
钢材利用率	%	69.48	73.49	66.19
七、建筑材料工业				
回转窑水泥熟料耗标准煤	千克/吨	202.52	169.62	
回转窑水泥综合耗电	千瓦小时/吨	103.74	107.14	
立窑水泥熟料耗标准煤	千克/吨	168.61	147.63	
立窑水泥综合耗电	千瓦小时/吨	97.15	94.35	
平板玻璃耗标准煤	千克/重量箱	33.21	38.17	
平板玻璃耗纯碱	千克/重量箱	10.94	10.28	
平板玻璃耗电	千瓦小时/重量箱	7.35	5.09	
八、纺织工业				
棉纱通扯净用棉量	公斤/吨	1084.43	1056	1042
棉纱耗电	千瓦小时/吨	2289.58	2390	2644
棉布用纱量	千克/百米		12.71	11.96
棉布耗电	千瓦小时/百米		24.39	23.18
印染布耗碱	千克/百米	1.35	1.10	1.33
印染布耗标准煤	千克/百米	45.80	46.36	55.47
九、森林工业				
锯材出材率	%	72.86	56.90	

11—18 独立核算工业企业主要经济效益指标

Main Economic Beneficial Indicators of Industrial Independent Accounting Enterprises

指　　标	单位	1994年	1996年	1997年
全部独立核算工业企业				
工业产品销售率	%	95.04	94.97	96.17
工业增加值率	%	29.43	29.6	28.9
工业成本费用利润率	%			−0.08
每百元固定资产原价实现的利税	元	13.82	9.54	9.06
每百元销售收入实现的利润	元	1.42	0.14	−0.08
产值利税率	%	10.06	8.17	8.63
资金利税率	%	10.55	7.59	7.16
流动资金周转天数	天	222	207	237
全员劳动生产率	元/年人		34823	41188
国有工业企业				
工业产品销售率	%	97.48	97.05	98.11
工业增加值率	%	30.03	29.4	29.0
工业成本费用利润率	%			−1.47
每百元固定资产原价实现的利税	元	12.69	9.03	8.03
每百元销售收入实现的利润	元	0.89	4.51	−1.40
产值利税率	%	11.09	12.02	11.57
资金利税率	%	10.30	5.65	6.81
流动资金周转天数	天	217	236	280
全员劳动生产率	元/年人		34158	39048
集体所有制工业企业				
工业产品销售率	%	89.70	92.06	93.99
工业增加值率	%	28.09	30.1	29.1
工业成本费用利润率	%			0.96
每百元固定资产原价实现的利税	元		13.38	13.35
每百元销售收入实现的利润	元	1.29	0.88	0.93
产值利税率	%		4.58	4.71
资金利税率	%	10.79	8.36	4.58
流动资金周转天数	天	206	154	170
全员劳动生产率	元/年人		31922	39158

注：该表全员劳动生产率按不变价工业总产值计算。

11—19 国有独立核算工业企业各种分组的主要经济效益指标(1997年)

Main Economic Beneficial Indicators of State—Owned Industrial Independent Accounting Enterprises by Various Characteristies

指　　标	工业增加值率(%)	每百元固定资产实现的利税(元)	每百元销售收入现的利税(元)	流动资金周转天数(天)	全部资金利税率(%)	产值利税率(%)
总　计	29.04	8.03	−1.40	280	6.81	11.57
中央企业	33.45	16.21	2.06	229	14.68	22.96
地方企业	25.23	1.31	−4.60	327	1.05	1.91
#省属企业	23.60	2.94	−1.90	296	2.53	4.28
地属企业	24.06		−7.08	387		−0.01
县(旗)属企业	28.97	1.30	−4.91	288	1.04	1.72
在总计中:轻工业	37.49	28.48	0.14	245	20.36	25.33
重工业	24.86	2.71	−2.14	296	2.42	4.66
在总计中:大型企业	28.90	14.22	2.05	245	12.35	17.75
中型企业	25.27	0.87	−8.81	376	0.68	1.43
小型企业	33.36	−0.45	−8.05	323	−0.39	−0.87
煤炭采选业	32.88	4.40	0.94	370	3.49	8.41
黑色金属矿采选业	16.90	0.42	−4.32	491	0.31	0.67
有色金属矿采选业	29.79	0.06	−5.36	288	0.06	0.11
非金属矿采选业	32.58	3.09	−2.89	341	2.85	6.54
食品加工业	27.20	−1.38	−2.94	209	−0.80	−0.74
饮料制造业	39.45	33.22	13.60	417	18.60	32.30
烟草加工业	51.81	117.50	4.74	179	69.13	57.67
纺织业	24.91	−1.56	−7.65	342	−1.17	−1.92
服装及其他纤维制品制造业	25.31	−0.58	−2.88	227	−0.44	−0.60
造纸及纸制品业	24.26	3.79	−2.37	301	3.11	5.13
印刷业、记录媒介的复制	32.73	2.49	−4.32	314	2.07	3.12
化学原料及化学制品制造业	21.08	0.43	−3.19	229	0.38	0.53
医药制造业	22.82	3.52	−1.55	352	2.55	3.92
塑料制品业	29.38	−9.01	−21.09	355	−6.82	−12.15
黑色金属冶炼及压延加工业	20.59	2.60	−1.03	248	2.41	3.76
有色金属冶炼及压延加工业	19.86	4.71	−1.08	231	3.62	4.20
普通机械制造业	25.12	−3.52	−11.84	549	−2.19	−5.85
交通运输设备制造业	22.34	9.00	0.28	302	5.62	8.20
电气机械及器材制造业	20.05	0.56	−3.77	420	0.36	0.69
电子及通信设备制造业	16.28	0.42	−4.55	599	0.28	0.33
电力、蒸汽、热水的生产和供应业	51.96	5.22	5.18	320	5.69	23.60
煤气生产和供应业	−2.92	−4.37	−24.77	318	−3.99	−20.60
自来水的生产和供应业	52.60	0.50	−5.27	256	0.57	1.74

11—20 国有独立核算工业企业各种分组的全员劳动生产率

Overall Labor Productivity of State-Owned Industrial Independent Accounting Enterprises by Various Characteristics

单位:元/人.年

项　　目	1993年	1995年	1996年	1997年
总　　计	31043	33067	34157.87	39048
一、按隶属关系分:				
中央企业	46665	51806	57660.11	63800
地方企业	26416	27264	27115.20	30652
#省　　属	34907	32900	33598.36	40381
地(市)属	28097	29160	26444.63	29425
县(市)属	20588	21613	24460.43	25492
二、按轻重工业分:				
轻工业	36882	40476	37076.88	46366
重工业	28338	29757	32814.07	36313
三、按企业规模分:				
大型企业	43375	46054	46446.29	56812
中型企业	31756	29832	27596.70	29092
小型企业	21044	21831	23060.29	21771
四、按工业行业分:				
煤炭采选业	5133	5487	6176.01	6068
黑色金属矿采选业	26008	18141	15564.08	22790
有色金属矿采选业	13015	15116	15150.05	16298
非金属矿采选业	16471	17766	22131.57	21116
食品加工业	54058	58421	48967.20	63061
饮料制造业	28722	29320	32432.50	39882
烟草加工业	214696	241443	254596.42	249928
纺织业	19845	19088	14235.40	21596
服装及其他纤维制品制造业	23752	13296	18692.80	16361
造纸及纸制品业	32674	35211	34106.77	32493
印刷业、记录媒介的复制	28700	23464	23357.51	24705
化学原料及化学制品制造业	35056	40200	43947.53	43135
医药制造业	50384	52591	59049.72	71710
塑料制品业	26920	22017	31023.81	24708
黑色金属冶炼及压延加工业	43456	32306	38998.10	45368
有色金属冶炼及压延加工业	56957	56885	61144.04	67495
普通机械制造业	23285	24923	22938.81	23056
交通运输设备制造业	38532	42513	47895.29	61872
电气机械及器材制造业	35192	35650	45100.34	40845
电子及通信设备制造业	30007	36928	47586.08	103352
电力蒸气热水生产和供应业	34579	38128	40408.63	39721
煤气生产和供应业	11349	14610	14560.45	15388
自来水生产和供应业	28733	24215	24024.97	21134

注:本表按不变价产值计算。

11—21 大中型工业企业主要指标(1997年)

Main Indicators of Large and Medium—Sized Industrial Enterprises

指　　标	企业单位数(个)	工业总产值(现价亿元)	工业增加值(生产法亿元)	全部职工年平均人数(万人)	固定资产原价合计(亿元)	全部资金(亿元)	利税总额(亿元)
总　　计	723	796.22	260.86	121.49	1050.37	1245.75	107.87
在总计中:轻工业	254	268.55	119.66	31.78	224.04	319.85	78.59
重工业	469	527.67	141.21	89.71	826.32	925.90	29.58
在总计中:大型企业	209	616.50	208.70	75.81	774.99	888.03	105.73
中型企业	514	179.72	52.16	45.68	275.38	357.72	2.14
煤炭采选业	14	17.87	6.90	10.36	33.19	44.20	1.95
黑色金属矿采选业	5	4.02	0.79	1.39	6.62	8.86	0.03
有色金属矿采选业	20	7.31	2.21	3.62	15.41	16.11	10.09
非金属矿采选业	11	4.31	1.59	1.28	8.59	9.22	0.36
木材及竹材采运业	1	0.40	0.14	0.19	0.24	0.76	—0.02
食品加工业	25	26.14	6.34	1.49	10.65	18.82	1.34
食品制造业	11	3.47	1.07	0.88	3.65	5.12	—0.15
饮料制造业	13	13.25	7.04	1.27	10.32	20.02	5.42
烟草加工业	17	119.83	73.10	2.62	58.77	100.33	69.40
纺织业	45	28.78	8.42	10.69	35.32	46.98	—0.84
服装及其他纤维制品制造业	3	1.19	0.32	0.23	1.04	1.29	—0.02
皮革、毛皮、羽绒及其制品业	6	0.68	0.13	0.27	2.09	3.15	—0.16
木材加工及竹藤棕草制品业	8	2.20	0.55	0.66	7.46	9.28	—0.03
造纸及纸制品业	25	15.32	4.57	2.57	19.81	23.82	1.0
印刷业、记录媒介的复制	14	3.52	1.41	0.79	4.64	4.90	0.28
石油加工及炼焦业	3	82.97	14.55	3.90	101.88	88.35	2.45
化学原料及化学制品制造业	86	69.85	16.53	10.29	83.40	92.61	2.13
医药制造业	19	11.80	3.74	1.66	12.19	17.07	1.10
化学纤维制造业	4	6.50	0.97	0.94	12.36	10.75	0.06
橡胶制品业	10	8.23	1.94	1.53	6.02	9.07	0.24
塑料制品业	10	2.23	0.49	0.50	4.58	5.42	—0.38
非金属矿物制品业	26	15.51	5.17	3.63	30.00	33.34	0.61
黑色金属冶炼及压延加工业	20	68.08	16.82	8.68	98.58	105.99	2.84
有色金属冶炼及压延加工业	18	47.82	10.95	4.67	40.66	53.42	2.25
金属制品业	7	1.76	0.39	0.66	2.29	3.14	—0.08
普通机械制造业	20	7.68	2.07	2.89	13.55	22.07	—0.67
专用设备制造业	44	16.52	5.03	6.63	31.53	44.36	—1.06
交通运输设备制造业	44	65.60	17.84	9.29	59.25	95.10	5.97
电气机械及器材制造业	37	26.48	6.71	4.92	29.79	49.94	0.20
电子及通信设备制造业	20	19.97	3.20	2.08	14.65	21.68	—0.01
仪器仪表及文化办公用机械制造业	6	2.34	0.70	0.88	3.39	4.87	—0.06
其他制造业	1	0.07	0.02	0.01	0.15	0.18	—0.01
电力蒸气热水生产和供应业	30	46.03	24.72	3.65	196.78	162.66	1.52
自来水生产和供应业	10	5.04	3.16	0.72	17.35	15.40	0.01

11—22 大中型工业企业主要指标在工业中的地位(1997年)

The Position of Main Indicators of Large and Midium－Sized Industrial Enterprises Among All Industrial Enterprises

单位:%

指标	企业单位数	工业总产值	工业增加值	全部职工年平均人数	固定资产原价合计	全部资金	利税总额
总计	3.15	45.74	45.67	40.50	63.37	59.33	71.80
在总计中:轻工业	2.58	40.30	48.12	31.82	56.43	52.98	80.25
重工业	3.59	49.12	43.77	44.83	65.56	61.90	55.98
煤炭采选业	1.49	35.11	37.16	41.69	60.31	60.47	45.96
黑色金属矿采选业	3.50	41.57	30.95	48.34	87.16	78.47	5.04
有色金属矿采选业	4.60	20.72	21.22	46.46	71.44	56.11	
非金属矿采选业	1.50	17.31	18.71	22.87	57.02	44.71	20.36
木材及竹材采运业	0.84	15.24	13.12	23.47	17.88	29.85	
食品加工业	1.86	23.42	18.33	20.83	29.44	27.18	56.13
食品制造业	2.18	17.84	16.16	21.62	21.76	22.33	
饮料制造业	1.96	45.82	58.04	29.15	51.10	55.18	92.77
烟草加工业	68.00	97.99	98.64	93.27	97.93	97.37	98.54
纺织业	8.12	44.63	42.24	56.44	64.30	60.08	160.58
服装及其他纤维制品制造业	0.69	9.45	8.11	6.85	19.39	13.49	
皮革、毛皮、羽绒及其制品业	1.46	3.09	2.01	7.91	23.19	18.29	
木材加工及竹藤棕草制品业	0.76	8.27	6.19	14.37	45.31	39.01	
造纸及纸制品业	3.17	33.67	31.41	29.21	56.18	50.22	39.90
印刷业、记录媒介的复制	1.91	14.98	16.38	17.74	28.44	22.98	12.62
石油加工及炼焦业	9.68	98.29	97.01	93.21	99.13	98.73	100.07
化学原料及化学制品制造业	6.77	48.24	39.05	48.07	68.11	60.71	47.77
医药制造业	11.38	57.89	59.65	54.68	66.04	62.64	84.92
化学纤维制造业	10.81	67.86	63.14	72.82	74.67	68.10	38.43
橡胶制品业	7.52	61.13	54.83	54.50	70.81	67.38	52.82
塑料制品业	1.68	10.92	7.12	11.64	35.00	28.84	
非金属矿物制品业	1.84	19.83	20.30	20.06	36.92	37.24	238.56
黑色金属冶炼及压延加工业	7.91	77.64	77.00	77.38	91.55	87.35	93.00
有色金属冶炼及压延加工业	5.19	58.43	54.90	61.18	70.32	67.32	64.33
金属制品业	0.80	4.47	3.53	10.09	13.30	10.27	
普通机械制造业	20.00	65.89	68.06	72.55	82.85	82.88	96.36
专用设备制造业	6.78	41.77	39.19	52.74	70.45	65.78	
交通运输设备制造业	5.58	65.96	68.60	62.67	79.24	77.80	80.34
电气机械及器材制造业	5.58	38.60	34.95	44.68	66.00	62.46	5.81
电子及通信设备制造业	10.81	73.86	55.82	49.84	45.74	47.03	
仪器仪表及文化办公用机械制造业	5.31	44.86	71.43	45.90	50.28	46.44	38.00
其他制造业	0.10	0.21	0.16	0.16	2.14	1.31	
电力蒸气热水生产和供应业	2.97	53.14	50.04	39.64	56.08	51.74	84.62
自来水生产和供应业	3.21	50.91	62.07	34.36	60.10	60.02	19.21

十二、建筑业

CONSTRUCTION

12—1 建筑企业概况

General Survey of Construction Enterprises

	1996年	1997年		1996年	1997年
一、总产值(亿元)	2783849	2965005	外商投资	·	167
#国有	1241762	1297126	港澳台投资	215	403
集体	1512196	1641797	其他	2668	365
私营	6380	7792	三、资本金合计(万元)	651672	852714
联营	304	3710	国有	230177	288337
股份制	13855	8815	集体	411711	553030
外商投资		239	私营	2267	4628
港澳台投资	480	1100	联营	550	1319
其他	8871	4426	股份制	3932	2183
#土木工程	2588195	2720824	外商投资		480
房屋建筑	2111522	2167863	港澳台投资	100	1150
矿山建筑	6579	7500	其他	2935	1587
铁路隧道公路桥梁	282220	303949	四、资产合计(万元)	2438586	2884855
线路管道设备安装	180871	220206	#流动资产	1660376	1921599
设备安装	131157	151564	#固定资产	636269	780695
建筑物装修、装饰	14783	23975	#专项工程	48930	50353
二、增加值(万元)	804491	870288	#无形及递延资产	30374	37365
#本年内提取的固定资产折旧	43003	59098	#国有	1293366	1516437
应付工资	405012	425762	集体	1129798	1343597
应付福利费	44454	49781	私营	2624	8345
管理费中的劳动待业保险费	19663	26703	联营	577	1609
工程结算税金及附加	77193	84575	股份制	8662	7540
工程结算利润	211819	218303	外商投资		759
管理费用中的税金	6962	8093	港澳台投资	303	3507
转作奖金的利润	3614	2029	其他	3257	3057
#国有	393729	395196	五、负债合计(万元)	1677962	2138120
集体	400891	468559	#流动负债	1566034	1945431
私营	1790	2255	长期负债	111928	192689
联营	189	934	六、所有者权益(万元)	760624	746734
股份制	5009	2407	#股本	11871	930

12—1 续表

	1996年	1997年		1996年	1997年
#国有	325741	351273	八、利税总额合计(万元)	119595	122323
集体	424446	386927	#利润总额	35440	29655
私营	2150	3206	工程结算税金及附加	77193	84575
联营	492	396	管理费用中的税金	6962	8093
股份制	5392	2356	产值利税率(%)	4.3	4.1
外商投资		429	资产利税率(%)	4.9	4.6
港澳台投资	269	926	#国有	39559	32969
其他	2133	1218	集体	77538	88236
负债合计	1677962	2138120	私营	504	213
#国有	967624	1165164	联营	15	424
集体	705352	956669	股份制	1081	493
私营	474	5139	外商投资		—25
联营	85	1212	港澳台投资	118	—39
股份制	3270	5184	其他	777	52
外商投资		330	九、利润总额合计(万元)	35440	29655
港澳台投资	33	2581	#国有	5981	—37
其他	1123	1839	集体	28592	29384
七、企业总收入(万元)	2480482	2616748	私营	100	59
#工程结算收入	2390946	2502880	联营	10	232
#工程结算成本	2101935	2200000	股份制	562	176
工程结算利润	211819	218303	外商投资		—46
其他业务收入	89535	113868	港澳台投资	100	—98
#其他业务利润	14586	18062	其他	94	—15
#国有	1214618	1193052	十、工程结算利润总计(万元)	211819	218303
集体	1237609	1405154	#国有	118513	108923
私营	6522	4802	集体	90704	107739
联营	125	3322	私营	526	525
股份制	13103	6594	联营	14	391
外商投资		524	股份制	1490	426
港澳台投资	480	1392	外商投资		70
其他	8024	1906	港澳台投资	119	105
			其他	453	119

12—2 建筑施工企业个数和平均人数

Number of Construction Enterprises and Its Average Annual Staff and Workers

年份	总计	国有	集体经济	其他经济	建筑业活动单位
一、施工企业个数(个)					
1995	1283	216	1023	3	41
1996	1811	278	1347	31	155
1997	1748	296	1425	27	…
二、施工企业人数(万人)					
1995	61.33	22.29	38.52	0.16	0.36
1996	78.88	24.32	50.72	0.90	2.94
1997	81.22	25.08	55.37	0.77	…

注:建筑施工企业均指资质等级四级及以上的建筑企业,下同。

12—3 国有建筑企业职工构成

Category of Staff and workers of State－Owned Consteuction Enterprises

类别	人数(万人)		构成(%)	
	1996年	1997年	1996年	1997年
总计	24.32	25.08	100.0	100.0
工人和学徒	16.19	16.20	66.6	64.6
工程技术人员	2.07	2.38	8.5	9.5
管理人员	2.70	2.88	11.1	11.5
服务人员	1.52	1.45	6.3	5.8
其他人员	1.84	2.17	7.5	8.6

注:本表不包括非独立核算的自营施工企业。

12—4 建筑施工企业固定资产、流动资产及利润(1997年)

Fixed Assets, Circulating Funds and Profits of Construction Enterprises

指标	单位	总计	国有	集体经济	其他经济
固定资产原值(年底数)	万元	1035794	538349	488068	9377
固定资产净值(年底数)	万元	753840	377558	368507	7775
流动资产年末合计	万元	1921599	1047711	859033	14855
利润总额	万元	29655	－37	29384	308
利税总额	万元	122323	32969	88235	1119
资金利润率	元/百元	1.1		2.4	1.4
产值利润率	%	1.0		1.8	1.2
产值利税率	%	4.1	1.1	5.4	4.3

注:本表不包括建筑业活动单位。

12—5 建筑施工企业工程质量(1997年)

Quality of Construction Works of Contruction Enterprises

指　标	单位	总计	国有	集体	其他经济
竣工产值	万元	1983323	791463	1167428	24432
验收鉴定的单位工程	个	12524	3730	8643	151
#优良品	个	3772	1898	1834	40
验收鉴定的单位工程优良品率	%	30.1	50.9	21.2	26.5
验收鉴定的房屋建筑竣工面积	万平方米	2279.9	466.0	1783.4	30.5
#优良品	万平方米	772.7	222.0	538.9	11.8
验收鉴定的房屋建筑竣工面积优良品率	%	33.9	47.6	30.2	38.7

12—6 建筑施工企业技术装备情况(1997年)

Technical Equipments of Local Construction Enterprises

指　标	单位	总计	国有	集体	其他经济
年底自有机械设备	台	259409	70605	186382	2422
年底自有机械设备净值	万元	321180	182564	134488	4128
技术装备率(全部职工)	元/人	3954	7279	2429	5361
动力装备率(全部职工)	千瓦/人	4.1	6.0	3.3	3.3

12—7 建筑施工企业劳动生产率(1997年)

Overal Labor Productivity of Construction Enterprises

单位:元/人

指　标	总计	国有	集体	其他经济
按施工产值计算的劳动生产率	36506	51720	29651	33873
按增加值计算的劳动生产率	10715	15757	8462	8484
人均竣工面积(平方米/人)	28.1	18.6	32.2	39.6

12—8 国有建筑企业主要经济指标

Main Economic Indicators of State－Owned Construction Enterprises

指　标	单　位	1995 年	1996 年	1997 年
国有建筑施工企业				
施工产值	亿元	106.70	124.18	129.71
全员劳动生产率	元/人	47871	51059	51720
计算劳动生产率的平均人数	万人	22.29	24.32	25.08
房屋建筑施工面积	万平方米	1094.53	1285.2	1236.7
房屋建筑竣工面积	万平方米	361.18	467.0	466.0
#住　宅	万平方米	156.74	199.4	209.81
地方国有建筑施工企业				
施工产值	亿元	47.44	58.08	63.57
全员劳动生产率	元/人	36328	39114	40620
计算劳动生产率的平均人数	万人	13.06	14.85	15.65
房屋建筑施工面积	万平方米	760.60	924.7	930.6
房屋建筑竣工面积	万平方米	278.22	363.7	372.8
#住　宅	万平方米	121.85	167.5	181.32

12—9 建筑业总产值和增加值(1997 年)

Gross Output Value and Added Value of Construction Enterprises

单位:万元

指　标	总　计	国　有	集　体	其他经济
一、建筑业总产值(施工产值)	2965005	1297126	1641797	26082
建筑安装	2850577	1269899	1555325	25353
房屋构筑物修理	83697	5752	77216	729
非标准设备制造	30731	21475	9256	
二、增加值	870288	395196	468559	6533
本年提取折旧	59098	33417	25238	443
应付工资	425762	171943	250932	2887
应付福利费	49781	24472	24602	707
管理费用中劳动待业保险费	26703	23504	3141	58
工程结算税金及附加	84575	30709	53218	648
管理费用中:税金	8093	2297	5633	163
扣除转作奖金部分后的工程结算利润	216274	108851	105792	1631

12—10 建筑企业分行业

Production Indicators of Construction

	单位	一、土木工程建筑业	1.房屋建筑业	2.矿山建筑业	3.铁路公路隧道桥梁建筑业
企业个数	个	1636	1530	3	39
建筑业总产值	万元	2720823.9	2167862.9	7500.1	303949.1
1.建筑工程	万元	2503438.7	1988552.4	7105.0	299229.8
2.安装工程	万元	110633.7	94037.7	251.3	4709.3
3.房屋构筑物修理	万元	78339.5	75327.0	15.8	6.0
4.非标准设备制造	万元	28412.0	9945.8	128.0	4.0
竣工产值	万元	1807480.5	1519657.5	1610.3	218264.1
单位工程施工个数	个	18702	16245	46	1654
#本年新开工个数	个	10881	9452	13	916
#投标承包个数	个	7236	6150	33	850
#本年新开工	个	4623	4001	16	503
单位工程竣工个数	个	10818	9590	15	740
#优良工程个数	个	3024	2367	5	579
房屋建筑施工面积	万平方米	4666.99	4606.71	3.50	25.91
#本年新开工面积	万平方米	2149.78	2122.83	1.41	10.18
#投标承包的面积	万平方米	2005.50	1985.33	2.41	6.81
#本年新开工	万平方米	1072.96	1064.84	1.41	2.07
房屋建筑竣工面积	万平方米	2244.48	2216.59	2.00	8.03
#优良工程面积	万平方米	763.82	754.84		6.43
自有机械设备年末总台数	台	242259	219698	797	9450
自有机械设备年末总功率	万千瓦	316.93	229.46	2.03	39.57
#施工机械功率	万千瓦	265.03	192.00	1.78	31.65
自有机械设备净值	万元	298225.5	188008.1	1722.1	58074.2
计算建筑业劳动生产率的平均人数	万人	76.59	68.72	0.40	4.00

生　产　指　标(1997年)

Enterprises by Sector

4.堤坝电站码头建筑业	5.其他土木工程建筑业	二、线路管道设备安装业	1.线路管道安装业	2.设备安装业	三、建筑物装修装饰业
22	42	81	43	38	31
179264.9	62246.9	220205.5	68641.6	151563.9	23975.2
154677.3	53874.2	66413.1	33366.6	33046.5	18753.5
7458.4	4177.0	149653.0	33452.4	116200.6	1685.3
813.0	2177.7	1820.8	1254.3	566.5	3536.4
16316.2	2018.0	2318.6	568.3	1750.3	
36406.4	31542.2	156833.9	52412.9	104421.0	19008.2
268	489	2199	915	1284	274
137	363	1444	673	771	180
127	76	495	238	257	40
56	47	403	221	182	20
134	339	1478	667	811	228
23	50	723	205	518	25
14.09	16.78	27.84	6.97	20.87	24.75
5.51	9.86	12.66	4.99	7.68	12.18
4.22	6.73	14.20	3.18	11.02	5.13
2.73	1.91	4.13	2.12	2.01	3.82
7.89	9.98	15.76	2.66	13.10	19.65
1.38	1.17	3.77	1.93	1.84	5.06
8403	3911	15509	6902	8607	1641
35.39	10.48	17.20	5.94	11.26	1.36
30.81	8.80	10.95	4.40	6.55	1.17
40696.0	9725.1	21600.3	5882.8	15717.5	1354.0
2.24	1.24	4.10	1.64	2.46	0.53

12—11 国有、集体建筑企业生产指标(1997年)

Basic Indicators of State－Owned Large and Medium－Sized Construction Enterprises

	单位	总计	一、二级企业	# 国有经济	中央企业	地方企业	# 集体经济
企业个数	个	1748	254	296	51	245	1425
建筑业总产值	万元	2965004.6	1758970.8	1297125.5	661420.6	635704.9	1641797.1
1.建筑工程	万元	2588605.3	1512042.2	1095884.6	521158.4	574726.2	1469592.9
2.安装工程	万元	261972.0	191444.3	174014.0	119923.6	54090.4	85732.3
3.房屋构筑物修理	万元	83696.7	30624.4	5751.7	2535.4	3216.3	77216.5
4.非标准设备制造	万元	30730.6	24859.9	21475.2	17803.2	3672.0	9255.4
竣工产值	万元	1983322.6	1076834.6	791463.3	369639.0	421824.3	1167427.9
单位工程施工个数	个	21175	8260	7149	3489	3660	13836
#本年新开工个数	个	12505	4315	3941	1861	2080	8450
#投标承包个数	个	7771	3336	2899	1379	1520	4803
#本年新开工	个	5046	1960	1674	824	850	3328
单位工程竣工个数	个	12524	4165	3730	1681	2049	8643
#优良工程个数	个	3772	2167	1898	1285	613	1834
房屋建筑施工面积	万平方米	4719.57	2135.54	1236.68	306.12	930.56	3444.90
#本年新开工面积	万平方米	2174.63	774.33	435.22	76.16	359.06	1718.53
#投标承包的面积	万平方米	2024.82	1030.92	723.08	184.57	538.51	1281.93
#本年新开工	万平方米	1080.91	438.67	272.92	45.78	227.15	794.13
房屋建筑竣工面积	万平方米	2279.89	811.47	465.95	93.18	372.77	1783.44
#优良工程面积	万平方米	772.65	413.60	221.97	51.59	170.38	538.94
自有机械设备年末总台数	台	259409	109238	70605	25795	44810	186382
自有机械设备年末总功率	万千瓦	335.48	190.14	149.57	74.39	75.18	183.39
#施工机械功率	万千瓦	277.15	152.53	116.25	56.00	60.25	158.82
自有机械设备净值	万元	321179.8	215147.0	182564.2	93815.7	88748.5	134487.9
计算建筑业劳动生产率的平均人数	万人	81.22	38.27	25.08	9.43	15.65	55.37

12—12 城镇集体建筑业固定资产投资(1997年)

Investment in Fixed Assets of Urban Collective－Owned Construction Enterprises

指标名称	单位	合计	一、土木工程建筑业	1.房屋建筑业	2.矿山建筑业	二、线路管道设备安装业	三、建筑物装修装饰业
本年施工项目个数	个	36	36	36			
其中:本年新开工	个	24	24	24			
本年投产项目个数	个	29	29	29			
计划总投资	万元	6092	6092	6092			
实际需要的总投资	万元	6283	6283	6283			
累计完成投资	万元	5704	5704	5704			
累计新增固定资产	万元	4878	4878	4878			
本年底未完工程累计投资	万元	426	426	426			
本年计划投资	万元	3934	3934	3934			
本年完成投资	万元	3992	3992	3992			
一、按构成分:							
1.建筑工程	万元	3828	3828	3828			
2.安装工程	万元	10	10	10			
3.设备、工具器具购置	万元						
4.其他费用	万元	154	154	154			
二、按工程用途分:							
1.农林牧渔业用	万元						
2.工业建筑业用	万元	143	143	143			
3.商业运输邮电业用	万元	476	476	476			
4.住宅	万元	3137	3137	3137			
5.其他	万元	236	236	236			
三、按隶属关系分:							
1.中央项目	万元						
2.地方项目	万元	3992	3992	3992			
省属	万元	180	180	180			
地市属	万元	466	466	466			
县属	万元	3346	3346	3346			
3.其他	万元						
四、按建设性质分:							
1.新建	万元	196	196	196			
2.扩建	万元	1292	1292	1292			
3.改建	万元	195	195	195			
4.单纯建造生活设施	万元	2309	2309	2309			
5.迁建	万元						
6.恢复	万元						
7.单纯购置	万元						
本年新增固定资产	万元	4588	4588	4588			
本年施工房屋面积	平方米	114585	114585	114585			
#:住宅	平方米	96180	96180	96180			
本年竣工房屋面积	平方米	85609	85609	85609			
#:住宅	平方米	71804	71804	71804			
本年竣工房屋价值	万元	4545	4545	4545			
#:住宅	万元	3712	3712	3712			

12—13 国 有 建 筑 业

Investment in Fixed Assets

指标名称	单位	合计	一、土木工程建筑业	1.房屋建筑业	2.矿山建筑业	3.铁路公路隧道桥梁建筑业
本年施工项目个数	个	60	47	30	1	11
其中:本年新开工	个	26	15	8		6
本年投产项目个数	个	39	32	21		8
计划总投资	万元	72908	68272	15522	5046	36783
实际需要总投资	万元	76381	71468	17603	5050	37767
累计完成投资	万元	60918	56472	14060	1596	32127
累计新增固定资产	万元	28384	24517	7822	1420	9573
本年底未完工程累计投资	万元	32523	31944	6238	165	22554
本年计划投资	万元	25417	20892	8868	140	9975
本年完成投资	万元	23710	19447	7860	400	9681
一、按构成分:						
1.建筑工程	万元	19926	17863	7193	400	8839
2.安装工程	万元	97	89	59		
3.设备、工具器具购置	万元	2906	714	578		120
4.其他费用	万元	781	781	30		722
二、按工程用途分:						
1.农林牧渔业用	万元					
2.工业、建筑业用	万元	5159	3019	965	80	1958
3.商业、运输邮电业用	万元	5553	5553	1776		3757
4.住宅	万元	8366	6698	4968	320	407
5. 其他	万元	4632	4177	151		3559
三、按隶属关系分:						
1.中央项目	万元	8850	5230	1192	400	2220
2.地方项目	万元	14809	14166	6617		7461
省属	万元	4357	3729	3527		202
地市属	万元	4157	4157	2765		1304
县属	万元	6295	6280	325		5955
3.其他	万元	51	51	51		
四、按建设性质分:						
1.新建	万元	1371	1371	315		
2.扩建	万元	8909	8894	1938		6634
3.改建	万元	6722	3328	488	400	2400
4.单纯建造生活设施	万元	5547	5547	4812		647
5.迁建	万元					
6.恢复	万元					
7.单纯购置	万元	1161	307	307		
本年新增固定资产	万元	19262	15395	5039	363	9079
本年施工房屋面积	平方米	316816	280273	191364	11245	26045
#住宅	平方米	217638	186959	132645	9860	7172
本年竣工房屋面积	平方米	115907	108953	84669	6560	7172
#住宅	平方米	93470	88621	70435	5460	7172
本年竣工房屋价值	万元	6539	6104	4648	359	407
#住宅	万元	4993	4689	3688	280	407

固 定 资 产 投 资(1997 年)

of State—Owned Construction Enterprises

4. 堤坝电站码头建筑业	5. 其他土木工程建筑业	二、线路管道设备安装业	1. 线路管道安装业	2. 设备安装业	三、建筑物装修装饰业
3	2	13	1	12	
1		11		11	
1	2	7	1	6	
10691	230	4636	593	4043	
10691	357	4913	593	4320	
8332	357	4446	593	3853	
5345	357	3867	593	3274	
2987		579		579	
1869	40	4525	529	3996	
1438	68	4263	529	3734	
1379	52	2063	7	2056	
30		8	8		
	16	2192	514	1678	
29					
	16	2140	514	1626	
	20				
971	32	1668	8	1660	
467		455	7	448	
1378	40	3620	514	3106	
60	28	643	15	628	
		628		628	
60	28				
		15	15		
1056					
322		15	15		
	40	3394		3394	
60	28				
		854	514	340	
557	357	3867	593	3274	
45955	5664	36543	1570	34973	
33028	4254	30679	1279	29400	
4888	5664	6954	1570	5384	
1300	4254	4849	1279	3570	
349	341	435	79	356	
60	254	304	64	240	

12—14 房屋建筑面积(1997年)

Floor Space of Building Construction

单位:万平方米

	房屋建筑面积		国有经济		集体经济	
	施工面积	竣工面积	施工面积	竣工面积	施工面积	竣工面积
1990	1159.10	558.70	572.40	233.50	586.70	325.20
1991	1282.70	653.20	577.20	269.50	705.50	383.70
1992	1554.00	711.30	699.40	279.80	854.60	431.50
1993	1869.50	802.20	867.90	334.60	1001.60	467.60
1994	2081.50	868.30	1011.10	378.40	1068.40	489.30
1995	4507.41	2313.70	1094.50	361.20	3223.05	1835.33
1996	4662.00	2393.05	1285.16	467.04	3333.59	1898.28
1997	4719.57	2279.89	1236.68	465.95	3444.90	1783.44
长　沙	1581.34	590.84	342.04	115.61	1236.91	473.64
株　洲	345.12	183.10	117.99	38.25	223.91	142.45
湘　潭	336.82	164.56	95.21	35.78	239.30	127.51
衡　阳	562.78	273.81	124.83	44.88	437.95	228.93
邵　阳	351.79	168.07	117.75	40.35	234.04	127.73
岳　阳	351.94	194.90	123.97	34.41	225.61	158.33
常　德	247.74	136.73	21.73	11.59	225.45	124.58
张家界	44.27	25.54	15.63	8.05	28.64	17.49
益　阳	153.51	89.83	23.49	10.99	111.95	62.11
郴　州	254.63	163.05	93.57	50.84	155.68	108.91
永　州	153.74	93.15	25.34	13.02	126.56	79.02
娄　底	179.73	111.28	67.66	27.16	112.07	84.12
怀　化	90.67	53.02	46.44	25.73	44.24	27.29
湘西自治州	65.49	32.01	21.03	9.29	42.59	21.33

注:1995年、1996年、1997年为资质等级四级及以上企业数据。

十三、运输、邮电

TRANSPORTATION, POST AND TELECOMMUNICATION SERVICES

13—1 运输线路里程

Length of Transportation Routes

单位:公里

年份	铁路营业里程	#地方铁路	#电气化里程	公路	内河航道	民用航空	国际航线	管道
1995	2293	329	349	59125	10050	17	1	
1996	2293	329	349	59125	10050	20	1	136
1997	2269	344.7	477.3	59761	10050	11		137.5

注:1996 年铁路正线延展里程为 3120 公里,1997 年为 3617.4 公里。

13—2 陆上运输线路质量

Quality of Overland Transportation Routes

单位:公里

	1995 年	1996 年	1997 年
铁路营业里程	2273	2273	2269
#复线里程	642	642	819.55
#自动闭塞里程	627	627	705
#电气化线路里程	349	349	477.3
#内燃机牵引线路里程	1862	1862	1601.3
#无缝线路里程	173	173	632
公路线路里程	59125	59554	59761
有路面里程	58191	58620	58827
#高级次高级路面	13137	14219	15242
无路面里程	934	934	934
等级公路	30383	31159	31674
#高速		45	45
一级	109	163	207
二级	122	161	155
等外路	28742	28395	28087

13—3 铁路机车拥有量

Number of Railway Locomotives

	单位	1995 年	1996 年	1997 年
一、中央铁路				
蒸汽机车	台	152	90	120
内燃机车	台	413	404	483
客车	辆	1329	1246	1697
电力机车	辆	34		61
二、地方铁路(窄轨)				
蒸汽机车	台	35	11	19
内燃机车	台	10	10	13
客车	辆	37	26	30
货车	辆	558	439	421

13—4 民用车辆、船舶拥有量

Number of Civil Motor Vehicles and Civilian Vessels

	单位	全省总计		一、交通部门	
		1996年	1997年	1996年	1997年
一、公路					
民用汽车	辆	374846	381216	10636	11168
#载货汽车	辆	217847	210202	2938	2538
载重量	吨位	878978	779062	16313	15451
载客汽车	辆	145473	163899	7698	8630
载客量	客位	1827459	2021420	276348	284884
特种车	辆	6016	4549		
轮胎式拖拉机	辆	206945	207053	231	208
摩托车	辆	408677	524068		
其他机动车	辆	40576	52350	415	353
载货挂车	辆	4198	3210	626	
二、水运					
货船	艘	8061	7610	2563	2254
载重量	吨位	382315	380745	213970	215424
客货船	艘	1	6		
载重量	吨位	13	71		
载客量	客位	30	110		
客船	艘	953	1116	185	187
载客量	客位	43356	47967	20314	19800
拖船	艘	181	183	132	129
功率	千瓦	25781	25370	21131	20746
驳船	艘	1098	969	878	744
载重量	吨位	151447	145801	145068	139725
载客量	客位				
其他非机动船	艘				
载重量	吨位				

13—4 续表

	单位	二、非交通部门		三、城乡个体	
		1996年	1997年	1996年	1997年
一、公路					
民用汽车	辆	197971	204555	166261	165493
#载货汽车	辆	149727	106657	65182	101007
载重量	吨位	558289	429059	304376	334552
载客汽车	辆	48244	91291	89531	63978
载客量	客位	632981	984477	918130	752059
特种车	辆	5982	4496	34	53
轮胎式拖拉机	辆	9944	8158	196770	198687
摩托车	辆	115941	51988	292736	472080
其他机动车	辆	40161	3584		48413
载货挂车	辆	3291	2623	281	587
二、水运					
货船	艘	5498	697		4659
载重量	吨位	168345	28165		137156
客货船	艘	1	1		5
载重量	吨位	13	13		58
载客量	客位	30	15		95
客船	艘	768	60		869
载客量	客位	23042	1220		26947
拖船	艘	49	39		15
功率	千瓦	4650	3727		897
驳船	艘	220	91		134
载重量	吨位	63779	4648		1428
载客量	客位				
其他非机动船	艘				
载重量	吨位				

13—5 旅客运量和旅客周转量

Passenger Traffic and Turnover Volume of Passenger Traffic

年份	合计	铁路			公路	水运	民用航空
			国家	地方			
客运量(万人)							
1980	32776	3434	3271	163	27590	1750	2
1981	33546	3723	3520	203	27871	1950	2
1982	37286	3898	3677	221	31380	2006	2
1983	40380	4117	3895	222	33955	2306	2
1984	43333	4368	4154	214	36497	2466	2
1985	48666	4686	4461	225	41520	2458	2
1986	50903	4368	4159	209	44464	2066	5
1987	53600	4586	4397	189	47071	1935	8
1988	56236	4937	4739	198	49182	2109	8
1989	54084	4357	4205	152	47865	1855	7
1990	54161	3474	3389	85	49112	1568	7
1991	54710	3514	3437	77	49566	1621	9
1992	52641	3638	3564	74	47366	1615	22
1993	55896	4022	3949	73	50252	1562	60
1994	64757	4176	4105	71	59028	1481	72
1995	71566	4135	4083	52	65971	1375	85
1996	76377	3892	3846	46	71087	1298	100
1997	79250	4488	4444	44	73233	1357	172
周转量(亿人公里)							
1980	133.68	65.47	65.12	0.35	62.90	5.25	0.06
1981	149.19	73.21	72.80	0.41	70.20	5.71	0.07
1982	159.66	78.05	77.61	0.44	75.62	5.92	0.07
1983	179.81	90.95	90.51	0.44	82.10	6.69	0.07
1984	204.68	104.85	104.42	0.43	93.08	6.68	0.07
1985	254.53	132.78	132.32	0.46	114.95	6.72	0.08
1986	275.38	140.09	139.65	0.44	128.68	6.38	0.23
1987	310.57	161.86	161.45	0.41	142.66	5.74	0.31
1988	354.23	191.21	190.79	0.42	156.57	6.11	0.34
1989	350.34	181.09	180.78	0.31	163.48	5.38	0.39
1990	339.86	162.32	162.17	0.15	172.73	4.25	0.56
1991	378.20	189.29	189.16	0.13	184.27	3.94	0.70
1992	435.19	228.39	228.24	0.15	200.09	4.87	1.84
1993	490.26	270.82	270.68	0.14	209.34	4.58	5.52
1994	539.02	291.44	291.29	0.15	237.00	3.90	6.68
1995	555.13	301.60	301.49	0.11	242.46	3.66	7.41
1996	538.29	262.99	262.89	0.10	263.48	3.45	8.37
1997	592.16	305.06	304.97	0.09	274.68	3.69	8.73

13—6 货物运量和货物周转量

Freight Traffic and Turnover Volume of Freight Traffic

年份	合计	铁路	国家	地方	公路	水运	民用航空
货运量(万吨)							
1980	23650	3778	3594	184	16576	3261	
1981	24633	3573	3408	165	18067	2955	
1982	26951	3783	3616	167	20054	3076	
1983	29100	3876	3710	166	22095	3089	
1984	31800	3977	3826	151	24655	3128	
1985	32902	4218	4092	126	35699	2945	
1986	34902	4346	4213	133	27140	3372	
1987	35747	4485	4354	131	27525	3693	
1988	39020	4522	4401	121	30922	3531	
1989	37842	4731	4567	164	29453	3671	
1990	37708	4771	4597	174	29679	3217	
1991	41219	4777	4614	163	33224	3177	
1992	42548	4906	4787	119	33788	3821	
1993	46040	4982	4886	96	37582	3441	1
1994	48413	4929	4841	88	39912	3536	1
1995	49853	5017	4904	113	41272	3531	1
1996	50420	4893	4830	63	42191	3301	1
1997	48946	4535	4495	40	41340	3034	2
周转量(亿吨公里)							
1980	331.43	272.42	271.02	1.40	33.95	24.98	
1981	340.22	274.11	272.87	1.24	39.57	26.54	
1982	359.71	286.44	285.24	1.20	43.83	29.35	
1983	388.55	302.28	301.10	1.18	50.56	35.61	
1984	435.78	335.83	334.83	1.00	59.70	40.15	
1985	512.03	392.52	391.73	0.79	75.55	43.86	
1986	582.44	438.71	437.83	0.88	91.91	51.72	
1987	637.60	481.87	480.96	0.91	103.91	51.66	
1988	690.60	504.58	503.74	0.84	134.16	51.76	
1989	730.40	544.44	543.57	0.87	129.58	56.29	
1990	774.81	590.33	589.44	0.89	137.02	47.37	
1991	830.64	621.98	621.18	0.80	164.42	44.15	
1992	901.85	656.29	655.50	0.79	191.53	53.95	
1993	951.77	683.10	682.49	0.61	209.85	58.66	0.07
1994	1003.38	720.46	719.87	0.59	221.78	60.98	0.07
1995	1043.59	751.84	751.24	0.60	235.52	56.06	0.09
1996	1029.25	728.91	728.46	0.45	240.13	60.10	0.11
1997	998.64	690.80	690.47	0.33	244.86	62.78	0.12

13—7 公路、水上客货运输量部门构成情况

Composition of Passenher and Freight Traffic by Sectors

	1996年				1997年			
	合计	交通系统	非交通系统	#私人	合计	交通系统	非交通系统	#私人
一、公路运输								
客运量(万人)	76377	25808	50569	45096	73233	20906	52327	47643
旅客周转量(亿人公里)	583	437	146.11	120.67	274.68	129.75	144.93	122.62
货运量(万吨)	50419	7725	42694	22561	41340	1065	40275	20273
货物周转量(亿吨公里)	1029	782	246.74	124.97	244.86	4.30	240.56	116.57
二、水上运输								
客运量(万人)	1298	517	704	701	1357	487	870	810
旅客周转量(万人公里)	34455	18973	14088	14020	36904	18184	18720	17820
货运量(万吨)	3301	1550	1527	1509	3034	1232	1802	1550
货物周转量(万吨公里)	600971	480823	114972	114684	627843	512384	115459	108500

13—8 交通运输邮电通讯业单位数和职工人数

Number and Staff and Workers of Transportation and Postal and Telecommunications

	1996年		1997年	
	单位数(个)	职工人数(人)	单位数(个)	职工人数(人)
铁路运输业	118	94000	110	108791
公路运输业	227	97000	247	66212
水上运输业	14	39000	14	7680
航空运输业	5	1000	4	1130
交通运输辅业	402	59000	400	44864
其他运输业	1	67	1	73
邮电通讯业	167	57610	150	59510

13—9 内河航运主要港口概况(1997年)

Major Indicators of principal ports in Navigable Inland Waterways

港口名称	主管单位	码头总延长(米)	泊位个数(个)	货物吞吐量(万吨)	旅客吞吐量(万人)
株洲港	株洲市交通局	2019	65	131.4	4
衡阳港	衡阳市交通局	411	45	151.4	6.4
岳阳港	岳阳市交通局	4248	71	213.2	68.9
城陵矶港	岳阳市交通局	712	11	581.4	50.9

注:本表只含独立核算内河港口企业。

13—10 独立核算交通运输企业财务状况(1997年)

Finaneinl Situation of Transportation Enterprises With Independnet Accouning Systems

单位:万元

	合计	公路运输	水路运输
企业个数(个)	343	262	77
#亏损企业(个)	191	131	56
资本金合计	148546	93994	50174
流动资产合计	128586	82258	42477
#存货	16830	11395	5030
固定资产合计	284689	205908	65269
固定资产原价	404313	267003	119029
#生产经营用	277719	178272	86541
累计折旧	152178	88859	57899
#本年折旧	24283	18684	5125
资产合计	430051	299068	113380
流动资产合计	197708	135855	56325
长期负债合计	62768	37734	22184
所有者权益合计	166232	123688	33319
#股本	2156	2156	
营运业务收入	176660	134128	38006
营运业务成本	131008	93865	33174
营运费用	885	765	120
营运税金及附加	5654	4301	1207
营运业务利润	36947	33326	3211
管理费用	57517	42682	12979
#税金	2068	1778	229
劳动待业保险金	13570	7850	4977
利润总额	-14723	-5613	-8241
#应交所得税	335	315	20
转作奖金利润	22	22	
本年应付工资	50981	35956	13100
本年应付福利费总额	7713	5286	2142

13—11 运输企业主要技术经济指标和财务指标

Main Economic and Technical Indicators and Financial Indicators of Transportation Enterprises

指　　标	单　位	1997年	指　　标	单　位	1997年
一、主要技术经济指标			2.地方铁路		
			营业收入	万元	3217
1.地方铁路			营业成本	万元	2053
旅客列车始发正点率	%	71	运输万换算吨公里综合成本	元	487.7
货运机车日产量	万吨公里	3.73	利润总额	万元	-1033.52
2.公　　路			税　　金	万元	119.56
载货汽车完好率	%	86.6			
载货汽车车吨年产量	吨公里	18960	3.公　　路		
载货汽车单车年产量	吨公里	114268	营业收入	万元	120909
载货汽车百吨公里耗汽油	升	7.2	营业成本	万元	85040
载货汽车百吨公里耗柴油	升	4.5	汽车千换算吨公里成本	元	
3.水　　运			利润总额	万元	-4393
内河拖轮营运率	%	24	税　　金	万元	3731
内河拖轮每千瓦年产量	吨公里	68025			
			4.水　　运		
二、主要财务指标			营业收入	万元	38265
			营业成本	万元	34070
1.中央铁路			轮驳船千换算吨公里成本	元	
运输收入	万元	425486	利润总额	万元	-9675
运输支出	万元	729829	税　　金	万元	1194
利　　润	万元	-36285			
税　　金	万元	13786			

13—12 邮　电　通　信　网

Postal and Telecommunication Services Network

年　份	邮电局、所（处）	邮路及农村投递线路总长度（万公里）	长话电路（路）	电报电路（路）	本地网为县市中继电　路
1990	2612	28.44	3114	472	
1995	3210	29.45	24621	428	19746
1996	11396	29	61024	430	
1997	14676	30.73	49349	398	31428

13—13 邮电业务量

Volume of Postal and Telecommunication Services

年份	邮电业务总量(万元)	函件(万件)	报刊期发数(万份)	电报(万份)	长途电话(万张)	市内电话(万户)	农村电话(万户)
1980	7627	13498	839	537	980	4.69	3.00
1985	10412	19266	1465	847	1270	6.81	2.88
1986	11330	19842	1432	793	1323	7.27	2.91
1987	12723	21330	1410	946	1483	8.03	3.05
1988	16263	23523	1331	1180	1875	9.62	3.26
1989	20126	22330	1153	896	2162	10.88	3.67
1990	44425	20015	979	1094	2629	12.38	4.20
1991	57066	19197	1255	1156	3504	15.55	5.20
1992	77181	22184	1371	1253	5692	26.30	7.29
1993	128071	27643	1652	1142	12035	50.73	9.81
1994	215397	36004	1395	887	22782	89.62	16.70
1995	314794	34412	1485	566	34246	131.71	30.72
1996	427332	29556	1790	351	41474	163.74	47.03
1997	522447	21979	1369	253	42847	199.60	66.26
长沙市	154281	6120	155	39	11348	38.53	8.57
株洲市	39711	920	103	11	3365	19.67	3.86
湘潭市	25239	1100	275	8	2256	12.45	2.73
衡阳市	42024	2421	88	29	3539	17.87	7.01
邵阳市	32764	1991	123	26	2509	13.25	5.98
岳阳市	46795	1221	121	20	4963	16.78	6.21
常德市	42124	1402	90	20	3365	18.91	8.51
张家界市	9370	387	18	8	851	3.96	1.34
益阳市	24948	1025	61	11	2230	10.44	5.28
郴州市	27025	2233	75	15	2017	10.53	4.85
永州市	24518	948	105	23	2235	10.84	3.58
娄底地区	18719	726	67	12	1546	8.95	2.62
怀化地区	22841	1015	50	23	1607	11.43	4.14
湘西自治州	12088	470	38	8	1016	5.99	1.58

13—14 邮电通信企业主要财务指标

Main Financial Indicators of Postal and Telecommunication Enterprises

单位:万元

指标	邮电企业合计		中央邮电		地方邮电	
	1996年	1997年	1996年	1997年	1996年	1997年
业务收入	382934	523545	342550	465333	40384	58212
业务支出	380291	406421	338932	353301	41359	53120
营业外损益净额	—661	—5184	—5536	—4883	—125	—301
税金及附加费	1529	20734	13724	18419	1535	2315
收支差额	—62895	—48504	—47379	—37292	—15516	—11212

13—15 邮 电 通 信 水 平

Level of Postal and Telecommunication Services

指　　标	单 位	1990 年	1995 年	1996 年	1997 年
平均每人每年发函件数	件	3.33	5.42	4.99	3.68
平均每万人每年订报刊数	份	1628	2338	1370	2141
平均每万人拥有电话机部数	部	55.00	256.74	367.41	450.11
设有邮电局所乡(镇)的比重	%	62.2	83.7	85	87.41
通邮路的乡(镇)比重	%	100.0	100.0	100.0	100.0
通电话的乡(镇)比重	%	99.3	99.6	98.0	97.1
进入长话自动网的乡(镇)比重	%				90.9
长沙市区平均每百人拥有电话机部数	部	1.90	21.93	23.77	26.52
县以上城市装有自动电话交换机比重	%	70.12	100.0	100.0	100.1

13—16 邮电通信工具拥有量

Telecommunications Facilties

年　　份	市话交换机容量(门)	农话交换机容量(门)	电话机(部)		
				城市电话	农村电话
1980	67992	58081	74265	47089	27176
1985	108108	64816	91649	65537	26112
1986	110726	66075	96157	69769	26388
1987	127456	68020	104504	76808	27696
1988	133926	70698	120186	90477	29709
1989	146862	84337	137343	103708	33635
1990	177502	97496	156675	117418	39257
1991	267155	112352	200214	151299	48915
1992	424386	142578	326382	255934	70448
1993	791685	193605	599733	501930	97803
1994	1387209	363546	1055547	889262	166285
1995	2056510	680974	1630988	1322387	308601
1996	2670499	914843	2348882	1864761	484121
1997	2985936	1124934	2652809	1989519	663290

注:以上数字均系邮电部门经营的。

十四、国内、外贸易 对外经济和旅游

DOMESTIC TRAOE, FOREIGN TRADE, FOREIGN ECONOMY AND TOURISM

14—1 国内贸易基本情况

Basic Statistics on Domestic Trade

项　　目	1995 年	1996 年	1997 年	1997 年为 1996 年%
全省批发零售贸易业				
商品购进总额(万元)	11746354	12143391	11967783	98.6
＃国有经济	7722308	8102743	7733387	95.4
集体经济	3443314	3459551	3492156	100.9
商品销售总额(万元)	12829514	13021788	12876203	98.9
＃国有经济	8403608	8642698	8290228	95.9
集体经济	3736433	3708974	3481907	93.9
商品库存总额(万元)	2540432	2833913	2977970	105.1
＃国有经济	1602806	1852770	1892817	102.2
集体经济	837234	878055	956294	108.9
社会消费品零售总额(万元)	8374141	9473952	10415984	109.9
按地区分				
市	4282864	4729279	5231554	110.6
县	1663110	1820303	2054568	112.9
县以下	2428166	2924369	3129861	107.0
按经济类型				
国有经济	2137278	2044868	1987272	97.2
集体经济	1174948	1203225	1323507	110.0
个体经济	3265804	4078435	4645601	113.9
按行业分				
批发零售贸易业	5548796	6226582	6780975	108.9
餐饮业	546355	711376	821886	115.5
制造业	532370	577520	620306	107.4
其他行业	1746619	1958473	2192816	112.0
城乡商品交易市场个数(个)	3905	3989	3869	97.0
城市	834	861	914	106.2
乡村	3071	3128	2955	94.5
城乡市场贸易成交额(亿元)	453.43	581.12	672.05	115.6
城市	230.91	306.64	354.15	115.5
乡村	222.52	274.48	317.90	115.8

14—2 批发零售贸易业商品购进、销售、库存总额(1997 年)

Gross Valne of Purchases,Sales and Inrentory of Wholesale and Retail Trade

计量单位:万元

	商品购进总额	商品销售总额			年末库存总额
		合　计	批　发	零　售	
总　　计	11967783	12876203	10054969	2821233	2977970
一、按经济类型分组:					
国有经济	7733387	8290228	6693296	1596932	1892817
集体经济	3492156	3701585	2812244	889341	952111
私营经济	352211	442687	301600	141087	66342
联营经济	21136	22600	20084	2515	4229
股份制经济	351615	406588	224504	182084	59281
外商投资经济	13507	5841	1477	4364	1906
港澳台投资经济	2429	5138	786	4351	906
其他经济	1337	1532	976	556	375

14—3 大中型批发零售贸易企业购进、销售、库存总额(1997年)

Gross Value of Purchases, Sales and Inventory of Large and Medium－Sizd Wholesale and Retail Trade Enterprises

单位:万元

项目	商品购进总额	商品销售总额			年末库存额
		合计	批发	零售	
总计	7192875	7815302	6633198	1182104	1256891
一、按经济类型分:					
国有经济	5618847	6198320	5336476	861843	797711
集体经济	1268968	1258719	1113449	145269	410464
私营经济					
联营经济					
股份制经济	302201	352636	183039	169596	46967
外商投资经营	1285	1316	232	1084	1157
港、澳、台投资经济	1573	4309		4309	590
其他经济					
二、按国民经济行业分:					
食品、饮料、烟草和家庭用品批发业	3918792	4210515	3922332	288182	709962
食品、饮料、烟草批发业	2724379	2995918	2900398	95519	355624
棉麻、土畜产品批发业	376188	297635	291373	6262	225271
纺织品、服装和鞋帽批发业	139830	139637	136436	3201	18810
日用百货批发业	273048	342408	275170	67238	49506
日用杂品批发业	4343	5528	4664	863	1472
五金、交电、化工批发业	282101	280187	246426	33761	25405
药品及医疗器械批发业	118901	149199	67862	81337	33871
能源、材料和机械电子设备批发业	1479628	1621585	1490894	130691	159228
能源批发业	567141	619285	550357	68927	58377
化工材料批发业	80505	115671	115014	656	6070
木材批发业	3720	8143	6734	1409	1214
建筑材料批发业	47886	50692	50550	142	2209
矿产品批发业	19535	22846	22846		2046
金属材料批发业	384593	378298	367938	10360	33143
机械、电子设备批发业	106804	137752	119736	18015	13307
汽车、摩托车及零配件批发业	228137	236767	210278	26489	37525
再生物资回收批发业	41303	52126	47438	4688	5333
其他批发业	765731	820618	797757	22860	130894
工艺美术品批发业	48542	52925	50928	1997	2203
图书报刊批发业	141898	143745	139336	4409	4132
农业生产资料批发业	547831	592616	581921	10694	122365
其他类未包括的批发业	27459	31330	25570	5760	2193
零售业	1028723	1162583	422213	740369	256805
食品、饮料和烟草零售业	138174	139773	49205	90568	67329
日用百货零售业	652530	754276	323129	431147	128292
纺织品、服装和鞋帽零售业	13729	17913	2397	15515	6364
日用杂品零售业	2002	3261	1137	2124	1651
五金、交电、化工零售业	53612	64849	19476	45373	17606
药品及医疗器械零售业	32032	46400	8320	38079	12953
图书报刊零售业	107396	102272	6902	95370	15449
其他零售业	29245	33835	11645	22190	7157

14—4 大中型批发零售贸易企业商品购进总额构成(1997年)

Composition of Commodities Purchases Value of Large and Medium－Sizd Wholesale and Retail Trade Enterprises

单位:万元

项目	合计	从生产者购进	农副产品购进	从批发零售贸易业购进	进口	其他
总计	7192875	4407713	468687	2554625	177769	52767
一、按经济类型分:						
国有经济	5618847	3671385	331448	1764319	151947	31195
集体经济	1268968	555640	136698	682995	21797	8534
私营经济						
联营经济						
股份制经济	302201	179931	541	105206	4025	13038
外商投资经营	1285	465		819		
港、澳、台投资经济	1573	289		1283		
其他经济						
二、按国民经济行业分:						
食品、饮料、烟草和家庭用品批发业	3918792	2353586	386551	1421598	121605	22002
食品、饮料、烟草批发业	2724379	1696714	259220	999501	7587	20575
棉麻、土畜产品批发业	376188	108469	85077	254893	11761	1064
纺织品、服装和鞋帽批发业	139830	126192	5	4817	8821	
日用百货批发业	273048	196395	33938	76218	137	297
日用杂品批发业	4343	3636	14	706		
五金、交电、化工批发业	282101	146330	6891	42451	93298	21
药品及医疗器械批发业	118901	75847	1404	43010		43
能源、材料和机械电子设备批发业	1479628	1046923	679	379361	30341	23001
能源批发业	567141	472452	143	90898		3790
化工材料批发业	80505	51574		13080	15850	
木材批发业	3720	3513	389	173		33
建筑材料批发业	47886	32683		15203		
矿产品批发业	19535	14730		4804		
金属材料批发业	384593	300353	147	82922		1318
机械、电子设备批发业	106804	32970		59342	14491	
汽车、摩托车及零配件批发业	228137	129649		98488		
再生物资回收批发业	41303	8995		14447		17859
其他批发业	765731	481552	10115	260297	21772	2108
工艺美术品批发业	48542	48542				
图书报刊批发业	141898	137291		4604		
农业生产资料批发业	547831	272714	9329	252744	21772	600
其他类未包括的批发业	27459	23004	786	2946		1508
零售业	1028723	525649	71341	493368	4049	5655
食品、饮料和烟草零售业	138174	71773	53316	66351		49
日用百货零售业	652530	377094	16380	270921	4049	465
纺织品、服装和鞋帽零售业	13729	4963	42	8766		
日用杂品零售业	2002	737		1265		
五金、交电、化工零售业	53612	19995		33595		21
药品及医疗器械零售业	32032	17985	956	14041		5
图书报刊零售业	107396	19593		82689		5113
其他零售业	29245	13507	646	15738		

14—5 大中型批发零售贸易企业商品批发销售总额构成(1997年)

Composition of Total Value of Wholesale in Large and Medium－Sizd Wholesale and Retail Trade Enterprises

单位:万元

项目	合计	对生产者的批发	对农民农业生资销售	对批发零售贸易业批发	出口
总计	6633198	1415350	209233	4559034	658813
一、按经济类型分:					
国有经济	5336476	1061944	68877	3621008	653523
集体经济	1113449	292842	140356	820585	22
私营经济					
联营经济					
股份制经济	183039	60564		117208	5267
外商投资经营	232			232	
港、澳、台投资经济					
其他经济					
二、按国民经济行业分:					
食品、饮料、烟草和家庭用品批发业	3922332	387099	47579	3023519	511714
食品、饮料、烟草批发业	2900398	227248	23827	2538251	134899
棉麻、土畜产品批发业	291373	81413	3147	160875	49084
纺织品、服装和鞋帽批发业	136436	4552		13173	118710
日用百货批发业	275170	47084	6818	170168	57916
日用杂品批发业	4664	12		4652	
五金、交电、化工批发业	246426	24000	13750	90890	131535
药品及医疗器械批发业	67862	2787	35	45507	19567
能源、材料和机械电子设备批发业	1490894	792977	16567	604499	93417
能源批发业	550357	319151	10932	231205	
化工材料批发业	115014	40909	1491	27811	46294
木材批发业	6734	1559		5175	
建筑材料批发业	50550	28224		20875	1451
矿产品批发业	22846	14886		1432	6528
金属材料批发业	367938	234556	1112	128607	4774
机械、电子设备批发业	119736	64906	2870	20692	34137
汽车、摩托车及零配件批发业	210278	61265	160	148780	232
再生物资回收批发业	47438	27518		19919	
其他批发业	797757	170600	119202	580129	47027
工艺美术品批发业	50928	3901			47027
图书报刊批发业	139336			139336	
农业生产资料批发业	581921	162621	119202	419300	
其他类未包括的批发业	25570	4078		21492	
零售业	422213	64672	25884	350887	6653
食品、饮料和烟草零售业	49205	7667	725	41537	
日用百货零售业	323129	45031	24469	271466	6631
纺织品、服装和鞋帽零售业	2397	344		2053	
日用杂品零售业	1137			1137	
五金、交电、化工零售业	19476	3704		15749	22
药品及医疗器械零售业	8320	517	2	7803	
图书报刊零售业	6902	11		6890	
其他零售业	11645	7395	687	4249	

14—6 大中型批发零售贸易企业商品销售、库存类值(1997 年)

Sales and Inrentory Value by Category of Commodities of Large and Medium－sized Wholesale and Retail Trade Entetprises

单位:万元

项目	销售额					年末库存额
	合计	批发	对生产经营单位批发	出口	零售额	
类值合计	7815302	6633198	1415350	658813	1182104	1256891
食品、饮料、烟酒类	3177324	2951330	204782	129602	225994	421111
针、纺织品类	139399	93217	1404	74913	46181	24740
服装、鞋帽类	218193	108463	922	81757	109730	38242
化妆品类	49695	23707	21		25987	9973
钟表、眼镜类	18020	4597			13423	6516
日用品类	170805	107432	6585	49832	63373	26052
五金、电工器具类	31961	15071	4315	1393	16890	11558
生活电器类	338263	216775	8497	1198	121487	50171
录像器材类	112021	72544	56	2900	39477	13339
自行车、摩托车类	62509	38893	5101	417	23616	7192
体育、娱乐用品类	26670	13620	401	6603	13049	6710
文化、办公用品类	68679	43885	27432	2362	24794	15351
金银珠宝类	49324	11645		1543	37678	11496
家具类	3624	201	2		3423	929
中西药品类	205557	87411	3040	30838	118145	50038
书报杂志类	251298	146306			104992	20106
汽车类	265058	234373	90610		30684	32143
建筑材料类	34014	30643	18055	6048	3370	1915
木材类	12053	8554	2531	1305	3498	1501
化工材料及制品类	696467	689747	206952	65090	6719	119942
黑色金属材料类	344647	332883	183411	31630	11764	29578
有色金属材料类	146405	141154	52714	64363	5250	6554
机电设备及零件类	178481	169763	73511	48405	8717	29055
煤炭及制品类	36347	33250	32266	4	3096	17731
石油及制品类	588397	512378	281334		76018	41835
种子饲料类	39539	36205	30188	3	3333	4176
棉麻、土畜产品类	304502	301950	78755	29891	2552	221384
再生资源类	37307	36815	21804	2570	492	3624
其他类	208730	170372	80649	26135	38357	33918

14—7 小型批发零售贸易企业商品销售、库存类值(1997年)

Sales and Inrentory Value by Category of Commodities of Small－sized and Subsidiary Wholesale and Retail Trade Enterpises

单位:万元

项目	销售额			年末库存额
	合计	批发	零售	
类值合计	5060900	3421771	1639129	1721078
食品、饮料、烟酒类	1164308	662359	501949	856268
针、纺织品类	171859	84708	87151	48265
服装、鞋帽类	168634	72684	95950	45680
化妆品类	39476	12346	27130	11191
钟表、眼镜类	36886	21099	15787	8577
日用品类	223809	117535	106274	55968
五金、电工器具类	84882	44115	40767	27592
生活电器类	170730	73992	96738	40213
录像器材类	83461	33044	50417	21127
自行车、摩托车类	103739	70641	33097	14551
体育、娱乐用品类	33070	22131	10938	10012
文化、办公用品类	49627	25103	24523	16005
金银珠宝类	15382	3264	12118	5314
家具类	39808	21189	18619	8759
中西药品类	75628	25025	50602	27709
书报杂志类	75813	20116	55696	15058
汽车类	76624	68422	8202	16975
建筑材料类	286117	236364	49753	54196
木材类	47284	31153	16131	9094
化工材料及制品类	434869	397649	37220	80685
黑色金属材料类	170589	141920	28668	27970
有色金属材料类	68280	65713	2566	9614
机电设备及零件类	202397	180202	22195	39839
煤炭及制品类	60646	40985	19661	9059
石油及制品类	170780	111896	58883	20525
种子饲料类	152158	143119	9038	35403
棉麻、土畜产品类	249935	227176	22758	56237
再生资源类	65546	59850	5695	13307
其他类	538551	407960	130591	135873

14—8 批发零售贸易企业商品销售、库存类值构成(1997年)

Sales and Inrentory Value and their Composition by Category of Commodities of Wholesale and Retail Trade Enterpises

项目	大中型企业、活动单位				小型企业、活动单位			
	销售额			年末库存额	销售额			年末库存额
	合计	批发	零售		合计	批发	零售	
合计	100.0	100.0	100.0	100.0	100.0	100.0	100.0	100.0
食品、饮料、烟酒类	40.7	44.5	19.1	33.5	23.0	19.4	30.6	49.8
针、纺织品类	1.8	1.4	3.9	2.0	3.4	2.5	5.3	2.8
服装、鞋帽类	2.8	1.6	9.3	3.0	3.3	2.1	5.9	2.7
化妆品类	0.6	0.4	2.2	0.8	0.8	0.4	1.7	0.7
钟表、眼镜类	0.2	0.1	1.1	0.5	0.7	0.6	1.0	0.5
日用品类	2.2	1.6	5.4	2.1	4.4	3.4	6.5	3.3
五金、电工器具类	0.4	0.2	1.4	0.9	1.7	1.3	2.5	1.6
生活电器类	4.3	3.3	10.3	4.0	3.4	2.2	5.9	2.3
录像器材类	1.4	1.1	3.3	1.1	1.6	1.0	3.1	1.2
自行车、摩托车类	0.8	0.6	2.0	0.6	2.0	2.1	2.0	0.8
体育、娱乐用品类	0.3	0.2	1.1	0.5	0.7	0.6	0.7	0.6
文化、办公用品类	0.9	0.7	2.1	1.2	1.0	0.7	1.5	0.9
金银珠宝类	0.6	0.2	3.2	0.9	0.3	0.1	0.7	0.3
家具类			0.3	0.1	0.8	0.6	0.1	0.5
中西药品类	2.6	1.3	10.0	4.0	1.5	0.7	3.1	1.6
书报杂志类	3.2	2.2	8.9	1.6	1.5	0.6	3.4	0.9
汽车类	3.4	3.5	2.6	2.6	1.5	2.0	0.5	1.0
建筑材料类	0.4	0.5	0.3	0.2	5.7	6.9	3.0	3.1
木材类	0.2	0.1	0.3	0.1	0.9	0.9	1.0	0.5
化工材料及制品类	8.9	10.4	0.6	9.5	8.6	11.6	2.3	4.7
黑色金属材料类	4.4	5.0	1.0	2.4	3.4	4.1	1.7	1.6
有色金属材料类	1.9	2.1	0.4	0.5	1.3	1.9	0.2	0.6
机电设备及零件类	2.3	2.6	0.7	2.3	4.0	5.3	1.4	2.3
煤炭及制品类	0.5	0.5	0.3	1.4	1.2	1.2	1.2	0.5
石油及制品类	7.5	7.7	6.4	3.3	3.4	3.3	3.6	1.2
种子饲料类	0.5	0.5	0.3	0.3	3.0	4.2	0.6	2.1
棉麻、土畜产品类	3.9	4.6	0.2	17.6	4.9	6.6	1.4	3.3
再生资源类	0.5	0.6		0.3	1.3	1.7	0.3	0.8
其他类	2.7	2.6	3.2	2.7	10.6	11.9	8.0	7.9

14—9 大中型批发零售贸易企业商品销售、库存数量(1997 年)

Sales and Inventory Quantity of Large and Medium-sized Wholesale and Retail Trade Enterprises

项目	单位	销售量					年末库存
		合计	批发	对生产经营单位批发	出口	零售	
粮食	吨	735396	503000	71632	2050	232396	1007191
食用植物油	吨	35457	20809	3585	148	14648	11130
猪和猪肉	吨	225818	188745	5392	45098	37073	14967
食糖	吨	81111	68673	11098		12438	4348
棉花	吨	172106	172027	75800		79	141339
布	百米	397957	334516	7889	281126	63441	85488
#棉布	百米	97728	69775	6910	37625	27953	21433
呢绒	百米	6438	1430	197		5008	4425
绸缎	百米	8862	2200	35		6662	14833
各种服装	百件	167713	105652	52	97838	62061	32462
鞋	百双	262115	161270	6238	36958	100845	127584
#皮鞋	百双	34204	6783	6	2559	27421	16379
黄金饰品	千元	424169	100271			323898	106618
照相机	架	37260	9114	141		28146	16021
自行车	辆	274964	147808	49	18007	127156	71148
摩托车	辆	68690	42546	959		26144	11081
电视机	台	834686	632562	139	11150	202124	109804
#彩色电视机	台	666034	513331	101		152703	82898
录音机	台	390974	338418	3	328300	52556	35938
#组合音响	台	9822	3819			6003	8480
摄像机	台	664	192	13		472	197
录像机	台	7824	2104	10		5720	3401
影碟机	台	13221	6240			6981	4176
#进口影碟机	台	679				679	99
家用电脑	台	3333	1708			1625	175
家用电风扇	台	659246	391172	5199		268074	282363
家用洗衣机	台	492851	343120	1564		149731	79875
家用电冰箱	台	265645	168698	1385		96947	57027
房间空调器	台	122890	66270	509		56620	26730
微波炉	台	9573	1926			7647	4420
抽油烟机	台	24563	3699	81		20864	13881
化学肥料	吨	4057701	4057701	1225814			693043
化学农药	吨	50672	50672	19835	68		11187
农用塑料薄膜	吨	5360	5360	2408			4089
汽车	辆	25851	23811	9046		2040	4232
#轿车	辆	7700	6693	2262		1007	1115

14—9　续表

项　　目	单位	销售量					年末库存
		合　计	批　发	对生产经营单位批发	出　口	零　售	
生铁	吨	142527	142518	69624	66459	9	2358
钢材	吨	971851	958528	542157	3000	13323	89126
普通中型钢材	吨	46133	46133	25045			6952
普通小型钢材	吨	247244	247244	141073	3000		17323
钢带	吨	908	908	619			40
线材	吨	340398	327075	222657		13323	11691
中厚钢板	吨	108204	108204	61434			16276
薄钢板	吨	123387	123387	43809			12454
硅钢片	吨	2254	2254	1257			402
铜	吨	11131	11131	6145	91		275
铝	吨	4551	4551	3513	16		178
铅	吨	698	698	422			128
锌	吨	5668	5668	629	3530		62
锡	吨	382	382	13	368		4
铜材	吨	1690	1690	441			97
铝材	吨	529	529	513			76
硫酸	吨	843	842	715		1	399
烧碱	吨	16117	16095	4259	8820	22	1542
纯碱	吨	41881	41844	26726		37	3302
天然橡胶	吨	895	895	872			243
合成橡胶	吨	1724	1724	1534			781
水泥	吨	253824	243871	153642		9953	10219
平板玻璃	重量箱	113060	112863	62580		197	20416
原木	立方米	154603	109255	64127		45348	34011
锯材	立方米	15756	15751	6987	32	5	1328
煤炭	万吨	70	63	44		7	6
焦炭	吨	24413	24413	21454			3109
汽油	吨	1180856	1024599	492603		156257	83521
柴油	吨	1061721	965645	501543		96076	57488
煤油	吨	22833	21653	9299		1180	5798
燃料油	吨	180	143	135		37	222

14—10 大中型批发零售贸易企业财务状况(1997年)

Financial Indicators of Large and Medium－sized Wholesale and Retail Trade Enterprises

(按经济类型分)

单位:万元

项目	合计	国有经济	集体经济	股份制经济	外商投资经济	港澳台经济
资本金合计	613128	400978	131544	74395	4758	1452
#国家资本金	486948	384890	59251	41988	87	730
外商资本金	5921	250	277		4670	722
流动资产合计	3028814	2100535	762964	161074	3772	467
#存货	1162654	709653	401752	50182	606	460
长期投资	276682	249544	21217	5917	2	
固定资产合计	1194749	904606	145635	139982	4509	16
固定资产原值	1206846	916969	172869	112006	4969	32
#生产经营用	876701	664648	107966	99207	4846	32
累计折旧	261837	185512	46607	29201	500	16
#本年提取折旧	35844	26800	4713	3888	435	6
无形及递延资产合计	107515	70793	19221	15820	1591	88
#无形资产	52442	38145	3648	10648		
资产总计	4861813	3411579	1063169	362495	23997	572
流动负债合计	3539281	2518802	811365	203376	5415	321
长期负债合计	477648	261529	179316	22516	14285	
负债合计	4016930	2780332	990682	225892	19701	321
所有者权益合计	844882	631246	72487	136602	4296	250
#股本	79328	19315	13319	46694		
商品销售收入(营业收入)	6588756	5166106	1101973	315379	983	4313
商品销售收入净额	6531655	5116331	1098203	311836	983	4301
商品销售成本(营业成本)	5983880	4697113	1010963	271539	833	3430
经营费用(营业费用)	246986	182650	50032	13728	227	349
#运杂装卸费	69586	50804	15892	2874	8	6
商品销售税金及附加费	15026	9489	4080	1450	6	
商品销售利润	285762	227078	33127	25118	－83	521
代购代销收入	2378	2340	38			
主营业务利润	288141	229418	33165	25118	－83	521
其他业务利润	16704	14132	797	1732	35	5
管理费用	260396	201388	43055	15056	393	504
#税金	9730	6857	1759	1113		
财产保险费	4528	3340	831	302	53	
劳动、待业保险费	18426	14302	2402	1663	3	54
财务费用	146728	103204	41651	1849	18	4
#利息支出	140255	100903	37525	1806	17	3
营业利润	－102023	－61076	－50449	9945	－461	18
补贴收入	31628	29475	1285	867		
利润总额	－56138	－22524	－48163	14969	－460	40
#应交所得税	30300	27506	795	1996		2
转作奖金的利润	619	109	76	420		12
应付利润	17066	10184	627	6250		4
已分配股利	1669	13	57	1598		
本年应付工资总额	134013	98960	25510	9057	235	250
#主营业务应付工资	125946	93102	23597	8817	179	250
本年应付福利费总额	17386	12934	3182	1213	30	25
#主营业务应付福利费	16555	12272	3037	1198	22	25
本年应缴增加值税额	65346	53017	6856	5403		68
本年进项增值税额	799023	681145	75808	41374	143	552
本年销项增值税额	819559	698222	73662	46913	134	626

14—10 续表 （按行业分） 单位:万元

项目	食品、饮料烟草和家用品批发业	能源、材料和机械电子设备批发业	其他批发业	零售业
资本金合计	242044	144352	45099	181631
#国家资本金	218977	135871	25764	106334
外商资本金		137		5783
流动资产合计	1770560	471651	255269	531332
#存货	700511	141938	118485	201720
长期投资	196137	59036	8447	13060
固定资产合计	555181	211661	49550	378356
固定资产原值	538260	246145	57212	365228
#生产经营用	384259	183503	33933	275005
累计折旧	112736	66984	17129	64987
#本年提取折旧	15926	6961	1588	11367
无形及递延资产合计	34920	28295	4621	39679
#无形资产	11720	26301	3129	11290
资产总计	2722458	787736	324024	1027594
流动负债合计	2073378	556934	243187	665782
长期负债合计	344431	27029	6189	99998
负债合计	2417809	583963	249377	765780
所有者权益合计	304648	203772	74647	261814
#股本	10281	17979	6490	44578
商品销售收入(营业收入)	3437202	1387105	775570	987778
商品销售收入净额	3433773	1386214	738817	972820
商品销售成本(营业成本)	3178620	1285306	680453	839499
经营费用(营业费用)	102646	54591	27625	62124
#运杂装卸费	26343	22698	12826	7718
商品销售税金及附加费	5789	1595	561	7079
商品销售利润	146716	44722	30206	64117
代购代销收入	1515	506	5	351
主营业务利润	148231	45228	30212	64468
其他业务利润	3338	5229	646	7489
管理费用	118540	50831	22273	68751
#税金	4806	1700	619	2605
财产保险费	2462	828	293	944
劳动、待业保险费	7977	2624	1247	6577
财务费用	96547	21191	8655	20333
#利息支出	95686	18182	8528	17858
营业利润	－64004	－21037	－12	－16968
补贴收入	21306	1589	249	8482
利润总额	－36361	－16531	707	－3953
#应交所得税	23294	1233	1408	4363
转作奖金的利润	107	23	18	469
应付利润	9500	2366	85	5113
已分配股利	57	1567	12	31
本年应付工资总额	53863	24033	12163	43953
#主营业务应付工资	51742	21595	10845	41762
本年应付福利费总额	6831	3312	1537	5705
#主营业务应付福利费	6528	3087	1466	5474
本年应缴增加值税额	36847	12432	2161	13906
本年进项增值税额	457523	213164	29314	99022
本年销项增值税额	455263	220033	26062	118200

14—11 大中型餐饮企业财务状况(1997年)

Financial Indicators of Large and Medium－sized Catering Enterprises

单位:万元

项　　目	合　计	按经济类型分			按行业分类		
		国　有	集　体	港澳台合　资	正　餐	快　餐	其他餐饮　业
资本金合计	14902	10763	975	1700	13027	524	1350
#国家资本金	11390	10185	205	1000	9849	524	1017
外商资本金	2475	312		700	2475		
流动资产合计	17035	12910	1981	1309	13628	603	2802
#存货	1272	1113	158		1166	86	19
长期投资	2374	2373			2373		
固定资产合计	37716	31886	4504	1054	33601	1586	2528
固定资产原值	36714	33004	1945	1341	32180	2244	2288
#生产经营用	30105	26762	1749	1170	25910	2037	2157
累计折旧	6824	5941	445	286	5712	760	351
#本年提取折旧	1363	871	268	163	1212	79	72
无形及递延资产合计	5902	3009	594	2200	4883	340	678
#无形资产	670	458	211		497		172
资产总计	65113	51756	7081	4792	56572	2531	6010
流动负债合计	29936	22258	3302	3728	24896	1433	3606
长期负债合计	10984	9324	361	200	10625	77	282
负债合计	40920	31583	3664	3928	35521	1510	3888
所有者权益合计	24193	20173	3417	863	21050	1020	2121
#股本	1009		233		1009		
商品销售收入(营业收入)	39604	31270	4137	2130	26541	4364	8698
商品销售收入净额							
商品销售成本(营业成本)	20883	16750	1878	8923	12986	2631	5265
经营费用(营业费用)	11790	8629	1242	970	9192	731	1866
#运杂装卸费							
商品销售税金及附加费	2022	1587	211	116	1334	209	479
商品销售利润							
代购代销收入							
主营业务利润	4906	4302	805	150	3028	792	1086
其他业务利润	1292	651	87	554	1272		20
管理费用	7065	4779	1142	1051	5340	700	1025
#税金	257	217	40		248	4	3
财产保险费	36	31		1	35		
劳动、待业保险费	601	565	34	2	421	59	120
财务费用	1877	1296	261	288	1664	89	123
#利息支出	1626	1070	237	288	1450	53	123
营业利润	－2743	－1122	－511	－634	－2704	2	－41
补贴收入	20	20			20		
利润总额	－1253	－117	－393	－639	－1449	13	182
#应交所得税	132	129	2		83	8	40
转作奖金的利润	20	20			20		
应付利润	66	41			54		12
已分配股利							
本年应付工资总额	5162	3540	691	571	4204	277	679
#主营业务应付工资	4856	3370	691	463	3899	277	679
本年应付福利费总额	602	467	69	14	472	31	98
#主营业务应付福利费	583	448	69	14	453	31	98

14—12 国有商业和供销合作社农业生产资料销售量

Sales of Agricultural Producer Goods of State-Owned Trade and Supply and Marketing Cooperative

年份	化学肥料（万吨）	化学农药（万吨）	大中型拖拉机（台）	手扶拖拉机（万台）	农用动力机械（万台/万千瓦）	农药械（万架）
1985	358.42	6.45	99	1.73	4.33/48.26	102.28
1986	481.96	5.97	103	1.72	4.45	103.44
1987	478.77	6.20	175	2.30	5.91	99.63
1988	517.84	5.71	134	2.22	7.32	73.57
1989	491.50	4.53	63	1.23	6.76	39.63
1990	508.76	4.45	45	1.30	8.28/42.57	48.51
1991	570.34	5.22	257	2.17	9.65/49.90	49.70
1992	539.68	4.00	147	2.23	7.61/44.89	46.23
1993	420.11	3.85	251	1.57	6.50/40.21	42.80
1994	332.48	3.67	216	2.1	8.03/46.39	35.42
1995	404.67	4.10	194	2.24	10.25/55.89	30.12
1996	408.31	3.81	118	1.04	10.65/49.07	43.32
1997	393.41	4.40	91	0.58	10.6/43.18	26.24

14—13 大中型贸易、餐饮企业增加值

Added Value of Large and Medium-Sized Trade and Catering Enterprise

单位:万元

指标	1995年	1996年	1997年	1997年为1996年%
批发零售贸易业				
增加值合计	303223.8	313729.1	223448.9	71.2
本年提取的固定资产折旧	34489.9	39240.8	35844.1	91.3
本年应付工资总额	193776.9	135687.5	134016.0	98.8
本年应付福利费总额	21237.4	19899.9	17393.9	87.4
劳动就业保险费	14721.7	17739.8	18426.4	103.9
商品销售税金及附加	15250.8	19001.6	15026.4	79.1
利润总额	-5638	4704.6	-56138.7	
管理费用中税金额	7254.1	10259.6	9730.9	94.8
餐饮业				
增加值合计	5590.4	6209.1	7286.5	117.4
本年提取的固定资产折旧	999.5	768.5	1363.6	177.4
本年应付工资总额	2930.8	4636	5162.0	111.3
本年应付福利费总额	459	589.1	602.0	102.2
劳动就业保险费	179.4	398.9	601.8	150.9
商品销售税金及附加	1314.7	1974.7	2022.9	102.4
利润总额	88.5	-652	-12535	
管理费用中税金额	72.9	376.1	257.2	68.4

14—14 社会消费品零售总额

Total Value of Retail Sales of Consumer Goods

单位:亿元

项目	1993年	1994年	1995年	1996年	1997年
总计	486.67	659.69	837.41	947.40	1041.60
一、按销售地区分:					
(1)市	228.66	323.17	428.29	472.93	523.15
(2)县	108.09	134.83	166.31	182.03	205.46
(3)县以下	149.72	201.69	242.81	292.44	312.99
二、按经济类型分:					
国有经济	157.23	183.03	213.73	204.49	198.73
集体经济	101.31	111.00	117.49	120.32	132.35
私营经济	0.33	9.12	13.26	18.78	24.81
个体经济	130.65	224.32	326.58	408.84	464.56
联营经济	0.08	0.25	1.07	1.19	1.23
股份制经济	6.94	6.48	8.07	12.48	18.90
外商投资经济	0.29	0.18	1.14	1.58	0.94
港澳台投资经济	0.24	0.45	0.26	0.67	1.40
其他经济	89.59	124.85	155.81	180.04	198.68
三、按行业分:					
批发、零售贸易业	329.29	432.24	554.88	622.66	678.10
餐饮业	21.46	39.17	54.63	71.14	82.19
制造业	36.20	47.11	53.24	57.75	62.03
其他	10.22	23.65	174.66	195.85	219.28
#农民对非农业居民零售	89.50	117.52	149.63	165.37	191.00

14—15 商品交易市场情况

Basic Statistics of Commodity Market

项目	1993年	1994年	1995年	1996年	1997年
市场个数(个)	4040	4060	3905	3989	3869
城市	721	738	834	861	914
农村	3319	3322	3071	3128	2955
商品交易市场成交额(亿元)	236.39	358.59	453.43	581.12	672.05
城市	110.82	170.82	230.91	306.64	354.15
农村	125.57	187.77	222.52	274.48	317.90
#粮食类	8.18	13.45	22.95	30.48	32.96
油脂油料类	3.32	7.09	14.30	17.74	23.22
棉烟麻类	1.08	1.94	2.32	5.20	6.94
肉食禽蛋类	38.26	56.36	126.57	138.97	160.93
水产品类	8.53	12.49	31.38	38.51	44.24
蔬菜类	11.81	16.82	42.85	55.29	62.62
干鲜果类	8.82	11.78	33.27	47.24	52.09
饲料农具种苗类	2.17	3.39	6.66		
大牲畜类	3.28	5.02	6.26	8.77	8.01
家畜类	8.90	13.13	15.93	17.45	21.91
工业品类	19.41	30.10	109.26	135.80	172.52
其他类	6.61	9.14	20.61	30.96	24.11
成交额为社会消费品零售总额%	48.57	54.36	54.15	61.34	64.52

14—16 对外经济贸易和旅游概况

A Surrey Foreign and Tourists

指　　标	1996年	1997年	1997年比1996年±(%)
进出口总额(人民币万元)	2666234	2718200	1.9
出口总额	1841305	1928300	4.7
进口总额	824929	289900	-4.2
进出口差额	1016376	1138400	12.0
进出口总额(亿美元)	32.12	32.83	2.2
出口总额	22.18	23.29	5.0
初级产品		2.98	
工业制成品		20.31	
进口总额	9.94	9.54	-4.0
初级产品		1.44	
工业制成品		8.10	
进出口差额	12.24	13.75	12.3
对外签订利用外资协议项目(个)	729	1080	48.1
对外借款	11	21	90.9
外商直接投资	437	407	-6.9
外商其他投资	281	652	132.0
对外签订利用外资协议金额(亿美元)	9.37	12.93	38.0
对外借款	3.80	4.02	5.8
外商直接投资	4.69	8.60	83.4
外商其他投资	0.88	0.31	-64.8
实际利用外资(亿美元)	11.25	13.57	20.6
对外借款	3.80	4.02	5.8
外商直接投资	7.03	9.17	30.4
外商其他投资	0.42	0.38	-9.5
外商投资企业基本情况			
年底登记户数(户)	3249	2756	-15.2
投资总额(亿美元)	74.67	74.53	-0.2
注册资本	46.38	46.33	-0.1
#外方	27.51	26.83	-2.5
对外经济合作合同金额(亿美元)	1.39	2.26	62.6
对外承包工程	1.21	2.04	68.6
对外劳务合作	0.13	0.13	
设计咨询	0.05	0.09	80.0
国际旅游人数总计(万人)	22.87	30.16	31.9
外国人	10.12	12.20	20.6
华侨	0.47	0.60	27.7
港澳台同胞	12.28	17.36	41.4
旅游外汇收入总额(亿美元)	1.02	1.40	37.3
涉外饭店(个)	114	142	24.6

14—17 外贸部门出口商品在1000万美元以上的国家、地区

Countries (Regions) to Which The Foreign Trade Depatment Exported Goods 10 Million $ and Over

国别(地区)	金额(万美元)		国别(地区)	金额(万美元)	
	1996年	1997年		1996年	1997年
香港	93134	75678	德国	7242	9085
澳门	1586	1587	法国	1474	1738
台湾省	4183	6697	意大利	2552	3795
日本	24128	20946	荷兰	5204	5797
泰国	2902	3734	英国	6679	8610
马来西亚	3074	4000	美国	21670	27810
新加坡	4477	6581	澳大利亚	2468	2406
印度尼西亚	3046	3173	埃及	1166	1211
孟加拉国	2053	2089	俄罗斯联邦	1592	2014
阿联酋	1976	1976	加拿大	1504	2182
印度	1511	3665			
巴基斯坦	1077	1537			
韩国	8993	11415			

14—18 各地区外贸部门出口商品总额

Total Value of Exports of The Foreign Trade Department by Region

	金额(万美元)		按人民币计算(万元)	
	1996年	1997年	1996年	1997年
长沙市	7251	18293	60183	151702
株洲市	2813	37844	23348	313837
湘潭市	4044	7516	33565	62329
衡阳市	2263	6746	18783	55944
邵阳市	899	2603	7462	21586
岳阳市	1023	3585	8491	29730
常德市	1198	4506	9943	37368
张家界市	62	144	515	1194
益阳市	708	2912	5876	24149
郴州市	3458	8272	28701	68599
永州市	475	2581	3943	21404
娄底地区	877	2510	7279	20815
怀化地区	1394	1308	11570	10847
湘西自治州	669	2069	5553	17158

14—19 外贸部门进出口总额及主要商品数量和金额

Total Value of Imports and Exports, Imports and Exports of Major Commodities of The Foreign Trade Department in Quantity and Value

项目	单位	1996年		1997年	
		数量	金额	数量	金额
进出口总额	万美元		321233.41		328323.00
进口总额	万美元		99389.04		95401.00
#钢材	万吨	14.73	6023.84	3.18	1330.69
纸张	吨	14605.18	1258.07	6396.99	652.99
有色金属	万美元		18101.05		18266.26
化肥	万吨	6.04	1237.72	12.17	2520.28
农药	万美元		707.79	3.83	469.13
计算机	万美元		5132.81		198.96
家用电器	万美元		540.47		1339.86
电视机及音响设备	万美元		446.52		726.72
化工原料	万美元		3829.96		1571.03
西成药	万美元		0.21		4.86
烟类	万美元		3314.87		1419.12
胶合板	万美元		34.00		
出口总额	万美元		221844.37		232922.00
活大猪	万头	42.80	6686.98	39.05	6346.28
冻猪肉	万吨	0.66	1066.84	0.59	1296.70
罐头	万吨	1.44	1752.60	2.34	2494.44
茶叶	万吨	1.18	2274.26	1.41	2298.20
饲料	万美元		345.80		146.60
鞭炮烟花	万箱	446.35	8655.36	307.01	7672.81
纺织品	万美元		23500.91		20019.65
麻制品	万美元		310.80		
丝织品	万美元		524.43		536.14
羽绒及制品	万美元		754.31		371.31
革皮及制品	万美元		773.88		1581.43
服装	万美元		22160.68		21698.92
鞋类	万美元		6168.36		6444.68
陶瓷类	万美元		7460.52		8179.10
锑	万吨	0.18	370.24	0.41	702.95
铁合金	万吨	4.88	3294.40	3.84	3127.82
各类机械	万美元		9468.61		6824.79
钢材	万吨	6.89	2546.14	5.84	1951.32
硬质合金	万美元				958.59

注:1997年在进口总额中,初级品1.44亿美元,工业制成品8.10亿美元;在出口总额中,初级品2.98亿美元,工业制成品20.31亿美元。

14—20 长沙海关进出口商品总值

Total Value of Imports and Exports (Changsha Customs Statistics)

单位:万美元

项目	1996年	1997年	比上年同期(+、-)%
进出口总值	176299	189445	7.5
其中:出口	129074	144796	12.2
进口	47225	44649	-5.4
进出口差额	81849	100147	22.4

14—21 长沙海关进出口商品主要产销国别(地区)总值

Value of Imports and Exports by Main Producer and Sales Countries (Regions)

(Changsha Customs Statistics)

单位:万美元

国家(地区)	1996年		1997年		比上年(+、-)%	
	进口	出口	进口	出口	进口	出口
合计	47225	129074	44649	144796	-5.5	12.2
香港	799	25334	552	28298	-30.9	11.7
日本	6641	17625	4373	14685	-34.2	-16.7
菲律宾	126	2630	47	1037	-62.7	-60.6
新加坡	333	4596	427	15031	28.2	227.0
韩国	6398	10917	7378	9665	15.3	-11.5
台湾省	4398	1979	3134	2313	-28.7	16.9
英国	1836	2686	896	2724	-51.2	1.4
德国	2602	5421	2367	7156	-9.0	32.0
法国	492	1230	1590	1277	223.2	3.8
意大利	1562	1737	386	1840	-75.3	5.9
荷兰	115	5225	1115	6585	869.6	26.0
俄罗斯	807	732	691	1556	-14.4	112.6
加拿大	996	1642	960	1964	-3.6	19.6
美国	6232	13800	3205	15494	-48.6	12.3
澳大利亚	2241	1572	3615	1712	61.3	8.9
沙特阿拉伯		1379		1045		-24.2
阿联酋		1382		1502		15.2
比利时	141	692	25	782	-82.3	13.1
西班牙	54	755	73	951	35.2	26.0
马来西亚	268	2034	346	1845	29.1	-9.3

14—22 长沙海关进出口商品机电电子产品情况

Import and Export Value of Machinery and eletron Commodities

(Changsha Custcoms Statistics)

单位:万美元

商 品 名 称	1996年		1997年		比上年(+、-)%	
	进 口	出 口	进 口	出 口	进 口	出 口
机电产品	19966	13056	23767	21780	19.0	66.8
#金属制品(不包括来料加工装配)	350	4751	158	7898	-54.9	66.2
机电仪器产品及设备(不包括来料加工装配)	19553	8220	23539	13422	20.4	63.3
#机械及设备	11358	3097	9248	4502	-18.6	45.4
电器及电子产品	6902	4173	11300	6638	63.7	59.1
运输工具	239	509	1656	1366	592.9	168.4
仪器仪表	1000	211	1142	639	14.2	202.8
其他	54	230	193	227	257.4	-1.3
来料加工装配出口产品	63	85	71	461	12.7	442.4

14—23 长沙海关进出口商品贸易方式

Value of Imports and Exports by Trade ways (Changsha Customs Statistics)

单位:万美元

国 家 (地区)	1996年		1997年		比上年(+、-)%	
	进 口	出 口	进 口	出 口	进 口	出 口
一般贸易	20389	106876	24284	127191	19.1	19.0
国家间、国际组织无偿援助和赠送的物资	12	30	4	18	-66.7	-40.0
华侨、港、澳同胞、外籍华人捐赠物资	14		1		-92.9	
补偿贸易	64	306		1294		322.9
来料加工装配贸易	3940	4551	3763	5201	-4.5	14.3
进料加工贸易	6612	17064	9230	10900	39.6	-36.1
寄售、代销贸易						
边境小额贸易(边民互市贸易除外)						
来料加工装配进口的设备						
对外承包工程货物				4		
租赁贸易						
外商投资企业作为投资进口的设备、物品	15806		7156		-54.7	
出料加工贸易			1			
易货贸易	84	126		49		-61.1
免税外汇商品	81		34		-58.0	
保税仓库进出境货物(95年增加)	134	121	136	138	1.5	14.0
其它贸易	89		41		-53.9	

14—24 长沙海关主要出口商品总值

Major Exports Commodities in Value (Changsha Customs Statistics)

单位:万美元

商品名称	1995年	1996年	1997年
合计	112570.04	98887.92	113020.38
活猪	5507.46	5298.11	5920.73
鲜、冻猪肉	1408.27	1014.29	1929.12
猪鬃	405.81	339.47	453.03
肠衣	855.23	921.90	564.10
茶叶	1711.12	2139.21	2404.36
大米			1751.56
药材	204.22	146.09	151.46
植物榨油后的剩余物	147.49	424.64	44.05
纸烟	8890.73	10108.35	410.21
氧化锑	2364.00	1827.95	1381.26
仲钨酸铵	1476.33	744.76	738.14
柠檬酸盐和酯	1548.55	798.58	1132.81
医药品	3011.07	2368.85	3524.65
烟花爆竹	3639.67	4902.88	5711.69
橡胶及其制品	579.17	821.09	790.44
木制餐具及厨房用具	705.23	576.65	635.11
棉机织物	6277.26	2614.26	3145.67
亚麻及苎麻机织物	3195.23	2454.71	2575.83
合成短纤与棉混纺机织物	1587.55	731.34	1081.23
人造纤维短纤机织物	759.27	357.45	214.92
服装及衣着附件	15554.51	12638.71	13700.72
其中:皮革制服装	2617.35	1619.54	2079.36
织物制服装	11028.62	9594.15	9985.38
棉浴巾	637.90	947.92	1103.10
鞋类	5223.34	3360.16	3252.16
其中:皮面鞋	1055.85	443.43	297.53
家用陶瓷器皿	7358.25	5960.95	6880.06
硅锰铁	505.59	983.95	1047.67
钢铁制品	2904.77	2064.19	2867.73
未锻造的铅	4290.99	6175.59	3481.52
未锻造的锌及锌合金	3323.55	5940.44	22991.35
未锻造的锡及锡合金	1425.19	1235.42	937.40
未锻造的锑	721.28	117.09	
未锻造的锰	3449.94	2938.28	4039.77
手用或机用工具	4770.75	4689.90	4266.20
轴承	871.49	859.49	901.16
录音机,收录机及音响	1452.09	112.03	118.99
电容器	466.96	140.76	22.56
通断及保护电路装置	637.98	475.34	487.37

14—25 长沙海关主要进口商品总值

Major Imports Commodities in Value (Changsha Customs Statistics)

单位:万美元

商品名称	1995年	1996年	1997年
合计	43456.12	19376.45	20107.89
食用植物油(包括棕榈油)	809.86	1323.97	1378.86
饲料用鱼粉	691.17	954.09	2066.15
铁矿砂	2374.84	2472.60	4878.26
成品油	120.71	1032.75	965.32
医药品	408.82	43.59	47.36
肥料	4128.43	1552.82	2394.99
天然橡胶	587.05	359.43	238.19
纸及纸板	1019.07	689.28	314.55
二醋酸纤维丝束	2190.10	2066.31	1282.97
涂覆或浸渍塑料的机织物	192.42	82.12	36.16
钢材	1118.45	1528.17	1268.66
建筑及采矿用机械	588.49	82.78	10.39
食品加工机械	381.57	1238.80	238.49
印刷、装订机械	966.12	731.04	65.60
纺织机械	6971.10	316.25	111.98
工业用缝纫机	114.16	30.72	4.42
金属轧机	77.05	27.28	169.51
金属加工机床	2511.20	2210.82	1206.93
橡胶或塑料加工机械	822.68	758.17	738.75
烟草加工机械	3780.23	514.18	820.69
型模及金属铸造用型箱	318.99	108.48	310.66
电动机及发电机	1507.72	180.15	130.57
有线电话电报设备	8755.90	452.23	894.18
彩色显像管	526.32	102.14	136.54
汽车及汽车底盘	1760.90	86.76	17.58
医疗仪器及器械	732.77	431.52	380.10

14—26 长沙海关进出口商品经营单位情况

Import and Expert Value by Manage Unit ((Changsha Customs Statistics)

单位:万美元

	进出口总值	进口	出口	总值比上年±%
总计	189445	44649	144796	7.5
长沙地区	126636	30422	96214	-4.1
株洲地区	31772	2345	29427	80.3
湘潭地区	8797	4029	4768	19.8
衡阳地区	4643	1139	3504	23.8
邵阳地区	1054	72	982	-4.9
岳阳地区	5021	4059	962	24.6
常德地区	2931	596	2335	60.4
张家界地区	74	50	24	-79.9
益阳地区	1445	117	1328	71.4
郴州地区	1537	67	1470	64.9
娄底地区	3048	1496	1552	-38.7
永州地区	470	156	314	11.9
怀化地区	819	99	720	-51.1
湘西自治州	1180		1180	133.2
其它地区	18	2	16	

注:"其它地区"指名称不详的进出口。

14—27 利 用 外 资 概 况

Utilization of Foreign Capital

项目单位:个

金额单位:万美元

项　　目	1995 年	1996 年	1997 年
一、利用外资签订合同项目	726	729	1080
对外借款	15	11	21
外商直接投资	574	437	407
外商其他投资	137	281	652
二、协议利用外资合同金额	174427	93670	129295
对外借款	37000	38000	40200
外商直接投资额	135462	46893	86013
外商其他投资额	1965	8777	3082
三、实际利用外资金额	87104	112530	135777
对外借款	37000	38000	40200
外商直接投资额	48802	70344	91702
外商其他投资额	1302	4186	3875

14—28 外商直接投资签订合同情况(分国别、地区)(1997 年)

Basic Statisics on Signed Contracts of Foreign Direct Investment

项目单位:个

金额单位:万美元

国别(地区)	合　计			合资经营			合作经营			独资经营		
	项目(合同)个数	合同外资金额	实际外资金额	项目(合同)个数	合同外资金额	实际外资金额	项目(合同)个数	合同外资金额	实际外资金额	项目(合同)个数	合同外资金额	实际外资金额
总　　计	407	86013	91702	167	24536	47460	57	35186	19208	183	26291	25034
香港(地区)	210	35950	42470	87	8480	22496	27	13211	7198	96	14259	12776
澳门(地区)	9	2338	1277	2	19	692	3	1499	78	4	820	507
台湾(地区)	74	6750	10688	29	2287	2522	4	1932	2201	41	2531	5965
日　　本	8	2020	3651	3	1848	3302			139	5	172	210
泰　　国	2	131	958	1	13	102	1	118	135			721
新 加 坡	13	2290	5627	8	859	5205	1	5	100	4	1426	322
加 拿 大	10	1425	809	5	166	395	1	200	314	4	1059	100
美　　国	30	6303	5100	15	1581	1371	5	2390	966	10	2332	2763
澳大利亚	5	1801	504	1	29	170	1	1000	174	3	772	160
马来西亚	8	2554	2280	1	983	2223	1	325		6	1246	57
英　　国	1	12	723	1	12				723			
韩　　国	6	2037	7182	3	1986	6986			195	3	51	1
荷　　兰	2	134	108	2	134	108						
维尔京群岛	16	18221	7513	1	2386	71	12	14376	6145	3	1459	1297

14—29 对外承包工程、劳务合作和设计咨询

Contracted Projects 、Labor Service Cooperation，
Designs and Advisory Service with Forgegn Countries

项　目	单 位	1995 年	1996 年	1997 年
对外承包工程、劳务合作和设计咨询合同	个	86	110	322
对外承包工程、劳务合作和设计咨询合同金额	万美元	4092	13900	22646
实际完成营业额	万美元	3451	7288	8333
年末在外人数	人	1102	1765	2584
全年派出人次	人次	515	1229	1630

14—30 国际技术贸易情况

Statistics on Cooperation With International Economy and Fechnology

项　目	单 位	1995 年	1996 年	1997 年
1. 技术引进合同	个	62	86	90
技术引进合同金额	万美元	21382	22671	22709
2. 技术出口合同	个	35	46	60
技术出口合同金额	万美元	5729	6077	6330

14—31 国际旅游人数和人天数

Foreign Tourists and Foreign Tourist—days

项　目	1995 年	1996 年	1997 年
接待国际旅游人数合计（人次）	177303	228703	301600
1. 外 国 人	71800	101201	122000
2. 华　侨	2883	4665	6100
3. 港澳台同胞	102620	122837	173500
#台　胞	50020	53943	76000
国际旅游人天数合计（人天）	496900	693213	1024245
1. 外 国 人	201200	326754	579357
2. 华　侨	8801	12986	11918
3. 港澳台同胞	286899	353473	432970
#台　胞	140001	144841	183709

14—32 旅游外汇收入

Income of Foreign Exchange Through Tourism

项目	1990年	1995年	1996年	1997年
旅游外汇收入合计(万美元)	1002.32	6499.45	10179.64	14003.93
1.商品性收入	491.95	1520.87	3165.87	3265.82
(1)商品销售收入	444.91	669.44	1964.67	2041.03
(2)饮食销售收入	47.04	851.43	1201.20	1224.79
2.劳务性收入	510.37	4978.58	7013.77	10738.11
(1)旅行社、旅游业务费收入	71.18	440.00	305.39	415.73
(2)宿费	179.54	2092.82	1781.44	1819.05
(3)长途交通费	228.89	1488.37	2717.96	4062.33
#民航	174.58	1345.39	1292.81	2037.46
铁道	53.79	64.99	692.22	812.34
公路	0.52	77.99	213.77	507.01
(4)市内交通费	15.17	194.99	183.23	352.78
(5)邮政电讯费	14.21	422.46	692.22	958.41
(6)文化娱乐费	0.40	129.99	692.21	1021.67
(7)其他	0.98	209.95	641.32	2108.14

注:1996年长途交通费中含轮船费519.16万美元。

14—33 接待外国人按国别分组

Foreign Tourists Arrived by Countries

单位:人次

国别	1990年	1995年	1996年	1997年
外国人合计	16544	71800	101201	122000
#日本	6545	16789	23739	20848
菲律宾	76	762	931	1260
新加坡	793	6692	11131	6510
泰国	224	1028	1694	1754
印度尼西亚	68	1247	2407	1205
美国	2084	13425	14372	16229
加拿大	639	1934	3351	5974
德国	1414	4172	3134	2515
英国	1163	2566	3301	4346
法国	331	1182	2487	2618
意大利	237	936	2307	2186
俄罗斯	141	384	2022	6947
澳大利亚	449	1468	4016	8862
新西兰	142	451	766	2013
其他	2238	18764	25543	38733

14—34　接待境外游客人数按地区分

Foreign Tourists by Prefecture

单位:人次

地　　区	1996年	1997年	1997年比1996年±　%
合　计	228703	301631	31.9
长沙市	149910	194664	29.8
株洲市	2726	1678	－93.9
湘潭市	1215	1218	0.2
衡阳市	1748	7474	327.6
邵阳市	121	335	176.9
岳阳市	33439	36290	8.5
常德市	4443	4060	－8.6
益阳市	2778	296	
郴州市	800	13935	1641.9
张家界	22876	38892	70.0
娄底地区	2806	401	
永州市	1531	973	－36.4
怀化市	2398	294	
湘西自治州	1912	1121	－41.4

十五、教育和科技

EDUCATION AND SCIENCE

15—1 各级学校单位数及教职工人数

Schools and School Staff by Level of School

年份	普通高等学校	普通中等专业学校	职业中学	技工学校	普通中学	普通小学（万所）	特殊教育学校	幼儿园
一、单位数(所)								
1995	49	150	567	161	4863	4.41	54	2226
1996	48	157	572	166	4722	4.23	48	2806
1997	48	164	613	166	4559	4.04	53	3396
二、教职工(万人)								
1995	3.95	2.29	2.01	1.22	21.77	31.79	932(人)	5.34
1996	3.95	2.45	2.14	1.23	22.60	31.85	1017(人)	5.18
1997	3.89	2.55	2.33	1.17	23.28	31.89	3888(人)	4.90
三、专任教师(万人)								
1995	1.53	1.06	1.39	0.59	17.91	29.80	642(人)	4.52
1996	1.57	1.16	1.49	0.60	18.71	29.85	676(人)	4.39
1997	1.59	1.23	1.64	0.62	19.48	29.95	803(人)	4.32

注：本表高等学校包括经省教委批准但未经国家教委批准而实际在进行教学的高等学校(含分校)。

15—2 各级学校在校学生、招生数及毕业生数

Student Enrollment, New Student Enrollment and Graduates by Level of School

单位：万人

年份	普通高等学校	普通中等专业学校	职业中学	技工学校	普通中学	高中	初中	普通小学	特殊教育学校(人)	幼儿园
一、在校学生										
1995	13.04	18.61	19.93	8.50	285.41	38.73	246.68	736.65	6819	131.60
1996	13.57	21.25	21.16	8.31	305.22	40.87	264.35	765.91	6725	117.27
1997	14.37	23.73	23.17	6.99	323.24	43.92	279.31	787.13	9304	94.80
二、招生数										
1995	4.06	6.63	8.75	3.78	111.17	15.05	96.12	137.63	2239	122.71
1996	4.21	7.13	9.49	3.40	113.84	16.02	97.82	141.55	1557	111.84
1997	4.51	8.24	10.40	2.89	119.04	17.20	101.84	128.76	2182	91.14
三、毕业生										
199	3.29	3.30	4.78	3.50	71.77	10.70	61.07	106.67	317	
1996	3.64	4.46	5.50	3.58	77.03	10.79	66.24	105.13	700	
1997	3.64	5.70	5.59	3.78	87.07	11.33	75.74	106.86	961	

15—3 研　　究　　生

Postgraduats

单位:人

年　份	招生数	毕业生数	在学人数	年　份	招生数	毕业生数	在学人数
1980	77		347	1991	687	783	2035
1985	1104	296	2016	1992	734	543	2168
1986	950	377	2583	1993	911	668	2357
1987	874	666	2771	1994	1209	630	2864
1988	769	1067	2538	1995	1209	710	3307
1989	600	862	2311	1996	1400	876	3775
1990	705	812	2165	1997	1383	1087	4027

15—4 普通高等学校分科在校学生、招生数及毕业生数

Student Enrollment, New Student Enrollment and Graduates of General Institutions of Higher Learning by Field of Study

单位:人

项目类别	在校学生		招收学生人数		毕业生人数	
	1996年	1997年	1996年	1997年	1996年	1997年
合　　计	135709	143654	42089	45111	36416	36381
哲　　学	108	107	20	30	18	32
经 济 学	20246	20997	6368	5823	5046	5445
法　　学	3738	4380	1267	1657	1108	1010
教 育 学	5475	5689	1893	1818	1582	1600
文　　学	22416	23804	7584	7415	6554	6042
历 史 学	2108	2061	608	660	692	567
理　　学	15833	16671	4873	5440	4647	4555
工　　学	50153	53763	15172	17489	13028	13364
农　　学	5190	5133	1450	1734	1527	1401
医　　学	10442	11049	2854	3045	2214	2365

15—5 普通中等专业学校分科在校学生、招生及毕业生人数

Student Enrollment, New Student Enrollment and Graduates of General Specialized Secondary Schools by Field of Study

单位：人

年份	合计	中等技术学校	工业	农业	林业	医药
一、在校学生						
1995	186108	150986	58698	29716	1631	20233
1996	212467	174840	70212	34065	1824	21722
1997	237270	198017	81824	37816	2138	23336
二、招生数						
1995	66337	52220	19769	10393	542	6520
1996	71324	56984	22572	9945	658	6929
1997	82375	67733	27514	11553	792	7537
三、毕业生						
1995	32999	21919	7996	3730	294	4072
1996	44633	33443	11399	5484	467	5399
1997	56967	43982	15426	7914	477	5822

年份	财经	政法	体育	艺术	其他	中等师范学校
一、在校学生						
1995	28978	3085	1180	2360	5105	35122
1996	30769	4624	1306	2823	7495	37627
1997	32376	6052	1731	3505	9239	39253
二、招生数						
1995	9970	1135	383	772	2736	14114
1996	9760	2213	498	996	3413	14340
1997	12013	2545	730	1561	3488	14642
三、毕业生						
1995	4099	500	155	238	835	11080
1996	7863	976	337	515	1003	11190
1997	10454	1103	291	863	1632	12985

15—6 普通中学、小学按城乡和主办部门分组的情况(1997年)

Basic Statistics on General Secondary Schools, Primary Schools by Urban and Rural Areas and by Department

单位:人

类别	合计	按城乡分			按主办部门分	
		城市	县镇	农村	教育部门和集体办	其他部门和民办
一、普通中学						
学校(所)	4559	595	1385	2579	4150	409
教职工	232769	44141	83107	105521	209203	23566
#专任教师	194835	33371	68785	92679	117230	17605
招生数	1190366	160958	413713	615695	1144272	46094
毕业生	870717	136689	294266	439762	829997	40720
在校学生	3232356	456411	1126442	1649503	3104036	128320
普通中学中:高中						
学校(所)	215	15	102	87	191	24
专任教师	31867	9487	16105	6275	28934	2933
招生数	172011	50535	86882	34594	159296	12715
毕业生	113299	31916	57725	23658	105631	7668
在校学生	439249	127422	223880	87947	408083	31166
普通中学中:初中						
学校(所)	3886	373	1085	2428	3597	289
专任教师	162968	23884	52680	86404	148296	14672
招生数	1018355	110423	326831	581101	984976	33379
毕业生	757418	104773	236541	416104	724366	33052
在校学生	2793107	328989	902562	1561556	2695953	97154
二、小学						
学校(所)	40403	1651	10783	27969	39661	722
教职工	318937	41105	97678	180154	239578	79359
#专任教师	299453	36658	92238	170557	223837	75616
招生数	1287597	127155	382436	778006	1241399	46198
毕业生	1068587	104947	291134	672506	1035039	33548
在校学生	7871345	781980	2364062	4725303	7602701	268644

15—7 普通高等学校、中等专业学校教职工

Staff and Workers in General Institutions of Higher Learning and Specialized Secondary Shools

单位:人

	高等学校			中等专业学校		
	1995 年	1996 年	1997 年	1995 年	1996 年	1997 年
教职工	39519	39456	38783	22869	24454	25463
#校部教职工	32108	32406	32811	20944	22598	23529
#专任教师	15307	15683	15894	10559	11618	12300
教辅人员	4247	4315	4212	2276	2414	2309
行政人员	6398	6418	6686	4232	4443	4727
工勤人员	6156	5990	6019	3877	4123	4193

15—8 普通高等学校分科专任教师(1997 年)

Full-Time Teachers of General Institutions of Higher Learning by Field of Study

单位:人

	合计	正高级	副高级	中级	初级	无职称
总计	15894	1170	4788	6036	2899	1001
哲学	507	30	151	217	83	26
经济学	1409	94	353	590	305	67
法学	303	16	73	127	64	23
教育学	912	21	190	424	212	65
文学	2882	168	675	1076	721	242
历史学	280	23	93	115	36	13
理学	3335	215	1212	1203	543	162
工学	4464	398	1425	1675	717	249
农学	619	73	233	222	57	34
医学	1183	132	383	387	161	120

15—9 各类普通中等专业学校专任教师

Full-Time Teachers of General Specialized Secondary Schools by Type of School

单位:人

	1995 年	1996 年	1997 年
总计	10559	11618	12300
中等技术学校	8533	9534	10155
工业学校	3769	4383	4662
农业学校	1413	1460	1575
林业学校	102	109	110
医药学校	1160	1225	1234
财经学校	1409	1520	1752
政法学校	105	180	231
体育学校	133	137	182
艺术学校	215	239	229
其他	227	281	180
中等师范学校	2026	2084	2145

15—10 各级学校在校女学生和女教师

Female Students and Teachers by Level of School

类　　别	1995年	1996年	1997年
一、女学生(万人)	500.38	526.62	549.53
普通高等学校	4.10	4.45	4.90
普通中等专业学校	8.14	9.85	11.92
普通中学	126.28	135.88	144.40
职业中学	9.95	10.26	11.22
普通小学	351.91	366.18	377.09
二、女学生占全部学生%	46.61	46.72	46.90
普通高等学校	31.44	32.79	34.09
普通中等专业学校	43.75	46.35	50.25
普通中学	44.25	44.52	44.67
职业中学	49.93	48.49	48.41
普通小学	47.77	47.81	47.91
三、女教师(万人)	20.59	21.35	22.14
普通高等学校	0.45	0.47	0.50
普通中等专业学校	0.39	0.44	0.48
普通中学	5.54	5.96	6.45
职业中学	0.45	0.52	0.59
普通小学	13.76	13.96	14.12
四、女教师占全部教师%	39.83	40.45	41.09
普通高等学校	29.57	29.94	31.57
普通中等专业学校	37.22	37.93	38.68
普通中学	30.91	31.85	33.13
职业中学	32.21	34.90	35.83
普通小学	46.18	46.77	47.17

15—11 平均每万人口中在校学生

Student Enrollment Per 10,000 Population

年　份	各类普通学校在校学生占全省人口%	平均每万人口中在校学生(人)			占各类学校在校学生总计%		
		普通高等学校学生	中等学校学生	普通小学学生	普通高等学校学生	中等学校学生	普通小学学生
1995	16.9	20.6	512.0	1164.2	1.2	30.2	68.6
1996	17.5	21.1	540.8	1191.5	1.2	30.8	68.0
1997	18.1	22.2	572.5	1217.5	1.2	31.6	67.2

注:1. 本表未包括技工学校在校学生。

2. 各类普通学校在校学生数包括普通高校、普通中专、职业中学、普通中小学的在校学生数。

15—12 民办（私立）学校情况

Statistics on Private Schools

单位:人

项目	单位	1996年	1997年	项目	单位	1996年	1997年
普通中学				普通小学			
学校数	所	72	65	学校数	所	49	32
教职工数	人	1257	1101	教职工数	人	502	951
专任教师数	人	850	731	专任教师数	人	282	597
毕业生数	人	3594	3343	毕业生数	人	202	365
招生数	人	6505	7730	招生数	人	2813	1641
在校学生数	人	16407	16016	在校学生数	人	5790	8692

15—13 各类学校代课教师及临时工人数

rovisional Teachers and Temporay Workers by Type of School

单位:人

项目	1996年	1997年	项目	1996年	1997年
普通中学			技工学校		
代课教师	7557	7669	兼职教师	899	1108
临时工	2936	2906	临时工	730	686
兼任教师	366	542			
职业中学			普通小学		
代课教师	653	722	代课教师	38306	38782
临时工	664	642	临时工	4176	4384
兼任教师	1601	1386	兼任教师	118	495

15—14 各类成人学历教育在校学生

Student Enrollment in Adult Education Schools by Type of School

单位:万人

项目	1996年	1997年	项目	1996年	1997年
			干部中专	0.66	0.80
总计	72.16	81.06	农民中专	1.86	1.66
一、成人高等教育	13.34	13.67	教师进修	4.62	3.56
1.广播电视大学	3.30	3.23	函授中专	0.53	0.22
2.职工大学	1.56	1.71	2.成人中学	2.54	4.97
3.管理干部学院	0.73	0.70	职工中学	0.92	1.01
4.教育学院	1.17	1.26	农民中学	1.62	3.96
5.函授干部专修、夜大学	6.58	6.77	三、成人初等教育	40.72	45.88
二、成人中等教育	18.1	21.51	1.职工初等学校	0.41	0.59
1.中等专业学校	15.56	16.54	2.农民初等学校	40.31	45.29
广播电视中专	3.33	5.37	小学班	13.81	22.38
职工中专	4.56	4.93	扫盲班	26.50	22.91

15—15 平均每一教职工负担学生

Student / Staff and Worker Ratio

单位:人

年份	平均每一教职工负担的学生				平均每一专任教师负担的学生			
	普通高等学校	普通中等专业学校	普通中学	普通小学	普通高等学校	普通中等专业学校	普通中学	普通小学
1995	3.3	8.1	13.1	23.2	8.5	17.6	15.9	24.7
1996	3.4	8.7	13.5	24.0	8.6	18.3	16.3	25.7
1997	3.7	9.3	13.9	24.7	9.0	19.3	16.6	26.3

15—16 初中和小学毕业生升学率

Percentage of Graduates of Junior Middle Schools and Primary Schools Entering Higher Level Schools

年份	初中			小学		
	毕业生(万人)	高级中等学校招生数(万人)	升学率(%)	毕业生(万人)	初级中等学校招生数(万人)	升学率(%)
1995	61.32	29.24	47.7	106.67	96.66	90.6
1996	66.46	35.21	53.0	105.13	98.38	93.6
1997	76.03	37.98	50.0	106.86	102.26	95.7

注:高级中等学校招生数包括中专招收初中毕业生数、普通高中和农、职业高中的招生数、技工学校的招生数;初级中等学校招生数包括普通初中和农、职业初中招生数。初中毕业生包括普通初中和农、职业初中毕业生。

15—17 小学学龄儿童入学率

Percentage of School－Age Children Enrolled

单位:万人

年份	学龄儿童	已入学学龄儿童	入学率(%)
1995	705.30	691.49	98.0
1996	729.68	716.66	98.2
1997	754.60	743.69	98.6

15—18 幼儿园基本情况

Basic Statistics on Kindergartens

年份	园数(所)	班数(个)	幼儿数(万人)	教职工数(万人)	#教师
1995	2226	42809	131.60	5.34	4.52
1996	2806	41175	117.27	5.18	4.39
1997	3396	38957	94.80	4.90	4.16

15—19 成 人 其 他 教 育

Statistics on Other Adult Education

单位:万人

项　　目	在校学生		结业学生	
	1996年	1997年	1996年	1997年
一、高等学校	1.14	0.93	6.13	3.15
1.证书教育	0.24	0.12	0.45	0.14
单科班	0.13		0.09	
专业证书班	0.11	0.12	0.36	0.14
2.岗位培训	0.70	0.43	4.90	2.33
资格培训	0.35	0.12	1.83	0.65
适应培训	0.35	0.31	3.07	1.68
3.大学后继续教育	0.04	0.17	0.15	0.32
4.其　　他	0.16	0.21	0.63	0.36
二、中等学校	5.99	7.59	6.41	14.73
1.单科班	0.12	0.34	0.12	0.34
2.专业证书班	0.43	0.58	0.62	0.64
3.岗位培训	3.63	3.18	4.46	6.77
资格培训班	1.97	1.57	2.61	2.54
适应培训班	1.58	1.50	1.73	3.95
工人技术培训班	0.08	0.12	0.12	0.27
4.农村技术培训班	0.08	0.52	0.23	5.63
5.文化补习班	0.12	0.18	0.15	0.17
6.其　　他	1.61	2.79	0.83	1.19
三、成人技术培训学校	198.23	207.71	209.91	294.52
1.职工技术培训学校	13.86	10.61	19.78	13.85
2.农民技术培训学校	184.37	197.10	190.13	280.67
#县　办	1.24	1.05	0.87	0.86

15—20 特殊教育学校基本情况(1997年)

Basic Statistics on Schools for Special Education

单位:人

年　　份	学校数(所)	毕业生	招生数	在校学生	教职工	#专任教师
总　　计	53	961	2182	9304	3888	803
其中:盲聋哑学校	49	479	1177	4080	1078	710
弱智儿童学校	4	482	1005	5224	2810	93

15—21 县级以上政府部门科研与科技开发机构、人员及经费(1997年)

Units, Personnel and Funds of Research, Development Institutions Attached to Local Governments at County Level and Above

项目	机构(个)	职工(人)	#科学家工程师	经费收入总额(万元)	#政府拨款	经费支出总额(万元)	#劳务费
一、自然科学	180	26676	8304	184491	35234	166667	26869
中央单位	22	9902	3781	99482	17397	86344	13326
地方单位	158	16774	4523	85009	17837	80323	13543
二、社会科学(地方)	2	234	139	938	738	827	321
三、科技情报与文献机构	13	253	137	636	435	553	260

15—22 各类专业技术人员

Various Specialized Technical Personnel

单位:人

项目	1996年	国有	集体	1997年	国有	集体
总计	1058329	1025584	32745	1116432	1082796	33636
一、自然科学	855722	838728	16994	910510	892974	17536
中央	130276	130276		138093	138093	
地方	725446	708452	16994	772417	754881	17536
二、社会及人文科学	202607	186856	15751	205922	189822	16100
地方	202607	186856	15751	205922	189822	16100

注:此表未包括国家机关与人民团体中的专业技术人员;中央在湘单位系估计数。

15—23 大中型工业企业科技活动情况(1997年)

项目类别	从事技术开发活动人员(人)	技术开发项目数(个)	技术开发经费筹集额(万元)	技术开发经费使用额(万元)	企业办科技机构(个)	技术改造经费支出(万元)
总计	53789	2196	113820	102389	407	308642
一、按经济类型分组						
国有经济	50293	2008	107369	96265	360	286021
集体经济	1090	87	1535	1384	14	1434
联营经济						
股份制经济	1868	96	4696	4520	30	19221
中外合资经济	492	3	43	43	1	1909
中外合作经济	29		117	117	1	57
港澳台与大陆合资经济	17	2	60	60	1	
二、按企业规模分:						
大型	39566	1497	85006	79029	203	262390
中型	14223	699	28814	23360	204	46252
三、按工业行业分:						
采掘业	3044	55	3833	3288	16	4798
制造业	48942	2011	107054	95711	383	289838
电力、煤气及水的生产供应业	1803	130	2933	3390	8	14006

15—24 大中型工业企业科技活动情况(1997 年度)

Basic Statistics for Scientific and Technogical Activities of Large and Medium Industrial Enterprises

行业	从事技术开发活动人员(人)	技术开发项目数(个)	技术开发经费筹集额(万元)	技术开发经费使用额(万元)	企业办科技机构(个)	技术改造经费支出(万元)
总计	53789	2196	113820	102389	407	308642
煤炭采选业	2057	28	3302	2792	6	818
黑色金属矿采选业	17	2	30	30		518
有色金属矿采选业	698	15	452	417	6	2800
非金属矿采选业	272	10	49	49	3	602
木材及竹材采运业					1	60
食品加工业	181	24	1410	1133	8	1665
食品制造业	61	5	170	170	2	141
饮料制造业	691	27	1092	1218	11	630
烟草加工业	678	27	1887	1886	14	12618
纺织业	1430	77	5494	892	18	1418
服装及其他纤维制品制造业	19	9	109	109	1	10985
皮革、毛皮、羽绒及其制品业	50	2	32	32	2	
木材加工及竹、藤、棕、草制品业	54	6	259	179	2	25
造纸及纸制品业	706	8	352	413	11	480
印刷业						106
石油加工及炼焦业	1393	109	8612	8036	12	80764
化学原料及化学制品制造业	2729	108	9929	12265	48	16755
医药制造业	656	51	4634	1949	19	3734
化学纤维制造业	347	10	4014	4014	3	17468
橡胶制品业	313	24	34	34	2	13
塑料制品业	18	1	40	40		
非金属矿物制品业	1813	200	1421	1284	27	4307
黑色金属冶炼及压延加工业	2076	117	2763	2667	7	59623
有色金属冶炼及压延加工业	3665	93	3001	2948	10	26404
金属制品业	304	13	86	85	3	856
普通机械制造业	9093	324	12346	12072	55	10790
专用设备制造业	4281	167	8700	8780	35	3138
交通运输设备制造业	8067	242	23724	18985	45	24024
电气机械及器材制造业	2868	159	3671	3645	20	4361
电子及通信设备制造业	2817	103	6654	6186	13	3683
仪器仪表及文化、办公用机械制造	1025	24	1084	1171	5	3194
其他制造	3607	81	5536	5518	10	2657
电力、蒸汽、热水的生产和供应	1803	130	2933	3390	8	13415
自来水的生产和供应业						590

注:1997 年全省大中型工业企业 723 家。

15—25 地方国有单位各行业自然科学技术人员(1997年)

Natural Scientific and Technical Personnel in Local State－Owned Units by Sector

单位:人

行业	自然科学技术人员	工程技术人员	农业技术人员	科学研究人员	卫生技术人员	教学人员
合计	754881	129268	20159	5256	112521	487677
农林牧渔水利	38920	14008	18482	101	1521	4808
工业	63850	49777	70	9	6288	7706
地质勘探	8732	7994	114		145	479
建筑业	9144	7828	1		858	457
运输邮电	8542	6873	36	99	618	916
商业、饮食业、物资供销	5910	4019	342	24	1160	365
房地产、公用、服务业	18449	14366	302	53	2308	1420
卫生、体育、福利	98467	1012	26	145	96050	1234
教育、文化	475429	3569	171	1183	1761	468745
科研和技术服务	10918	6179	480	3601	426	232
金融保险	118	89	6	2	4	17
机关团体						
其他	16402	13554	129	39	1382	1298
在合计中:						
高级职称	30924	5630	886	1222	4598	18588
中级职称	243867	33923	5303	2398	33506	168737

15—26 地方集体单位各行业自然科学技术人员(1997年)

Natural Scientific and Technical Personnel in Local Collective－Owned Units by Sector

单位:人

行业	自然科学技术人员	工程技术人员	农业技术人员	科学研究人员	卫生技术人员	教学人员
合计	17536	8358	495	4	7701	978
农林牧渔水利	464	90	364	2	3	5
工业、运输、建筑业	5997	5633	10		289	65
商业	396	162	83		118	33
文化教育卫生	7801	78	1		6990	732
其他	2878	2395	37	2	301	143
合计中:女性	4406	1508	48	1	2617	232

15—27 地方国有单位各行业社会、人文科学专业人员(1997年)

Specialized Personnel Engaged in Society and Humane Studies in Local State—Owned

单位:人

行业	社会、人文科学专业人员	民航飞行、船舶技术人员	经济、会计、统计、海关人员	翻译、图书、档案、文博、新闻出版、播音人员	工艺美术体育人员	律师公证人员	政工人员
合计	189822	95	143479	12807	5601	980	26860
农林牧渔水利	13539		10752	249	53	27	2458
工业	45482	1	34644	1436	344	32	9025
地质勘探	2783		1930	166	2	3	682
建筑业	5387		4149	94	29	5	1110
运输邮电	13736	85	10908	239	12	15	2477
商业、饮食业、物资供销	35389	1	32034	267	130	11	2946
房地产、公用、服务业	23188		17692	803	145	529	4019
卫生、体育、福利	5874	7	4375	471	768	4	249
教育、文化	18748		6373	7910	3785	13	667
科研和技术服务	2740		1905	495	122	11	207
金融保险	1213		1166	23	1		23
机关团体							
其他	21743	1	17551	654	210	330	2997

15—28 地方集体单位各行业社会、人文科学专业人员

Specialized Personnel Engaged in Society and Humane Studies in Local Collective—Owned Units by Sector

单位:人

行业	1995年	1996年	1997年
合计	18403	15751	16100
农林牧渔水利	326	217	162
工业、建筑、运输业	12131	6680	5945
商业	3789	2112	2342
文化、教育、卫生	482	625	683
其他	1675	6117	6968
合计中:女性	7316	6628	7203

15—29 自然科学研究获奖成果

Number of Achievements in Natural Scientific Research

单位:项

项目	1995年	1996年	1997年
一、省科技进步奖	329	277	309
二、国家科学技术进步奖	19	29	16
三、国家批准授予的发明奖	6	3	9
四、国家自然科学奖			

15—30 科技成果情况(1997年)

Statistics on Achievements of Science and Technology

单位:项

项目	合计	独立科研机构	大专院校	工矿企业	集体与个体机构	其他
一、项目基本情况						
鉴定项目数	916	356	224	214	92	122
省部登记项目数	604	214	193	168	12	29
省部级奖励项目数	309	92	72	80	6	65
二、项目计划管理情况						
国家计划项目	199	86	70	41	12	2
省部计划项目	248	119	42	87		
计划外项目	157	9	81	40		27
三、成果水平						
国际首创或领先	38	20	18			
国际先进	87	37	38	12		
国内首创或领先	213	101	52	44		16
国内先进	266	56	85	112		13
省部先进						
四、成果应用领域						
工业、交通、邮电、建筑、地质	360	50	2	285		23
农林牧渔水利	88	48	30			10
医药、卫生	46	10	17	12		7
商业、金融、文教	51	12	15	20		4
科学研究和综合技术服务	44	16	13	15		
其它行业	15			10		5

15—31 三种专利申请与批准项数

Three Types of Patent Applications Examined and Certified

单位:项

项目	申请数		批准数	
	1996年	1997年	1996年	1997年
总计	2968	3069	1256	1333
一、按种类分				
发明	460	513	40	66
实用新型	2119	2179	1023	1074
外观设计	389	377	193	193
二、按申请人类别分				
个人	2479	2611	1020	1066
大专院校	44	42	25	26
科研单位	105	46	43	55
工矿企业	319	345	125	167
机关团体	21	25	43	19

15—32 各类技术合同签订及执行情况(1997年)

Statistics on Contracts Signed and Performed

项目	合同数(项)	合同金额(万元)	#技术交易额	实现金额(万元)	#技术交易额
总计	14848	161392	96133	129683	78716
一、技术开发合同	1586	57440	32883	44860	27193
二、技术转让合同	2269	26559	20936	23993	17460
三、技术服务合同	8475	59719	33101	51239	27277
四、技术咨询合同	2518	17674	9213	9591	6786

15—33 各级科技计划项目进入技术市场情况(1997年)

Statistics on Different Levels Scientific Plan Items Put into Technical Markets

单位:项,万元

计划类别 卖方类别	合计		国家、部门计划		省级计划		地、市、县计划	
	项数	金额	项数	金额	项数	金额	项数	金额
合计	1321	38633	128	12024	139	5144	1054	21465
科研机构	129	4833	41	3544	32	661	56	628
大中专院校	88	1842	2	335	29	794	57	713
工业企业	377	14872	67	7490	64	3320	246	4062
技术贸易机构	478	10639	10	205	9	277	459	10157
个人及个人合伙	186	1273	3	40	2	62	181	1171
其他	63	5174	5	410	3	30	55	4734

湖南科学技术出版社

湖南科学技术出版社是湖南省新闻出版局直属的出版社之一。作为一家地方科技出版社，该社设有理工、农业、医卫、管理、科普、综合、对外合作、职教、装帧等九个编辑室，全社现有职工107人，其中具有正高职称的2人，具有副高职称的19人。

建社以来，该社本着"弘扬科学精神，推动科技发展"办社宗旨，推出了一大批高品味、高格调、重实用、讲实效的科技佳作。《杂交水稻育种栽培学》一书荣获我国图书最高奖——首届国家图书奖，在获奖十种技术图书中名列第一;《科学的历程》获95年度中宣部"五个一工程"一本好书奖。建社19年，有近400种图书获国家、省部级优秀图书奖。以引进世界科学名著编辑而成的《第一推动丛书》为代表的一大批畅销书满足了广大读者的需求，产生了显著的社会效益和经济效益。

97—98年，该社继续实施"出精品，夺大奖，创双效"的经营战略，取得了可喜成绩。《九亿农民健康教育读本》再次夺得湖南省宣传部1996年度全省精神文明建设"五个一工程"优秀作品一等奖，中宣部第六届精神文明建设"五个一工程"一本好书奖。《有限元高精度理论》获第八届全国优秀科技图书二等奖。《守望家园》、《爱因斯坦全集》也即将面世。1997年度各项生产计划均超额完成：出版品种总数为515种，其中初版195种，出版总字数5700万字，总印数550万册，发行总码洋9760万元，利润总额比去年增加80%。

目前，我国政府实施"科教兴国"的伟大发展战略，该社决定抓住机遇，为迎接新世纪的曙光，为让科学的理性普照人寰，竭尽全力，再创辉煌。

社长：汪华
地址：湖南省长沙市展览馆路66号
电话：2231182
邮编：410005

岳阳县畜牧水产局

岳阳县地处湘北，北临长江、西跨洞庭，境内湖泊、水库、池塘星罗棋布，河流、沟港纵横交错，水产资源十分丰富。有各种鱼类157种，主要经济鱼类有青、草、鲢、鲤、鲫、鳊、刁、鳜、乌鳢、银鱼、鳗鱼、黄颡鱼等，名贵水产动物有白鳖豚、中华鲟等均有分布，此外龟、鳖、贝类等也较丰富，发展水产具有得天独厚的自然条件。

全县水产技术力量雄厚，现已形成国营中洲渔场为龙头的64个乡镇村级渔场的产业群。全县现有水产技术人员675人，其中中专以上的专业人员40人，中级职称的10人，助理工程师12人。县农科教中心，农广校两所职中每年面向农村培养一大批水产养殖实用人才。1997年全县完成水产品产量3.4万吨。目前，通过加大招商引资力度，增加渔业生产投入，推广名贵鱼养殖和鱼类病害综合防治技术等措施进一步促进全县渔业生产的发展。

十六、文化、体育、卫生

CULTURE, SPORTS, PUBLIC HEALTH

16—1 文化产业机构和人员(1997年)

Cultural Institutions and Personnel

单位:个、人

类　　别	合　　计		文化部门		其他部门	
	机　构	人　员	机　构	人　员	机　构	人　员
总　　计	26058	103713	5347	41012	20711	62701
电影业	5909	15174	839	7793	5070	7381
出版发行业	5700	25754	593	10285	5107	15469
艺术业	206	6637	206	6637		
图书馆业	115	1827	115	1827		
群众文化业	2651	6383	2651	6383		
艺术教育业	7	555	7	555	8092	33239
娱乐业	8250	34680	158	1441		
文艺科研业	2	44	2	44		
文物业	198	2053	195	1946	3	107
其他文化产业	3020	10606	581	4101	2439	6505

16—2 电影业机构和人员(1997年)

Film Institutions and Personnel

单位:个、人

类　　别	合　　计		文化部门		其他部门	
	机　构	人　员	机　构	人　员	机　构	人　员
总　　计	5909	15174	839	7793	5070	7381
电影制片厂	1	473	1	473		
电影发行放映管理机构	275	3283	272	3280	3	3
电影院	355	3170	247	2928	108	242
影剧院	28	840	25	778	3	62
开放礼堂、俱乐部	29	260	1	3	28	257
放映队	4805	6235	244	248	4561	5987
其　他	416	913	49	83	367	830

16—3 电影制片及放映情况

Statistics on Production and Projection of Films

项　　目	单　位	1995年	1996年	1997年
一、摄制电影片	部	6	6	3
#故事片	部	6	6	3
二、电影放映情况				
放映单位	个	6440	5067	5633
放映场数	万场	47.20	42.69	35.20
观众人次	亿人次	1.76	1.44	1.09
放映收入	万元	6435	6222	5617.38
发行收入	万元	2914	2959	2767.61

16—4 艺术业机构和人员

Art Institutions and Personnel

单位:个、人

类别	1996年		1997年	
	机构	人员	机构	人员
总计	216	6764	206	6637
一、艺术表演团体	88	4347	86	4414
1.话剧团	1	96	1	95
2.歌剧、舞剧、歌舞剧团	7	391	7	615
3.歌舞团、轻音乐团	3	334	3	137
4.文工团、文宣队	5	141	7	314
5.戏曲剧团	70	3162	66	3022
6.曲艺、杂技、木偶、皮影团	2	223	2	231
二、艺术表演场所(剧场、影剧院)	103	2282	97	2095
三、艺术创作机构	19	111	18	104
四、艺术展览机构	2	11	4	21
五、其他	4	13	1	3

16—5 出版发行、文物、图书馆、群众文化业机构人员(1997年)

Institutions and Personnel of Publishing, Distribution, Cultural Relics, Library and Mass Culture

单位:个、人

类别	合计		文化部门		其他部门	
	机构	人员	机构	人员	机构	人员
一、出版发行事业	5700	25754	593	10285	5107	15469
1.出版社	15	1231	10	944	5	287
2.书刊印刷厂	14	7434	3	3291	11	4143
3.书　店	119	2667	114	2637	5	30
4.图书发行网点	5548	14046	462	3037	5086	11009
5.其　他	4	376	4	376		
二、文物事业	198	2053	195	1946	3	107
#文物保护管理机构	129	932	129	932		
博物馆	67	1017	64	910	3	107
#综合性的	28	643	28	643		
纪念性的	37	363	34	256	3	107
文物商店	2	104	2	104		
三、图书馆事业	115	1827	115	1827		
四、群众文化事业	2651	6383	2651	6383		
1.群众艺术馆	15	510	15	510		
2.文化馆	124	1834	124	1834		
3.文化站	2512	4039	2512	4039		

注:文物保护管理机构的人员包含文物行政主管机关中文物事业编制的人员。

16—6 图书、杂志、报纸出版情况

Statistics on Books, Magazines and Newspapers Published

年 份	图书			杂志			报纸		
	种 数（种）	总印数（万册）	总印张（亿印张）	种 数（种）	总印数（万册）	总印张（亿印张）	种 数（种）	总印数（万份）	总印张（亿印张）
1995	2357	33677	14.90	208	7768	1.75	63	62425	6.90
1996	2734	39393	16.74	212	7844	1.80	63	63585	7.15
1997	2856	37494	14.92	212	7686	1.83	61	68726	8.58

注：图书种数不包括租型图书。

16—7 广播、电视业情况

Statistics on Broadcasting Stations and Television

项 目	单 位	1997年	项 目	单 位	1997年
一、广播电视系统全部职工	万人	1.97	三、电 视		
二、广 播			电视中心台数	座	28
广播电台数	座	12	电视节目套数	套	31
广播电台节目套数	套	19	平均每周播出时间	时：分	1734：02
平均每日播出时间	时：分	224：45	电视发射台、转播台数	座	664
中、短波发射台、转播台数	座	26	#1千瓦以上	座	46
中、短波发射机功率	部/千瓦	36/578	电视发射机功率	部/千瓦	875/272.86
覆 盖 率	%	78.62	覆 盖 率	%	87.71

16—8 体 育 业 情 况

Statistics on Sports

项 目	单 位	1997年	项 目	单 位	1997年
一、体委系统固定和合同制职工	人	5052	少 年 级	人	1233
#体育运动学校	人	413	八、等级裁判员发展人数	人	2337
业余体校	人	1189	#国家级裁判员	人	
训练基地	人	165	九、打破纪录情况		
公共体育场、馆	人	420	世界纪录	人/次/项	8/56/17
优秀运动队	人	1366	亚洲纪录	人/次/项	8/46/17
二、体育场	个	36	全国纪录	人/次/项	2/2/3
三、体育馆	个	52	十、获奖情况		
四、游泳池、馆	个	110	1. 参加全国比赛获奖		
五、举办县级以上运动会次数	次	2134	金 牌	枚	35.5
六、国家体育锻炼标准达标人数	万人	800.32	银 牌	枚	27
七、等级运动员发展人数	人	3937	铜 牌	枚	33.5
#国际级运动健将	人		2. 参加国际比赛获奖		
国家级运动健将	人		金 牌	枚	12
一 级	人	88	银 牌	枚	5
二 级	人	523	铜 牌	枚	5
三 级	人	2093			

注：1. 体育场、体育馆、游泳池只包括体委系统的。

2. 参加全国比赛指参加全国性的成人竞技比赛。参加国际比赛指参加世界锦标赛、世界杯赛、奥运会、亚洲锦标赛和亚运会，奖牌数包括我省运动员参加国家队集体项目所得的奖牌。

16—9 卫 生 机 构

Health Care Institutions

单位:个

年 份	卫生机构总 计	医 院	#县及县以上 医 院	疗养院、所	门诊部、所
1995	9137	3879	641	12	4417
1996	9031	3423	674	10	178
1997	9177	3349	688	10	134

年 份	专科防治所 、站	卫生防疫站	妇幼保健所 、站	药品检验所 、室	医学科学研究机构	其 他卫生机构
1995	115	151	125	112	4	322
1996	106	166	123	112	7	4906
1997	108	146	123	111	7	5189

16—10 卫 生 工 作 人 员

Personnel in Health Care Institutions

单位:万人

年 份	卫生工作人 员	#卫生技术人员	#医 生	中 医	西医师	西医士	#护师、护士
1995	23.64	19.25	8.46	1.94	4.92	1.56	4.92
1996	24.64	20.22	9.57	2.03	5.76	1.78	5.15
1997	25.08	20.56	10.61	1.93	7.02	1.66	5.33

注:表中“中医”包括中医师、中医士和其他中医;“西医”包括西医师、西医士。中西结合高级医师 1996 年为 223 人,1997 年为 247 人。

16—11 卫 生 机 构 床 位

Hospital Beds in Health Care Institutions

单位:万张

年 份	卫生机构床位总计	医 院	#县及县以上 医 院	疗养院、所	其 他卫生机构	每万人口中拥有医院病床数 (张)
1995	14.95	13.52	9.04	0.28	1.15	21.28
1996	14.44	13.36	9.08	0.27	0.81	20.79
1997	14.44	13.47	9.24	0.23	0.74	20.84

16—12 各类卫生机构、床位和人员(1997年)

Health Care Institutions, Beds and Personnel by Type

类别	机构(个)	床位(张)	卫生工作人员(人)	#卫生技术人员
总计	9177	144550	250829	205576
一、医院	3349	134723	195513	161749
1.县及县以上医院	683	92268	126065	97700
综合医院	488	63018	86421	67391
中医院	115	14258	20411	16492
医学院校附属医院	8	4933	8272	5900
传染病院	3	426	569	398
精神病院	19	4033	3015	2013
结核病院	6	1078	948	661
妇幼保健院	13	988	1888	1440
儿童医院	1	300	549	383
职业病院	2	205	242	163
肿瘤医院	3	946	1153	853
康复医院	5	570	464	340
口腔医院	2	33	267	195
整形医院	1	100	161	130
中西医结合医院	4	533	735	589
其他专科医院	13	847	970	752
2.区、乡(镇)卫生院	2639	41770	68483	63209
3.其他医院	27	685	965	840
二、疗养院、所	10	2325	1518	897
三、门诊部、所	134	1500	2442	2114
四、专科防治所、站	108	3349	3934	3070
五、卫生防疫站	146	40	8971	7122
六、妇幼保健所、站	123	1295	4032	3405
七、药品检验所、室	111		1360	1011
八、医学科学研究机构	7	225	918	556
九、高等医药院、校	5		4202	1227
十、中等医药学校	103	384	5242	2421
十一、其他卫生事业机构(含诊所、医务室、卫生室等)	5081	709	22697	22004

16—13 卫生机构各类卫生人员

dPersonnel in Health Care Institutions by Type of Personnel

单位:人

类　　别	1995 年	1996 年	1997 年
一、卫生工作人员	236447	246382	250573
#卫生技术人员	192526	202245	205576
中医师	13750	13571	13258
西医师	49216	48882	49527
中、西医结合高级医师	349	597	494
护　师	25445	27266	29404
中药师	6087	6537	6839
西药师	4827	5394	5858
检验师	4432	4688	5083
其他技师	3765	4145	4268
中医士	4455	5314	5290
西医士	15603	17831	20634
护　士	23790	24206	23845
助产士	2100	2324	2385
中药剂士	5915	6110	6316
西药剂士	3518	3708	4011
检验士	2917	2991	3129
其他技士	2038	2234	2275
其他中医	1223	1463	747
护理员	3495	3190	2919
中药剂员	3650	3367	3015
西药剂员	1316	1296	1262
检验员	872	960	850
其他初级卫生技术人员	13763	16171	14167
二、平均每万人口中卫生技术人员	30.31	31.46	31.8
#医　生	13.32	13.64	13.9

16—14 农村卫生人员

Health Care Personnel in Rural Areas

单位:人

类　　别	1995 年	1996 年	1997 年
一、乡村医生和卫生员	64121	64423	64019
#乡村医生	47571	47837	47300
二、乡村接生员	40234	38677	38155

16—15 县及县以上医院病床使用情况

Utilization of Hospital Beds at County Level and Above

指标	1995年	1996年	1997年
病床周转率(次)	15.2	16	14.71
病床工作日数(日)	236.5	238	206.89
病床使用率(%)	64.6	65	56.68
出院者平均住院日数(日)	14.8	14	13.53

16—16 医院诊疗人次及入院人数(1997年)

Hospital Patients

类别	诊疗人次（万人次）	门、急诊人次（万人次）	入院人数（万人）	每百诊次的入院人数（人）	每百门、急诊人次的入院人数（人）
总计	10137.40	8625.86	219.90	2.17	2.55
1. 县及县以上医院	4083.86	3667.12	130.92	3.21	3.57
#卫生部门	2491.18	2322.95	107.86	4.33	4.64
工业及其他部门	1569.61	1322.10	22.71	1.45	1.72
集体所有制	23.06	22.07	0.35	1.52	1.59
2. 卫生院	6020.25	4925.56	88.59	1.47	1.80
3. 其他医院	33.30	33.18	0.39	1.17	1.18

16—17 城乡主要疾病死亡构成(1997年)

Death Rate of Major Diseases in Urban and Rural Areas

单位:%

类别	城市			农村		
	合计	男	女	合计	男	女
传染病和寄生虫病	1.89	2.34	1.30	5.62	6.09	5.05
#传染病	1.87	2.30	1.30	5.34	5.76	4.82
#肺结核	1.21	1.51	0.80	3.07	3.41	2.64
肿瘤	20.06	22.11	17.32	11.63	11.80	11.41
#恶性肿瘤	19.52	21.48	16.91	11.47	11.64	11.26
循环系统	44.35	43.52	45.46	31.57	30.93	32.37
#心脏病	20.67	19.40	22.36	14.84	13.80	16.15
脑血管病	20.81	21.51	19.88	13.36	13.81	12.80
呼吸系统	12.13	10.85	13.83	21.71	21.61	21.85
消化系统	3.45	3.40	2.99	4.75	5.22	4.15
泌尿生殖系统	1.52	1.55	1.48	1.50	1.56	1.43
新生儿病	0.63	0.64	0.62	1.35	1.29	1.43
损伤和中毒	8.86	9.71	7.73	15.60	16.10	14.97
内分泌、营养和代谢及免疫疾病	1.51	1.28	1.82	0.72	0.64	0.83
其他	5.60	4.60	7.45	5.55	4.76	6.51

十七、党群、政法和社会福利

PARTY AND MASS, POLITICS AND LAW, SOCIAL WELFARE

17—1 历届省人民代表大会的代表人数

Deputies to Our Province People's Congress Over The Sessions

单位:人

指　标	第一届（1954年）	第二届（1958年）	第三届（1964年）	省革命委员会（1968年）	第五届（1977年）	第六届（1983年）	第七届（1988年）	第八届（1993年）	第九届（1997年）
代表总数	552	552	662	160	1252	988	874	870	763
在代表总数中:									
女代表	36	36	148		274	225	210	191	175
占代表总数%	6.5	6.5	22.4		21.9	22.8	24.0	22.0	22.9
在代表总数中:									
少数民族代表	9	9	57		72	84	78	87	85
占代表总数%	1.6	1.6	8.6		5.8	8.5	8.9	10.0	11.14
在代表总数中:									
中青年代表	399	399	409		966	570	529	587	488
占代表总数%	72.3	72.3	61.8		77.2	57.7	60.5	62.0	64.0

注:1968年省革命委员会召开了全体委员会议,代表人数为委员人数。

17—2 历届省政治协商会议的委员人数

Deputies to Our Province People's Political Consultative Conferences Over The Sessions

单位:人

指　标	第一届（1955年）	第二届（1959年）	第三届（1964年）	第四届（1977年）	第五届（1983年）	第六届（1988年）	第七届（1993年）	第八届（1997年）
委员总数	175	396	398	500	732	703	724	716
在委员总数中:								
中国共产党委员	39	131	134	222	270	280	288	280
占委员总数%	22.3	33.1	33.7	44.4	36.9	39.8	39.8	39.1
在委员总数中:								
少数民族委员	6	15	20	26	38	58	61	70
占委员总数%	3.4	3.8	5.0	5.2	5.2	8.3	8.4	9.8

17—3 工 会 工 作 情 况

Labor Union Work

项　　目	1997年	项　　目	1997年
一、工会组织情况		民主评议领导干部的单位数(个)	6936
工会基层组织个数(万个)	1.95	被评议的领导干部人数(万人)	6.91
基层单位的职工人数(万人)	396	三、职工开展劳动竞赛情况	
#女职工	154	开展劳动竞赛的单位数(个)	4790
基层单位的会员数(万人)	364	参加技术比赛的人数(万人次)	75.00
#女会员	142	参加劳动竞赛的人次数(万人次)	234.00
工会专职工作人员(万人)	2.20	四、职工合理化建议情况	
工会专职干部数(万人)	2.10	提出的建议数(万件)	43.19
#女干部(人)	5800	已采纳的建议数(万件)	21.17
二、职工代表大会情况		已实施(执行)的建议数(万件)	13.91
已建立职工代表大会制的单位数(万个)	1.14	创造价值(亿元)	8.85
召开职工代表大会基层单位数(万个)	1.07	五、工会劳动保护工作情况	
职工代表数(万人)	54.63	劳动保护监督检查委员会(个)	4980
#女代表	17.54	车间工会劳保委员会(个)	17695
职代会提出提案数(万件)	23.51	工会小组劳保检查员(万人)	7.57
#实现提案数	13.99	从事工会劳保工作的专职干部(人)	3474

注:本表指标分组按工会现行统计报表制度作了修改。

17—4 历 届 省 妇 代 会 情 况

Our Province Women's Congress Over The Sessions

单位:人

类　　别	第一届(1953年)	第二届(1955年)	第三届(1962年)	第四届(1973年)	第五届(1978年)	第六届(1984年)	第七届(1989年)	第八届(1994年)
妇代会代表	520	520	686	1500	1548	1000	650	650
妇联执委	59	55	55	125	115	109	86	93
候补执委		6	4		20	20		
常务委员	17			25	17		12	15

17—5 社会福利、优抚事业单位机构和人员

Institutions and Personnel in Social Welfare and Special Care

单位:机构(个)、人员(人)

类别	1996年		1997年	
	机构	人员	机构	人员
一、收养性事业单位总计	1937	6548	1756	6291
总计中:1.优抚事业单位	200	1390	197	1443
城镇	165	1319	144	1341
乡村	35	71	53	102
2.社会福利事业单位	1737	5158	1559	4848
城镇	699	3168	644	3100
乡村	1038	1990	915	1748
总计中:1.民政部门举办	211	3028	213	3150
2.社会举办	1726	3520	1543	3141
二、社会福利企业单位总计	1632	50293	1282	37943
总计中:1.工厂	1499	49077		
2.商业服务业	133	1216		
总计中:1.民政部门举办	138	9692	135	8071
2.社会举办	1494	40601	1147	29872
三、流浪乞讨收容遣送安置单位	105	1587	97	1877
1.收容遣送站	50	631	51	663
2.不设站的收容遣送工作处	49	124	40	112
3.安置农场	6	832	6	1102
四、烈士纪念建筑物管理单位	21	219	23	254
五、殡葬事业单位	43	743	50	788

注:1.社会福利企业单位总数中未含安置农场。

2.民政部门举办的社会福利企业单位人员数1995年修改为9620人。

17—6 享受补助、救济人员情况

Persons Accessing Subsidies or Relief Funds

类别	单位	1995年	1996年	1997年
一、乡村社会困难户得到救济人次数	万人次	76.49	209.43	97.47
#得到国家定期定量救济人数	万人	1.59	1.66	0.28
二、城镇社会困难户得到救济人次数	万人次	15.72	25.02	39.42
#得到国家定期定量救济人数	万人	0.88	0.86	2.20
三、社会散居孤老残幼人数	万人	38.89	39.66	24.93
#得到国家定期定量救济人数	万人	2.19	2.28	2.10
#城镇	万人	1.16	1.31	1.24
乡村	万人	1.03	0.97	0.86
得到集体给予供养人数	万人	23.93	24.86	22.83
#城镇	万人	3.20	3.30	
乡村	万人	20.73	21.56	
四、精减退职老弱残职工得到救济人数	万人	5.17	5.15	5.13
#享受原工资40%救济人数	万人	1.54	1.52	1.50
享受定期定量救济人数	万人	3.64	3.64	3.63
五、当年扶贫户数	万户	35.75	33.44	36.89
#脱贫户数	万户	9.41	7.50	10.26

注:1、本表中各类优抚救济人数,均不包括优抚、社会福利事业单位的在院收养人员数。

2、第4列第1、2、3、4、6行数,本次年鉴作了修正。

17—7 收养性社会福利、优抚事业单位基本情况(1997年)

Basic Statistics on Adoption Social Welfare and Special Care Units

项　目	机　构 (个)	职　工 (人)	床　位 (张)	年末在院人数 (人)
总　计	1756	6291	34069	26645
一、民政部门举办	213	3150	10939	7660
残废军人休养院	1	133	110	89
光　荣　院	129	630	3956	2835
复退军人精神病院	6	549	893	422
社会福利院	64	851	4061	2954
社会儿童福利院	7	104	517	389
社会精神病人福利院	6	883	1402	971
二、城镇社会举办	575	1291	10130	9234
光　荣　院	8	29	192	132
敬　老　院	567	1262	9938	9102
三、乡村社会举办	968	1850	13000	9751
光　荣　院	53	102	299	238
敬　老　院	915	1748	12701	9513

17—8 社会救济和福利主要费用

Value of Major Social Relief and Welfare Funds

单位:万元

项　目	1995年	1996年	1997年
总　计	63354	78474	73790
一、国家支出	42681	53779	48234
1.抚恤事业费	10896	12717	13820
2.社会救济福利事业费	8106	8662	9952
3.离休、退休费	6398	6633	7452
4.自然灾害救济费	13030	20885	11198
5.其他民政事业费	4251	4882	5812
二、集体供给	20673	24695	25556
1.优抚对象优待总金额	5824	7587	8417
2.社会困难户集体补助金额	2254	2238	1724
3.社会散居孤、老、残、幼集体供养金额	11296	13230	13041
4.集体办光荣院集体供给金额	58	57	55
5.集体办敬老院集体供给金额	1241	1583	2319

17—9 律师、公证、调解工作基本情况

Basic Statistics on Lawyers，Notarization and Mediation

类　别	单　位	1995 年	1996 年	1997 年
一、律师工作				
律师事务所	个	309	333	327
律　　师	人	3824	4178	4006
专职律师	人	1731	1872	1879
兼职律师	人	1554	1714	1591
特邀律师	人	539	592	536
聘请常年法律顾问单位	个	7713	8037	8587
刑事案件代理及辩护	件	10414	11847	12431
民事诉讼代理	件	16271	19951	21720
经济案件诉讼代理	件	14179	17129	13977
非诉讼代理	件	30335	34272	29160
行政诉讼代理	件	1441	2027	1939
解答法律询问	人次	93608	95287	345646
代写法律事务文书	件	21494	24144	28728
二、公证工作				
公 证 处	个	136	137	137
公证人员	人	613	576	581
受理公证文书	件	462267	229812	321877
#出证文书	人次	305904	223914	319527
总计中：国内经济合同公证	件	105233	102942	113713
三、人民调解工作				
专职司法助理员	人	3952	4323	3943
人民调解委员会	个	60358	59232	60064
调解人员	人	846129	861867	865865
调解民间纠纷	件	353996	302971	333376

注：第 4 列第 7 行“律师工作人员”、“其他工作人员”数，本次年鉴作了修正。

17—10 调解各类民间纠纷

Civil Disputes Mediated by Type

单位：万件

类　别	1995 年	1996 年	1997 年
总　计	35.40	30.3	33.35
婚　姻	6.85	5.20	5.56
继　承	1.81	1.74	1.92
赡抚、扶养	1.87	1.73	1.77
房屋、宅基地	3.84	2.58	3.05
债　务	3.30	3.28	3.63
生产经营	4.83	4.18	4.60
损害赔偿	2.67	3.02	3.24
邻　里	5.02	4.33	4.44
其　他	5.21	4.24	5.14

17—11 婚姻登记情况

Marriage Registration

项　目	单　位	1995 年	1996 年	1997 年
一、准予登记结婚	万对	43.77	42.92	41.48
初　婚	万人	82.96	82.00	78.88
再　婚	万人	4.58	3.85	4.08
二、离婚人数	万对	6.33	6.69	5.39

17—12 干部队伍人数

Personnel of Cadres

单位：人

指标名称	1978 年	1985 年	1990 年	1995 年	1997 年
干部人数总计	682206	979549	1148581	1252668	1383075
※女干部	164375	243165	307504	380816	437466
※少数民族干部	19562	45204	69256	96304	114767
※行政机关人员	142916	214093	275152	286790	292525
※大中专以上文化程度人数	112967	484999	818483	948306	1105360
※专业技术人员数	239841	538844	963166	872631	951380
#女性	71173	177981		308512	350335
#高级职称		805	26463	32317	35706
#中级职称		26807	218257	240221	299248
#初级职称				531668	530414

17—13 档案机构、人员、资料及其利用情况

Archies Institntions, Personnal, Dossier and Their Utlization

年份	档案馆数（个）	档案干部数（人）	馆(室)藏档案资料（卷件册）	利用档案资料（卷件册）	利用档案资料人次（人次）
1991	192	5927	8739555	1781405	835891
1992	192	8109	9201022	1550718	652878
1993	190	5549	9583931	31326127	867594
1994	191	5236	9814369	2782614	790192
1995	195	5396	9936543	1462105	767924
1996	200	5434	21497431	1007613	547977
1997	200	5130	12355432	877476	395361

17—14 妇联及其所属组织机构数

Women's Federation and It's Insitutions

单位：个、所

类别	1997年	类别	1997年
一、各级妇联		六、妇女干部及女子职业学校	
地、州、市	14	妇女干部学校(大专)	1
县(市)	122	女子职业学校	5
乡(镇)	2435	大专	1
街道	345	中专	4
二、基层妇代会		七、妇女律师事务所	13
城市	3993	省级	1
农村	55799	地级	4
乡镇企业	1228	县级	8
个体劳动者协会	58	八、其他组织	
三、机关、事业单位妇委会		妇女基金会	13
省直系统	104	儿童基金会	41
地直系统	409	妇儿活动阵地	57
县直系统	3021	家庭教育场所	16833
四、团体会员		家长学校	11387
女职工委员会	11250	广播父母学校	3283
类妇女组织	2592	家教咨询	2163
五、研究机构		妇联办托幼园	74
妇女理论研究会	6	为妇女儿童服务的单位	99
婚姻家庭研究会	2	企业	61
家庭教育研究会	92	事业	38

17—15 交通事故发生情况

Basic Statistics on Traffic Accidents

指　　标	年　份	合　计	按事故发生程度分			按发生地分	
			特　大	重　大	一　般	城　市	乡　村
次数(起)	1995年	10361	151	3082	7128	1578	8783
	1996年	10994	148	3113	7733	2007	8987
	1997年	10401	155	2981	7265	1977	8424
死亡(人)	1995年	3428	440	2983	5	517	2911
	1996年	3368	346	3022		525	2843
	1997年	3308	422	2882	4	510	2798
受伤(人)	1995年	9176	697	2200	6279	1035	8141
	1996年	10448	518	2614	7316	1640	8808
	1997年	9978	742	2336	6900	1474	8304
损失折款(万元)	1995年	6202.99	1122.50	1660.69	3419.8	693.17	5509.82
	1996年	6967.38	1048.38	1961.14	3957.86	915.44	6051.95
	1997年	6586.39	1183.34	1795.00	3608.05	955.47	5630.92
平均每起损失(元)	1995年	5986.86	74337.75	5388.36	4797.7	4392.71	6273.28
	1996年	6337.44	70836.49	6299.84	5118.14	4561.24	6734.12
	1997年	6332.46	76343.52	6021.47	4966.35	4832.92	6684.38

17—16 火灾发生情况

Basic Statistics on Fires

指　　标	年　份	合　计	按事故发生程度分			按发生地分	
			特　大	重　大	一　般	城　市	乡　村
发生(起)	1995年	1128	18	133	977	816	312
	1996年	1087	19	127	941	1042	45
	1997年	2467	6	29	2432	2180	287
死亡(人)	1995年	73	9	21	43	39	34
	1996年	106	16	36	54	95	11
	1997年	130	41	33	56	105	25
受伤(人)	1995年	266	41	70	155	152	114
	1996年	195	21	84	90	191	4
	1997年	328	96	45	187	267	61
损失折款(万元)	1995年	6824.18	3157.17	2490.81	1176.20	5439.39	1384.79
	1996年	5271.00	1894.18	2179.35	1197.47	5116.75	154.25
	1997年	7666.43	2802.15	1186.95	3677.33	6336.28	1330.15
平均每起损失(万元)	1995年	6.05	175.40	18.73	1.20	6.67	4.44
	1996年	4.85	99.69	17.16	1.27	4.91	3.42
	1997年	3.11	467.03	40.93	1.51	2.91	4.63

十八、各地、市、县主要经济和社会统计指标

MAIN ECONOMIC AND SOCIAL STATISTICS INDICATORS BY PREFECTURE, CITY AND COUNTY

18—1 各 地、市、县 人 口(1997年)

Population by Prefecture, City and County

单位:万人

名 称	总户数(万户)	总人口	总人口中		总人口中		总人口中	
			男	女	市 镇	乡 村	农业人口	非农业人口
长沙市	164.78	571.91	296.07	275.84	209.09	362.82	400.93	170.98
长沙市区	49.71	163.44	84.87	78.57	163.44		31.01	132.43
芙蓉区	9.16	29.89	15.37	14.52	29.89		3.69	26.20
天心区	10.03	32.46	17.06	15.40	32.46		3.13	29.33
岳麓区	8.11	28.32	14.92	13.40	28.32		8.79	19.53
开福区	12.24	37.45	18.93	18.52	37.45		8.58	28.87
雨花区	10.17	35.32	18.59	16.73	35.32		6.82	28.50
浏阳市	35.22	133.01	68.98	64.03	14.11	118.90	120.58	12.43
长沙县	21.69	74.10	38.33	35.77	11.34	62.76	68.66	5.44
望城县	19.76	71.39	36.42	34.97	6.71	64.68	63.07	8.32
宁乡县	38.40	129.97	67.47	62.50	13.49	116.48	117.61	12.36
株洲市	97.83	365.65	188.52	177.13	102.48	263.17	278.02	87.63
株洲市区	20.99	71.19	36.90	34.29	71.19		19.52	51.67
荷塘区	5.77	19.90	10.34	9.56	19.90		5.55	14.35
芦淞区	5.65	19.15	9.88	9.27	19.15		2.45	16.70
石峰区	6.99	23.45	12.34	11.11	23.45		5.45	18.00
天元区	2.58	8.69	4.34	4.35	8.69		6.07	2.62
醴陵市	25.98	100.37	51.92	48.45	12.39	87.98	87.02	13.35
株洲县	11.87	44.54	23.07	21.47	3.90	40.64	39.91	4.63
攸 县	19.94	73.82	37.79	36.03	8.31	65.51	64.79	9.03
茶陵县	14.20	58.12	29.80	28.32	4.31	53.81	51.83	6.29
炎陵县	4.85	17.61	9.04	8.57	2.38	15.23	14.95	2.66
湘潭市	81.15	276.18	142.40	133.78	82.30	193.88	205.87	70.31
湘潭市区	19.60	64.62	33.56	31.06	64.62		14.04	50.58
雨湖区	10.07	32.80	16.99	15.81	32.80		5.41	27.39
岳塘区	9.53	31.82	16.57	15.25	31.82		8.63	23.19
湘乡市	26.78	88.94	45.69	43.25	9.56	79.38	78.67	10.27
韶山市	3.07	10.05	5.11	4.94	1.49	8.56	8.50	1.55
湘潭县	31.70	112.57	58.04	54.53	6.63	105.94	104.66	7.91
衡阳市	181.99	692.42	361.90	330.52	149.98	542.44	560.69	131.73
衡阳市区	23.34	77.50	40.07	37.43	77.50		19.91	57.59
江东区	4.91	15.73	8.28	7.45	15.73		0.07	15.66
城南区	4.39	17.87	9.40	8.47	17.87			17.87
城北区	6.22	19.83	10.43	9.40	19.83			19.83
郊 区	6.00	18.93	9.36	9.57	18.93		16.55	2.38
南岳区	1.82	5.14	2.60	2.54	5.14		3.29	1.85
耒阳市	29.87	120.47	63.36	57.11	13.13	107.34	104.59	15.88

18—1 续表 1　　(1997 年)　　单位:万人

名　称	总户数(万户)	总人口	总人口中		总人口中		总人口中	
			男	女	市　镇	乡　村	农业人口	非农业人口
常宁市	20.64	83.19	43.80	39.39	17.40	65.79	70.42	12.77
衡阳县	27.51	114.21	59.39	54.82	11.66	102.55	101.45	12.76
衡南县	25.75	101.53	52.71	48.82	10.62	90.91	90.18	11.35
衡山县	10.40	39.70	20.63	19.07	3.79	35.91	34.98	4.72
衡东县	18.36	65.14	34.19	30.95	6.47	58.67	57.99	7.15
祁东县	26.12	90.68	47.75	42.93	9.41	81.27	81.17	9.51
邵阳市	197.39	711.04	369.05	341.99	117.14	593.90	620.09	90.95
邵阳市区	17.51	58.11	29.78	28.33	58.11		27.92	30.19
双清区	7.66	24.49	12.70	11.79	24.49		9.31	15.18
大祥区	7.65	26.62	13.61	13.01	26.62		12.75	13.87
北塔区	2.20	7.00	3.47	3.53	7.00		5.86	1.14
武冈市	20.28	71.09	37.03	34.06	8.05	63.04	63.41	7.68
邵东县	31.26	115.90	59.33	56.57	9.39	106.51	105.43	10.47
新邵县	20.01	72.32	38.53	33.79	8.13	64.19	65.70	6.62
邵阳县	24.10	92.41	47.77	44.64	6.31	86.10	85.64	6.77
隆回县	30.10	107.11	55.90	51.21	6.58	100.53	100.10	7.01
洞口县	22.24	76.99	40.29	36.70	8.28	68.71	68.93	8.06
绥宁县	9.34	34.37	17.82	16.55	3.11	31.26	30.29	4.08
新宁县	16.09	57.89	29.77	28.12	5.47	52.42	51.75	6.14
城步县	6.46	24.85	12.83	12.02	3.71	21.14	20.92	3.93
岳阳市	151.88	510.35	266.46	243.89	132.92	377.43	415.64	94.71
岳阳市区	30.16	82.95	43.52	39.43	82.95		39.48	43.47
岳阳楼区	18.26	46.53	24.62	21.91	46.53		14.73	31.80
云溪区	5.13	15.56	8.10	7.46	15.56		8.15	7.41
君山区	6.77	20.86	10.80	10.06	20.86		16.60	4.26
汨罗市	20.89	69.94	36.33	33.61	8.88	61.06	61.06	8.88
临湘市	13.26	46.94	24.51	22.43	8.82	38.12	37.82	9.12
岳阳县	20.69	74.51	38.99	35.52	6.85	67.66	66.76	7.75
华容县	19.21	70.94	36.54	34.40	10.18	60.76	62.54	8.40
湘阴县	20.85	67.88	35.46	32.42	7.87	60.01	58.84	9.04
平江县	26.82	97.19	51.11	46.08	7.37	89.82	89.14	8.05
常德市	173.57	593.32	306.29	287.03	194.23	399.09	482.23	111.09
常德市区	40.29	131.45	67.15	64.30	131.45		93.98	37.47
武陵区	14.87	43.79	22.52	21.27	43.79		16.70	27.09
鼎城区	25.42	87.66	44.63	43.03	87.66		77.28	10.38
津市市	8.30	25.35	13.38	11.97	11.19	14.16	15.52	9.83
安乡县	14.41	57.44	29.24	28.20	8.42	49.02	45.66	11.78

18—1 续表 2 (1997 年) 单位:万人

名称	总户数(万户)	总人口	总人口中		总人口中		总人口中	
			男	女	市镇	乡村	农业人口	非农业人口
汉寿县	21.21	80.09	41.88	38.21	8.07	72.02	69.02	11.07
澧县	25.59	87.72	45.12	42.60	10.43	77.29	74.86	12.86
临澧县	13.24	43.43	22.01	21.42	5.61	37.82	37.28	6.15
桃源县	28.92	97.54	50.87	46.67	9.73	87.81	86.11	11.43
石门县	21.61	70.30	36.64	33.66	9.33	60.97	59.80	10.50
张家界市	46.78	153.77	79.84	73.93	56.09	97.68	130.86	22.91
张家界市区	14.12	44.60	23.13	21.47	44.60		33.36	11.24
永定区	12.69	40.14	20.79	19.35	40.14		30.72	9.42
武陵源区	1.43	4.46	2.34	2.12	4.46		2.64	1.82
慈利县	20.42	67.02	34.71	32.31	6.87	60.15	60.07	6.95
桑植县	12.24	42.15	22.00	20.15	4.62	37.53	37.43	4.72
益阳市	125.43	446.87	231.23	215.64	164.83	282.04	371.07	75.80
益阳市区	35.01	124.25	63.73	60.52	124.25		95.05	29.20
资阳区	11.65	40.55	20.81	19.74	40.55		31.54	9.01
赫山区	23.36	83.70	42.92	40.78	83.70		63.51	20.19
沅江市	21.35	74.03	38.11	35.92	13.88	60.15	60.14	13.89
南县	20.88	72.70	37.55	35.15	7.73	64.97	60.57	12.13
桃江县	22.04	81.54	42.68	38.86	8.19	73.35	72.61	8.93
安化县	26.15	94.35	49.16	45.19	10.78	83.57	82.70	11.65
郴州市	121.99	444.76	231.46	213.30	108.86	335.90	364.35	80.41
郴州市区	17.83	61.24	32.26	28.98	61.24		34.36	26.88
北湖区	8.46	27.48	14.42	13.06	27.48		13.93	13.55
苏仙区	9.37	33.76	17.84	15.92	33.76		20.43	13.33
资兴市	10.74	35.82	18.70	17.12	11.65	24.17	23.67	12.15
桂阳县	20.34	75.97	39.48	36.49	7.50	68.47	67.41	8.56
永兴县	15.90	62.02	32.02	30.00	7.82	54.20	53.11	8.91
宜章县	13.22	54.13	28.05	26.08	6.17	47.96	47.23	6.90
嘉禾县	9.77	33.01	17.10	15.91	3.08	29.93	29.40	3.61
临武县	8.89	30.69	16.12	14.57	3.39	27.30	26.76	3.93
汝城县	9.82	36.02	18.88	17.14	3.00	33.02	32.59	3.43
桂东县	4.61	16.85	8.78	8.07	1.53	15.32	14.99	1.86
安仁县	10.87	39.01	20.07	18.94	3.48	35.53	34.83	4.18
永州市	144.48	550.07	287.35	262.72	156.89	393.18	475.02	75.05
永州市区	28.15	103.24	53.69	49.55	103.24		76.30	26.94
芝山区	14.31	56.86	29.56	27.30	56.86		45.65	11.21
冷水滩区	13.84	46.38	24.13	22.25	46.38		30.65	15.73
东安县	14.84	57.22	29.36	27.86	5.41	51.81	51.55	5.67

18－1 续表 3 (1997 年) 单位:万人

名 称	总户数(万户)	总人口	总人口中 男	总人口中 女	总人口中 市镇	总人口中 乡村	总人口中 农业人口	总人口中 非农业人口
道 县	16.21	64.05	34.31	29.74	15.05	49.00	55.03	9.02
宁远县	18.86	75.34	39.89	35.45	5.19	70.15	69.87	5.47
江永县	6.33	24.33	12.57	11.76	2.71	21.62	21.35	2.98
江华县	11.35	43.88	23.43	20.45	3.98	39.90	39.68	4.20
蓝山县	9.05	34.20	17.77	16.43	2.56	31.64	31.37	2.83
新田县	10.44	36.87	19.22	17.65	2.77	34.10	33.80	3.07
双牌县	4.90	16.64	8.79	7.85	2.48	14.16	13.82	2.82
祁阳县	24.35	94.30	48.32	45.98	13.50	80.80	82.25	12.05
娄底地区	110.45	392.13	203.58	188.55	64.17	327.96	319.21	72.92
娄底市	12.91	37.77	19.53	18.24	19.96	17.81	16.21	21.56
冷水江市	11.19	34.39	17.81	16.58	14.40	19.99	17.11	17.28
涟源市	30.21	104.93	54.36	50.57	9.92	95.01	91.93	13.00
双峰县	24.75	88.84	46.11	42.73	8.14	80.70	79.95	8.89
新化县	31.39	126.20	65.77	60.43	11.75	114.45	114.01	12.19
怀化地区	128.98	476.62	247.80	228.82	79.23	397.39	388.78	87.84
怀化市	16.53	54.96	28.56	26.40	22.45	32.51	32.07	22.89
洪江市	3.31	9.49	4.76	4.73	5.64	3.85	3.37	6.12
黔阳县	11.78	40.48	20.87	19.61	6.24	34.24	33.71	6.77
沅陵县	16.89	63.25	33.02	30.23	8.22	55.03	51.97	11.28
辰溪县	12.89	50.32	25.93	24.39	8.22	42.10	41.26	9.06
溆浦县	21.55	83.40	43.28	40.12	7.38	76.02	75.27	8.13
麻阳县	8.64	35.16	18.26	16.90	3.08	32.08	31.48	3.68
新晃县	6.60	24.99	13.75	11.24	2.49	22.50	22.04	2.95
芷江县	9.93	34.48	18.11	16.37	3.47	31.01	30.50	3.98
会同县	9.36	33.81	17.49	16.32	2.78	31.03	30.47	3.34
靖州县	6.32	24.95	12.74	12.21	7.45	17.50	17.35	7.60
通道县	5.18	21.33	11.03	10.30	1.81	19.52	19.29	2.04
湘西自治州	64.89	253.83	130.96	122.87	35.32	218.51	216.00	37.83
吉首市	8.02	26.05	13.61	12.44	9.92	16.13	14.92	11.13
泸溪县	6.68	26.79	13.91	12.88	4.96	21.83	22.81	3.98
凤凰县	7.95	35.80	18.53	17.27	3.21	32.59	32.21	3.59
花垣县	6.35	26.08	13.59	12.49	3.15	22.93	22.69	3.39
保靖县	6.83	27.47	14.42	13.05	2.70	24.77	24.13	3.34
古丈县	4.23	13.38	6.88	6.50	1.97	11.41	11.15	2.23
永顺县	11.53	47.41	23.74	23.67	4.32	43.09	42.32	5.09
龙山县	13.30	50.85	26.28	24.57	5.09	45.76	45.77	5.08

18—2 各地、市、县、区计划生育指标(1997年)

Indicators of Family Plan by Prefecture, City and County

名　称	出生率 (‰)	死亡率 (‰)	自然增长率 (‰)	计划内生育率 (%)	多孩率 (%)	已婚育龄妇女人数 (人)	节育率 (%)	措施落实率 (%)	措施及时率 (%)	节育手术 (例)
长沙市	10.70	6.89	3.81	98.02	0.05	1220766	89.67	98.11	85.02	94727
芙蓉区	9.86	5.11	4.75	98.51	0.00	60817	88.75	98.47	85.77	2058
天心区	8.58	6.50	2.08	98.59	0.00	52339	90.26	98.57	86.39	3277
岳麓区	8.67	5.59	3.08	98.52	0.00	54201	88.62	98.52	84.77	3773
开福区	9.62	6.82	2.80	98.50	0.00	73510	88.62	98.32	86.12	2870
雨花区	9.50	5.73	3.77	98.47	0.00	73650	90.64	98.42	85.37	4723
长沙县	11.66	7.38	4.28	98.27	0.04	167685	90.54	98.03	85.16	14275
望城县	11.56	7.05	4.51	97.73	0.01	160582	88.77	98.22	83.26	10381
浏阳市	10.80	7.50	3.30	96.74	0.16	290240	90.22	97.93	83.92	28938
宁乡县	11.50	7.13	4.37	98.71	0.05	287742	89.40	97.93	86.47	24432
株洲市	12.08	6.76	5.32	96.36	0.25	833432	89.55	97.49	81.01	66156
荷塘区	11.99	5.03	6.96	97.94	0.64	34451	88.54	97.93	86.84	2228
芦淞区	10.87	4.92	5.95	97.71	0.00	28883	88.16	98.22	87.32	1507
石峰区	12.13	5.00	7.13	97.73	0.00	36297	88.37	97.86	87.10	1748
天元区	12.78	5.82	6.96	96.52	1.61	47104	88.43	97.56	82.30	2859
醴陵市	12.06	7.16	4.90	94.64	0.23	225003	90.22	96.36	78.97	24933
株洲县	11.26	6.80	4.47	96.75	0.21	110658	88.95	98.40	79.76	6605
攸　县	12.87	7.03	5.84	96.87	0.09	187796	88.76	98.28	82.17	15478
茶陵县	11.96	7.28	4.68	96.95	0.17	124396	91.65	97.11	79.58	7952
炎陵县	12.03	7.62	4.41	96.75	0.05	38844	88.80	97.79	79.68	2846
湘潭市	13.03	7.05	5.98	95.10	0.29	606236	90.95	97.34	81.01	41337
雨湖区	12.51	6.17	6.33	98.38	0.02	72554	91.71	97.78	88.23	4307
岳塘区	11.84	6.79	5.05	97.91	0.03	78011	90.30	97.77	86.93	4961
韶山市	13.16	6.85	6.31	98.57	0.15	22311	91.77	97.89	86.23	1686
湘乡市	14.41	7.41	7.00	95.03	0.42	190067	90.25	97.70	79.06	13161
湘潭县	12.42	7.10	5.32	93.13	0.33	243293	91.41	96.76	78.70	17222
衡阳市	13.47	7.06	6.41	92.30	0.23	1494882	90.96	97.48	76.16	135350
江东区	10.83	5.19	5.64	97.35	0.00	42312	88.76	97.22	80.59	1438
城南区	11.12	4.80	6.32	97.32	0.00	43339	90.20	97.11	81.21	1414
城北区	11.56	4.98	6.57	97.30	0.00	49597	92.72	97.97	80.65	1546
郊　区	12.49	6.32	6.17	97.07	0.17	44193	91.92	96.91	80.61	3885
南岳区	13.21	6.40	6.81	95.30	0.15	11172	91.29	98.10	79.19	985

注:1.本表按照计划生育责任区划填列。

2.表中所列资料系根据抽样调查数推算。

18—2 续表1 (1997年)

名称	出生率 (‰)	死亡率 (‰)	自然增长率 (‰)	计划内生育率 (%)	多孩率 (%)	已婚育龄妇女人数 (人)	节育率 (%)	措施落实率 (%)	措施及时率 (%)	节育手术 (例)
耒阳市	11.94	7.21	4.73	92.60	0.50	238538	91.62	97.74	78.07	18343
衡阳县	14.30	7.50	6.80	92.99	0.13	250271	90.94	97.07	78.27	20715
衡南县	14.48	7.13	7.35	93.02	0.11	225162	91.45	97.69	77.09	19332
衡山县	13.96	7.05	6.91	92.37	0.04	86326	91.01	97.27	77.02	8376
衡东县	13.55	6.98	6.57	90.16	0.15	142610	90.27	97.89	76.00	11824
常宁市	14.16	7.59	6.57	86.74	0.33	171759	90.59	97.15	66.53	31889
祁东县	14.00	7.24	6.76	93.32	0.35	189603	90.41	97.60	76.68	15603
邵阳市	13.15	7.06	6.09	93.82	0.81	1466694	90.69	98.13	76.75	119235
双清区	13.01	5.55	7.45	97.50	0.37	42673	89.41	97.45	80.26	1961
大祥区	12.73	4.76	7.97	97.11	0.36	31923	91.88	97.36	80.89	1471
北塔区	12.67	6.87	5.80	92.30	1.37	62334	91.86	97.16	74.80	4472
邵东县	13.56	6.76	6.80	95.73	0.65	251533	92.16	98.15	81.09	20971
新邵县	12.92	7.05	5.87	89.99	1.76	144635	91.75	98.72	70.59	11607
邵阳县	13.37	7.17	6.21	92.92	0.51	171235	92.21	98.43	79.35	14722
隆回县	13.44	7.46	5.98	95.21	0.73	222546	88.74	97.58	80.90	18736
洞口县	13.59	6.95	6.64	94.29	0.67	161851	90.98	98.41	75.35	13079
武冈市	13.89	7.30	6.58	94.78	0.56	150316	89.02	98.34	76.75	14245
绥宁县	12.46	7.37	5.08	92.70	0.89	66542	92.03	98.19	69.68	7072
新宁县	11.78	7.14	4.64	91.69	0.84	114549	88.63	98.45	73.08	7715
城步县	11.30	7.74	3.56	91.97	1.32	46557	89.64	97.57	64.93	3184
岳阳市	13.00	7.16	5.84	93.85	0.50	1030222	90.61	97.36	76.74	102729
岳阳楼区	12.93	4.74	8.19	96.26	0.02	87842	91.39	97.26	79.16	8293
云溪区	11.63	6.25	5.38	96.51	0.22	33088	89.20	97.17	79.95	3615
汨罗市	13.43	7.46	5.98	95.22	0.35	144269	91.32	96.41	78.38	15628
岳阳县	13.28	7.62	5.65	92.11	0.77	184622	89.20	97.11	74.86	15959
临湘市	13.48	7.32	6.16	93.16	0.89	98627	90.53	97.92	77.04	9889
华容县	11.65	7.53	4.12	96.45	0.04	147015	88.92	98.13	79.91	16047
湘阴县	14.07	7.60	6.47	93.11	0.55	145281	92.73	97.07	76.25	18207
平江县	12.84	7.31	5.53	91.67	0.79	189478	91.08	97.75	73.58	15091
常德市	12.31	7.25	5.06	97.55	0.03	1350826	92.19	97.73	82.76	102795
武陵区	13.45	6.45	7.01	97.02	0.05	97602	91.43	97.51	82.04	6779
鼎城区	12.55	7.28	5.27	97.10	0.03	210537	92.78	97.03	79.74	18651
津市市	12.20	6.93	5.28	98.49	0.00	56429	92.64	97.79	83.02	3732
安乡县	11.61	7.25	4.37	98.86	0.00	119135	92.69	97.83	87.35	8505

18－2 续表 2 (1997 年)

名 称	出生率 (‰)	死亡率 (‰)	自然增长率 (‰)	计划内生育率 (%)	多孩率 (%)	已婚育龄妇女人数 (人)	节育率 (%)	措施落实率 (%)	措施及时率 (%)	节育手术 (例)
汉寿县	11.60	7.12	4.48	96.40	0.01	160302	91.26	97.74	78.35	17842
澧 县	12.93	7.56	5.37	98.03	0.05	228427	92.44	98.66	86.21	16101
临澧县	12.16	7.41	4.75	98.86	0.00	92477	92.69	98.58	89.01	6744
桃源县	12.17	7.14	5.03	97.54	0.06	211744	92.73	97.36	83.61	12743
石门县	12.48	7.66	4.82	97.34	0.03	174173	91.04	97.36	81.49	11698
张家界市	13.48	7.33	6.15	92.05	1.34	321641	89.17	96.64	71.83	30759
永定区	14.51	6.66	7.85	94.10	0.99	82784	88.48	96.06	73.52	10179
武陵源区	15.19	6.94	8.26	93.11	1.80	9476	88.75	96.51	73.83	1204
慈利县	12.79	7.50	5.30	93.55	1.04	146683	89.85	97.26	73.93	12559
桑植县	13.40	7.74	5.66	87.57	2.09	82698	88.69	96.14	66.58	6817
益阳市	10.91	7.05	3.87	96.35	0.14	924673	90.10	97.64	78.64	61167
资阳区	11.11	7.25	3.86	96.51	0.15	85400	90.60	97.17	79.35	5726
沅江市	10.76	6.87	3.88	95.79	0.12	152853	91.17	97.69	79.43	9031
赫山区	10.87	6.58	4.29	96.53	0.15	171342	89.60	97.60	79.47	11186
南 县	11.71	7.23	4.48	96.57	0.15	153511	88.98	97.95	79.18	11920
桃江县	10.93	6.96	3.97	95.88	0.14	177554	90.78	97.54	77.20	11369
安化县	10.35	7.44	2.92	96.81	0.13	184013	89.71	97.70	77.87	11935
娄底地区	13.04	7.07	5.97	92.36	0.20	790125	90.86	97.05	75.81	72085
娄底市	12.96	6.26	6.71	96.39	0.08	80876	91.62	97.90	81.25	6347
冷水江市	12.36	6.31	6.04	96.43	0.12	73353	91.11	97.45	81.79	4586
涟源市	13.27	6.71	6.56	90.69	0.21	210239	92.38	96.14	75.74	20485
双峰县	13.40	7.11	6.30	93.06	0.17	192375	89.66	97.07	78.18	14438
新化县	12.81	7.80	5.01	91.00	0.26	233282	90.14	97.45	71.68	26229
郴州市	10.87	7.26	3.61	95.53	0.11	883021	91.22	97.34	78.20	64636
北湖区	11.00	5.93	5.07	97.51	0.03	59445	88.50	97.32	81.36	3332
资兴市	10.76	7.55	3.21	97.49	0.03	76845	90.32	97.45	79.77	6749
苏仙区	10.28	7.19	3.09	97.95	0.03	70702	90.85	97.58	84.22	5323
桂阳县	10.83	7.29	3.54	95.21	0.10	144110	92.62	97.52	77.52	9044
永兴县	10.69	7.55	3.14	95.87	0.08	121296	91.50	98.64	77.71	8044
宜章县	10.83	7.22	3.61	94.74	0.10	99637	90.93	96.39	73.14	8368
嘉禾县	12.05	7.24	4.81	92.43	0.05	68132	92.58	96.14	78.66	5154
临武县	10.53	7.64	2.89	96.19	0.19	59062	91.31	97.97	80.53	4399
汝城县	11.05	7.80	3.25	95.64	0.33	70760	89.87	96.87	78.72	5731
桂东县	11.24	7.78	3.46	94.36	0.11	32048	88.73	96.94	77.51	3193
安仁县	10.75	6.49	4.26	94.39	0.19	80984	92.76	97.07	77.86	5299

18—2 续表 3 (1997 年)

名称	出生率(‰)	死亡率(‰)	自然增长率(‰)	计划内生育率(%)	多孩率(%)	已婚育龄妇女人数(人)	节育率(%)	措施落实率(%)	措施及时率(%)	节育手术(例)
永州市	12.56	7.23	5.33	92.47	0.69	1051080	90.91	96.22	74.19	100718
芝山区	11.28	6.85	4.43	96.39	0.28	110293	91.27	97.07	79.34	8696
冷水滩区	11.93	6.66	5.27	95.22	0.48	90252	92.68	96.68	75.60	12606
东安县	12.17	7.34	4.83	97.36	0.22	114745	90.78	96.23	79.56	7526
道县	13.32	7.84	5.49	90.99	1.06	115208	91.55	95.32	74.08	10243
宁远县	12.02	7.68	4.34	90.31	1.22	140300	88.66	94.49	73.33	12962
江永县	12.73	6.90	5.83	94.48	0.65	44535	91.12	96.94	73.49	4959
江华县	14.40	6.92	7.48	82.86	1.48	84211	90.11	96.51	67.60	10240
蓝山县	13.95	6.79	7.15	88.47	1.27	67023	92.59	95.34	69.79	6543
新田县	13.14	7.53	5.61	91.54	0.31	68220	92.73	96.52	71.90	6712
双牌县	11.84	8.06	3.78	94.93	0.31	29547	91.63	97.48	75.33	2481
祁阳县	12.33	7.07	5.27	95.04	0.23	186746	90.17	97.08	75.56	17750
怀化地区	13.04	7.22	5.82	93.58	0.57	1002272	88.64	95.85	73.39	82288
怀化市	14.01	6.67	7.34	94.32	0.51	117703	89.25	95.19	77.31	7125
洪江市	13.83	7.16	6.67	96.50	0.39	25849	88.64	95.89	79.65	1394
黔阳县	13.78	7.25	6.53	96.12	0.32	95171	88.73	97.18	72.60	7897
沅陵县	11.87	7.84	4.03	92.96	0.35	119671	88.73	97.17	70.76	11212
辰溪县	11.24	6.96	4.28	87.87	1.04	99767	88.66	98.63	70.32	7118
溆浦县	11.78	6.93	4.85	95.48	0.29	170827	88.69	94.67	75.81	11544
麻阳县	14.90	7.29	7.61	93.35	0.48	70013	88.31	94.58	73.31	6801
新晃县	13.42	7.83	5.59	92.99	0.30	53787	87.88	94.05	72.38	5250
芷江县	16.85	7.30	9.54	94.43	0.68	80792	88.77	96.34	74.88	8449
会同县	13.07	7.47	5.60	94.53	0.93	76476	88.28	94.67	71.34	7130
靖州县	12.77	7.22	5.55	94.37	0.51	50613	88.60	97.27	74.26	3620
通道县	12.24	7.10	5.15	88.22	1.77	41603	88.20	93.43	68.39	4748
湘西自治州	15.05	7.29	7.76	83.06	3.23	469225	90.05	97.02	67.15	82929
吉首市	14.03	6.36	7.67	91.68	1.19	47621	92.76	97.38	73.36	8982
泸溪县	15.68	7.30	8.38	80.58	3.80	49167	89.86	97.33	67.19	9306
凤凰县	13.98	7.23	6.75	80.07	4.60	62945	89.75	96.13	64.98	12047
花垣县	15.56	7.65	7.91	81.52	3.10	47647	90.39	97.36	65.73	8091
保靖县	15.34	7.68	7.66	81.71	3.52	53419	88.99	96.67	66.09	9240
古丈县	15.35	8.00	7.34	81.41	3.61	23777	88.98	95.62	66.89	4662
永顺县	15.52	7.13	8.39	83.05	3.12	84250	89.06	97.27	66.67	14367
龙山县	15.05	7.36	7.69	84.28	2.89	100399	90.53	97.41	67.79	16234

18—3　各地、市、县从业人员人数(1997年底)

Laborers by Prefecture, City and County

单位:万人

名　　称	从业人员人数	职　工	#国有经济单位	#城镇集体经济单位	城镇个体劳动者	城镇私营企业从业人员	农村社会劳动者	其他社会劳动者
长沙市	341.89	89.92	66.77	19.40	21.55	3.47	225.35	1.60
长沙市区	99.59	68.98	51.73	14.15	14.94	3.06	11.82	0.79
浏阳市	76.10	5.72	4.39	1.23	1.58	0.19	68.18	0.43
长沙县	44.45	4.50	3.22	0.96	0.37	0.04	39.50	0.04
望城县	40.20	4.04	2.40	1.45	0.79	0.05	35.09	0.23
宁乡县	81.55	6.68	5.03	1.61	3.87	0.13	70.76	0.11
株洲市	197.50	45.84	34.30	9.38	4.75	1.90	144.00	1.01
株洲市区	40.64	28.27	21.68	5.32	2.37	1.06	8.36	0.58
醴陵市	52.93	6.17	3.84	1.69	1.16	0.51	44.87	0.22
株洲县	22.41	2.24	1.55	0.66	0.47	0.10	19.51	0.09
攸　县	43.20	4.58	3.51	0.96	0.29	0.18	38.09	0.06
茶陵县	28.85	3.22	2.63	0.54	0.37	0.04	25.17	0.05
炎陵县	9.47	1.36	1.09	0.21	0.09	0.01	8.00	0.01
湘潭市	162.84	36.99	27.62	8.40	9.73	1.31	114.33	0.48
湘潭市区	42.75	26.39	19.86	5.57	8.72	1.26	6.16	0.22
湘乡市	50.35	5.50	3.87	1.63	0.33	0.02	44.49	0.01
韶山市	5.71	1.06	0.80	0.25	0.01	0.02	4.62	
湘潭县	64.03	4.04	3.09	0.95	0.67	0.01	59.06	0.25
衡阳市	366.75	60.07	46.90	12.07	15.20	1.30	289.02	1.16
衡阳市区	38.61	26.91	20.94	5.09	2.74	0.50	8.30	0.16
#南岳区	2.35	0.49	0.40	0.08	0.06	0.02	1.77	0.01
耒阳市	63.43	7.47	6.52	0.88	3.69	0.21	51.82	0.24
常宁市	46.88	5.84	4.58	1.26	4.65	0.23	36.06	0.10
衡阳县	63.73	4.52	3.36	1.16	1.04	0.03	58.01	0.13
衡南县	49.72	5.48	4.02	1.44	0.55	0.03	43.49	0.17
衡山县	22.73	2.32	1.75	0.50	1.38	0.14	18.79	0.10
衡东县	34.18	3.06	2.29	0.74	0.91	0.09	30.04	0.08
祁东县	47.47	4.47	3.44	1.00	0.24	0.07	42.51	0.18

注:职工中包括其他各种经济类型单位的人数。

18—3 续表1　　(1997年底)　　单位:万人

名　　称	从业人员人数	职　工	#国有经济单位	#城镇集体经济单位	城镇个体劳动者	城镇私营企业从业人员	农村社会劳动者	其他社会劳动者
邵阳市	399.34	45.76	35.16	8.71	17.21	2.74	332.22	1.41
邵阳市区	35.56	17.35	13.79	2.99	2.28	0.69	15.11	0.13
武冈市	42.15	3.56	2.45	0.85	1.90	0.17	36.45	0.07
邵东县	58.40	4.93	3.85	1.08	3.49	0.18	49.58	0.22
新邵县	42.75	3.08	2.48	0.60	4.16	0.91	34.29	0.31
邵阳县	53.54	3.36	2.57	0.72	0.48	0.07	49.40	0.23
隆回县	55.64	3.24	2.52	0.65	0.49	0.16	51.53	0.22
洞口县	46.02	3.79	2.84	0.94	1.66	0.11	40.36	0.10
绥宁县	18.70	1.98	1.17	0.28	0.92	0.30	15.44	0.06
新宁县	32.16	2.38	1.93	0.40	1.31	0.07	28.37	0.03
城步县	14.42	2.09	1.56	0.20	0.52	0.08	11.69	0.04
岳阳市	259.98	54.21	43.63	9.27	15.95	1.10	186.69	2.03
岳阳市直	20.99	18.58	14.83	2.93	1.13	0.40		0.88
岳阳楼区	10.31	1.18	0.55	0.61	5.73	0.02	3.33	0.05
云溪区	4.21	0.77	0.56	0.22	0.26	0.02	3.12	0.04
君山区	8.38	6.30	6.23	0.04	0.46		1.42	0.20
汨罗市	35.24	7.59	6.36	1.06	1.73	0.20	25.68	0.04
临湘市	23.03	4.04	3.44	0.57	1.58	0.27	16.86	0.28
岳阳县	33.19	3.40	2.66	0.66	1.05	0.05	28.66	0.03
华容县	36.54	4.65	3.03	1.60	0.92	0.02	30.77	0.18
湘阴县	38.13	4.09	3.16	0.93	1.71	0.05	32.13	0.15
平江县	49.96	3.61	2.81	0.65	1.38	0.07	44.72	0.18
常德市	319.87	48.13	37.89	9.70	17.78	3.78	249.03	1.15
常德市区	73.01	17.58	14.32	2.98	8.54	1.32	45.43	0.14
武陵区	11.17	2.31	0.87	1.38			8.82	0.04
鼎城区	51.08	6.45	5.14	1.31	6.96	0.96	36.61	0.10
津市市	12.63	3.62	2.66	0.89	0.99	0.24	7.74	0.04
安乡县	29.50	3.51	2.36	1.05	2.19	0.39	23.12	0.29
汉寿县	44.83	7.30	6.09	1.17	1.65	0.19	35.54	0.15
澧　县	44.43	4.61	3.47	1.14	0.68	0.41	38.60	0.13
临澧县	24.73	2.64	1.85	0.78	0.87	0.52	20.61	0.09
桃源县	52.03	4.65	3.67	0.98	0.92	0.23	46.00	0.23
石门县	38.71	4.22	3.47	0.71	1.94	0.48	31.99	0.08

18—3 续表 2　　(1997 年底)　　单位:万人

名　　称	从业人员人数	职　工	#国有经济单位	#城镇集体经济单位	城镇个体劳动者	城镇私营企业从业人员	农村社会劳动者	其他社会劳动者
张家界市	80.71	10.22	8.08	1.84	3.16	0.24	66.78	0.31
张家界市直	1.46	1.39	1.32	0.02		0.06		0.01
永定区	18.12	2.67	1.95	0.66	1.58	0.07	13.76	0.04
武陵源区	2.54	0.38	0.35		0.15	0.01	1.94	0.06
慈利县	38.21	3.50	2.43	0.91	0.96	0.09	33.54	0.12
桑植县	20.38	2.28	2.03	0.25	0.47	0.01	17.54	0.08
益阳市	249.96	40.93	31.34	8.62	10.33	2.71	194.81	1.18
益阳市直	18.60	15.58	13.91	1.21	2.00	0.64		0.38
资阳区	22.31	3.20	2.09	1.10	1.10	0.10	17.82	0.09
赫山区	38.61	3.59	2.40	1.02	1.46	0.03	33.41	0.12
沅江市	40.37	5.67	4.23	1.42	2.70	1.10	30.76	0.14
南　县	35.34	3.82	2.52	1.17	0.90	0.24	30.26	0.12
桃江县	46.04	4.41	3.30	0.94	1.24	0.40	39.79	0.20
安化县	48.69	4.66	2.89	1.76	0.93	0.20	42.77	0.13
郴州市	243.74	34.15	28.90	4.37	12.75	0.53	195.23	1.08
郴州市直	9.18	7.92	7.20	0.39	0.94	0.29		0.03
北湖区	10.10	2.55	1.64	0.75	0.04		7.50	0.01
苏仙区	13.06	1.68	1.35	0.26	0.20	0.06	11.03	0.09
资兴市	21.29	5.73	5.04	0.53	1.23	0.03	14.23	0.07
桂阳县	42.74	3.72	3.04	0.59	1.82	0.03	37.02	0.15
永兴县	29.17	2.34	1.84	0.49	0.30		26.26	0.27
宜章县	32.14	2.56	2.13	0.38	3.53	0.02	25.86	0.17
嘉禾县	18.25	1.55	1.35	0.20	1.36	0.03	15.26	0.05
临武县	16.72	1.71	1.52	0.18	0.39		14.53	0.09
汝城县	17.93	1.56	1.38	0.18	0.32		15.99	0.06
桂东县	9.45	0.94	0.81	0.13	0.13	0.01	8.36	0.01
安仁县	23.71	1.89	1.60	0.29	2.49	0.06	19.19	0.08
娄底地区	223.04	34.68	28.32	6.07	15.47	2.15	169.44	1.30
娄底市	23.41	10.50	9.09	1.35	3.08	0.92	8.73	0.18
冷水江市	20.59	8.29	6.90	1.32	2.84	0.30	8.98	0.18
涟源市	57.64	5.96	4.69	1.27	4.06	0.51	46.64	0.47
双峰县	51.76	3.94	3.08	0.86	2.08	0.11	45.44	0.19
新化县	69.64	5.99	4.56	1.27	3.41	0.31	59.65	0.28

18－3 续表3 (1997年底) 单位:万人

名称	从业人员人数	职工	#国有经济单位	#城镇集体经济单位	城镇个体劳动者	城镇私营企业从业人员	农村社会劳动者	其他社会劳动者
永州市	301.47	32.75	27.81	4.52	10.89	2.00	254.65	1.18
永州市直	6.52	5.75	5.36	0.10	0.03	0.32	0.37	0.05
芝山区	26.87	2.33	1.95	0.38	1.38	0.04	23.07	0.05
冷水滩区	21.05	2.53	1.98	0.54	1.63	0.50	16.26	0.13
东安县	26.16	2.55	2.05	0.48	1.33	0.03	22.01	0.24
道县	35.30	3.12	2.70	0.41	0.53	0.06	31.42	0.17
宁远县	46.40	2.61	2.09	0.51	0.73	0.02	42.98	0.06
江永县	12.91	1.87	1.71	0.15	0.51	0.01	10.49	0.03
江华县	23.51	2.01	1.82	0.19	0.56	0.06	20.83	0.05
蓝山县	19.92	1.46	1.35	0.11	1.08	0.31	17.01	0.06
新田县	21.35	1.56	1.34	0.20	0.56	0.08	19.12	0.03
双牌县	8.48	1.34	1.19	0.16	0.40	0.04	6.64	0.06
祁阳县	53.00	5.62	4.27	1.29	2.15	0.53	44.45	0.25
怀化地区	260.19	33.38	26.90	5.69	13.26	0.93	211.13	1.49
怀化市	31.02	6.94	5.47	0.91	4.52	0.29	18.98	0.29
洪江市	5.36	2.48	1.86	0.54	0.53	0.14	2.12	0.09
黔阳县	23.07	2.92	2.42	0.45	0.78	0.07	19.20	0.10
沅陵县	31.91	3.82	3.19	0.61	1.42	0.02	26.56	0.09
辰溪县	26.87	4.05	3.32	0.73	0.97	0.02	21.60	0.23
溆浦县	43.05	3.94	3.18	0.73	1.98	0.13	36.90	0.10
麻阳县	18.83	1.72	1.42	0.29	0.87	0.03	16.14	0.07
新晃县	15.68	1.44	1.15	0.29	0.55	0.09	13.50	0.10
芷江县	19.14	1.72	1.33	0.38	0.58	0.04	16.70	0.10
会同县	19.59	1.65	1.41	0.23	0.37	0.02	17.37	0.18
靖州县	13.56	1.60	1.26	0.33	0.51	0.05	11.31	0.09
通道县	12.11	1.10	0.89	0.20	0.18	0.03	10.75	0.05
湘西自治州	135.27	17.53	14.98	2.44	5.39	0.51	111.65	0.19
吉首市	15.27	4.92	4.42	0.44	1.43	0.25	8.64	0.03
泸溪县	15.15	1.75	1.55	0.21	0.72	0.05	12.61	0.02
凤凰县	19.07	1.59	1.35	0.24	0.74	0.03	16.71	
花垣县	14.35	1.77	1.38	0.39	0.55	0.07	11.95	0.01
保靖县	14.86	1.55	1.27	0.28	0.32	0.01	12.96	0.02
古丈县	7.60	0.91	0.79	0.12	0.10	0.01	6.57	0.01
永顺县	22.25	2.52	2.21	0.31	0.61	0.03	19.08	0.01
龙山县	26.72	2.52	2.01	0.45	0.92	0.06	23.13	0.09
未列入地区的单位	17.74	12.92	12.92			2.27		2.55

18—4 各地、市、县国有单位各行业职工人数(1997年底)

Staff and Workers in State－Owned Units by Sector and by Prefecture, City and County

单位:人

名称	农林牧渔业	采掘业	制造业	电力、煤气及水的生产和供应业	建筑业	地质勘查业、水利管理业	交通运输仓储及邮电通信业	批发和零售贸易、餐饮业
长沙市	23434	14747	190805	7026	50916	10654	34527	77381
长沙市区	21785	499	156184	4978	50799	7986	26906	61352
浏阳市	872	6311	5559	1307		596	1247	5454
长沙县	27	197	11286	85		492	3451	2192
望城县	320	156	8515	108		155	997	2225
宁乡县	430	7584	9261	548	117	1425	1926	6158
株洲市	13955	11406	150910	7665	21162	2958	10084	28764
株洲市区	8250	1769	120308	5232	20741	1759	5703	11966
醴陵市	364	1701	13198	472	328	377	1586	5264
株洲县	149	684	3490	241	52	138	701	1985
攸县	1152	2217	10530	702	29	356	992	4886
茶陵县	3229	4922	2701	303	12	266	746	3204
炎陵县	811	113	683	715		62	356	1459
湘潭市	1681	13215	136916	3836	16994	2872	6749	17853
湘潭市区	386	7224	114274	3293	14676	2057	5129	11434
湘乡市	957	332	16784	496		496	1011	3173
韶山市	47		1965	47	1300		108	654
湘潭县	291	5659	3893		1018	319	501	2592
衡阳市	6867	50942	163203	10088	19279	7081	15714	43316
衡阳市区	1630	3579	103816	4733	13342	2594	11471	17904
耒阳市	504	30966	5205	2217	648	1751	716	5060
常宁市	662	7388	15722	820	906	182	578	4092
衡阳县	585	469	10365	368		769	765	2981
衡南县	1382	4237	5805	142	3962	1145	377	4509
衡山县	530	1505	4387	242	404	151	494	2045
衡东县	779	1062	5860	1546		212	482	3127
祁东县	795	1736	12043	20	17	277	831	3598

18—4 续表1 (1997 年底) 单位:人

名称	农林牧渔业	采掘业	制造业	电力、煤气及水的生产和供应业	建筑业	地质勘查业、水利管理业	交通运输仓储及邮电通信业	批发和零售贸易、餐饮业
邵阳市	22535	19367	85933	9153	16164	5132	14136	39597
邵阳市区	2293	2345	62513	3174	14936	1053	8105	12408
武冈市	2974	1214	1789	1578	192	1323	525	3423
邵东县	366	9420	3838	301	719	227	919	4331
新邵县	1298	1660	6974	194		170	774	2523
邵阳县	3416	2120	1587	992	72	167	553	3232
隆回县	623	971	2697	316		565	880	3456
洞口县	5316	1290	2785	1099		700	569	3965
绥宁县	985		18	672	62	119	584	1491
新宁县	2149	347	1941	62		800	617	2987
城步县	3115		1791	765	183	8	610	1781
岳阳市	101288	5462	135720	5326	14912	3908	13714	43838
岳阳市直	2558		86137	3130	8922	314	7977	15330
岳阳楼区	21		533					157
云溪区	2196		226	22	27	78	22	522
君山区	43434		8533	184	5074	7	19	1796
汨罗市	36487	235	7944	161	526	233	411	4407
临湘市	5564	4159	8103	162	313	509	967	4165
岳阳县	2781		4155	163	26	701	842	4448
华容县	2844	47	5126	230		1347	1397	5168
湘阴县	3093		10741	207		710	731	5021
平江县	2310	1021	4222	1067	24	9	1348	2824
常德市	65382	10895	97661	7265	3906	7778	15241	46417
常德市区	19539	532	47448	3366	3130	1845	10070	16371
武陵区	40		670		122	3	18	2622
鼎城区	19226	532	8376	217	353	1842	542	4614
津市市	2373	2226	9079	523		244	1779	3127
安乡县	2578	38	4863	219	28	676	697	4848
汉寿县	32320		8174	137	324	803	669	5029
澧县	2887	2719	7022	127	22	1941	499	5345
临澧县	211	401	3690	311	87	448	332	3737
桃源县	1816		11215	566		1070	448	4324
石门县	3658	4979	6170	2016	315	751	747	3636

18—4 续表 2　　(1997 年底)　　单位:人

名　称	农林牧渔业	采掘业	制造业	电力、煤气及水的生产和供应业	建筑业	地质勘查业、水利管理业	交通运输仓储及邮电通信业	批发和零售贸易、餐饮业
张家界市	4545	2379	10463	4003	2432	1363	3903	10216
张家界市直			1168	756	1449		1063	1350
永定区	2021		3666	342	503	351	663	3185
武陵源区		167	127	54		51	141	115
慈利县	1279	652	3043	990	43	849	1313	3152
桑植县	1245	1560	2459	1861	437	112	723	2414
益阳市	79619	4086	78167	4936	2081	5149	13160	33631
益阳市直	64426		41429	2294	2052	510	9077	4336
资阳区	1710		5502			511	27	4711
赫山区	1889	8	3265	153		265	591	4163
沅江市	8650		9368	119		1619	993	6848
南　县	459	21	4810	373		1494	849	5400
桃江县	1899	2049	8738	676		363	917	5036
安化县	586	2008	5055	1321	29	387	706	3137
郴州市	8894	54412	48076	9300	6823	5077	10289	32144
郴州市直	135	9845	24370	2107	2344	2821	4629	6921
北湖区		147	4371		1024	73	63	2866
苏仙区	611	506	1987	582	453	47	154	1715
资兴市	1036	22300	7691	2550	2056	250	703	3879
桂阳县	1726	8538	841	353	303	571	827	3942
永兴县	418	1665	890	647	441	298	645	2618
宜章县	318	4040	2872	604		140	924	2273
嘉禾县	801	1680	1074	419		160	527	1333
临武县	1050	3571	546	609		152	432	1841
汝城县	1221	1374	628	647		141	540	1695
桂东县	552	434	656	304			383	864
安仁县	1026	312	2150	478	202	424	462	2197
娄底地区	7763	47403	90027	4418	16652	4100	5904	25597
娄底市	723	3063	40370	2057	11694	1760	3518	8036
冷水江市	137	26363	21401	1928	1195	355	540	4626
涟源市	1655	6352	14576	257	1593	856	675	4506
双峰县	907	7597	2963	76	86	211	346	3777
新化县	4341	4028	10717	100	2084	918	825	4652

18—4　续表 3　　(1997 年底)　　单位:人

名　称	农林牧渔业	采掘业	制造业	电力、煤气及水的生产和供应业	建筑业	地质勘查业、水利管理业	交通运输仓储及邮电通信业	批发和零售贸易、餐饮业
永州市	19161	8542	65998	7723	5267	3175	11076	30221
永州市直	1021	735	23896	1971	3119	835	4251	3930
芝山区	434	901	2429	192	590		508	3419
冷水滩区	358	377	3910		630	95	561	3208
东安县	990		4831	718		235	673	2655
道　县	1497	544	9725	115		93	793	2801
宁远县	1026		2951	550		549	790	3269
江永县	5107	582	2172	296	70	137	378	1561
江华县	2502	2387	1244	588		18	706	1459
蓝山县	744		1354	908	510	687	479	1188
新田县	287	72	2081	140		58	550	1771
双牌县	1245	188	2975	476			354	1442
祁阳县	3950	2756	8430	1769	348	468	1033	3518
怀化地区	7340	14453	69270	13109	2496	1428	12143	29358
怀化市	1214	957	9334	3023	1695	700	4277	7785
洪江市	108		11866	540	34		437	1132
黔阳县	624	1114	8196	1239	15	48	941	2525
沅陵县	1165	1259	7437	2553	179	52	1238	4063
辰溪县	578	4137	12913	762	91	212	994	3016
溆浦县	336	3265	8767	1441	37		913	2507
麻阳县	697	1617	1583	795			648	1621
新晃县	241	854	2447	428		91	377	1032
芷江县	412	282	2152	546		133	544	815
会同县	797	558	1771	878	107	50	441	1952
靖州县	820	410	1934	517	258	142	770	1873
通道县	348		870	387	80		563	1037
湘西自治州	2593	2377	38484	7360	1275	1859	7314	16355
吉首市	437		12818	1450	1004	843	3895	5567
泸溪县	561		5625	850	12	105	872	1594
凤凰县	127	220	2346	557	98	93	440	1063
花垣县	129	437	3349	1173		499	391	1184
保靖县	400	153	2824	824			386	1198
古丈县	193		1867	300		53	233	961
永顺县	632	651	4762	1003	59	205	595	2497
龙山县	114	916	4893	1203	102	61	502	2291
未列入地区的在湘单位								
广州铁路公司			1632		4242		86408	8230
铁五局			248		5482			307
总后非企业								

18—4 续表 4 (1997 年底) 单位:人

名称	金融保险业	房地产业	社会服务业	卫生、体育和社会福利业	教育、文化艺术及广播电影电视业	科学研究和综合技术服务业	国家机关、政党机关和社会团体	其他行业
长沙市	13851	3324	26780	27670	93716	26723	60400	5738
长沙市区	11204	2987	24900	21331	57433	25727	38257	5018
浏阳市	848	195	949	2367	10820	129	7116	83
长沙县	440	53	82	635	7736	666	4409	416
望城县	582		88	1066	6131	89	3525	38
宁乡县	777	89	761	2271	11596	112	7093	183
株洲市	6643	1148	7555	7876	37008	5304	29503	1108
株洲市区	4376	524	6412	3724	10307	4357	11244	218
醴陵市	708	285	244	1337	7317	491	4425	254
株洲县	318	77	166	624	4060	111	2667	18
攸县	495	92	309	798	7064	187	5334	
茶陵县	405	109	128	837	5722	101	3599	8
炎陵县	341	61	296	556	2538	57	2234	610
湘潭市	4612	1186	5727	7458	30549	1744	23081	1774
湘潭市区	3369	1074	4467	4830	12607	1652	10936	1282
湘乡市	661	112	653	1213	7798	34	4510	465
韶山市	131		548	404	1381	16	1408	
湘潭县	451		59	1011	8763	42	6227	27
衡阳市	7947	2938	10721	19496	59831	3716	45809	2061
衡阳市区	4401	2295	8316	7779	12937	2010	11807	776
耒阳市	619	243	810	2246	8730	35	5243	164
常宁市	486	98	543	1639	6393	141	5691	438
衡阳县	592	39	165	3046	6706	168	6447	158
衡南县	489	47	139	1727	9108	940	6092	129
衡山县	464	62	201	731	3515	150	2559	87
衡东县	425	84	263	985	4662	51	3329	67
祁东县	471	70	284	1343	7780	221	4641	242

18—4 续表5　　(1997年底)　　单位:人

名 称	金融保险业	房地产业	社会服务业	卫生、体育和社会福利业	教育、文化艺术及广播电影电视业	科学研究和综合技术服务业	国家机关、政党机关和社会团体	其他行业
邵阳市	6952	1255	6770	13746	63773	1980	44050	1038
邵阳市区	3059	638	4843	3475	7986	1207	9563	265
武冈市	399	148	208	1275	5762	138	3543	52
邵东县	656	57	77	1228	10657	283	5330	105
新邵县	358	17	227	1176	5632	35	3721	48
邵阳县	521	61	149	990	7577	49	4131	105
隆回县	498	53	132	1512	8305	82	5067	30
洞口县	437	145	309	1403	6461	20	3784	84
绥宁县	335	33	243	920	3412	50	2752	45
新宁县	343	71	289	1136	4709	77	3645	112
城步县	346	32	293	631	3272	39	2514	192
岳阳市	5896	692	6521	11673	45025	1703	38770	1812
岳阳市直	3204	293	3101	2467	4787	910	8358	649
岳阳楼区		113	91	517	1943	87	2055	17
云溪区			567	222	495		1164	18
君山区			408	236	396		1985	250
汨罗市	381		388	749	6884	147	4486	216
临湘市	462	49	281	933	4318	239	3894	274
岳阳县	383	26	427	1624	6388	58	4379	221
华容县	461	18	701	1364	7259	43	4272	34
湘阴县	424	85	240	1331	5342	106	3578	
平江县	581	108	317	2230	7213	113	4599	133
常德市	6645	1458	7715	13323	50329	2477	40545	1845
常德市区	3007	609	4641	4436	12979	1076	12955	1157
武陵区	231	88	496	755	2033	42	1467	115
鼎城区	629	152	578	1398	6773	227	5959	
津市市	502	202	687	833	2764	79	2093	105
安乡县	441	29	246	883	4647	82	3289	42
汉寿县	492	118	284	1404	6035	597	4456	8
澧 县	605	168	393	1073	6393	171	5348	49
临澧县	471	149	524	792	3972	120	3206	16
桃源县	619	67	549	2465	8069	246	5106	166
石门县	508	116	391	1437	5470	106	4092	302

18—4 续表 6 （1997 年底） 单位：人

名称	金融保险业	房地产业	社会服务业	卫生、体育和社会福利业	教育、文化艺术及广播电影电视业	科学研究和综合技术服务业	国家机关、政党机关和社会团体	其他行业
张家界市	2022	418	4982	4544	14965	480	13997	98
张家界市直	805	99	1623	950	1027	163	2658	15
永定区	364	154	627	608	4170	179	2695	
武陵源区	98	7	1519	72	3	6	1136	20
慈利县	436	106	730	1826	5456	91	4316	41
桑植县	319	52	483	1088	4309	41	3192	22
益阳市	4572	1263	3352	10774	39959	1634	30560	511
益阳市直	1417	432	2223	1276	3169	588	5806	68
资阳区	562		147	1275	3966	11	2509	13
赫山区	559	49	197	1408	7365	94	3966	57
沅江市	524	239	406	2043	6450	596	4430	
南县	462	217	95	1195	5769	47	3861	81
桃江县	568	152	132	1448	6996	78	3737	187
安化县	480	174	152	2129	6244	220	6251	105
郴州市	5877	795	6758	11549	45043	1373	41645	988
郴州市直	1732	330	3905	2623	3567	781	5627	310
北湖区	718	10	414	790	3189	6	2632	48
苏仙区	351	20	141	627	3380	114	2773	62
资兴市	497	72	555	1011	4133	46	3467	176
桂阳县	373	99	306	1167	6760	67	4417	97
永兴县	348	55	346	1048	4879	96	3953	27
宜章县	454	44	322	925	4074	26	4298	24
嘉禾县	317	32	258	786	2748	20	3235	107
临武县	330	37	179	548	3217	39	2585	32
汝城县	304	29	60	688	2661	68	3602	92
桂东县	172	26	113	438	2044	27	2134	
安仁县	281	41	159	898	4391	83	2922	13
娄底地区	3661	929	5211	9419	31977	688	28163	1281
娄底市	1711	525	2151	1687	6090	339	6754	373
冷水江市	550	153	1996	816	4660	141	4013	141
涟源市	514	87	504	2885	6848	50	5461	73
双峰县	417	38	169	1355	6905	72	5797	115
新化县	469	126	391	2676	7474	86	6138	579

18－4 续表7 (1997年底) 单位:人

名称	金融保险业	房地产业	社会服务业	卫生、体育和社会福利业	教育、文化艺术及广播电影电视业	科学研究和综合技术服务业	国家机关、政党机关和社会团体	其他行业
永州市	5271	1377	6947	14182	52783	1539	44236	553
永州市直	1036	269	3195	1927	2220	632	4168	335
芝山区	538	28	166	1505	5163	18	3539	32
冷水滩区	527	38	563	1190	4768	26	3559	
东安县	401	168	309	1092	4726	123	3576	
道县	379	209	239	844	5045	19	4726	
宁远县	387	91	521	1267	5719	21	3794	
江永县	273	74	321	473	3140	71	2343	106
江华县	293	49	300	1136	4281	36	3168	
蓝山县	420	51	171	619	3096	32	3238	33
新田县	261	61	328	740	4247	24	2799	
双牌县	187	23	154	619	1631	209	2311	30
祁阳县	569	316	680	2770	8747	328	7015	17
怀化地区	6074	1132	6513	11626	46995	2261	43823	1028
怀化市	1982	164	3529	2837	7995	791	8109	357
洪江市	348	211	439	845	1085	53	1434	82
黔阳县	388	43	126	1054	3926	32	3850	52
沅陵县	557	197	640	950	6019	179	5148	287
辰溪县	399	68	430	1004	4297	88	4184	32
溆浦县	484	108	282	1127	6608	861	5044	23
麻阳县	267	89	206	802	3120	89	2590	47
新晃县	338	39	285	672	2170	59	2388	30
芷江县	344	68	276	615	3418		3579	68
会同县	324	105	102	498	3372	39	3067	
靖州县	350	33	121	652	2482	12	2250	
通道县	293	7	77	570	2503	58	2180	50
湘西自治州	3405	392	3740	7432	28700	1101	27086	372
吉首市	1416	213	1410	2249	5736	629	6374	151
泸溪县	309	26	225	761	2313	74	2087	70
凤凰县	283	50	238	508	3842	75	3586	32
花垣县	225	11	264	679	2641	91	2675	16
保靖县	250	6	213	556	3048	49	2793	28
古丈县	171		173	456	1595	27	1827	28
永顺县	383	40	763	1067	5371	101	3924	
龙山县	368	46	454	1156	4154	55	3820	47
未列入地区的在湘单位								
广州铁路公司				3570	4507	77		
铁五局				552	64			
总后非企业								13754

18—5 各地、市、县城镇集体单位各行业职工人数(1997年底)

Staff and Workers in Urban Collective－Owned Units by Sector and by Prefecture,City and County

单位:人

名 称	农林牧渔业	采掘业	制造业	电力、煤气及水的生产和供应业	建筑业	地质勘查业、水利管理业	交通运输仓储及邮电通信业	批发和零售贸易、餐饮业
长沙市	672	229	100886	52	29988	117	7362	38608
长沙市区	59		76725		28975	7	3444	23319
浏阳市			4894	52	495		606	3989
长沙县	560		2897		89		853	3740
望城县	3	94	8346			110	2025	2782
宁乡县	50	135	8024		429		434	4778
株洲市	816	103	48907		10355		6317	18225
株洲市区			32406		7789		3678	5812
醴陵市			8423		589		772	4888
株洲县	226		2447		828		502	1801
攸 县	311		3993		568		408	2989
茶陵县	248	95	1073		401		874	1910
炎陵县	31	8	565		180		83	825
湘潭市	22	352	42944	77	12441	166	6772	15360
湘潭市区			35400		7439	64	3222	7616
湘乡市	22	352	6360	77	2799	76	1921	3115
韶山市			279		1635	26		293
湘潭县			905		568		1629	4336
衡阳市	969	367	48849		18615		7763	31090
衡阳市区	18	367	27285		8905		1864	8631
耒阳市			2107		200		2366	3458
常宁市	330		6702		137		1299	2597
衡阳县			3771		428		245	5363
衡南县	595		1601		4391		561	5486
衡山县	26		2541		438		504	1020
衡东县			3065		715		823	1821
祁东县			1777		3401		101	2714

18—5 续表 1 (1997 年底) 单位:人

名　称	农林牧渔业	采掘业	制造业	电力、煤气及水的生产和供应业	建筑业	地质勘查业、水利管理业	交通运输仓储及邮电通信业	批发和零售贸易、餐饮业
邵阳市	397	690	31453	25	13051	58	4001	23919
邵阳市区	397	66	12435	25	6616		2017	3899
武冈市		14	3907		1483		285	2056
邵东县		417	2871		1358		677	3673
新邵县		34	1840		924		170	1967
邵阳县			2213		299		225	3247
隆回县			1913		911		134	2415
洞口县		159	4633		414		261	2822
绥宁县			436		243	58	137	1169
新宁县			636		538		95	1931
城步县			569		265			740
岳阳市	2457	778	31832	205	17531	85	5916	24972
岳阳市直			15282		8082		1991	2419
岳阳楼区	76	109	1828		2090	6	353	916
云溪区			609	36	377		110	874
君山区	18		121	31				196
汨罗市	1050	124	1997		1212		1140	2788
临湘市	879		1537		270		293	1941
岳阳县		247	2060		800	79	110	2782
华容县			4571	64	3877		855	5387
湘阴县	274		2233		221		1064	4517
平江县	160	298	1594	74	602			3152
常德市	1568	215	31255	119	8948	1156	9267	33206
常德市区	336	193	13008		3268	188	2512	7180
武陵区			8053		1247		1224	2231
鼎城区	336	193	3251		1915		1215	4092
津市市	98		4977		812		628	1888
安乡县	269		1695		846	517	963	4895
汉寿县	367		3004		1046	428	1159	4112
澧　县	325		2830		476		1221	4826
临澧县	173		1987	119	432	23	911	2918
桃源县			2518		1165		1247	4132
石门县		22	1236		903		626	3255

18—5 续表 2　　(1997 年底)　　单位:人

名　称	农林牧渔业	采掘业	制造业	电力、煤气及水的生产和供应业	建筑业	地质勘查业、水利管理业	交通运输仓储及邮电通信业	批发和零售贸易、餐饮业
张家界市	518	178	5522		4007		742	5812
张家界市直			11					107
永定区		178	1220		2116		189	2254
武陵源区								
慈利县	311		4082		1557		370	2186
桑植县	207		209		334		183	1265
益阳市	499	359	37326	338	6780	436	9115	23092
益阳市直	28		4345		1248		3762	2548
资阳区			7306		24			2524
赫山区	315		4519			369		3570
沅江市	24	5	6066		1041	67	1950	3666
南　县	38		3858		818		295	5153
桃江县	19		2139		1490		1750	2350
安化县	75	354	9093	338	2159		1358	3281
郴州市	530	950	13795		3610	69	2076	14783
郴州市直		342	790		949		93	1487
北湖区		33	3938		462	51	629	1847
苏仙区			914		209		60	827
资兴市	193		2530				325	1842
桂阳县		75	2575		256		118	1771
永兴县	177		863		23	18	524	1271
宜章县			522		630		98	1398
嘉禾县	98		644		120		66	683
临武县		480	19		223			772
汝城县		9	266		156			999
桂东县	62	11	119		400			491
安仁县			615		182		163	1395
娄底地区	876	1168	29643	24	4286		6671	13973
娄底市		50	8498		619		1236	2270
冷水江市		717	5901	24	1644		2125	2029
涟源市	476	174	6552		133		952	3883
双峰县	400		2027		1155		928	2845
新化县		227	6665		735		1430	2946

18—5 续表 3 (1997 年底) 单位:人

名 称	农林牧渔业	采掘业	制造业	电力、煤气及水的生产和供应业	建筑业	地质勘查业、水利管理业	交通运输仓储及邮电通信业	批发和零售贸易、餐饮业
永州市	1120	337	14185		5796	88	2729	14942
永州市直			241				97	409
芝山区			1153		418		87	1743
冷水滩区	152	153	2066		747	42	581	1364
东安县	264	154	1264		591		71	1615
道 县	68		710		818	33	449	1450
宁远县	281		595		660		183	2503
江永县	70		179		410			545
江华县	119		254		215	13		681
蓝山县			111		279		25	365
新田县	166		176		507			896
双牌县			560		273		55	161
祁阳县		30	6876		878		1181	3210
怀化地区	364		18050	544	5277	418	6310	15622
怀化市			2271		642		374	4004
洪江市			3693		342		630	421
黔阳县			1434		467		413	1270
沅陵县			1492	356	335	58	628	1932
辰溪县			3372	85	549		1023	1265
溆浦县			1323		393	360	1530	2564
麻阳县			818		532		416	674
新晃县			1131	20	373		301	84
芷江县	129		1384	83	512		82	724
会同县	216		256		161		84	928
靖州县			649		574		615	978
通道县	19		227		397		214	778
湘西自治州	511	100	8096	99	3113		1520	8422
吉首市	30		1022	51	878		390	1602
泸溪县			533		125		454	814
凤凰县	253		759		195			924
花垣县		100	2545	48	76		60	739
保靖县			875		529		110	946
古丈县			329		105		310	361
永顺县			716		659		18	1271
龙山县	228		1317		546		178	1765

18—5 续表 4 (1997 年底) 单位:人

名称	金融保险业	房地产业	社会服务业	卫生、体育和社会福利业	教育、文化艺术及广播电影电视业	科学研究和综合技术服务业	国家机关、政党机关和社会团体	其他行业
长沙市	2468	223	6178	5118	840	91	577	563
长沙市区	340	223	5931	1202	581	36	429	252
浏阳市	748			1409	25		39	31
长沙县	421		17	798		55	38	24
望城县	350			560	234		29	
宁乡县	609		230	1149			42	256
株洲市	3118	58	1543	3577	72	216	233	253
株洲市区	1393	53	1119	568	16	33	213	109
醴陵市	528		348	1063	52	174		26
株洲县	303			506		9	20	
攸县	358			925				
茶陵县	361	5	76	351				43
炎陵县	175			164	4			75
湘潭市	1469	27	940	2722	229	26	45	369
湘潭市区	213	27	830	292	180	26	18	332
湘乡市	533		110	893	45			27
韶山市	101			111				10
湘潭县	622			1426	4		27	
衡阳市	5396	127	2031	4814	101		343	194
衡阳市区	994	127	1456	841	101		314	8
耒阳市	362		108	135				40
常宁市	353		223	939				29
衡阳县	1816							
衡南县	722			1027				
衡山县	204			289			15	31
衡东县	243			721			10	30
祁东县	702		244	862			4	56

18—5 续表 5

(1997 年底)

单位:人

名称	金融保险业	房地产业	社会服务业	卫生、体育和社会福利业	教育、文化艺术及广播电影电视业	科学研究和综合技术服务业	国家机关、政党机关和社会团体	其他行业
邵阳市	3636	89	4448	4579	208		69	522
邵阳市区	378	89	3332	193	145		37	211
武冈市	328		180	259				35
邵东县	629		106	967	49			63
新邵县	354		65	566	3			48
邵阳县	283		299	635				39
隆回县	438			644			32	11
洞口县	436		289	361	4			43
绥宁县	296		58	386				32
新宁县	262		74	431				40
城步县	232		45	137	7			
岳阳市	3006	139	1390	2453	81		563	1334
岳阳市直		139	1213		44			104
岳阳楼区	111		67	220			283	26
云溪区				176				
君山区				50			40	
汨罗市	728			489			67	965
临湘市	369			326			28	36
岳阳县	508							42
华容县	400		15	634	37		145	69
湘阴县	382		90	514				38
平江县	508		5	44				54
常德市	3930	67	826	5245	406	21	493	272
常德市区	983	30	111	1593	176	21	54	146
武陵区	364	30	56	279				99
鼎城区	619		38	1314	65		54	
津市市	189		3	229	14		23	
安乡县	333	37	49	739	55		99	13
汉寿县	540		148	757	62		90	
澧　县	416		186	945	53			77
临澧县	406		160	637			95	
桃源县	606		57		29		69	
石门县	457		112	345	17		63	36

18－5　续表 6　　(1997 年底)　　单位:人

名　称	金融保险业	房地产业	社会服务业	卫生、体育和社会福利业	教育、文化艺术及广播电影电视业	科学研究和综合技术服务业	国家机关、政党机关和社会团体	其他行业
张家界市	836		271	370			30	83
张家界市直	14		29					20
永定区	259		52	317			30	
武陵源区								
慈利县	329		190	53				35
桑植县	234							28
益阳市	3426		590	3595	143	11	237	221
益阳市直	96						37	
资阳区	474		22	459	51		124	
赫山区	704			646	32			40
沅江市	521		283	492	20		76	11
南　县	548		179	659				121
桃江县	618		106	920	30	11		
安化县	465			419	10			49
郴州市	2893	16	623	2209	6	14	384	1785
郴州市直	131		5					109
北湖区	237	16		128	6		126	23
苏仙区	268			205		14	118	28
资兴市	413							
桂阳县	417		4	483			48	111
永兴县	253		14	352				1382
宜章县	311		600	235			39	
嘉禾县	131			186				61
临武县	171			140			9	27
汝城县	200			187				32
桂东县	114			79			10	12
安仁县	247			214			34	
娄底地区	1983		411	1283	81	43	230	28
娄底市	329		101	328		23	68	
冷水江市	233		80	410		20	28	
涟源市	395				46		58	
双峰县	488		111	545	35		35	
新化县	538		119				41	28

18—5 续表 7 (1997 年底) 单位:人

名　称	金　融 保险业	房　地 产　业	社　会 服务业	卫生、体 育和社会 福利业	教育、文 化艺术及 广播电影 电视业	科学研究 和综合技 术服务业	国家机 关、政党 机关和 社会团体	其　他 行　业
永州市	2974		320	1694	74		133	860
永州市直	60		77		31			44
芝山区	402		5					
冷水滩区	236							32
东安县	406			441			25	
道　县	226			285			51	
宁远县	264		144	401	43		3	55
江永县	142		69	67				31
江华县	236			391			20	
蓝山县			25					290
新田县	144			109			34	
双牌县	110							408
祁阳县	748							
怀化地区	4272	23	949	3414	121	69	620	858
怀化市	722	14	281	599			114	67
洪江市	175		22	92			31	5
黔阳县	532		69	322			23	
沅陵县	386		108	590			215	37
辰溪县	468		167	283	38		75	10
溆浦县	395		80	549	52		53	34
麻阳县	272			141	31		31	6
新晃县	294		62					652
芷江县	228		114	475			29	23
会同县	371			228			24	
靖州县	262		12	135		69		24
通道县	167	9	34				25	
湘西自治州	1449		157	689	45		70	156
吉首市	249		49	17	45			42
泸溪县	135							
凤凰县	203							40
花垣县	119		14	137			28	
保靖县	149		9	178				23
古丈县	82							19
永顺县	249		15	159			42	
龙山县	263		70	198				32

18—6 各地、市、县职工工资总额和年平均工资（1997年）

Total Wage Bill and Average Annual Wage of Staff and Workers by Prefecture, City and County

名称	工资总额（万元）	国有单位	城镇集体单位	年平均工资（元）	国有单位	城镇集体单位	年平均工资为上年%
长沙市	557968	454437	78629	6281	6867	4124	107.4
长沙市区	447508	369084	58259	6565	7180	4213	107.7
浏阳市	31146	24798	5851	5536	5763	4830	101.6
长沙县	24801	18543	3952	5600	5887	4169	114.4
望城县	19511	13754	4055	4835	5767	2764	114.6
宁乡县	35002	28258	6512	5321	5727	4044	101.5
株洲市	275721	217099	44062	6062	6362	4784	103.6
株洲市区	198230	156634	30667	7046	7254	5801	106.1
醴陵市	24759	17522	4499	4021	4581	2667	91.5
株洲县	10174	7769	2246	4593	5021	3527	98.9
攸县	21562	16877	4262	4886	4910	4923	98.8
茶陵县	13644	11991	1488	4217	4523	2801	102.1
炎陵县	7352	6306	900	5534	5868	4413	111.3
湘潭市	207442	170533	31807	5600	6146	3824	102.3
湘潭市区	149205	124549	19672	5654	6269	3534	103.3
湘乡市	33810	25806	7996	6204	6740	4936	100.3
韶山市	5377	4322	945	5243	5571	4034	110.7
湘潭县	19050	15856	3194	4773	5216	3356	101.1
衡阳市	282995	237667	38690	4752	5105	3246	101.1
衡阳市区	131511	109850	16009	4897	5243	3154	102.0
耒阳市	34547	31834	2407	4731	5016	2742	104.2
常宁市	27850	23605	4245	4756	5153	3329	98.6
衡阳县	19795	16271	3524	4412	4865	3086	104.4
衡南县	23814	18696	5071	4418	4705	3628	101.6
衡山县	11701	9399	1940	5147	5442	4001	101.8
衡东县	13477	11059	2317	4521	4881	3344	91.3
祁东县	20300	16953	3177	4605	5006	3267	97.9

注：工资总额中包括其他各种所有制单位的资料。

18—6　续表1　(1997年)

名　称	工资总额(万元)	国有单位	城镇集体单位	年平均工资(元)	国有单位	城镇集体单位	年平均工资为上年%
邵阳市	198435	163428	27893	4394	4717	3227	103.2
邵阳市区	72170	60571	9274	4243	4495	3120	99.0
武冈市	14020	11333	2329	4012	4719	2769	100.5
邵东县	23721	19748	3973	4742	5005	3762	111.8
新邵县	13881	11852	2029	4563	4834	3440	105.2
邵阳县	13940	11239	2273	4197	4419	3193	109.7
隆回县	15967	13278	2311	5026	5386	3624	112.1
洞口县	15772	13320	2405	4222	4791	2555	103.3
绥宁县	10322	6898	1205	5238	6019	4132	106.5
新宁县	10074	8566	1410	4263	4494	3494	100.4
城步县	8568	6623	684	4178	4327	3446	94.5
岳阳市	273633	230959	34258	5038	5282	3683	101.8
岳阳市直	117294	98100	12529	6293	6603	4225	100.6
岳阳楼区	5496	3524	1849	4684	6441	3058	
云溪区	3613	2801	812	4728	5124	3734	
君山区	26754	26529	152	4271	4283	3376	
汨罗市	35410	30676	4112	4626	4973	3889	112.7
临湘市	17055	15255	1640	4313	4627	2882	105.9
岳阳县	13612	10702	2409	4023	4048	3643	102.3
华容县	19707	13429	6236	4260	4460	3884	133.1
湘阴县	16297	13822	2475	4028	4430	2671	101.9
平江县	18395	16121	2044	4670	5115	3152	106.9
常德市	237933	200651	34833	5004	5357	3647	109.4
常德市区	94228	83682	9003	5353	5844	2995	107.7
武陵区	7947	4544	3285	3393	5228	2333	109.2
鼎城区	30617	26495	4122	4772	5181	3168	108.0
津市市	17572	14756	2643	4836	5510	2976	114.8
安乡县	16089	10780	4880	4674	4607	4865	119.7
汉寿县	26450	22647	3698	3830	3907	3486	105.9
澧　县	20928	16659	4269	4595	4867	3773	106.7
临澧县	14183	10941	3241	5538	6054	4302	106.8
桃源县	24454	20415	4039	5266	5587	4081	115.1
石门县	24029	20771	3060	5714	6043	4252	110.0

18—6 续表 2 (1997年)

名称	工资总额(万元)	国有单位	城镇集体单位	年平均工资(元)	国有单位	城镇集体单位	年平均工资为上年%
张家界市	50071	43034	5851	5047	5437	3364	104.6
张家界市直	9706	9185	99	7051	7061	5294	145.9
永定区	11979	9547	2198	4667	4977	3716	95.1
武陵源区	2162	2015		5814	5711		137.3
慈利县	15616	12465	2768	4631	5289	3137	93.2
桑植县	10608	9822	786	4750	4945	3183	103.3
益阳市	167632	136429	27000	4110	4364	3151	105.5
益阳市直	61493	55868	3363	3910	3972	2782	108.6
资阳区	9438	7096	2291	3050	3564	2099	95.4
赫山区	15265	10726	3928	4279	4492	3904	106.2
沅江市	24166	19390	4735	4294	4626	3324	102.9
南县	17348	12362	4389	4592	4939	3848	117.0
桃江县	18794	15261	2900	4280	4686	3012	96.1
安化县	21128	15726	5394	4582	5469	3112	105.1
郴州市	189506	167223	17912	5604	5832	4158	103.7
郴州市直	52069	47783	2231	6566	6640	5670	106.0
北湖区	10210	7412	2149	4061	4610	2891	96.7
苏仙区	8723	7341	1112	5379	5538	4345	100.3
资兴市	35088	31265	3143	6162	6233	5945	101.9
桂阳县	20680	18061	2142	5671	6047	3684	114.7
永兴县	11411	10019	1357	4973	5560	2813	111.4
宜章县	12900	11131	1636	5082	5249	4325	97.5
嘉禾县	8151	7334	799	5424	5645	3964	100.7
临武县	9131	8233	844	5449	5468	5411	108.7
汝城县	7948	7163	785	5155	5269	4299	95.7
桂东县	4558	4066	492	4932	5102	3866	106.4
安仁县	8637	7415	1222	4470	4478	4423	93.8
娄底地区	170919	149309	20535	5106	5434	3580	100.8
娄底市	63449	56765	6356	6217	6440	4761	104.5
冷水江市	42705	37374	5097	5362	5598	4176	99.1
涟源市	23553	20121	3412	4090	4406	2874	96.5
双峰县	17509	15178	2331	4562	5070	2759	101.1
新化县	23703	19871	3339	4152	4491	2899	100.9

18－6　续表 3　　(1997 年)

名　称	工资总额(万元)	国有单位	城镇集体单位	年平均工资(元)	国有单位	城镇集体单位	年平均工资为上年%
永州市	148219	130427	15538	4598	4771	3471	105.0
永州市直	30560	28431	442	5481	5485	4703	118.1
芝山区	9991	8571	1420	4325	4441	3734	89.6
冷水滩区	9780	8152	1567	3909	4155	2942	106.8
东安县	11945	10007	1798	4729	4936	3745	103.4
道　县	14229	12611	1556	4605	4708	3872	101.3
宁远县	11549	9771	1778	4505	4749	3514	104.0
江永县	8211	7692	505	4522	4633	3308	103.6
江华县	8486	7580	905	4230	4185	4653	94.0
蓝山县	7134	6731	403	4921	5092	3150	100.2
新田县	7503	6489	935	4922	4973	4755	112.0
双牌县	5061	4589	472	3796	3901	3009	98.4
祁阳县	23770	19803	3757	4292	4686	2996	105.6
怀化地区	159846	134911	20921	4827	5066	3681	102.3
怀化市	36844	30019	3663	5405	5623	4022	105.1
洪江市	9517	8218	1148	3775	4358	2077	99.7
黔阳县	13949	12091	1617	4820	5052	3596	101.5
沅陵县	18634	16046	2489	4940	5103	4057	103.2
辰溪县	15529	13236	2293	3843	3996	3146	98.8
溆浦县	17586	15078	2445	4504	4781	3369	97.1
麻阳县	8738	7640	1043	5112	5413	3629	106.2
新晃县	8034	6750	1284	5612	5928	4384	110.9
芷江县	8814	7209	1572	5195	5515	4143	104.4
会同县	8664	7603	958	5291	5447	4335	102.4
靖州县	8238	6591	1588	5163	5259	4762	98.9
通道县	5299	4430	821	4851	4941	4376	103.9
湘西自治州	85322	75729	9081	4949	5146	3757	102.4
吉首市	28340	25870	2179	5845	5941	5066	108.1
泸溪县	6797	6329	468	3955	4169	2335	89.2
凤凰县	8160	7425	735	5104	5456	3089	94.2
花垣县	8901	7041	1841	5125	5198	4852	108.1
保靖县	6570	5508	1062	4322	4423	3863	106.1
古丈县	3649	3239	410	4099	4180	3556	99.2
永顺县	11716	10582	1134	4706	4878	3542	103.6
龙山县	11189	9735	1252	4594	5031	2728	98.1
未列入地区的在湘单位							
广州铁路公司	129468	129468		12048	12048		111.9
铁五局	5872	5872		8748	8748		99.8
总后非企业	8168	8168		5985	5985		138.7

18—7 各地、市、县国内生产总值(1997年)

Gross Domestic Product by Prefecture, City and County

名　称	国内生产总　值(万元)	第一产业	第二产业	第三产业	国内生产总值为上年%	人均国内生产总值(元)
长沙市	4828691	687320	2075005	2066366	115.9	8476
长沙市区	3021813	64427	1328853	1628533	116.5	18664
浏阳市	527278	158072	244223	124983	115.8	3970
长沙县	643768	138000	378550	127218	118.9	8707
望城县	409975	123257	172390	114328	110.7	5745
宁乡县	535155	189449	201100	144606	112.0	4117
株洲市	2397033	491597	1155827	749609	111.5	6557
株洲市区	1181518	39847	702124	439547	109.7	16564
醴陵市	415904	122247	212373	81284	116.4	4153
株洲县	195812	72342	62068	61402	109.9	4402
攸　县	368622	143196	122800	102626	114.1	4971
茶陵县	172211	86586	43239	42386	109.2	2972
炎陵县	62966	27379	13223	22364	106.3	3576
湘潭市	1875000	371431	824000	679569	110.0	6801
湘潭市区	918472	26340	510849	381283	104.8	14289
湘乡市	444436	144055	167827	132554	115.2	5000
韶山市	59595	13793	24434	21368	109.3	5936
湘潭县	452497	187243	120890	144364	115.5	4023
衡阳市	2643541	902091	899373	842077	110.5	3832
衡阳市区	676619	37217	284852	354550	108.9	8794
耒阳市	436388	138596	182809	114983	109.5	3637
常宁市	329048	109051	135634	84363	102.8	3972
衡阳县	378355	213145	81334	83876	110.4	3325
衡南县	395698	174058	142390	79250	111.8	3912
衡山县	154059	56971	49135	47953	109.1	3894
衡东县	303058	101148	108818	93092	108.5	4660
祁东县	340837	117894	117430	105513	112.3	3762

注:价值指标按当年价格计算,为上年%按可比价格计算。

18—7 续表1 (1997年)

名称	国内生产总值(万元)	第一产业	第二产业	第三产业	国内生产总值为上年%	人均国内生产总值(元)
邵阳市	2046973	868752	598265	579956	112.1	2888
邵阳市区	293120	22577	120942	149601	92.7	5132
武冈市	189405	98893	43921	46591	116.6	2675
邵东县	550858	185590	206710	158558	114.3	4765
新邵县	189840	73049	59800	56991	116.8	2638
邵阳县	214986	107393	50000	57593	115.0	2332
隆回县	244122	107171	69299	67652	115.5	2291
洞口县	239657	127095	39771	72791	113.4	3125
绥宁县	147957	70795	42014	35148	120.8	4314
新宁县	151095	84190	24184	42721	112.3	2605
城步县	50279	23648	11801	14830	111.2	2036
岳阳市	2795623	866303	1018464	910856	113.2	5505
岳阳市区	1112182	60486	572196	479500	111.1	15017
汨罗市	245697	100125	102115	43457	106.7	3885
临湘市	180164	59718	73898	46548	111.7	3850
岳阳县	275000	123000	74000	78000	106.5	3544
华容县	287801	166217	67896	53688	129.7	4070
湘阴县	320664	157446	105498	57720	113.0	4723
平江县	245199	121387	55490	68322	107.8	2525
常德市	2831623	1073300	1019340	738983	109.3	4787
常德市区	772229	230386	305353	236490	100.7	5974
武陵区	376537	26375	200603	149559	91.1	9049
鼎城区	395692	204011	104750	86931	110.2	4514
津市市	91359	33505	35647	22207	110.0	3627
安乡县	206400	112616	40430	53354	93.7	3605
汉寿县	259227	149014	52057	58156	111.7	3237
澧县	349555	136865	74563	138127	100.5	3993
临澧县	220480	70008	100150	50322	105.3	5077
桃源县	469080	209435	139535	120110	118.8	4821
石门县	235879	93813	82806	59260	110.0	3365

18—7 续表 2 (1997年)

名 称	国内生产总值(万元)	第一产业	第二产业	第三产业	国内生产总值为上年%	人均国内生产总值(元)
张家界市	475513	140111	136040	199362	112.2	3107
永定区	96111	47939	14339	33833	110.6	2400
武陵源区	14000	4447	1120	8433	118.3	3139
慈利县	148003	64717	34624	48662	110.0	2208
桑植县	68555	30700	15528	22327	106.6	1629
益阳市	1730754	560146	574249	596359	111.9	3880
资阳区	145341	43972	53745	47624	114.2	3584
赫山区	283428	93300	103130	86998	111.6	3386
沅江市	270858	112403	75879	82576	126.0	3659
南 县	238859	131797	53086	53976	118.0	3285
桃江县	200164	89456	59892	50816	105.0	2460
安化县	240026	85145	86452	68429	109.2	2547
郴州市	1895096	550074	694007	651015	112.6	4276
北湖区	267574	24471	145122	97981	113.2	9765
苏仙区	177203	34776	71776	70651	112.9	5301
资兴市	234398	57740	114069	62589	117.5	6544
桂阳县	262108	106547	74463	81098	113.7	3453
永兴县	219242	71051	82503	65688	114.8	3549
宜章县	190762	57212	61642	71908	111.7	3524
嘉禾县	122297	38444	43302	40551	116.2	3717
临武县	99215	34089	38767	26359	113.4	3239
汝城县	101352	38562	32583	30207	112.0	2824
桂东县	33493	15094	7580	10819	112.5	1988
安仁县	114236	65661	27210	21365	115.5	2938
永州市	2138027	802124	720042	615861	112.7	3887
芝山区	326886	83543	149965	93378	111.8	5649
冷水滩区	252184	66653	107987	77544	111.2	5456
东安县	221597	92392	75726	53479	109.4	3884
道 县	232579	103550	75727	53302	108.0	3657
宁远县	170036	74009	59573	36454	105.1	2272

18—7 续表3 （1997年）

名称	国内生产总值（万元）	第一产业	第二产业	第三产业	国内生产总值为上年%	人均国内生产总值（元）
江永县	83768	39502	18255	26011	115.7	3454
江华县	107783	60369	24651	22763	105.3	2456
蓝山县	90722	37551	28584	24587	115.0	2664
新田县	81618	37481	25049	19088	113.1	2215
双牌县	59796	25210	19838	14748	104.0	3602
祁阳县	324976	144854	90115	90007	108.1	3459
娄底地区	1660841	426968	773730	460143	110.8	4246
娄底市	347994	31009	193986	122999	113.6	9263
冷水江市	263294	21566	152993	88735	109.9	7676
涟源市	310839	96512	144255	70072	110.1	2968
双峰县	396138	170674	158532	66932	112.6	4463
新化县	302146	112403	95904	93839	108.9	2401
怀化地区	1900695	613734	611875	675086	111.7	4000
怀化市	432872	51994	127657	253221	119.1	7924
洪江市	45624	6045	25878	13701	103.5	4869
黔阳县	139451	57174	42533	39744	107.8	3446
沅陵县	241310	62417	136204	42689	109.7	3824
辰溪县	108468	44344	28419	35705	111.6	2162
溆浦县	221641	106030	74755	40856	110.5	2663
麻阳县	78432	32463	23189	22780	120.3	2240
新晃县	79102	29423	28656	21023	110.4	3173
芷江县	98399	42472	24321	31606	108.1	2867
会同县	113200	47732	39002	26466	111.7	3349
靖州县	104736	40007	31340	33389	112.1	4220
通道县	41985	18971	10086	12928	105.1	1968
湘西自治州	570515	206829	191457	172229	103.0	2259
吉首市	142752	23832	64831	54089	110.8	5527
泸溪县	54351	24774	13283	16294	99.6	2041
凤凰县	69905	25303	19052	25550	80.3	1966
花垣县	48422	21216	15081	12125	106.7	1867
保靖县	41075	17317	12070	11688	109.4	1503
古丈县	23984	11208	4281	8495	101.3	1798
永顺县	80217	38872	21615	19730	106.0	1702
龙山县	109809	44307	41244	24258	106.8	2163

18—8 各地、市、县耕地面积及播种面积(1997年)

Cultivated Area and Sown Area by Prefecture, City and County

单位:千公顷

名称	耕地面积	水田	旱地	播种面积	粮食作物	经济作物
长沙市	244.07	216.70	27.37	629.15	433.67	27.70
芙蓉区	0.81	0.32	0.49	2.82	0.52	0.01
天心区	1.23	1.05	0.18	3.19	1.85	0.02
岳麓区	2.36	1.81	0.55	6.20	3.27	0.04
开福区	4.17	3.57	0.60	11.76	7.25	0.05
雨花区	3.09	2.34	0.75	7.45	2.65	0.07
浏阳市	65.42	56.26	9.16	167.31	109.31	12.19
长沙县	49.37	45.94	3.43	128.77	87.03	6.22
望城县	40.12	36.80	3.32	104.38	77.57	2.75
宁乡县	77.50	68.61	8.89	197.27	144.22	6.35
株洲市	159.83	141.34	18.49	360.57	253.33	38.82
荷塘区	3.03	2.74	0.29	6.93	5.04	0.09
芦淞区	0.63	0.46	0.17	1.82	1.24	0.02
石峰区	3.01	2.57	0.44	10.34	4.98	0.26
天元区	3.50	3.06	0.44	7.79	5.23	0.28
醴陵市	37.91	33.80	4.11	81.38	63.82	5.43
株洲县	27.32	24.38	2.94	61.65	43.83	3.15
攸县	44.04	38.63	5.41	100.92	62.86	16.28
茶陵县	28.43	24.76	3.67	65.59	47.93	10.91
炎陵县	11.96	10.94	1.02	24.15	18.40	2.40
湘潭市	121.84	110.36	11.48	265.69	201.94	4.77
雨湖区	1.47	1.13	0.34	3.53	1.79	
岳塘区	3.46	2.90	0.56	7.80	5.34	0.19
湘乡市	43.54	38.77	4.77	103.39	74.42	1.78
韶山市	5.22	4.68	0.54	11.99	9.21	0.19
湘潭县	68.15	62.88	5.27	138.98	111.18	2.61
衡阳市	306.05	266.23	39.82	792.43	518.34	138.01
衡阳市郊区	7.77	6.02	1.75	15.60	9.72	1.18
南岳区	1.85	1.61	0.24	4.45	2.79	0.74
耒阳市	49.31	38.67	10.64	127.24	82.27	17.50
常宁市	37.90	33.01	4.89	100.92	70.52	10.85
衡阳县	58.82	52.47	6.35	164.34	98.57	49.07
衡南县	60.54	56.16	4.38	165.11	99.28	38.94
衡山县	17.48	16.20	1.28	39.02	29.55	2.29
衡东县	33.41	29.65	3.76	88.90	60.38	11.53
祁东县	38.97	32.44	6.53	86.85	65.26	5.91

18—8 续表1　　　　(1997年)　　　　单位:千公顷

名称	耕地面积	水田	旱地	播种面积	粮食作物	经济作物
邵阳市	322.23	243.33	78.90	768.49	545.15	94.20
双清区	3.21	2.33	0.88	5.91	4.96	0.35
大祥区	6.20	4.20	2.00	11.92	9.21	0.90
北塔区	2.27	1.69	0.58	6.39	4.17	0.56
武冈市	36.50	29.52	6.98	92.99	67.95	10.32
邵东县	46.27	31.12	15.15	111.07	76.46	6.98
新邵县	29.09	21.00	8.09	71.18	57.18	4.01
邵阳县	45.50	32.90	12.60	106.96	76.05	17.51
隆回县	50.15	38.37	11.78	119.73	80.75	17.97
洞口县	38.12	30.38	7.74	106.57	74.27	18.43
绥宁县	19.97	18.22	1.75	39.50	23.69	6.90
新宁县	32.56	22.81	9.75	71.84	52.77	6.50
城步县	12.39	10.79	1.60	24.43	17.69	3.77
岳阳市	286.65	208.03	78.62	721.04	432.21	150.90
岳阳楼区	1.75	1.14	0.61	4.40	2.91	0.37
云溪区	5.68	3.88	1.80	14.61	8.76	2.42
君山区	25.03	12.50	12.53	50.65	21.52	19.64
汨罗市	42.36	34.41	7.95	98.51	67.70	12.61
临湘市	30.90	22.24	8.66	83.95	51.50	13.63
岳阳县	40.48	31.62	8.86	118.50	77.14	17.93
华容县	54.13	30.68	23.45	141.97	59.96	57.07
湘阴县	38.35	33.00	5.35	99.08	65.18	12.39
平江县	47.97	38.56	9.41	109.37	77.54	14.84
常德市	433.23	316.45	116.78	1101.45	599.22	349.45
武陵区	8.31	5.40	2.91	21.08	9.58	4.55
鼎城区	75.00	59.51	15.49	200.73	112.17	47.35
津市市	16.12	11.25	4.87	40.82	21.03	15.42
安乡县	42.82	24.45	18.37	106.57	45.40	50.41
汉寿县	57.15	44.04	13.11	150.51	81.74	41.57
澧县	67.87	48.87	19.00	157.76	79.72	62.77
临澧县	35.26	28.77	6.49	95.58	54.73	31.58
桃源县	89.12	68.07	21.05	210.37	118.29	62.58
石门县	41.58	26.09	15.49	118.03	76.56	33.22

18－8　续表 2　　(1997 年)　　单位:千公顷

名　　称	耕地面积	水　田	旱　地	播种面积	粮食作物	经济作物
张家界市	88.00	55.77	32.23	245.10	153.39	68.32
永定区	23.17	17.15	6.02	62.52	35.12	19.36
武陵源区	2.07	1.73	0.34	5.60	3.35	1.72
慈利县	41.41	24.46	16.95	106.11	67.41	28.34
桑植县	21.35	12.43	8.92	70.87	47.51	18.90
益阳市	246.48	175.33	71.15	588.12	359.53	115.75
资阳区	19.61	17.20	2.41	49.79	34.34	4.53
赫山区	37.76	33.62	4.14	89.83	63.44	3.54
沅江市	57.74	32.62	25.12	121.32	66.19	36.19
南　县	57.35	35.44	21.91	136.96	57.28	53.57
桃江县	40.69	33.79	6.90	95.81	70.18	3.81
安化县	33.33	22.66	10.67	94.41	68.10	14.11
郴州市	207.17	168.30	38.87	467.87	316.96	64.85
北湖区	8.71	7.19	1.52	17.88	10.00	1.71
苏仙区	15.46	13.32	2.14	27.40	21.74	1.57
资兴市	17.74	16.05	1.69	39.75	28.85	1.96
桂阳县	39.64	27.17	12.47	86.04	51.54	23.64
宜章县	23.05	18.06	4.99	58.32	39.62	4.68
永兴县	25.86	22.13	3.73	64.71	43.77	9.01
嘉禾县	14.12	10.09	4.03	34.82	23.58	5.21
临武县	13.79	10.49	3.30	30.14	19.64	3.83
汝城县	19.29	17.02	2.27	42.33	31.23	1.87
桂东县	9.04	8.28	0.76	15.81	10.53	1.06
安仁县	20.47	18.50	1.97	50.67	36.46	10.31
永州市	283.11	232.67	50.44	720.54	470.10	79.46
芝山区	33.31	30.30	3.01	85.67	59.78	4.70
冷水滩区	24.35	21.82	2.53	65.53	46.29	5.76
祁阳县	43.98	38.93	5.05	118.79	87.65	12.14
东安县	34.67	30.62	4.05	89.85	58.74	6.02
双牌县	7.02	6.14	0.88	18.05	12.52	0.50
道　县	37.29	26.53	10.76	101.72	56.50	9.39
江永县	16.25	12.43	3.82	35.40	20.13	9.36

18—8 续表 3 (1997 年) 单位:千公顷

名称	耕地面积	水田	旱地	播种面积	粮食作物	经济作物
宁远县	32.95	25.38	7.57	71.58	48.06	9.98
蓝山县	16.09	12.62	3.47	34.78	20.40	4.81
新田县	15.28	11.49	3.79	42.90	24.84	7.48
江华县	21.92	16.41	5.51	56.27	35.19	9.32
娄底地区	146.29	107.33	38.96	364.41	282.10	26.30
娄底市	8.57	6.15	2.42	23.91	16.94	0.98
冷水江市	5.50	3.67	1.83	12.65	9.51	0.33
涟源市	42.76	28.37	14.39	104.42	84.99	2.78
双峰县	40.92	33.68	7.24	119.79	89.30	14.57
新化县	48.54	35.46	13.08	103.64	81.36	7.64
怀化地区	242.81	206.86	35.95	585.45	352.37	99.07
怀化市	23.26	21.06	2.20	50.90	29.41	7.52
洪江市	1.80	1.54	0.26	4.24	2.22	0.59
黔阳县	22.14	19.99	2.15	50.63	31.39	6.25
沅陵县	33.22	29.51	3.71	96.21	56.78	18.94
辰溪县	21.47	18.34	3.13	53.51	32.01	7.60
溆浦县	40.70	29.40	11.30	101.84	67.77	19.87
麻阳县	15.93	13.63	2.30	44.80	24.17	9.10
新晃县	13.73	9.71	4.02	34.88	22.63	5.09
芷江县	25.09	21.59	3.50	54.31	32.42	9.18
会同县	17.15	15.67	1.48	36.47	22.39	6.38
靖州县	15.27	14.16	1.11	33.26	16.65	5.91
通道县	13.05	12.26	0.79	24.40	14.53	2.64
湘西自治州	142.34	96.09	46.25	398.67	236.95	108.78
吉首市	9.49	6.27	3.22	29.44	13.12	8.58
泸溪县	13.98	10.48	3.50	39.74	19.40	11.48
凤凰县	23.20	17.54	5.66	63.01	30.69	18.80
花垣县	17.25	10.23	7.02	36.84	24.33	8.00
保靖县	16.64	9.03	7.61	42.75	27.02	10.86
古丈县	7.82	5.69	2.13	20.47	11.51	5.34
永顺县	27.85	21.00	6.85	83.68	56.62	22.95
龙山县	26.11	15.85	10.26	82.74	54.26	22.77

18—9 各地、市、县机耕、灌溉面积及水库、塘坝和堤防(1997年)

Tractor—Ploughed Area and Irrigated Area, Reservoirs, Small Reservoirs and Dikes by Prefecture, City and County

名称	机耕面积(千公顷)	有效灌溉面积(千公顷)	水库(座)	水库库容量(万立方米)	塘坝(座)	塘坝库容量(万立方米)	堤防长度(公里)
长沙市	140.23	224.41	767	116138	235493	98723	512
芙蓉区	0.20	0.75	2	155	75	65	19
天心区	1.00	1.06	2	48	707	252	11
岳麓区	1.02	2.28	17	592	1992	1356	32
开福区	2.82	4.11	17	708	3926	3955	75
雨花区	1.25	2.70	8	543	1850	1025	26
浏阳市	28.60	63.96	177	56930	55172	16170	
长沙县	31.44	45.03	173	18120	61341	20200	98
望城县	36.00	37.73	90	6794	37330	15400	201
宁乡县	37.90	66.79	281	32248	73100	40300	50
株洲市	98.98	146.90	885	89459	97327	43170	157
荷塘区	1.80	3.03	17	571	2098	1289	
芦淞区	0.60	0.63	3	51	931	318	7
石峰区	1.88	3.01	13	668	2753	1506	7
天元区	1.78	3.24	12	157	2071	1386	32
醴陵市	26.37	34.68	193	27146	26050	6541	
株洲县	17.68	24.76	144	10408	17202	11700	111
攸县	28.59	42.53	299	41268	21820	15430	
茶陵县	16.66	24.21	193	8560	22302	4780	
炎陵县	3.62	10.81	11	630	2100	220	
湘潭市	72.53	115.54	380	95945	137333	56162	277
雨湖区	0.76	1.47	1	20	1760	1256	17
岳塘区	2.38	3.06	6	362	3406	2084	30
湘乡市	22.00	43.54	181	73700	72600	18900	78
韶山市	4.13	4.31	49	1976	4600	1372	
湘潭县	43.26	63.16	143	19887	54967	32550	152
衡阳市	122.69	252.59	1529	192430	428272	78045	386
衡阳市郊区	6.00	5.93	24	900	9830	3614	92
南岳区	1.00	0.88	8	568	1700	210	
耒阳市		39.01	275	60447	28000	7400	15
常宁市	16.94	30.06	180	19424	40640	7045	
衡阳县	48.15	50.88	235	30979	109698	19990	29
衡南县	3.00	51.73	348	25920	97250	15520	118
衡山县	13.20	13.92	109	10840	22550	4570	41
衡东县	15.20	29.68	189	20772	35468	10621	91
祁东县	19.20	30.50	161	22580	83136	9075	

18—9 续表1 (1997年)

名称	机耕面积(千公顷)	有效灌溉面积(千公顷)	水库(座)	水库库容量(万立方米)	塘坝(座)	塘坝库容量(万立方米)	堤防长度(公里)
邵阳市	112.53	252.93	1245	138934	260644	60757	
双清区	0.38	2.82	15	667	5450	746	
大祥区	2.13	3.73	27	2143	8230	1112	
北塔区	0.63	2.03	13	367	2176	442	
武冈市	4.49	28.56	120	14289	24900	3700	
邵东县	17.67	38.76	126	19860	73900	12800	
新邵县	10.10	20.78	106	12486	30127	6590	
邵阳县	8.53	32.15	270	17600	44000	12000	
隆回县	20.27	35.93	245	32563	27518	5204	
洞口县	22.33	36.08	151	16410	17570	3963	
绥宁县	13.81	17.93	39	2850	6500	3630	
新宁县	8.70	24.80	107	17660	18000	8200	
城步县	3.49	9.36	26	2039	2273	2370	
岳阳市	161.44	247.26	1457	166023	120436	37396	1062
岳阳楼区	0.41	1.57	21	899	1669	333	8
云溪区	3.68	4.13	47	2127	2537	2143	35
君山区	11.92	22.65					155
汨罗市	40.19	36.14	283	23110	28470	3410	110
临湘市	16.35	25.94	299	19067	17500	10500	53
岳阳县	9.52	37.70	381	84700	27090	10640	106
华容县	34.59	49.13	59	3820	6390	1700	348
湘阴县	32.49	35.30	75	4270	7900	2550	247
平江县	12.29	34.70	292	28030	28880	6120	
常德市	264.53	393.60	1217	255345	186381	74957	1259
武陵区	7.40	7.90					14
鼎城区	58.83	74.44	189	31165	18256	8040	127
津市市	7.54	11.89	31	2415	8246	3715	56
安乡县	41.85	40.15					393
汉寿县	46.57	45.80	211	12300	8602	4190	178
澧　县	35.00	59.36	117	58706	42146	16957	275
临澧县	13.11	35.26	138	28170	26430	9600	49
桃源县	45.20	81.58	352	97144	58990	14630	167
石门县	9.03	37.22	179	25445	23711	17825	

18—9 续表 2 (1997 年)

名 称	机耕面积(千公顷)	有效灌溉面积(千公顷)	水库(座)	水库库容量(万立方米)	塘坝(座)	塘坝库容量(万立方米)	堤防长度(公里)
张家界市	7.63	48.53	241	36589	17716	5841	17
永定区	3.00	13.70	88	13096	2793	1500	
武陵源区	0.30	0.93	5	750	221	380	
慈利县	3.96	26.58	104	19635	13618	3686	16
桑植县	0.37	7.32	44	3108	1084	275	1
益阳市	160.15	217.15	548	412184	50026	17929	1002
资阳区	15.69	17.40	29	3998	2900	654	133
赫山区	27.00	34.47	138	10678	10956	6793	159
沅江市	38.02	54.11	3	9177	1409	414	308
南 县	51.74	55.81					361
桃江县	24.00	35.19	210	19264	13126	5003	41
安化县	3.70	20.17	168	369067	21635	5065	
郴州市	112.00	167.82	900	916159	87761	22753	
北湖区	4.00	8.10	13	4162	2502	910	
苏仙区	10.00	13.88	43	7673	6287	2225	
资兴市	12.00	15.12	61	817840	4847	2550	
桂阳县	15.00	26.52	187	17917	23205	3210	
宜章县	7.00	17.99	126	7360	4872	3400	
永兴县	16.00	20.72	126	21380	13145	3338	
嘉禾县	7.00	11.11	74	9556	8909	1100	
临武县	1.00	9.83	66	8531	4805	864	
汝城县	12.00	19.16	62	6340	1352	956	
桂东县	4.00	6.32	30	1120	2950	500	
安仁县	24.00	19.07	112	14280	14887	3700	
永州市	138.17	234.39	1259	180339	172018	51325	
芝山区	14.43	29.00	146	13290	10000	6500	
冷水滩区	9.52	21.45	137	7099	19350	13160	
祁阳县	31.51	38.20	206	15187	72250	12000	
东安县	20.09	30.29	262	11492	18005	3750	
双牌县	4.17	6.40	20	72080	1615	642	

18—9 续表3 (1997年)

名 称	机耕面积（千公顷）	有效灌溉面积（千公顷）	水库（座）	水库库容量（万立方米）	塘坝（座）	塘坝库容量（万立方米）	堤防长度（公里）
道县	8.34	28.81	100	9310	17100	5770	
江永县	5.55	14.42	101	9257	2016	1184	
宁远县	21.97	25.13	87	10997	11896	3500	
蓝山县	9.23	12.14	33	2455	1201	516	
新田县	3.26	11.53	72	13282	16520	1833	
江华县	10.10	17.02	95	15890	2065	2470	
娄底地区	46.68	112.11	710	62531	179356	33149	
娄底市	2.26	6.00	51	1351	15200	2970	
冷水江市	0.95	5.29	30	2419	6041	1055	
涟源市	7.85	33.12	154	16428	57500	7080	
双峰县	28.24	32.80	204	13003	71865	13844	
新化县	7.38	34.90	271	29330	28750	8200	
怀化地区	50.58	182.35	1577	245593	71797	41471	
怀化市		17.05	182	11700	3457	1847	
洪江市	0.37	1.44	12	654	768	200	
黔阳县	12.00	17.72	130	9400	4352	1735	
沅陵县	3.73	24.16	194	158100	4840	6214	
辰溪县	0.06	17.69	238	9890	3100	2297	
溆浦县	11.63	27.53	153	16557	21116	14500	
麻阳县	5.00	13.00	258	13080	8852	2938	
新晃县	2.35	7.61	66	3300	1198	422	
芷江县	3.20	16.42	135	11900	5848	1560	
会同县		14.86	129	5812	6373	1448	
靖州县	8.24	13.66	46	4300	7513	4600	
通道县	4.00	11.21	34	900	4380	3710	
湘西自治州	6.42	76.80	612	44309	6027	5338	
吉首市	0.50	4.99	23	3500	500	420	
泸溪县	1.16	8.01	127	8750	1520	1860	
凤凰县	1.07	13.17	92	8200	790	630	
花垣县	0.01	8.36	55	3315	328	200	
保靖县	0.50	7.25	57	5200	516	310	
古丈县	0.01	4.56	47	1800	333	208	
永顺县	2.17	13.07	146	8200	1091	1270	
龙山县	1.00	17.39	65	5344	949	440	

18—10 各地、市、县主要农业机械年底拥有量(1997年)

Year－End Possession of Major Agriculture Machinery by Prefecture, City and County

名　称	农业机械总动力(千瓦)	大中型拖拉机		小型及手扶拖拉机		排灌机械		农用载重汽车(辆)
		台	千瓦	台	千瓦	台	千瓦	
长沙市	1728939	272	16028	16867	146891	103261	430916	7272
芙蓉区	31987	11	1495	71	627	403	5521	270
天心区	22307	7	361	37	327	1854	3384	129
岳麓区	45267	4	221	227	2003	1030	8651	350
开福区	61302	7	375	219	1871	1736	17097	454
雨花区	46226	6	191	86	758	1102	5894	353
浏阳市	336916	31	1745	5352	45073	12264	66314	1305
长沙县	498080	96	5390	2959	26111	44774	141236	1795
望城县	312698	73	4406	2938	25943	21701	115550	994
宁乡县	374156	37	1844	4978	44178	18397	67269	1622
株洲市	860047	275	12896	13828	123981	25909	143008	3869
荷塘区	21855	55	1838	104	1092	1184	4025	125
芦淞区	14198	10	552	13	114	35	176	184
石峰区	27006	39	1832	173	1525	1025	4576	186
天元区	29083	28	1718	185	1656	1155	5864	63
醴陵市	216651	21	1147	5425	48839	5736	36064	593
株洲县	131353	31	1265	996	9245	7898	36121	516
攸　县	258994	77	3489	3460	29998	5937	32131	1652
茶陵县	118564	8	779	2222	20492	2294	20523	484
炎陵县	42343	6	276	1250	11020	645	3528	66
湘潭市	802516	18	957	11557	102241	79848	198627	2260
雨湖区	13520			171	1490	824	3159	105
岳塘区	45198	8	514	882	7788	2649	9062	255
湘乡市	261540	8	391	3021	26683	34930	70743	570
韶山市	44202			959	8560	6216	12613	50
湘潭县	438056	2	52	6524	57720	35229	103050	1280
衡阳市	1352341	109	3083	17374	156281	66183	326422	5255
衡阳市郊区	70846	2	110	576	5278	4998	25523	231
南岳区	6460	1	22	148	1503	511	1288	16
耒阳市	196164	34	800	4953	43581	6166	34210	640
常宁市	106943			1800	15894	5965	36822	195
衡阳县	175048	7	170	2675	24199	10604	36238	779
衡南县	298239			2211	20552	14064	76853	1370
衡山县	150928			1224	10808	4963	21942	765
衡东县	188498	1	26	2706	24416	7128	34204	702
祁东县	159215	64	1955	1081	10050	11784	59342	557

18—10 续表 1

(1997 年)

名称	农业机械总动力(千瓦)	大中型拖拉机		手扶拖拉机		排灌机械		农用载重汽车(辆)
		台	千瓦	台	千瓦	台	千瓦	
邵阳市	1342441	100	3550	20765	187337	67091	281773	4341
双清区	39876	4	239	400	3532	2130	8726	230
大祥区	29550	6	246	319	2838	1735	11420	79
北塔区	25768	31	947	226	1995	1088	6912	65
武冈市	132249	5	89	3516	31744	7148	26364	330
邵东县	253105	11	422	3148	28340	16986	54905	862
新邵县	124783	8	275	1684	16279	583	5347	406
邵阳县	142312			1623	15223	10563	48888	424
隆回县	106835	13	691	2032	17954	11403	44621	167
洞口县	200505	22	641	3494	30828	9460	38924	977
绥宁县	148794			2424	21964	2827	18093	427
新宁县	98712			951	8233	2181	11691	298
城步县	39952			948	8407	987	5882	76
岳阳市	2022729	1672	69317	17236	161554	70368	458257	5209
岳阳楼区	37351	4	210	128	1133	397	3457	426
云溪区	59246	8	441	225	1987	1277	13415	355
君山区	113837	474	20601	1094	9549	2044	27041	266
汨罗市	341324	520	24043	3744	35723	10584	67196	932
临湘市	258447	372	13526	1923	21493	8602	44718	939
岳阳县	202149	48	2221	1826	16082	4547	36573	1035
华容县	400627	177	4906	2631	23263	24171	150844	274
湘阴县	374636	50	2755	2971	27952	12223	64967	320
平江县	235112	19	614	2694	24372	6523	50046	662
常德市	1902134	725	30666	22717	203929	115886	724971	5262
武陵区	78791			979	8755	2805	18640	260
鼎城区	355891	257	10406	3887	34778	22905	147429	1376
津市市	62667	29	1371	991	8970	6580	37921	100
安乡县	210905	152	7961	2439	21934	15575	105973	151
汉寿县	308819	73	2073	2801	24118	12091	127677	409
澧　县	313645	116	3951	2901	26212	24357	137870	986
临澧县	189118			3158	28412	14595	64043	520
桃源县	245166	70	3853	3302	30649	11743	65005	949
石门县	137132	28	1051	2259	20101	5235	20413	511

18—10 续表 2 (1997 年)

名称	农业机械总动力(千瓦)	大中型拖拉机		手扶拖拉机		排灌机械		农用载重汽车(辆)
		台	千瓦	台	千瓦	台	千瓦	
张家界市	326761	22	780	6799	59986	5947	37302	1764
永定区	110916			2060	18079	1727	16967	839
武陵源区	6298	2	37	277	2446	50	241	20
慈利县	133108	11	541	3373	29839	2750	15166	487
桑植县	76439	9	202	1089	9622	1420	4928	418
益阳市	1628297	924	45723	19598	182579	102257	526667	2812
资阳区	147331	110	4372	2175	19569	10992	54184	161
赫山区	309381	103	4156	5074	45659	22628	100991	825
沅江市	395374	351	17452	3209	36689	28570	159185	368
南县	397255	360	19743	4277	37576	27590	155083	209
桃江县	183533			2640	23441	7739	35977	522
安化县	195423			2223	19645	4738	21247	727
郴州市	1274071	70	3856	16361	146791	22258	142012	6532
北湖区	64453			478	4221	414	3002	432
苏仙区	107136	8	482	975	10309	2135	16071	523
资兴市	86697	2	114	1454	12915	1091	6282	249
桂阳县	180838	16	856	2960	26181	3866	22622	864
宜章县	247673	20	1145	1789	15666	7040	45071	1385
永兴县	116359			1694	15281	3149	17869	534
嘉禾县	123636	20	1074	1610	14367	1705	10909	748
临武县	163857	2	114	949	8481	968	6527	1213
汝城县	73732	1	20	1990	17617	470	4174	188
桂东县	26465			670	5916	315	1805	58
安仁县	83225	1	51	1792	15837	1105	7680	338
永州市	1175899	145	5605	8840	77669	62682	326465	3448
芝山区	130744	19	1122	325	2870	10611	57056	198
冷水滩区	132723	2	59	837	7407	13697	45698	241
祁阳县	239089	30	1658	1338	11789	15969	89886	575
东安县	119890			749	6669	9585	42634	189
双牌县	32983			257	2226	587	5120	14

18—10 续表 3

(1997 年)

名称	农业机械总动力(千瓦)	大中型拖拉机		手扶拖拉机		排灌机械		农用载重汽车(辆)
		台	千瓦	台	千瓦	台	千瓦	
道县	77709	18	452	484	4146	2146	22150	355
江永县	41637	19	823	1055	9435	2166	13313	171
宁远县	142496	4	91	93	799	3314	20196	477
蓝山县	102223	49	1190	1324	11691	862	4551	652
新田县	74563			1667	14534	2193	11370	434
江华县	81842	4	210	711	6103	1552	14491	142
娄底地区	1020855	121	4106	8563	76611	62293	254259	4933
娄底市	92471	22	1503	1070	9448	4694	16720	508
冷水江市	77974	3	169	205	1799	1650	16517	521
涟源市	311243			3459	30543	14348	65306	1651
双峰县	359245	96	2434	2150	19004	33546	105947	1601
新化县	179922			1679	15817	8055	49769	652
怀化地区	1003240	19	1254	9011	80576	33322	219619	4030
怀化市	142339	12	894	841	7454	3016	19520	839
洪江市	13114			266	2470	200	2109	31
黔阳县	91850			716	6418	2519	16166	216
沅陵县	135437			678	5991	4608	31522	583
辰溪县	121142			961	9100	5631	34909	678
溆浦县	118116			1428	12679	3365	28575	445
麻阳县	47197			374	3302	2065	19917	102
新晃县	42964	1	26	346	3017	1048	6004	139
芷江县	87227			1012	9015	4903	33830	275
会同县	72670	3	169	926	8187	2014	9480	178
靖州县	80750	3	165	832	7312	3200	12429	369
通道县	50434			631	5631	753	5158	175
湘西自治州	488126	150	3996	7070	62332	10057	67419	1371
吉首市	44046	19	1048	691	6102	594	5080	230
泸溪县	57906	1	162	543	4796	1388	12800	172
凤凰县	68555	5	276	602	5316	2515	20767	88
花垣县	41239			807	7126	1038	5483	156
保靖县	41865			683	5888	401	2754	95
古丈县	36217			297	2623	530	2534	178
永顺县	72483	7	253	1602	14146	2102	6223	105
龙山县	125815	118	2257	1845	16335	1489	11778	347

18—11 各地、市、县农村用电及化肥农药施用量(1997年)

Electricity Consumed and Chemical Fertilizer, Pesticide Applied in Rural Areas by Prefecture, City and County

名称	农村小水电		农村用电(万千瓦小时)	化肥施用实物量		农药施用量(吨)
	处	容量(千瓦)		合计(吨)	每公顷播种面积施用化肥(公斤)	
长沙市	188	7451	68316	558285	887	8915
芙蓉区			2643	1471	522	38
天心区			1886	2343	734	41
岳麓区			4201	5351	863	186
开福区			1906	4286	364	234
雨花区			3791	6220	835	111
浏阳市	156	4053	10775	147906	884	2380
长沙县	4	1105	18733	104557	812	1654
望城县	4	538	14035	88220	845	1360
宁乡县	24	1755	10346	197931	1003	2911
株洲市	636	47260	36181	321934	893	3714
荷塘区			2278	310	45	8
芦淞区			1500	713	392	20
石峰区			3249	1134	110	70
天元区			634	3760	483	85
醴陵市	339	16795	8510	72590	892	1450
株洲县	9	337	4681	61150	992	650
攸县	44	12230	4681	105741	1048	710
茶陵县	63	3010	3024	65038	992	623
炎陵县	181	14888	7624	11498	476	98
湘潭市	24	1745	21722	296801	1117	4425
雨湖区			1155	3695	1047	50
岳塘区			1692	7956	1020	83
湘乡市	2	70	7230	102386	990	1118
韶山市			2330	8685	724	92
湘潭县	22	1675	9315	174079	1253	3082
衡阳市	154	11409	26586	660164	833	12381
衡阳市郊区			2262	18688	1198	276
南岳区	4	680	238	3375	758	35
耒阳市	31	883	4085	106992	841	1598
常宁市	50	4533	2123	95860	950	4072
衡阳县	7	891	6350	124163	756	1523
衡南县	10	849	4583	129286	783	2148
衡山县	17	2508	2295	39505	1012	567
衡东县	14	890	1632	77824	875	908
祁东县	21	175	3019	64468	742	1254

18—11 续表 1 (1997 年)

名　　称	农村小水电		农村用电（万千瓦小时）	化肥施用实物量		农药施用量（吨）
	处	容量（千瓦）		合计（吨）	每公顷播种面积施用化肥（公斤）	
邵阳市	457	33207	33364	606642	789	6570
双清区			447	4791	811	65
大祥区			532	8734	733	106
北塔区			441	6108	956	40
武冈市	21	1912	1562	68156	733	649
邵东县	5	920	7538	119632	1077	955
新邵县	18	2433	2893	50971	716	351
邵阳县	5	263	2902	84627	791	760
隆回县	60	4168	6244	91934	768	1194
洞口县	17	5573	4300	83209	781	1322
绥宁县	40	8125	3250	25057	634	318
新宁县	128	5624	2550	51748	720	700
城步县	163	4189	704	11675	478	110
岳阳市	84	15167	28364	739589	1026	4795
岳阳楼区			798	4700	1068	26
云溪区			1029	16148	1105	59
君山区			2337	67660	1336	421
汨罗市	3	547	5066	82955	842	479
临湘市	20	4005	3051	60194	717	398
岳阳县	11	1523	3166	85978	726	512
华容县			2987	206872	1457	1279
湘阴县			6250	117065	1182	764
平江县	50	9092	3680	98017	896	857
常德市	69	14867	54374	1065864	968	8953
武陵区			2598	19907	944	194
鼎城区	3	250	10898	171416	854	1618
津市市			1329	43128	1057	421
安乡县			6808	155048	1455	991
汉寿县	1	10	7281	175380	1165	1713
澧　县	7	1046	5982	186995	1185	1529
临澧县	2	1260	9483	70623	739	514
桃源县	41	9587	7122	129560	616	1166
石门县	15	2714	2874	113807	964	807

18—11　续表 2　　　　　　　　　　（1997 年）

名　称	农村小水电		农村用电（万千瓦小时）	化肥施用实物量		农药施用量（吨）
	处	容量（千瓦）		合计（吨）	每公顷播种面积施用化肥（公斤）	
张家界市	56	10165	4512	149608	610	1266
永定区	14	2555	955	34123	546	417
武陵源区			166	3217	574	18
慈利县	34	5985	2657	74444	702	599
桑植县	8	1625	734	37824	534	232
益阳市	300	18188	34894	596217	1014	6721
资阳区	1	26	3361	55200	1109	1173
赫山区	5	600	7762	95526	1063	1298
沅江市			5618	159268	1313	1744
南　县			9697	176651	1290	1614
桃江县	48	3559	6874	63220	660	500
安化县	246	14003	1582	46352	491	392
郴州市	1191	100876	22925	454515	971	5509
北湖区	43	9167	1263	15383	860	239
苏仙区	108	18875	3711	26345	961	360
资兴市	129	17448	3608	33726	848	590
桂阳县	280	13276	4258	89181	1037	964
宜章县	53	10417	2710	50258	862	1036
永兴县	222	3528	1779	60741	939	503
嘉禾县	9	2005	1287	36145	1038	286
临武县	133	5718	1506	29102	966	250
汝城县	93	14388	1168	50451	1192	611
桂东县	44	3766	583	18447	1167	142
安仁县	77	2288	1052	44736	883	528
永州市	1792	37717	24327	636088	883	7181
芝山区	111	4515	2164	55135	644	619
冷水滩区	6	1280	2049	51967	793	471
祁阳县	74	5079	7459	105842	891	1205
东安县	142	7088	3989	58084	646	980
双牌县	145	6283	582	13128	727	135

18—11 续表 3 (1997 年)

名 称	农村小水电 处	农村小水电 容量 (千瓦)	农村用电 (万千瓦小时)	化肥施用实物量 合计 (吨)	化肥施用实物量 每公顷播种面积施用化肥(公斤)	农药施用量 (吨)
道 县	154	1467	1165	96617	950	629
江永县	55	147	413	71525	2020	775
宁远县	479	3110	1812	64064	895	811
蓝山县	306	3283	1445	36207	1041	540
新田县	132	693	1055	45139	1052	441
江华县	188	4772	2195	38380	682	575
娄底地区	86	19154	26614	319085	876	3860
娄底市	8	3940	3792	18341	767	226
冷水江市	3	570	5600	9000	711	270
涟源市	23	7154	6501	79914	765	940
双峰县	2	85	6559	137868	1151	1812
新化县	50	7405	4162	73962	714	612
怀化地区	186	38418	24880	299139	511	4968
怀化市	17	3967	3694	24640	484	562
洪江市			419	1812	427	66
黔阳县	27	10185	2127	34204	676	757
沅陵县	14	4315	4919	23112	240	403
辰溪县	8	1452	1829	29373	549	615
溆浦县	42	2238	3019	79325	779	1066
麻阳县	2	130	1430	19648	439	375
新晃县	6	2230	1862	12983	372	157
芷江县	11	2333	1401	27913	514	408
会同县	27	5260	2125	18172	498	180
靖州县	14	3850	1143	17148	516	241
通道县	18	2458	912	10809	443	138
湘西自治州	127	24583	9699	168404	422	1593
吉首市	10	2345	892	12745	433	206
泸溪县	11	1891	782	12204	307	244
凤凰县	19	3536	770	19078	303	282
花垣县	21	4583	1614	37538	1019	101
保靖县	16	2801	2179	15430	361	120
古丈县	16	1754	261	3732	182	69
永顺县	16	2603	913	30329	362	286
龙山县	18	5070	2289	37348	451	285

18—12 各地、市、县农林牧渔业总产值(1997年)

Gross Output Value of Farming, Forestry, Animal Husbandry, Fishery by Prefecture, City and County

单位:万元

名称	农林牧渔业总产值		农业产值	种植业产值	林业产值	牧业产值	渔业产值
	绝对数	为上年%					
长沙市	1114485	7.8	561705	526753	41906	460042	50832
芙蓉区	15958	7.1	7006	6076	66	7521	1365
天心区	8955	9.4	4955	3865	103	3023	874
岳麓区	24357	10.3	10049	8325	973	12235	1100
开福区	28565	10.8	12974	9805	809	11616	3166
雨花区	27106	6.4	15216	13886	353	10584	953
浏阳市	254905	7.6	125535	116886	17807	99987	11576
长沙县	257858	6.4	124119	117617	4539	121824	7376
望城县	184388	8.4	89874	85124	3773	80170	10571
宁乡县	312393	8.4	171977	165169	13483	113082	13851
株洲市	749052	5.6	367125	351667	36339	312450	33138
荷塘区	17525	11.9	8619	8490	679	7682	545
芦淞区	8644	16.6	4043	3948	1034	2788	779
石峰区	19982	1.0	8538	8370	546	9861	1037
天元区	16344	20.1	7794	7495	216	7724	610
醴陵市	179555	4.7	93582	88308	4116	71433	10424
株洲县	113358	3.4	58037	56651	3645	46128	5548
攸县	213466	6.0	106403	101538	9779	89452	7832
茶陵县	137881	6.7	60195	57487	7424	64204	6058
炎陵县	42297	0.4	19914	19380	8900	13178	305
湘潭市	584913	6.1	254467	242486	8662	286897	34887
雨湖区	20823	6.5	4963	4793	561	14164	1135
岳塘区	23155	7.7	9071	8455	217	12703	1164
湘乡市	217197	5.8	87798	83693	3032	112439	13928
韶山市	21687	3.3	10207	9886	115	10174	1191
湘潭县	302051	6.4	142428	135659	4737	137417	17469
衡阳市	1468959	6.8	651098	608601	36769	675499	105593
衡阳市郊区	48516	3.5	24818	24247	746	17832	5120
南岳区	13095	8.3	8048	4296	762	4010	275
耒阳市	203725	5.3	78582	76722	12122	101014	12007
常宁市	159629	3.7	72788	66436	5990	70092	10759
衡阳县	328248	12.4	135594	127410	5179	162546	24929
衡南县	286968	7.6	137291	130537	2398	126346	20933
衡山县	93125	5.6	46271	39593	1578	40144	5132
衡东县	152210	-0.9	67235	63666	6028	72443	6504
祁东县	183443	8.3	80471	75694	1966	81072	19934

注:总产值按当年价格计算,为上年%按可比价格计算。

18—12 续表1 (1997年) 单位:万元

名称	农林牧渔业总产值		农业产值	种植业产值	林业产值	牧业产值	渔业产值
	绝对数	为上年%					
邵阳市	1345207	10.0	687324	651410	57562	558790	41531
双清区	12530		5479	5009	12	6343	696
大祥区	19869		10880	10758	244	7998	747
北塔区	7228		4393	4293	66	2515	254
武冈市	159505	11.9	80961	80405	1319	72714	4511
邵东县	260208	8.7	139298	131459	727	106831	13352
新邵县	130949	9.2	69625	62165	2580	55770	2974
邵阳县	161107	8.0	91821	88911	2708	60077	6501
隆回县	161608	13.9	76376	71162	4202	78765	2265
洞口县	175514	13.4	87469	86677	4474	79599	3972
绥宁县	115821	18.6	50349	43370	35367	28548	1557
新宁县	102893	8.6	50724	49328	2464	45328	4377
城步县	37975	8.2	19949	17873	3399	14302	325
岳阳市	1357948	14.8	606498	588388	23378	591543	137529
岳阳楼区	33727	19.5	6236	5813	35	18339	9117
云溪区	31247	16.4	12421	11968	496	12509	5821
君山区	106171	79.9	56821	55602	307	35584	13459
汨罗市	220554	13.9	80380	77456	941	130245	8988
临湘市	107890	—1.8	61449	58321	4611	33194	8636
岳阳县	200558	5.5	92647	89949	3428	85036	19447
华容县	260646	18.8	137412	135840	2306	90949	29979
湘阴县	228118	5.8	81638	79581	955	105205	40320
平江县	169037	—1.1	77494	73858	9299	80482	1762
常德市	1627799	5.2	849795	817580	32807	602572	142625
武陵区	41087	0.2	19507	19177	126	15589	5865
鼎城区	305771	11.1	155029	151478	6477	110849	33416
津市市	63810	9.5	31731	30921	504	25414	6161
安乡县	166619	—8.9	101356	100492	558	42667	22038
汉寿县	215677	14.3	125613	123655	4450	48605	37009
澧县	214879	—6.6	123472	121384	1321	78052	12034
临澧县	169188	4.7	75757	67777	4628	79922	8881
桃源县	305745	13.8	144739	135344	10742	136319	13945
石门县	145023	1.8	72591	67352	4001	65155	3276

18—12 续表 2 (1997 年) 单位:万元

名称	农林牧渔业总产值		农业产值	种植业产值	林业产值	牧业产值	渔业产值
	绝对数	为上年%					
张家界市	226939	10.2	140281	128771	14432	68602	3624
永定区	75049	11.5	48225	44447	3193	22324	1307
武陵源区	7013	32.2	3571	3431	1308	2121	13
慈利县	100792	8.8	59236	54939	6413	33230	1913
桑植县	44085	9.4	29249	25954	3518	10927	391
益阳市	860760	13.2	510627	464079	28882	248703	72548
资阳区	66204	16.7	41262	39856	743	18340	5859
赫山区	146510	5.1	79370	60680	2638	56314	8188
沅江市	180972	20.9	103760	101253	3784	40030	33398
南县	209132	19.3	142668	137422	695	47703	18066
桃江县	134485	9.9	80966	65305	8005	43413	2101
安化县	123457	5.3	62601	59563	13017	42903	4936
郴州市	864476	11.1	418605	387819	53492	359764	32615
北湖区	39000	14.2	18643	17540	2250	16465	1642
苏仙区	60192	12.1	23726	22320	3967	28764	3735
资兴市	86723	14.7	30503	29528	14278	36305	5637
桂阳县	159497	11.7	105920	98773	5716	43391	4470
宜章县	88442	10.4	40724	38105	2686	42024	3008
永兴县	115365	14.8	53500	49095	7562	47931	6372
嘉禾县	75811	14.0	32224	30713	1820	40791	976
临武县	55339	9.2	27467	25275	1796	24391	1685
汝城县	58868	0.5	24254	22260	8016	26116	482
桂东县	22512	2.8	11115	10507	2546	8534	317
安仁县	102737	10.4	50530	43706	2863	45049	4295
永州市	1252235	8.1	621918	551857	56550	519165	54602
芝山区	139664	8.1	82636	71574	1842	51249	3937
冷水滩区	107376	16.4	52830	45895	4308	43313	6925
祁阳县	213367	10.2	108865	104612	7964	82505	14033
东安县	140851	7.6	73512	61789	5212	55338	6789
双牌县	37423	5.7	17521	13881	5459	13608	835

18—12 续表 3 (1997 年) 单位:万元

名称	农林牧渔业总产值		农业产值		林业产值	牧业产值	渔业产值
	绝对数	为上年%		种植业产值			
道县	155734	3.4	74944	71299	4497	66892	9401
江永县	63760	18.4	34272	31911	2540	25273	1675
宁远县	137354	5.2	63745	57835	4298	63314	5997
蓝山县	87084	9.2	29149	23305	3411	53284	1240
新田县	60300	5.1	32838	27804	1018	24537	1907
江华县	109322	3.0	51606	41952	16001	39852	1863
娄底地区	638899	8.7	299321	288887	9619	305345	24614
娄底市	45950	9.9	20987	20405	765	21386	2812
冷水江市	29742	6.7	11910	11207	500	16015	1317
涟源市	140655	4.1	76348	73769	1838	58752	3717
双峰县	253140	4.4	114501	111730	4581	123071	10987
新化县	169412	19.8	75575	71776	1935	86121	5781
怀化地区	812982	6.2	442571	403710	63159	289343	17909
怀化市	78731	4.7	34128	32793	8315	33049	3239
洪江市	9604	5.0	4883	4095	583	3793	345
黔阳县	72242	6.1	40970	36244	4349	25877	1046
沅陵县	104603	8.1	55168	48281	11863	35271	2301
辰溪县	61729	5.5	36385	34013	2257	22194	893
溆浦县	158253	4.6	90461	83246	5165	59212	3415
麻阳县	56337	8.3	37422	34119	1753	16418	744
新晃县	34829	5.1	18108	16883	898	15255	568
芷江县	70675	3.9	38374	35685	3596	27287	1418
会同县	71960	7.3	39321	34396	8041	23254	1344
靖州县	58834	9.9	30252	28346	8241	18428	1913
通道县	35184	6.4	17098	15609	8098	9305	683
湘西自治州	323455	6.2	207223	186186	17249	90029	8954
吉首市	38049	6.2	26056	23082	1144	9964	885
泸溪县	37017	11.4	23282	21655	960	12130	645
凤凰县	36848	2.7	26919	23520	626	8627	676
花垣县	31687	4.1	18322	16414	387	11736	1242
保靖县	28215	11.8	18371	16151	1731	7614	499
古丈县	16522	6.5	10567	9217	1448	3515	992
永顺县	62131	9.6	40417	37645	4370	16708	636
龙山县	72986	2.6	43289	38502	6583	19735	3379

18—13 各地、市、县主要农产品产量(1997 年)

Output of Major Farm Products by Prefecture, City and County

单位:吨

名　称	粮食合计	稻　谷	小　麦	薯　类	杂　粮	玉　米	大　豆
长沙市	2928132	2757668	9551	85889	58636	21124	16388
芙蓉区	2493	2444		36	13		
天心区	13817	13808			9		
岳麓区	21793	20843		908	22		20
开福区	46169	44795		877	165		332
雨花区	18841	18314		330	145		52
浏阳市	701247	672411	3880	11621	10899	3559	2436
长沙县	595636	561329	211	14489	16899	5264	2708
望城县	537871	492846	765	27657	14306	10572	2297
宁乡县	990265	930878	4695	29971	16178	1729	8543
株洲市	1828686	1761508	278	41935	12213	6439	12752
荷塘区	38580	37153		1342	14		71
芦淞区	9603	9344		241			18
石峰区	37412	35160		1421	81		750
天元区	36479	36320		129	30		
醴陵市	485955	470474	74	8241	5574	4013	1592
株洲县	321426	307519	108	8520	3580	1223	1699
攸　县	469387	454872	96	10795	923	357	2701
茶陵县	312039	298697		7555	1274	631	4513
炎陵县	117805	111969		3691	737	215	1408
湘潭市	1491803	1469589	1377	12801	6140	1469	1896
雨湖区	13492	13492					
岳塘区	39477	39009		400	43		25
湘乡市	537858	526768	839	6420	2791	380	1040
韶山市	67242	66232	122	603	231	153	54
湘潭县	833734	824088	416	5378	3075	936	777
衡阳市	3181775	3028717	12712	73383	36243	5241	30720
衡阳市郊区	58440	56710		849	758	422	123
南岳区	18182	16994		1032	121	37	35
耒阳市	437153	408231	3779	17514	3715	124	3914
常宁市	367624	340393	4485	12689	4610	917	5447
衡阳县	676779	641896	1533	15610	11149	2481	6591
衡南县	568105	546149	542	5960	9124	857	6330
衡山县	217789	213717	35	2239	1078	60	720
衡东县	384527	371812		9108	1961	234	1646
祁东县	453176	432815	2338	8382	3727	109	5914

18—13 续表 1 (1997 年) 单位:吨

名称	粮食合计	稻谷	小麦	薯类	杂粮	玉米	大豆
邵阳市	3166749	2726376	75413	172168	135447	112385	57345
双清区	29638	27575	181	1230	210	50	442
大祥区	52234	48013	400	2132	474	313	1215
北塔区	20628	17563	748	1743	224		350
武冈市	434942	377695	6924	13310	30848	29565	6165
邵东县	493856	427106	11077	30610	15038	10730	10025
新邵县	318417	250438	13724	39519	9002	2918	5734
邵阳县	407129	360429	5572	18502	10566	5465	12060
隆回县	425356	366010	14551	27608	10230	8711	6957
洞口县	447962	387277	17196	14771	22766	19728	5952
绥宁县	155943	141701	767	6273	4979	4216	2223
新宁县	287942	239482	3230	14403	25188	25064	5639
城步县	92702	83087	1043	2067	5922	5625	583
岳阳市	2602316	2417613	7765	86204	64212	45592	26522
岳阳楼区	11685	8970	10	838	1055	800	812
云溪区	42154	38397	65	1478	834	420	1380
君山区	131486	125700	778	1219	3451	1587	338
汨罗市	418292	384627	217	8992	22673	21426	1783
临湘市	245698	217127	379	14586	7528	6013	6078
岳阳县	419020	371093	1259	23938	14274	11050	8456
华容县	399772	385067	650	4555	7000	2000	2500
湘阴县	486065	471049	1062	10505	2274	756	1175
平江县	448144	415583	3345	20093	5123	1540	4000
常德市	3231683	3030079	25378	90930	53287	38209	32009
武陵区	50156	49715			173	63	268
鼎城区	666242	650991	71	6378	1151	68	7651
津市市	113241	109293	135	1857	494	187	1462
安乡县	279923	274772		1767	2122	211	1262
汉寿县	496237	486796		5194	2136	308	2111
澧县	449846	423009	6051	7216	11388	8683	2182
临澧县	305804	289169	6799	4639	1878	112	3319
桃源县	591270	553043	212	21168	7560	4336	9287
石门县	278964	193291	12110	42711	26385	24241	4467

18—13 续表 2 (1997 年) 单位:吨

名称	粮食合计	稻谷	小麦	薯类	杂粮	玉米	大豆
张家界市	597467	389735	29105	87792	74674	69552	16161
永定区	165024	128438	4698	17706	10326	8416	3856
武陵源区	13693	9854	235	1305	1921	1738	378
慈利县	275233	175917	18037	35546	39611	36937	6122
桑植县	143517	75526	6135	33235	22816	22461	5805
益阳市	2070773	1910110	4812	107330	33606	15336	14915
资阳区	208250	198932		8270	816	772	232
赫山区	381085	369815	270	9500	600	150	900
沅江市	408270	387012	1554	9508	9198	725	998
南县	413514	408974	242	645	3085	470	568
桃江县	379094	350735	767	22779	2446	1053	2367
安化县	280560	194642	1979	56628	17461	12166	9850
郴州市	1707587	1496867	4098	106151	75611	64437	24860
北湖区	58934	54334		3279	643	377	678
苏仙区	112880	105476		4580	1703	1300	1121
资兴市	157167	141948	18	5112	8729	7081	1360
桂阳县	283840	231366	1374	30949	9329	6880	10822
宜章县	200516	164509		15957	18308	17899	1742
永兴县	239006	211460	1875	11218	12278	8856	2175
嘉禾县	134141	109845	752	9504	11562	10618	2478
临武县	107270	89014	46	9560	7703	7205	947
汝城县	127373	117910	18	5597	3020	2457	828
桂东县	49984	45855	15	2403	1195	790	516
安仁县	236476	225150		7992	1141	974	2193
永州市	2475333	2236527	14623	123553	55383	31531	45247
芝山区	318290	299889	2616	6375	5289	1228	4121
冷水滩区	234358	222158	94	4633	2434	499	5039
祁阳县	510022	460923	9696	14738	13838	5358	10827
东安县	311603	292455	265	9988	3489	1901	5406
双牌县	57177	51455	67	3545	1166	726	944

18—13 续表 3 (1997 年) 单位:吨

名称	粮食合计	稻谷	小麦	薯类	杂粮		大豆
						玉米	
道县	294681	246348	587	35478	4493	2208	7775
江永县	103451	91683	55	8443	1714	1460	1556
宁远县	251906	227105	1206	17856	3831	624	1908
蓝山县	114029	106285		6307	673	470	764
新田县	128566	107396	37	6740	10929	10609	3464
江华县	151250	130830		9450	7527	6448	3443
娄底地区	1640522	1363505	70398	103288	72312	23272	31019
娄底市	99841	86794	1588	4556	3981	70	2922
冷水江市	58426	48412	2693	5676	1427	612	218
涟源市	454256	348876	30970	43258	21501	5895	9651
双峰县	577377	501950	19583	19301	23777	3555	12766
新华县	450622	377473	15564	30497	21626	13140	5462
怀化地区	1758610	1530013	25306	109279	69685	55606	24327
怀化市	177730	163014	436	7826	4342	2680	2112
洪江市	12286	11739	25	454	63	35	5
黔阳县	154255	143981	373	7327	2054	1387	520
沅陵县	225480	186357	102	14185	14695	11894	10141
辰溪县	155266	137819	4048	9722	1347	1079	2330
溆浦县	336983	278161	10312	22882	19759	16195	5869
麻阳县	120746	111740	1209	4643	2818	1542	336
新晃县	95947	59438	5470	15429	15355	14535	255
芷江县	160717	142855	1141	12318	3661	3022	742
会同县	125480	114043	2116	5553	2993	1306	775
靖州县	113701	107043	74	4476	1238	571	870
通道县	80019	73823		4464	1360	1360	372
湘西自治州	851325	563465	40317	120402	109714	100996	17427
吉首市	53735	41444	84	3249	7326	6178	1632
泸溪县	79818	68531	3061	3716	2983	1345	1527
凤凰县	119893	97397	2269	8214	9816	9361	2197
花垣县	102849	65000	3724	12275	20500	20250	1350
保靖县	88952	54056	4130	11320	17310	16352	2136
古丈县	38018	30760	540	1137	4873	4517	708
永顺县	189504	118392	8398	36117	22860	19884	3737
龙山县	178556	87885	18111	44374	24046	23109	4140

18—13　续表 4　　　　　　　　　　　　(1997 年)　　　　　　　　　　　　单位:吨

名　称	棉　花	油　料		黄红麻	苎　麻	烤　烟	茶　叶	柑　桔
			油菜籽					
长沙市	1424	29201	20945	28	103	3032	6060	28990
芙蓉区		16	5				32	793
天心区		13	13					73
岳麓区		92	92				45	535
开福区		44	44				7	583
雨花区		84	84				1	88
浏阳市	526	9738	8927	20	38	2518	639	5387
长沙县	65	7522	6814	8	8	9	3768	6569
望城县		2750	2214			31	544	5186
宁乡县	833	8942	2752		57	474	1024	9776
株洲市	4407	37009	27080		1095	1518	1451	28319
荷塘区		82	62				19	192
芦淞区		29	29				14	148
石峰区		408	169				14	463
天元区	200	223	76				29	226
醴陵市	139	5923	4737		11	73	255	4152
株洲县	829	2931	993		15	101	264	4640
攸　县	2604	16480	12777		67	157	310	2090
茶陵县	597	8801	6690		1002	1187	432	11953
炎陵县	38	2132	1547				114	4455
湘潭市	530	5297	1181		28		936	5269
雨湖区							2	314
岳塘区		504	22				56	495
湘乡市	375	1469	121		20		529	1374
韶山市	11	270	124				54	75
湘潭县	144	3054	914		8		295	3011
衡阳市	26736	161475	134487	43	193	5324	1451	67581
衡阳市郊区		1445	830			60	72	8485
南岳区	15	271	158				37	580
耒阳市	1950	17800	15936	25	38	2430	171	5540
常宁市	209	11454	6280	8	86	176	335	6795
衡阳县	12249	58725	52180	8	43	135	30	10305
衡南县	11860	50250	44357			1896	268	9037
衡山县	277	2602	1610		8		205	8858
衡东县	121	12378	9891		8		274	8514
祁东县	55	6550	3245	2	10	627	59	9467

18—13　续表 5　　(1997 年)　　单位:吨

名　称	棉　花	油　料		黄红麻	苎　麻	烤　烟	茶　叶	柑　桔
			油菜籽					
邵阳市	829	114033	84432	20	246	9690	2742	223131
双清区	25	465	275				11	12457
大祥区	35	1425	686				32	19227
北塔区		545	430					2682
武冈市	90	13304	10944		38	889	825	12274
邵东县	141	9171	4338		64		153	20750
新邵县	141	2966	2102	20	21	2305	106	8015
邵阳县	160	24313	15860		67	2135	90	21846
隆回县	105	16046	13430			4036	294	13174
洞口县	90	23536	20646		40	33	1000	52766
绥宁县	41	9132	8019		16		135	26253
新宁县	1	9136	4591			292	5	32080
城步县		3994	3111				91	1607
岳阳市	63544	124587	110724	1824	1871		12462	41431
岳阳楼区	3	414	384		1		77	1016
云溪区	372	2306	1915		6		483	683
君山区	15577	9976	9965	20	37		3	5853
汨罗市	1878	8282	6976		33		1497	3224
临湘市	3420	13033	12023		892		4376	1196
岳阳县	4950	18880	10297		30		1689	12993
华容县	35002	50216	50001	1679	834		362	8229
湘阴县	1540	9137	7799	125	20		2150	2900
平江县	802	12343	11364		18		1825	5337
常德市	103523	366067	344198	949	11932	4818	7385	204404
武陵区	807	5195	4467				70	9310
鼎城区	14921	41814	36514	175	573	13	217	31907
津市市	5278	15920	13388	35			84	3645
安乡县	27775	55843	55763	285	1746	454	16	19725
汉寿县	12796	37388	35153	435	5145	10	2436	21734
澧　县	21113	72710	71786	19	75		190	8038
临澧县	8514	33299	31269		15	936	169	2649
桃源县	7176	72654	67223		4273	974	2181	42698
石门县	5143	31244	28635		105	2431	2022	64698

18—13 续表 6 (1997 年) 单位:吨

名 称	棉 花	油 料		黄红麻	苎 麻	烤 烟	茶 叶	柑 桔
			油菜籽					
张家界市	3765	66711	48254		6921	15869	916	67214
永定区	347	18062	11035		4826	3769	109	7291
武陵源区	10	1935	1444		64	566	4	328
慈利县	3380	27756	23985		1697	6189	693	56692
桑植县	28	18958	11790		334	5345	110	2903
益阳市	41457	82587	72060	648	24674	2484	10778	100289
资阳区	749	3632	3275		582		433	15229
赫山区	25	3171	2500		87		1812	4102
沅江市	11589	25343	25113	229	11401		126	55294
南 县	28480	27690	27549	419	12457			13659
桃江县	458	4352	3123		143		3185	3153
安化县	156	18399	10500		4	2484	5222	8852
郴州市	411	29933	12493		84	91455	1104	75325
北湖区		767				3334	20	2756
苏仙区	45	1018	31		1	1747	70	4686
资兴市	67	1953	513		12	321	175	28642
桂阳县		3963			5	50703	170	8371
宜章县	4	3042	1275			4880	42	5788
永兴县	49	3195	2363		57	11144	124	7508
嘉禾县	7	2897			9	9181	29	4528
临武县	9	1561				7293	12	8665
汝城县	171	2034	726			153	68	1823
桂东县	12	585				206	118	567
安仁县	47	8918	7585			2493	276	1991
永州市	4967	49775	17721	62	36	49587	1548	214754
芝山区	544	4824	431	8	7	857	36	22000
冷水滩区	2012	2831	1212			770	837	19438
祁阳县	660	14553	9146			490	203	47396
东安县	1157	4968	669	12	18	1496	2	25245
双牌县	6	384	28			9	29	6960

名称	棉花	油料	油菜籽	黄红麻	苎麻	烤烟	茶叶	柑桔
道县	68	6858	310			4909	31	27101
江永县	8	4833	2890			5415	34	37245
宁远县	504	3702	1275	42	11	10989	100	15000
蓝山县		1333				5707	62	7561
新田县		1750				11012	58	3068
江华县	8	3739	1760			7933	156	3740
娄底地区	648	34572	21488		242	1533	6553	22856
娄底市	31	1321	381		7		1063	3006
冷水江市	12	481	52			5	37	5513
涟源市	109	3392	785		47	528	1091	4129
双峰县	460	20180	16330		188	89	3172	4599
新化县	36	9198	3940			911	1190	5609
怀化地区	2457	95543	78042	14	111	5475	1471	199244
怀化市	394	9459	7384			50	21	8539
洪江市		755	755				34	2945
黔阳县	11	5553	5230			372	12	42995
沅陵县	87	17474	13506			50	427	3850
辰溪县	392	7785	5148			120	8	15452
溆浦县	1398	15600	13647			596	930	27135
麻阳县	53	12382	7880		15			24460
新晃县		3641	3348		36	1955	2	3117
芷江县	22	8093	7163			1988	9	21850
会同县	56	6331	6119	14	10	246	24	30874
靖州县	13	6384	5776		50	12	1	14487
通道县	31	2086	2086			86	3	3540
湘西自治州	1004	95791	74807		1131	33970	636	62593
吉首市	138	7253	6024		392	1418	2	13205
泸溪县	262	11912	9682		164	1229	4	6308
凤凰县	42	12095	10113		216	6745	39	7344
花垣县	11	8548	5488		30	1450	7	985
保靖县	181	8582	5382		29	1647	51	13409
古丈县	101	4017	3714			576	310	2234
永顺县	175	25248	18877		298	7094	148	13689
龙山县	94	18136	15527		2	13811	75	5419

18—14 各地、市、县主要林产品产量(1997年)

Output of Major Forest Products by Prefecture, City and County

名　称	油茶籽（吨）	油桐籽（吨）	松　脂（吨）	板　栗（吨）	棕　片（吨）	竹笋干（吨）	木材采伐量（万立方米）	竹　材采伐量（万根）
长沙市	56157	1159	768	680	779	1927	18.18	908.86
芙蓉区								0.10
天心区	3						0.05	
岳麓区			30	3			0.08	
开福区	9	5	27		6		0.06	3.20
雨花区	15	2	15	1	1	1	0.01	0.20
浏阳市	48500	700	310	480	300	400	7.10	401.00
长沙县	2144	110	283	108	12	6	2.54	20.36
望城县	591	44	20	7	80	670	1.24	150.00
宁乡县	4895	298	83	81	380	850	7.10	334.00
株洲市	42063	663	729	962	352	2978	17.25	211.20
荷塘区	902				37	5	0.08	1.20
芦淞区	2000						0.01	0.70
石峰区	1000			2	29	2	0.03	
天元区	750						0.01	1.00
醴陵市	8167	35	90	80	12	30	2.29	18.00
株洲县	6000	20	100	180	20	25	0.92	31.50
攸　县	12000	60		24	50	200	3.76	40.00
茶陵县	9588	508	408	558	128	249	2.35	46.80
炎陵县	1656	40	131	118	76	2467	7.80	72.00
湘潭市	6782	217	356	110	115	120	5.44	45.10
雨湖区	2		8				0.01	0.30
岳塘区	356		6		1		0.17	0.35
湘乡市	1890	125	60	10	28	61	2.33	17.80
韶山市	100	2		1			0.09	1.00
湘潭县	4434	90	282	99	86	59	2.84	25.65
衡阳市	57061	1852	836	2009	559	790	11.16	1672.60
衡阳市郊区	190			1			0.25	
南岳区	370	8		42		98	0.30	105.00
耒阳市	18000	375	280	1080	210	220	1.20	1200.00
常宁市	9851	19		260	25	400	3.63	34.90
衡阳县	8887	50	40	50	80	20	1.08	110.00
衡南县	3560	915	36	110	72	10	0.95	35.00
衡山县	2450	150	400	180	135	15	0.45	110.00
衡东县	11653	270	80	256	30	7	2.50	69.20
祁东县	2100	65		30	7	20	0.80	8.50

18—14 续表1 (1997年)

名称	油茶籽(吨)	油桐籽(吨)	松脂(吨)	板栗(吨)	棕片(吨)	竹笋干(吨)	木材采伐量(万立方米)	竹材采伐量(万根)
邵阳市	5810	606	1807	490	300	969	42.96	452.78
双清区								
大祥区	398	16					0.03	2.03
北塔区	75							
武冈市	43	25		8	47	2	0.74	19.14
邵东县	155	11	36	13	6	1	1.00	8.00
新邵县	18	27		6	50	21	1.59	12.80
邵阳县	4219	128		286	5	16	1.71	3.80
隆回县	343	122		30	91	103	3.46	29.73
洞口县	8	16		19	64	13	7.38	48.28
绥宁县	336	54	1309	44	7	686	19.00	200.00
新宁县	56	31	434	33	17	95	3.75	48.00
城步县	159	176	28	51	13	32	4.30	81.00
岳阳市	9011	657	763	579	106	176	7.73	1080.60
岳阳楼区							0.04	
云溪区				35	2		0.10	25.50
君山区							0.31	
汨罗市	170	19	300	8		7	0.59	25.00
临湘市	75	22		84	8	14	1.81	244.00
岳阳县	889	70	300	252		9	0.85	57.00
华容县	96	171	3	50			0.98	99.70
湘阴县	200	60	160		2	10	0.34	30.00
平江县	7581	315		150	94	136	2.71	599.40
常德市	28491	2650	332	785	442	122	10.40	569.86
武陵区	64						0.10	
鼎城区	10985	26		22	24	6	0.75	139.04
津市市	139	113	16	9	13		0.20	5.35
安乡县							0.38	0.42
汉寿县	3474	18	10	2	3		3.39	50.24
澧　县	130	153		14	12		0.49	9.61
临澧县	2956	32	20	94	114	15	1.46	1.83
桃源县	9645	827	256	277	119	100	2.25	255.73
石门县	1098	1481	30	367	157	1	1.38	107.64

18—14　续表 2　　　　　　　　　　　　(1997 年)

名　称	油茶籽（吨）	油桐籽（吨）	松　脂（吨）	板　栗（吨）	棕　片（吨）	竹笋干（吨）	木材采伐量（万立方米）	竹　材采伐量（万根）
张家界市	2532	4421	120	893	1117	128	8.39	604.06
永定区	1159	1911		169	101	5	3.50	53.00
武陵源区	14	238	22	4	42		0.76	75.12
慈利县	889	1944	28	368	883	23	2.24	206.94
桑植县	470	328	70	352	91	100	1.89	269.00
益阳市	9573	474	185	217	830	386	24.34	865.20
资阳区	1712	1		1	4	4	0.21	14.00
赫山区	3015	15		8	50	21	0.70	70.00
沅江市	8						5.96	
南　县					46		0.82	
桃江县	1280	150		50	280	180	1.35	580.00
安化县	3558	308	185	158	450	181	15.30	201.20
郴州市	29043	408	590	993	407	1156	46.16	320.86
北湖区	1321	1		64	8	74	1.85	46.26
苏仙区	2039	34		8	2	10	2.26	95.00
资兴市	3384	75	150	362	53	391	18.15	65.00
桂阳县	6750	90	35	90	110	114	2.65	9.80
宜章县	829	4	41	7	56	11	3.12	27.60
永兴县	6713	6	24	26	57	3	1.51	16.00
嘉禾县	2150	95	10	40	3	1	1.20	4.00
临武县	400	20	40	3	3	10	1.85	5.00
汝城县	2568	20	280	280	70	312	10.72	31.00
桂东县	340	12		10	25	165	1.65	21.00
安仁县	2549	51	10	103	20	65	1.20	0.20
永州市	53449	1193	6887	831	515	991	35.97	270.54
芝山区	2890	24	50	24	131	90	0.75	12.00
冷水滩区	10235	10	189	97	4	10	0.91	1.50
祁阳县	9376	170		420	44	263	4.70	18.50
东安县	2175	56		11	122	20	1.46	12.47
双牌县	146	48	103	33	58	30	6.08	66.42

18—14 续表 3　　　　　(1997 年)

名　称	油茶籽（吨）	油桐籽（吨）	松　脂（吨）	板　栗（吨）	棕　片（吨）	竹笋干（吨）	木材采伐量（万立方米）	竹　材采伐量（万根）
道　县	12087	149	150	129	21	52	0.90	5.00
江永县	1203	176	414	17		15	3.01	2.70
宁远县	3300	20	108	20	25	6	4.30	24.00
蓝山县	1270	15	73	4	33	35	3.55	103.95
新田县	2000	10		5		4	0.84	5.00
江华县	8767	515	5800	71	77	466	9.47	19.00
娄底地区	5138	527	55	87	154	234	5.78	178.50
娄底市	367	4	9	4	2	6	0.52	3.30
冷水江市	32	11		7	17	6	0.14	12.00
涟源市	780	1			52	10	1.07	20.00
双峰县	3620	178	46	36	53	62	2.05	77.20
新化县	339	333		40	30	150	2.00	66.00
怀化地区	22211	12669	2965	2925	1331	387	79.95	581.54
怀化市	7150	3850		750	900	50	8.00	10.00
洪江市	271	99		2			0.47	24.34
黔阳县	1566	920	12	70	1	165	5.14	66.56
沅陵县	1034	741	15	1250	229	24	18.20	59.20
辰溪县	1740	220		50	19	11	2.18	16.51
溆浦县	1452	498		12	20	5	9.30	20.00
麻阳县	214	309		328			1.62	2.00
新晃县	87	1327	1	75	89	2	1.22	13.47
芷江县	751	717	15	225	17	5	3.88	15.28
会同县	5044	3272	674	132	55	81	9.16	80.41
靖州县	502	28	1030	10		31	9.06	17.00
通道县	2400	688	1218	21	1	13	11.72	256.77
湘西自治州	13112	22611	133	2477	161	95	15.41	38.19
吉首市	505	378		556	3		0.54	0.10
泸溪县	690	520		280	20	12	0.48	
凤凰县	446	256		18		4	0.59	
花垣县	378	530		35	20	50	0.06	
保靖县	418	2607		400	16	8	1.18	9.36
古丈县	1060	1040	25	63	14		2.60	
永顺县	5374	9961	103	356	28	8	1.96	3.64
龙山县	4241	7319	5	769	60	13	8.00	25.09

18—15 各地、市、县牲畜头数、畜产品及水产品产量(1997年)

Number of Livestocks, Output of Livestock Products and Aquatic Products by Prefecture, City and County

名称	大牲畜年底头数(头)	耕牛	猪、牛、羊肉产量(吨)	猪年底头数(万头)	肉猪年内出栏头数(万头)	水产品(吨)	鱼
长沙市	331238	296353	393202	355.90	608.33	75529	73663
芙蓉区	223	75	6103	4.02	9.24	1588	1577
天心区	392	184	2911	3.59	4.34	1534	1534
岳麓区	858	858	11019	8.86	18.20	1896	1896
开福区	2196	1878	9938	11.10	18.16	4907	4879
雨花区	734	635	10547	9.56	15.21	1300	1296
浏阳市	85557	84100	80450	80.80	120.40	16320	15700
长沙县	105750	105600	114085	99.80	170.62	11234	11129
望城县	23187	23187	64890	56.67	108.43	14280	13541
宁乡县	112341	79836	93259	81.50	143.73	22470	22111
株洲市	169157	167901	218979	206.40	328.65	39177	37584
荷塘区	785	785	5855	3.70	8.84	738	738
芦淞区	486	281	1820	2.05	2.65	920	912
石峰区	1070	1056	7143	6.08	10.69	1403	1382
天元区	658	658	3772	3.60	5.90	871	871
醴陵市	24750	24206	52096	54.28	77.82	10236	9836
株洲县	10871	10820	34869	27.44	52.50	7006	6239
攸县	58098	58008	62312	56.00	94.00	9341	9098
茶陵县	48614	48262	41893	42.47	62.43	8330	8177
炎陵县	23825	23825	9219	10.78	13.82	332	331
湘潭市	68242	67939	225351	199.84	362.31	53000	51931
雨湖区	155	117	10857	9.72	18.79	1750	1728
岳塘区	514	494	10521	8.55	16.74	1683	1596
湘乡市	54560	54560	91752	83.10	141.33	21050	20520
韶山市	2000	2000	7805	12.73	12.45	1800	1748
湘潭县	11013	10768	104416	85.74	173.00	26717	26339
衡阳市	246841	245858	491619	383.58	717.39	151349	143698
衡阳市郊区	2604	2593	13953	18.16	19.05	7388	7196
南岳区	5570	5570	3673	2.52	4.40	337	327
耒阳市	37850	37850	81378	58.36	113.38	17270	16931
常宁市	31449	31314	50152	56.48	76.13	13259	12422
衡阳县	58125	58125	101384	78.00	150.10	34000	32880
衡南县	59330	59330	91311	59.80	119.98	31803	29550
衡山县	8249	8249	35861	24.80	59.47	7760	7270
衡东县	30123	29354	56434	40.98	83.67	10836	8753
祁东县	13541	13473	57473	44.48	91.21	28696	28369

18—15 续表1 (1997年)

名称	大牲畜年底头数(头)	耕牛	猪、牛、羊肉产量(吨)	猪年底头数(万头)	肉猪年内出栏头数(万头)	水产品(吨)	鱼
邵阳市	896401	817632	458626	437.39	716.43	53342	51482
双清区	2913	2881	4080	3.25	5.45	1077	1063
大祥区	6863	6494	7519	4.46	9.69	1181	1089
北塔区	4042	4036	1599	1.06	2.07	328	318
武冈市	87386	86700	83858	71.79	126.02	6000	5779
邵东县	29055	28937	78579	58.20	115.76	18800	17648
新邵县	77145	76751	42720	34.77	60.36	3647	3578
邵阳县	120646	114668	7737	42.38	82.30	7241	7166
隆回县	119648	118893	53176	53.18	67.67	3850	3783
洞口县	84244	84119	95748	91.10	152.00	5720	5676
绥宁县	115564	91250	34867	30.10	41.56	1302	1284
新宁县	174858	131529	32941	32.00	39.00	3876	3802
城步县	74037	71374	15802	15.10	14.55	320	296
岳阳市	227904	226313	413254	331.79	661.80	225481	211610
岳阳楼区	1359	1359	13348	4.93	21.48	16496	16376
云溪区	5548	5423	9169	10.44	14.49	9945	9563
君山区	11780	11775	25186	16.29	40.41	23137	22686
汨罗市	45717	45717	100956	67.07	164.66	13019	11411
临湘市	20551	20288	22976	19.04	36.84	13917	13523
岳阳县	43590	43588	58689	63.41	92.56	34348	33725
华容县	25520	24400	44189	30.21	71.06	50521	47883
湘阴县	18500	18500	74831	72.50	120.00	60900	53277
平江县	55339	55263	63910	47.90	100.30	3198	3166
常德市	334291	313182	327436	284.07	416.19	198042	188961
武陵区	3325	3179	9502	5.45	12.60	9733	9692
鼎城区	39664	37620	56872	52.44	76.31	51093	49952
津市市	9834	8927	15359	10.17	19.08	9550	9159
安乡县	14148	7442	21860	31.74	29.62	32675	31950
汉寿县	27627	27050	30743	33.49	42.97	35672	31639
澧县	39079	33812	37150	35.94	48.06	18014	17749
临澧县	33188	33018	34865	23.54	41.98	13377	12666
桃源县	87401	82664	83599	51.53	100.73	22391	20732
石门县	80025	79470	37486	39.77	44.84	5537	5422

18—15　续表 2　　　　　　　(1997 年)

名　　称	大牲畜年底头数（头）	耕　牛	猪、牛、羊肉产量（吨）	猪年底头数（万头）	肉猪年内出栏头数（万头）	水产品（吨）	鱼
张家界市	167265	166066	69082	66.05	87.89	5309	5185
永定区	43356	43337	19572	16.82	24.52	1872	1827
武陵源区	3019	3018	1589	1.02	2.40	26	26
慈利县	63425	62618	29670	27.90	39.08	3030	2971
桑植县	57465	57093	18251	20.31	21.89	381	361
益阳市	253434	251911	187107	168.65	251.47	113779	109139
资阳区	5284	5284	13691	11.55	20.04	8500	7817
赫山区	13765	13731	42279	33.80	48.70	12120	11863
沅江市	14095	14095	29397	29.97	44.48	50058	47522
南　县	16168	14989	34326	21.63	45.45	33107	32270
桃江县	34322	34012	29819	32.70	44.80	3050	2970
安化县	169800	169800	37595	39.00	48.00	6944	6697
郴州市	347181	343157	286204	264.68	394.26	43271	41941
北湖区	21409	20792	12570	8.34	16.78	2100	2069
苏仙区	49800	49800	22575	16.89	29.21	5003	4952
资兴市	27607	27535	29686	23.98	41.86	7562	7439
桂阳县	46614	46508	33121	36.30	47.45	6010	5913
宜章县	46981	46436	31334	36.87	46.01	4040	3982
永兴县	45740	45283	36466	38.88	51.29	8570	8368
嘉禾县	15552	14471	36221	26.16	47.02	1316	1250
临武县	14741	14657	19137	18.06	26.65	2602	2082
汝城县	28100	28100	20685	24.00	28.44	650	635
桂东县	21294	21294	7887	7.79	9.59	406	385
安仁县	29343	28281	36522	27.41	49.96	5012	4866
永州市	531401	526811	378530	330.10	494.68	74949	68588
芝山区	53337	53225	37989	30.23	52.18	5800	5324
冷水滩区	28900	28730	34771	24.60	45.88	10462	9941
祁阳县	17268	17238	59188	40.16	78.68	22823	20872
东安县	73286	71560	41220	30.40	46.60	7748	7310
双牌县	23544	23544	7332	6.90	9.45	1117	1017

18—15 续表 3 (1997 年)

名称	大牲畜年底头数(头)	耕牛	猪、牛、羊肉产量(吨)	猪年底头数(万头)	肉猪年内出栏头数(万头)	水产品(吨)	鱼
道县	111610	109400	45702	50.01	54.26	12052	11467
江永县	80434	80187	24087	16.71	28.10	2085	1906
宁远县	33958	33958	49651	42.42	64.23	7891	5920
蓝山县	24820	24732	33668	30.50	46.10	1378	1374
新田县	14774	14767	20864	26.47	31.00	1886	1858
江华县	69470	69470	24058	31.70	38.20	1707	1599
娄底地区	315189	314684	258739	249.02	402.53	38625	35853
娄底市	17574	17504	13182	15.32	20.08	4039	3625
冷水江市	18155	18137	11077	13.62	16.16	1952	1908
涟源市	52000	51760	50090	54.87	77.96	5770	5413
双峰县	40103	40103	107148	97.26	172.02	16600	15200
新化县	187357	187180	77242	67.95	116.31	10264	9707
怀化地区	639284	635662	248616	234.81	289.12	23481	22430
怀化市	50120	49600	31284	21.70	35.90	6777	6257
洪江市	3287	3202	3665	2.36	4.26	451	391
黔阳县	39678	39491	19543	17.84	21.84	1317	1287
沅陵县	101955	101955	30624	28.63	31.71	3250	3132
辰溪县	49700	49700	14001	21.74	23.02	1052	1033
溆浦县	70567	70418	51122	40.20	57.59	3769	3748
麻阳县	43701	43701	10682	14.23	15.12	1240	1108
新晃县	74117	73200	19308	18.58	26.30	670	662
芷江县	42728	42565	24806	22.35	27.57	1422	1418
会同县	69211	68999	18283	19.25	19.10	1384	1290
靖州县	52260	51000	18272	16.80	17.55	1461	1425
通道县	41960	41831	7026	11.13	9.16	688	679
湘西自治州	437979	436432	83496	119.73	106.55	12276	12069
吉首市	35144	34789	8225	7.46	10.66	1088	1025
泸溪县	46499	46499	7433	10.35	10.85	864	846
凤凰县	71678	71668	7727	16.88	10.43	1433	1423
花垣县	49320	49320	12278	20.22	13.30	1768	1754
保靖县	52825	52795	8356	13.58	12.65	750	733
古丈县	34204	34090	3388	5.40	4.57	1167	1167
永顺县	98380	97399	15515	23.10	19.58	924	905
龙山县	49929	49872	20574	22.74	24.51	4282	4216

18—16 各地、市、县工业、轻工业、重工业总产值(1997年)

Gross Output Value of Industry, Light Industry and Heavy Industry by Prefecture, City and County

单位:万元

名 称	全部工业总产值	#乡及乡以上	轻 工 业	重 工 业	工业总产值为上年%
长沙市	6008035	3620568	3142252	2865783	121.3
长沙市区	2602271	2120199	1521945	1080326	116.7
浏阳市	790658	287669	542100	248558	115.4
长沙县	1204466	674074	496817	707649	129.5
望城县	626530	237128	282812	343718	121.2
宁乡县	784109	301497	298578	485531	134.1
株洲市	3528681	2002825	1232651	2296030	119.1
株洲市区	1865512	1512806	364750	1500762	120.0
醴陵市	741707	232360	470158	271549	116.9
株洲县	267686	85997	108366	159320	105.2
攸 县	340989	98064	154895	186094	112.8
茶陵县	247582	52600	99214	148368	141.8
炎陵县	65205	20998	35268	29937	152.1
湘潭市	2342194	1435100	754570	1587624	116.9
湘潭市区	1240622	995794	397736	842886	112.0
湘乡市	509428	260050	166498	342930	125.3
韶山市	121244	41504	46742	74502	131.8
湘潭县	470901	137753	143596	327305	119.5
衡阳市	3977847	1621283	1513137	2464710	119.7
衡阳市区	1034836	672707	366949	667887	120.0
耒阳市	543450	155989	153650	389800	130.3
常宁市	418610	168106	136397	282213	98.6
衡阳县	507106	176068	292628	214478	124.4
衡南县	550077	119174	208581	341496	126.7
衡山县	145780	59710	74320	71460	96.0
衡东县	309360	110694	147194	162166	132.4
祁东县	468629	158836	133420	335209	121.4

18—16 续表1 (1997年) 单位:万元

名称	全部工业总产值	#乡及乡以上	轻工业	重工业	工业总产值为上年%
邵阳市	2538482	771146	1288731	1249751	121.0
邵阳市区	337287	229666	154859	182428	75.2
武冈市	242250	48341	134933	107317	172.6
邵东县	690890	97384	381708	309182	102.8
新邵县	236167	95501	134337	101830	114.3
邵阳县	292604	56198	126189	166415	160.4
隆回县	141492	56302	90686	50806	138.6
洞口县	169514	72626	85250	84264	175.1
绥宁县	236217	57758	85713	150504	200.5
新宁县	120458	26599	45282	75176	212.8
城步县	71603	30781	49775	21828	142.6
岳阳市	4435869	2602471	2163887	2271982	123.3
岳阳市区	1954144	1601054	733646	1250498	126.1
汨罗市	725109	258130	394107	331002	133.5
临湘市	267195	156741	127029	140166	91.5
岳阳县	324827	126464	226469	98358	98.9
华容县	389579	203979	272187	117392	128.8
湘阴县	488080	195955	272741	215339	145.2
平江县	256935	60148	137707	119228	117.4
常德市	3323160	1668730	2099902	1223258	100.2
常德市区	1245713	728770	877072	368641	110.6
武陵区	570117	488115	453781	116336	96.4
鼎城区	675596	240655	423291	252305	126.1
津市市	155143	121374	98702	56441	107.3
安乡县	143630	90055	123042	20588	79.7
汉寿县	195662	106524	130596	65066	104.7
澧县	407197	148439	230331	176866	95.3
临澧县	206225	173541	106973	99252	41.7
桃源县	740949	166869	484370	256579	138.9
石门县	228640	133157	48813	179827	105.9

18－16　续表 2　　　　　　(1997 年)　　　　　　单位:万元

名　　称	全部工业总产值	#乡及乡以上	轻　工　业	重　工　业	工业总产值为上年%
张家界市	323169	125429	187306	135863	122.7
张家界市区	80878	37862	43453	37425	116.9
永定区	74050	36322	38105	35945	124.2
武陵源区	6828	1540	5348	1480	72.7
慈利县	161816	47517	94761	67055	126.4
桑植县	80475	40050	49092	31383	121.4
益阳市	1891694	763970	1116057	775637	121.9
益阳市区	638780	288248	342171	296609	106.2
资阳区	103857	47186	62378	41479	66.0
赫山区	534923	241062	279793	255130	184.7
沅江市	324517	138948	247997	76520	137.7
南　县	223066	130944	172393	50673	109.3
桃江县	399613	96964	201350	198263	128.2
安化县	305718	108866	152145	153573	154.4
郴州市	2965897	996652	1028480	1937417	140.4
郴州市区	741275	437622	260135	481140	123.6
北湖区	436611	312532	219071	217540	151.9
苏仙区	304664	125090	41064	263600	94.4
资兴市	312583	164570	59892	252691	144.0
桂阳县	411527	96010	264036	147491	165.7
宜章县	407720	76549	83049	324671	241.7
永兴县	280701	49011	54689	226012	96.1
嘉禾县	231357	34697	93653	137704	130.8
临武县	267487	37212	63531	203956	159.5
汝城县	122906	60227	42105	80801	113.3
桂东县	38199	12790	13625	24574	129.7
安仁县	152144	27966	93765	58379	155.5
永州市	2508321	879302	1062408	1445913	128.9
芝山区	424842	250653	238495	186347	117.3
冷水滩区	402103	169409	114031	288072	142.6
祁阳县	553436	153542	211351	342085	142.6
东安县	129492	64129	32704	96788	67.6
双牌县	81182	30013	34764	46418	157.0

18—16 续表 3 (1997 年) 单位:万元

名 称	全部工业总产值	#乡及乡以上	轻 工 业	重 工 业	工业总产值为上年%
道 县	288918	66742	125270	163648	142.0
江永县	81659	25222	40536	41123	144.8
宁远县	213881	19369	115783	98098	142.7
蓝山县	140182	26170	38366	101816	168.0
新田县	105903	45624	77735	28168	123.2
江华县	86725	28431	33374	53351	99.1
娄底地区	2100613	1079300	407766	1692847	118.4
娄底市	623002	431146	40199	582803	134.7
冷水江市	422300	258782	19965	402335	109.2
涟源市	302786	177077	73595	229191	85.0
双峰县	487769	110159	185138	302631	134.9
新化县	264756	102136	88870	175886	133.2
怀化地区	1711083	961153	751149	959934	117.4
怀化市	254541	175879	122093	132448	82.2
洪江市	114157	72543	69844	44313	120.4
黔阳县	173745	85590	89801	83944	134.7
沅陵县	231727	204084	30846	200881	111.1
辰溪县	145917	64258	60775	85142	141.7
溆浦县	138042	82557	54041	84001	109.5
麻阳县	86229	37015	56674	29555	118.4
新晃县	61373	49065	37259	24114	77.6
芷江县	103223	60376	46079	57144	121.4
会同县	168267	49382	43272	124995	156.2
靖州县	175935	61612	96006	79929	167.3
通道县	57927	18792	44457	13470	150.0
湘西自治州	516435	321976	309365	207070	104.9
吉首市	169915	121557	124059	45856	104.4
泸溪县	41402	26778	10569	30833	82.4
凤凰县	40483	20890	30067	10416	64.2
花垣县	48367	38471	5313	43054	123.9
保靖县	38551	16176	18333	20218	125.6
古丈县	11329	7384	4394	6935	106.8
永顺县	58440	30063	39408	19032	116.4
龙山县	107949	60658	77222	30727	119.9

18—17 各地、市、县按经济类型分工业总产值(1997年)

Gross Output Value of Industry by Ownership and by Prefecture, City and County

单位:万元

名称	国有	集体	#乡办工业	#村办工业	城镇个体工业	农村个体工业
长沙市	1599622	2025937	903308	558330	86737	1662317
长沙市区	1397771	686758	1102651	122490	21276	306021
浏阳市	48611	247617	122986	106233	60467	336289
长沙县	28224	506185	361395	137704		392688
望城县	28313	242335	93531	99403	138	289419
宁乡县	96704	343043	126054	92500	4856	337900
株洲市	1208213	1053380	324084	448413	75440	970921
株洲市区	1095698	360466	54712	123998	33639	192981
醴陵市	31577	345380	145458	158982	6136	328029
株洲县	11590	119815	57088	41649	14639	119167
攸县	43764	111888	29424	54396	7352	174617
茶陵县	17005	93757	28880	59046	9614	126322
炎陵县	8579	22076	8521	10342	4060	29805
湘潭市	751030	871968	293290	207417	23980	620008
湘潭市区	580877	437107	125943	56108	17924	145009
湘乡市	134927	202059	65011	55333	986	165887
韶山市	6023	46346	26436	11091		68649
湘潭县	29204	186456	75900	84885	5070	240463
衡阳市	764455	1291311	601652	465260	79127	1716871
衡阳市区	440194	236487	84575	64390	332	297407
耒阳市	90818	137900	51159	67030	4560	301451
常宁市	105685	95958	48415	34195	50079	166230
衡阳县	27771	201847	127389	71523	21058	238457
衡南县	14311	195390	87637	104317		326586
衡山县	15632	70374	35727	25961	631	57486
衡东县	27020	185161	72621	23726	2467	93579
祁东县	43023	169104	94130	74118		235675

注:按当年价格计算。

18—17 续表1 (1997年) 单位:万元

名称	国有	集体	#乡办工业	#村办工业	城镇个体工业	农村个体工业
邵阳市	295913	674773	299264	230440	137647	1336070
邵阳市区	154844	71641	25427	4272	30650	64699
武冈市	9335	78436	31827	40761	33693	119455
邵东县	23939	72199	39678	23127	6266	559983
新邵县	30909	103524	56355	41402	17112	80838
邵阳县	6252	120751	36376	45020	24039	137160
隆回县	16964	40067	19851	8821	1900	66746
洞口县	21915	73184	36789	21804	2265	69924
绥宁县	2842	66103	28522	31535	13911	133013
新宁县	11817	30096	13203	7003	1095	76960
城步县	17096	18772	11237	6695	6716	27292
岳阳市	1406750	1344694	609880	312027	146348	1174781
岳阳市区	1083712	268290	64491	79518	70027	227835
汨罗市	143651	274208	81686	101518	6550	291583
临湘市	56164	131513	87864	33977	10750	65727
岳阳县	9956	147903	76658	35410	17831	144346
华容县	51200	155976	115549		30281	141399
湘阴县	42146	302419	151229	36395	9867	133355
平江县	19923	64385	32402	25209	1042	170536
常德市	818400	1250932	532310	458825	145222	1050197
常德市区	462228	406192	166740	174932	25605	316406
武陵区	410631	97288	19199	54266	3033	24703
鼎城区	51597	308904	147541	120666	22572	291703
津市市	71319	58664	21914	13607	3089	17073
安乡县	25692	58336	19665	3864	8206	41505
汉寿县	38984	90809	42957	26884	4153	58101
澧县	38104	192971	73617	85306	60480	112972
临澧县	43375	141819	97760	11467	4150	16881
桃源县	37866	244906	87395	115903	31437	426740
石门县	100832	57234	22262	26862	8102	60519

18—17 续表 2 (1997 年) 单位:万元

名称	国有	集体	#乡办工业	#村办工业	城镇个体工业	农村个体工业
张家界市	68198	79484	30049	31830	25009	138975
张家界市区	24246	20682	3823	9973	17492	13744
永定区	23656	17797	3051	9767	16097	11864
武陵源区	590	2885	772	206	1395	1780
慈利县	14186	43172	16840	16530	6737	91032
桑植县	29767	15629	9386	5327	780	34299
益阳市	286873	839047	283610	251970	108236	597725
益阳市区	122954	279687	52647	119854	36867	161444
资阳区	8885	69456	18294	33026	4994	18651
赫山区	114069	210231	34353	86828	31873	142793
沅江市	57146	142681	61024	43267	48639	67932
南县	45579	102870	50970	27321	3330	61471
桃江县	27402	162260	62784	27397	6750	199599
安化县	33790	151549	56185	34131	12650	107279
郴州市	459406	1189468	359170	296413	101273	1144141
郴州市区	230592	90625	37291	25578	14887	70962
北湖区	230592	90625	37291	25578	14887	70962
苏仙区	49171	119292	51366	49670		129904
资兴市	114643	115408	33760	38604	21397	55902
桂阳县	18376	180959	48809	23848	2600	196473
永兴县	13098	247215	40666	46801	9786	127095
宜章县	2270	84738	36669	25462	5448	185188
嘉禾县	5528	95750	20274	46733	18749	110772
临武县	9680	142554	24616	10754		112948
汝城县	5606	58756	46236	5105	5754	51820
桂东县	2386	11885	8540	1481	2459	21469
安仁县	8057	42285	10943	22377	20193	81608
永州市	469757	707483	262999	140679	213613	1055866
芝山区	171591	99720	63975	15334	14961	129722
冷水滩区	110050	104220	30847	31093	24561	156717
祁阳县	45462	260406	77083	69500	58000	177394
东安县	16061	59482	37415	1490	1336	4949
双牌县	15060	25649	8690	249	8136	32336

18—17 续表 3 (1997 年) 单位:万元

名称	国有	集体	#乡办工业	#村办工业	城镇个体工业	农村个体工业
道县	33732	70883	21581	9626	12574	169821
江永县	12190	13736	4802	2690	10323	38904
宁远县	7795	30556	6305	6960	1055	174475
蓝山县	4028	8735	4080	1385	51388	59962
新田县	34922	27957	4698	241	17755	24381
江华县	18866	6141	3524	2111	13524	42659
娄底地区	666537	721838	282943	182972	56240	651518
娄底市	355988	153433	33080	40535	12282	100795
冷水江市	194049	106281	33756	41548	22044	99926
涟源市	65041	173632	86069	25800	12407	51568
双峰县	12637	174785	88877	39182	4267	296080
新化县	38821	113707	41160	35907	5240	103149
怀化地区	429397	597581	311601	94519	77501	517165
怀化市	54095	111629	36801	23198	36750	7424
洪江市	36041	35079	18700	1024	14292	26298
黔阳县	24058	54099	46118	1756	5258	81141
沅陵县	180862	29085	9347	7121	305	20217
辰溪县	32832	44157	24065	12731	6358	62570
溆浦县	17410	51840	31839	15248	287	39904
麻阳县	12365	31010	19517	2846	1460	41394
新晃县	24269	26224	21577	1428	3458	7422
芷江县	13079	56597	25021	6631	3980	29520
会同县	12973	55644	31299	12601	2137	97093
靖州县	14962	81245	37405	5040	3205	74848
通道县	6450	20974	9913	4895	11	29334
湘西自治州	233659	87345	53566	6699	15321	169572
吉首市	100239	18495	10578	861	2169	43764
泸溪县	22466	5260	3248	948	1990	11686
凤凰县	15530	5648	3342	1036	1701	16856
花垣县	17022	23341	10914	1891	617	7388
保靖县	8460	8728	6420	275	732	20065
古丈县	5069	2363	903	48	385	3512
永顺县	23440	6587	4671	741	4104	23532
龙山县	41433	16923	13489	899	3623	42769

18—18 各地、市主要工业产品产量(1997 年)

Output of Major Industrial Products by Prefecture, City and County

名称	纱(万吨)	布(亿米)	针棉织品(折用纱线)(万吨)	机制纸及纸板(万吨)	缝纫机(万架)	自行车(万辆)	日用陶瓷器(亿件)	灯泡(万只)
长沙市	1.49	0.49	0.18	1.01	0.10	0.02	1.25	416.50
株洲市	0.13	0.01	0.22	5.01		1.36	3.85	5184
湘潭市	1.52	0.78		4.68	0.10		0.21	
衡阳市	0.81	0.15		4.03		0.27	2.84	3977.82
邵阳市	0.66	0.38		13.94			0.08	3.60
岳阳市	1.49	0.34	0.07	15.87			0.60	35.24
常德市	3.59	0.99	0.08	15.93	0.91		0.11	1794.77
张家界市		0.03	0.05	0.28				
益阳市	0.96	0.07	0.02	8.86	3.05		0.71	2350.70
郴州市	0.51	0.20	0.08	3.36			0.19	
永州市	0.57	0.41	0.01	5.62			0.40	
娄底地区	0.35	0.00	0.05	1.51			0.94	277.76
怀化地区	0.86	0.42	0.02	6.30			1.00	1379
湘西自治州	0.32	0.15	0.03	0.59			0.20	

名称	糖(万吨)	卷烟(万箱)	化学原料药(吨)	饮料酒(混合量)(万吨)	食用植物油(万吨)	配混合饲料(万吨)	钢(万吨)	生铁(万吨)
长沙市	0.03	72.67	2649	7.12	0.24	18.02	0.93	0.01
株洲市			452	1.37	0.48	15.77	2.77	0.37
湘潭市				5.45	0.07	1.92	100.78	114.81
衡阳市		4.80	14	12.58	1.63	20.30	13.37	5.64
邵阳市		7.30	407	2.00	0.97	18.78		3.18
岳阳市	2.82		320.83	6.78	5.18	38.25		
常德市	1.28	68.00	93	5.39	15.10	3.96	0.02	
张家界市		2.20		0.28	1.27	1.17		
益阳市	2.83			3.51	5.45	5.37		
郴州市		32.00		1.04	0.23	6.00		
永州市	0.75	32.34	1	4.44	0.75	6.58		5.96
娄底地区				0.39	0.09	5.27	123.93	134.73
怀化地区		3.70	84	1.75	3.29	8.28	1.93	
湘西自治州		10.40		4.20	1.30	0.07		

18—18 续表 (1997年)

名　　称	原　煤（万吨）	发电量（亿千瓦小时）	#水　电	成品钢材（万吨）	水　泥（万吨）	平板玻璃（万重量箱）	硫　酸（万吨）	烧　碱（万吨）
长沙市	207.81	2.83	1.33	3.26	283.82		14.42	
株洲市	260.44	19.90	4.03	2.48	133.88	294.63	44.17	9.50
湘潭市	65.98	8.60	1.44	75.74	189.42		0.21	0.57
衡阳市	635.18	31.16	9.58	21.58	82.27		19.71	2.08
邵阳市	356.82	9.53	6.71		121.20	51.15	2.31	1.07
岳阳市		43.24	1.98		65.78	0.66	1.72	4.24
常德市	166.09	23.94	4.95		272.35	12.27	7.00	0.01
张家界市	52.69	3.34	2.85		34.95			
益阳市	29.76	30.44	29.29		177.65		1.25	0.01
郴州市	1267.63	42.69	32.41		221.40	182.78	13.00	1.04
永州市	84.64	15.55	15.31	2.18	249.76		0.59	
娄底地区	976.31	31.92	2.35	93.73	238.05		3.83	0.25
怀化地区	278.48	76.61	74.82	0.05	107.48			0.47
湘西自治州	28.00	6.22	5.94		30.61		2.15	0.06

名　　称	化学农药（原药）（万吨）	化学肥料（折纯量）（万吨）	#氮　肥	#磷　肥	电　石（万吨）	塑料树脂及共聚物（吨）	矿山设备（吨）	金属切削机床（台）
长沙市	0.22	10.35	6.50	3.84	0.73	0.02	1395	1013
株洲市	0.47	19.27	15.15	4.12	3.46	2.16	440	12
湘潭市	0.60	2.94	2.34	0.61		0.01	54	
衡阳市	0.92	11.20	7.44	3.76	1.47		1532	
邵阳市	0.30	4.75	3.72	1.03	0.22	0.01	169	
岳阳市	0.69	45.59	44.50	0.95		5.72		58
常德市	0.04	12.88	8.21	4.67	0.17		846	
张家界市		1.38	1.33	0.05				
益阳市	0.56	4.33	3.70	0.13		0.03		20
郴州市	0.28	13.01	9.90	3.10	0.60	0.74	538	
永州市	0.08	4.34	4.21	0.13	0.26			
娄底地区	0.04	14.34	13.33	1.02	0.21	0.03	3120	
怀化地区		4.18	1.50	2.67	6.61		223	24
湘西自治州		1.92	0.20	1.72	0.08			

18—19 各地、市乡及乡以上独立核算工业主要经济指标(1997年)

Main Ecomomic Indicators of Independent Accounting Industrial Enterprises at Township Level and Above by Prefecture,City and County

单位:亿元

名称	企业单位数(个)	亏损企业	工业总产值(现价)	工业增加值(生产法)	销售产值
长沙市	3360	835	330.26	114.22	316.71
株洲市	1470	500	186.01	51.46	180.12
湘潭市	1179	466	116.30	31.54	112.08
衡阳市	2297	444	154.53	44.22	147.70
邵阳市	2043	442	71.82	25.53	68.82
岳阳市	1720	224	251.25	77.00	244.95
常德市	1800	532	148.92	52.20	143.20
张家界市	427	131	11.34	5.37	10.59
益阳市	1678	487	71.07	18.57	65.35
郴州市	1616	243	96.82	29.77	94.13
永州市	1678	199	79.55	33.26	74.70
娄底地区	1232	488	104.20	31.63	101.52
怀化地区	1810	401	88.91	43.99	86.44
湘西自治州	609	240	29.60	12.44	27.54

名称	资本金	#外商资本金	工业中间投入合计	全部职工年平均人数(人)
长沙市	119.62	17.09	234.07	48.40
株洲市	74.37	6.12	144.78	29.29
湘潭市	47.66	2.75	89.41	23.84
衡阳市	58.73	2.77	115.02	33.95
邵阳市	20.92	0.28	49.37	21.17
岳阳市	43.49	2.55	185.23	23.84
常德市	44.33	1.10	104.01	21.23
张家界市	6.79	0.67	6.48	3.02
益阳市	26.72	0.72	55.01	16.98
郴州市	45.54	1.33	71.57	17.91
永州市	23.66	0.40	50.86	14.79
娄底地区	38.82	0.19	77.77	22.97
怀化地区	31.83	0.92	47.68	16.32
湘西自治州	10.65	0.08	19.28	6.32

18－19　续表 1　　　　(1997 年)　　　　单位:亿元

名　　称	流动资产	存　货	产成品	流动资产年平均余额
长沙市	207.49	87.60	33.49	196.09
株洲市	130.44	48.74	19.52	123.36
湘潭市	89.45	34.69	11.96	87.89
衡阳市	88.90	35.91	16.09	84.73
邵阳市	39.12	16.58	7.28	43.46
岳阳市	96.63	37.26	15.07	109.21
常德市	81.55	39.53	10.36	77.88
张家界市	6.46	2.14	0.76	6.56
益阳市	41.61	16.89	8.47	41.37
郴州市	50.59	15.50	6.10	52.08
永州市	42.85	17.78	5.72	41.35
娄底地区	64.31	23.41	10.49	63.03
怀化地区	38.92	12.52	5.29	39.69
湘西自治州	37.36	11.11	4.74	34.16

名　　称	固定资产	固定资产原价合计	生产经营用固定资产	累计折旧	本年折旧
长沙市	199.42	233.17	171.88	68.00	13.49
株洲市	120.68	169.17	136.25	54.99	8.57
湘潭市	123.17	150.10	121.04	47.57	5.24
衡阳市	115.84	143.17	110.98	44.81	5.83
邵阳市	52.94	69.47	49.86	21.48	2.42
岳阳市	159.14	209.67	172.77	74.02	11.67
常德市	116.54	140.84	117.76	32.57	6.28
张家界市	19.13	14.82	9.08	3.76	0.64
益阳市	52.97	71.83	56.64	23.35	2.52
郴州市	85.60	104.36	74.71	29.52	3.96
永州市	48.03	56.88	40.09	15.79	2.67
娄底地区	85.26	113.77	89.17	42.04	5.27
怀化地区	120.30	143.39	109.56	26.94	6.81
湘西自治州	33.27	36.78	29.36	7.22	1.20

18—19 续表 2 (1997年) 单位:亿元

名　称	固定资产净值年平均余额	无形及递延资产合计	资产总计	流动负债合计
长沙市	153.05	19.81	456.69	218.92
株洲市	110.90	6.60	281.82	135.86
湘潭市	92.30	4.00	224.46	107.20
衡阳市	96.19	4.67	213.85	101.52
邵阳市	46.45	1.68	96.71	51.98
岳阳市	117.30	17.16	281.98	110.25
常德市	96.94	4.56	205.66	92.00
张家界市	10.58	0.71	27.25	9.91
益阳市	47.12	3.23	100.35	52.30
郴州市	78.77	4.91	150.21	53.73
永州市	39.95	2.01	95.13	50.05
娄底地区	67.03	4.49	160.19	74.70
怀化地区	113.75	1.99	165.11	49.43
湘西自治州	28.39	1.88	73.70	42.01

名　称	长期负债	所有者权益	产品销售收入	#产品销售费用	#产品销售税金及附加
长沙市	61.48	172.58	296.06	12.19	26.79
株洲市	41.91	103.77	172.89	4.75	2.68
湘潭市	40.50	76.44	104.16	3.01	0.75
衡阳市	43.63	67.97	129.78	3.93	2.44
邵阳市	18.61	24.20	59.68	2.70	1.78
岳阳市	83.41	87.47	221.48	6.34	1.09
常德市	55.72	57.42	128.90	3.24	14.53
张家界市	9.78	7.31	9.51	0.33	0.73
益阳市	19.49	26.04	56.90	1.95	0.67
郴州市	31.84	64.38	85.58	3.17	6.28
永州市	16.75	27.71	68.36	2.27	7.11
娄底地区	33.48	51.13	97.26	2.02	0.58
怀化地区	86.96	27.42	61.68	3.31	1.42
湘西自治州	14.64	16.94	27.91	1.07	3.44

18—19 续表 3 (1997 年) 单位:亿元

名称	产品销售利润	管理费用	利息支出	营业利润	利润总额
长沙市	39.37	25.42	11.23	3.33	7.65
株洲市	23.11	16.58	6.76	0.21	1.81
湘潭市	10.39	10.01	5.11	—4.63	—2.81
衡阳市	15.45	12.73	5.75	—3.01	—0.59
邵阳市	5.16	7.14	2.44	—4.66	—3.63
岳阳市	22.08	14.70	7.96	—0.64	1.86
常德市	13.26	8.54	6.20	—1.87	—1.07
张家界市	0.40	0.96	0.63	—1.32	—0.59
益阳市	4.94	5.36	2.66	—3.08	—2.28
郴州市	10.35	7.37	2.40	0.30	0.87
永州市	6.83	5.05	2.40	—0.52	0.13
娄底地区	10.82	9.11	3.92	—2.25	—1.06
怀化地区	3.96	6.28	3.30	—5.81	—1.54
湘西自治州	2.82	2.69	1.81	—1.19	0.03

名称	利税总额	应交所得税	应付利润	本年应付工资	本年应付福利费
长沙市	52.46	2.60	3.77	23.42	3.48
株洲市	14.72	0.64	0.71	17.64	2.21
湘潭市	2.59	0.18	0.08	11.03	1.75
衡阳市	6.56	0.54	1.26	14.56	1.82
邵阳市	1.22	0.15	0.19	8.07	1.08
岳阳市	13.94	0.75	1.23	13.10	1.71
常德市	20.76	0.46	0.27	9.62	1.37
张家界市	0.66	0.15	0.07	1.24	0.14
益阳市	0.89	0.02	0.18	6.22	0.70
郴州市	11.66	0.46	0.70	10.26	1.37
永州市	11.81	0.24	0.87	6.32	0.77
娄底地区	4.72	0.21	0.05	14.43	1.58
怀化地区	2.65	0.59	0.17	7.01	0.80
湘西自治州	5.59	0.37	0.13	3.87	1.19

18—20 各地、市、县国有经济固定资产投资、新增固定资产及房屋竣工面积(1997年)

Investment in Fixed Assets, Newly Increased Fixed Assets and Completed Building Floor Space of State－Owned Units by Prefecture, City and County

名称	固定资产投资(万元)	基本建设	更新改造	其他投资	房地产开发	新增固定资产(万元)	房屋建筑竣工面积(平方米)	住宅(平方米)
长沙市	643556	444061	126945	5747	66803	434869	1953396	984250
芙蓉区	143669	98735	13299		31635	64081	383045	169722
天心区	202536	114050	77832	100	10554	168413	494698	258736
岳麓区	50053	37749	8904		3400	32223	166150	96166
开福区	94653	73296	11917		9440	58702	277898	154034
雨花区	55021	34771	5131	5311	9808	46240	218933	153337
浏阳市	31291	29133	1305		853	12612	88112	41448
长沙县	19135	18121	969		45	11637	100342	44623
望城县	21717	16482	3831	336	1068	14546	26282	16486
宁乡县	25481	21724	3757			26415	197936	49698
株洲市	171290	83740	69708	7390	10452	193305	776701	449195
荷塘区	22163	8517	13611		35	36484	162411	124478
芦淞区	41014	12538	24532	3909	35	46879	104147	59671
石峰区	48698	18944	27115		2639	49225	149756	88367
天元区	29709	23725			5984	23408	183624	110146
醴陵市	9418	5722	2976		720	5094	38266	25770
株洲县	6303	5282	324	540	157	17919	30018	12970
攸　县	6689	3280	380	2831	198	5901	46484	12971
茶陵县	3653	2765	688		200	3942	30380	5064
炎陵县	3643	2967	82	110	484	4453	31615	9758
湘潭市	251128	185263	50809	5594	9462	196039	633415	375621
雨湖区	24598	10601	6770	987	6240	28390	237629	169890
岳塘区	196624	161596	32729	252	2047	94893	233508	95473
湘乡市	20610	6194	9186	4355	875	66113	103473	74418
韶山市	2015	1335	680			2285	12650	12000
湘潭县	7281	5537	1444		300	4358	46155	23840
衡阳市	187739	98595	72176	8721	8247	217590	1027179	666466
江东区	9020	2466	5717	505	332	6745	34935	21754
城南区	39386	8587	25984	689	4126	122493	245493	168104
城北区	47918	25570	17014	3878	1456	27919	155415	104075
郊　区	8476	6207	979		1290	3595	43251	38441
南岳区	5593	5229	364			1571	17531	5807
耒阳市	18830	11837	6797	96	100	5776	49337	44969
常宁市	10607	5166	3818	1593	30	9086	73096	23437
衡阳县	9773	7395	2378			9706	100389	63311

18—20 续表 1 (1997 年)

名　称	固定资产投资（万元）	基本建设	更新改造	其他投资	房地产开发	新增固定资产（万元）	房屋建筑竣工面积（平方米）	住宅（平方米）
衡南县	15949	14595	1084		270	6378	75497	53293
衡山县	4692	1844	1156	1295	397	5803	61974	36265
衡东县	5344	3087	2151		106	5225	12885	6947
祁东县	12151	6612	4734	665	140	13293	157376	100063
邵阳市	118432	94305	14614	2103	7410	92965	727606	396701
双清区	15988	6992	6493	1577	926	14698	90056	64120
大祥区	17018	10213	2726		4079	13046	116366	79793
北塔区	1470	535	15		920	1469	20900	16900
武冈市	11451	9340	1130	450	531	7964	59337	31263
邵东县	18912	18812	100			15577	115405	82217
新邵县	3792	2872	880		40	2927	24450	13700
邵阳县	7600	6628	652		320	7231	79430	23420
隆回县	13214	12505	563		146	7706	47713	17885
洞口县	8866	6868	1666	76	256	5552	42263	14951
绥宁县	8068	7979	89			8089	85356	30893
新宁县	4852	4732			120	4989	11216	8486
城步县	7201	6829	300		72	3717	35114	13073
岳阳市	356613	188775	147091	16889	3858	281229	661898	431356
岳阳楼区	304062	152100	134618	14346	2998	239107	279865	182039
云溪区	712	712				310	5480	4280
君山区	1844	1844				1445	19496	15344
汨罗市	6420	4837	1413		170	5036	65517	35728
临湘市	11410	7789	3191		430	10423	64518	48942
岳阳县	9365	5190	4075		100	6805	59837	34482
华容县	12971	8447	2621	1743	160	10650	64468	42443
湘阴县	3591	2791		800		3061	31016	16722
平江县	6238	5065	1173			4392	71701	51376
常德市	322619	226360	73579	9457	13223	308281	1063448	490196
武陵区	127426	60744	48058	7810	10814	101297	369377	198466
鼎城区	22667	16100	5253	500	814	15043	106535	48234
津市市	6524	5080	1214		230	5351	44167	35037
安乡县	12439	10866	1313		260	10899	89145	10298
汉寿县	6975	5572	973		430	5762	62798	25905
澧　县	12920	12920				11654	153971	68412

18—20 续表 2 (1997 年)

名称	固定资产投资（万元）	基本建设	更新改造	其他投资	房地产开发	新增固定资产（万元）	房屋建筑竣工面积（平方米）	住宅（平方米）
临澧县	9242	5070	4032		140	10575	38010	8376
桃源县	106767	102237	4155	270	105	31575	101179	45182
石门县	17659	7771	8581	877	430	116125	98266	50286
张家界市	79157	71179	7317	393	268	35309	153408	61162
永定区	19960	16453	3507			11034	72783	16092
武陵源区	1780	590	1190			1972	8100	5100
慈利县	41049	40577	204		268	2876	46409	24010
桑植县	16368	13559	2416	393		19427	26116	15960
益阳市	133836	78528	27060	21398	6850	85347	458213	263415
资阳区	8808	4036	303		4469	5932	50382	42417
赫山区	59507	40473	16110	1358	1566	39274	210875	122466
沅江市	9220	5147	2988	910	175	13303	58448	29869
南　县	6297	2475	3124	698		3131	47250	16128
桃江县	14904	12623	1641		640	5433	41232	24479
安化县	35100	13774	2894	18432		18274	50026	28056
郴州市	154923	102746	41626	4031	6520	166026	1089475	611718
北湖区	49621	27304	17733	3305	1279	48969	223825	132933
苏仙区	22899	17542	3219		2138	14993	192842	142854
资兴市	22752	9899	11914	102	837	36785	131648	91320
桂阳县	15883	12643	2360		880	15499	151456	57770
宜章县	8060	6228	1322	120	390	10108	108306	56286
永兴县	5057	3357	1545		155	4086	30440	20831
嘉禾县	7408	6687	521		200	6433	66530	51592
临武县	5806	3745	916	504	641	6223	50260	18080
汝城县	9767	9067	700			11588	49599	22197
桂东县	2655	2200	455			2540	42591	9961
安仁县	5015	4074	941			8802	41978	7894
永州市	133765	88676	28442	8259	8388	113037	1040854	523997
芝山区	16051	10129	4937	143	842	9334	106966	43100
冷水滩区	48746	23808	20008	440	4490	39958	299231	146391
祁阳县	21155	16700	1403	2361	691	16471	115832	43628
东安县	14823	14033			790	18557	120770	63650
双牌县	3880	2439	214	1227		2628	23095	18095
道　县	8012	4390		2647	975	7332	44571	28763

18—20 续表 3 (1997 年)

名 称	固定资产投资（万元）	基本建设	更新改造	其他投资	房地产开发	新增固定资产（万元）	房屋建筑竣工面积（平方米）	住宅（平方米）
江永县	7073	5302	100	1221	450	7705	121125	76787
宁远县	2832	2682			150	2961	63840	30700
蓝山县	3592	3281	311			3331	63705	34675
新田县	4305	3781	304	220		3141	61435	35248
江华县	3296	2131	1165			1619	20284	2960
娄底地区	118301	54307	56275	1655	6064	118321	424427	209091
娄底市	54314	24347	26871	130	2966	55496	184615	103502
冷水江市	29640	10647	18933	60		32953	57807	23623
涟源市	10564	4979	4870	430	285	8801	76111	28972
双峰县	8048	6105	217	893	833	5787	28178	9128
新化县	15735	8229	5384	142	1980	15284	77716	43866
怀化地区	134369	100066	27034		7269	107527	535845	269037
怀化市	24946	16901	5260		2785	11537	104504	53947
洪江市	1835	1276	174		385	3897	36143	23636
黔阳县	2918	1798	1120			1868	18997	8148
沅陵县	52179	49589	2372		218	40698	66273	39865
辰溪县	11976	7220	2265		2491	5502	45970	34122
溆浦县	14653	4674	9979			20964	38486	6910
麻阳县	2513	1640	873			2669	25358	10668
新晃县	3132	2353	535		244	2565	44562	18159
芷江县	4167	3734	396		37	2876	37539	10185
会同县	6655	3430	2312		913	6150	39838	28094
靖州县	6239	5023	1020		196	4289	46536	20116
通道县	3156	2428	728			4512	31639	15187
湘西自治州	67880	38298	26071	454	3057	61255	450049	149941
吉首市	30776	14532	13699		2545	28536	239277	77544
泸溪县	7671	6492	1129		50	8188	56579	28060
凤凰县	2159	1701		104	354	1991	19247	9171
花垣县	7151	2473	4678			7026	15318	3874
保靖县	2641	1396	1245			1818	10875	7801
古丈县	2202	1230	972			1483	16935	7101
永顺县	6380	5103	1169		108	4370	42535	4160
龙山县	8900	5371	3179	350		7843	49283	12230
不分地区	666126	525241	125485	15400		280922	431282	328550

18—21 各地、市、县社会消费品零售总额(1997年)

Total Value of Retail Sales of Consumer Goods by Prefecture, City and County

单位:万元

名称	社会消费品零售总额	国有	集体	私营个体	农对非
长沙市	2050280	496713	395560	790277	258760
长沙市区	1564902	430129	297943	559471	179640
浏阳市	151639	21342	30936	82970	16390
长沙县	111763	14039	21023	47395	18579
望城县	104380	11640	27386	34649	30180
宁乡县	117595	19561	18270	65792	13970
株洲市	876029	107706	87029	452331	184582
株洲市区	473431	65377	24809	231129	109431
醴陵市	169248	13276	19592	104539	30145
株洲县	66997	6013	13341	34326	13316
攸县	95769	11786	17590	50091	16302
茶陵县	51335	6400	7825	27122	9988
炎陵县	19247	4852	3870	5124	5400
湘潭市	548066	79531	101555	294237	63193
湘潭市区	311224	39245	39006	176244	47509
湘乡市	110764	14866	24323	64468	7107
韶山市	20688	2979	1873	13487	2349
湘潭县	105389	22440	36352	40038	6228
衡阳市	948150	162526	103532	374774	279462
衡阳市区	466276	62222	25318	169315	183441
#南岳区	20465	1348	1461	12421	5234
耒阳市	86362	22523	16060	23305	23308
常宁市	74323	19659	16756	28443	9464
衡阳县	74555	15676	8932	26148	23798
衡南县	61651	10866	5956	29227	15602
衡山县	43651	7831	9048	20232	6344
衡东县	71956	10504	7792	45100	8560
祁东县	69376	13245	13670	33004	8945

18—21 续表 1 (1997 年) 单位:万元

名 称	社会消费品零售总额	国 有	集 体	私营个体	农 对 非
邵阳市	697499	126536	83761	366052	103543
邵阳市区	145536	24495	6847	56800	57002
武冈市	53793	6863	6432	33016	7263
邵东县	167999	16390	11210	119362	6111
新邵县	63035	12856	11623	32196	6330
邵阳县	73827	14966	14097	37747	4923
隆回县	61445	12627	8226	34632	5959
洞口县	57909	14373	10981	27600	4954
绥宁县	30444	7435	8075	10857	4305
新宁县	24144	7331	3173	9753	3756
城步县	19365	9198	3093	4088	2940
岳阳市	995402	132127	59662	458303	332641
岳阳市区	510929	43736	24505	220049	216628
汨罗市	78344	23539	10551	33115	10790
临湘市	66018	15197	3082	28215	19524
岳阳县	103357	11151	3116	47418	40593
华容县	91917	17408	8219	55090	10000
湘阴县	72483	10298	5077	27299	26521
平江县	72354	10798	5112	47117	8585
常德市	905297	151571	113352	481089	141785
常德市直	136770	38975	333	57261	37120
武陵区	6342	2347	3797		
鼎城区	141844	13499	8940	113117	6100
津市市	61068	6690	5380	20708	21657
安乡县	63208	12919	20399	21269	9028
汉寿县	80545	9769	15865	48100	6810
澧 县	102019	10901	12552	60014	18552
临澧县	68774	18737	12174	27005	8917
桃源县	149713	19426	19427	90363	18471
石门县	95010	18303	14481	43252	15130

18—21 续表 2 (1997 年) 单位:万元

名称	社会消费品零售总额	国有	集体	私营个体	农对非
张家界市	147379	42786	13987	66605	23808
张家界市直	9027	9027			
永定区	56010	9799	6114	29445	10467
武陵源区	334	148	7	171	
慈利县	54800	16510	3937	29731	4621
桑植县	27206	7300	3928	7257	8719
益阳市	574342	128593	89909	209655	137287
资阳区	102292	18270	957	30845	47879
赫山区	127959	28086	19763	55984	24126
沅江市	72496	15179	2532	28870	25914
南县	104764	20311	19140	37859	27340
桃江县	78064	23402	18207	24589	7506
安化县	88764	23343	29308	31508	4522
郴州市	787754	195213	112319	339233	131438
市直	230937	96176	8270	55380	69669
北湖区	75323	9896	51074	11924	2323
苏仙区	40462	4288	4037	25387	5841
资兴市	76887	13350	3234	44210	16093
桂阳县	71622	8340	5655	51081	6340
永兴县	74180	16331	8289	43556	3843
宜章县	98425	19704	21275	45807	11180
嘉禾县	36818	3430	1602	25439	2095
临武县	20351	7853	1638	6609	4250
汝城县	25346	7463	803	14385	2695
桂东县	9714	2201	2061	3078	2373
安仁县	27685	6177	4378	12376	4734
永州市	537504	118591	48222	257855	102184
永州市直	36855	12964	70	21000	
芝山区	81046	10371	10038	36966	21384
冷水滩区	79545	7309	3924	43702	21228
东安县	49608	8248	3892	30238	7230
道县	44161	15526	4468	18377	5790
宁远县	61376	11900	5395	31263	12817

名　称	社会消费品零售总额	国　有	集　体	私营个体	农对非
江永县	23501	3655	957	10064	8825
江华县	29916	7264	2625	15484	4501
蓝山县	20901	9754	2234	4233	3033
新田县	17351	9334	1732	4391	1894
双牌县	13785	5381	2303	4139	1485
祁阳县	79455	16880	10581	37997	13997
娄底地区	519779	104181	62158	302239	38946
娄底市	108789	35331	15619	48577	8620
冷水江市	104407	17245	8275	66188	4822
涟源市	122533	20653	17887	68447	11808
双峰县	88040	15524	10545	49475	12496
新化县	96008	15426	9831	69550	1200
怀化地区	536278	93974	40038	317956	75730
怀化市	121824	24996	6141	61173	30764
洪江市	29953	4089	1003	19773	4572
黔阳县	45913	5089	2149	30048	6673
沅陵县	65505	13749	5287	40704	5535
辰溪县	46446	5453	1725	37120	2100
溆浦县	75019	11998	10196	44682	8000
麻阳县	25500	5269	2769	15644	1776
新晃县	18098	3641	1974	8608	3875
芷江县	29788	6467	3148	13162	7010
会同县	27992	6755	2629	9858	2067
靖州县	29399	4470	1454	19998	3258
通道县	20837	1992	1559	17186	100
湘西自治州	287492	41434	13506	183045	49084
吉首市	98075	19113	2179	61837	14944
泸溪县	21143	2083	1172	15335	2142
凤凰县	34767	2130	1756	25991	4890
花垣县	18773	3539	1323	9922	3989
保靖县	16648	2448	2000	7628	4572
古丈县	10739	859	697	7355	1815
永顺县	45507	6252	2234	25974	11046
龙山县	41837	5006	2141	29003	5686

18—22 各地、市、县财政收入与支出(1997年)

Goverment Revenue and Expenditures by Prefecture, City and County

单位:万元

名 称	财政收入	财政支出	名 称	财政收入	财政支出
长沙市	256384	280728	邵阳市	85154	129437
本 级	140486	130987	本 级	9097	23140
芙蓉区	9992	9368	邵阳市区	5180	6494
天心区	6551	7809	东 区	1818	1515
岳麓区	7021	9324	西 区	1585	1599
开福区	11469	11068	郊 区	1777	3380
雨花区	6146	10963	武冈市	7972	9775
浏阳市	21465	31842	邵东县	15320	18868
长沙县	22765	29929	新邵县	6575	9320
望城县	13967	17533	邵阳县	6977	9907
宁乡县	16522	21905	隆回县	9654	15864
株洲市	105634	131002	洞口县	8299	11976
本 级	37255	56451	绥宁县	7728	9664
天元区	8298	10752	新宁县	5156	7360
芦淞区	7037	3810	城步县	3196	7069
荷塘区	4995	3344	岳阳市	93422	136619
石峰区	5897	3185	本 级	31412	51844
醴陵市	13975	16074	岳阳市区	15490	13909
株洲县	5979	8377	岳阳楼区	9111	7266
攸 县	10778	13058	君山区	1787	2614
茶陵县	7438	10000	云溪区	4592	4029
炎陵县	3982	5951	汨罗市	9338	13206
湘潭市	51806	66982	临湘县	7777	9929
本 级	19180	26962	岳阳县	5565	10662
雨湖区	4234	4961	华容县	7725	11514
岳塘区	3901	4010	湘阴县	8026	11073
湘乡市	11005	14639	平江县	8089	14482
韶山市	2193	3506	常德市	99988	142806
湘潭县	11293	12904	本 级	25593	45047
衡阳市	102171	139829	常德市区	15422	21335
本 级	22302	39216	武陵区	4525	5711
南岳区	1648	2337	鼎城区	10897	15624
江东区	2114	1929	津市市	5744	6743
城南区	2457	2451	安乡县	6887	9370
城北区	2851	2807	汉寿县	9144	11618
郊 区	3322	3756	澧 县	10442	13546
耒阳市	12918	16179	临澧县	6535	8700
常宁市	10197	11684	桃源县	11953	14334
衡阳县	11422	13602	石门县	8268	12113
衡南县	10675	14037			
衡山县	5089	6251			
衡东县	7856	9029			
祁东县	9320	16551			

18—22 续表 (1997年) 单位:万元

名　称	财政收入	财政支出	名　称	财政收入	财政支出
张家界市	24807	46813	永州市	72114	111591
本　级	3759	10059	本　级	14439	24946
张家界市区	8918	12373	芝山区	4284	8055
永定区	5126	7931	冷水滩区	3985	7967
武陵源区	3792	4442	东安县	5778	7327
慈利县	7763	10676	道　县	7006	8646
桑植县	4367	13705	宁远县	6650	8876
益阳市	49764	86134	江永县	3967	5182
本　级	3737	19302	江华县	4201	8734
益阳市区	14953	17567	蓝山县	5035	6110
资阳区	4146	7423	新田县	3145	7621
赫山区	10807	10144	双牌县	2835	4313
沅江市	8391	12943	祁阳县	10789	13814
南　县	7306	10724	怀化地区	76098	115791
桃江县	7431	11119	本　级	4333	15411
安化县	7946	14479	怀化市	14358	15806
郴州市	98348	128866	洪江市	2450	3433
本　级	19047	28085	黔阳县	5978	7445
郴州市区	12612	17728	沅陵县	8712	14208
北湖区	6476	9901	辰溪县	5694	7934
苏仙区	6136	7827	溆浦县	7973	10371
资兴市	8935	11280	麻阳县	4364	8082
桂阳县	12410	13165	新晃县	3280	7495
永兴县	8314	9850	芷江县	4895	6922
宜章县	8740	10589	会同县	4957	6093
嘉禾县	7581	8657	靖州县	5678	7016
临武县	6891	7995	通道县	3426	5575
汝城县	5668	8858	湘西自治州	32077	101968
桂东县	1609	5139	本　级	6416	22189
安仁县	6541	7520	吉首市	5500	11839
娄底地区	57630	85771	泸溪县	2101	6788
本　级	1804	12860	凤凰县	3452	14326
娄底市	15817	16949	花垣县	2841	8625
冷水江市	11079	12551	保靖县	1687	7805
涟源市	10455	12899	古丈县	995	4635
双峰县	9114	13145	永顺县	3564	11620
新化县	9361	17367	龙山县	5521	14141

18—23 各地、市、县各级学校(1997年)

Schools by Level and by Prefecture, City and County

单位:所

名称	普通高等学校	中等学校	普通中等专业学校	职业中学	普通中学	普通小学
长沙市	20	519	47	93	379	2779
长沙市区	20	188	44	53	91	317
浏阳市		118	1	26	91	884
长沙县		60		7	53	434
望城县		55	1	5	49	416
宁乡县		98	1	2	95	728
株洲市	2	276	12	25	239	2145
株洲市区	2	68	10	9	49	172
醴陵市		63		3	60	528
株洲县		36		3	33	322
攸县		55	2	6	47	537
茶陵县		36		3	33	377
炎陵县		18		1	17	209
湘潭市	5	256	14	27	215	1359
湘潭市区	5	60	12	11	37	133
湘乡市		96	1	5	90	485
韶山市		13		2	11	56
湘潭县		87	1	9	77	685
衡阳市	6	549	13	42	494	3724
衡阳市区	6	89	10	25	54	203
耒阳市		78	1	2	75	632
常宁市		71		2	69	440
衡阳县		97		3	94	592
衡南县		69	2	4	63	538
衡山县		30		1	29	276
衡东县		45		3	42	514
祁东县		70		2	68	529

18—23 续表 1 (1997 年) 单位:所

名称	普通高等学校	中等学校	普通中等专业学校	职业中学	普通中学	普通小学
邵阳市	2	627	11	72	544	3753
邵阳市区	2	75	9	21	45	127
武冈市		61	1	3	57	362
邵东县		124	1	30	93	427
新邵县		46		1	45	330
邵阳县		72		2	70	505
隆回县		85		2	83	477
洞口县		69		6	63	477
绥宁县		36		3	33	369
新宁县		42		2	40	426
城步县		17		2	15	253
岳阳市	2	491	11	80	400	3082
岳阳市区		101	10	25	66	230
汨罗市		87	1	29	57	403
临湘市		40		6	34	302
岳阳县		63		5	58	648
华容县		62		4	58	365
湘阴县		59		3	56	406
平江县		79		8	71	728
常德市	2	386	11	53	322	2789
常德市区	2	107	8	21	78	669
武陵区				11	25	111
鼎城区				10	53	558
津市市		19	2	2	15	113
安乡县		28		2	26	226
汉寿县		44		4	40	532
澧县		53		9	44	310
临澧县		26		3	23	267
桃源县		65	1	7	57	381
石门县		44		5	39	291

18—23　续表 2　　　　(1997 年)　　　　单位:所

名　称	普　通 高等学校	中等学校	普通中等 专业学校	职业中学	普通中学	普通小学
张家界市	1	117	1	11	105	1462
张家界市区	1	42	1	5	36	350
永定区				5	34	314
武陵源区					2	36
慈利县		45		4	41	588
桑植县		30		2	28	524
益阳市	2	352	6	33	313	3215
益阳市区	2	94	5	15	74	655
沅江市		68	1	5	62	413
南　县		58		5	53	388
桃江县		61		4	57	658
安化县		71		4	67	1101
郴州市	2	377	7	28	342	3005
郴州市区	2	71	5	13	53	339
北湖区				12	24	146
苏仙区				1	29	193
资兴市		44	1	2	41	305
桂阳县		53		2	51	551
永兴县		43	1	1	41	358
宜章县		44		2	42	335
嘉禾县		24		2	22	233
临武县		25		1	24	176
汝城县		29		2	27	331
桂东县		15		1	14	139
安仁县		29		2	27	238
娄底地区	1	369	8	50	311	2018
娄底市	1	46	5	19	22	108
冷水江市		44	3	6	35	131
涟源市		77		8	69	556
双峰县		87		11	76	471
新化县		115		6	109	752

18—23　续表 3　　(1997 年)　　单位:所

名　　称	普　通 高等学校	中等学校	普通中等 专业学校	职业中学	普通中学	普通小学
永州市	1	427	8	44	375	4642
市　区	1	112	5	24	83	852
芝山区	1	73	3	22	48	540
冷水滩区		39	2	2	35	312
东安县		46		3	43	493
道　县		44	2	2	40	537
宁远县		50		4	46	676
江永县		17		2	15	147
江华县		24		1	23	451
蓝山县		25		2	23	414
新田县		23		1	22	363
双牌县		13		1	12	228
祁阳县		73	1	4	68	481
怀化地区	1	412	7	25	380	3995
怀化市	1	58	4	8	46	321
洪江市		6		1	5	36
黔阳县		32	2	2	28	287
沅陵县		65		4	61	660
辰溪县		41		3	38	379
溆浦县		64		1	63	672
麻阳县		27		1	26	293
新晃县		26		1	25	3011
芷江县		33	1	1	31	308
会同县		28		1	27	344
靖州县		21		1	20	184
通道县		11		1	10	210
湘西自治州	1	178	8	30	140	2435
吉首市	1	30	7	5	18	201
泸溪县		11		1	10	221
凤凰县		30		5	25	397
花垣县		12		3	9	229
保靖县		20		3	17	288
古丈县		10		2	8	180
永顺县		35	1	7	27	516
龙山县		30		4	26	403

18—24 各地、市、县各级学校教职工(1997年)

School Staff and Workers by Level and by Prefecture, City and County

单位:人

名　称	普　通 高等学校	中等学校	普通中等 专业学校	职业中学	普通中学	普通小学
长沙市	22624	34090	7732	2621	23737	28373
长沙市区	22624	16534	7319	1731	7484	7778
浏阳市		6502	85	336	6081	7533
长沙县		3282		179	3103	3561
望城县		3184	205	239	2740	3319
宁乡县		4588	123	136	4329	6182
株洲市	1876	17446	2464	1140	13842	16509
株洲市区	1876	6300	2191	448	3661	3340
醴陵市		3142		230	2912	3839
株洲县		1706		77	1629	1982
攸　县		3149	273	204	2672	3553
茶陵县		2240		121	2119	2682
炎陵县		909		60	849	1113
湘潭市	5094	13792	1763	1088	10941	12559
湘潭市区	5094	5558	1619	673	3266	3262
湘乡市		3688	85	162	3441	4236
韶山市		489		59	430	518
湘潭县		4057	59	194	3804	4543
衡阳市	2859	28021	1907	2066	24048	33713
衡阳市区	2633	5994	1466	830	3698	3757
耒阳市		4300	150	84	4066	6180
常宁市		2909		158	2751	4353
衡阳县	226	3617		199	3418	5027
衡南县		3784	291	299	3194	5237
衡山县		1605		127	1478	1871
衡东县		2008		195	1813	2970
祁东县		3804		174	3630	4318

18—24 续表1 (1997年) 单位:人

名　　称	普　通 高等学校	中等学校	普通中等 专业学校	职业中学	普通中学	普通小学
邵阳市	849	27887	1490	2282	24115	30700
邵阳市区	849	4680	1188	725	2767	2801
武冈市		2443	154	214	2075	2926
邵东县		4949	148	478	4323	4401
新邵县		2650		112	2538	3161
邵阳县		2712		85	2627	3810
隆回县		3458		197	3261	4400
洞口县		2642		176	2466	3081
绥宁县		1515		162	1353	2019
新宁县		1731		76	1655	2425
城步县		1107		57	1050	1676
岳阳市	765	23042	1572	2026	19444	23861
岳阳市区	765	6283	1460	667	4156	4496
汨罗市		3523	112	449	2962	3309
临湘市		2086		187	1899	2473
岳阳县		2838		178	2660	3233
华容县		2887		217	2610	3065
湘阴县		2479		98	2381	3413
平江县		2946		230	2716	3872
常德市	807	23695	1544	2414	19737	27990
常德市区	807	6604	1076	854	4674	6127
武陵区				474	1699	2047
鼎城区				380	2975	4080
津市市		1471	323	147	1001	1223
安乡县		2133		143	1990	2547
汉寿县		2686		185	2501	4103
澧　县		3115		269	2846	3781
临澧县		1933		208	1725	2333
桃源县		3464	145	338	2981	4651
石门县		2289		270	2019	3225

18—24 续表 2 (1997 年) 单位:人

名 称	普通高等学校	中等学校	普通中等专业学校	职业中学	普通中学	普通小学
张家界市	297	6017	496	508	5013	8114
张家界市区	297	2385	496	205	1684	2651
永定区	297	2249	496	205	1548	2374
武陵源区		136			136	277
慈利县		2236		216	2020	3139
桑植县		1396		87	1309	2324
益阳市	828	18430	853	1480	16097	23574
益阳市区	828	6537	753	660	5124	6775
沅江市		3009	100	207	2702	3857
南 县		3283		170	3113	4303
桃江县		2924		204	2720	4184
安化县		2677		239	2438	4454
郴州市	683	19686	1056	1617	17013	25379
郴州市区	683	4615	781	705	3129	3828
北湖区				598	1494	1913
苏仙区				107	1635	1915
资兴市		2219	151	189	1879	2325
桂阳县		2833		163	2670	4548
永兴县		2728	124	124	2480	2820
宜章县		1724		87	1637	3109
嘉禾县		1128		98	1030	1638
临武县		964		50	914	1775
汝城县		1262		78	1184	1849
桂东县		603		41	562	943
安仁县		1610		82	1528	2544
娄底地区	424	18945	1437	1975	15533	18940
娄底市	424	3562	886	646	2030	2126
冷水江市		2862	551	301	2010	2690
涟源市		4435		344	4091	4353
双峰县		4058		452	3606	4295
新化县		4028		232	3796	5476

18—24 续表 3 (1997 年) 单位:人

名称	普通高等学校	中等学校	普通中等专业学校	职业中学	普通中学	普通小学
永州市	410	22679	1171	1291	20217	27414
永州市区	410	5950	816	423	4711	5215
芝山区	410	3271	506	304	2461	2713
冷水滩区		2679	310	119	2250	2502
东安县		2201		134	2067	2845
道　县		2452	261	139	2052	3472
宁远县		2374		115	2259	3646
江永县		1169		111	1058	1205
江华县		1573		90	1483	2435
蓝山县		1103		65	1038	1744
新田县		1137		77	1060	1676
双牌县		671		36	635	1048
祁阳县		4049	94	101	3854	4128
怀化地区	489	18598	1039	1513	16046	27937
怀化市	489	3495	568	536	2391	3286
洪江市		433		50	383	550
黔阳县		1886	348	151	1387	2185
沅陵县		2214		95	2119	3871
辰溪县		1808		111	1697	3899
溆浦县		2736		115	2621	4386
麻阳县		1148		51	1097	2047
新晃县		743		57	686	1294
芷江县		1342	123	180	1039	1887
会同县		1281		55	1226	1846
靖州县		916		60	856	1535
通道县		596		52	544	1151
湘西自治州	778	9247	939	1322	6986	13874
吉首市	778	2051	815	193	1043	1607
泸溪县		859		47	812	1473
凤凰县		1049		257	792	1735
花垣县		788		91	697	1553
保靖县		863		147	716	1563
古丈县		410		69	341	775
永顺县		1782	124	296	1362	2545
龙山县		1445		222	1223	2623

18—25 各地、市、县各级学校在校学生(1997年)

Student Enrollment by Level and by Prefecture, City and County

单位:人

名称	普通高等学校	中等学校	普通中等专业学校	职业学校	普通中学	高中	初中	普通小学
长沙市	72020	409909	76808	23686	309415	52263	257152	642950
长沙市区	72020	162113	70624	15010	76479	20043	56436	133022
浏阳市		88768	1407	4294	83067	9972	73095	169285
长沙县		45712	1040	1692	42980	5897	37083	87546
望城县		46365	2373	1479	42513	5031	37482	95224
宁乡县		66951	1364	1211	64376	11320	53056	157873
株洲市	6807	227772	18963	12846	195963	26100	169863	467938
株洲市区	6807	58671	16984	6343	35344	7810	27534	68540
醴陵市		52339		1887	50452	5953	44499	137586
株洲县		26889		535	26354	2693	23661	62180
攸县		41070	1979	2428	36663	5103	31560	90917
茶陵县		36849		1203	35646	3387	32259	84952
炎陵县		11954		450	11504	1154	10350	23763
湘潭市	19655	187636	19837	10310	157489	22103	135386	338061
湘潭市区	19655	54683	18210	5179	31294	7627	23667	56983
湘乡市		53453	936	1431	51086	7220	43866	118823
韶山市		6000		661	5339	711	4628	10466
湘潭县		73500	691	3039	69770	6545	63225	151789
衡阳市	12736	402587	15681	28227	358679	41928	316751	831630
衡阳市区	11362	63739	11684	11690	40365	9139	31226	83119
耒阳市		60140	1258	1770	57112	4829	52283	156455
常宁市		50946		1867	49079	4736	44343	102591
衡阳县	1374	57585		3367	54218	5573	48645	120995
衡南县		61353	2739	3317	55297	5542	49755	114817
衡山县		23440		1230	22210	2437	19773	48129
衡东县		34322		2504	31818	2883	28935	86646
祁东县		51062		2482	48580	6789	41791	118878

18－25　续表 1　(1997 年)　单位:人

名　　称	普　　通 高等学校	中等学校	普通中等 专业学校	职业学校	普通中学	高　中	初　中	普通小学
邵阳市	4841	410068	12547	20117	377404	54081	323323	936976
邵阳市区	4841	46098	9760	5524	30814	6712	24102	67577
武冈市		37364	1369	2170	33825	4370	29455	82378
邵东县		74379	1418	4548	68413	10153	58260	151420
新邵县		38043		1004	37039	5805	31234	92373
邵阳县		43168		407	42761	5679	37082	122513
隆回县		57422		1778	55644	6950	48694	151636
洞口县		46532		2206	44326	6918	37408	92888
绥宁县		22790		1377	21413	2881	18532	51334
新宁县		30222		736	29486	2973	26513	88911
城步县		14050		367	13683	1640	12043	35946
岳阳市	3748	282842	11574	17585	253683	34610	219073	622448
岳阳市区	3748	57808	11391	4930	41487	8521	32966	90620
汨罗市		44263	183	3604	40476	4551	35925	84009
临湘市		25324		1711	23613	3553	20060	58761
岳阳县		42021		1774	40247	4795	35452	95698
华容县		35248		2017	33231	4668	28563	86557
湘阴县		35762		1102	34660	3957	30703	89881
平江县		42416		2447	39969	4565	35404	116922
常德市	4690	263869	15206	20725	227938	41491	186447	580490
常德市区	4690	70652	10249	6633	53770	11019	42751	141421
武陵区				4155	19004	4414	14590	42543
鼎城区				2478	34766	6605	28161	98878
津市市		13927	3476	833	9618	2428	7190	22500
安乡县		25709		1301	24408	4166	20242	63328
汉寿县		34719		1728	32991	5125	27866	86951
澧　县		35304		3876	31428	5207	26221	80590
临澧县		20233		1915	18318	3516	14802	37808
桃源县		40274	1481	2456	36337	6326	30011	90417
石门县		23051		1983	21068	3704	17364	57475

18—25 续表 2 (1997 年) 单位:人

名称	普通高等学校	中等学校	普通中等专业学校	职业学校	普通中学	高中	初中	普通小学
张家界市	1073	63947	3090	3589	57268	8436	48832	164064
张家界市区	1073	21556	3090	1047	17419	2280	15139	50340
永定区	1073			1047	15926	2051	13875	45820
武陵源区					1493	229	1264	4520
慈利县		26422		2062	24360	4047	20313	61688
桑植县		15969		480	15489	2109	13380	52036
益阳市	4537	232759	9306	17009	206444	32363	174081	547459
益阳市区	4537	79376	8147	7959	63270	11364	51906	148344
沅江市		37711	1159	1981	34571	5255	29316	92244
南　县		37865		2018	35847	5404	30443	93240
桃江县		40521		2113	38408	5730	32678	98990
安化县		37286		2938	34348	4610	29738	114641
郴州市	3035	279345	12690	16660	249995	24257	225738	611989
郴州市区	3035	56429	11109	9717	35603	6308	29295	71127
北湖区				8671	17077	3136	13941	34152
苏仙区				1046	18526	3172	15354	36975
资兴市		24050	1450	1114	21486	2574	18912	39332
桂阳县		43304		1735	41569	3090	38479	103982
永兴县		39790	131	946	38713	2869	35844	90551
宜章县		27802		744	27058	2173	24885	82381
嘉禾县		17225		826	16399	1121	15278	46134
临武县		18567		310	18257	1108	17149	45890
汝城县		16938		357	16581	1758	14823	49828
桂东县		7944		231	7713	745	6968	23867
安仁县		27296		680	26616	2511	24105	58897
娄底地区	2289	237529	11735	20032	205762	31728	174034	528094
娄底市	2289	34421	7881	6791	19749	4135	15614	42039
冷水江市		27671	3854	2609	21208	4152	17056	48337
涟源市		63747		3935	59812	7875	51937	146293
双峰县		56713		4790	51923	7997	43926	120793
新化县		54977		1907	53070	7569	45501	170632

名称	普通高等学校	中等学校	普通中等专业学校	职业学校	普通中学	高中	初中	普通小学
永州市	2399	359308	10496	15187	333625	36826	296799	705551
永州市区	2399	87403	8034	6774	72595	10236	62359	117816
芝山区	2399	51197	4954	6088	40155	5009	35146	66946
冷水滩区		36206	3080	686	32440	5227	27213	50870
东安县		41857		1216	40641	4258	36383	78238
道县		34262	1344	1638	31280	2441	28839	90943
宁远县		41219		1378	39841	3508	36333	99824
江永县		17386		429	16957	1608	15349	30906
江华县		26321		439	25882	1469	24413	58486
蓝山县		20261		876	19385	1905	17480	49946
新田县		20804		357	20447	1975	18472	59868
双牌县		10861		281	10580	1368	9212	23226
祁阳县		58934	1118	1799	56017	8058	47959	96298
怀化地区	2690	234427	11065	13194	210168	23398	186770	569678
怀化市	2690	39984	6058	4996	28930	3524	25406	75815
洪江市		4330		437	3893	585	3308	7952
黔阳县		24646	3708	834	20104	2300	17804	45389
沅陵县		28766		652	28114	3020	25094	70043
辰溪县		20684		1109	19575	2755	16820	59582
溆浦县		35539		2434	33105	3993	29112	89155
麻阳县		13669		166	13503	1545	11958	41539
新晃县		9661		257	9404	742	8662	30363
芷江县		14919	1299	1526	12094	1631	10463	37039
会同县		17069		293	16776	1574	15202	42029
靖州县		17359		214	17145	1188	15957	38754
通道县		7801		276	7525	541	6984	32018
湘西自治州	3054	107171	8272	12553	86346	9665	76681	322082
吉首市	3054	18952	7288	1464	10200	1915	8285	31847
泸溪县		10480		286	10194	915	9279	35482
凤凰县		13627		2614	11013	896	10117	47297
花垣县		10243		902	9341	745	8596	29604
保靖县		9622		1233	8389	905	7484	33283
古丈县		5051		540	4511	504	4007	16556
永顺县		19953	984	3038	15931	2160	13771	56269
龙山县		19243		2476	16767	1625	15142	71744

18—26 各地、市、县卫生机构、人员与床位(1997年)

Health Care Institutions, Personnel and Beds by Prefecture, City and County

名　　称	机　　构(个)	#医　院	卫生工作人　员(人)	#卫生技术人　员	#医　生	床　　位(张)	#医　院床　位
长沙市	368	246	35167	25026	10180	20751	18240
长沙市区	186	94	24954	16545	6541	13434	11906
浏阳市	58	51	2989	2550	1084	1971	1935
长沙县	31	27	1641	1402	628	1361	1361
望城县	38	28	2110	1719	767	1476	1216
宁乡县	55	46	3473	2810	1160	2509	1822
株洲市	226	193	14097	11569	4743	9544	9455
株洲市区	49	36	7023	5583	2200	4774	4724
醴陵市	51	48	2500	2076	946	1590	1590
株洲县	29	25	788	670	315	506	493
攸　县	41	37	1830	1569	630	1255	1249
茶陵县	34	30	1326	1116	403	988	968
炎陵县	22	17	630	555	249	431	431
湘潭市	161	116	12072	9727	3832	7745	7558
湘潭市区	53	43	6801	5139	1942	4636	4554
湘乡市	38	33	2373	2084	890	1464	1434
韶山市	11	8	506	393	147	340	325
湘潭县	59	32	2392	2111	853	1305	1245
衡阳市	406	354	26943	20972	8892	14842	
衡阳市区	89	67	10834	7545	3069	6768	
#郊区	11	9	545	477	219	515	
南岳区	10	7	521	339	110	620	
耒阳市	56	49	3059	2479	974	1644	
常宁市	72	69	2649	2131	942	1343	
衡阳县	34	30	3014	2561	1049	1007	
衡南县	42	36	2601	2194	1103	1314	
衡山县	33	31	979	853	340	634	
衡东县	37	32	1704	1408	577	791	
祁东县	43	40	2103	1801	838	1341	

注:本表资料未含医务室、卫生室、诊所。

18—26　续表 1　　(1997 年)

名　称	机　构(个)	#医　院	卫生工作人　员(人)	#卫生技术人　员	#医　生	床　位(张)	#医　院床　位
邵阳市	341	284	17673	14427	5933	12092	11350
邵阳市区	49	38	4187	3191	1277	2877	2749
武冈市	28	23	1390	1172	414	902	902
邵东县	45	41	2336	1992	902	1610	1610
新邵县	29	24	1565	1188	526	1584	1178
邵阳县	34	27	1538	1287	548	1005	888
隆回县	42	37	1919	1647	687	1231	1201
洞口县	37	32	1671	1395	592	968	959
绥宁县	33	28	827	713	336	552	512
新宁县	27	22	1504	1226	356	848	836
城步县	17	12	736	616	295	515	515
岳阳市	328	216	16460	13812	5650	10409	8535
岳阳市区	71	34	5820	4623	2019	3707	3058
汨罗市	51	33	1737	1529	649	1189	963
临湘市	34	27	1344	1143	441	1011	903
岳阳县	34	25	1454	1308	558	982	732
华容县	48	26	2089	1801	645	1376	1036
湘阴县	55	42	1719	1431	575	1202	947
平江县	35	29	2297	1977	763	942	896
常德市	381	279	19575	16277	6900	12552	11308
常德市区	98	64	6596	5262	2136	4078	3727
武陵区	41	23	3632	2685	1095	2321	2271
鼎城区	57	41	2964	2577	1041	1757	1456
津市市	23	17	1151	901	341	811	721
安乡县	36	26	1691	1452	565	1192	1096
汉寿县	60	37	2233	1890	809	1561	1231
澧　县	50	39	2289	1947	854	1434	1230
临澧县	25	20	1307	1172	456	723	663
桃源县	53	48	2371	1992	937	1494	1458
石门县	36	28	1937	1661	802	1259	1182

18—26 续表 2 (1997 年)

名　称	机　构（个）	#医　院	卫生工作人员（人）	#卫生技术人员	#医　生	床　位（张）	#医院床位
张家界市	87	61	4671	3987	1754	3203	3051
张家界市区	37	24	1841	1522	752	1133	1111
永定区	29	18	1722	1425	704	1090	1068
武陵源区	8	6	119	97	48	43	43
慈利县	25	19	1809	1590	606	1287	1167
桑植县	25	18	1021	875	396	783	773
益阳市	249	192	14972	12588	5526	8582	7498
益阳市区	70	52	4986	3997	1773	2825	2446
沅江市	60	43	3101	2674	1112	1756	1346
南　县	41	30	2240	1854	787	1385	1200
桃江县	39	34	2162	1878	901	1203	1123
安化县	39	33	2483	2185	953	1413	1383
郴州市	359	294	15153	12240	5091	10420	9932
郴州市区	68	45	4857	3693	1541	3219	2963
北湖区	39	21	3110	2343	1017	1717	1511
苏仙区	29	24	1747	1350	524	1502	1452
资兴市	45	40	1652	1342	537	1196	1190
桂阳县	48	44	1699	1413	652	1202	1167
永兴县	33	28	1565	1284	478	941	929
宜章县	34	30	1390	1187	398	1147	1112
嘉禾县	23	19	873	728	299	493	471
临武县	25	20	740	634	263	503	497
汝城县	30	24	889	748	397	747	636
桂东县	24	20	432	364	180	318	313
安仁县	29	24	1056	847	346	654	654
娄底地区	172	144	13421	11303	4841	8157	7958
娄底市	36	27	3317	2491	1044	1985	1965
冷水江市	34	28	2265	1883	694	1596	1536
涟源市	35	31	3031	2605	1133	2100	2016
双峰县	24	20	2077	1863	891	1122	1102
新化县	43	38	2731	2461	1079	1354	1339

18－26　续表 3　　　　　　　　(1997 年)

名　　称	机　　构(个)	#医　院	卫生工作人　员(人)	#卫生技术人　员	#医　生	床　　位(张)	#医　院床　位
永州市	369	313	15462	12917	5999	9182	8884
永州市区	57	43	4751	3767	1736	2596	2489
东安县	42	38	1539	1342	696	657	649
道　县	47	40	1402	1183	469	927	881
宁远县	53	49	1578	1378	587	1293	1257
江永县	19	16	538	462	206	462	432
江华县	34	29	1150	974	406	754	754
蓝山县	32	28	776	662	293	443	443
新田县	27	23	826	729	307	552	538
双牌县	18	14	468	383	192	307	307
祁阳县	40	33	2434	2037	1107	1191	1134
怀化地区	487	414	15899	13164	5517	11309	11110
怀化市	63	51	4084	3115	1298	2269	2217
洪江市	19	15	986	788	259	707	707
黔阳县	36	30	1340	1126	441	1094	1074
沅陵县	76	63	1694	1417	666	1393	1339
辰溪县	43	38	1557	1334	617	1213	1200
溆浦县	68	63	1758	1531	674	1340	1330
麻阳县	34	28	875	770	333	574	574
新晃县	31	26	638	526	192	655	635
芷江县	36	31	1059	911	401	607	607
会同县	33	29	695	618	266	545	535
靖州县	21	17	706	611	207	503	503
通道县	27	23	507	417	163	409	389
湘西自治州	299	243	7999	6568	3116	5762	5668
吉首市	35	20	2144	1641	684	1376	1330
泸溪县	27	22	715	581	271	491	491
凤凰县	40	34	827	683	359	602	584
花垣县	28	22	728	614	316	529	529
保靖县	32	27	730	635	306	531	525
古丈县	22	16	373	318	172	291	276
永顺县	55	49	1213	1003	524	1039	1039
龙山县	60	53	1269	1083	484	903	894

18—27 各地、市、县农民平均每人纯收入(1997年)

Net Income of Peasant Household Per Capita by Prefecture, City and County

名称	调查户数(户)	调查户常住人口(人)	平均每人全年纯收入(元)	劳动者报酬收入	家庭经营收入	转移性收入	财产性收入
长沙市	550	2191	2649.27	717.78	1817.69	79.64	34.16
雨花区	30	123	3327.22	637.35	2571.13	74.88	43.86
芙蓉区	30	113	3348.95	468.74	2804.67	2.37	73.17
天心区	30	112	3270.25	1142.99	1857.37	161.58	108.31
岳麓区	30	114	3028.62	645.84	1953.66	96.32	332.81
开福区	30	128	2891.68	949.16	1857.88	56.95	27.70
浏阳市	100	418	2442.32	933.95	1447.64	45.63	15.09
长沙县	100	390	2991.70	839.02	2053.72	69.25	29.72
望城县	100	385	2720.00	470.14	2146.13	88.20	15.53
宁乡县	100	408	2328.06	532.65	1647.51	120.23	27.67
株洲市	600	2519	2285.08	546.93	1604.52	118.86	14.76
荷塘区	20	86	2761.14	507.08	2052.37	97.41	104.28
石峰区	50	190	2775.52	942.57	1550.67	154.46	127.83
芦淞区	30	116	2651.75	1466.03	1012.42	105.91	67.39
醴陵市	100	442	2528.66	713.70	1724.73	79.12	11.12
株洲县	100	427	2408.93	505.98	1813.72	84.47	4.76
攸　县	100	410	2598.95	843.39	1614.54	128.07	12.94
茶陵县	100	427	1936.35	262.56	1404.86	259.84	9.10
炎陵县	100	421	1745.14	272.68	1405.05	56.68	10.72
湘潭市	330	1308	2531.57	685.76	1763.41	63.14	19.26
雨湖区	30	127	3337.07	745.57	2415.68	152.28	23.54
岳塘区	40	184	3257.41	670.27	2356.89	229.45	0.80
湘乡市	100	376	2383.25	684.60	1636.47	42.89	19.29
韶山市	60	235	2788.45	371.30	2215.69	150.13	51.33
湘潭县	100	386	2524.99	710.78	1742.84	53.42	17.94
衡阳市	790	3223	2285.15	693.90	1520.26	64.51	6.47
衡阳市郊	60	251	2848.98	1280.15	1517.96	40.52	10.36
南岳区	50	198	2612.25	582.18	1749.10	255.72	25.25
耒阳市	100	455	2180.47	849.47	1310.07	20.93	
常宁市	100	409	2208.49	1097.12	1017.14	93.30	0.92
衡阳县	100	397	2318.75	552.55	1718.84	31.70	15.66
衡南县	100	373	2260.45	641.07	1538.51	80.72	0.15
衡山县	80	346	2316.16	379.02	1798.20	115.17	23.77
衡东县	100	396	2298.25	438.44	1720.61	132.50	6.70
祁东县	100	398	2322.05	617.18	1655.82	43.88	5.18

注:本表系农村住户抽样调查数字,与历年资料对比时请注意价格的可比性。

18—26 续表1 (1997年)

名称	调查户数（户）	调查户常住人口（人）	平均每人全年纯收入（元）	劳动者报酬收入	家庭经营收入	转移性收入	财产性收入
邵阳市	930	3812	1825.40	496.10	1205.77	103.47	20.06
北塔区	70	278	2109.65	467.33	1481.41	158.85	2.06
武冈市	100	426	1795.65	145.07	1350.88	289.29	10.41
邵东县	100	380	2481.78	937.24	1399.04	72.58	72.93
新邵县	100	390	1874.23	526.19	1162.78	158.63	26.63
邵阳县	100	424	1706.64	507.73	1141.98	49.88	7.05
隆回县	100	388	1267.81	426.75	804.18	35.52	1.36
洞口县	100	377	1966.93	543.51	1326.11	83.97	13.34
绥宁县	80	364	2032.73	354.05	1506.49	157.11	15.09
新宁县	100	420	1511.40	291.47	1173.53	44.64	1.76
城步县	80	365	1228.31	124.86	975.03	125.34	3.07
岳阳市	630	2591	2077.89	329.44	1630.50	113.20	4.75
岳阳楼区	30	112	3219.97	853.49	2229.97	131.33	5.18
汨罗市	100	380	2188.21	288.57	1836.34	54.28	9.01
临湘市	100	406	2047.42	457.27	1481.84	103.88	4.43
岳阳县	100	407	2002.01	57.41	1761.73	176.01	6.86
华容县	100	420	2072.09	102.17	1838.42	128.95	2.55
湘阴县	100	426	2122.27	555.85	1518.27	42.46	5.72
平江县	100	440	1280.49	376.24	796.21	107.99	0.04
常德市	850	3096	2054.71	421.33	1544.57	73.89	14.92
武陵区	70	273	3069.89	646.18	2187.47	80.18	156.06
鼎城区	100	374	2022.32	589.69	1392.67	29.72	10.24
津市市	80	272	2080.88	247.76	1798.25	28.73	6.14
安乡县	100	375	1979.53	173.38	1771.30	24.54	10.31
汉寿县	100	374	1984.55	578.51	1308.48	89.86	7.70
澧县	100	353	2015.01	456.56	1525.25	31.27	1.92
临澧县	100	363	2319.98	436.56	1802.86	55.78	24.78
桃源县	100	354	2145.45	467.49	1481.34	184.53	12.09
石门县	100	358	1691.85	82.61	1535.67	64.56	9.02

名 称	调查户数(户)	调查户常住人口(人)	平均每人全年纯收入(元)	劳动者报酬收入	家庭经营收入	转移性收入	财产性收入
张家界市	310	1222	1440.55	254.67	1125.64	51.26	8.98
武陵源区	30	123	1589.39	46.17	1496.88	45.93	0.41
永定区	100	400	1587.54	295.35	1242.16	39.45	10.58
慈利县	100	375	1576.67	337.97	1185.42	39.75	13.54
桑植县	80	324	1090.30	101.76	907.76	79.85	0.93
益阳市	600	2429	1760.97	361.26	1317.49	68.65	13.56
资阳区	100	422	1871.73	197.06	1524.87	128.06	21.74
赫山区	100	405	2138.08	539.07	1545.37	34.88	18.76
沅江市	100	372	1861.65	90.22	1612.41	144.51	14.51
南 县	100	421	1910.03	239.78	1649.90	11.11	9.25
桃江县	100	381	2069.32	613.90	1314.04	122.66	18.72
安化县	100	428	985.22	334.87	634.71	11.47	4.18
郴州市	890	3998	1911.84	363.32	1475.43	64.66	8.43
北湖区	60	263	2026.67	365.35	1482.44	178.56	0.32
苏仙区	60	243	2254.32	377.21	1680.01	181.18	15.92
资兴市	100	398	2212.29	400.83	1665.56	113.61	32.30
桂阳县	100	406	2148.01	267.74	1862.89	11.96	5.42
永兴县	100	420	1964.43	490.47	1408.73	60.61	4.62
宜章县	100	463	2003.80	394.34	1510.49	97.73	1.24
嘉禾县	80	326	2003.00	485.91	1476.99	35.16	4.94
临武县	100	408	1943.41	312.10	1563.13	40.63	27.55
汝城县	80	352	1144.95	353.67	705.69	80.97	4.62
桂东县	70	304	1064.88	187.98	836.33	39.38	1.19
安仁县	100	415	1803.66	297.24	1474.73	24.04	7.66
娄底地区	480	1913	1725.50	554.38	1069.14	95.35	6.64
娄底市	100	372	2480.94	699.57	1668.54	105.65	7.18
冷水江市	80	329	2083.47	677.39	1176.06	226.51	3.51
涟源市	100	397	2206.92	850.21	1298.12	47.31	11.28
双峰县	100	394	1994.05	490.52	1282.05	211.86	9.61
新化县	100	421	1005.30	329.37	642.00	32.48	1.45

18—27　续表 3　　(1997 年)

名　　称	调查户数(户)	调查户常住人口(人)	平均每人全年纯收入(元)	劳动者报酬收入	家庭经营收　入	转移性收　入	财产性收　入
永州市	1020	4393	1858.79	447.69	1355.85	49.08	6.16
芝山区	100	446	1999.87	431.53	1485.72	81.15	1.47
冷水滩区	100	385	1951.49	314.59	1522.71	88.96	25.22
东安县	100	391	1993.98	308.14	1600.89	81.16	3.79
道　县	100	453	2015.14	635.40	1337.66	38.69	3.39
宁远县	100	403	1547.58	359.71	1151.39	24.65	11.84
江永县	100	456	1929.10	127.90	1768.35	29.00	3.85
江华县	90	440	1260.55	375.53	851.65	29.11	4.26
蓝山县	70	316	1858.70	557.99	1255.02	42.35	3.34
新田县	80	362	1009.29	221.51	768.25	19.52	
双牌县	80	340	1914.37	357.39	1424.89	131.64	0.45
祁阳县	100	401	2017.08	641.36	1340.21	30.00	5.51
怀化地区	1000	4320	1525.24	242.54	1173.04	104.43	5.23
怀化市	90	365	1750.31	198.70	1125.95	417.38	8.27
洪江市	40	177	2025.99	190.09	1817.18	12.92	5.80
黔阳县	80	327	1828.38	345.30	1406.94	61.58	14.57
沅陵县	100	423	1023.68	71.94	802.44	133.68	15.62
辰溪县	90	433	1468.91	203.59	1133.77	130.40	1.15
溆浦县	100	402	1677.51	416.32	1239.66	19.99	1.54
麻阳县	90	418	1268.73	175.04	976.30	115.96	1.42
新晃县	70	312	1293.81	116.54	1058.46	117.64	1.17
芷江县	100	381	1752.13	147.88	1537.68	63.41	3.16
会同县	100	413	1747.88	561.64	1147.17	35.49	3.59
靖州县	70	321	1888.08	158.40	1724.69	4.98	
通道县	70	348	976.67	27.46	888.41	60.61	0.19
湘西自治州	700	3231	1079.27	111.49	890.54	75.01	2.23
吉首市	70	325	1508.21	0.86	1443.86	63.49	
泸溪县	80	388	953.18	192.24	720.24	40.70	
凤凰县	100	508	1046.54	91.48	899.57	54.09	1.40
花垣县	70	311	1018.26	228.13	713.55	73.04	3.54
保靖县	100	441	1062.07	192.90	855.76	10.47	2.93
古丈县	70	300	974.85	113.81	692.27	167.64	1.13
永顺县	100	448	1027.82	24.32	835.72	165.05	2.73
龙山县	100	510	1093.17	74.19	961.27	52.72	4.98

十九、各地、市、县主要指标排序

RANKING OF MAIN INDICATOR BY PREFECTURE, CITY AND COUNTY

19—1 各地市县主要指标排序(1997年)

Main economic indicators and their ranks

县市名称	年末人口		从业人员		职工人数		工资总额		职工平均工资	
	绝对数（万人）	位次	绝对数（万人）	位次	绝对数（万人）	位次	绝对数（万元）	位次	绝对数（元）	位次
长沙市	571.91		341.89		89.92		557968		6281	
长沙市区	163.44		99.59		68.98		447508		6565	
芙蓉区	29.89	89								
天心区	32.46	86								
岳麓区	28.32	90								
开福区	37.45	71								
雨花区	35.32	76								
浏阳市	133.01	1	76.10	2	5.72	15	31146	9	5536	11
长沙县	74.10	31	44.45	26	4.50	28	24801	15	5600	9
望城县	71.39	36	40.20	34	4.04	36	19511	32	4835	40
宁乡县	129.97	2	81.55	1	6.68	7	35002	6	5321	18
株洲市	365.65		197.50		45.84		275721		6062	
株洲市区	71.19		40.64		28.27		198230		7046	
荷塘区	19.90	106								
芦淞区	19.15	108								
石峰区	23.45	103								
天元区	8.69	119								
醴陵市	100.37	11	52.93	12	6.17	10	24759	16	4021	94
株洲县	44.54	60	22.41	63	2.24	74	10174	69	4593	61
攸　县	73.82	33	43.20	28	4.58	26	21562	25	4886	37
茶陵县	58.12	47	28.85	51	3.22	52	13644	55	4217	85
炎陵县	17.61	111	9.47	95	1.36	95	7352	92	5534	12
湘潭市	276.18		162.84		36.99		207442		5600	
湘潭市区	64.62		42.75		26.39		149205		5654	
雨湖区	32.80	85								
岳塘区	31.82	87								
湘乡市	88.94	18	50.35	16	5.50	18	33810	8	6204	2
韶山市	10.05	117	5.71	100	1.06	99	5377	97	5243	21
湘潭县	112.57	7	64.03	4	4.04	35	19050	33	4773	42
衡阳市	692.42		366.75		60.07		282995		4752	
衡阳市区	77.50		38.61		26.91		131511		4897	
江东区	15.73	114								
城南区	17.87	110								
城北区	19.83	107								
郊　区	18.93	109								
南岳区	5.14	121	2.35	104	0.49	103				
耒阳市	120.47	4	63.43	6	7.47	4	34547	7	4731	47

19—1 续表 1 (1997 年)

县市名称	年末人口		从业人员		职工人数		工资总额		职工平均工资	
	绝对数（万人）	位次	绝对数（万人）	位次	绝对数（万人）	位次	绝对数（万元）	位次	绝对数（元）	位次
常宁市	83.19	24	46.88	21	5.84	13	27850	12	4756	44
衡阳县	114.21	6	63.73	5	4.52	27	19795	30	4412	72
衡南县	101.53	10	49.72	18	5.48	19	23814	20	4418	71
衡山县	39.70	68	22.73	62	2.32	71	11701	62	5147	26
衡东县	65.14	43	34.18	44	3.06	56	13477	57	4521	67
祁东县	90.68	17	47.47	20	4.47	29	20300	29	4605	57
邵阳市	711.04		399.34		45.76		198435		4394	
邵阳市区	58.11		35.56		17.35		72170		4243	
双清区	24.49	101								
大祥区	26.62	94								
北塔区	7.00	120								
武冈市	71.09	37	42.15	32	3.56	46	14020	51	4012	95
邵东县	115.90	5	58.40	7	4.93	20	23721	22	4742	46
新邵县	72.32	35	42.75	30	3.08	55	13881	54	4563	64
邵阳县	92.41	16	53.54	10	3.36	50	13940	53	4197	86
隆回县	107.11	8	55.64	9	3.24	51	15967	44	5026	31
洞口县	76.99	27	46.02	24	3.79	41	15772	45	4222	84
绥宁县	34.37	80	18.70	76	1.98	77	10322	67	5238	22
新宁县	57.89	48	32.16	45	2.38	68	10074	70	4263	81
城步县	24.85	100	14.42	85	2.09	75	8568	82	4178	87
岳阳市	510.35		259.98		54.21		273633		5038	
岳阳市区(市直)	82.95		20.99		18.58		117294		6293	
岳阳楼区	46.53	58	10.31	93	1.18	97	5496	96	4684	51
云溪区	15.56	115	4.21	102	0.77	102	3613	102	4728	49
君山区	20.86	105	8.38	98	6.30	9	26754	13	4271	80
汨罗市	69.94	40	35.24	42	7.59	3	35410	4	4626	56
临湘市	46.94	57	23.03	61	4.04	34	17055	41	4313	75
岳阳县	74.51	30	33.19	44	3.40	49	13612	56	4023	93
华容县	70.94	38	36.54	39	4.65	23	19707	31	4260	82
湘阴县	67.88	41	38.13	38	4.09	32	16297	42	4028	92
平江县	97.19	13	49.96	17	3.61	44	18395	36	4670	53
常德市	593.32		319.87		48.13		237933		5004	
常德市区	131.45		73.01		17.58		94228		5353	
武陵区	43.79	62	11.17	92	2.31	72	7947	90	3393	102
鼎城区	87.66	21	51.08	15	6.45	8	30617	10	4772	43
津市市	25.35	97	12.63	90	3.62	43	17572	38	4836	39
安乡县	57.44	49	29.50	49	3.51	47	16089	43	4674	52

19--1　续表 2　　　　　　　　　　(1997 年)

县市名称	年末人口		从业人员		职工人数		工资总额		职工平均工资	
	绝对数（万人）	位次	绝对数（万人）	位次	绝对数（万人）	位次	绝对数（万元）	位次	绝对数（元）	位次
汉寿县	80.09	26	44.83	25	7.30	5	26450	14	3830	99
澧　县	87.72	20	44.43	27	4.61	25	20928	27	4595	59
临澧县	43.43	63	24.73	56	2.64	59	14183	50	5538	10
桃源县	97.54	12	52.03	13	4.65	24	24454	17	5266	20
石门县	70.30	39	38.71	35	4.22	31	24029	19	5714	6
张家界市	153.77		80.71		10.22		50071		5047	
张家界市区(市直)	44.60		1.46		1.39		9706		7051	
永定区	40.14	67	18.21	78	2.67	58	11979	59	4667	54
武陵源区	4.46	122	2.54	103	0.38	104	2162	103	5814	5
慈利县	67.02	42	38.21	37	3.50	48	15616	46	4631	55
桑植县	42.15	64	20.38	70	2.28	73	10608	66	4750	45
益阳市	446.87		249.96		40.93		167632		4110	
益阳市区(市直)	124.25		18.60		15.58		61493		3910	
资阳区	40.55	65	22.31	64	3.20	53	9438	74	3050	103
赫山区	83.70	22	38.61	36	3.59	45	15265	48	4279	79
沅江市	74.03	32	40.37	33	5.67	16	24166	18	4294	76
南　县	72.70	34	35.34	40	3.82	40	17348	40	4592	62
桃江县	81.54	25	46.04	23	4.41	30	18794	34	4280	78
安化县	94.35	14	48.69	19	4.66	22	21128	26	4582	63
郴州市	444.76		243.74		34.15		189506		5604	
郴州市区(市直)	61.24		9.18		7.92		52069		6566	
北湖区	27.48	91	10.10	94	2.55	63	10210	68	4061	91
苏仙区	33.76	83	13.06	88	1.68	85	8723	79	5379	16
资兴市	35.82	74	21.29	67	5.73	14	35088	5	6162	3
桂阳县	75.97	28	42.74	31	3.72	42	20680	28	5671	7
永兴县	62.02	46	29.17	50	2.34	69	11411	64	4973	32
宜章县	54.13	53	32.14	46	2.56	61	12900	58	5082	30
嘉禾县	33.01	84	18.25	77	1.55	91	8151	87	5424	14
临武县	30.69	88	16.72	80	1.71	84	9131	75	5449	13
汝城县	36.02	73	17.93	79	1.56	90	7948	89	5155	25
桂东县	16.85	112	9.45	96	0.94	100	4558	100	4932	34
安仁县	39.01	69	23.71	57	1.89	78	8637	81	4470	70
永州市	550.07		301.47		32.75		148219		4598	
永州市区(市直)	103.24		6.52		5.75		30560		5481	
芝山区	56.86	51	26.87	52	2.33	70	9991	71	4325	73
冷水滩区	46.38	59	21.05	68	2.53	64	9780	72	3909	97
东安县	57.22	50	26.16	55	2.55	62	11945	60	4729	48

19—1　续表 3　　(1997 年)

县市名称	年末人口		从业人员		职工人数		工资总额		职工平均工资	
	绝对数（万人）	位次	绝对数（万人）	位次	绝对数（万人）	位次	绝对数（万元）	位次	绝对数（元）	位次
道　县	64.05	44	35.30	41	3.12	54	14229	49	4605	58
宁远县	75.34	29	46.40	22	2.61	60	11549	63	4505	68
江永县	24.33	102	12.91	89	1.87	79	8211	85	4522	66
江华县	43.88	61	23.51	58	2.01	76	8486	83	4230	83
蓝山县	34.20	81	19.92	71	1.46	93	7134	93	4921	36
新田县	36.87	72	21.35	66	1.56	89	7503	91	4922	35
双牌县	16.64	113	8.48	97	1.34	96	5061	99	3796	100
祁阳县	94.30	15	53.00	11	5.62	17	23770	21	4292	77
娄底地区	392.13		223.04		34.68		170919		5106	
娄底市	37.77	70	23.41	59	10.50	1	63449	1	6217	1
冷水江市	34.39	79	20.59	69	8.29	2	42705	2	5362	17
涟源市	104.93	9	57.64	8	5.96	12	23553	24	4090	90
双峰县	88.84	19	51.76	14	3.94	37	17509	39	4562	65
新化县	126.20	3	69.64	3	5.99	11	23703	23	4152	88
怀化地区	476.62		260.19		33.38		159846		4827	
怀化市	54.96	52	31.02	48	6.94	6	36844	3	5405	15
洪江市	9.49	118	5.36	101	2.48	67	9517	73	3775	101
黔阳县	40.48	66	23.07	60	2.92	57	13949	52	4820	41
沅陵县	63.25	45	31.91	47	3.82	39	18634	35	4940	33
辰溪县	50.32	55	26.87	53	4.05	33	15529	47	3843	98
溆浦县	83.40	23	43.05	29	3.94	38	17586	37	4504	69
麻阳县	35.16	77	18.83	75	1.72	83	8738	78	5112	28
新晃县	24.99	98	15.68	81	1.44	94	8034	88	5612	8
芷江县	34.48	78	19.14	73	1.72	82	8814	77	5195	23
会同县	33.81	82	19.59	72	1.65	86	8664	80	5291	19
靖州县	24.95	99	13.56	87	1.60	87	8238	84	5163	24
通道县	21.33	104	12.11	91	1.10	98	5299	98	4851	38
湘西自治州	253.83		135.27		17.53		85322		4949	
吉首市	26.05	96	15.57	82	4.92	21	28340	11	5845	4
泸溪县	26.79	93	15.15	83	1.75	81	6797	94	3955	96
凤凰县	35.80	75	19.07	74	1.59	88	8160	86	5104	29
花垣县	26.08	95	14.35	86	1.77	80	8901	76	5125	27
保靖县	27.47	92	14.86	84	1.55	92	6570	95	4322	74
古丈县	13.38	116	7.60	99	0.91	101	3649	101	4099	89
永顺县	47.41	56	22.25	65	2.52	66	11716	61	4706	50
龙山县	50.85	54	26.72	54	2.52	65	11189	65	4594	60

19—1　续表 4　　　　　　　　　　(1997 年)

县市名称	国内生产总值		第一产业		第二产业		第三产业		人均国内生产总值	
	绝对数（万元）	位次	绝对数（万元）	位次	绝对数（万元）	位次	绝对数（万元）	位次	绝对数（元）	位次
长沙市	4828691		687320		2075005		2066366		8476	
长沙市区	3021813		64427		1328853		1628533		18664	
芙蓉区										
天心区										
岳麓区										
开福区										
雨花区										
浏阳市	527278	4	158072	9	244233	2	124983	8	3970	27
长沙县	643768	1	138000	16	378550	1	127218	7	8707	2
望城县	409975	11	123257	20	172390	8	114328	12	5745	7
宁乡县	535155	3	189449	3	201100	5	144606	3	4117	22
株洲市	2397033		491597		1155827		749609		6557	
株洲市区	1181518		39847		702124		439547		16564	
荷塘区										
芦淞区										
石峰区										
天元区										
醴陵市	415904	10	122247	22	212373	3	81284	22	4153	21
株洲县	195812	48	72342	46	62068	43	61402	35	4402	18
攸　县	368622	15	143196	14	122800	18	102626	14	4971	11
茶陵县	172211	53	86586	41	43239	55	42386	56	2972	58
炎陵县	62966	80	27379	77	13223	85	22364	74	3576	42
湘潭市	1875000		371431		824000		679569		6801	
湘潭市区	918472		26340		510849		381283		14289	
雨湖区										
岳塘区										
湘乡市	444436	7	144055	13	167827	9	132554	6	5000	10
韶山市	59595	82	13793	88	24434	74	21368	77	5936	6
湘潭县	452497	6	187243	4	120890	19	144364	4	4023	24
衡阳市	2643541		902091		899373		842077		3832	
衡阳市区	676619		37217		284852		354550		8794	
江东区										
城南区										
城北区										
郊　区										
南岳区										
耒阳市	436388	8	138596	15	182809	7	114983	11	3637	38

19—1　续表 5　　　　(1997 年)

县市名称	国内生产总值		第一产业		第二产业		第三产业		人均国内生产总值	
	绝对数（万元）	位次	绝对数（万元）	位次	绝对数（万元）	位次	绝对数（万元）	位次	绝对数（元）	位次
常宁市	329048	19	109051	28	135634	16	84363	19	3972	26
衡阳县	378355	14	213145	1	81334	31	83876	20	3325	52
衡南县	395698	13	174058	6	142390	13	79250	24	3912	28
衡山县	154059	55	56971	58	49135	52	47953	50	3894	29
衡东县	303058	23	101148	34	108818	22	93092	16	4660	16
祁东县	340837	18	117894	24	117430	20	105513	13	3762	34
邵阳市	2046973		868752		598265		579956		2888	
邵阳市区	293120		22577		120942		149601		5132	
双清区										
大祥区										
北塔区										
武冈市	189405	51	98893	36	43921	53	46591	51	2675	63
邵东县	550858	2	185590	5	206710	4	158558	2	4765	14
新邵县	189840	50	73049	45	59800	46	56991	40	2638	66
邵阳县	214986	45	107393	29	50000	51	57593	39	2332	73
隆回县	244122	33	107171	30	69299	40	67652	31	2291	74
洞口县	239657	36	127095	19	39771	60	72791	26	3125	57
绥宁县	147957	58	70795	48	42014	57	35148	62	4314	19
新宁县	151095	56	84190	43	24184	76	42721	54	2605	67
城步县	50279	84	23648	82	11801	87	14830	83	2036	82
岳阳市	2795623		866303		1018464		910856		5505	
岳阳市区	1112182		60486		572196		479500		15017	
岳阳楼区										
云溪区										
君山区										
汨罗市	245697	31	100125	35	102115	24	43457	53	3885	30
临湘市	180164	52	59718	54	73898	39	46548	52	3850	32
岳阳县	275000	26	123000	21	74000	38	78000	25	3544	44
华容县	287801	25	166217	8	67896	41	53688	43	4070	23
湘阴县	320664	21	157446	10	105498	23	57720	38	4723	15
平江县	245199	32	121387	23	55490	48	68322	30	2525	69
常德市	2831623		1073300		1019340		738983		4787	
常德市区	772229		230386		305353		236490		5974	
武陵区	376537		26375		200603		149559		9049	
鼎城区	395692		204011		104750		86931		4514	
津市市	91359	71	33505	72	35647	63	22207	76	3627	39
安乡县	206400	46	112616	25	40430	59	53354	45	3605	40

19—1 续表 6 (1997 年)

县市名称	国内生产总值		第一产业		第二产业		第三产业		人均国内生产总值	
	绝对数（万元）	位次	绝对数（万元）	位次	绝对数（万元）	位次	绝对数（万元）	位次	绝对数（元）	位次
汉寿县	259227	30	149014	11	52057	50	58156	37	3237	55
澧　县	349555	16	136865	17	74563	36	138127	5	3993	25
临澧县	220480	43	70008	49	100150	25	50322	48	5077	9
桃源县	469080	5	209435	2	139535	14	120110	10	4821	13
石门县	235879	38	93813	38	82806	29	59260	36	3365	50
张家界市	475513		140111		136040		199362		3107	
张家界市区										
永定区	96111		47939		14339		33833		2400	
武陵源区	14000		4447		1120		8433		3139	
慈利县	148003	57	64717	51	34624	64	48662	49	2208	78
桑植县	68555	79	30700	75	15528	82	22327	75	1629	89
益阳市	1730754		560146		574249		596359		3880	
益阳市区										
资阳区	145341		43972		53745		47624		3584	
赫山区	283428		93300		103130		86998		3386	
沅江市	270858	27	112403	26	75879	32	82576	21	3659	36
南　县	238859	37	131797	18	53086	49	53976	42	3285	53
桃江县	200164	47	89456	40	59892	45	50816	47	2460	70
安化县	240026	35	85145	42	86452	28	68429	29	2547	68
郴州市	1895096		550074		694007		651015		4276	
郴州市区										
北湖区	267574		24471		145122		97981		9765	
苏仙区	177203		34776		71776		70651		5301	
资兴市	234398	39	57740	55	114069	21	62589	34	6544	5
桂阳县	262108	29	106547	31	74463	37	81098	23	3453	48
永兴县	219242	44	71051	47	82503	30	65688	33	3549	43
宜章县	190762	49	57212	56	61642	44	71908	27	3524	45
嘉禾县	122297	61	38444	68	43302	54	40551	58	3717	35
临武县	99215	69	34089	71	38767	62	26359	67	3239	54
汝城县	101352	68	38562	67	32583	65	30207	65	2824	62
桂东县	33493	89	15094	87	7580	89	10819	89	1988	83
安仁县	114236	62	65661	50	27210	70	21365	78	2938	60
永州市	2138027		802124		720042		615861		3887	
永州市区										
芝山区	326886		83543		149965		93378		5649	
冷水滩区	252184		66653		107987		77544		5456	
东安县	221597	42	92392	39	75726	34	53479	44	3884	31

19—1 续表 7 (1997 年)

县市名称	国内生产总值		第一产业		第二产业		第三产业		人均国内生产总值	
	绝对数（万元）	位次	绝对数（万元）	位次	绝对数（万元）	位次	绝对数（万元）	位次	绝对数（元）	位次
道 县	232579	40	103550	33	75727	33	53302	46	3657	37
宁远县	170036	54	74009	44	59573	47	36454	60	2272	75
江永县	83768	73	39502	65	18255	81	26011	68	3454	47
江华县	107783	66	60369	53	24651	73	22763	73	2456	71
蓝山县	90722	72	37551	69	28584	68	24587	70	2664	64
新田县	81618	74	37481	70	25049	72	19088	81	2215	77
双牌县	59796	81	25210	79	19838	79	14748	84	3602	41
祁阳县	324976	20	144854	12	90115	27	90007	17	3459	46
娄底地区	1660841		426968		773730		460143		4246	
娄底市	347994	17	31009	74	193986	6	122999	9	9263	1
冷水江市	263294	28	21566	83	152993	11	88735	18	7676	4
涟源市	310839	22	96512	37	144255	12	70072	28	2968	59
双峰县	396138	12	170674	7	158532	10	66932	32	4463	17
新化县	302146	24	112403	27	95904	26	93839	15	2401	72
怀化地区	1900695		613734		611875		675086		4000	
怀化市	432872	9	51994	59	127657	17	253221	1	7924	3
洪江市	45624	86	6045	90	25878	71	13701	85	4869	12
黔阳县	139451	60	57174	57	42533	56	39744	59	3446	49
沅陵县	241310	34	62417	52	136204	15	42689	55	3824	33
辰溪县	108468	65	44344	61	28419	69	35705	61	2162	80
溆浦县	221641	41	106030	32	74755	35	40856	57	2663	65
麻阳县	78432	77	32463	73	23189	77	22780	72	2240	76
新晃县	79102	76	29423	76	28656	67	21023	79	3173	56
芷江县	98399	70	42472	63	24321	75	31606	64	2867	61
会同县	113200	63	47732	60	39002	61	26466	66	3349	51
靖州县	104736	67	40007	64	31340	66	33389	63	4220	20
通道县	41985	87	18971	85	10086	88	12928	86	1968	84
湘西自治州	570515		206829		191457		172229		2259	
吉首市	142752	59	23832	81	64831	42	54089	41	5527	8
泸溪县	54351	83	24774	80	13283	84	16294	82	2041	81
凤凰县	69905	78	25303	78	19052	80	25550	69	1966	85
花垣县	48422	85	21216	84	15081	83	12125	87	1867	86
保靖县	41075	88	17317	86	12070	86	11688	88	1503	90
古丈县	23984	90	11208	89	4281	90	8495	90	1798	87
永顺县	80217	75	38872	66	21615	78	19730	80	1702	88
龙山县	109809	64	44307	62	41244	58	24258	71	2163	79

19—1 续表 8 (1997 年)

县市名称	年末耕地面积		农业机械总动力		化肥施用量		农村用电量		农林牧渔业总产值	
	绝对数（千公顷）	位次	绝对数（千瓦）	位次	绝对数（折纯量吨）	位次	绝对数（万千瓦时）	位次	绝对数（万元）	位次
长沙市										
长沙市区										
芙蓉区	0.81	118	31987	107	439	116	2643	58	15958	112
天心区	1.23	117	22307	113	568	115	1886	75	8955	116
岳麓区	2.36	110	45267	93	1236	108	4201	34	24357	102
开福区	4.17	103	61302	87	1353	105	1906	74	28565	99
雨花区	3.09	107	46226	92	1409	104	3791	39	27106	101
浏阳市	65.42	6	336916	11	40065	7	10775	4	254905	10
长沙县	49.37	14	498080	1	24300	26	18733	1	257858	9
望城县	40.12	32	312698	13	18381	41	14035	2	184388	22
宁乡县	77.50	2	374156	7	45987	1	10346	5	312393	2
株洲市										
株洲市区										
荷塘区	3.03	108	21855	114	143	119	2278	65	17525	109
芦淞区	0.63	119	14198	115	288	118	1500	86	8644	117
石峰区	3.01	109	27006	110	371	117	3249	46	19982	107
天元区	3.50	104	29083	109	1287	106	634	109	16344	111
醴陵市	37.91	37	216651	26	19690	36	8510	9	179555	25
株洲县	27.32	54	131353	51	19472	38	4681	29	113358	51
攸　县	44.04	20	258994	19	26788	21	4681	30	213466	17
茶陵县	28.43	52	118564	58	15311	50	3024	49	137881	44
炎陵县	11.96	90	42343	98	4129	90	7624	11	42297	85
湘潭市										
湘潭市区										
雨湖区	1.47	116	13520	116	1000	111	1155	95	20823	106
岳塘区	3.46	105	45198	94	1988	102	1692	80	23155	103
湘乡市	43.54	22	261540	18	28649	16	7230	15	217197	14
韶山市	5.22	102	44202	95	2425	100	2330	62	21687	105
湘潭县	68.15	4	438056	2	40668	5	9315	8	302051	5
衡阳市										
衡阳市区										
江东区										
城南区										
城北区										
郊　区	7.77	97	70846	83	5113	86	2261	66	48516	82
南岳区	1.85	113	6460	118	781	113	238	118	13095	113
耒阳市	49.31	15	196164	30	26692	22	4085	36	203725	20

19—1　续表 9　　　　　　　　　　　　(1997 年)

县市名称	年末耕地面积		农业机械总动力		化肥施用量		农村用电量		农林牧渔业总产值	
	绝对数（千公顷）	位次	绝对数（千瓦）	位次	绝对数（折纯量吨）	位次	绝对数（万千瓦时）	位次	绝对数（万元）	位次
常宁市	37.90	38	106943	64	23092	27	2123	72	159629	33
衡阳县	58.82	8	175048	37	30983	15	6350	21	328248	1
衡南县	60.54	7	298239	17	31228	14	4583	31	286968	6
衡山县	17.48	73	150928	40	10149	68	2295	63	93125	60
衡东县	33.41	44	188498	33	19511	37	1632	81	152210	38
祁东县	38.97	34	159215	39	16640	47	3019	51	183443	23
邵阳市										
邵阳市区										
双清区	3.21	106	39876	103	1213	109	447	113	12530	114
大祥区	6.20	99	29550	108	2431	99	532	112	19869	108
北塔区	2.27	111	25768	112	1877	103	441	114	7228	118
武冈市	36.50	41	132249	50	17389	44	1562	84	159505	34
邵东县	46.27	18	253105	21	31454	13	7538	12	260208	8
新邵县	29.09	51	124783	54	14495	52	2893	54	130949	47
邵阳县	45.50	19	142312	45	22511	28	2902	53	161107	32
隆回县	50.15	13	106835	65	25135	24	6244	23	161608	31
洞口县	38.12	36	200505	29	21415	31	4300	32	175514	26
绥宁县	19.97	69	148794	41	8437	75	3250	45	115821	49
新宁县	32.56	49	98712	67	13965	54	2550	60	102893	57
城步县	12.39	89	39952	102	2919	98	703	108	37975	89
岳阳市										
岳阳市区										
岳阳楼区	1.75	115	37351	104	1210	110	798	104	33727	95
云溪区	5.68	100	59246	88	3516	96	1029	99	31247	97
君山区	25.03	58	113837	61	15450	49	2337	61	106171	55
汨罗市	42.36	25	341324	10	17749	42	5066	27	220554	13
临湘市	30.90	50	258447	20	13409	55	3051	48	107890	53
岳阳县	40.48	31	202149	28	19850	35	3166	47	200558	21
华容县	54.13	12	400627	3	42389	3	2987	52	260646	7
湘阴县	38.35	35	374636	6	25592	23	6250	22	228118	12
平江县	47.97	17	235112	25	25074	25	3680	42	169037	29
常德市										
常德市区										
武陵区	8.31	95	78791	75	4932	87	2598	59	41087	86
鼎城区	75.00	3	355891	9	41839	4	10898	3	305771	3
津市市	16.12	78	62667	86	10178	67	1329	90	63810	72
安乡县	42.82	23	210905	27	33738	11	6808	18	166619	30

19—1 续表10 (1997年)

县市名称	年末耕地面积		农业机械总动力		化肥施用量		农村用电量		农林牧渔业总产值	
	绝对数（千公顷）	位次	绝对数（千瓦）	位次	绝对数（折纯量吨）	位次	绝对数（万千瓦时）	位次	绝对数（万元）	位次
汉寿县	57.15	11	308819	16	38316	9	7281	14	215677	15
澧　县	67.87	5	313645	12	45409	2	5982	24	214879	16
临澧县	35.26	42	189118	32	19452	39	9483	7	169188	28
桃源县	89.12	1	245166	23	35509	10	7122	16	305745	4
石门县	41.58	26	137132	46	28523	17	2874	55	145023	40
张家界市										
张家界市区										
永定区	23.17	62	110916	62	10086	69	955	100	75049	66
武陵源区	2.07	112	6298	119	971	112	166	119	7013	119
慈利县	41.41	27	133108	48	21214	32	2657	57	100792	59
桑植县	21.35	67	76439	78	10717	66	733	107	44085	84
益阳市										
益阳市区										
资阳区	19.61	70	147331	42	12803	58	3361	44	66204	71
赫山区	37.76	39	309381	15	21999	30	7762	10	146510	39
沅江市	57.74	9	395374	5	32122	12	5618	25	180972	24
南　县	57.35	10	397255	4	40351	6	9697	6	209132	19
桃江县	40.69	30	183533	34	15255	51	6874	17	134485	46
安化县	33.33	45	195423	31	11873	62	1582	83	123457	48
郴州市										
郴州市区										
北湖区	8.71	93	64453	85	4230	89	1263	92	38783	87
苏仙区	15.46	81	107136	63	6744	80	3711	40	59770	77
资兴市	17.74	72	86697	71	9109	73	3608	43	86155	63
桂阳县	39.64	33	180838	35	27562	20	4258	33	158738	35
宜章县	23.05	63	247673	22	14052	53	2710	56	87784	61
永兴县	25.86	56	116359	60	17313	45	1779	79	114531	50
嘉禾县	14.12	84	123636	55	11905	61	1287	91	75372	65
临武县	13.79	86	163857	38	8204	77	1506	85	54983	81
汝城县	19.29	71	73732	80	12692	59	1168	93	58414	79
桂东县	9.04	92	26465	111	4574	88	583	110	22328	104
安仁县	20.47	68	83225	72	11856	63	1052	98	101836	58
永州市										
永州市区										
芝山区	33.31	46	130744	52	15545	48	2164	69	139664	43
冷水滩区	24.35	59	132723	49	12892	57	2049	73	107376	54
祁阳县	43.98	21	239089	24	28470	18	7459	13	213367	18

19—1 续表 11 (1997 年)

县市名称	年末耕地面积		农业机械总动力		化肥施用量		农村用电量		农林牧渔业总产值	
	绝对数（千公顷）	位次	绝对数（千瓦）	位次	绝对数（折纯量吨）	位次	绝对数（万千瓦时）	位次	绝对数（万元）	位次
东安县	34.67	43	119890	57	16791	46	3989	37	140851	41
双牌县	7.02	98	32983	106	3930	92	582	111	37423	90
道　县	37.29	40	77709	77	27821	19	1165	94	155734	37
江永县	16.25	77	41637	100	19940	34	413	116	63760	73
宁远县	32.95	48	142496	43	17573	43	1812	78	137354	45
蓝山县	16.09	79	102223	66	9445	71	1445	87	87084	62
新田县	15.28	82	74563	79	12960	56	1054	97	60300	76
江华县	21.92	65	81842	73	12403	60	2194	67	109322	52
娄底地区										
娄底市	8.57	94	92471	68	5345	85	3792	38	45950	83
冷水江市	5.50	101	77974	76	3428	97	5600	26	29742	98
涟源市	42.76	24	311243	14	22333	29	6500	20	140655	42
双峰县	40.92	28	359245	8	38826	8	6558	19	253140	11
新化县	48.54	16	179922	36	18451	40	4162	35	169412	27
怀化地区										
怀化市	23.26	60	142339	44	7711	78	3693	41	78731	64
洪江市	1.80	114	13114	117	624	114	419	115	9604	115
黔阳县	22.14	64	91850	69	11812	64	2127	70	72242	68
沅陵县	33.22	47	135437	47	7537	79	4919	28	104603	56
辰溪县	21.47	66	121142	56	9164	72	1829	77	61729	75
溆浦县	40.70	29	118116	59	20354	33	3018	50	158253	36
麻阳县	15.93	80	47197	91	5391	84	1430	88	56337	80
新晃县	13.73	87	42964	97	2407	101	1862	76	34829	94
芷江县	25.09	57	87227	70	8403	76	1401	89	70675	70
会同县	17.15	75	72670	81	5532	83	2124	71	71960	69
靖州县	15.27	83	80750	74	5965	81	1143	96	58834	78
通道县	13.05	88	50434	90	3561	95	911	102	35184	93
湘西自治州										
吉首市	9.49	91	44046	96	3925	93	892	103	38049	88
泸溪县	13.98	85	57906	89	3689	94	781	105	37017	91
凤凰县	23.20	61	68555	84	5784	82	769	106	36848	92
花垣县	17.25	74	41239	101	9761	70	1614	82	31687	96
保靖县	16.64	76	41865	99	4107	91	2178	68	28215	100
古丈县	7.82	96	36217	105	1256	107	261	117	16522	110
永顺县	27.85	53	72483	82	8850	74	913	101	62131	74
龙山县	26.11	55	125815	53	10753	65	2288	64	72986	67

19—1 续表 12 (1997 年) 单位:吨

县市名称	粮食产量		棉花产量		油料产量		猪牛羊肉产量		水产品产量	
	绝对数	位次	绝对数	位次	绝对数	位次	绝对数	位次	绝对数	位次
长沙市										
长沙市区										
芙蓉区	2493	119			16	117	6103	109	1588	84
天心区	13817	113			13	118	2911	116	1534	85
岳麓区	21793	109			92	112	11019	89	1896	76
开福区	46169	101			44	115	9938	94	4907	60
雨花区	18841	111			84	113	10547	92	1300	95
浏阳市	701247	3	526	33	9738	39	80450	13	16320	23
长沙县	595636	6	65	66	7522	54	114085	1	11234	31
望城县	537871	10			2750	83	64890	17	14280	24
宁乡县	990265	1	833	25	8942	46	93259	7	22470	15
株洲市										
株洲市区										
荷塘区	38580	104			82	114	5855	110	738	108
芦淞区	9603	118			29	116	1820	117	920	104
石峰区	37412	106			408	107	7143	107	1403	89
天元区	36479	107	200	45	223	111	3772	112	871	105
醴陵市	485955	16	139	54	5923	60	52096	26	10236	35
株洲县	321426	38	829	26	2931	80	34869	45	7006	49
攸　县	469387	17	2604	18	16480	25	62312	19	9341	39
茶陵县	312039	41	597	31	8801	48	41893	35	8230	42
炎陵县	117805	78	38	75	2132	86	9219	96	332	116
湘潭市										
湘潭市区										
雨湖区	13492	115				119	10857	90	1750	81
岳塘区	39477	103			504	103	10521	93	1683	83
湘乡市	537858	11	375	39	1469	93	91752	8	21050	17
韶山市	67242	92	11	88	270	110	7805	101	1800	79
湘潭县	833734	2	144	51	3054	77	104416	3	26717	12
衡阳市										
衡阳市区										
江东区										
城南区										
城北区										
郊　区	58440	94			1445	94	13953	82	7388	47
南岳区	18182	112	15	84	271	109	3673	113	337	115
耒阳市	437153	24	1950	20	17800	23	81378	12	17270	20

19—1 续表 13 (1997 年) 单位:吨

县市名称	粮食产量		棉花产量		油料产量		猪牛羊肉产量		水产品产量	
	绝对数	位次	绝对数	位次	绝对数	位次	绝对数	位次	绝对数	位次
常宁市	367624	36	209	44	11454	37	50152	28	13259	27
衡阳县	676779	4	12249	8	58725	3	101384	4	34000	7
衡南县	568104	9	11860	9	50250	5	91311	9	31803	10
衡山县	217789	57	277	42	2602	84	35861	44	7760	44
衡东县	384527	33	121	56	12378	33	56434	24	10836	32
祁东县	453176	19	55	68	6550	57	57473	22	28696	11
邵阳市										
邵阳市区										
双清区	29638	108	25	81	465	105	4080	111	1077	101
大祥区	52234	98	35	77	1425	95	7519	104	1181	97
北塔区	20628	110			545	102	1599	118	328	117
武冈市	434942	25	90	62	13304	30	83858	10	6000	53
邵东县	493856	14	141	52	9171	42	78579	14	18800	18
新邵县	318417	39	141	53	2966	79	42720	33	3647	67
邵阳县	407129	31	160	49	24313	15	7737	102	7241	48
隆回县	425356	26	105	58	16046	26	53176	25	3850	65
洞口县	447962	23	90	61	23536	16	95748	6	5720	56
绥宁县	155943	66	41	74	9132	45	34867	46	1302	94
新宁县	287942	45	1	99	9136	44	32941	52	3876	64
城步县	92702	88			3994	68	15802	78	320	118
岳阳市										
岳阳市区										
岳阳楼区	11685	117	3	98	414	106	13348	84	16496	22
云溪区	42154	102	372	40	2306	85	9169	97	9945	36
君山区	131486	72	15577	5	9976	38	25186	61	23137	13
汨罗市	418292	28	1878	21	8282	51	100956	5	13019	28
临湘市	245698	52	3420	16	13033	31	22976	65	13917	25
岳阳县	419020	27	4950	15	18880	19	58689	21	34348	6
华容县	399772	32	35002	1	50216	6	44189	32	50521	3
湘阴县	486065	15	1540	22	9137	43	74831	16	60900	1
平江县	448144	22	802	28	12343	34	63910	18	3198	69
常德市										
常德市区										
武陵区	50156	99	807	27	5195	62	9502	95	9733	37
鼎城区	666242	5	14921	6	41814	7	56872	23	51093	2
津市市	113241	81	5278	13	15920	27	15359	80	9550	38
安乡县	279923	48	27775	3	55843	4	21860	67	32675	9

19—1 续表 14 (1997年) 单位:吨

县市名称	粮食产量		棉花产量		油料产量		猪牛羊肉产量		水产品产量	
	绝对数	位次	绝对数	位次	绝对数	位次	绝对数	位次	绝对数	位次
汉寿县	496237	13	12796	7	37388	8	30743	55	35672	5
澧　县	449846	21	21113	4	72710	1	37150	40	18014	19
临澧县	305804	43	8514	11	33299	9	34865	47	13377	26
桃源县	591270	7	7176	12	72654	2	83599	11	22391	16
石门县	278964	49	5143	14	31244	10	37486	39	5537	57
张家界市										
张家界市区										
永定区	165024	63	347	41	18062	22	19572	71	1872	78
武陵源区	13693	114	10	91	1935	90	1589	119	26	119
慈利县	275233	50	3380	17	27756	11	29670	59	3030	71
桑植县	143517	70	28	80	18958	18	18251	77	381	114
益阳市										
益阳市区										
资阳区	208250	58	749	29	3632	73	13691	83	8500	41
赫山区	381085	34	25	82	3171	76	42279	34	12120	29
沅江市	408270	30	11589	10	25343	13	29397	60	50058	4
南　县	413514	29	28480	2	27690	12	34326	49	33107	8
桃江县	379094	35	458	36	4352	66	29819	57	3050	70
安化县	280560	47	156	50	18399	20	37595	38	6944	50
郴州市										
郴州市区										
北湖区	58934	93			767	99	12570	86	2100	73
苏仙区	112880	82	45	72	1018	98	22575	66	5003	59
资兴市	157167	65	67	65	1953	89	29686	58	7562	46
桂阳县	283840	46			3963	69	33121	51	6010	52
永兴县	200516	59	4	97	3042	78	31334	53	4040	62
宜章县	239006	53	49	70	3195	75	36466	42	8570	40
嘉禾县	134141	71	7	95	2897	81	36221	43	1316	93
临武县	107270	83	9	92	1561	92	19137	74	2602	72
汝城县	127373	74	171	48	2034	88	20685	69	650	111
桂东县	49984	100	12	86	585	101	7887	100	406	113
安仁县	236476	54	47	71	8918	47	36522	41	5012	58
永州市										
永州市区										
芝山区	318290	40	544	32	4824	65	37989	37	5800	54
冷水滩区	234358	55	2012	19	2831	82	34771	48	10462	33
祁阳县	510022	12	660	30	14553	29	59188	20	22823	14

19—1 续表 15　　(1997 年)　　单位:吨

县市名称	粮食产量		棉花产量		油料产量		猪牛羊肉产量		水产品产量	
	绝对数	位次	绝对数	位次	绝对数	位次	绝对数	位次	绝对数	位次
东安县	311603	42	1157	24	4968	63	41220	36	7748	45
双牌县	57177	96	6	96	384	108	7332	106	1117	99
道　县	294681	44	68	64	6858	56	45702	31	12052	30
江永县	103451	84	8	93	4833	64	24087	63	2085	74
宁远县	251906	51	504	34	3702	71	49651	30	7891	43
蓝山县	114029	79			1333	96	33668	50	1378	91
新田县	128566	73			1750	91	20864	68	1886	77
江华县	151250	69	8	94	3739	70	24058	64	1707	82
娄底地区										
娄底市	99841	86	31	78	1321	97	13182	85	4039	63
冷水江市	58426	95	12	87	481	104	11077	88	1952	75
涟源市	454256	18	109	57	3392	74	50090	29	5770	55
双峰县	577377	8	460	35	20180	17	107148	2	16600	21
新化县	450622	20	36	76	9198	41	77242	15	10264	34
怀化地区										
怀化市	177730	62	394	37	9459	40	31284	54	6777	51
洪江市	12286	116			755	100	3665	114	451	112
黔阳县	154255	68	11	89	5553	61	19543	72	1317	92
沅陵县	225480	56	87	63	17474	24	30624	56	3250	68
辰溪县	155266	67	392	38	7785	53	14001	81	1052	102
溆浦县	336983	37	1398	23	15600	28	51122	27	3769	66
麻阳县	120746	76	53	69	12382	32	10682	91	1240	96
新晃县	95947	87			3641	72	19308	73	670	110
芷江县	160717	64	22	83	8093	52	24806	62	1422	88
会同县	125480	75	56	67	6331	59	18283	75	1384	90
靖州县	113701	80	13	85	6384	58	18272	76	1461	86
通道县	80019	90	31	79	2086	87	7026	108	688	109
湘西自治州										
吉首市	53735	97	138	55	7253	55	8225	99	1088	100
泸溪县	79818	91	262	43	11912	36	7433	105	864	106
凤凰县	119893	77	42	73	12095	35	7727	103	1433	87
花垣县	102849	85	11	90	8548	50	12278	87	1768	80
保靖县	88952	89	181	46	8582	49	8356	98	750	107
古丈县	38018	105	101	59	4017	67	3388	115	1167	98
永顺县	189504	60	175	47	25248	14	15515	79	924	103
龙山县	178556	61	94	60	18136	21	20574	70	4282	61

19—1　续表 16　　　　　　　　　(1997 年)

县市名称	工业总产值		总产值增长速度		国有单位固定资产投资		国有单位房屋竣工面积	
	绝对数(万元)	位次	比上年增长(%)	位次	绝对数(万元)	位次	绝对数(平方米)	位次
长沙市								
长沙市区								
芙蓉区					143669	4	383045	2
天心区					202536	2	494698	1
岳麓区					50053	12	166150	18
开福区					94653	7	277898	6
雨花区					55021	9	218933	12
长沙县	1204466	1	29.5	41	19135	36	100342	39
望城县	626530	8	21.2	54	21717	32	26282	104
宁乡县	784109	3	34.1	33	25481	25	197936	14
浏阳市	790658	2	15.4	63	31291	21	88112	43
株洲市								
株洲市区								
荷塘区					22163	31	162411	19
芦淞区					41014	18	104147	35
石峰区					48698	15	149756	24
天元区					29709	23	183624	17
株洲县	267686	38	5.2	74	6303	88	30018	102
攸　县	340989	28	12.8	66	6689	83	46484	76
茶陵县	247582	44	41.8	25	3653	103	30380	101
炎陵县	65205	83	52.1	15	3643	104	31615	98
醴陵市	741707	4	16.9	61	9418	62	38266	91
湘潭市								
湘潭市区								
雨湖区					24598	27	237629	9
岳塘区					196624	3	233508	10
湘潭县	470901	17	19.5	57	7281	78	46155	78
湘乡市	509428	13	25.3	47	20610	34	103473	36
韶山市	121244	71	31.8	37	2015	117	12650	118
衡阳市								
衡阳市区								
江东区					9020	66	34935	96
城南区					39386	19	245493	7
城北区					47918	16	155415	21
郊　区					8476	70	43251	83
南岳区					5593	93	17531	114
衡阳县	507106	14	24.4	48	9773	60	100389	38

19—1　续表 17　　(1997 年)

县市名称	工业总产值		总产值增长速度		国有单位固定资产投资		国有单位房屋竣工面积	
	绝对数（万元）	位次	比上年增长（%）	位次	绝对数（万元）	位次	绝对数（平方米）	位次
衡南县	550077	11	26.7	44	15949	44	75497	48
衡山县	145780	64	—4.0	82	4692	98	61974	60
衡东县	309360	32	32.4	36	5344	94	12885	117
祁东县	468629	18	21.4	53	12151	54	157376	20
耒阳市	543450	12	30.3	39	18830	38	49337	71
常宁市	418610	21	—1.4	80	10607	58	73096	49
邵阳市								
邵阳市区								
双清区					15988	43	90056	41
大祥区					17018	40	116366	28
北塔区					1470	121	20900	109
邵东县	690890	7	2.8	77	18912	37	115405	30
新邵县	236167	47	14.3	64	3792	102	24450	107
邵阳县	292604	35	60.4	9	7600	76	79430	45
隆回县	141492	66	38.6	28	13214	50	47713	73
洞口县	169514	58	75.1	4	8866	68	42263	86
绥宁县	236217	46	100.5	3	8068	71	85356	44
新宁县	120458	72	112.8	2	4852	97	11216	119
城步县	71603	82	42.6	21	7201	79	35114	95
武冈市	242250	45	72.6	5	11451	56	59337	63
岳阳市								
岳阳市区								
岳阳楼区					304062	1	279865	5
云溪区					712	122	5480	122
君山区					1844	118	19496	111
岳阳县	324827	29	—1.1	79	9365	63	59837	62
华容县	389579	27	28.8	42	12971	51	64468	56
湘阴县	488080	15	45.2	17	3591	106	31016	99
平江县	256935	42	17.4	59	6238	91	71701	51
汨罗市	725109	6	33.5	34	6420	86	65517	54
临湘市	267195	40	—8.5	84	11410	57	64518	55
常德市								
常德市区								
武陵区					127426	5	369377	3
鼎城区					22667	30	106535	33
安乡县	143630	65	—20.3	88	12439	53	89145	42
汉寿县	195662	54	4.7	75	6975	82	62798	59

19—1 续表 18 (1997 年)

<table>
<tr><th rowspan="2">县市名称</th><th colspan="2">工业总产值</th><th colspan="2">总产值增长速度</th><th colspan="2">国有单位固定资产投资</th><th colspan="2">国有单位房屋竣工面积</th></tr>
<tr><th>绝对数(万元)</th><th>位次</th><th>比上年增长(%)</th><th>位次</th><th>绝对数(万元)</th><th>位次</th><th>绝对数(平方米)</th><th>位次</th></tr>
<tr><td>澧 县</td><td>407197</td><td>24</td><td>-4.5</td><td>83</td><td>12920</td><td>52</td><td>153971</td><td>22</td></tr>
<tr><td>临澧县</td><td>206225</td><td>53</td><td>-58.3</td><td>92</td><td>9242</td><td>64</td><td>38010</td><td>92</td></tr>
<tr><td>桃源县</td><td>740949</td><td>5</td><td>38.9</td><td>27</td><td>106767</td><td>6</td><td>101179</td><td>37</td></tr>
<tr><td>石门县</td><td>228640</td><td>50</td><td>5.9</td><td>73</td><td>17659</td><td>39</td><td>98266</td><td>40</td></tr>
<tr><td>津市市</td><td>155143</td><td>61</td><td>7.3</td><td>71</td><td>6524</td><td>85</td><td>44167</td><td>82</td></tr>
<tr><td>张家界市</td><td></td><td></td><td></td><td></td><td></td><td></td><td></td><td></td></tr>
<tr><td>张家界市区</td><td></td><td></td><td></td><td></td><td></td><td></td><td></td><td></td></tr>
<tr><td>永定区</td><td></td><td></td><td></td><td></td><td>19960</td><td>35</td><td>72783</td><td>50</td></tr>
<tr><td>武陵源区</td><td></td><td></td><td></td><td></td><td>1780</td><td>120</td><td>8100</td><td>121</td></tr>
<tr><td>慈利县</td><td>161816</td><td>60</td><td>26.4</td><td>45</td><td>41049</td><td>17</td><td>46409</td><td>77</td></tr>
<tr><td>桑植县</td><td>80475</td><td>81</td><td>21.5</td><td>51</td><td>16368</td><td>41</td><td>26116</td><td>105</td></tr>
<tr><td>益阳市</td><td></td><td></td><td></td><td></td><td></td><td></td><td></td><td></td></tr>
<tr><td>益阳市区</td><td></td><td></td><td></td><td></td><td></td><td></td><td></td><td></td></tr>
<tr><td>资阳区</td><td></td><td></td><td></td><td></td><td>8808</td><td>69</td><td>50382</td><td>67</td></tr>
<tr><td>赫山区</td><td></td><td></td><td></td><td></td><td>59507</td><td>8</td><td>210875</td><td>13</td></tr>
<tr><td>南 县</td><td>223066</td><td>51</td><td>9.3</td><td>69</td><td>6297</td><td>89</td><td>47250</td><td>74</td></tr>
<tr><td>桃江县</td><td>399613</td><td>26</td><td>28.2</td><td>43</td><td>14904</td><td>47</td><td>41232</td><td>88</td></tr>
<tr><td>安化县</td><td>305718</td><td>33</td><td>54.4</td><td>14</td><td>35100</td><td>20</td><td>50026</td><td>69</td></tr>
<tr><td>沅江市</td><td>324517</td><td>30</td><td>37.7</td><td>29</td><td>9220</td><td>65</td><td>58448</td><td>64</td></tr>
<tr><td>郴州市</td><td></td><td></td><td></td><td></td><td></td><td></td><td></td><td></td></tr>
<tr><td>郴州市区</td><td></td><td></td><td></td><td></td><td></td><td></td><td></td><td></td></tr>
<tr><td>北湖区</td><td></td><td></td><td></td><td></td><td>49621</td><td>13</td><td>223825</td><td>11</td></tr>
<tr><td>苏仙区</td><td></td><td></td><td></td><td></td><td>22899</td><td>28</td><td>192842</td><td>15</td></tr>
<tr><td>桂阳县</td><td>411527</td><td>22</td><td>65.7</td><td>8</td><td>15883</td><td>45</td><td>151456</td><td>23</td></tr>
<tr><td>宜章县</td><td>407720</td><td>23</td><td>141.7</td><td>1</td><td>8060</td><td>72</td><td>108306</td><td>31</td></tr>
<tr><td>永兴县</td><td>280701</td><td>37</td><td>-3.9</td><td>81</td><td>5057</td><td>95</td><td>30440</td><td>100</td></tr>
<tr><td>嘉禾县</td><td>231357</td><td>49</td><td>30.8</td><td>38</td><td>7408</td><td>77</td><td>66530</td><td>52</td></tr>
<tr><td>临武县</td><td>267487</td><td>39</td><td>59.5</td><td>10</td><td>5806</td><td>92</td><td>50260</td><td>68</td></tr>
<tr><td>汝城县</td><td>122906</td><td>70</td><td>13.3</td><td>65</td><td>9767</td><td>61</td><td>49599</td><td>70</td></tr>
<tr><td>桂东县</td><td>38199</td><td>91</td><td>29.7</td><td>40</td><td>2655</td><td>112</td><td>42591</td><td>84</td></tr>
<tr><td>安仁县</td><td>152144</td><td>62</td><td>55.5</td><td>13</td><td>5015</td><td>96</td><td>41978</td><td>87</td></tr>
<tr><td>资兴市</td><td>312583</td><td>31</td><td>44.0</td><td>19</td><td>22752</td><td>29</td><td>131648</td><td>25</td></tr>
<tr><td>永州市</td><td></td><td></td><td></td><td></td><td></td><td></td><td></td><td></td></tr>
<tr><td>永州市区</td><td></td><td></td><td></td><td></td><td></td><td></td><td></td><td></td></tr>
<tr><td>芝山区</td><td>424842</td><td>19</td><td>17.3</td><td>60</td><td>16051</td><td>42</td><td>106966</td><td>32</td></tr>
<tr><td>冷水滩区</td><td>402103</td><td>25</td><td>42.6</td><td>23</td><td>48746</td><td>14</td><td>299231</td><td>4</td></tr>
<tr><td>祁阳县</td><td>553436</td><td>10</td><td>42.6</td><td>22</td><td>21155</td><td>33</td><td>115832</td><td>29</td></tr>
</table>

(1997 年)

县市名称	工业总产值		总产值增长速度		国有单位固定资产投资		国有单位房屋竣工面积	
	绝对数（万元）	位次	比上年增长（%）	位次	绝对数（万元）	位次	绝对数（平方米）	位次
东安县	129492	69	－32.4	90	14823	48	120770	27
双牌县	81182	80	57.0	11	3880	101	23095	108
道　县	288918	36	42.0	24	8012	74	44571	80
江永县	81659	79	44.8	18	7073	81	121125	26
宁远县	213881	52	42.7	20	2832	111	63840	57
蓝山县	140182	67	68.0	6	3592	105	63705	58
新田县	105903	75	23.2	50	4305	99	61435	61
江华县	86725	77	－0.9	78	3296	107	20284	110
娄底地区								
娄底市	623002	9	34.7	31	54314	10	184615	16
冷水江市	422300	20	9.2	70	29640	24	57807	65
涟源市	302786	34	－15.0	85	10564	59	76111	47
双峰县	487769	16	34.9	30	8048	73	28178	103
新化县	264756	41	33.2	35	15735	46	77716	46
怀化地区								
怀化市	254541	43	－17.8	87	24946	26	104504	34
洪江市	114157	73	20.4	55	1835	119	36143	94
黔阳县	173745	56	34.7	32	2918	110	18997	113
沅陵县	231727	48	11.1	67	52179	11	66273	53
辰溪县	145917	63	41.7	26	11976	55	45970	79
溆浦县	138042	68	9.5	68	14653	49	38486	90
麻阳县	86229	78	18.4	58	2513	114	25358	106
新晃县	61373	84	－22.4	89	3132	109	44562	81
芷江县	103223	76	21.4	52	4167	100	37539	93
会同县	168267	59	56.2	12	6655	84	39838	89
靖州县	175935	55	67.3	7	6239	90	46536	75
通道县	57927	86	50.0	16	3156	108	31639	97
湘西自治州								
吉首市	169915	57	4.4	76	30776	22	239277	8
泸溪县	41402	88	－17.6	86	7671	75	56579	66
凤凰县	40483	89	－35.8	91	2159	116	19247	112
花垣县	48367	87	23.9	49	7151	80	15318	116
保靖县	38551	90	25.6	46	2641	113	10875	120
古丈县	11329	92	6.8	72	2202	115	16935	115
永顺县	58440	85	16.4	62	6380	87	42535	85
龙山县	107949	74	19.9	56	8900	67	49283	72

19—1　续表 20　　　　　　　　(1997 年)

县市名称	地方财政收入		地方财政支出		社会消费品零售总额		农民全年人均纯收入	
	绝对数（万元）	位次	绝对数（万元）	位次	绝对数（万元）	位次	绝对数（元）	位次
长沙市	256384		280728		2050280		2649.27	
长沙市区								
芙蓉区	9992	25	9368	61			3348.95	1
天心区	6551	63	7809	80			3270.25	4
岳麓区	7021	56	9324	62			3028.62	8
开福区	11469	12	11068	44			2891.68	10
雨花区	6146	67	10963	45			3327.22	3
浏阳市	21645	2	31842	1	151639	3	2442.32	23
长沙县	22765	1	29929	2	111763	10	2991.70	9
望城县	13967	8	17533	5	104380	16	2720.00	15
宁乡县	16522	3	21905	3	117595	9	2328.06	26
株洲市	105634		131002		876029		2285.08	
株洲市区								
天元区	8298	39	10752	46				
芦淞区	7037	55	3810	109			2651.75	16
荷塘区	4995	84	3344	114			2761.14	14
石峰区	5897	71	3185	115			2775.52	13
醴陵市	13975	7	16074	10	169248	1	2528.66	19
株洲县	5979	69	8377	72	66997	49	2408.93	24
攸　县	10778	20	13058	29	95769	23	2598.95	18
茶陵县	7437	52	10000	53	51335	62	1936.35	68
炎陵县	3982	96	5951	97	19247	92	1745.14	83
湘潭市	51806		66982		548066		2531.57	
湘潭市区								
雨湖区	4234	92	4961	103			3337.07	2
岳塘区	3901	98	4010	108			3257.41	5
湘乡市	11005	16	14639	14	110764	11	2383.25	25
韶山市	2193	112	3506	111	20688	88	2788.45	12
湘潭县	11293	14	12904	31	105389	13	2524.99	20
衡阳市	102171		139829		948150		2285.15	
衡阳市区								
南岳区	1648	119	2337	119			2612.25	17
江东区	2114	113	1929	120				
城南区	2457	110	2451	118				
城北区	2851	107	2807	116				
郊　区	3322	103	3756	110	20465	89	2848.96	11
耒阳市	12918	9	16179	9	86362	28	2180.47	38

19—1　续表 21　(1997 年)

县市名称	地方财政收入		地方财政支出		社会消费品零售总额		农民全年人均纯收入	
	绝对数(万元)	位次	绝对数(万元)	位次	绝对数(万元)	位次	绝对数(元)	位次
衡阳县	11422	13	13602	24	74555	38	2318.75	29
衡南县	10675	21	14037	21	61651	54	2260.45	32
衡山县	5089	82	6251	94	43651	68	2316.16	30
衡东县	7856	46	9029	64	71956	45	2298.25	31
常宁市	10197	24	11684	37	74323	39	2208.49	35
祁东县	9320	29	16551	8	69376	47	2322.05	27
邵阳市	85154		129437		697499		1825.40	
邵阳市区	5180		6494					
双清区	1818	115	1515	122				
大祥区	1585	121	1599	121				
北塔区	1777	117	3380	113			2109.65	43
武冈市	7972	44	9775	58	53793	61	1795.65	79
邵东县	15320	5	18868	4	167999	2	2481.78	21
新邵县	6575	62	9320	63	63035	53	1874.23	73
邵阳县	6977	58	9907	55	73827	41	1706.64	84
隆回县	9654	26	15864	11	61445	55	1267.81	97
洞口县	8299	38	11976	35	57909	58	1966.93	64
绥宁县	7728	49	9664	59	30444	73	2032.73	49
新宁县	5156	80	7360	87	24144	83	1511.40	91
城步县	3196	105	7069	90	19365	91	1228.31	99
岳阳市	93422		136619		995402		2077.89	
岳阳市区	15490		13909					
岳阳楼区	9111	32	7266	89				
云溪区	1787	116	2614	117				
君山区	4592	87	4029	107			3219.97	6
汨罗市	9338	28	13206	26	78344	33	2188.21	37
临湘市	7777	47	9929	54	66018	50	2047.42	48
岳阳县	5565	77	10662	49	103357	17	2002.01	58
华容县	7725	50	11514	40	91917	25	2072.09	46
湘阴县	8026	42	11073	43	72483	43	2122.27	42
平江县	8089	41	14482	15	72354	44	1280.49	95
常德市	99988		142806		905297		2054.71	
常德市区	15422		21335					
武陵区	4525	88	5711	98	6342	100	3069.89	7
鼎城区	10897	17	15624	13	141844	5	2022.32	52
津市市	5744	73	6743	93	61068	57	2080.88	45
安乡县	6887	60	9370	60	63208	52	1979.53	63

19—1 续表 22 (1997 年)

县市名称	地方财政收入		地方财政支出		社会消费品零售总额		农民全年人均纯收入	
	绝对数（万元）	位次	绝对数（万元）	位次	绝对数（万元）	位次	绝对数（元）	位次
汉寿县	9144	30	11618	39	80545	30	1984.55	62
澧 县	10442	23	13546	25	102019	19	2015.01	55
临澧县	6535	65	8700	68	68774	48	2319.98	28
桃源县	11953	11	14334	17	149713	4	2145.45	40
石门县	8268	40	12113	34	95010	24	1691.85	85
张家界市	24807		46813		147379		1440.55	
张家界市区	8918		12373					
永定区	5126	81	7931	78	56010	59	1589.39	87
武陵源区	3792	99	4442	105	334	101	1587.54	88
慈利县	7763	48	10676	48	54800	60	1576.67	89
桑植县	4367	89	13705	23	27206	80	1090.30	102
益阳市	49764		86134		574342		1760.97	
益阳市区	14953		17567					
资阳区	4146	94	7423	86	102292	18	1871.73	74
赫山区	10807	18	10144	52	127959	6	2138.08	41
沅江市	8391	36	12943	30	72496	42	1861.65	75
南 县	7306	54	10724	47	104764	14	1910.03	71
桃江县	7431	53	11119	42	78064	34	2069.32	47
安化县	7946	45	14479	16	88764	26	985.22	111
郴州市	98348		128866		787754		1911.84	
郴州市区	12612		17728					
北湖区	6476	66	9901	56	75323	36	2026.67	50
苏仙区	6136	68	7827	79	40462	70	2254.32	33
资兴市	8935	33	11280	41	76887	35	2212.29	34
桂阳县	12410	10	13165	27	71622	46	2148.01	39
永兴县	8314	37	9850	57	74180	40	1964.43	65
宜章县	8740	34	10589	50	98425	20	2003.80	56
嘉禾县	7581	51	8657	69	36818	71	2003.00	57
临武县	6891	59	7995	75	20351	90	1943.41	67
汝城县	5668	76	8858	66	25346	82	1144.95	100
桂东县	1609	120	5139	101	9714	99	1064.88	103
安仁县	6541	64	7520	83	27685	79	1803.66	78
娄底地区	57630		85771		519779		1725.50	
娄底市	15817	4	16949	7	108789	12	2480.94	22
冷水江市	11079	15	12551	33	104407	15	2083.47	44
涟源市	10455	22	12899	32	122533	7	2206.92	36
双峰县	9114	31	13145	28	88040	27	1994.05	60

县市名称	地方财政收入		地方财政支出		社会消费品零售总额		农民全年人均纯收入	
	绝对数（万元）	位次	绝对数（万元）	位次	绝对数（万元）	位次	绝对数（元）	位次
新华县	9361	27	17367	6	96008	22	1005.30	110
永州市	72114		111591		537504		1858.79	
永州市区								
芝山区	4284	91	8055	74	81046	29	1999.87	59
冷水滩区	3985	95	7967	76	79545	31	1951.49	66
东安县	5778	72	7327	88	49608	63	1993.98	61
道　县	7006	57	8646	70	44161	67	2015.14	54
宁远县	6650	61	8876	65	61376	56	1547.58	90
江永县	3967	97	5182	100	23501	84	1929.10	69
江华县	4201	93	8734	67	29916	75	1260.55	98
蓝山县	5031	83	6110	95	20901	86	1858.70	76
新田县	3145	106	7621	82	17351	95	1009.29	109
双牌县	2835	109	4313	106	13785	97	1914.37	70
祁阳县	10789	19	13814	22	79455	32	2017.08	53
怀化地区	76098		115791		536278		1525.24	
怀化市	14358	6	15806	12	121824	8	1750.31	81
洪江市	2450	111	3433	112	29953	74	2025.99	51
黔阳县	5978	70	7445	85	45913	65	1828.38	77
沅陵县	8712	35	14208	19	65505	51	1023.68	107
辰溪县	5694	74	7934	77	46446	64	1468.91	93
溆浦县	7973	43	10371	51	75019	37	1677.51	86
麻阳县	4364	90	8082	73	25500	81	1268.73	96
新晃县	3280	104	7495	84	18098	94	1293.81	94
芷江县	4895	86	6922	91	29788	76	1752.13	80
会同县	4957	85	6093	96	27992	78	1747.88	82
靖州县	5678	75	5016	102	29399	77	1888.08	72
通道县	3426	102	5575	99	20837	87	976.67	112
湘西自治州	32077		101968		287492		1079.27	
吉首市	5500	79	11839	36	98075	21	1508.21	92
泸溪县	2101	114	6788	92	21143	85	953.18	114
凤凰县	3452	101	14326	18	34767	72	1046.54	105
花垣县	2841	108	8625	71	18773	93	1018.26	108
保靖县	1687	118	7805	81	16648	96	1062.07	104
古丈县	995	122	4635	104	10739	98	974.85	113
永顺县	3564	100	11620	38	45507	66	1027.82	706
龙山县	5521	78	14141	20	41837	69	1093.17	101

19—2 城乡个体工商业分县排序(1997年)

Basic Statistics Industry and Commerce in Crban and Rural Areasby Counry

县市名称	个体工商户		从业人员(人)	注册资本(万元)	销售总额或营业收入(万元)
	位次	户数(户)			
合　计		1800927	4294156	1656926	7375451
邵东县	1	57120	95682	58565	350788
新化县	2	43000	127200	21180	146990
鼎城区	3	39018	101446	46822	103968
双峰县	4	38762	112229	26054	131309
浏阳市	5	38167	133245	74633	64095
涟源县	6	37528	92000	30086	164045
桃源县	7	37070	99070	20116	124998
岳阳楼区	8	36911	108515	41376	95841
耒阳市	9	36628	91916	30075	47349
醴陵县	10	34324	74152	31555	143819
宁乡县	11	30010	96705	27852	153033
新邵县	12	28657	57245	27807	71275
祁东县	13	28321	69937	52973	95710
澧　县	14	28038	63834	28891	35642
溆浦县	15	27096	8819	11196	43899
常宁县	16	26770	69970	15001	74346
湘潭县	17	25305	51992	25310	79594
攸　县	18	24824	61263	31937	138925
怀化市	19	24463	62387	19924	50586
衡南县	20	24287	72665	15920	32179
汉寿县	21	24277	43591	19614	51031
衡阳县	22	23385	83193	24943	165922
娄底市	23	22580	55260	11670	96330
临澧县	24	22000	53300	16301	30000
石门县	25	21260	47800	17900	78900
邵阳县	26	21076	47612	8067	48552
武冈县	27	21016	51312	14959	67530
洞口县	28	21004	45582	13331	81593
衡东县	29	20770	64996	19035	136790
湘乡县	30	20040	43428	29813	119455
祁阳县	31	20004	49908	17722	41511
冷水江市	32	19927	51228	15652	162582
宜章县	33	19550	57585	36086	162711
慈利县	34	18896	36760	13588	40273

注:本表由省工商管理局提供。

19—2 续表 1

(1997 年)

县市名称	个体工商户		从业人员	注册资本	销售总额或营业收入
	位次	户数(户)	(人)	(万元)	(万元)
	35	18445	36911	17877	69194
永兴县	36	18267	45828	11705	117697
桂阳县	37	17926	37590	14822	8039
沅陵县	38	17750	20239	15561	34979
茶陵县	39	17608	44020	8860	44000
安乡县	40	17437	52340	18367	21164
安仁县	41	16031	31036	10218	17476
湘阴县	42	16006	59748	16008	69892
资兴市	43	15878	32453	8779	93667
嘉禾县	44	15451	37617	8587	30485
益阳赫山区	45	15074	29845	8469	35964
安化县	46	15017	27997	5778	71164
吉首市	47	15002	33129	6739	37846
龙山县	48	14475	39169	22250	53879
长沙县	49	14302	26909	4294	33474
辰溪县	50	14018	29175	7333	47135
永顺县	51	13993	30620	18721	49338
长沙天心区	52	13782	23712	12251	46166
黔阳县	53	13745	29684	8372	25812
桃江县	54	13500	27000	6325	40290
永定区	55	13370	30231	7064	19443
临湘市	56	13184	26771	14997	21354
新宁县	57	13176	46000	5644	11602
望城县	58	12621	33999	9785	9746
汝城县	59	12181	27033	14785	51353
隆回县	60	12110	28621	12225	37238
湘潭雨湖区	61	12050	43732	47236	116880
凤凰县	62	12001	21721	3709	17403
汨罗市	63	11985	28417	6387	50889
沅江县	64	11792	24673	8328	33695
平江县	65	11270	26754	2880	14718
冷水滩	66	11056	30305	22730	66207
郴州苏仙区	67	10867	23497	11027	53906
长沙芙蓉区	68	10738	31305	6370	121600
麻阳县	69	10725	23815	7279	51250

19—2　续表 2　　(1997 年)

县市名称	个体工商户		从业人员	注册资本	销售总额或营业收入
	位次	户数(户)	(人)	(万元)	(万元)
绥宁县	70	10559	26153	7560	21591
岳阳县	71	10318	20203	2755	2789
东安县	72	10161	23463	9390	41915
长沙开福区	73	9981	34000	7326	6616
芷江县	74	9980	239008	3047	17473
南　县	75	9862	21552	6574	25486
衡山县	76	9753	27621	19784	20846
益阳资阳区	77	9714	20594	5085	28366
蓝山县	78	9608	23050	15086	133087
华容县	79	9518	17956	5494	35960
湘潭岳塘区	80	9505	32919	7723	79841
花垣县	81	8298	15472	4637	22495
郴州直属所	82	8279	18736	9791	136282
靖州县	83	8230	14300	4230	32270
新晃县	84	8210	13188	4088	21166
株洲县	85	8172	16664	2476	30852
津市市	86	8035	18292	6219	41215
益阳运管所	87	8023	23412	12860	15505
长沙岳麓区	88	7860	31000	3930	57633
永州芝山分局	89	7465	16418	3061	23043
通道县	90	7287	12271	3589	23546
新田县	91	7208	13000	1461	9222
泸溪县	92	6911	12036	3499	28683
道　县	93	6817	15375	5310	22799
保靖县	94	6742	9745	2183	3051
邵阳市东区	95	6255	14645	8340	113579
宁远县	96	6058	16699	5224	30125
城步县	97	5988	12145	4393	13956
桑植县	98	5892	11610	2197	14589
岳阳市场分局	99	5805	13768	3306	31244
会同县	100	5481	10829	5498	18625
江永县	101	5005	9071	5445	12811
江华县	102	4638	8690	5495	14893
洪江市	103	4129	7832	3521	36497
衡阳市郊区	104	4085	8476	4441	7609

19—2　续表 3　　(1997 年)

县市名称	个体工商户		从业人员	注册资本	销售总额或营业收入
	位次	户数(户)	(人)	(万元)	(万元)
双牌县	105	4002	5252	3266	3435
邵阳市西区	106	3749	7207	2463	42304
岳阳云溪区	107	3583	4607	1679	4664
常德城西分局	108	3518	4668	5183	9442
常德城东分局	109	3512	8779	3056	13286
炎陵县	110	3492	5232	1959	8215
衡阳城北区	111	3480	13780	3700	24058
衡阳市直管局	112	3447	10140	8162	99433
桂东县	113	3329	5340	1770	9424
邵阳市郊区	114	3193	9194	3211	50521
益阳市农场分局	115	3162	6928	2103	5807
衡阳江东区	116	2907	11432	3674	140560
岳阳开发区	117	2911	4783	4588	12500
岳阳君山区	118	2680	4321	900	8540
韶山市	119	2514	5505	2349	7603
岳阳屈原分局	120	2421	3882	1535	2558
岳阳市钱粮湖	121	2413	3484	1893	8011
长沙市直属局	122	2200	5000	1400	1360
郴州北湖区	123	2188	4096	3259	14281
湘潭个体分局	124	2100	5670	16066	25076
古丈县	125	1886	2354	639	5671
湘潭布市分局	126	1863	3471	3724	59300
张家界武陵源	127	1830	3980	1296	4525
衡阳南岳区	128	1698	2925	1985	6306
常德西洞庭农场	129	1625	2633	3873	5560
长沙东塘分局	130	1231	2115	720	646
常德西湖农场	131	1120	1456	660	2400
衡阳市城南区	132	970	3937	374	6465
常德生资分局	133	931	1831	8295	216400
常德德山分局	134	570	1454	624	2851
湘潭市高新区	135	456	896	202	2695
湘潭民主路分局	136	289	487	82	990
永州凤凰园分局	137	267	523	509	8568
常德贺家山农场	138	205	333	201	409
衡阳市开发区	139	175	334	236	796

二十、各行业按主要指标企业排序

RANKING OF ENTERPRISES BY MAIN INDICATOR BY SECTOR

20—1 十强工业企业(1997年)

The 10 Most Powerful Industrial Enterprises Among All Industrial Enterprises

名次	法人单位名称	名次	法人单位名称
	工业总产值最高十企业		**销售收入最多十企业**
1	中国巴陵石油化工公司	1	中国巴陵石油化工公司
2	长沙卷烟厂	2	长沙卷烟厂
3	常德卷烟厂	3	常德卷烟厂
4	涟钢股份有限公司	4	涟钢股份有限公司
5	中国南方航空动力机械公司	5	湘潭钢铁公司
6	株洲冶炼厂	6	中国南方航空动力机械公司
7	湘潭钢铁公司	7	株洲冶炼厂
8	远大空调有限公司	8	零陵卷烟厂
9	湖南曙光电子集团公司	9	乐金曙光电子有限公司
10	零陵卷烟厂	10	郴州卷烟厂
	增加值最高十企业		**实现利税最多十企业**
1	长沙卷烟厂	1	长沙卷烟厂
2	常德卷烟厂	2	常德卷烟厂
3	中国巴陵石油化工公司	3	零陵卷烟厂
4	零陵卷烟厂	4	郴州卷烟厂
5	涟钢股份有限公司	5	中国南方航空动力机械公司
6	中国南方航空动力机械公司	6	湘西自治州湘泉酒总厂
7	湘潭钢铁公司	7	中国巴陵石油化工公司
8	郴州卷烟厂	8	远大空调有限公司
9	远大空调有限公司	9	湖南旺旺食品有限公司
10	湘西自治州湘泉酒总厂	10	涟钢股份有限公司
	固定资产规模最大十企业		**容纳劳动最多十企业**
1	中国巴陵石油化工公司	1	中国巴陵石油化工公司
2	湘潭钢铁公司	2	涟邵矿务局
3	涟钢股份有限公司	3	湘潭钢铁公司
4	长沙卷烟厂	4	涟钢股份有限公司
5	中国南方航空动力机械公司	5	湖南省白沙矿务局
6	株洲冶炼厂	6	资兴矿务局
7	常德卷烟厂	7	中国南方航空动力机械公司
8	乐金曙光电子有限公司	8	南方通用电气集团公司
9	涟邵矿务局	9	株洲电力机车厂
10	衡阳钢管厂	10	江南机器厂

20—2 十强交通运输企业(1997年)

The 10 Most Powerfnl Transportation Enterprises Amorg All Transportation Enterprises

名次	法人单位名称	名次	法人单位名称
	旅客周转量最大的公路运输企业前十名		**货物周转量最大的水运企业前十名**
1	常德汽车运输总公司	1	湖南省远洋运输公司
2	邵阳汽车运输总公司	2	岳阳市水运总公司
3	湖南省衡阳汽车运输总公司	3	常德市水运公司
4	长沙汽车客运发展(集团)公司	4	湖南岳阳港务总公司
5	湖南省怀化汽车运输总公司	5	常德轮船运输总公司
6	郴州市汽车运输总公司	6	津市轮船总公司
7	湖南省永州汽车运输总公司	7	湘阴县航运总公司
8	湖南省益阳汽车运输总公司	8	湖南省望城航运总公司
9	株洲运输集团有限责任公司	9	湖南长沙运贸总公司
10	湖南岳阳汽车运输总公司	10	湖南省益阳市轮船实业总公司
	货物周转量最大的公路运输企业前十名		**主营业务收入最多的交通运输企业前十名**
1	长沙长途汽车货运公司	1	邵阳汽车运输总公司
2	长沙市第二运输公司	2	长沙汽车客运发展(集团)公司
3	常德汽车运输总公司	3	湖南省怀化汽车运输总公司
4	长沙市联运总公司	4	湖南省衡阳汽车运输总公司
5	湖南省怀化汽车运输总公司	5	株洲运输集团有限责任公司
6	湖南岳阳汽车运输总公司	6	常德汽车运输总公司
7	湖南外运衡阳市公司	7	湖南省远洋运输公司
8	湖南省衡阳汽车运输总公司	8	湖南省益阳汽车运输总公司
9	湖南省益阳市陆运公司	9	长沙市联运总公司
10	郴州市第一运输公司	10	郴州市汽车运输总公司
	旅客周转量最大的水运企业前十名		
1	长沙市港务局		
2	湖南省安乡县拾比佰航运有限公司		
3	湖南省安乡县航运总公司		
4	沅江市运输处		
5	华容县航运公司		
6	湖南省益阳市轮船实业总公司		
7	沅江市水运公司		
8	安化县航运总公司		
9	湖南省益阳市水运公司		
10	溆浦县航运公司		

20—3 50强建筑施工企业(1997年)

The 50 Most Powerful Construction Enterprises

名次	法人单位名称	名次	法人单位名称
	完成施工产值前50名企业		**实现利税总额前50名企业**
1	中国水利水电第八工程局	1	中国水利水电第八工程局
2	湖南省公路桥梁建设总公司	2	铁道部第五工程局新线铁路运输处
3	中建五局第二建筑安装公司	3	中国建筑第五工程局第三建筑安装公司
4	湖南省第六工程公司	4	铁道部第五工程局电务工程处
5	中国建筑第五工程局第三建筑安装公司	5	湖南省火电建设公司
6	湖南省火电建设公司	6	中建五局第二建筑安装公司
7	湖南省第三工程公司	7	湖南省第六工程公司
8	湖南省第四工程公司	8	湖南省第三工程公司
9	中国化学工程第四建设公司	9	衡阳县第二建筑工程公司
10	中国有色第二十三冶金建设公司	10	湖南省第四工程公司
11	湖南省建工集团第五工程公司	11	岳阳市公路桥梁基建总公司
12	铁道部第五工程局新线铁路运输处	12	长沙高岭建筑总公司
13	湖南建工程集团工业设备安装公司	13	长沙望新建筑工程公司
14	湖南省送变电建设公司	14	中国化学工程第四建设公司
15	中国建筑第五工程局第五工程公司	15	长沙市基建工程公司
16	广州铁路第三工程公司	16	广州铁路第三工程公司
17	铁道部第五工程局机械筑路工程处	17	湖南建工集团工业设备安装公司
18	铁道部第五工程局电务工程处	18	澧县第三建筑工程公司
19	铁道部第五工程局第二工程处	19	湖南省送变电建设公司
20	中建五局机械施工公司	20	铁道部第五工程局机械筑路工程处
21	长沙市建筑工程公司	21	中国建筑第五工程局工业设备安装有限公司
22	湖南环达公路桥梁建筑总公司	22	湖南省公路桥梁建设总公司
23	岳阳市公路桥梁基建总公司	23	长沙县螺丝塘建筑工程总公司
24	长沙高岭建筑总公司	24	湘乡市新研建筑工程公司
25	长沙望新建筑工程公司	25	常德市第四建筑工程公司
26	长沙洞井建筑公司	26	湖南省水电安装工程公司
27	中国第五工程局第一建筑安装公司	27	中国建筑第五工程局第五工程公司
28	湖南省水电安装工程公司	28	长沙县黄花建筑机械化施工公司
29	衡阳县第二建筑工程公司	29	长沙格塘建筑工程公司
30	长沙黎托建筑工程公司	30	铁道部第五工程局第二工程处
31	长沙市建筑安装工程公司	31	湖南省耒阳市城关建筑公司
32	中国建筑第五工程局工业设备安装有限公司	32	湖南省水利水电第二工程公司
33	郴州工程公司	33	长沙望城建筑安装工程公司
34	长沙县黄花建筑机械化施工公司	34	长沙北山建筑工程公司
35	长沙北山建筑工程公司	35	长沙洞井建筑公司
36	长沙县暮云镇南托建筑公司	36	湖南长大建设集团公司
37	长沙南托建筑工程公司	37	祁东县华厦建筑安装工程公司
38	长沙望城建筑安装工程公司	38	湖南省建工集团第五工程公司
39	浏阳市永安建筑工程公司	39	长沙市市政工程公司
40	长沙市捞刀河建筑有限公司	40	岳阳市云溪区第一建筑工程公司
41	祁东县华厦建筑安装工程公司	41	道县道江镇建筑公司
42	湘乡市新研建筑工程公司	42	浏阳市永安建筑工程公司
43	长沙县星沙建筑集团公司	43	长沙县星沙镇建筑工程公司
44	湖南长大建设集团公司	44	湘潭县狮山建筑公司
45	广州铁路第六工程公司	45	郴州工程公司
46	湖南省邮电建设工程局	46	广州铁路第六工程公司
47	长沙沙坪建筑总公司	47	广州铁路长沙电务工程公司
48	澧县第三建筑工程公司	48	双峰县花门镇建筑工程公司
49	湖南省水利水电第二工程公司	49	长沙友仁建筑公司
50	娄底地区建筑工程公司	50	醴陵市东富建筑工程公司

20—4 50强房地产开发企业(1997年)

The 50 Most Powerful Real Estute Development Enterprises

名次	法人单位名称	名次	法人单位名称
	完成投资前50名		**房屋销售面积前50名**
1	湖南湘迪置业发展有限公司	1	岳阳市华厦苑置业有限公司
2	湖南新华联置业有限公司	2	衡阳市城市建设开发总公司
3	湖南铁银房地产开发人司	3	衡阳市华达房地产开发公司
4	岳阳市华厦苑置业有限公司	4	湘潭信泰物业开发有限公司
5	长沙市城市建设开发公司	5	永州市三泰房地产开发总公司
6	长沙市天心区城市建设开发公司	6	湘潭市城郊房地产开发总公司
7	益阳市房地产开发投资公司	7	长沙市城市建设开发公司
8	长沙通发房地产开发总公司	8	鸿铭(湖南)置业发展有限公司
9	长沙房地产开发承包公司	9	长沙市旧城改建开发公司
10	鸿铭(湖南)置业发展有限公司	10	常德市房地产开发公司
11	湖南安基房地产开发有限公司	11	新化县城建开发公司
12	长沙市房地产开发公司	12	湖南鸿都房地产开发有限公司
13	湖南金敏物业开发有限公司	13	湘潭市汇丰房地产综合开发公司
14	湖南中意集团房地产开发公司	14	凯达(湖南)房地产开发有限公司
15	中房集团株洲房地产开发公司	15	湘潭市房地产开发公司
16	湖南省振中房地产开发公司	16	保利实业发展有限公司
17	湖南佳程房地产开发有限公司	17	常德市华达建设开发总公司
18	凯达(湖南)房地产开发有限公司	18	衡阳市房地产综合开发总公司
19	湖南新富城房地产开发公司	19	邵阳市住宅建设开发公司
20	湖南银港房地产开发有限公司	20	湘乡市城市建设综合开发公司
21	湖南高宝利房地产开发有限公司	21	衡阳市湘衡房地产开发公司
22	湖南日恒物业开发有限公司	22	永州市财盛房地产开发总公司
23	长沙咸嘉房地产开发有限公司	23	长沙恒达房地产开发有限公司
24	常德市华达建设开发总公司	24	新晃县开发区房地产公司
25	长沙市福利房地产开发公司	25	湖南常德湘北房地产开发公司
26	湖南省安居房地产开发有限公司	26	衡阳市天创房地产综合开发公司
27	湖南省建筑房地产开发公司	27	常德市武陵房地产综合开发公司
28	粤湘邵阳公司	28	邵阳市泰诚投资开发有限公司
29	湖南拓展集团有限公司	29	湘西自治州城乡建设综合开发公司
30	怀化铁路总公司房地产开发公司	30	常德市城市建设综合开发公司
31	湖南石油房地产开发公司	31	深圳安华衡阳房地产开发公司
32	新化县城建开发公司	32	祁阳县房地产公司
33	怀化九龙物业发展有限公司	33	湖南省华侨住宅开发总公司
34	永州市三泰房地产开发总公司	34	衡阳科欣置业有限公司
35	湖南富华房地产开发公司	35	湘潭大同世界实业股份有限公司
36	湘潭市城郊房地产开发总公司	36	郴州市华成房地产开发公司
37	岳阳康泽置业有限公司	37	湖南省同发置业有限公司
38	长沙望城坡房地产开发总公司	38	湖南日恒物业开发有限公司
39	常德市城市建设综合开发公司	39	常德实通房地产开发公司
40	株洲市家园房地产开发有限公司	40	桃江县房改办
41	长沙建银房地产开发公司	41	衡阳市永兴建设开发有限公司
42	长沙四方房地产开发公司	42	衡阳百事泰房地产股份有限公司
43	邵阳市房地产开发总公司	43	湖南省华航房地产开发公司
44	衡阳市雁城房地产综合开发公司	44	石门县房地产管理局
45	邵阳市泰诚投资开发有限公司	45	常德华星宇房产物业开发公司
46	长沙新大新置业有限公司	46	湖南泰华房地产开发有限公司
47	衡阳科欣置业有限公司	47	郴州市城市建设综合开发实业总公司
48	长沙市公用设施建设开发公司	48	益阳市城建综合开发公司
49	永州市财盛房地产开发总公司	49	岳阳银威房地产有限公司
50	湖南对外建设总公司	50	湖南高新实业股份有限公司

20—5 50强国内商业企业(1997年)

The 50 Most Powerful Wholesale and Retail Trade Enterprise

名次	法人单位名称	名次	法人单位名称
	批发企业按完成销售额排序		**零售企业按完成销售额排序**
1	中国烟草总公司湖南省公司	1	长沙友谊(集团)有限公司
2	长沙市烟草公司	2	湖南五一文实业股份有限公司
3	湖南省农业生产资料总公司	3	长沙通程实业(集团)有限公司
4	湖南省粮油食品进出口公司	4	长沙阿波罗商业城
5	湖南省机电设备总公司	5	长沙中山商业(集团)股份有限公司
6	株洲市烟草公司	6	衡阳市金果实业股份有限公司
7	湖南省新华书店	7	长沙市粮食连锁店
8	湖南省金属材料总公司	8	衡阳市供销大厦股份有限公司
9	长沙县烟草专卖局	9	株洲百货股份有限公司
10	湖南省进出口总公司	10	湖南省岳阳市九洲大厦
11	湖南省商业集团总公司	11	衡阳市食品总公司
12	湖南汽车贸易(集团)总公司	12	长沙大厦
13	湘潭市烟草公司	13	岳阳九龙商厦
14	长沙泰阳商城	14	长沙县路口区供销合作社
15	湖南长沙市石油总公司	15	株洲庆云发展股份有限公司
16	长沙市物资集团公司	16	株洲市前进百货股份有限公司
17	岳阳市第一百货大楼	17	娄底地区湘中商业大厦
18	桂阳县烟草公司	18	华容县粮油总公司
19	湖南省机械设备进出口公司	19	长沙市新华书店
20	湖南省轻工业总公司进出口公司	20	湖南省岳阳商大实业有限公司
21	湖南省国际经济开发(集团)公司	21	双峰县食品公司
22	湖南省工艺品进出口公司	22	桃源县陬溪中心供销社
23	湖南华升工贸进出口(集团)公司	23	长沙县榔梨区供销社
24	湖南省烟草公司衡阳市公司	24	株洲市蔬菜食品总公司
25	湖南省纺织品进出口公司	25	湖南国储实业有限公司国储商业城
26	湖南省物资建材(集团)总公司	26	湘潭百货大楼集团公司
27	湖南省烟草公司浏阳市卷烟经理部	27	株洲市宏源商业物资公司
28	湖南省土产畜产进出口公司	28	株洲市药业有限责任公司
29	湖南省华湘进出口(集团)公司	29	长沙县福临区供销社
30	湖南省石油总公司	30	长沙新兴发展有限公司购物中心
31	湖南省医药保健品进出口公司	31	长沙市黄花区供销社
32	湖南省常德市安乡县棉麻总公司	32	株洲申湘汽车有限责任公司
33	华容县棉麻土产公司	33	冷水江锑都大厦股份有限公司
34	益阳市烟草公司	34	长沙吉申百货公司
35	邵东县百货股份有限公司	35	郴州市燃料贸易总公司
36	龙山县烟草公司	36	桃源县漆河中心供销合作社
37	湖南省物资贸易中心	37	衡阳县西渡供销社
38	湖南省印刷物资总公司	38	湖南省衡阳市新华书店
39	湖南省化工轻工总公司	39	洞口县药材公司
40	衡阳市物资产业集团公司	40	祁东县商城大厦
41	湖南省邮电器材公司	41	衡阳市蒸湘粮贸公司
42	湖南省石油总公司岳阳市公司	42	长沙市医药总公司中华医药器械公司
43	衡阳市飞龙实业有限公司	43	邵阳县药材公司
44	中国土产畜产湖南茶叶进出口公司	44	娄底市新世纪商业大厦
45	南县棉麻总公司	45	常德市新化书店
46	中国物资武汉储运衡阳公司	46	吉首市吉首商场
47	湖南省棉麻总公司	47	常德市中心商贸总公司
48	湖南省医药公司	48	株洲市建设百货商场
49	湖南省金环进出口总公司	49	新化县新华书店
50	澧县棉麻公司	50	祁阳县石油公司

20—6 外经外贸骨干企业(1997年)

Core Enterprise in Foregh Trade

名次	法人单位名称	名次	法人单位名称
	三资企业按销售收入排序前40家		**外贸按进出口总值排序前10家**
1	乐金曙光电子有限公司	1	株洲冶炼厂进出口公司
2	株洲南方雅马哈摩托车有限公司	2	湖南省进出口集团有限公司
3	湖南火炬有色金属有限公司	3	湖南省粮油食品进出口公司
4	岳阳正大有限公司	4	湖南省华隆进出口公司
5	湘钢华光线材有限公司	5	湖南省轻工业品进出口公司
6	株洲南方摩托车制造有限公司	6	湖南工艺品进出口公司
7	湖南旺旺食品有限公司	7	湖南省土产畜产进出口公司
8	湖南光南摩托车有限公司	8	湖南国际经济开发集团公司
9	衡阳市钢管有限公司	9	湖南省金环进出口总公司
10	湖南湘大实业有限公司	10	湖南省化工进出口公司
11	湖南金湘铜业有限公司		**按营业额及外派人员排序前10家**
12	湖南斯伦贝谢通信设备有限公司	1	湖南交通国际工程合作公司
13	湖南金沙彩色印刷有限公司	2	湖南国际经济技术合作公司
14	怀化正大有限公司	3	中国化学工程第四化工建设公司
15	长沙旺旺食品有限公司	4	湖南建筑工程集团总公司
16	岳阳巴陵油脂工业有限公司	5	湖南环球集团公司
17	常德金鹏凹版印刷有限公司	6	湖南省公路桥梁建设总公司
18	湖南长沙华天大酒店	7	中国水利水电第八工程局
19	伊莱克斯中意电冰箱有限公司	8	冶金部长沙冶金设计院
20	株洲南方雅马哈减震器有限公司	9	长沙轻工总会长沙设计院
21	长沙味康食品有限公司	10	湖南省进出口总公司
22	南岳油泵油嘴有限公司		**按业务收入旅行社排序前10家**
23	湖南金狮啤酒有限公司	1	湖南中国国际旅行社
24	岳阳正大农牧发展有限公司	2	湖南华天国际旅行社
25	湖南光远铜管有限公司	3	湖南中国青年旅行社
26	湖南富丽华大酒店	4	长沙中国国际旅行社
27	庆达纺织有限公司	5	衡阳中国国际旅行社
28	株洲普兰特油脂有限公司	6	湖南省中国旅行社
29	长沙正大有限公司	7	长沙电信旅行社
30	衡阳宏湘化工有限公司	8	长沙铁路旅行社
31	湖南中太化纤制品有限公司	9	湖南妇女国际旅行社
32	湖南莱孪铝业有限公司	10	湖南邮电旅行社
33	湖南关西汽车涂料有限公司		
34	湖南三安纺织品有限公司		
35	长沙湘威锦纶制品有限公司		
36	湘潭大阳电磁线有限公司		
37	安乡恒安卫生用品有限公司		
38	岳阳中显房地产公司		
39	湖南江麓一浩利工程有限公司		
40	株洲穗屏饲料有限公司		

20—7　湖南股市20个挂牌上市公司及全省最大的10个餐饮企业名单(1997年)

The 20 Marketable Corporation of HUNAN Provincestock Exchange and The 10 Most Powerful Catering Enterprise of Whole Province

名次	法人单位名称	名次	法人单位名称
	湖南挂牌上市公司名单		**餐饮企业销售收入最高的10家**
1	长沙中意集团股份有限公司	1	长沙市饮食公司玉楼东酒家
2	株洲火炬火花塞股份有限公司	2	长沙市又一村大酒店
3	衡阳古汉集团股份有限公司	3	湖南天心炸鸡实业发展公司
4	湖南海利化工股份有限公司	4	长沙市饮食公司火宫殿酒家
5	湖南华天大酒店股份有限公司	5	株洲车站旅行服务公司
6	长沙东塘百货股份有限公司	6	湖南凤凰餐饮有限公司
7	张家界旅游开发股份有限公司	7	衡阳市穗丰大厦
8	湖南华银电力股份有限公司	8	长沙县开元大酒店
9	岳阳恒立冷气设备股份有限公司	9	衡阳市饮食服务总公司
10	衡阳飞龙实业股份有限公司	10	长沙市二饮食公司新华楼削面馆
11	株洲庆云发展股份有限公司		
12	湖南正虹饲料股份有限公司		
13	衡阳金果农工商实业股份有限公司		
14	南方摩托股份有限公司		
15	湖南五一文实业股份有限公司		
16	岳阳兴长石化股份有限公司		
17	湖南计算机股份有限公司		
18	湖南酒鬼酒股份有限公司		
19	湖南金健米业股份有限公司		
20	湖南华升集团益鑫泰股份有限公司		

长沙市芙蓉区简介

芙蓉区位于古城长沙的东部，与风景秀丽的岳麓山隔江相望。全区现辖8个街道办事处和4个乡镇场。总面积40.8平方公里，人口30万。其中农村面积23.2平方公里，耕地面积10256.5亩，农业人口29469人，1997年乡镇企业总产值36.8亿元，农业总产值1.6亿元，农村人平纯收入3348元。

一、努力发展农村经济，夯实奔小康的经济基础

实现小康，经济是基础。该区把努力发展农村经济，放在奔小康的首要位置，合理调整农村经济结构，促进一、二、三产业的协调发展，加大对外开放和招商引资力度，初步形成了一个以“一优两高”农业为基础，乡镇企业、外向型经济、个体私营经济三足鼎立的乡村经济发展新格局。

第一，强农固本，坚持科技兴农。引导农民走农业产业化的发展道路，逐步形成了粮、菜、猪、鱼、禽、草莓、花卉等七大产业，扶持特种养殖基地年产值达100万元或200万元以上的种养大户5户，全区农业产业化逐步走上了产品市场化、布局区域化、生产科学化、经营企业化的轨道。

第二，大力发展乡镇企业，增强经济实力。先后引进了振升铝材、亚大化工企业、佳亨钢厂等工业企业，并在东岸乡张公岭建成工业小区，形成了以机械、建材、鞋业、医药、消防、软件为重点的产业优势，1997年全区完成乡镇企业总产值现行价　　　亿元，比上年增长　　　%。

第三，加强市场建设，大力发展第三产业。全区各乡临近城区，是长沙市今后重点发展的商住区之一。各乡充分利用这些优势，积极兴办各种娱乐、服务业，建成了东大门市场、三湘大市场、南湖大市场、湘华陶瓷市场、蔬菜批发市场、果品批发市场等大型专业化市场，带动了全区第三产业和区域经济的健康发展。

二、加强基础设施建设，改善农村的生产条件和生活环境

基础设施建设是衡量小康建设的重要标志之一。近三年来，该地区农村投入公益事业资金累计达2.2亿多元，完成水利工程2450处，修建乡村公路120余公里，新改建各类校舍面积3500m^2，实现了村村通公路、通电、通电话，100%的农民饮用安全水，100%的农户通电，程控电话拥有率为60%，农村的面貌得到了很大的改善。

三、努力推进农村精神文明建设，不断优化社会环境

精神文明，既是小康目标的重要内容，又是实现小康的保证。我们在抓精神文明建设中突出抓好了以下几方面的工作：一是努力提高人口素质。全面推行“三优”(优生、优育、优教)工程，培养了一大批少生快富的典型，全区计生率、晚育率、节育率均达100%。同时，全面推行九年制义务教育，学龄儿童入学率达100%，中学入学率达100%。二是丰富农民精神生活。该区每年定期举办文艺汇演，开展卡拉OK、乒乓球、拔河赛等一系列活动，农民家庭对文化生活的投入也大幅度增加，电视机普及率为100%。三是建立社会保障制度，加快扶贫帮困工作。全区对贫困户实行定期跟踪调查，并通过对口扶贫使其全面实现脱贫。全区实行了退休养老金制度和对五保户实行敬老供养制，所有的五保人口生活均得到保障。四是整治社会秩序，使农民群众安居乐业。从1995年开始，该区广泛开展创社会治安模范单位、模范乡镇、模范村活动，强化农村社会治安综合管理，严厉打击各种违法犯罪，切实保障了人民群众的生命财产安全。

二十一、各省市主要经济社会统计指标

MAIN ECONOMIC AND SOCIAL INDICATORS BY PROVINCES

21—1 各省市国内生产总值和人均国内生产总值(1997年)

GDP and Per Capta GDP by Region(1997)

地　　区	国内生产总值(亿元)	第一产业	第二产业	第三产业	国内生产总值比上年增长(%)	人均国内生产总值(元/人)
北　京	1807.5	85.0	750.8	971.7	9.5	16658
天　津	1240.3	74.5	643.9	521.9	12.1	13700
河　北	3950.5	760.0	1927.3	1263.1	12.5	6073
山　西	1480.0	189.9	797.7	492.4	10.5	4736
内蒙古	1088.0	317.0	443.0	328.0	9.1	4663
辽　宁	3501.2	474.0	1737.2	1290.0	9.0	8519
吉　林	1450.4	375.1	570.1	505.2	9.5	5515
黑龙江	2710.0	500.0	1460.0	750.0	10.0	7246
上　海	3360.2	75.80	1754.4	1530.0	12.7	25739
江　苏	6685.6	1010.9	3414.6	2260.1	12.0	9352
浙　江	4600.0	635.0	2460.0	1505.0	11.0	10400
安　徽	2670.6	722.0	1270.6	678.0	13.0	4359
福　建	3000.4	619.5	1247.9	1133.0	14.3	9173
江　西	1715.0	475.0	670.0	570.0	11.5	4155
山　东	6650.0	1195.0	3185.1	2270.0	11.2	7590
河　南	4080.5	1050.1	1879.5	1150.9	10.5	4432
湖　北	3450.2	767.9	1607.0	1075.3	13.0	5899
湖　南	2993.0	855.7	1167.0	970.3	10.8	4643
广　东	7308.2	986.9	3666.3	2655.0	10.6	10400
广　西	2065.2	658.0	771.1	636.1	9.1	4469
海　南	418.0	158.4	84.3	175.3	6.7	5816
重　庆	1375.0	308.0	582.0	485.0	11.5	4535
四　川	3320.1	919.3	1385.4	1015.5	10.2	4027
贵　州	790.3	278.4	284.3	227.6	9.0	2207
云　南	1625.5	398.6	724.5	502.3	9.3	3996
西　藏						
陕　西	1345.0	286.9	552.2	505.9	10.0	3760
甘　肃	781.3	192.6	343.4	245.3	8.8	3137
青　海	202.0	40.6	79.1	82.3	9.0	4065
宁　夏	211.4	44.8	86.6	80.0	7.6	4018
新　疆	1050.0	280.0	413.0	357.0	10.8	5856

注:1. 本表绝对数按当年价格计算,指数按可比价格计算。

2. 由于四舍五入的原因,各项相加不完全等于总计。

21—2 各省市总人口和出生率、死亡率、自然增长率(1997年)

Total Poputation and Birth Rate. Death Rate and Natural Growth Rate by Region(1997)

地区	年底总人口(万人)	出生率(‰)	死亡率(‰)	自然增长率(‰)
北京	1240	7.91	6.02	1.89
天津	953	9.98	6.95	3.03
河北	6525	13.11	6.82	6.29
山西	3141	16.18	6.06	10.12
内蒙古	2326	15.21	6.96	8.25
辽宁	4138	11.78	6.38	5.40
吉林	2628	12.22	5.42	6.80
黑龙江	3751	12.02	5.17	6.85
上海	1457	5.50	6.80	—1.30
江苏	7148	11.43	6.84	4.59
浙江	4435	11.41	6.48	4.93
安徽	6127	15.80	6.50	9.30
福建	3282	12.41	6.09	6.32
江西	4150	17.43	6.56	10.87
山东	8785	11.28	6.65	4.63
河南	9243	13.97	6.30	7.67
湖北	5873	14.81	6.69	8.12
湖南	6465	12.59	6.99	5.60
广东	7051	16.90	5.40	11.50
广西	4633	15.93	6.40	9.53
海南	743	19.18	5.62	13.56
重庆	3042	13.60	7.36	6.24
四川	8430	15.75	7.00	8.75
贵州	3606	22.15	7.67	14.48
云南	4094	20.82	7.91	12.91
西藏	248	23.90	7.90	16.00
陕西	3570	13.91	6.29	7.62
甘肃	2494	17.22	6.20	11.02
青海	496	21.80	6.95	14.85
宁夏	530	18.90	5.43	13.47
新疆	1718	19.66	6.55	13.11

21—3 各省市职工人数(1997年)

Namber of Staff and Workers by Region(1997)

单位:万人

地　　区	年末人数	国有经济单位	集体经济单位	联营经济单位	股份制经济单位	外商投资经济单位	港澳台投资经济单位	其他经济单位
北　　京	465.3	348.7	65.0	3.0	18.4	20.2	9.6	0.5
天　　津	281.3	191.6	55.3	1.9	6.0	17.5	8.2	0.9
河　　北	676.7	531.5	112.1	0.8	16.6	7.9	7.5	0.3
山　　西	455.9	364.3	82.3	0.2	5.8	1.8	1.4	0.1
内 蒙 古	363.9	291.9	59.4	0.2	7.1	2.8	2.1	0.3
辽　　宁	969.4	651.3	257.0	4.6	29.4	18.6	8.5	0.1
吉　　林	500.9	375.9	100.2	0.4	15.1	7.3	1.8	0.2
黑 龙 江	797.0	608.2	157.9	0.5	20.4	4.6	4.6	0.7
上　　海	435.3	292.8	71.2	2.0	30.3	25.8	11.9	1.3
江　　苏	893.7	577.5	239.6	8.6	21.4	23.2	20.2	3.3
浙　　江	482.3	285.0	144.5	2.2	23.0	14.4	12.7	0.4
安　　徽	502.6	353.1	119.7	0.8	21.4	3.9	2.3	1.5
福　　建	357.7	215.6	54.8	2.7	8.8	31.8	43.7	0.3
江　　西	409.4	334.0	67.7	0.1	2.5	2.4	2.4	0.3
山　　东	937.6	665.6	190.9	1.4	38.5	28.5	12.8	…
河　　南	841.3	602.8	176.9	0.9	44.2	7.1	8.6	0.9
湖　　北	735.4	560.1	126.5	1.8	36.2	4.6	5.4	0.8
湖　　南	597.5	471.5	110.5	0.4	8.5	3.5	2.9	0.2
广　　东	897.3	544.5	179.6	5.8	28.4	42.4	95.6	1.1
广　　西	340.0	280.7	42.6	0.4	7.3	6.4	2.0	0.5
海　　南	102.6	86.5	8.3	0.8	3.0	2.2	1.8	0.1
重　　庆	289.3	211.1	61.6	0.4	11.6	2.7	1.8	0.1
四　　川	681.6	506.2	131.0	0.6	35.8	3.6	1.8	2.5
贵　　州	232.8	196.1	31.3	0.5	2.7	1.4	0.6	0.3
云　　南	313.7	265.1	39.1	0.4	5.7	1.4	1.9	0.1
西　　藏	16.7	15.4	1.1	…	…	0.1	—	…
陕　　西	396.2	335.1	52.4	0.3	6.0	1.3	0.8	0.5
甘　　肃	246.7	208.1	35.2	0.1	1.5	1.1	0.3	0.3
青　　海	63.7	55.5	7.5	0.3	0.2	0.1	0.2	—
宁　　夏	73.9	61.7	8.6	0.1	2.0	1.1	0.3	…
新　　疆	310.7	278.5	27.2	0.4	2.6	0.6	1.3	…

21—4 各省市职工工资总额(1997年)

Total Wages of Staff and Workers by Region(1997)

单位:亿元

地区	工资总额	国有经济单位	集体经济单位	联营经济单位	股份制经济单位	外商投资经济单位	港澳台投资经济单位	其他经济单位
北京	514.8	383.6	53.8	3.0	22.1	36.3	14.2	1.7
天津	223.3	160.5	26.5	1.1	7.1	20.2	7.5	0.5
河北	386.0	321.8	44.1	0.4	9.9	4.9	4.6	0.2
山西	240.0	209.2	25.6	0.1	3.1	1.1	0.9	…
内蒙古	185.4	158.6	21.0	0.1	3.1	1.5	1.0	0.1
辽宁	544.5	408.1	92.4	1.8	19.5	16.5	6.3	…
吉林	274.5	221.4	35.3	0.3	11.1	5.1	1.2	0.1
黑龙江	382.8	318.2	42.4	0.2	16.5	2.5	2.7	0.3
上海	510.1	353.7	53.7	1.8	39.4	43.0	16.9	1.6
江苏	635.4	447.0	124.9	6.5	19.7	20.6	14.7	2.2
浙江	402.0	251.8	100.1	1.7	21.2	14.8	12.0	0.3
安徽	273.8	212.2	43.4	0.4	13.5	2.3	1.3	0.8
福建	263.4	160.4	29.5	2.8	7.3	26.1	37.0	0.2
江西	194.4	166.7	21.9	0.1	2.0	1.9	1.7	0.1
山东	580.5	450.0	79.7	0.9	23.8	18.7	7.4	…
河南	434.1	336.3	66.0	0.5	21.8	4.5	4.5	0.4
湖北	391.0	317.8	45.7	0.8	19.2	3.8	3.4	0.4
湖南	314.9	265.5	40.7	0.2	4.2	2.7	1.4	0.1
广东	858.4	539.9	120.4	6.2	35.0	50.1	105.8	0.9
广西	184.9	155.9	18.4	0.2	4.7	4.2	1.1	0.3
海南	58.1	47.5	3.4	0.5	3.2	1.9	1.5	0.1
重庆	158.2	122.7	24.4	0.2	6.9	2.5	1.5	…
四川	380.6	302.0	51.4	0.3	22.5	2.4	1.0	1.1
贵州	119.9	105.6	11.0	0.2	1.7	1.0	0.4	0.1
云南	219.1	190.8	21.0	0.2	4.3	1.2	1.5	0.2
西藏	17.0	16.4	0.5	…	…	0.1	—	…
陕西	204.6	182.3	16.4	0.1	4.2	0.8	0.4	0.3
甘肃	153.1	134.5	16.4	…	0.8	1.1	0.2	0.1
青海	45.9	43.0	2.6	0.1	0.1	0.1	0.1	—
宁夏	44.9	38.0	4.4	0.1	1.3	1.0	0.2	…
新疆	209.8	189.9	16.4	0.2	1.9	0.4	1.1	…

21—5 各省市职工平均工资(1997年)

Average Wage of Staff and Workers by Region(1997)

单位:元

地　区	平均工资	国有经济单位	集体经济单位	联营经济单位	股份制经济单位	外商投资经济单位	港澳台投资经济单位	其他经济单位
北　京	11019	10907	8259	9917	12864	18058	14945	37096
天　津	8238	8689	5083	5667	11829	11797	8950	5109
河　北	5692	6066	3843	5073	6029	6323	6186	7125
山　西	5320	5791	3177	3349	5267	6367	6290	5044
内蒙古	5124	5462	3551	5290	4407	5512	4599	3581
辽　宁	5591	6226	3583	3789	6618	9158	7417	4899
吉　林	5664	6017	3813	7403	7471	7402	6659	6811
黑龙江	4889	5323	2747	4472	8066	5513	5933	3266
上　海	11425	11733	7329	8746	12698	16857	14175	12720
江　苏	7108	7745	5183	7390	9144	9153	7352	6864
浙　江	8386	8847	7026	7346	9356	10417	9500	8178
安　徽	5492	6039	3692	4830	6306	6042	5511	5605
福　建	7559	7621	5582	11124	8556	8336	8732	7507
江　西	5089	5303	3636	6056	7987	8545	7535	4465
山　东	6241	6817	4186	6420	6257	6782	5826	2351
河　南	5225	5643	3797	5912	4989	6409	5307	4995
湖　北	5401	5741	3731	5193	5319	8237	6769	4963
湖　南	5326	5683	3736	6218	5027	7929	5224	3713
广　东	9698	10032	6814	11036	12475	12410	11140	7713
广　西	5542	5654	4437	5296	6536	6765	5577	6189
海　南	5664	5468	4208	7010	11062	9077	8373	8462
重　庆	5502	5828	4016	3852	6166	9114	8361	7025
四　川	5626	5996	3982	4642	6333	6707	5568	4509
贵　州	5206	5434	3556	3778	6686	7313	7048	3661
云　南	7037	7237	5473	5065	7710	8388	8109	11793
西　藏	10098	10524	4588	5918	9558	7114	—	6292
陕　西	5184	5452	3177	4482	7067	6613	5621	7030
甘　肃	6182	6445	4598	4356	5146	10043	6272	3296
青　海	7091	7623	3419	2248	5701	5391	4979	—
宁　夏	6073	6206	4831	4144	6446	9512	4716	1042
新　疆	6644	6709	5849	5258	7460	6754	8324	4351

21—6 各省市固定资产及基本建设投资(1997年)

Investnvent in Fixed Assets and Captal Construction by Region(1997)

地　　区	固定资产投资额(亿元)	地方项目	1997年比1996年增长(%)	地方项目	基本建设投资额(亿元)	地方项目	1997年比1996年增长(%)	地方项目
东部地区	10962.5	8563.8	8.0	7.8	5216.8	3703.6	14.3	18.1
北　京	905.9	567.7	9.9	7.8	374.3	151.3	20.5	28.1
天　津	429.2	308.9	18.9	23.2	200.6	119.7	18.6	18.8
河　北	829.0	618.1	22.8	23.4	482.1	333.1	28.9	28.2
辽　宁	833.5	505.0	12.6	8.2	396.1	205.8	17.8	9.5
上　海	1807.7	1528.0	0.9	2.7	748.8	555.7	11.7	24.3
江　苏	1373.6	1129.2	17.3	15.7	581.9	434.9	27.2	27.3
浙　江	936.0	755.4	15.6	9.0	507.0	368.9	28.9	19.8
福　建	623.6	572.2	18.5	18.3	265.1	229.8	22.6	22.4
山　东	1030.6	711.2	8.7	4.3	493.9	333.0	11.2	15.6
广　东	1778.0	1514.4	−4.4	−0.2	874.2	718.7	−2.2	10.8
广　西	298.4	252.1	1.4	6.5	189.9	162.4	8.9	13.7
海　南	116.9	101.6	−21.2	−19.2	102.9	90.6	−17.8	−14.9
中部地区	4034.3	2511.4	9.6	11.1	2369.8	1353.9	16.7	21.0
山　西	316.2	184.3	26.7	18.1	195.0	97.4	36.4	18.4
内蒙古	222.5	120.3	9.0	0.5	156.5	73.7	16.7	10.8
吉　林	293.7	184.1	−4.6	16.4	179.8	89.5	−6.2	28.0
黑龙江	571.8	224.4	18.9	11.9	341.9	145.8	53.3	41.0
安　徽	398.0	296.2	10.0	16.4	210.7	147.8	9.2	23.7
江　西	236.5	185.8	15.9	18.2	133.6	100.3	18.6	22.9
河　南	776.7	559.8	7.7	13.8	478.1	335.1	16.6	33.9
湖　北	820.6	523.1	9.9	9.5	436.4	214.9	11.0	7.7
湖　南	398.3	233.5	−1.9	−4.9	238.0	149.4	3.1	2.3
西部地区	2555.6	1584.5	20.9	23.9	1549.8	888.3	28.5	33.1
重　庆	256.9	199.5	17.7	16.8	118.8	83.5	38.5	23.3
四　川	673.7	452.1	23.4	23.2	425.7	249.5	30.3	27.8
贵　州	163.2	109.0	15.2	9.8	88.6	57.4	7.8	0.9
云　南	408.7	306.2	26.7	30.0	235.2	181.7	40.9	46.1
西　藏	21.9		−29.3		21.3		−27.8	
陕　西	280.9	182.3	15.2	14.6	174.0	100.4	31.4	32.5
甘　肃	191.5	84.2	10.9	29.8	116.8	46.7	14.5	42.5
青　海	82.4	39.2	21.9	3.1	60.0	25.4	15.4	2.1
宁　夏	72.0	42.2	25.1	23.9	47.1	24.7	30.8	31.2
新　疆	404.6	169.8	29.7	54.0	262.2	119.0	36.3	67.9

注:本表不含农村集体及城乡个人投资。

21—7 各省市更新改造投资及房地产开发、商品房销售情况（1997年）

Investment in Innovation. Red Estate Development. Sales of Commerical Houses by Region(1997)

地区	更新改造投资额（亿元）	地方项目	1997年比1996年增长（%）	地方项目	房地产开发投资额（亿元）	地方企业	商品房销售额（亿元）
东部地区	2295.4	1636.9	7.9	4.1	2451.4	2345.9	1248.5
北京	191.7	101.8	13.6	−3.1	323.4	298.0	145.2
天津	134.3	108.4	24.5	36.9	80.9	78.7	43.0
河北	242.8	185.5	15.4	19.2	47.1	43.6	23.8
辽宁	241.4	133.3	21.5	14.6	136.2	127.3	67.1
上海	389.3	334.1	−8.3	−9.8	629.9	598.5	199.3
江苏	274.4	191.5	16.7	10.6	234.1	231.6	133.6
浙江	116.5	83.2	23.5	26.9	209.9	209.6	153.8
福建	123.4	107.4	35.3	38.4	135.7	135.7	72.7
山东	268.3	178.8	7.1	−3.9	105.6	102.9	54.4
广东	245.6	165.9	−6.8	−13.2	509.8	481.9	338.1
广西	61.5	43.7	−15.1	−6.5	31.7	31.7	14.2
海南	6.1	3.5	−32.3	−44.5	7.0	6.6	3.3
中部地区	982.3	582.5	5.5	5.9	380.0	356.5	175.7
山西	87.3	54.8	7.8	9.5	17.2	15.6	12.5
内蒙古	48.2	29.5	−9.1	−21.8	10.5	10.2	7.9
吉林	57.5	39.7	−6.3	2.6	24.5	23.3	10.4
黑龙江	111.6	34.4	−5.0	−11.6	44.8	34.8	26.4
安徽	115.6	80.1	15.3	14.0	44.2	42.3	24.2
江西	66.1	50.5	12.9	10.0	26.5	25.9	12.0
河南	179.7	117.9	18.7	17.7	52.8	52.2	19.3
湖北	211.7	141.7	10.3	16.5	126.5	122.9	49.5
湖南	104.6	33.9	−10.2	−27.5	33.1	29.4	13.5
西部地区	570.1	329.9	9.0	14.7	275.0	266.7	139.3
重庆	60.3	39.2	−16.1	−12.4	66.8	66.2	30.8
四川	117.1	85.0	17.8	26.5	98.0	97.5	54.3
贵州	53.6	33.6	32.1	39.3	14.1	13.8	6.3
云南	111.3	65.2	13.6	16.5	36.6	36.5	17.6
西藏	0.6		−59.9		—	—	—
陕西	61.8	37.8	−9.5	−10.1	27.5	26.9	13.8
甘肃	58.0	25.6	9.5	21.3	12.2	8.9	5.0
青海	14.1	10.1	41.1	32.8	2.3	2.1	1.0
宁夏	17.7	10.3	14.8	13.4	5.7	5.7	4.8
新疆	75.7	23.1	16.1	46.1	11.7	9.0	5.7

21—8 各省市财政收入决算情况(1997年)

Final Statement of Government Revenue by Region(1997)

单位:万元

地 区	收入合计	工商税收	农牧业税 耕地占用税	企 业 所得税	国有企业 上缴利润
北 京	1823161	2146081	23652	221613	-261
天 津	899082	714212	9511	130950	
河 北	1760742	1100859	131656	266240	7846
山 西	928131	697329	49803	90183	4867
内 蒙 古	660777	418572	130023	60554	5964
辽 宁	2281632	1804507	109382	245470	9929
吉 林	828508	559589	72396	81024	8366
黑 龙 江	1361550	1014154	186279	67905	7815
上 海	3324672	3036435	112933	606551	
江 苏	2555850	1894651	210933	378324	5295
浙 江	1573296	1499230	100949	322316	52
安 徽	1405216	844461	214664	172868	10064
福 建	1629149	1013838	142031	176459	32140
江 西	884409	513134	121168	78419	10755
山 东	2903955	1917073	250978	484919	10885
河 南	1857268	1023862	212677	284316	37132
湖 北	1398901	850609	183581	131061	9707
湖 南	1371557	818836	170727	67967	9601
广 东	5439453	3978163	220843	748574	56446
广 西	991568	562252	154817	88657	22143
海 南	308698	198604	34512	17388	1356
重 庆	593060	397321	89715	47486	2112
四 川	1728966	1026119	240055	260616	24420
贵 州	558833	325758	147678	40549	3384
云 南	1504181	849048	405940	96969	7565
西 藏	29537	24045	50	7401	908
陕 西	765492	526603	113937	70073	7087
甘 肃	469143	318493	59291	39864	2671
青 海	109200	76885	12269	8824	1765
宁 夏	140738	97673	11832	15071	323
新 疆	545248	413106	50442	40746	217

21—9 各省市财政支出决算情况(1997年)

Final Statement of Government Expenditure by Region(1997)

单位:万元

地区	支出合计	基本建设	支援农业生产	农林水利气象部门事业费	城市维护费	文教事业费	科学事业费
北京	2363940	248948	53245	31793	104397	428888	37386
天津	1227843	226899	14579	18185	122987	226318	10240
河北	2704603	161698	57501	96471	104639	577931	16947
山西	1435129	44982	56048	56559	62660	312327	8939
内蒙古	1429118	91114	57202	79116	64198	256833	9707
辽宁	3406269	390169	109788	100455	259497	517827	29719
吉林	1677548	84950	34904	73687	80929	323529	18050
黑龙江	2203829	120542	61750	98039	122456	384101	21887
上海	4088139	826992	55996	35763	141474	673554	49045
江苏	3643605	258811	104408	107399	250839	885530	35274
浙江	2401592	107594	83420	87882	195982	548741	24096
安徽	2072408	149498	63479	75657	110992	433157	10467
福建	2243565	214088	63424	79047	92967	480838	22069
江西	1501570	70314	51072	57747	73326	297370	8795
山东	4077878	239629	127832	173176	281070	907792	34974
河南	2843717	134963	73752	92972	119483	600801	16961
湖北	2236993	92140	59598	85564	95476	444320	12509
湖南	2308151	137783	71111	105453	121088	460079	15416
广东	6826619	955334	196287	164767	365354	1167240	86120
广西	1708345	123278	67092	69415	52655	339884	13634
海南	478408	51760	13466	17406	14956	84784	3695
重庆	1010110	77654	19243	29320	62833	201359	7618
四川	2750975	206420	89047	111692	119317	500557	25290
贵州	1118288	57088	49569	55060	45190	216644	10173
云南	3132012	442387	206819	131334	110414	536132	33122
西藏	381952	48980	14169	13788	2752	57051	1055
陕西	1377240	78518	78835	71715	57491	305599	9481
甘肃	1043042	63183	35758	57389	45679	201086	10342
青海	364713	18037	8291	20880	4503	61603	1986
宁夏	336300	27550	18657	20595	12658	58260	2823
新疆	1233534	91767	28789	65230	46674	252958	12317

21—10 各省市居民消费价格指数和商品零售价格指数(1997年)

Consumer Price Indices and Retail Price Indices of Commodities by Region(1997)

(上年＝100)

地　　区	居民消费价格指数			商品零售价格指数		
	全　省(区、市)	城　市	农　村	全　省(区、市)	城　市	农　村
北　　京	105.3			103.8		
天　　津	103.1			100.7		
河　　北	103.5	103.7	103.4	102.1	102.0	102.1
山　　西	103.1	103.1	103.0	101.3	100.9	101.7
内 蒙 古	104.5	104.6	104.3	102.3	102.4	101.9
辽　　宁	103.1	103.8	102.1	101.0	101.0	100.5
吉　　林	103.7	103.7	103.7	101.8	101.7	102.0
黑 龙 江	104.4	104.5	103.8	102.2	102.0	102.6
上　　海	102.8			98.8		
江　　苏	101.7	101.3	102.0	99.3	99.1	99.5
浙　　江	102.8	104.1	102.1	100.3	100.9	99.4
安　　徽	101.3	101.9	100.7	99.4	100.1	98.9
福　　建	101.7	102.5	101.3	99.8	99.6	100.1
江　　西	102.0	103.0	101.2	99.6	100.1	99.3
山　　东	102.8	103.2	102.4	100.8	100.8	100.7
河　　南	103.5	102.4	103.9	100.5	99.8	101.2
湖　　北	103.2	102.6	103.6	101.5	100.8	102.2
湖　　南	102.8	103.0	102.5	100.3	100.6	99.8
广　　东	101.9	102.1	101.5	99.8	99.8	99.8
广　　西	100.8	100.7	100.8	99.6	99.9	99.4
海　　南	100.8	101.5	100.3	99.4	99.6	99.1
重　　庆	103.1			101.6		
四　　川	105.1	105.1	105.0	102.9	102.8	102.9
贵　　州	103.4	103.4	103.4	101.5	101.4	101.7
云　　南	104.3	104.6	103.9	102.3	101.6	103.2
西　　藏						
陕　　西	104.8	105.2	104.0	101.6	101.3	101.8
甘　　肃	102.9	102.8	102.9	101.6	101.4	101.9
青　　海	104.8	105.1	104.2	103.0	103.2	102.7
宁　　夏	103.8	103.9	103.5	102.2	102.2	102.1
新　　疆	103.7	103.5	103.9	101.8	101.3	102.5

21—11 各省市城镇居民家庭人均收支情况(1997年)

Per Capita Annual Income and Expenditure of Urban Households by Region(1997)

单位:元

地　区	全部收入	可支配收入	实际支出	消费性支出	非消费性支出	恩格尔系数(%)
北　京	7862	7813	7091	6532	560	43.7
天　津	6621	6608	6029	5204	825	46.7
河　北	4982	4959	4988	4004	979	42.0
山　西	4008	3990	4029	3229	795	43.3
内蒙古	3968	3945	3582	3032	540	43.5
辽　宁	4547	4518	4558	3720	838	48.1
吉　林	4206	4191	4012	3408	603	47.0
黑龙江	4110	4091	3839	3213	623	45.9
上　海	8476	8439	7377	6820	557	51.5
江　苏	5807	5765	5425	4534	885	47.7
浙　江	7366	7359	7117	6170	945	43.9
安　徽	4620	4599	4405	3694	710	52.4
福　建	6201	6144	5867	4936	925	52.8
江　西	4091	4071	3824	3200	620	50.6
山　东	5217	5191	4773	4041	731	41.0
河　南	4112	4094	3946	3378	565	44.6
湖　北	4694	4673	4550	3856	691	46.0
湖　南	5249	5210	5302	4317	978	45.7
广　东	8646	8562	7985	6853	1128	46.0
广　西	5140	5110	5522	4453	1061	47.5
海　南	4918	4850	4551	3909	592	57.0
重　庆	5343	5323	5431	4938	492	46.5
四　川	4788	4763	5024	4093	930	49.1
贵　州		4442	4275	3556	715	51.1
云　南	5616	5558	5681	4537	1126	46.5
西　藏						
陕　西	4022	4001	3955	3462	492	43.0
甘　肃	3613	3592	3392	2946	444	48.9
青　海	4016	3999	3781	3300	480	48.3
宁　夏	3864	3837	3967	3271	687	43.4
新　疆	4879	4845	4581	3887	686	43.3

21—12 各省市农民家庭收支情况(1997年)

Per Capita Annual Income and Expenditure of Rural Households by Region(1997)

单位:元

地区	总收入	现金	纯收入	总支出	生活消费	现金支出	恩格尔系数(%)
北京	4273	3818	3662	3392	2693	3333	44.8
天津	4387	3532	3244	3041	1882	2730	50.9
河北	3169	2311	2286	2283	1395	1839	50.3
山西	2151	1526	1738	1575	1145	1210	57.0
内蒙古	2991	1874	1780	2799	1560	1978	55.9
辽宁	3387	2561	2301	2905	1790	2393	55.4
吉林	3292	2107	2186	2772	1624	2218	55.1
黑龙江	3745	2430	2308	3077	1549	2574	54.8
上海	5933	5512	5277	4953	4228	4899	41.5
江苏	4193	3271	3270	3456	2488	2936	48.9
浙江	4722	4144	3684	3945	2839	3602	48.5
安徽	2550	1805	1809	2097	1337	1602	56.5
福建	3478	2845	2786	2736	1994	2379	55.2
江西	2963	2068	2107	2452	1569	1806	58.8
山东	3469	2363	2292	2855	1626	2112	53.6
河南	2502	1598	1734	2070	1271	1469	54.6
湖北	2913	1822	2102	2498	1660	1827	55.9
湖南	3061	2218	2037	2853	1816	2188	59.4
广东	4517	3747	3468	3746	2618	3178	52.3
广西	2679	2040	1875	2207	1376	1717	58.2
海南	2540	1785	1917	1929	1287	1350	63.0
重庆	2422	1372	1643	2186	1390	1307	65.8
四川	2636	1655	1681	2381	1440	1569	62.4
贵州	1813	1044	1299	1594	1066	944	69.6
云南	2197	1437	1376	2171	1318	1364	62.1
西藏	1555	843	1198	1121	805	775	66.2
陕西	1813	1307	1273	1778	1215	1327	52.8
甘肃	1713	879	1185	1522	976	859	57.5
青海	1862	982	1321	1633	1085	972	66.3
宁夏	2509	1899	1513	2314	1250	1717	55.8
新疆	3162	2571	1504	3161	1395	2703	48.0

21—13 各省市农林牧渔业总产值和指数(1997年)

Gross Output Value of Farming. Forestry. Animal Husbandry and Fisherg and the Related Indices(1997)

地区	农林牧渔业总产值(亿元)	农业	林业	牧业	渔业	农林牧渔业总产值指数(上年=100)
北京	171.0	90.2	2.9	71.9	6.0	101.3
天津	144.3	91.9	1.0	40.6	10.8	100.9
河北	1433.9	832.5	26.3	524.2	50.8	107.3
山西	346.9	237.3	15.1	93.2	1.4	94.6
内蒙古	463.7	298.5	13.9	148.0	3.3	99.6
辽宁	922.1	427.8	14.7	342.4	137.2	100.6
吉林	577.7	311.4	8.2	249.8	8.4	95.7
黑龙江	862.6	592.0	18.0	237.0	15.6	105.2
上海	211.3	88.3	0.7	92.3	30.0	113.0
江苏	1893.2	1078.4	27.6	523.9	263.3	106.7
浙江	1009.5	524.5	59.4	197.3	228.4	103.9
安徽	1220.3	723.7	48.2	340.5	107.9	109.3
福建	991.8	421.4	75.3	231.2	263.8	110.2
江西	795.0	400.0	48.2	257.3	89.5	107.0
山东	2150.0	1028.8	50.0	750.1	321.2	100.5
河南	1785.8	1088.6	47.0	638.0	12.2	108.7
湖北	1215.4	703.8	36.1	363.8	111.7	108.5
湖南	1322.3	618.5	48.0	538.2	76.1	108.3
广东	1625.2	850.1	54.8	411.5	309.2	105.6
广西	980.6	487.2	41.2	357.2	95.0	110.9
海南	239.8	112.9	42.0	46.0	38.8	108.6
重庆	459.5	267.9	11.9	167.8	11.9	103.4
四川	1414.8	831.1	43.3	511.5	29.0	104.6
贵州	430.0	287.9	15.5	123.1	3.5	104.3
云南	620.4	399.1	46.8	164.2	10.4	106.8
西藏	39.5	19.2	0.9	19.3	0.0	102.7
陕西	466.5	322.3	18.4	122.9	3.0	102.8
甘肃	333.0	231.0	8.2	93.0	0.8	106.5
青海	58.1	31.1	0.9	26.0	0.1	102.9
宁夏	70.0	48.0	1.2	19.5	1.3	100.3
新疆	455.0	352.7	6.5	92.5	3.3	107.5

注:本表绝对数按当年价格计算,指数按可比价格计算。

21—14 各省市主要农产品产量(1997年)

Yiald of Maior Farm Crops(1997)

单位:万吨

地区	粮食	棉花	油料	糖料	水产品
北京	237.5	0.2	2.7		7.7
天津	206.2	0.4	3.0		19.0
河北	2746.7	24.9	118.0	7.1	60.6
山西	901.4	4.4	28.1	66.8	2.1
内蒙古	1421.0	0.1	73.1	306.4	5.5
辽宁	1313.5	1.5	16.1	40.1	285.1
吉林	1808.3		15.9	32.9	13.2
黑龙江	3104.5		18.2	447.7	32.3
上海	230.2	0.4	10.7	6.2	30.2
江苏	3563.8	50.7	141.9	23.3	265.7
浙江	1493.5	4.8	48.9	60.0	377.7
安徽	2802.7	30.1	205.0	19.9	135.2
福建	961.8		24.4	249.9	429.3
江西	1767.7	13.2	105.6	220.6	115.1
山东	3852.2	35.4	240.9	1.5	610.3
河南	3894.7	79.0	276.7	17.3	23.9
湖北	2634.4	58.1	195.5	100.9	202.4
湖南	2877.0	25.6	129.3	174.5	110.8
广东	1897.7		75.5	1764.3	521.0
广西	1544.8	0.1	55.5	3242.4	191.7
海南	213.9		8.4	377.5	52.3
重庆	1157.7	0.1	23.3	8.1	15.8
四川	3461.3	10.7	134.2	155.8	37.2
贵州	1025.9	0.1	59.0	37.1	4.2
云南	1271.9	0.1	17.4	1435.2	11.9
西藏	77.3		3.4		0.2
陕西	1044.4	2.1	36.7	3.4	4.5
甘肃	766.2	3.4	35.6	139.1	0.9
青海	127.6		18.4		0.2
宁夏	256.6		6.2	59.8	2.2
新疆	830.0	115.0	30.0	388.7	5.2

21—15 各省市工业总产值和指数(1997年)

Gross Industrial Output Value and It's Indices by Region(1997)

地　区	工业总产值(亿元)	国有工业	集体工业	乡办工业	其他经济类型工业	工业总产值指数(上年=100)
北　京	1716.9	943.3	190.4	142.4	583.2	110.9
天　津	1772.9	614.7	335.7	276.6	822.4	110.4
河　北	3046.7	1372.1	1214.7	881.1	459.8	116.4
山　西	1207.2	777.3	390.1	270.1	39.8	108.6
内蒙古	705.6	472.0	144.2	70.9	89.4	110.1
辽　宁	3651.6	2022.1	925.7	512.0	703.8	110.1
吉　林	1356.5	907.3	236.0	121.3	213.2	111.8
黑龙江	2180.9	1485.8	513.9	289.3	181.1	110.1
上　海	4691.0	1668.4	610.4	1115.4	2412.2	113.8
江　苏	8332.6	2344.4	4137.2	3168.8	1851.1	114.0
浙　江	4319.5	1000.3	2593.1	1929.8	726.1	110.0
安　徽	2697.2	959.3	1394.6	1201.2	343.3	118.0
福　建	2035.9	447.7	357.4	230.8	1230.8	115.3
江　西	1076.2	656.9	364.1	244.2	55.3	113.2
山　东	6460.6	2511.9	2947.0	2170.9	1001.8	113.8
河　南	3065.2	1608.4	1000.5	594.2	456.3	110.9
湖　北	3426.9	1532.8	1414.9	1002.4	479.1	116.3
湖　南	1898.9	953.0	790.9	554.7	155.1	112.1
广　东	8406.1	1811.4	1844.5	1005.2	4750.2	115.7
广　西	1105.1	582.2	365.9	222.0	156.9	106.5
海　南	178.9	79.8	11.2	2.4	88.0	114.3
重　庆	932.5	510.8	241.6	138.7	180.1	111.4
四　川	2347.2	1194.1	834.5	617.3	318.6	116.1
贵　州	580.9	424.1	135.0	101.8	21.8	113.1
云　南	1056.2	804.3	172.4	92.6	79.5	103.7
西　藏						
陕　西	1029.2	715.2	220.1	128.4	93.8	111.0
甘　肃	713.8	525.1	161.7	99.9	27.0	108.2
青　海	140.3	115.2	20.2	9.9	4.8	111.0
宁　夏	186.0	130.0	25.5	14.9	30.5	105.1
新　疆	709.6	589.8	88.7	25.4	31.1	110.7

注:本表绝对数按当年价格计算;指数按可比价格计算;统计范围为乡及乡以上工业的数字。

21—16 各省市工业主要经济指标(1997年)

Main Indicators of Industrial Economy by Region(1997)

单位:亿元

地区	产品销售收入	利税总额	利润总额	亏损企业亏损额	应收帐款净额	产成品
北京	1442.43	107.32	21.13	36.99	259.19	176.82
天津	1654.18	133.39	56.06	49.78	340.39	164.86
河北	2733.37	287.39	125.32	35.25	438.98	280.27
山西	994.69	111.15	29.51	21.04	241.63	132.03
内蒙古	647.27	67.95	18.72	12.51	121.08	81.37
辽宁	3214.81	221.69	25.46	97.31	708.54	341.23
吉林	1180.62	77.16	−9.75	47.92	333.10	158.59
黑龙江	1845.07	311.82	133.29	44.80	400.72	193.90
上海	4485.12	433.95	193.83	90.67	1006.82	346.50
江苏	7374.02	511.99	181.22	95.09	1120.87	580.64
浙江	3720.19	309.54	122.51	49.41	573.99	361.21
安徽	1321.72	126.68	24.62	26.72	220.67	131.46
福建	1571.08	142.03	45.01	27.88	209.51	126.46
江西	829.22	61.01	6.15	21.98	141.55	89.65
山东	5653.26	571.34	232.39	56.15	804.90	584.66
河南	2341.21	229.21	57.71	39.08	421.21	263.59
湖北	2707.38	240.15	69.47	41.67	487.96	227.75
湖南	1493.43	150.08	−0.34	47.51	263.64	150.47
广东	7307.14	524.27	222.69	196.61	1259.34	611.05
广西	859.59	54.11	−10.15	40.60	150.31	115.41
海南	118.46	7.65	−0.15	6.38	23.18	13.79
重庆	761.41	32.63	−22.03	53.73	198.84	91.26
四川	1943.66	172.41	36.63	64.96	373.01	233.88
贵州	382.89	51.41	−1.12	17.60	132.93	55.44
云南	914.44	318.17	83.84	23.73	172.02	72.55
西藏						
陕西	825.46	61.25	−6.68	40.17	223.64	129.57
甘肃	608.40	46.68	0.75	18.84	135.93	93.85
青海	118.95	−0.03	−8.55	9.65	44.47	18.36
宁夏	163.02	14.03	1.32	6.19	49.71	22.63
新疆	558.27	50.97	−2.14	21.15	97.76	71.98

21—17 各省市工业经济效益综合指数(1997年)

Main Indicators on Economic Benfit of Industrial Enterprises by Region(1997)

地区	综合指数(%)	产品销售率(%)	资金利税率(%)	成本费用利润率(%)	劳动生产率(元/人)	流动资产周转次数(次)	增加值率(%)
北京	90.90	97.58	4.77	1.46	24821.86	1.25	26.27
天津	86.35	98.54	5.77	3.46	19131.85	1.33	19.92
河北	98.34	97.21	8.23	4.81	17892.93	1.63	28.81
山西	78.46	98.64	5.71	3.14	12514.19	1.16	35.35
内蒙古	78.66	97.32	5.96	2.95	12767.00	1.20	33.47
辽宁	70.61	96.02	4.18	0.80	14473.26	1.23	24.30
吉林	62.25	95.28	3.44	—0.82	13037.21	1.07	25.31
黑龙江	109.19	95.58	11.66	8.01	16428.38	1.36	37.81
上海	125.50	98.31	8.18	4.46	38107.53	1.37	22.97
江苏	100.03	95.59	7.04	2.52	23883.45	1.78	21.16
浙江	102.87	95.92	8.38	3.41	23060.97	1.74	21.14
安徽	88.81	95.12	7.88	1.94	16831.30	1.55	26.70
福建	98.08	96.63	8.09	2.99	19290.05	1.78	27.35
江西	66.79	97.31	4.85	0.75	10630.35	1.28	24.99
山东	104.85	96.62	9.19	4.35	20932.41	1.74	26.46
河南	87.95	96.66	7.18	2.57	16583.29	1.44	29.39
湖北	95.14	96.55	7.38	2.66	19932.12	1.58	28.45
湖南	78.31	96.28	7.91	—0.02	11922.25	1.59	27.34
广东	101.85	95.82	6.18	3.15	26439.13	1.58	22.98
广西	73.62	94.52	4.02	—1.19	17834.15	1.31	26.79
海南	73.75	92.73	3.62	—0.12	19383.53	1.22	20.60
重庆	54.69	95.43	2.67	—2.83	12009.50	1.11	22.20
四川	79.18	94.88	5.79	1.97	15692.07	1.19	28.88
贵州	77.36	93.96	6.69	—0.33	17069.12	0.89	33.18
云南	171.53	96.55	24.31	12.21	31193.44	1.37	45.90
西藏							
陕西	63.07	94.60	4.15	—0.82	12054.22	1.05	28.67
甘肃	70.03	93.76	4.57	0.13	13267.18	1.24	29.93
青海	43.96	95.02	—0.01	—6.85	13404.98	0.90	29.41
宁夏	66.90	93.99	4.45	0.82	12561.72	1.07	26.62
新疆	78.92	94.16	4.57	—0.39	18306.55	1.24	34.67

21—18 各省市全社会货物周转量(1997年)

Freight Ton—Kilometers by Region(1997)

单位:亿吨公里

地区	合计	国家铁路	地方铁路	公路	水运
北京	366.2	289.2	0.1	76.9	
天津	364.5	254.7	3.6	44.0	62.2
河北	2059.7	1529.4	4.5	455.0	70.8
山西	773.2	553.6	0.9	218.6	…
内蒙古	813.5	631.4	…	182.2	
辽宁	1375.0	1040.4	1.0	226.4	107.2
吉林	520.7	440.9	0.4	78.3	1.1
黑龙江	957.1	813.9	3.8	133.7	5.7
上海	170.8	42.1		47.1	81.6
江苏	1096.4	355.7	0.2	303.4	437.1
浙江	914.8	172.2	…	262.3	480.2
安徽	876.1	550.7	0.8	192.9	131.7
福建	617.1	143.0		151.2	322.9
江西	500.2	358.1	0.3	109.7	32.1
山东	1290.8	729.1	4.1	349.0	208.6
河南	1607.6	1237.4	7.3	352.7	10.2
湖北	854.9	559.4	1.1	180.5	113.9
湖南	985.9	677.9	0.3	244.9	62.8
广东	911.7	234.6	2.5	310.6	364.1
广西	613.4	321.0	16.8	183.5	92.1
海南	309.4	1.6		34.2	273.6
重庆	128.5			62.5	66.0
四川	741.7	502.3	1.5	219.5	18.4
贵州	332.3	278.0		50.3	4.1
云南	384.6	132.4	0.5	250.6	1.2
西藏	18.9			18.9	
陕西	529.8	421.1		108.5	0.2
甘肃	526.0	428.9		97.1	…
青海	69.7	39.1		30.7	
宁夏	156.9	112.3	1.0	43.6	
新疆	443.0	196.2		246.8	
不分地区	16871.7			4.3	16259.3

注:不分地区合计中,包括公路和水运部门的直属企业、民航、管道完成数。

21—19 各省市社会消费品零售总额(1997年)

Total Retail Sales of Consumer Goods by Region(1997)

(按行业分)

单位:亿元

地区	社会消费品零售总额	批发零售贸易业	餐饮业	制造业	农民对非农业居民
北京	1051.5	709.4	72.5	56.3	142.6
天津	535.0	295.3	46.1	41.3	66.3
河北	1195.0	833.4	91.0	107.7	127.7
山西	503.1	323.5	39.9	37.2	76.6
内蒙古	364.5	235.0	31.7	31.8	50.6
辽宁	1450.1	1034.5	134.5	56.0	195.1
吉林	620.3	392.3	59.0	28.4	132.7
黑龙江	860.2	668.4	62.1	36.7	78.7
上海	1325.2	1077.3	87.6	38.0	109.4
江苏	2106.6	1422.5	153.5	202.0	262.8
浙江	1717.9	1184.7	107.6	110.8	246.7
安徽	849.2	540.2	65.8	81.6	133.2
福建	986.0	706.3	99.0	49.8	87.8
江西	552.3	332.2	41.2	42.7	119.8
山东	1906.5	1209.7	166.8	236.5	204.8
河南	1364.0	835.8	161.0	193.2	127.5
湖北	1348.6	843.1	120.0	80.2	247.1
湖南	1037.6	673.0	80.4	62.0	189.9
广东	2907.1	1892.0	404.5	149.3	340.3
广西	666.3	430.2	63.8	46.4	104.5
海南	129.0	74.0	14.9	2.9	27.8
重庆	507.9	280.6	49.1	30.9	117.9
四川	1144.6	673.3	114.5	92.5	219.6
贵州	264.8	182.6	18.2	17.0	36.8
云南	433.8	295.1	33.0	23.7	70.3
西藏					
陕西	483.5	310.5	37.5	42.6	78.8
甘肃	271.4	170.8	32.1	19.5	34.6
青海	66.9	46.9	6.5	3.9	8.1
宁夏	71.4	45.6	5.2	3.8	15.8
新疆	296.3	182.7	22.0	20.3	45.4

注:因部分地区统计不全,各地区之和不等于全国总计。

21—20 各省市国际旅游业基本情况

Basic Indicators of International Tourism by Region

地区	1996年			1997年		
	旅游人数（万人次）	外国人	旅游收汇总额（亿美元）	旅游人数（万人次）	外国人	旅游收汇总额（亿美元）
北京	218.89	176.16	22.52	229.84	186.86	22.48
天津	23.33	20.02	1.52	28.04	23.10	1.80
河北	25.42	22.53	0.74	32.17	27.38	0.97
山西	9.70	6.95	0.27	12.53	8.76	0.37
内蒙古	31.50	31.09	0.94	34.84	34.24	1.07
辽宁	29.79	24.25	2.20	38.80	31.07	2.60
吉林	18.83	17.59	0.53	20.04	18.09	0.59
黑龙江	25.90	22.47	0.78	34.19	30.37	1.05
上海	143.19	115.48	11.71	165.35	129.99	13.17
江苏	88.69	57.74	3.17	101.70	64.26	4.08
浙江	72.90	41.30	2.92	81.15	45.34	3.45
安徽	17.38	9.17	0.42	29.04	11.80	0.64
福建	104.57	27.57	5.55	115.05	31.62	6.14
江西	9.90	2.59	0.34	13.34	3.23	0.45
山东	53.16	36.37	1.96	58.50	34.44	2.04
河南	24.21	11.46	0.73	26.44	13.54	0.95
湖北	36.89	24.12	1.25	58.02	35.31	1.70
湖南	22.87	10.12	1.01	30.16	12.20	1.40
广东	691.10	123.66	26.38	739.16	134.66	28.01
广西	52.05	36.06	1.54	57.31	34.05	1.78
海南	33.90	7.03	0.85	41.28	10.03	1.02
重庆				26.12	15.57	1.05
四川	45.47	30.60	1.62	27.13	14.81	0.79
贵州	12.53	6.67	0.38	15.02	7.81	0.44
云南	74.25	57.11	2.11	80.54	58.03	2.64
西藏	7.50	7.26	0.30	8.18	7.30	0.32
陕西	50.03	42.24	1.98	53.94	43.70	2.25
甘肃	10.45	7.64	0.19	11.63	8.40	0.28
青海	1.04	0.73	0.02	1.28	0.94	0.03
宁夏	0.42	0.33	0.01	0.42	0.33	0.01
新疆	17.69	16.05	0.68	17.25	15.71	0.71

企业简介

1997年我省各行业不少基层企业取得了很大成绩，本《年鉴》对部分企业就有关情况进行简要介绍，以交流信息，供有关部门、企业参考。

长沙卷烟厂

长沙卷烟厂是中国烟草行业大型骨干企业，占地面积51万平方米，现有员工3350余人，其中大中专以上毕业生近1000人，总资产53亿元，拥有国际先进水平的制丝、卷接、包装设备，以及各种先进的科研、检测等仪器。主要产品有“金沙”、“精品白沙”、“白沙”、“长沙”、“特制湘烟”、“DUOROU”、“NISE”等，产品畅销国内外市场，企业经济效益连续十年快速增长，实现税利以平均每年2个亿的速度递增。

1988年，长沙卷烟厂登上了国家二级企业台阶，1989年晋升为国家一级计量单位，1994年被国家统计局、技术监督局和中国质量管理协会评为全国100家“质量效益型”先进企业。1995年通过了ISO9002国际标准体系的国内外认证，再次被评为“全国质量效益型先进企业”，一举荣获全国优秀企业“金马奖”。1996年该厂进入300家重点国有企业行列，全年完成产量87万箱，实现销售收入46亿元，实现税利26亿元，产品创汇1.13亿美元。1997年，该厂实现销售收入52.7亿元，税利达32.6亿元，并且已连续多年成为湖南省利税首户。企业综合实力大大增强，名列全国烟草行业前列。

十多年来，在以厂长肖寿松同志为核心的企业决策层领导下，长沙卷烟厂坚持以市场为导向，以科研为龙头，深化改革，强化管理，拓展国内外市场，加快外向型发展，积极转换企业经营机制，先后完成了从生产型向生产经营型，从内向型向外向型，从外向型向企业集团过渡的“三级跳”。

在振兴和发展过程中，长沙卷烟厂注重实施“名牌战略”，坚持“科技兴烟”，促进技术进步，提高产品的技术含量，致力于提高经济增长的质量和效益。在产品开发上，以生物生化为主线，以追赶国际名牌为目标，将传统经验和科学技术相结合。传统产品“白沙”系列香烟，畅销南方各省，并已在全国市场铺开；新产品“金沙”，充分运用多项最新科研成果，品味一流，焦油含量在12毫克/克以下，在国内低焦油烤烟型产品中处于领先地位。在技术改造上，坚持高起点、高标准、“七五”、“八五”以来，该厂技术改造取得了较大的进展，企业硬件环境得到极大改善，拥有从德国、意大利进口的COMAS制丝线、PROTOS、GD卷包机以及PM5N成型机，生产能力达到90万大箱，特别是卷包机型全部是统一的PROTOS、GD机，标志着该厂设备已达到世界先进水平。

长沙卷烟厂加强企业管理，独创并推行“人才、信息、决策、开发、管理”五要素全方位优化管理模式，全面推行ISO9000标准，于1995年一次性通过英国标准化协会、香港品质保证局、中国商检质量认证中心的国内外认证，成为国内烟草行业第一家同时通过国内外认证的企业；为促进管理手段的现代化，该厂引进并实施美国SSA公司的小型机系统和BPCS软件，安装了工业闭路电视，促进了物流、信息流和行为流的有效管理，实现了生产全过程的自动控制，确保了企业管理水平的稳步提高。

在加强物质文明建设的同时，长沙卷烟厂积极推进社会主义精神文明建设，创建以人力资源开发为龙头，对外树立企业形象，对内振奋人心的具有长烟特色的企业文化，形成和谐、竞争、向上的人文环境。在人才培养方面，注重内引外联，大量吸收大中专毕业生，加强人才的送外培训，每年培训达3000余人次，先后派出300余人到国外学习深造，选派50名骨干人员参加MBA高层管理培训。为丰富职工文化生活，宣传企业形象，该厂组建了“金沙”艺术团，嘉沙少儿艺术团，赴意大利、德国演出，双双获奖。在“上为国家作贡献，下为职工谋福利”的治厂方针指导下，该厂决策层注重提高职工生活福利水平，兴建养殖场，推行自助餐，修建高层住宅，提高了广大员工的生产干劲和工作热情。

当前，长沙卷烟厂正积极向资产经营型转轨，先后投资并发展了制药、储运、印刷、金融、房地产、广告、装饰等新兴产业，盘活了大量资产，优化了产业结构，提高了企业综合竞争实力。为进一步推进企业集团化发展，该厂已进入烟草行业的现代企业制度试点企业之列，正积极进行公司制改造，加快组建“一业为主、多种经营”的白沙集团。(供稿人：唐忠保)

地址：湖南省长沙市劳动东路346号

电话：(0731)5559112

传真：(0731)5559175

邮编：410014

岳阳恒立冷气设备股份有限公司

岳阳恒立冷气设备股份有限公司1996年经中国证监会批准，成为中国汽车空调业第一家上市公司。公司现有职工1700人，固定资产7000万元是国家规划生产汽车空调的专业厂家，中国汽车空调协会理事长单位。

公司在“七五”、“八五”期间投资1200万美元，从德、美、日、英等国家引进平流式换热器、管带式换热器、管片式换热器、大中型客车空调机、小轿车空调机、风机盘管等产品的制造技术与设备，形成了年产大中型客车空调机5000台套、小轿车空调机20万台套的生产能力，为国内数十家重点客车厂和上海大众桑塔纳桥车配套。

公司坚持“管理从严、科技领先、质量第一、用户满意”的质量方针，1997年汽车空调产品正式取得中国机械工业质量体系认证中心和德国TUV莱茵公司按ISO9001标准进行的质量体系认证。并在全国各大中城市设有特约维修点，确保产品的销后服务。公司致力于中国汽车空调技术的研究和应用，力争为中国汽车空调行业的发展作出新的贡献。

湖南通用电气集团

湖南通用电气集团是经湖南省人民政府批准，于1997年3月组建成立的大型企业集团。集团现有职工11517人，占地面积236万平方米，总资产13.51亿元，拥有主要生产设备2899台，其中进口九十年代设备117台，已成为跨行业、跨部门、集科、工、贸多元化经营为一体的大型国有企业集团。

集团主要生产交直流电动机、工矿电机车、电动轮自卸车、牵引电气和电气成套设备、城市交通轨道车辆、军工产品等20个大类产品。其中自主开发的108吨自卸车是国内独家产品、进口替代品，80吨、100吨、200吨大型准轨工矿电机车国内独家生产，市场占有率为100%，电机产品具有八十年代末、九十年代初国际水平，市场占有率达25%以上。先后创国优产品3项，部优和省优产品13项，96年公司被评为“机械工业企业技术进步示范工程试点企业”；304KWGTO直流斩波调速系统获国家“八五”科技攻关一等奖，97年获国家科技进步二等奖；200吨机车被评为国家级97年新产品；039产品充电发电机和定子冲片模、30立升热水器前罩拉模和1.5匹空调室外机前罩成形模，被中国模具工业协会评为97年国产优质模具。

法人代表：戴志强

总经理：陈广摄

地址：湘潭市下摄司街302号

电话：(0732)8595919

邮编：411101

长沙通大(集团)有限公司

长沙通大(集团)有限公司是1996年11月注册成立的大型国有独资公司。下辖长沙水泵厂、长沙电机厂和长沙化工机械厂。注册资本1.04亿元,1997年末资产总值6.63亿元,销售收入2.97亿元,利税总额4067.67万元,其中利润1309.34万元,资产负债率为56%,职工总数5830人。主要从事泵、电机、化工设备、建材设备及其它通用机械和电气产品的生产、销售和进出口,并提供相应的工程设计、设备成套、技术培训和安装服务。

公司生产的泵类产品67.6%的品种达到国际80年代水平,其中大型立式涡壳泵、中开泵、大型立式斜流泵、熔融尿素泵、高温油泵、矿井排水泵等产品多次荣获国家和省科技成果奖。

此外,泵类产品的生产已于1997年11月取得ISO9001质量体系认证;电机产品采用IEC国际标准生产,目前正在进行ISO9001质量体系认证;化机产品的生产有化工部等颁发的一、二、三类压力容器设计、制造许可证,并获得美国机械工程师学会ASME规范容器制造授权证及U、U_2相应的钢印。

法人代表:吴京生

详细地址:长沙市芙蓉南路99号

联系电话:(0731)5218290

邮政编码:410007

长丰(集团)有限责任公司

长丰集团是1996年10月由中国人民解放军第七三一九工厂按照建立现代企业制度的要求,改制而成的现代企业集团,下设五个子公司和三个分公司,属国家大二型企业。

长丰集团通过引进日本三菱PAJERO汽车生产技术,对现有汽车生产线进行技术改造,其主导产品猎豹(三菱)汽车达到90年代国际先进水平,现已形成一万辆整车和三万辆车身冲压件的生产能力,产品畅销28个省、市、自治区。"太阳神"汽车天然胶、丁基胶内胎系列被评为全军优质产品和名牌产品,年产量达到200万条,产品销往全国各地。

1997年长丰集团完成工业总产值3.42亿元(不变价),实现销售收入4.69亿元,分别是去年同期的2.9倍和3.8倍,实现利税9940万元,其中净利润2867万元,分别是去年同期的4.5倍和2.9倍,企业生产经营蓬勃发展。1995年名列湖南工业经济活力200强第19位,并先后荣获"全国五一劳动奖状"、"湖南省先进企业"、"广州军区生产经营先进单位"等40多项省、军以上单位授予的荣誉称号。

法人代表:李建新

地址:湖南省永州市冷水滩区

电话:(0746)8456019—3068

邮编:425101

湖南省建华机械厂

该厂系湖南省科工办领导的大型二档工业企业,始建于1966年,位于永州市南郊,占地面积121平方米,建筑面积9.5万平方米,其中生产用建筑面积4.7万平方米。现有资产总额9639万元,固定资产原值5967万元,其中生产经营用固定资产原值4875万元,拥有各类设备892台(套),现有职工1843人,各类专业技术人员415人。1997年军品通过了ISO9001质量体系认证,民品通过了ISO9002质量体系认证、1998年又通过了质量体系第二方认定。企业产品先进,设备精良,经济效益连续三年名列同行之首。

近年来,工厂坚持科技兴厂、狠抓新产品开发和技术改造,先后成功地开发了三大系列的军民品,其中军品有7个品种,民品有11个品种,并以一流的质量,良好的服务,占领了市场,振兴了企业。

工厂目前生产的主要民品有:"五岑"牌汽车真空助力器和液压制动主缸系列产品,该产品吸收了国际上先进国家汽车制动——真空助力与双管路制动的先进技术,结合我国各类车型的特点自行研制生产的。该产品经中国汽车工业总公司重庆汽车研究所检测，其性能全部满足行业标准。其中寿命测试50万次，达到国内先进水平。

该厂还生产："雪雷"牌组合聚醚元醇、JM—821、822胶粘剂、特种胶、硝基磁漆等产品。

厂　址：湖南省永州市芝山区

联系电话：(0746)6731204

巴陵石化长岭炼油化工总厂

巴陵石化长岭炼油化工总厂是中国石化总公司在我国中南区的一座现代化大型炼油化工生产企业，也是全国最大、品种最全的炼油催化剂科研、生产基地，现有固定资产32亿元，占地面积8.6平方公里。

该厂具有加工原油500万吨、生产炼油催化剂2万吨、生产聚丙烯9万吨的能力。能生产汽油、煤油、石脑油、柴油、苯类、液化石油气、溶剂油以及催化裂化催化剂、催化重整催化剂、加氢精制催化剂、助燃剂、聚丙烯等70多种石油化工产品，其中0号轻柴油、6号抽提溶剂获国家产品质量金奖、石油甲苯、石油二甲苯、橡胶工业溶剂油、1号共Y催化裂化剂、6号重整催化剂获国家产品质量银奖。产品畅销全国17个省、市及港澳、东南亚地区。

法人代表：蒋信成

地　　址：湖南省岳阳市

电　　话：(0730)8451000

传　　真：(0730)8451010

邮　　编：414012

核工业二七二厂

核工业二七二厂是核工业总公司所属大型化工冶金企业。1989年晋升为国家二级企业。1992年被国家定为大型Ⅰ类企业。国家一级计量单位。年工业总产值5亿元以上。

工厂位于衡阳市南部，占地面积4.45平方公里，拥有资产总额5.39亿元，15公里专线铁路，9股道火车站，机车自备车厢及其它配套设备设施齐全，并且形成了设计、科研、咨询、生产等整套完善的生产经营管理体系。

现有在职职工3625人，中级以上各类专业技术人员600多人。主要产品有军用产品"121"、"181"；民用产品铁白粉、硝酸钠、硝酸钾、肌醇、中性蛋白酶、恒酸钙、纯碱等。其中，军用产品获国家质量金奖。销酸钠和钛白粉产品均畅销国内外。目前企业正朝着多产业、多机制、多产品的集团化公司方向发展。

地址：湖南省衡阳市江东区东阳渡

电话：(0734)8356541　8356300

传真：(0734)8356448

邮编：421004

湖南省湘江氮肥厂

湘氮位于中国南方最大的铁路交通枢纽株洲市。经过20余年的发展，现已形成以生产化肥、化工原料、有机化学品、建材、高新技术产品的大型企业。工厂现有职工5700余人，其中工程技术人员1300余人，拥有固定资产9.71亿元，年销售收入5.6亿元，年实现利税2100余万元，主要生产：合成氨17.6万吨、尿素25万吨、有机化学品11.2万吨(甲醇、甲醛、甲醇钠)、纯碱及氯化铵各4万吨、复肥15万吨、供热量550万百千焦、发电装机容量5.1万千瓦，同时还生产磁化肥、砖、砌块、钕铁硼磁性材料、工业氯化铵、水质稳定剂、工业及食品二氧化碳、工业及医用氧气、氮气、氢气、化学试剂等20余种产品。其中湘江牌尿素是部优产品，荣获国家金奖；甲醇为免检产品，同时为出口产品；复肥获97年度"湖南省首届农民满意肥"评比第一名。目前在同行企业中规模及效益处于领先地位，合成氨及尿素生产能力在全国55家中氮企业中排前6位，企业先后被评为化工部、省经贸委、省石化局授予各类多项荣誉称号。

随着生产规模的扩大，高新技术、高附加

值产品的进一步开发，湘氮将成为湖南重要的集化肥、无机化工、有机化工产品为一体的综合性生产基地。

厂长、党委书记：黄　斌

地　　址：湖南株洲建设北路 98 号

联系电话：(0733)8332500

传　　真：(0733)8361440

邮　　编：412005

湖南丽臣实业有限责任公司

湖南丽臣实业有限责任公司是湖南省规模最大的综合性日用化工大型企业。公司下设制皂、牙膏、合成洗涤剂、油化、热电、家化、包装材料等七个生产厂，一个科研所，二个中外合资企业，现有员工 2000 余人，固定资产 2.08 亿元。生产经营各类洗涤、护肤、化妆品及表面活性剂、食用油、塑料制品等。1997 年实现销售收入 3.05 亿元，利税 1680 万元。

公司技术力量雄厚，以“质量第一”为宗旨，生产的光辉增白洗衣粉、甲种工业甘油获部优名牌产品；马头洗衣皂、长沙药物牙膏、丽臣药物牙膏、光辉低泡洗衣粉、青春洗发膏、贝花洗洁精、坚尔齿牙膏、人造奶油获省优名牌产品。

法人代表、董事长：李丙均

总经理：贾齐正

厂址：长沙市浏阳河路 1 号

电话总机：(0731)4223211

电传：(0731)4223602

邮编：410003

长沙九芝堂(集团)有限公司

长沙九芝堂(集团)有限公司是国家重点中药企业。其前身“劳九芝堂药铺”创建于 1650 年，是中国著名老字号。公司下辖九芝堂制药厂、神箭制药厂、药材公司和供销公司四个骨干企业。并拥有经营生物制药、包装印刷、营养保健、进出口贸易等多家全资、控股子公司和参股企业。公司连续七年被评为“全国医药工业企业经济效益百强”和“湖南省工业企业经济效益百强”，其综合经济实力在湖南省医药行业排名第一，并已跻身于全国中药工业企业十强之列。

公司拳头产品神箭牌驴胶冲剂和芝牌乙肝宁冲剂及(颗粒剂)均是国家基本药物及国家中药保护品种，斯奇康、健胃愈疡片、肝立克、益龄精、偏瘫灵及浓缩丸系列产品，疗效确切，定位准确，市场前景广阔，新开发的天添营养保健食品，以其独特的效果，深受消费者喜爱。此外，公司年出口创汇在 150 万美元以上，产品远销日本、东南亚及美国。

“九洲同济，芝兰同芳”，公司力争 2000 年跻身中国医药 10 强和中国企业 500 强。

岳阳纸业集团有限公司

岳阳纸业集团公司兴建于 1958 年，占地面积 130 万平方米，现有职工 4500 人，总资产达 8 亿元，年生产能力 13 万吨，是目前国内最大的系列胶印书刊纸和低定量涂布纸生产厂家之一。主要产品有胶印书刊纸、新闻纸、双胶纸、高强中性印刷纸、书写纸、低定量涂布纸、箱板纸和制浆造纸设备，是湖南省最大制浆、造纸兼轻机制造的“国家大型一类”企业。1991 年晋升为国家二级企业。产品中 52g/M2“岳阳楼牌”胶印书刊纸荣获国家质量金奖。目前，企业正加快技改步伐，投资 20 亿元筹建年产 12 万吨彩色胶印书刊纸和低定量涂布纸项目，每年新增产值 10 亿元，整体经济实力大大增强，在国际国内市场竞争中一展中国国有纸业大公司的风采。

董事长、总经理：邱光林

党委书记、监事会主席：杨子文

地址：湖南省岳阳城陵矶

电话：(0730)8561622

传真：(0730)8561262

电挂：4786

邮编：414002

常德金鹏凹版印刷有限公司

常德金鹏凹版印刷有限公司是常德卷烟厂与香港贵联发展有限公司合资兴建的中外合资大型包装印刷企业。

公司位于湖南常德武陵经济技术开发区内，现拥有当今世界先进水平的六色凹版印刷生产线2条，西德产罗兰4色全电脑自动胶印机3台，德国产斯托拿与瑞士产博斯特全息镭射烫印模切两用机5台，并装备了英国产电脑自动分切机，日本产电脑全自动模切机、切纸机和全套进口制版印刷设备等20多台(套)，设备总值800多万美元，具有设计印刷100万大箱高中档次的烟用商标和其它各类纸质包装装潢产品的生产能力。97年底，中港双方总投资达9100万元，实现销售近2亿元，上缴增值税900万元。97年被评为湖南省先进技术型企业。

董事长：罗　毅

副董事长：蔡　得

总经理：蒋祥银

地址：湖南省常德武陵经济开发区(常挑路八号)

电话：(0736)7287028　7270376

传真：(0736)7280198

邮编：415000

中国水利水电第八工程局

中国水利水电第八工程局是集施工、科研、制造、安装于一体的工程施工总承包壹级企业，并具有对外经营合作权。拥有施工机械设备7000多台(套)。

该局先后在巴基斯坦、斯里兰卡、尼泊尔及国内17个省、市、自治区承建了大中型水利水电项目、工业民用建筑、桥梁、高速公路、港口、码头、机场等各类建筑工程。其中贵州乌江渡水电站等多项工程项目荣获优质工程奖。

该局始终坚持“科技兴局，质量取胜”的发展战略，在人工砂石系统安装与生产、高坝砼综合机械施工与砼温度控制、水下砼施工、砼实验研究、开挖工程、地下工程、预裂爆破、各类灌浆、大型金属结构制作安装、水轮发电机组安装及各种电压等级输变电设备安装等方面一直处于国内先进行列，尤其是碾压砼筑坝技术为国际先进水平。已有41项重大科研成果获国家、部、省级奖。先后被湖南省政府授予“文明建设先进单位”，98年全国总工会授予“五一劳动奖状”。

法人代表、局长：湛世明

地址：湖南省长沙市城南中路2号

联系电话：(0731)5563756

邮　　编：410007

湖南省第三工程公司

湖南省第三工程公司是国家一级大型施工企业。现有在职职工6877人，具有各类专业技术职称的1681人，其中高、中级职称的400多人。拥有固定资产9707万元，具有各种大、中型机械设备2218台(套)，有适应20层以上的施工塔吊20余台，具备完善的检验、测试点手段，建立有符合GB/T19002—1994标准要求的质量体系，具有承担各类工业与民用建筑(包括超高层建筑)和国外工程承包资质，具有建筑、水电、暖通、安装、房地产开发、装饰装璜、机械制造、路桥和基础工程、混凝土预制构件，上、下水泥制管等施工(生产)综合能力，年施工生产能力10亿元以上。

97年公司承担国家、省属重点工程7项，其中湘电30万千瓦机组17个月并网发电，聚炳稀工程正式投产，获省石化总公司等各级领导的高度赞扬，97年湘潭人民银行综合大楼项目被授予省“芙蓉奖”工程；湘潭行政办公大楼、长炼第二污水工程被评为省优质工程。省图书城工地综合考评在长沙市名列前茅。

公司经理、企业法人：董华生

地　　址：湘潭市解放南路289号

联系电话：8265467

邮　　编：410001

中国建筑第五工程第二建筑安装公司

该公司是国家直属大型一级建筑安装施工企业，现有正式职工 2500 人，各类专业技术人员 800 余人(其中高级技术职称 30 余人)；拥有固定资产 6900 万元，各类中外施工机械设备 1200 余台，具有承建各类工业与民用建筑安装工程、工业设备安装工程、市政工程、水利电力工程、公路桥梁工程等资质和经验，1997 年通过 ISO9002 质量体系认证，年施工能力 8 亿元以上。

30 年来，施工足迹遍布国内 12 个省、市和伊拉克、南也门等 3 个国家，先后承建了湖南柘溪水电站、华能岳阳电厂、岳阳 5 万吨己内酰胺工程、上海外高桥电厂、湖北襄樊电厂、湖南石门电厂、珠海斗门水厂、上海东方大厦、厦门兴鸿广场、泉州福华商厦、南京颐和商厦、长沙华天酒店、天都大厦等一系列国家、省级及市级重点工程和伊拉克阿巴西亚坝、库法坝等国外水电工程，创建省部级优质工程 10 余项，连续 11 年被岳阳市人民政府评为“特级重合同守信誉企业”，连续 3 年被湖南省评为“特级信用企业”。

法人代表：尤全文

公司地址：湖南省岳阳市新路口

电　　话：(0730)8222500

邮　　编：414000

铁道部第五工程局机械筑路工程处

铁道部第五工程局机械筑路工程处是铁道部审查、建设部核发证书，从事铁路、公路、市政、工民建工程施工的全民所有制企业，是国家首批大型建筑企业之一。

现有职工 1800 人，工程专业技术人员 404 人(具有高、中级技术职称的 70 人)，技术工人 1147 人，有与施工项目相适应的现代化配套机械 368 台，总功率 37160 千瓦。拥有资本金 4389.5 万元，固定资产原值 8734 万元，年产值 2.2 亿元。设有健全的质量管理机构和功能齐全经国家认证的一级工程试验室。

三十多年来先后参加了成昆、衡广、京九等 10 多条铁路干线和铁路枢纽建设；以及成渝、京沈等 10 多条高速公路及衡阳、岳阳等近 10 座城市的市政建设。曾荣获湖南省“百强企业”，铁道部“全国铁路安全先进单位”等多项荣誉称号，具有良好的社会信誉。

该处全体员工感谢全国各界朋友的大力支持，并愿与社会各界朋友真诚合作，在未来的建筑市场中再创辉煌。

法人代表：姜寿海

联系地址：衡阳市江东区洪塘冲 32 号

电话：传真：(0734)8311234

邮　　编：421002

铁道部第五工程局电务工程处

铁道部第五工程局电务工程处，是从事铁路通信、信号、电力及电气化工程施工的专业队伍。兼营房屋建筑。1995 年再次经国家建设部核准为铁路电务工程一级施工企业。现有员工 1880 人，专业技术干部 406 人，其中高级职称 28 人。固定资产 5320 万元。能承接铁路、公路、市政、地铁、机场、水利、码头等建筑项目的“四电”工程及其配套的房屋建筑工程的施工。

建处四十多年来，参加过国内外 20 多条铁路干线“四电”工程施工和上海引水电气控制工程、东莞邮电工程、广州地铁通信、信号、电气化工程施工。

该处 1990 年荣获国务院企业管理委员会和国务院生产委员会授予的“国家二级企业”称号及证书。98 年荣获中华全国总工会授予的“五一劳动奖”及证书。承建的工程多次被评为国家和部级优质工程。97 年企业通过了 IS09002 质量体系认证。

法人代表：张关生

地　　址：湖南省怀化市红星路4号
电　　话：(0745)2233351转65255
电　　挂：怀化6670
传　　真：2237056
邮　　编：418000

长沙市建筑工程公司

长沙市建筑工程公司系国家一级国有建筑施工中一型企业，具有承担各种类型、各种结构、高层次、大跨度的工业与民用建筑施工，室内外高、中档装饰装修施工和道路、桥梁施工的能力。公司现有职工3500多人，专业技术人员589人，其中工程师以上职称人员181人；注册资产5600万元，总资产3.2亿元；年产值近2亿元。1997年工程质量合格率100%，优良率71.4%，有两项工程荣获湖南省建筑工程芙蓉奖，施工的赤新路立交桥荣获全国市政工程质量最高奖——金杯奖。公司被建设部授予“全国工程建设管理先进单位”和“全国工程质量优秀企业”光荣称号。

长沙望城建筑安装工程公司

长沙望城建筑安装工程公司始建于1964年。1996年经国家建设部审核批准晋升为国家一级施工企业。公司注册资金3060万元，自有流动资金1600万元；现有职工2841人，其中各类工程经济技术职称人员488人，各类持证上岗人员298人，有58人有项目经理证书，技术工人平均5.2级；拥有各种施工机械设备1380台件、折合功率11450马力。可承担各种类型、各种规模、高层次、大跨度(包括桥梁、水库工程和各种高级装饰)的工业与民用建设项目的建筑施工。

近三年，公司年完成建安产值过亿元，近五年施工项目达160多项，建筑面积51万多平方米，工程合格率100%，其中省优质样榜工程10项，优良率年均为62%。公司连续20年被省、市、县主管部门评为“先进企业”，被省建行评定为“特级信用单位”，省工商局授予“重合同、守信用”企业。

公司秉承“以质量求生存，以信誉求发展”的宗旨，以优质、高速、安全、低耗的方式服务于用户。

总经理：魏俊杰
地址：长沙望城高塘岭镇郭亮北路84号
电话：(0731)8062140
邮编：410200

湖南新华联置业有限公司

湖南新华联置业有限公司(原振信置业)系马来西亚新华联集团有限公司，中国银行湖南省信托咨询公司合资组建的二级资质房地产开发企业，注册资金250万美元。现有员工76名，其中具有各类专业技术职称的技术、管理人员52名。下辖振信贸易有限公司、湖南九华物业管理有限公司。

公司成立五年来，取得了较快发展，先期征地近50亩，累计投入资金2.3亿元，先后建成九家湾高级华侨公寓、兰景花园高级商住区、华联大厦、湘春路商住楼、以及华联花园高级商住区等项目，总面积超过12万平方米。最近，又与三湘公司达成协议，在湘湖渔场征地80亩，拟开发总建筑面积达15万平方米的新华联花园。

公司全体员工信奉“团结、务实、开拓、奉献”的企业精神，坚持“信誉第一、质量第一、顾客至上”的经营宗旨，竭诚为所有客户创造最大价值，提供最佳服务。

董事长：傅　军
总经理：方明理
公司地址：湖南省长沙市芙蓉中路269号
　　　　　华联大厦23楼
电　　话：(0731)2233888转
传　　真：(0731)4434088
邮政编码：410011

湘潭信泰物业开发有限公司

湘潭信泰物业开发有限公司是由湖南电线电缆集团公司、湖南大阳实业股份有限公司、湘潭市外商投资服务公司、中国银行银鑫公司、香港信港贸易有限公司合资设立，注册资金1800万元人民币。经省、市建委、市经委、工商部门核准为二级开发企业，列为湖南省房地产开发企业百强之一。主要采用合资合作、自营等方式，从事国内的土地开发、各类房屋（写字楼、住宅楼、厂房、仓库、商厦）的规划设计、营造、出售、出租以及与之配套的物业管理、建筑装饰材料的经营等业务。

公司自成立以来，主要开发建造了湘潭明珠花园、大阳新村、东塘村住宅小区和长征新村住宅区、金凤住宅区、深圳沁园小区、红旗大厦、市老干二所公寓、湘潭师院学生公寓、岳塘国土局综合楼、湘潭市防汛指挥中心楼、湘潭市沥青厂宿舍等优秀物业，累计开发面积达12.8万平方米。1997年被省、市评为文明卫生先进单位、安居工程优秀住宅小区、房地产开发先进企业、外商投资先进企业。

总经理：朱红斌

地址：湘潭市建设南路1号

电话：(0732)8590592

电挂：5000

邮编：411101

长沙新大新置业有限公司

长沙新大新置业有限公司注册资本3600万元，现有员工30余人，其中具有中高级职称的技术、管理人员20余人。主营房地产开发，同时承担城市建设各项基础设施和配套公共设施的综合开发，代建房屋工程，综合开发土地房屋等业务。

公司正在兴建的“长沙新大新购物中心大厦”位于湖湘繁华的商业街——黄兴中路，是长沙市五一广场商业特区的重点建设项目。大厦由两层地下车库、七层商场、一层仓储、十八层高档商住楼组成。楼高86.8m，总建筑面积4.33万m^2。商场采用国际最流行的“城中城、街中街”商业布局理念，按立体商业街形式设计成精品商业城。商住楼的设计充分满足了当今成功人士对阳江与功能的追求，“厅有阳台，功能明晰”被专业人士称为不可多得的经典之作！长沙新大新购物中心大厦是您投资置业经营、创造辉煌人生的理想舞台。

法人代表：伍跃时

公司地址：长沙市人民路新59号投资银行大厦11楼

联系电话：2222988

图文传真：5501118

长沙工程置业有限公司

长沙工程置业有限公司是1993年经长沙市建委批准成立的全民所有制叁级房地产开发企业。公司先后参与金盆村小区项目建设开发和独立开发西文庙坪小区尚德街住宅，新生村住宅等项目。其中自行开发、设计、施工的解放路星光购物中心项目被评为市优良工程，并体现了公司开发、设计、施工的整体实力。公司始终以诚信、守义为经营宗旨，视造福市民为己任，注重经济效益和社会效益，合同履约率100%。公司不断进取，完善自我，成为长沙市首批改制企业之一，公司管理向现代企业制度迈进，给企业发展创造了新的机遇。

法人代表：蓝光明

地　　址：长沙市八一路149号

联系电话：4421190

邮政编码：410011

常德湘北房地产开发公司

常德湘北房地产开发公司是湖南省湘北工贸集团总公司创办的，以房地产开发为主兼营商贸建材等多种产业的综合型全民所有制企业，现有员工21人，公司设四部一室，各部门有较强的技术力量和精干的业务人员，具有高、中、初专业技术人员17人，占总数的80%以上。公司自93年成立以来，已开发商品房建筑面积76000平方米，定向开发建筑面积16000平方米，开发土地51000平方米，完成总投资4200万元，销售商品房总面积40000平方米，累计销售金额3500万元。经湖南省建委资质审查属国家开发资质三级企业。1995年经湖南省统计局评为湖南省房产开发“百强”企业，一九九七年获得常德市房地产综合开发“十佳”企业的光荣称号。

法人代表：席佑林

地址：常德市洞庭大道432号

电话：7715380

邮编：415000

湖南省耒阳电厂

湖南省耒阳电厂是国家电力公司下属的大二型企业，是国家“七五”期间的重点能源项目，规划装机容量100—120万千瓦。一期工程两台20万千瓦机组分别于1988年6月、1989年11月投产。企业先后荣获全国“五一”劳动奖状、全国电力系统安全文明生产达标企业、全国环境保护先进企业等地市以上各种奖牌65项。

该厂现有职工1530人，其中：专业技术人员374人，固定资产9亿元，占地3000亩。扩建两台30万千瓦机组工程，前期工作顺利进行，计划99年开工，2002年全部建成，届时耒阳电厂将成为100万千瓦的大型企业。

该厂地处古城耒阳，位于京广线、107国道、郴耒煤田旁，交通便利。是一个环境优美，生活福利娱乐设施一流的花园电厂。

厂长：彭俊清

厂址：湖南省耒阳市振兴路185号

电话：(0734)4302241

邮编：421800

长沙汽车客运发展(集团)公司

长沙汽车客运发展(集团)公司是湖南省交通运输跨地区、跨行业、跨所有制、集运、工、贸为一体的大型企业集团。

该公司下辖内部核算实体12个，全资、控购、参股的紧密型、半紧密型企业20家，已成为湖南省国有公路旅客运输历史最长、规模最大、效益最好的骨干企业。现有员工7000余人，固定资产原值2.52亿元，年营业收入1.57亿元，拥有各类营运车辆1000多台，经营长沙至全省82个地(州)、市、县以及毗邻9省35个城市、工业区、名胜风景旅游点的旅客运输、中巴、的士、市内公共运输以及四星客车制造厂和旅乐食宿全方位配套服务。

九六年、九七年实现利税过1000万元，受到长沙市人民政府的嘉奖。为增强竞争力，公司投资新建了长沙汽车东站、西站、南站三个大型客站和一个县级站星沙汽车站。该公司94年在全国500家最大服务企业的80家公路交通运输企业中名列13名，并名列湖南省大型公路交通运输企业榜首。(撰稿人：李中跃)

地址：长沙市八一路35号

电话：2233445—2445

邮编：410001

郴州市汽车运输总公司

郴州市汽车运输总公司是郴州市最大的国营专业运输企业，成立于1957年9月，现有职工4300余人，资产总额1.3亿元，占地总面积60.56万平方米，总建筑面积为21万平方米。下设25个单位，其中客车队11个，货车队3个，出租汽车公司和旅行社各一个；有17个车站及各类型车600辆，其中营运客车560辆，营运里程达15.64万公里，每天可发1056个班次。此外公司还拥有马家坪商品批发市场和副食水果批发市场，及机动车配件等三大商贸市场，共有各类商业门面、摊位2800余个。位于市区内投资2600多万元，占地15000平方米的郴州市中心汽车站正在兴建之中。与中国一汽集团联营兴办了湖南最大型的中国一汽服务站。公司已形成一个"一业为主，多业发展，大、中、小型，高、中、低档车相结合，运、工、商、贸为一体"的新型运输企业。1997年再次荣获郴州市"优秀领导班子"称号。

法人代表：黄兆林

地　　址：郴州市郴桂路

联系电话：(总机)2222911

衡阳市公共交通总公司

衡阳市公共交通总公司成立于1950年。主要经营公共汽车客运、轮渡和出租汽车业务和经营房地产开发、驾驶员培训、广告业、旅馆业、物业管理。该公司下设16个基层单位和14个职能处室，现有职工2633人，营运车辆230台(未含的士)，客轮3艘，营运(航)线路23条，线路总长181公里，线路总长122公里，固定资产原值5208万元，净值3424万元。

1997年完成营业收入4064万元，营运里程1148公里，客运总量4902万人次。1995年与新加坡客商合资兴办的狮城汽车服务有限公司拥有的士近百辆，现已取得了良好的经济效益。目前总公司尚有待开发土地100多亩，其中20多亩位于衡阳火车站前最繁华的街边，可兴建贸易市场、宾馆、住宅、工厂等。总公司愿以各种方式招商引资，共图大业。

法人代表：管志英

地址：衡阳市环城北路94号

电话：(0734)8223769

邮编：421001

湖南华天国际旅行社

湖南华天国际旅行社是湖南华天集团的直属企业，是经国家旅游局批准，可直接经营国际国内旅游业务的国际性旅游经济实体，是湖南省唯一进入全国百强的国际旅行社。

华天国旅主要组织办理国内公民赴国外及港、澳、台地区旅游、商务考察，为之办理因公、因私护照，代理各国的签证，承办外国人、华侨、港澳台同胞来中国旅游观光业务，为团体、散客安排观光旅游、商务旅游、文化、体育等多种特殊旅游项目。

华天国旅拥有一批从事多年旅游工作的管理人员和一支训练有素、经验丰富的英、日、德、法、俄导游翻译队伍；在世界各地都有信誉良好的旅行社负责接待；并拥有湖南国际包机公司15%的股份。

华天国旅长期以来坚持客户至上，信誉第一，以细致、优良、完善的服务赢得广大客户的一致好评，是值得您信赖的合作伙伴。伴您天涯行，华天国旅献真情！

法人代表：刘芬珍

地址：长沙市解放东路380号(华天大酒店内)

联系电话：(0731)4119138　4145872

(0744)8232858

传真：(0731)4118148　4462235

(0744)8233333

邮编：410001

湖南省中国青年旅行社

湖南省中国青年旅行社是经国家旅游局批准的可直接经营国内业务的旅游经济实体，创办于1984年。该社主要承办外国人、华侨、港澳台人士来中国旅游观光业务，为团体和散客安排观光旅游，商务旅游，文化、体育交流等多种旅游项目；组织办理国内公民赴境外(包括港澳台地区)和祖国各地的旅游考察；同时经营国际国内航空机票、火车票代售业务、出租车业务、因私出境(留学、劳务)咨询业务等，是湖南省最具实力的旅行社之一。

该社拥有一支经营旅游业务多年、素质精良的管理人员队伍，拥有一支语种齐全、训练有素的导游队伍，始终不渝地坚持"宾客至上，信誉第一”的宗旨，愿同海内外各界同仁竭诚合作，共同发展。

地址：长沙市展览馆路 46 号
电话：(0731)4434369　4447764
传真：(0731)4441866　4414946
邮编：410005

湖南衡山国际旅游股份有限公司

湖南衡山国际旅游股份有限公司以募集方式设立于 1993 年 5 月，经湖南省证券监督管理委员会确认，在湖南省工商行政管理局登记注册，注册资本为 5500 万元人民币。公司充分利用衡阳地区丰富的旅游资源，以维护股东权益，提高投资收益，实现资产保值增值为目的，立足于资本经营，形成了一个以旅游资源和旅游物业开发为主，旅游服务和旅游产品经销为辅的旅游产业集团，其经营和投资收益逐年稳步增长。

公司地址：湖南省衡阳市船山路 28 号
电话：(0734)8260888
邮编：421001

湘 江 宾 馆

湘江宾馆始建于 1950 年，1990 年被国家旅游局评定为湖南省首批涉外三星级宾馆。现有各类客房 300 间，床位 600 个，全部客房均有中央空调和 IDD、DDD 直拨电话以及可接收香港卫视台节目的闭路电视；有餐厅、酒吧 11 间，餐位 480 个，经营正宗湘菜及川菜、粤菜、西餐、自助餐，是宴请宾客、朋友聚餐、婚庆寿宴的理想场所；豪华会议室、国际会议厅适合于举行签字仪式和新闻发布会等重要活动；宾馆适宜于商务宾客、国内外旅游者和 200 人以下的会议住宿。此外，宾馆设有歌厅、舞厅、卡拉 OK 厅、桑拿、保健按摩，服务设施齐全。

湘江宾馆总经理文济资先生及全体员工，热忱欢迎您的光临！

地址：长沙市中山路 36 号
电话：(0731)4408888
传真：(0731)4448285

新 天 宾 馆

新天宾馆隶属湖南省军区五里牌干休所。93 年 11 月正式营业，1994 年被评为国家二星级涉外旅游饭店，95 年被评为大型服务企业，全省旅馆百强第 9 名，96 年被湖南省评为优秀星级宾馆，97 年普升为三星级，连续 4 年被评为省军区优秀企业。

宾馆位于远大一路 3 号，占地面积 14000 平方米，现有固定资产总额 1.45 亿元；高中档客房 210 套，写字楼一栋，有可供 400 人同时就餐的中餐酒楼、西餐厅各一个，各种大小会议室 6 个，有富丽堂皇的新闻发布中心和影视会议中心。歌舞厅、商场、桑拿保健药浴中心、咖啡厅、商务中心、票务中心、旅行社等服务设施配套齐全，还建成了拥有 8000 平方米营业场所的分店——新天高桥大酒店。近期，又投资 600 多万元对客房进行了改造，改造后客房接近四星标准。

宾馆秉行“宾客至上，服务第一”的宗旨，实行军事化管理，不断完善服务设施，提高服务质量，竭诚为广大宾客提供优质服务。

法人代表：高建平
地　　址：长沙市远大一路 3 号
联系电话：2299661(总机)
传　　真：2297736
邮政编码：410001

长 沙 大 厦

长沙大厦地处火车站、民航售票处“金三角地带”，占地面积 1.8 万平方米，建筑面积 4.3 万平方米；主楼 22 层，高 71.5 米；现有员工 1120 人，固定资产 2 亿元；是湖南省首家大型多功能、综合性商业企业。大厦拥有营业面积 11000 平方米的超市和一家涉外定点宾馆——银河酒店以及物业经营公司，并设有海鲜酒楼、旋转餐厅、红番的士高、影视城、卡拉 OK 包房、咖啡厅、西餐厅、鲜花屋、彩色扩印等一系列服务设施。

开业十年来，大厦累计实现营业收入 10 亿元，上缴国家税额 2100 万元，并荣获："全国商业计量先进单位"、"全国商业计量政策法规最佳单位"、"全国执行物价计量政策法规最佳单位"、"全国文明经营示范单位"、"湖南省执行物价政策法规信得过单位"、"湖南省零售商业综合实力百强企业（第八名）"、"湖南省百强旅馆企业（第二名）"、"省级重合同守信用企业"、"省百城万店无假货先进单位"。

法人代表：彭家顺

地址：长沙市五一东路 87 号

联系电话：4114408

邮编：410001

湖南太空世界实业有限公司

湖南太空世界实业有限公司是由湖南省展览总公司和香港惠基实业有限公司合资经营的集宾馆、酒楼、娱乐为一体的服务型企业。总投资 8000 万元，从业人员 400 余人，1997 年营业收入 2900 万元。

公司由太空大世界（原太空娱乐城）、太空宾馆、太空酒楼三大经营实体组成，其中：太空大世界是中南乃至全国一流的高档次、多功能的美食娱乐城，仅灯光、音响和装修就耗资人民币二千多万元。拥有八百餐位的美食啤酒广场、45 间音响一流、装修风格各异的豪华 KTV 包房和湖南省目前享有盛誉的 JJ 歌厅。1997 年被长沙市文化局授予"文明娱乐厅"的光荣称号。

湖南太空世界实业有限公司法人代表、董事长兼总经理朱冬余先生率全体员工恭候各位嘉宾的光临。

公司地址：长沙市展览路 50 号

电话：4421395

邮编：410005

湖南省工艺品进出口公司

湖南省工艺品进出口公司是一家拥有雄厚经济实力和良好信誉的国家外贸公司。1978 年成立以来，公司以经营湖南工艺品为基础，并采取灵活贸易措施，接受委托代理，开展中外合资经营，合作生产，承办"三来一补"等项业务，逐步发展成为多门类多品种的产品经营格局，连续五年名列中国进出口额最大的五百家企业并迈入全国省级工艺进出口公司前十名，雄跨湖南省外贸企业十强，连年被中国银行湖南省分行评为"AAA"特级信用企业，被长沙海关授予"信得过企业"称号，并先后被省外经贸委授予"创汇与效益一等奖"和省直机关工委授予"双文明建设先进单位"。目前公司经营的主要产品有"日用陶瓷，艺术陶瓷，鞋帽箱包，有色金属及矿产品，铸件产品，五金工具，工农具，纺织品，抽纱品及服装，夏布，圣诞树及其系列装饰产品，草柳竹藤，编织品，木框坐垫，各种伞、扇、软木画等工艺品，珠宝，纸制品。

法人代表、总经理：付　辉

单位地址：长沙市五一东路 80 号

电话：(0731)2283197

传真：(0731)2287869　2287981

邮编：410001

湖南省轻工业品进出口公司

公司成立于 60 年代初，现年进出口总额 1.378 亿美元，系中国进出口额最大的 500 家企业之一。

该司设有 12 个业务部，拥有 5 个独资子公司，自办厂 4 个，国内外合资合作企业 6 个，经营的主要出口产品有：鞋帽、箱包（袋）、文体器材、五金、纸制品、玩具、玻璃器皿、玻璃、搪瓷、铝制品、建筑材料、塑料制品、洗涤用品、轻工机械，日用百货，日用陶瓷，工艺品、家用电器，自行车，缝纫机等 20 多类 1000 多个品种。其中"DH"运动鞋、布胶鞋和"DEYI"鞋及 FEI-

TIEN 箱、包(袋)等花色繁多,款式新颖,选材考究,质地优良,饮誉国际市场,年创汇 2000 多万美元。"海鸥"、"WINCO"牌电池,"蓬蓬"牌热水瓶和"金宝"牌卫生纸、书写纸、打字纸等产品被评为省优、部优,深受用户好评。

公司在积极开展出口业务的同时,还承办地方进口业务,以及"三来一补"和房地产等业务。1997 年公司被评为全国外贸系统先进集体,总经理张华香被评为全国外经贸系统劳动模范。

湖南省土产畜产进出口公司

湖南省土产畜产进出口公司成立于 1950 年,是湖南外贸创建最早的专业骨干公司之一。四十多年来,公司一直奉行质量第一,信誉至上,优质服务,互惠互利的经营宗旨,积极发展同世界各国贸易往来,出口业务不断扩大。现已发展成为经营进出口业务、来料加工、进料加工、补偿贸易、转口贸易、易货贸易、提供代理、承办中外合资、合作和"三来一补"业务及仓储、运输、加工服务等项目的大型国有综合进出口公司。并连续 5 年名列全国进出口总额最大的 500 家企业之一。

公司主要经营的出口商品:京果类、食品罐头类、山货类、棉麻纺织类、饲料类、香料油类、林产竹木及制品类、小五金类、皮革及制品类,羽绒及制品类、毛、鬃、绒及制品类、各种肠衣以及工艺、轻工、纺织、机械电器、医药保健品、矿产品等 10 多类 80 多个品种。特别是"温尔康"牌羽绒制品、"斑马牌"蚊香、"白鹤牌"蚊香等名牌商品更是享誉海内外,深受广大消费者喜爱。

法人代表、总经理:周国权
地址:中国湖南长沙市五里牌
电话:(0731)4727265
传真:(0731)4726674
电传:98126 TUHSICN
电挂:"TUHSU"CHANG SHA
邮编:410001

湖南省金属材料总公司

湖南省金属材料总公司是湖南省首批大型Ⅰ类批发企业,注册资金 6478 万元,总资产 49584 万元,现有在职职工 680 人。

1997 年购销钢材、生铁、矿石、有色金属及原材料等总量近 85 万吨,购销总额近 20 亿元,进入中国 100 家最大物资流通企业行列,荣获湖南批发业销售收入净额第八名,并在 1996 年被国家确定为全国第一批钢材代理制试点企业。

总公司地处长沙市芙蓉路繁荣地段,拥有较高档次的办公楼两座,机械化程度较高的大型仓库两座,二条三股道 6 公里长的铁路专线以及各种装卸、运输设备和车辆共计 140 多台套,年吞吐能力在 70 万吨以上。

总公司本着信誉第一、质量第一、服务第一的经营宗旨,与广大客户携手共进,为湖南的经济腾飞作出贡献。

法人代表:李长保
地　　址:长沙市芙蓉中路 29 号
电话:2253310
传真:4441442　4495352
邮编:410005

湖南邵东百货股份有限公司

座落在全省第一个民营经济实验区的湖南邵东百货股份有限公司是一个以开拓农村市场闻名全国的跨省经营的大型商贸企业。现有员工 2452 人,在省内外拥有 7 座百货大楼,9 家专业批发公司,2 座工厂,2 个宾馆,有劳服公司,维修中心、车队、仓储和房地产开发公司等 23 个核算单位,总资产近 3 亿元。

公司经营百货、针纺、家电、文化用品、洗化用品、副食、家具等品种达 3 万余种,质量可靠,价格合理;97 年实现销售 25021 万元,98 年一季度销售突破 1 亿元,连续荣获湖南省商业"十佳",利税"十强"和省"文明建设先进单位"称号。

公司在未来发展战略中，以开拓农村市场为方向，组建“联合舰队”，共图伟业，苦练内功，深化改革，完善机制，抓住机遇，通过资产重组，扩大经营规模，积极向高科技工业，高效农业进军，沿着贸工农方向发展，向组建特大型企业集团迈进。

董事长、总经理、法人代表：张本善（湖南省人大代表、湖南省优秀企业家、中国商贸全国理事会百货分会副主任）

党委书记：李向阳

单位地址：湖南邵东县城解放路 6 号

联系电话：(0739)2721012

图文传真：(0739)2721826

邮　　编：422800

衡阳市供销大厦股份有限公司

衡阳市供销大厦股份有限公司是湘南地区最大的综合性大型商业企业。座落在国道、省道交汇处，地理位置优越。公司占地 2 万平方米，营业面积 17100 平方米，拥有商场 8000 平方米和一个二星级宾馆、大型停车场、船山酒家、翼星电影院及 8000 平方米标准仓库。总资产 2.5 亿元，净资产 8100 万元；经济实力雄厚；服务项目齐全，集商业贸易、生产加工、宾馆服务、影视娱乐为一体，自 93 年以来年销售连年过亿元，97 年达 2.4 亿元，雄居本市国合商界之首，列全省国合零售商界第八位，是全国供销系统“自强企业”、“全国商业信誉企业”、“商贸服务全国用户满意单位”。

地址：湖南省衡阳市蒸湘北路 30 号

电话：8221211　8221212

邮编：421001

湖南省医药公司

公司于 1949 年成立，是湖南成立最早、规模最大、实力最雄厚的国家医药商业企业。公司下属各类经营部门十六个，主营化学药品、医疗器械、化学试剂、玻璃仪器和麻精药品，并担负着全省灾情、疫情及突发事故的药械储备供应工作。公司先后被省政府评为“省级先进企业”，1991 年被国家医药管理局和国务院企业管理指导委员会批准为“国家二级企业”，被国家经贸委和外经贸委批准为享有直接进出口权的内贸企业。1997 年公司各经营部门年购销总额达 5 亿元，同比增长 51.66%。

从事医药商业工作近四十年的范良君总经理正率公司全体员工以人为本，建立全新的现代企业文化，全力实施国营医药商业企业全面质量管理规范(GSP)，建立全方位现代企业制度，为湖南医药经济和祖国医药卫生事业的发展作出新的贡献。

公司地址：长沙市芙蓉路 249 号

联系电话：4478010　4478034

邮　　编：410008

衡阳市饮食服务总公司

衡阳市饮食服务总公司座落在衡阳市繁华地段解放路 451 号，是湖南省地市餐饮业中唯一的一家大型企业。现有职工 2200 余人，下辖 21 个支部，68 个独立核算单位，有经营场地 2.1 万多 m^2，固定资产近亿元。经过几十年的努力，已形成以餐饮、旅店、冷饮为龙头，商业、娱乐业于一体的经营格局，并有一套精干、高效的决策班子和管理机构。1997 年，营业收入 1960 余万元，实现利税 160 万元。

法人代表：周宏达

单位地址：衡阳市解放路 451 号

联系电话：(0734)8225741

邮　　编：421001

怀化铁路总公司怀化医院

怀化铁路总公司怀化医院 1994 年被评为二级甲等医院，现有职工 498 人，其中副高级以上职称的 118 人，病床 300 张，拥有磁共振减像系统、彩色B超、全自动生化分析仪、人工肾、多参数摇控心电监护仪、500mAX光机、高压氧仓、系列内窥镜、麻醉机、心肺复苏仪、同光路手术显微镜、体外震波碎石机、依—192后装肿瘤治疗机等先进医疗设备。

该院技术力量雄厚、特色专科突出。能进行各类腔内检查和手术,包括复杂的肾癌、输尿管癌、膀胱癌的根治,大脑半球肿瘤切除,基底节区脑溢血的手术治疗等;流行性出血热的诊治方面有独到的经验;特别是拥有中华医学会湖南分会内科常务学术委员渝良波主任医师在治疗心血管疾病方面造诣较深,具有较高的知名度。1984年以来,获省、部级成果16项,总公司级成果82项,省部级以上发表交流论文460篇。

法人代表:姚湘澧

地址:怀化市武陵中路9号

电话:(0745)2760638

邮编:412001

株洲电力机车工厂职工医院

株洲电力机车工厂职工医院始建于1954年,占地面积近4万平方米,建筑面积14594平方米,门诊建筑面积6830平方米。现有固定资产2000余万元;病床200张;职工290人,其中卫技人员255人,高中级职称人员76人。每年门诊量30多万人次,收治住院病人2600多人。

目前,该院拥有全身CT、彩超、电视腹腔镜、500mAX光机、多功能麻醉机、生化分析仪、电解质分析仪、血气分析仪、前列腺电切镜、各类监护仪、动态心电分析系统等万元以上设备共计100余台套。现已成为中国铁路工业总公司五家重点医院之一。1994年被评为二级甲等医院,1996年通过爱婴医院的验收,1997年被评为铁道部卫生系统先进集体。

法人代表:陈　兵

地址:株洲田心东门

电话:(0733)8441341

邮编:412001

长岭炼油化工总厂职工医院

长岭炼油化工总厂职工医院隶属国家一级企业长岭炼油化工总厂,是湘北一所有名望的二级甲等医院和爱婴医院。

该院现有职工340人,其中主任医师2人,副主任医师15人,中级职称115人。开放病床250张,拥有核磁共振、血液透析机、彩色B超、前列腺射频治疗仪、1250mA带电视X线机等万元以上设备100余台件,固定资产原值2400万元。

年门、急诊量近20万人次,收治住院病人5000人次。特色重点专科建设成效显著,如术中、术后胆道镜检查和取石术、经尿道前列腺电镜切除术等日臻精湛,急性心肌梗塞治愈率达90%以上,烧伤治疗技术享誉湘北。近年在省以上医学刊物上发表论文60余篇,获省级科研成果奖3项。

法人代表、院长:林俊华(主任医师)

地址:岳阳市云溪区长岭炼油化工总厂职工医院

电话:(0730)8451000转52500

传真:(0730)8453040

邮编:414012

株洲三三一医院

中国南方航空动力机械集团株洲三三一医院创建于1951年。现有职工553人,其中主任医师16人,副主任医师(技、护)37人,拥有病床450张,拥有株洲市眼科中心、耳鼻喉科中心、白内障超声乳化中心、甲状腺外科中心。1992年晋升为“二甲”医院;1993年被列为衡阳医学院教学医院;1996年被评审为湖南省爱婴医院;1997年被评为湖南省、株洲市“四满意”服务竞赛活动先进单位。

该院先后开展和引进肾移植手术、腹腔镜手术、B超放射介入检查治疗、角膜移植、重症肝炎抢救等新诊疗项目300余项,引进高档全身CT机、腹腔手术镜、彩色B超等万元以上设备83台，总价值1200余万元。

法人代表：邓定安

地址：湖南省株洲市芦淞区董家段

电话：(0733)8550650

邮编：412002

核工业四一五医院

核工业四一五医院是中国核工业总公司直属的一所集医疗、教学、科研和药品生产为一体的大型综合性医院。现有职工1000余人，各级专业技术人员700余人，其中高级职称75人，享受国务院政府特殊津贴的专家13人。医院设病床600张，年门、急诊15万人次，收治住院病人8000余人次。医疗拥有设备1800多台件，其中包括：全身CT、八导生理记录仪、彩色多普勒超声诊断仪、麻醉监护仪、血气分析仪、血液透析机、全自动生化分析仪、800mA多功能数字减影X光机、各种内窥镜等。

该院是三级乙等医院、爱婴医院和衡阳医学院教学医院，获衡阳市"十佳医院"、"文明服务医院"、"药品质量信得过医院"等光荣称号。有11项科研成果分获全国科学大会和省部级"科技进步"奖。

法人代表：贺治溪

党委书记：陶荣安

地址：湖南省衡阳市江东区东风路390号

电话：(0734)8332851—2016

邮编：421002

湖南省邮电规划设计院

湖南省邮电规划设计院是经国家审查批准的甲级勘察、设计、施工总承包单位。该院高级工程师占21%，工程师占39%，大学本科及以上毕业者占72%，该院先后为省内外承担了程控交换、数字微波、移动通信、卫生通信、光纤通信、可视会议电话、图像通信、闭路电视、防磁电干扰、绿卡工程、200号业务、300号业务、综合智能布线、分组交换、7号信令网、计算机互联网、信息港、光同步(SDH)数字传输网、邮政机械、数字数据(DDN)网、帧中继网以及土木建筑等工程的规划、可行性研究、勘察、设计及施工。该院连续12年设计文件合格率稳定在100%，优良品率达95%以上，先后有49项工程设计荣获国家、部省、厅(局)优秀工程设计奖。

法人代表、院长：刘春鸣

地址：长沙市五一中路十二号

电话：(0731)2227208

邮编：440011

湖南省电力勘测设计院

该院具有电力系统规划设计、大型火力发电厂、超高压送变电工程及调度通信工程的勘测设计能力，是一所具有综合实力的甲级勘测设计院。该院专业配套齐全，技术力量雄厚，拥有各类专业人才500多人，其中教授级高级工程师和高级工程师120人。并建有覆盖全院的企业级ATM主干网络，拥有各类计算机300多台，CAD出图率达99.03%，拥有技术书刊、资料和工程档案49万余(册)份。

该院设计的大型电力工程主要有：湖南金竹山4X125MW和株洲2X125MW火电厂各一座；耒阳2X20MW火电厂一座；石门2X300MW、湘潭2X30MW、益阳2X30MW火电厂各一座；湖南云田、岗市、民丰500KV变电站三座，500KV送电线路773Km，220KV变电站56座，220KV送电线路88条。获国家级及省(部)级优质工程、优秀设计和优秀勘测奖40项，科技进步奖21项。

法人代表：谷建军

地址：长沙市劳动西路84号

电话(0731)5527700

邮编：410007

湖南省交通规划勘察设计院

该院创建于1960年，是首批获国家甲级

资质的勘察设计单位。现有职工近500人，各类专业技术干部占71%，其中高、中级职称技术人员214人。主要承担公路、桥遂、港口码头、航道、工业与民用建筑等工程的规划、可行性研究、勘察、设计、咨询、监理及工程承包等任务。

该院现在承担国家重点建设项目京珠高速公路(湖南段)和湘江大源渡枢纽工程的设计。在全长5747.82米、主孔为四跨(130+2×310+130)米、总投资近6亿元，由江泽民总书记题写桥名的"岳阳洞庭湖大桥"的设计中采用预应力砼三塔双索面全漂浮体系，属国内首创。

1978年以来该院获得国家、部、省级优秀工程勘察设计奖和科学技术进步奖共54项，其中获国家奖10项。承担的长沙湘江大桥设计、常德沅水大桥勘察与设计、长沙湘江北大桥设计获国家优秀工程设计金奖和勘察金质奖。经国家技术监督局和国家质量评审委员会审定，成为湖南省首家悬挂"国家质量奖"奖旗的勘察设计单位。

法人代表:虢代章

地址:长沙市八一路442号

电话:(0731)4416732

传真:(0731)4435804

邮编:410011

长沙冶金设计研究院

长沙冶金设计研究院成立于1957年，是冶金部直属甲级大型综合设计研究院，现有在职员工1091人，专业技术人员845人，其中教授级高级工程师32人，高级工程师217人，2人获国家设计大师称号，12人享受政府特殊津贴。

该院持有冶金、建筑、黄金、环保行业甲级设计证书和城市规划、勘察、市政、轻工、建材、有色、医药等行业乙级设计证书，具有工程承包、咨询、监理甲级资质，经国家对外贸易经济合作部批准，具有对外经济技术合作经营权，可承担国内外工程勘察、咨询、设计、监理和工程总承包。

建院以来，共荣获国家级、省部级优秀工程设计奖、发明奖、科技奖188项，其中国家级优秀设计金质奖5项，银质奖3项，国家科技进步特奖1项;97年综合实力名列全国工程勘察设计单位百强第74位，连续9年被长沙市授予"重合同守信用企业"称号，97年被授予省级"重合同守信用企业"称号;是湖南省10家CAD示范单位之一。

法人代表:高少青

地址:湖南省长沙市劳动东路33号

电话:(0731)5464911

传真:(0731)5468920

邮编:410007

湖南省建筑设计院

湖南省建筑设计院是国家建设部颁发甲级勘察设计证书并由外经贸部授予对外经营权的甲级勘察设计单位。成立于1952年，现有职工510人，其中高级建筑师与高级工程师128人。

该院主要从事国内外民用建筑工程的设计、勘察、咨询、监理服务，技术力量雄厚，工种配套齐全，设施装备完善。40多年来，在国内完成长沙火车站、中山商业大厦、贺龙体育馆、湖南革命烈士纪念塔、张家界机场等大、中型工程设计3000余项;在亚洲、非洲、拉丁美洲13个国家完成坦桑尼亚国会山建筑群、利比里亚体育场、也门共和国国家银行大厦、喀麦隆妇女儿童医院等重要工程150余项。近些年来，设计方案中标率达75%，设计成果优良品率在95%以上，先后获部优、省优设计奖80多项，省科技成果奖39项。省QC小组奖23项，国家专利4项。

法人代表、院长:程世陵

地址:湖南省长沙市人民中路140号

电话(0731)5166238

传真:(0731)5163176

电挂:5003
邮编:410011

中南工业大学

中南工业大学成立于1952年,1996年9月正式通过国家"211工程"立项审核,成为面向21世纪国家重点建设的大学之一。学校现设12个学院,52个研究所。有41个本科专业,36个硕士点,15个博士点;3个国家重点学科;3个博士后科研流动站;1个国家级工程研究中心,1个国家重点实验室和2个省重点实验室。是工商管理硕士(MBA)学位试点单位。现有在校学生11000余人,其中研究生982人;教职工3013人,其中教授及相应职称253人,付教授及相应职称554人,中国科学院士2人,中国工程院士7人,博士生导师74人。建校以来,学校已为国家培养各类学生55000余人,其中研究生3000余人。

中南工业大学作为我国有色金属行业高层次人才的培养基地和科学研究的主要基地,其优势学科为有色金属的地质、采矿、选矿、冶金材料及材料加工等构成的学科体系,同时建有与优势学科相配套的机械、自控、计算机、物理、化学、数学、力学、管理、经济、法律、社科、外语等学科,使学校成为多学科相结合的综合性工业大学。在学校41个学科专业中,矿产普查与勘探(含应用地球物理)、矿物加工工程、有色金属冶金和粉末冶金处于国内领先水平,在国际上也有较大影响。1996年,中南工业大学物理、化学学科被国家教委确定为国家级工科基地。1981年以来,学校每年承接600项科研项目,共取得重大科研成果近800项,有618项获部省级以上奖励,其中国家级三大奖(国家自然科学奖、国家发明奖、国家科技进步奖)43项,获得专利权177项,专利实施率65%,居全国高校首列。

近年来,学校积极开展对外交流与合作,接待来访外宾人次逐年增加。1997年共接待外宾105人次,比上年增加46%。学校教师中,每年大约有70—90人次出国进行学术访问、讲学、合作科研和攻读硕士、博士学位。学校已与国外40所高校和研究单位签订了合作协议或建立了友好合作关系。

校长、教授:黄伯云
党委书记、研究员:汪诗训
地址:湖南省长沙市麓山南路
电话:(0731)8826911(总机)
传真:(0731)8826136
电子邮件:office@csut edu.cn
邮编:410083

小天使报社
校园与家庭杂志社

小天使报社与校园与家庭杂志社是一个报刊联合体,现有员工20人。《小天使报》是为小学生素质教育服务的优秀少年报。《校园与家庭》杂志社顺应时代的潮流,竭力推崇大教育的观念,将学校、家庭、社会教育有机地结合起来,在全国刊林中独树一帜,填补了我国期刊界的空白。

目前,报刊已在全国20多个省市自治区发行,发行量分别达到26万和30万份。小天使报社与校园与家庭杂志社均为中国少年报刊协会成员单位。1998年,参加中国少年报刊协会与中央电视台联合举办的"我与电视"征文大赛中,《小天使报》的一位小作者荣获全国第一名。

法人代表:肖林图
地址:湖南长沙市德雅路邮电村
电话:(0731)4224181　4225142
邮编:410003

中学生化学报

本社出版、发行《中学生化学报》(初中内容)、(高中内容)及本报合订本和经营本报广告。

中学生化学报创办14年来，以服务中学师生、服务中学化学教学、全面提高中学生的化学素质为办报宗旨，紧扣中学化学教材，配合教学进度，联系教学实际，注重激发学生学习兴趣，重视培养学生学习能力。

中学生化学报内容广泛新颖，栏目丰富多彩，文章短小精悍，具有很强的针对性、实用性、可读性。目前，报纸订户遍及全国各地，发行量在全国同类报纸中名列前茅。

中学生化学报因具有发行量大、发行面广、时效较长、读者对象集中等优势，受到广大广告客户的垂青。本社热忱欢迎广告客户前来洽谈。

单位名称：中学生化学报社

法人代表：彭鸣凯

地址：长沙市岳麓区桃花坪1号

电话：8826692（总编室） 8826071（发行部） 8826492（广告部）

邮编：410012

衡阳会计师事务所

衡阳会计师事务所经湖南省财政厅批准，于1986年9月正式成立是湘南最早且规模最大的会计查帐、验证和会计咨询服务的社会中介机构。1993年在湘南率先获得资产评估资格，现有注册会计师26人，拥有高级会计师、高级经济师、高级工程师、资产评估师、律师以及电脑等专业技术人员共50人。执业人员平均年龄35岁。12年来，共为7000家客户提供了各种服务，实现业务总收入800多万元。逐步形成了以外商投资企业审计为龙头，以国有大中型企业审计为主体，以资产评估和房地产施工企业审计为两翼的业务体系。

所处、主任会计师：刘吉元

地址：湖南省衡阳市、环城北路96号

电话：(0734)8248997、8222291

邮编：421001

长沙中意集团股份有限公司

长沙中意集团股份有限公司是我国名优冰箱生产“五强”企业之一。1993年晋升国家大型一档企业，并成为深交所上市公司。现有职工1565人，其中大专以上学历的占员工总数的23%，具有中级以上专业技术职称的126人，占员工总数的9%。

公司自1985年转产家用电冰箱系列家用电器以来，以市场为导向，大力推进科技进步，通过多次较大的技术改造，现已形成年产电冰箱100万台，空调80万台，冰柜20万台的生产能力。中意冰箱1988年获部优和国家银质奖、全国轻工业企业出口创汇“金龙腾飞奖”，“中意”商标人选中国驰名商标。从1990年开始连续多年进入全国500家大工业企业行列，1992年被评为全国100家质量、效益优秀企业，1994年又荣获全国用户最信得过产品金桥奖、“三连冠”企业。1997年公司冷柜空调生产开发取得了长足的发展，开发了4个新产品，完善和改进了3个老产品，形成了中意冷柜五大系列23个品种。并与美国弗瑞吉代尔公司签订了技术服务协议，通过技术合作完善提高了KC—25窗机的质量，发行改进窗机生产线设备，达到单班生产窗机700台的潜力。

按照“到国家新的增长点上去找市场，到市场上去找企业新的经济点”的经营思路，公司抓住1997年房地产业从低谷复苏的契机，加大对房地产的投入，实现了走筑进度快、工程质量好、企业信誉高、房产销售畅、资金回宠快的良好局面，创造了良好的经济效益。公司现已发展成为以家电工业为主导，集生产、科研高贷、房地产开发为一体的多产业规模经济实体。

近几年来，公司在资本经营方面取得了较好的成效。1997年公司兼并市铝制品二厂，重组冷柜厂，理顺产权关系，增强了集团冷柜的生产能力；收购中外合资中南机电市场的外方投股份，新出租商业门面54间，面积4200平方米，收入360万元。

在深化企业改革过程中，公司大胆探索，已形成了一套具有中意特色的管理模式。质量管理、安全管理、现场管理、档案管理、标准化管理等曾被有关部门作为典型向全国推介。公司曾获省企业管理优秀企业奖、轻工部现代化管理成果奖和轻工部质量管理奖等多项荣誉。在以董事长邓文全为首和公司领导班子的率领下，在公司全体员工的努力下，中意集团将在迈向21世纪的道路上再创辉煌。

长常高速公路

长沙至常德高速公路是湖南省"九·五"期间的重点工程，是湖南省跨世纪的"一纵一横"公路规划主骨架网的"横"向主干道。长常高速公路与现有的厦门到成都319国道基本平行，它东起长沙延申至长沙黄花国际机扬，经浏阳与江西省交界，西至常德，向西可至桃花源和国家级森林公园张家界，经湘西与重庆直辖市、四川省、贵州省相连，是我省重要的交通主干道。

长常高速公路全长153.481公里，全线按平原微丘区一级汽车专用公路标准设计，计算行车速度100KM/H，桥涵设计荷载汽一超20，挂——120级，计算洪水频率1/100。全封闭、全立交，控制出入口。平曲线最小半径1890M，最大纵坡3.75，竖曲线最小半径10000M。

长常高速公路组织管理机构设长常公路建设指挥部及长常高速公路建设开发投资有限公司，一个部门，两块牌子。湖南省省委常委、常务副省长周伯华同志为长常公路建设指挥部指挥长，原省建委主任现省人大常委会主任高锦屏同志、省政府办公厅副秘书长唐见奎同志、省交通厅厅长李安同志为捌指挥长，张志超同志为长常公路建设指挥部办公室主任，主持日常工作长常高速公路建设开发有限公司总经理张志超同志、副总经理宁文高、李定国、何海鹰、刘代全等同志组成。在省交通厅、省高速公路建设开发总公司的直接领导下，进程进展顺利，质量稳步上升。1997年交通部在建重点工程全国大检查中，长常高速公路的质量得到了检查组的较好评价：有关建设各方在工程拆迁难度大，工期紧的情况下，合理安排，精心管理，克服了雨水多，施工期短，地质条件差，施工干扰多等困难，积极组织各方力量，相互配合努力工作，基本按计划完成了施工任务。

坚持工程招标投标制度，择优选用施工单位。长常公司坚持无论工程大小，一律采取招投标选择施工单位，其招标的公开、公正性受到了交通部检查组的高度评价；正确处理好进度和质量的关系，牢固树立进度服从质量的指导思想。抓好先进典型推广，提高施工工艺，基本上形成了全线工艺一致，标准统一；严把计量关，加强了工程费用控制；实现了益常段全线计算机联网，开通计算机电子邮件传递，依靠自身开发的"高速公路工程网络应用系统软件"将工程量化到每个实体，为提高工程建设管理水平创造了条件。

省委、省政府对长常高速公路的建设高度重视，省委书记王茂林、省长杨正午、省委常委副省委长周伯华、省人大副主任高锦屏等领导多次到工地视察现场办公，省交通厅厅长李安、副厅长马其伟、詹新华等同志直接参加了对工程的领导工作。同时长沙市、益阳市、常德市等地方政府和沿线广大人民群众，对长常高速公路的建设都给予了大力支持。由此为长常高速公路营造了良好的施工环境。

（撰稿人：宋文高、周亚夫）

益阳汽车运输总公司

湖南益阳运输总公司地处益阳风景秀丽的秀峰湖畔，是一个拥有68年悠久历史，资金雄厚的中型专业公路运输企业。现有职工3800多人，营运车辆645台，固定资产达1.13亿元。下设9个客货运输公司，1个修制厂4个生产辅助服务公司。客运开辟班线371条，遍布湖北、广东、广西、江苏、浙江、福建、江西、海南、上海等省、市，日发班次 1207 次，日接送旅客 45000 人。货运承接全国各地整车、零担运输，并实行了公铁联运。同时，在宾馆、餐饮、商业、汽车检测、车辆维修等行业都有较全面的开发，做到了主副业同步发展。

改革开放以来，该司法人代表、党委书记、总经理吴国强带领全司员工大胆改革、勇于创新，使企业走上了一要健康、快速、稳定发展的康庄大道。现在，企业各项事业空前发展，两个文明建设显著提高。总公司先后被授予全国优质运输先进集体、全国及全省交通系统先进单位、益阳市优秀政工企业、湖南省工交系统廉政建设先进单位等数十个荣誉称号；所属的益阳汽车站、安化汽车站被交通部授予“全国文明车站”称号，顺达车队被定全省公路运输行业唯一的“文明示范窗口”。

详细地址：湖南省益阳市长益路 81 号
联系电话：4219221
邮政编：413000

湖南省贸促会　湖南国际商会

湖南省贸促会、湖南国际商会是由湖南经贸界有代表性的人士、企业和团体组成的全省性正厅级民间对外经贸社团机构。其宗旨是：遵循中华人民共和国的法律法规，依照国际惯例，开展促进对外贸易、利用外资、引进国外先进技术及各种形式的中外经济技术合作等活动，促进湖南同世界各国、各地区之间的贸易与经济合作的发展，增进湖南人民与世界各国人民之间的相互了解和交流。湖南国际商会拥有企业和团体会员 1600 家，个人会员 100 多人；各地州市已设立了相应机构，并与世界 100 多个国家和地区的对口组织建立了密切联系。主要服务业务：对外联络、出国展览、经贸信息、涉外法律调解与仲裁、出证认证、商标代理等。

Hunan Trade Promoting Committee Hunan International Commercial Committee

Hunan Trade Promoting Committee (HTPC) and Hunan International Commercial Committee (HICC) is a non－governmental organization than composed by representative personages, enterprises and associations. Abiding by the law ofpeople's Republic of China and complying with the international practice, the purpose of HTRC and HICC is: to establish business relaions with foreign companies, to recommend foreign investment and technology, to develop various external economic and technological cooperation, to promote the economic cooperation and communication between Hunan and the outer world. The present president of HTPC and HTCC is Mr. Tang Deyuan. HTPC and HICC have 1600 enterprises and asspciations' me,ber and 100 individual members. HTPC and HICC set up equivalent agencies in a lot of districts and rehions in China and established close relations with more than 100 similar organizations all over the world. The business scope of HTPC and HICC includding external liaison, exhibition, trade information, consultation, reconciliation and arbitration of foreign case, attestation, trade mark attorney and so on. (8)

“社会力量办学的中坚”简介

湖南科技专修学院

湖南科技专修学院 1982 年经省教委批准创办，现有固定资产 500 多万元，在校学生 480 人。开设大、中专经贸英语、工商管理、电子技术、计算机应用、财会、中英文秘、工民建、机电一体化、计算机应用与维修等专业。学院创始人院长梁忠、董事长周政，历届毕业生 2000 多人。校址：长沙市岳麓山岳麓渔场四方塘，联系电话：(0731)8825053，邮编：410012。

湖南广益实验中学

湖南广益实验中学 1997 年经教委批准创办。现有固定资产 450 万元，在校学生 232 人。学校开普通教育课程。创始人董事长王慧松，校长江文笔，副校长何秋。校址：长沙市岳麓区二里半，联系电话：(0731)8884252，邮政编码：410006。

湖南振湘职业教育专修学院

湖南振湘职业教育专修学院 1994 年经教委批准创办，现有固定资产 142 万元，在校学生 350 人。该院开设中医疗、临床医学、针推美容、经贸英语、电子技术等专业。创始人董事长杨涛，创始人院长汪松葆，副院长廖转运、王旺梅。历届毕业生 260 人。院址长沙市树木岭 43 号，联系电话：(0731)5587119－3050、5584191，邮编：410014。

湖南潇湘文理专修学院

湖南潇湘文理专修学院 1997 年经教委批准创办。现有固定资产 150 万元，在校学生 100 人。学校开设中文教育、英语教育、数学教育、电子技术、中英文秘、律师等专业。创始人，校长陈宏能，副校长廖普成。校址：永州市芝山区杨梓塘，联系电话：(0746)6381394，邮政编码：425000。

长沙文理专修学院

长沙文理专修学院 1989 年经教委批准创办，现有固定资产 200 万元，在校学生 420 人。学院开设汉语言文学、英语、文秘、会计、计算机及应用、电子技术、经贸英语等专业。创始人蒋静、申思荣等，院长秦旭卿、副院长邹蕤宾、蒋静、李果因，历届毕业生 852 人。校址长沙市岳麓山阜埠河路，联系电话：(0731)8825644，邮编：410012。

湖南家长函授学校

湖南家长函授学校 1996 年经教委批准创办。现有固定资产 10 万元，在校函授学员 5300 人。学校开设婴幼儿家长培训。小学生家长培训、中学生家长培训课程。创始人，校长蒋伟杰，校务委员会主任刘先捍。历届结业学员 6200 人。校址：长沙市左家垅湖南教育学院内，联系电话：(0731)8825885，邮政编码：410012。

长沙经贸学院

长沙经贸学院 1994 年经教委批准创办。现有固定资产 40 万元，在校学生 424 人。学校开设计算机应用、英语、电算会计、文秘、企业管理等专业。创始人、董事长刘辉，院长刘流，副院长柴宗义、曹汝清。历届毕业生 824 人。校址：长沙市坪塘镇，联系电话：(0731)8500710，邮编：410208。

湖南郴州南方成人中等专业学校

湖南郴州南方成人中等专业学校 1991 年经教委批准创办。现有固定资产 300 余万元，在校学生 860 人。学校开设电算会计、电脑文秘、电子技术、机电、计算机应用、旅游服务管理、护士等专业。创始人、董事长周连生，创始人、副董事长、校长伍志宏。历届毕业生 2580 人。校址：郴州市人民西路 21 号，联系电话：(0735)2242972，邮编：423000。

衡阳文理专修学院

衡阳文理专修学院 1993 年经教委批准创办。现有固定资产 3261393 元，在校学生 906 人。学院设置工业与民用建筑、工商管理、电子技术、经贸英语、旅游管理、美术、财会、高师、高护、小教师资、广告装潢、汽修等大、中专专业。董事长周观茂，副董事长罗清福，创始人、副董事长兼院长李承志、副院长王焕、孙贺庭、刘仁达、许宏磊。历届毕业生 1163 人。校址：衡阳市黄茶岭拥军路 177 号，联系电话：(0734)8411610，邮编：421008。

宁远九嶷高等专科进修学校

宁远九嶷高等专科进修学校 1987 年经教委批准创立。现有固定资产 520 万元，在校学生 420 人。学校开设英语、汉语言文学、美术、医疗、电脑等专业。创始人郑国栋、周忠熙、何福思。历届毕业生 1900 人。校址：湖南宁远县城关东郊，联系电话：(0746)7222851，邮编：425600。

零陵九嶷山进修学院

零陵九嶷山进修学院 1981 年经教委批准创办，现有固定资产 1000 多万元，在校学生 756 人。开设经贸英语、企业管理、中文、医学、美术、幼师等专业。学校创始人乐天宇，董事长黄森，常务副董事长、党总支书记杜殿魁，校长蒋先哲，副校长唐正固、黄自尧。历届毕业生 4126 人。校址：湖南永州市冷水滩区，联系电话：(0746)8324184，邮编：425000。

屈原大学

屈原大学 1985 年经教委批准创办。现有固定资产 1000 万元，在校学生 240 人。学校开设电子技术、电子计算机、文秘、保安等专业。创始人赵觉民、屈正中，董事长兼校长赵觉民，常务副董事长兼常务副校长徐文彬，副董事长屈正中、高杨、李育斌、副校长汪荣甲、胡兆。历届毕业生 535 人。校址：岳阳市金鹗东路，联系电话：(0730)8612651，邮编：414000。

湖南省人民政府外事办公室简介

1997年,在省委、省政府和外交部的领导下,全省外事战线的广大干部职工紧密围绕省委、省政府"开放带动"战略的实施,围绕湖南外事工作"九五"规划,以"扩大对外开放的程度,提高对外开放的水平"为职志,抢抓机遇,求实进取,全省外事工作较为活跃,成效较为显著,具体体现出以下几个特点:

一、坚持扩大对外交往,提高对外开放程度

对外交往是对外开放的前提和基础。1997年,湖南对外交往日趋活跃,开放程度不断扩大。全年由省外办接待的团组达到156批1187人次,其特点是高规格团组、知名人士、重要外国财团和外交人员来访增长较快。与此同时,省外办积极贯彻省委、省政府扩大开放的决策,大力促进有实质性内容的团组出国考察访问。全年因公出国(境)2478批,8684人次,分别比上年增长3.6%和7.4%,其中经贸考察和劳务输出比上年增加7.2%,表明因公出国(境)的经济含量有所增加。

友城"主渠道"不断拓宽,全年派出各类团组38批271人,接待团组23批261人,人数之多和覆盖面之广均超过往年。民间外交取得突破性进展,全年接待来自美、日、丹麦等国来访团组23批208人次,派出团组12批96人次,均较上年有较大幅度的增长。此外,省外办还先后组织了原正市先生铜像揭幕仪式暨在华外国专家工作研讨会、欧洲国家驻华大使访湘、外交部驻外使节团访湘等大型活动,促进了湖南对外开放的进一步深入。

二、坚持外事服务经济,创办湖南特色外事

以经济外交为主题,突出服务经济建设,是湖南外事的鲜明特色。1997年,这一特色得到了更进一步凸现。一年来,共向国家外国专家局组织申报引智项目64个,国家外专局批准立项49个,共引进外国专家91名,创造了较好的社会效益和经济效益。如常德农校前些年从日本引进的幸水梨新水果品种和栽培技术,已于今年挂果,该项目有望成为我国水果行业继红富士之后的又一次成功引进。怀化安塑集团在引进外国专家之后,加快了技术改造步伐,增强了企业竞争力,1997年成功兼并了长沙塑料厂。

现在,外事工作为经济建设服务已成为全省各级外事部门的共识,地市州外办及工业、农业、科技、教育等各级外事部门围绕经济建设,做了大量工作,取得了显著效益。

三、坚持抓好归口管理,保证外事有序进行

管理出效益,提高对外开放的质量和水平重在加强管理。1997年,省外办根据中央和省里的要求,对没有实质性内容和有明显公费旅游倾向的因公出国(境)团组进行了控制,拟定了严格控制因公出国(境)10条意见,并制定具体规定下发地市州和省直部门。尤为值得一提的是,1997年9月,省委、省政府联合下发了《关于加强全省外事工作的意见》,为全省外事工作的有序进行、为外事工作更好地服务于地方对外开放和经济建设提供了强有力的保证。

在加强因公出国(境)归口管理的同时,我们还加强了涉外案件、外国专家、省级领导人外事活动、外国记者、领事认证等众多外事领域的归口管理工作,保证了外事工作的有序进行。

湖南省建筑消防设施监测服务中心

湖南省建筑消防设施监测服务中心是根据公安部《关于抓紧建立和认真落实建筑消防设施检查维修管理制度的通知》和《湖南省建筑消防设施管理规定》的文件精神，经省公安厅批准成立的，经湖南省公安消防总队严格资质审查，颁发了“建筑消防设施检测维护资质证”，是我省目前唯一具备对建筑消防设施测试资格的专业检测机构。

该监测中心承担着全省建筑消防设施的检测、技术咨询及管理维护人员培训工作。通过对建筑消防设施的竣工检测、定期检测、专项检测，来保证建筑消防设施的安全作用。检测范围包括防火门、窗、卷帘和消防电梯、消防给水系统、机械防排烟系统和通风空调系统、消防电气和消防通讯设施、自动喷水灭火系统、火灾自动报警系统、气体灭火系统、水喷雾自动灭火系统等。

地址：长沙市外湘春街 48 号

电话：4316391

邮编：410008

民办湖南景文学院

民办湖南景文学院 1997 年经教委批准创办。现有固定资产 2000 万元，在校学生 550 人（景文中学 1000 人）。学校开设英语、日语、计算机及应用、中文、工民建、公关文秘等专业。创始人，董事长钟鼎舜（台胞），院长王文，书记孙蒲英，副院长孙浩、刘绍亮。历届中学毕业生 1500 人。校址：邵阳市宝庆西路，联系电话：(0739)5357965(办)，邮编：422000。

常德经贸学院

常德经贸学院 1996 年经教委批准创办。现有固定资产 2500 万元，在校学生 300 人。学院开设：计算机及应用（本、专科）、计算机信息管理（本、专科）、机电一体化工程（本、专科）、市场营销（专科）、公共关系、法律汽车运用工程、汽车运输管理工程、工民建、计算机应用与维护、电算会计、法律、经济管理等专业。创始人、院长闵安稳，理事长车东万，副理事长闵安稳、黄崇林、刘安民，副院长倪桂林。历届毕业生 200 人，校址：常德高等专科学校内，联系电话：(0736)7796795(办)，7796872(院长办)，邮编：415000。

湖南太极码电脑专修学院

湖南太极码电脑专修学院 1993 年经教委批准创办。现有固定资产 124 万元，在校学生 580 人。学院开设计算机及应用、计算机信息管理、文秘、英语、会计、市场营销等专业。创始人戴顺天、曹逸兴，董事长兼院长曹逸兴，副董事长张兰天，副院长易显颐、曹勇。历届毕业生 1560 人。校址：长沙市咸家湖，联系电话：(0731)8803044，邮编：410008。

湖南经济社会发展进修学院

湖南经济社会发展进修学院 1994 年经教委批准创办。现有固定资产 120 万元，在校学生 689 人。学校设置经济管理文秘、经济管理、电子技术、经贸英语、中文、电算会计、计算机及应用等专业。创始人陆魁宏、何鹄志，院长陆魁宏，常务副院长、党支部书记曾郁园。历届毕业生 365 人。地址：长沙市德雅村省社会科学院内；联系电话：4211224、4224351；邮编：410003。

宁远九嶷山专修学院

该学院 1980 年经省教委批准创办。现有固定资产 466.85 万元，在校学生 516 人。学院开设中文、英语（经贸英语）、数理、医疗、美术等专业。创始人乐天宇，副董事长乐燕生，院长张克鼎。历届毕业生 3950 人。学院地址：湖南省宁远县舜陵镇九嶷南路。

长沙实验外国语专修学院

长沙实验外国语专修学院 1993 年经省教委批准创办。现有固定资产 50 万元，在校学生 309 人。学院开设英语专科及本科预科专业。创始人、院长胡亚元，副院长丁森林。历届毕业生 132 人。院址：长沙市留山南路宝马广场石马村，电话：（0731）5581672、5572179、4127087，邮编：410004。

三湘人杰

长沙市文化局文物工作队宋少华

宋少华同志 20 多年来，一直奋战在艰苦的考古工作第一线。他身先士卒，长期带病坚持工作，为完成大型墓葬的发掘坚持数月战斗在野外考古工地，为我国文博事业的发展做出了重要贡献。

他坚持贯彻“保护为主，抢救第一”的文物工作方针，20 多年来，抢救发掘的古墓葬、古遗址达 2000 余座（处），保护了数百件国家一、二级珍贵文物。10 多次受到建设单位的表扬和政府的表彰，特别是 1993—1996 年短短四年间，率领本单位的全体同志主动配合城市建设，取得了发掘“西汉长沙王室特大型古墓”、“长沙走马楼三国吴简”两项重大考古成果，分别被国家文物局评为’93、’96 年全国十大考古新发现之一，受到了党和国家领导的高度重视，在国内外引起了巨大轰动。特别是三国吴简的发现，被誉为世纪性的考古发现之一。

他在业务上勤奋学习，刻苦钻研，自学成才，先后被聘请参加“八·五”国家哲学社科重点课题《长沙楚墓》和国家重点图书《中国漆器——汉代卷）的科研编撰工作。多年来撰写并发表《湖南秦墓初论》、《长沙西郊桐梓坡汉墓》、《五弦筑研究》、《长沙文物志——历代藏品》、《走马楼简牍概述》等战国秦汉魏晋考古学论文、报告 40 余篇，20 余万字。他还主持参与《长沙走楼三国吴简暨历代精品展》、《长沙历史文物展》、《长沙文物普查成果展》等大型展览的内容设计和布展工作。其研究成果和工作实绩多次在省、市社科成果评选中获奖，受到专家学者、领导的好评。

衡阳静园宾馆

静园宾馆地处衡阳市中心。建筑熔古典风味与现代气息于一炉，飞檐峭壁，熠熠生辉。环境优雅、四季常青、闹中取静，故有“静园”的雅称。是国内外宾客的好住处，经贸洽谈的好窗口，是宴请宾朋和召开会议的好场所。

宾馆设有总统套房、豪华套间、标准间等舒适的高、中档客房300间，大小会议室16个及1个大型停车场。餐饮有中式、欧式、日式卡拉OK包厢，可同时供500人就餐。高档豪华的天霸夜总会、歌舞厅可同时容纳400余人陶冶美的心灵，辉映美的形象。附设的购物、商务、洗涤、票务、桑拿按摩、游泳健身、美容美发等项服务令来宾方便自如、宾至如归。

静园人崇尚“宾客至上、服务一流”的职业宗旨，以旺盛的精力、诚挚的热情、无微不至的服务为各位宾客营造一方温馨的世界。

总经理：丁冬生

书　记：尹运钧

电　话：8226713　8222971

湖南东风汽车销售有限责任公司

公司成立于1994年，注册资本300万元，系湖南物贸实业有限责任公司与东风汽车公司合资组建的紧密型联营企业，是国家经贸委正式批准的东风汽车在湖南地区的一级代理商。本公司仓储面积达28000平方米，专营正宗东风系列车、原厂配件，集整车销售、配件供应、维修服务、信息反馈于一体。本公司以批发为主，批零兼营；整车年销售量为800台，销售额达6000多万元。竭诚欢迎各界朋友光临惠顾。

总经理：吴钦松

岳阳巴陵油脂工业有限公司系中国石化总公司巴陵石化公司、马来西亚五洲控股有限公司共同投资兴建的中外合资企业，总投资1.5亿元人民币，注册资本6117万元人民币，占地面积48000平方米。年产桶装及各类小包装精炼食用植物油9万吨。

公司自1995年正式投产以来，每年均获得省市“消费者信得过单位”和“重合同守信用单位”称号，公司主导产品——“道道全”牌色拉油，调和油，荣获“全国第三届农业博览会金奖”、“96年度和97年度湖南省名牌产品品牌”；1998年2月产品正式通过ISO9002产品质量体系认证。

法人代表：黄景汉

公司地址：岳阳市经济技术开发区通海路

联系电话：(0730)8264100 8264116

邮　　编：414000

岳阳巴陵油脂工业有限公司

邵阳市公共交通总公司是一九六〇年成立的全民所有制城市公共服务性企业。现有固定职工1912人，拥有固定资产原值总额2968万元。公司下辖五个城市客运分公司及保养厂、广告公司、轮渡公司、劳服公司、城建发展公司、印刷厂、酱厂、东风市场、技校等十四个二级机构，经营范围涉及城市客运服务、轮渡、汽车维修保养、驾驶员培训、广告装潢、食品酿造等，拥有各类公交车辆300多台，经营27条城郊公司汽车线路，线路总长超过380公里，1997年共完成营运收入2600余万元，在1997年度全省市内公共汽车、电车行业中排序第四名。

一九九一年五月参加为期一年的全国城市公交优质服务竞赛活动，九二年六月被国家建设部授予“优胜企业”光荣称号，九三年被市人民政府授予“劳动就业工作先进单位”称号，九四、九五年度获省建委授予的“全省建设系统职业道德建设先进单位”称号，4－008号车荣获全国首批“青年文明号”称号。

企业法人代表：　魏仁发

公 司 地 址：　邵阳市宝庆中路185号

邮 政 编 码：　422000

邵阳市公共交通总公司

湖南省石油总公司衡阳市公司

湖南省优秀企业经营者，公司经理、党委书记：唐发锦

雄伟壮观的石油大厦

湖南省石油总公司衡阳市公司成立于1951年，现有职工800多人；油库10座、库容总量63000多M^3；加油站30余座，油罐车20多辆；固定资产6000多万元；下属七个县(市)公司和石油厂、运输公司共九个企业；年供油能力达60多万吨。公司在经理、党委书记劳动模范唐发锦同志的带领下，深化改革，拼博进取，各项工作取得了显著成绩。1997年实现利润居全省石油系统前列，近十年企业固定资产增加近5倍。并连续十年被省石油总公司和衡阳市政府评为"目标管理先进单位"、"双文明企业"。

宁远县电影发行放映公司

湖南省宁远县电影发行放映公司，现有在职职工83名，直辖影院三家，下设农村管理站九个，现有放映单位82个。

公司一直把工作重点放在农村，每年农村放映均在1.4万场左右，村平20场以上。近五年来，每年在全县102所中小学放映优秀影片100余部，年均放映4500余场，观看影片的学生均在100万余人次。此外，认真组织城镇广大干部职工观看诸如《鸦片战争》等优秀影片，取得了精神文明建设和物资文明建设双丰收。受到了中央、省、市、县各级各部门的表彰嘉奖。1997年被评为"湖南省96－97年度十佳电影公司"，同年在永州市迎香港回归电影展竞赛活动中被评为第一名。

法人代表：蒋人梁
地　　址：宁远县舜陵镇解放西路16号
联系电话：(0746)7223758
邮　　编：425600

高教改革与发展的新思路

何彬生

在改革开放的新形势下，全国各地的教育事业随之蓬勃发展，教学设备日新月异，不断更新；师资队伍日益壮大；教育教学质量不断提高；教学管理逐渐科学化，整个教育事业已进入了辉煌的发展时期。教育的发展促进了社会的稳定，民族的团结。在这红火的发展时期，我们要抓住机遇，认真贯彻党的十五大精神，坚定不移地学习《教育法》、《职业教育法》和国务院颁布的《社会力量办学条例》，共同探讨分析教育教学管理，为教育工作者和受教育者寻找一条更科学更符合我国国情的教育教学管理新途径，使我国的教育事业健康发展。为此就我国的高教改革与教育发展谈几点建议和体会，供领导在决策时参考。

一、发展民办医学教育事业刻不容缓

面临全国，特别是湖南广大基层严重缺医少药的局面，小道庸医充斥医疗市场，老百姓负病兴叹，得不到较高技术水平的医师及时诊治，小病变大，大病不治，此种情况长此以往，我们痛感农村基层高级医药人才的培养刻不容缓。根据湖南省卫生事业的发展对人才需求情况预测，到 2000 年全省共需要 10000 人以上，而我省现只有 5 所医学院校，其中本科院校只有 3 所(部属 1 所)，医学高等专科学校 2 所，而这 5 所学校每年面向我省的招生规模仅 3000 人左右，可见湖南的卫技人才供需矛盾非常突出，同时现有的卫技人才素质较低，据调查，湖南卫技人员中大专以上文化程度的仅占 15%，其中地市级 18%，县级 11%，乡镇级占 3.5%，高级卫技人才数量不足，质量不高的现状不能适应广大人民群众对医疗保健的需要。因此发展民办教育走自力更生的道路是我们的必经之路。

二、现行的教育环境

科教兴国靠人才，高科技人才来自于学校，我们讲爱国不能只是口头上喊一喊，搞一搞形式，在我们国家有相当一部分人过于追求超级享受，智力投资心痛，却拿钱尝洋味。现就调整国办教育的利弊分析和开创新的教育模式谈点建议：

(一)调整国办教育的利弊分析：近些年来我国的教育出现了一系列的法律法规政策性文件，从根本上奠定了教育发展的基础和方向。从表面上看教育在改革在发展，而实际是国办教育教学质量在滑坡，我们目前提倡高校调整合并，我认为有些合并是不妥的，为什么？①校址无法连在一起。如果二、三所学校并成一起，政府要拿出一笔资金搞硬件建设，同时荒废了原有的教学资源。如果硬拉在一起实际上是“一顶帽子大家戴”，牌子香了，名气大了，人才质量却提高不了多少。②教授多了素质低了，领导多了，教师少了。难免会出现庙大和尚小的局面，假如某专科学校与某大学合并，他们相隔近 10 余里，为了不浪费资源把另一所校址作为专科教学分部或做一个“二级仓库”，原有的国家资源被闲置，国家还要拿出一大笔资金来改善合并后的大学条件，而且大家都想挤到大学本部工作，我们想一想，这样的合并究竟好在哪里?! ③仪器设备增加，使用率降低，专科层次同样要按本科院校设置设备，但挂的是大学招牌，要按大学的要求设置，这样浪费了教学资源，同时淡化了专科层次的教学质量。为此建议按实事求是的原则进行调整，才是把握教育发展的方向和提高教学质量的手段。据了解，美国现有各类高等院校 10703 所，授学位的四年制大学 2190 所，其中私立的就有 1586 所，公立的仅 604 所，授学位 2 年制学院有 1503 所，其中公立的 1021 所，私立的 482 所；不具有学位授予权的职业学院有 7071 所，其中 6514 所是私立的。而我们国家在 1997 年 10 月前仅只有高等学校 2210 所(其中普通高校 1054 所，成人高校 1156 所)，而成人高校的 1156 所，在校生 300 人以下的有 465 所，100 人左右的有 197 所，有 96 所学校 1 个学生也没有。

从以上数据来看，中国的教育并不乐观，鉴于国家的财政压力来分析，发展民办教育和国办教育改民办，走公平竞争共同发展的道路是最适合中国教育发展实际的。

小平同志南巡讲话后，我国的民办教育如雨后春笋，蓬勃发展起来。全国现有各类民办学校 21502 所，其中幼儿园 18284 所，小学 1078 所，中学、职高、中专 1380 所，学历教育 20 余所，非学历教育 800 余所。湖南各类民办学校 1427 所，校舍面积 150 万平方米，教职工 9904 人，图书 357 万册，仪器设备价值 8529 万元，在校生 20.3 万人。民办学校虽然生机勃勃，但亟待着雨露滋润，更重要的是人们要尽快转变观念，解放思想，要鼓励学生去民办学校学习深造，民办学校要更新办学模式，大力推行教育教学管理的改革，挖掘办学潜力。

(二)开创新的教育模式

1、改革义务教育:①国家要尽快制定从小学到高中12年一贯制的义务教育硬性措施，其宗旨是保证人人享有平等的教育机会，国家要加大义务教育的投入，改善义务教育的办学条件。②加快义务教育教师的素质培训提高，制定教师素质标准，清理不合格的义务教育教师，提高义务教育教师待遇和改善工作生活环境。③取缔义务教育高收费和贵族学校。④为了使全国的义务教育落到实处，建议以县级为单位，责任层层直接下放到一把手身上，其经费概由受教育者的地区负责。⑤成立督导评估机构，要授予该机构相应的职权范围。一是对教师素质评估;二是对教学教育质量的评估;三是督导各地区经费的投入情况和使用情况，各级一把手的重视情况，并保持及时公布宣传与批评公开，要加大宣传力度。⑥小平同志在南巡讲话中指出“让一部分人先富起来”，我们国家现在的教育，也可不可以让一部分地区先富起来，谁有钱就让谁办大教育，发展教育，办好典型，带动落后地区教育的发展。现在提倡高校总体布局是势在必行，但切不可拉郎配！高校设置我认为应以大中城市为主且要看这个城市的教育资源优势而定。

2、改革单一的素质教育模式，解决文化素质教育存在的问题，首先要明确文化素质的基本要求，文化素质教育的基本目的是培养学生具有全面的、优良的素质。其基本内容:进行以弘扬爱国主义精神为主要内容的中国历史教育和中华民族的优秀文化教育、哲学教育，使学生具有一定的哲学修养，确立正确的世界观、人生观、价值观，养成科学的思维方式和工作方法。艺术教育，培养学生高尚的情操和审美情趣，了解和掌握现代科学技术的基本知识。其实施的途径有:增设人文艺术类课程，发挥课堂教学的主渠道作用，开设多种形式的讲座，丰富文化素质教育的内容，加强校园文化建设，营造校园文化气氛，实行一本一专制和双学位制等多种学制，培养复合型人才，组织社会实践，扩大文化素质教育阵地。

在我们国家大家坐到一起谈素质教育，纯单一的指中小学的素质教育，而且连中小学的素质教育也没有落实到实处而仅仅只是提提而已，基础教育的素质教育当然重要，如果在高等教育里忽视素质教育将是一个极大的失误，学校领导只顾往上面要钱，不重视对教师、学生的政治思想素质教育。倡导素质教育，就是要使学生的德、智、体、美、劳等各方面的基本素质得到全面的、充分的发展，有些中学为追求升学率，不开体育、音乐、美术课……普及素质教育，特别是对教师、机关干部的素质教育应摆在首位，他们的素质提高了，中国这个13亿人口大国才会有希望。

3、民办教育:发展民办教育是穷国办大教育，提高全民族人口素质的必经之路，要发展首先就必须要转变教育思想，更新教育观念。为此我提几点建议供参考:①中国的民办教育分为两类，一类是学历教育，另一类是非学历教育(即民办教育)，建议政府及教育部门还要加大放开力度，对民办教育不要管得太多，管得太死，出了问题不要大惊小怪，政府要协助调解。要鼓励机关、企事业单位，为民办学校大开方便之门。民办学校人才培养目标主要为基层和贫困地区，学校本身要加强自身建设，绝不能等、靠、要，必须发挥主动性，创造性才能增强其生存力，充分发挥民办学校的独特优势，以质量取胜，以特色求发展。②全国各行各业提倡持培训上岗证上岗，培训机构可采取多样化，在职的以业余为主，要制定无证不上岗的制度。③政府要加强对民办教育典型的宣传和奖励，吸收他们参政议政，免交民办学校征地、基建等规费，并向民办学校提供基建质量监督服务，保证民办教育机构用地，政府对民办学校免交各种税费、管理费、治安费、特困企业基金等，以示支持发展。④政府要制定民办学校毕业生与国办学校毕业生同等学历、就业同等的制度，对非学历的学生积极推荐就业制度，鼓励学生到民办学校学习，优惠向民办学校提供学生见习、实习场所。⑤民办学校财产应与私营企业一样，它的产权应属投资者(举办人)所有，这样才体现平等，投资者既然选择办教育，最起码他是爱国的，是想为提高全民族的文化素质和人口素质做点实事，他不会过多去考虑财产归谁。政府硬性规定学校停办后其财产不得转移、抵押、出卖、撤回资金，这样可能会影响整个民办学校对教育的投入，能否换一种说法促其发展。⑥建议政府设立民办学校教育专项贷款政策，并放开民办学校收费标准，由民办学校根据其办学条件和办学质量自己确定，促使它在大潮中快速发展和自我淘汰，这样才会充分体现出优胜劣汰，才符合市场经济改革与发展的需要。⑦规范民办学校名称。

三、改革教育管理

(一)“教”和“育”:如何科学办教育科学管理教育是我们全民族关注的大事。首先是要彻底改变旧的教育模式，树立新的教改意识。我们的教育、教学管理是按照孔子的教育管理模式，孔子过于强调“教”和“管”，对学生严教严管，死背硬记。科学的进步和发展主要还是想象力和创造力，我们要培养学生有良好的思维能力，教育一定要强调“育”，把“育”字推向首位。

（二）“管”和“理”：在教育教学管理或其它管理上，我们现在的模式是一管到底，我们的改革开放特别是教育正处于发展时期，在管理方面应多考虑“理”，而不是“管”，多“理”少“管”，把“理”字推向首位。

四、试行医学教育改革的几点体会

我是从国办教育走上民办教育的领导岗位的，我热爱教育事业，热爱学校的管理工作。自1988年至现在，我独资办起了一所医学高等专科学校。在政府和教育、计划、卫生行政部门的扶持之下，学校发展良好。学校现有占地面积200亩，建筑面积4万平方米，教学仪器400多万元，专职教师71名，兼职教师69名，在校学生2000余人，还有一所700张病床，800余名医护工作人员，医疗器械设备齐全的附属医院，给学生提供了良好的实习条件，我校是一所集教学科研于一体的民办医学高等专科学校。经过10年的教学管理和探索，制定了符合基层人才需求的培养目标和教学计划，通过几年的实施，毕业生倍受社会欢迎。

我校有普通中专和大专两个层次，开设有中专社区医学、妇幼卫生、药剂士、护士、检验士、皮肤医士、助产士、医学美容；大专设有：临床医学、高级护理、妇幼卫生、医学美容等专业。原先学校为了保证质量，不耽搁教学计划规定的理论教学，把实验课压到星期天和晚上，学生学得喘不过气来，虽然学生能够按计划大纲要求达到了毕业水平，但掌握的知识是单一的。鉴于这种状况，我们组织对毕业生进行跟踪调查，通过对3个县和69个乡镇调查，结果发现整个医学教育过于专业化，除了自己所学的专业之外，其余一窍不通。于是我们就认真研究、分析，决定在原有的大纲计划上增加其它门类专业课，培养应用型通科人才。

我们医卫类专业的培养目标，是为县以下医疗单位培养所需的各类医疗人才，招收对象为应届初中毕业生，学制四年。在教学上，除保证国家规定的主要课程之外，适当压缩文化课，增加计算机、英语授课时，增开外科护理、儿科护理、基础护理专业课，护理（护士）专业、药剂专业、检验专业增开诊断学、内、外科学、儿科学等专业课，在全校大、中专层次医学专业里增开护理专业课，护理、检验、药剂等专业开设医学专业课，而且确保英语、计算机过等级。使各专业毕业生学医的懂护理，学护理的懂医疗诊断，学药和检验的懂医疗和护理，在医护人员缺乏的紧急时候可单独治疗处理。通过几年这样的模拟试行，从目前看来是成功的，如96届的毕业生推荐在县乡镇基层工作倍受称赞，97年几十所乡镇以上的医疗单位来电来函来人向我们要毕业生，而绝大部分的毕业生在实习的医疗单位实习结束时就基本上被留用，到毕业时要学校推荐工作的几乎没有。

为了加速对湖南医学人才的培养，我校决定从98年起招收五年制大专临床医学专业班，招收对象为应届初中毕业生，分四个阶段完成全部教学任务，第一阶段（1—3学期）以外语、计算机课程为主，外语语种以英语为主，日、法、德、俄任选一门语种选修，重点培养听话能力，要求达到3级以上水平，计算机以文字处理、初级程序为主，要求达到3级以上水平。

本阶段课程安排：英语540学时，以普通英语为主，医用英语为辅，计算机340学时，语文216学时，数学184学时，化学100学时，政治100学时，生物60学时，物理84学时。

第二阶段（4—6学期）教学以基础课、临床公共课为主，目的在于培养各专业学生交叉动手能力，本阶段尽可能多一些为学生安排实验、见习时间，以使学生获得感性认识。课程安排解剖（组胚）180学时，生化72学时，生理96学时，针灸40学时，病理90学时，微寄86学时，诊断90学时，药理104学时，医学心理学40学时，卫生学80学时，X线诊断40学时，实验室诊断40学时，基础护理学180学时，内科学194学时，外科学194学时。

第三阶段（7—8学期）学生分专业进行授课，突出专业特点，培养动手能力。课程安排：护理学科突出医学、妇科学、产科学和学科教学，内科护理110学时，外科护理110学时，妇科护理120学时，儿科护理120学时，传染病护理90学时，五官科护理80学时，老年病护理60学时，中医护理80学时，常见急症80学时，妇科学130学时，产科学100学时，传染病120学时，中医244学时，五官科学60学时，皮肤性病学40学时，儿科学90学时，常见急症100学时，精神病护理100学时，老年病学100学时，授课教学5614学时。

第四阶段（9—10学期）毕业实习安排到医院全科生产实习2000学时，总学时7614学时。这样，使学生毕业具有一技多能的大学专科毕业水平，能独立从事医学各专业的工作能力。这种医学教育的改革模式能否值得借鉴，还有待于进一步在实践中去研究和挖掘。

（作者为湖南省湘南医学高等专科学校校长）

中国统计出版社

最新资料书简目